D0718167

DUNANT'S DREAM

Henri Dunant as a Young Man

Dunant's Dream

WAR, SWITZERLAND AND THE HISTORY OF THE RED CROSS

CAROLINE MOOREHEAD

HarperCollins*Publishers*

HarperCollins*Publishers*
77–85 Fulham Palace Road,
Hammersmith, London w6 8jb

Published by HarperCollins 1998
1 3 5 7 9 8 6 4 2

ISBN 0 00 255141 1

Set in Postscript Monotype Spectrum by
Rowland Phototypesetting Ltd,
Bury St Edmunds, Suffolk

Printed and bound in Great Britain by
Caledonian International Book Manufacturing Ltd, Glasgow

To Stephen

CONTENTS

LIST OF ILLUSTRATIONS   xi

ACKNOWLEDGEMENTS   xv

PREFACE   xxi

INTRODUCTION   xxv

1 Tutti Fratelli   1

2 Inhumanity Under Another Name   23

3 True Metal and Tinkling Brass   51

4 Stone Heaps Full of Snakes   87

5 Rebels, Barbarians and Perjurers   119

6 American Angels of Mercy   149

7 The Little Cushion of Europe   175

8 One of Us, Heart and Soul   207

9 The Greatest Mother in the World   231

10 The Amiable Gentlemen of Geneva   258

11 The Feet of Little Angels   292

12 Where a Savage Inquisition is Master   329

13 New and Old Instruments of Destruction   371

14 Keep the Fires Burning Under Those
    Old Gentlemen   411

15 Piercing the Darkness   471

16 Surviving the Cold Winter   500

17 One Reference to God   530

18 Affairs of the Heart   558

19 Men of the Red Cross   598

20 La Maison   640

21 The Landscape of War   682

APPENDIX ONE: The Geneva Conventions   717

APPENDIX TWO: Summary of the
   Fundamental Rules of Humanitarian
   Law Applicable in Armed Conflicts   718

APPENDIX THREE: Presidents of the
   International Committee of the Red
   Cross   719

CHRONOLOGY   721

NOTES   723

INDEX   745

LIST OF ILLUSTRATIONS

Frontispiece: Henri Dunant as a young man (*Photothèque CICR*)

Between pages 128 and 129

The founders (*Photothèque CICR*)

The attack on the tower of Solferino during the battle of 24 June 1859
by Gustave Doré (*L' IHD, Photothèque CICR*)

Red Cross volunteers during the Franco-Prussian war, 1870–71
(*DICA/CICR, Geneva*)

Dutch Red Cross medical team at Mannheim, 1870–71 (*CICR/Hist 177/8*)

The Hall of Mirrors in the Palace of Versailles, 1871 (*Bildarchiv Preussischer
Kulturbesitz, Berlin*)

One of the first Red Cross ambulances during the Franco-Prussian war
(*ND-Viollet, Paris*)

An ambulance train during the Boer War, 1899–1902 (*Photothèque CICR*)

Foreign Red Cross volunteers during the siege of Ladysmith
(*Photothèque CICR*)

The Empress Shôken visits the wounded during the Russo-Japanese war,
1904–5 (*CICR/Hist 311*)

Japanese Red Cross nurses (*Musée International de la Croix Rouge, Geneva*)

Clara Barton of the American Red Cross (*American Red Cross Society,
Washington*)

Mabel Boardman (*American Red Cross Society, Washington*)

'The Greatest Mother in the World' poster painted for the American Red
Cross by A. E. Foringer in 1918 (*Imperial War Museum, London*)

Shirley Temple fund-raising for the American Red Cross during the 1930s
(*American Red Cross Society, Washington*)

Henri Dunant shortly before his death on 30 October 1910 (*Photothèque
CICR*)

Between pages 288 and 289

Gustave Ador (*Photothèque CICR/Hist 656/15*)

Dr Frédéric Ferrière (*Photothèque CICR*)

Mlle Margarite Cramer (*Photothèque CICR/Hist 569/21*)

Madame Poincaré and friends engaged in war work, *c.* 1916 (*American Red Cross, Washington*)

The Tsarina of Russia with her daughters the Grand Duchesses Olga and Tatiana, *c.* 1916 (*American Red Cross, Washington*)

FANYs in action during the First World War (*Imperial War Museum, London*)

FANY drivers at the Front (*Imperial War Museum, London*)

An International Committee delegate visits a prisoner-of-war camp (*Photothèque CICR/Hist 617/14*)

Gustave Ador is greeted by Red Cross supporters in Geneva on 27 June 1917 (*Photothèque CICR/Hist 3117/5*)

Red Cross postcard commemorating the execution of Edith Cavell (*Photothèque CICR/Hist 1197/12A*)

A disinfection station in Poland (*Photothèque CICR/Hist 1716/10A*)

American Red Cross volunteers on their way to Europe, 1917 (*American Red Cross Society, Washington*)

Typists at work in the prisoner-of-war agency in the Musée Rath, Geneva (*Photothèque CICR/Hist 1816.13*)

The tracing service in the Musée Rath, Geneva (*Photothèque CICR/Hist 570/14*)

Dr Elsie Inglis (*Imperial War Museum, London*)

Mrs St Clair Stobbart (*Imperial War Museum, London*)

Two British Red Cross drivers in Pervyse, 1917 (*Imperial War Museum, London*)

German prisoners-of-war at a clearing depot in Abbeville, 2 October 1918 (*Imperial War Museum, London*)

Between pages 448 and 449

The British ambulance at Waldia during the Italian campaign in Ethiopia 1935–36 (*Photothèque CICR/Hist 688/29*)

Count Carl Gustav von Rosen (*Photothèque CICR/Hist 2753/24A*)

A woman wounded by phosgene gas in Ethiopia, 1935–36 (*Photothèque CICR/Hist 1940*)

International Committee delegates in Ethiopia (*Photothèque CICR/Hist 977/ 27*)

One of the International Committee offices in Madrid during the Spanish Civil War 1936–39 (*Photothèque CICR/Hist 1850/21*)

An ambulance carrying refugees is bombed during the Spanish Civil War (*Photothèque CICR/Hist 1860/17*)

A fund-raising poster of the German Red Cross from the 1930s (*DRK, Bonn*)

Cover of the German Red Cross magazine for May 1940 (*German Red Cross Society*)

A gathering of Red Cross nurses and auxiliaries in Hitler's Germany (*German Red Cross Society*)

Max Huber (*Photothèque CICR/Hist 656/11*)

Mlle Suzanne Ferrière (*Photothèque CICR/Hist 2909/11*)

Carl-Jacob Burkhardt and Mlle Lucie Odier (*Photothèque CICR/Hist 57/8A*)

Dr Fritz Paravicini (*Photothèque CICR*)

The delegate Dr Maurer with two members of the SS at the time of the liberation of Dachau, 29 April 1945 (*Photothèque CICR/Hist 3103/2*)

Red Cross lorries carry relief into devastated German cities (*Photothèque CICR/Hist 1651/56*)

An International Committee delegate at Buchenwald shortly after liberation (*Photothèque CICR/Hist 323/30*)

Children dying of hunger during the famine in Greece in 1942 (*Photothèque CICR/Hist 2525/38*)

Dr Junod in Japan, autumn 1945 (*Photothèque CICR/Hist 261/9A*)

Relief leaving a Red Cross depot in Geneva for the prisoner-of-war camps (*Photothèque CICR/Hist 3073/26*)

Dr Ernst Grawitz (*German Red Cross Society*)

British and Canadian prisoners-of-war examine their Red Cross parcels (*Imperial War Museum, London*)

Between pages 608 and 609

One of the posters of the lost and missing children from 1945 (*German Red Cross Society*)

Convoys carrying relief to Hungary during the Hungarian revolution (*Photothèque CICR/Hist Hu/14/4*)

Friedrich Born (*Photothèque CICR/Hist 976/17*)

Hungarian refugees in a camp at Tratzkirchen, Austria (*Votava/CICR*)

Jaques Moreillon (*Gassmann/CICR*)

Jean-Paul Hocké (*Gassmann/CICR*)

Jean Pictet (*Photothèque CICR*)

Melchior Borsinger (*Photothèque CICR*)

An exchange of wounded prisoners between North and South Korea, April 1953 (*United Press/CICR*)

American prisoners-of-war in North Korea, September 1950 (*Popperfoto*)

Frédéric Bieri distributing cigarettes in a camp in South Korea, July 1950 (*Photothèque CICR/Coree 17/3A*)

Women in Sana'a in the Yemen examining International Committee relief in 1964 (*Musée de la Croix Rouge, Geneva*)

Transporting relief into the Yemen in 1965 (*Boisard/CICR*)

The Swedish Red Cross distribute food at Udo, a camp in Biafra (*Vaterlaus/CICR*)

Biafra, where starvation prompted talk of genocide, 1967–70 (*Vaterlaus/CICR*)

The Cambodian refugee camp of Khao I Dang in Thailand (*Leblanc/CICR*)

Khmer refugees searching for their families at a missing persons centre in the camp of Nang Samet, 1980 (*Leblanc/CICR*)

Water tanks in a Cambodian refugee camp in Thailand during the 1970s (*Gaddis/CICR*)

An International Committee nurse-delegate monitoring the growth of children in Ethiopia in 1988 (Gassmann/CICR)

Families searching for disappeared relatives in Cyprus in 1974 (*Photothèque CICR/2558/2*)

The headquarters of the International Committee, Geneva (*Photothèque CICR/Hist 1818/3*)

ACKNOWLEDGEMENTS

Without the help of the International Committee of the Red Cross itself, President Sommaruga and the senior members of staff, as well as the librarians, historians and archivists, this book could never have been begun. Much of the material in *Dunant's Dream* is based on papers – reports, letters, minutes of meetings, cables, memos and notes on telephone calls, going back to the 1870s – that make up the exceptional archives of the International Committee in Geneva. These archives were closed to the public until January 1996; I was fortunate enough to be the first person granted unconditional access to virtually all papers up until the end of the Second World War. The later papers remain closed, as do all personal files on delegates. I would like to express my thanks to the organization both for their permission to consult the archives far beyond normal opening hours, and for the considerable amount of help I received. In particular, I would like to thank Françoise Perret for her endless help during the four years of research. Paul Reynard also gave me much time and information.

Within the International Committee archives and library I am extremely grateful for the patience, advice and help of Philippe Abplanalp, Verena Anne Bouladier, Sophie Coppex, the late Florianne Truniger, Martin Morger, Michel Clapasson. Within the press and publications departments I would like to thank Tony Burgener and Kim Gordon-Bates, Rebecca Irwin, Michèle Mercier and Cristina Fedele, now retired from the ICRC, provided help at the beginning of the project. François Bugnion, whose own book, *Le Comité International de la Croix-Rouge et la protection des victimes de la guerre*, was published in 1995, was unfailingly helpful.

I am particularly indebted to Jean-Claude Favez, Arieh Ben-Tov, Gerhart Riegner and Paul Stauffer for their help in understanding the events of the Second World War in Switzerland, and the role played by the ICRC. Much of my research on that period began with their books and information. Towards the end of the 1980s, Jean-Claude Favez, rector of the University of Geneva, was invited by the International Committee to produce an account of its work on behalf of those held by the Germans in concentration camps during the Second World War. To do this he was given full access to the archives, the only outsider ever to be given it before 1996. His book *Une Mission Impossible* remains essential reading for this period, as does *Facing the Holocaust in Budapest*, by Arieh Ben-Tov, who was given permission to consult the documents in the archives relating exclusively to his subject.

From the start, I received a great deal of encouragement and assistance from a number of people whether within the ICRC, retired from it, or who had worked closely with the organization in recent years. In particular I would like to thank Gian-Battista Bacchetta, Rainer Baudendistel, Melchior Borsinger, the late Alexandre Hay, Jacques Moreillon, Jean Pictet, and the late Sir Evelyn Shuckburgh.

Kathy Ramsperger and Lynda Allen of the Federation of Red Cross and Red Crescent Societies were extremely helpful, and gave me access to the Federation archives, though unfortunately some of the pre-Second World War files of what was then the League disappeared after 1939. A history of the Federation, *Beyond Conflict*, by Daphne A. Reid and Patrick F. Gilbo appeared at the end of 1997.

During the course of my research I visited the Red Cross Societies in Britain, the United States, France, Germany, Poland, Hungary and Italy. All were very generous with their time and help. I want to thank Alison Cox, Geoffrey Dennis, John Gray, Alison Kearns, Lady Limerick, Veronica Marchbanks, Michael Meyer, the late Muriel Monkhouse, Antonia Moon, Helen Pugh, Margaret Poulter, Sandra Singer and David Wyatt of the British Red Cross Society; Patrick Gilbo, Elizabeth Hooks and Barbara Pathe of the American Red Cross Society; Giorgio Salimei of the Italian Red Cross; Maria Garay of the French Red Cross; Dr Roman Hrabar, Alina Kusmierczyk, Eugeniusz Sztomberek of the Polish Red Cross, as well as Szymonik Boloslaw and the members of the Zamosc Survivors Association; and Frau Busse, Herr Mittermeier, and Anton Schöling of the German Red Cross. Vice-President Tadateru Konoe of the Japanese Red Cross patiently answered my many questions by letter.

I am also indebted to Alan Bell and the staff of the London Library, to William Creech of the National Archives in Washington, to Rodney Breen of the Save the Children Fund archives, to the archivists and librarians of the Imperial War Museum, the Public Record Office, and the British Library, and to Marie-Agnes Gainon-Court, and Jean-Pierre Gaume of the Museum of Red Cross and Red Crescent Societies in Geneva.

The following people, many of them delegates or former delegates, provided me with their memories of the Red Cross movement and the ICRC, and in some cases lent me their papers and unpublished documents. I am very grateful to all of them. They include: Bill Alexander, Francis Amar, Sally Ashburton, Carlos Bauverd, Sir Franklin Berman, Geoffrey Best, Charles Biedermann, Maggie Black, Urs Boegli, Rhiannon Boissier, Jean-Marc Bornet, Romy Brauman, Nicolas Burckhardt, Michel Cagneux, Dr Pierre Calpini, Vice President Claudio Caratsch, Massimo Cataldi, Meira Chand, Jean-David Chappuis, Olive Checkland, Paddy Coulter, Jean Courvoisier, Steve Davey, R.D. Davies, Felice Dindo, Louise Doswald-Beck, Dr Daniel Dufour, Peter van den Dungen, André Durand, Roger Durand, Charles Egger, Jeanne Egger, Glyn Evans, Pierre Gaillard, Hans-Peter Gasser, Pierre Gassmann, Thierry Germond, Suzanne Gunther Gillessen, Daniel Goldhagen, David Goodman, Philippe Grand d'Hauteville, Christopher Greenwood, Martin Griffiths, Paul Grossrieder, Dr Bartold Bierens de Haan, Claudine Haenni, Jon Halliday, Ceri Martyn Hammond, Françoise Hampson, Marion Harroff-Tavel, Didier Helg, the late Princess Margaret of Hesse, Jean-Pierre Hocké, Jean Hoefliger, François Jean, Dominique Debora Junod, June Kane, Timur Keckes, Anatol Ketuly, Geza Kiss, Christian Kornevall, René Kosirnik, Bob Kroon, Jean-Francois Labarthe, Maître Flavien Lalive, Karsai Laszlo, Andreas Lendorff, Dominic Lieven, Olivier Long, Laurent Marti, Jean-Pierre Maunoir, Béatrice Mégevand, Reto Meister, Marie Béatrice Meriboute, Martin Morland, André Pasquier, the late Jean-Pierre Pradervand, Professor Adam Roberts, André Rochat, Nigel Rodley, Major General Tony Rogers, Jean de Salis, Werner Salzmann, Yves Sandoz, Suzy Schumacher, Liliane de Siebenthal, Harry Shukman, Chris Smith, Nicolas Sommer, Clarissa Stacey, Jacques Stroun, Martha Swift, Richard Symonds, Jean-Daniel Tauxe, Cedric Thornberg, Anja Toivala, Jiri Toman, Theo Tschuy, Nicolas Vecsey, Jurg Vittani, Laurent Vust, Peter Walker, Dr de Watteville, Denise Werner, René-Jean Wilhelm, Georges Willemin, April Zinovieff.

I would like to thank Fran Hibberd, for her permission to quote from the letters of her father, Kenneth Kennedy in the First World War, and

Joan Couper for her permission to quote from her Second World War papers.

Particular thanks go to Paul Ress and Jane and Bob Geniesse for their hospitality, to Julia Neronova who interpreted for me in Russia, to Tomasz Potanski who made my trip to Poland possible, to my agent Anthony Sheil, and to Stuart Proffitt and Arabella Pike at HarperCollins. I am indebted to Prof. Hilaire McCoubrey, Alison Kearns, Dr Surya Subedi and François Perret for reading the manuscript, to Douglas Matthews for his invaluable help and index, and, as always, to Teddy Hodgkin, for his support and editing.

'The mission of the Red Cross is to serve, and only that. Neither attacks, nor thanks, nor prestige will alter anything.'

MAX HUBER, President of the International Committee

'La guerre est un élément de l'ordre du monde établi par Dieu.'

COUNT VON MOLTKE, Prussian Field Marshal,
11 December 1890

'There is a growing body of evidence to suggest that the world may have recently crossed the boundary into a state of permanent emergency.'

DONALD TANSLEY, 1975

PREFACE

The Red Cross is one of the most familiar of all modern images. Yet the organization which gave birth to it 130 years ago and today presides over a movement of 220 million people is in many ways almost entirely unknown.

The International Committee of the Red Cross, from its headquarters in Switzerland, monitors the laws of war; visits prisoners-of-war and political detainees; acts as go-between and negotiator during hijackings and hostage takings; campaigns to control weapons; takes relief and medical help to the victims of conflicts; traces the 'disappeared'; puts families separated by war in touch with each other and acts as custodian of the Geneva Conventions; and it does all these things silently, often in secret and without publicity.

Like a riddle, the signals it gives out are contradictory. The International Committee:

* calls itself international; yet is a private Swiss company, based in Geneva and governed by twenty-five Swiss citizens.

* prides itself on being closer to victims than any other humanitarian organization; yet does not speak for them.

* exists to help and heal the victims of war; yet does not itself lobby against war.

* has its roots in precedence and institutional memory; yet thrives on action and sometimes seems curiously uninterested in history.

* employs 'delegates' — some eight hundred in 1997, for the most part Swiss — who gather information about torture, 'disappearances' and summary executions that no one else has access to; yet under its mandate cannot reveal to the public or media what they know.

* fears the word 'politics'; yet is one of the shrewdest political actors of our day.

* has no enforceable authority; yet its moral power is, and always has been, considerable.

If the International Committee did not exist, no one would be able, in the 1990s, to invent it. Who today would put the power to monitor and criticize all the governments of the world in the hands of a small band of co-opted elderly Swiss lawyers and bankers? Its mandate is unique and its composition a quirk of history.

This book is not an institutional history of the Red Cross, nor of the national societies that make up its membership, nor even of the International Committee itself. Rather, it is the story of how a young speculator from Geneva called Henri Dunant had a dream and how five Swiss citizens, finding that they shared a conviction that it was the duty of states to mitigate the horrors of war, decided to found an organization that quickly became a movement larger, more varied and more influential than any other outside organized religion.

Dunant's Dream makes no attempt to be comprehensive – South America, the war in Vietnam, the work of the Federation of the Red Cross and Red Crescent Societies, the African famines are all barely touched on, and only some of the International Committee's many activities in the Second World War are covered – but chooses from 130 years of war and natural disasters those conflicts, issues and moral dilemmas which seem to have had the most determining effect on the growth of the modern Red Cross. Given the number of national societies, it has only been possible to describe a few of them in any detail: their stories will have to stand for the others.

Dunant's Dream is a book about the people – eccentric adventurers, moralists, visionaries and canny political manipulators – who shaped the International Committee's identity and saw and recognized their own dreams in Dunant's creation. There is something fascinating as well as admirable about those whose lives revolve around the misfortunes of others. It is also a book about war, and what successive generations have thought could and should be done to control it and to lessen the sufferings it causes.

For the sake of simplicity, the name 'International Committee of the

Red Cross' is throughout abbreviated to International Committee. Apart from official reports supplied by the International Committee already in English, the translations are all my own.

INTRODUCTION

To an outsider, the twenty-three men and women arriving at the Hôtel
Metropole in Geneva in the early afternoon of Wednesday 14 October
1942 would have looked like any other gathering of philanthropic, concerned citizens come to disburse charitable funds perhaps, or agree on
a new orphanage. They were all Swiss, all but a couple Protestant and
nearly all of them from the canton and republic of Geneva itself, the
twelve-mile enclave that had been home in the nineteenth century to
many of Europe's radicals and free-thinkers. None was very young,
and the eldest, Georges Wagnière, journalist, diplomat and expert on
international affairs, was in his eightieth year. All wore neat, dark clothes;
Mlle Odier, one of the four women present and a former nurse in her
late fifties, formidable behind a somewhat mouse-like appearance, was
wearing her invariable muted greys. All were comfortably off, some
exceedingly so, descendants of Switzerland's oldest and richest families.
The arts, the law, medicine, politics and the army were all well represented.

There was only one item on the agenda that day. These twenty-three
people had gathered together to decide whether or not to launch a
public appeal on behalf of the Jews of occupied Europe who were, by
the autumn of 1942, being systematically rounded up and deported to the
Nazi extermination camps. They were the members of the International
Committee of the Red Cross, the neutral, Swiss, private organization
founded in the wake of the battle of Solferino in 1859 to help the victims
of war, to act as keepers of the Geneva Conventions, and to inspire
and watch over the world's national Red Cross societies. The International Committee was — and is — one of the most exclusive clubs in
the world.

What was perhaps most surprising about the meeting and its most
telling characteristic was that these twenty-three men and women actually felt that, in the middle of a war already infamous for the atrocities
committed from one end of Europe to the other and rapidly spreading

throughout Asia, their word actually counted for something. By 1942 the International Committee was extremely busy looking after several million Axis and Allied prisoners-of-war, with so many staff and volunteers that they had accepted the city of Geneva's offer of the splendid Hôtel Metropole overlooking the lake as its wartime headquarters. Ever since the Franco-Prussian war of 1870, it had shown itself capable of transforming the lives of many millions of prisoners-of-war and its record, through the First World War, the Abyssinian conflict and the Spanish Civil War, had been excellent.

Its performance in the Second World War had, to date, also been good, except over the concentration camps of occupied Europe to which the delegates of the International Committee had consistently been denied all access. And this is what the members had come to discuss: whether they should break with over seventy years of their tradition of secrecy, neutrality and impartiality and speak out in public condemnation, broadcasting throughout the world, appealing to the Germans to respect the basic rights of the people whose countries they had invaded. Nothing in their history had quite prepared them for this.

The timing, furthermore, was crucial. Eight months had passed since the Wannsee conference, when Himmler had outlined plans to rid Europe of its Jews, discussing how quickly it would be possible to make the continent 'Judenfrei'. Though details of that meeting had been kept secret, rumours and more recently comprehensive reports of the deportations, the trains, the camps and the massacres had been reaching the Allies, the Vatican and the International Committee in Geneva. True, not all of them could be substantiated. But the Polish underground had, by the summer of 1942, furnished incontrovertible evidence of the deportations, while Jewish sources, in close contact with the World Jewish Congress in Geneva and its young general secretary Gerhart Riegner, were absolutely clear about what was happening. Riegner himself made sure the information reached the right places. In any case, the International Committee had a member who was extremely well placed to know. Carl-Jacob Burckhardt, historian and professor at the prestigious Institut Universitaire des Hautes Etudes Internationales in Geneva, where he had taught Riegner and got to know him well, had his own excellent contacts throughout Europe. He had been a student at German universities, was a friend of Ernst von Weizsäcker, the German deputy foreign secretary, and had been appointed the League of Nations high commissioner for the disputed territory of Danzig in 1937. The reports that had reached Burckhardt all that spring left no room for doubt. By August, Hitler's Final Solution was being widely discussed throughout Europe and North America.

What was in doubt, not just for the International Committee but for the Allies and the churches, was what could or should be done.

In the absence of the International Committee's ailing president, the pious, timid but revered Max Huber, who was holding himself ready at home to cast his vote in case of deadlock, the chair was taken by a diplomat called Edouard Chapuisat. The sixty-nine-year-old former journalist and politician active in Swiss public affairs was a very experienced chairman. He had an almost complete turnout, more members than had been seen together for many months, drawn by the gravity of the decision to be made. Even Philippe Etter, president of the Swiss Confederation, had decided to come from Berne to attend though he had never been to a meeting of the Committee before and would not attend one again. His presence had been judged crucial by Huber, so essential in fact that Etter had been allowed to dictate the day and time. Etter, as would become clear, had brought his own concerns. Just two months earlier he, as president of the Confederation, had been the person to sign a decree making entry to Switzerland all but impossible to the Jews seeking asylum across its borders. Despite widespread fears of being overwhelmed by Europe's refugees and still greater fears of invasion by Germany, that decision had not been altogether popular among the Swiss, and there was a feeling in government circles that a measure of moderation and discretion would be politic on the part of the International Committee, Switzerland's most prized institution, and that more public furore could only be harmful to the country.

The meeting opened with a reminder by Chapuisat that the issue at stake was fundamentally one of both morality and pragmatism. Would the International Committee *really* be able to help the Jews by speaking out? And if they did so, would they jeopardize their work with prisoners-of-war which, after all, lay at the very heart of their mandate? Each member, in turn, was asked to give an opinion. They had come prepared. In September they had all been consulted by post on their views and sent the draft of a possible appeal to the German government. Huber and Burckhardt were known to prefer silence. But twenty-two out of twenty-four — the full Committee, including Huber and honorary members, stood at twenty-six — had pronounced themselves in favour of doing at least something. It was this unexpectedly high number suggesting that action was needed that had prompted the October meeting.

The first to speak was Paul des Gouttes, a seventy-three-year-old lawyer, active inside the organization for almost fifty years and christened by Huber the 'legal conscience' of the Committee. Des Gouttes had no doubts: he felt that the Committee must express its disapproval at the way the most fundamental principles of humanity were being violated. Edouard de Haller, politician and public figure, and at forty-five one of the youngest present, was eager to respond, but not publicly. A public appeal, he said, was 'neither the most efficacious, nor the most opportune' way to go about things.

Next to speak came Mme Margarite Frick-Cramer, a lawyer by training and widely regarded as the cleverest of the four women present, valued by her colleagues for her sympathy and understanding. She too had no doubts. It would be cowardly to stay silent. Not speaking out, she said, would be a 'negative act' and as such so profoundly harmful that it would threaten the very existence of the organization. Two other women on the Committee, Mlle Suzanne Ferrière and Mlle Lucie Odier, agreed with her, as did several of the men. Dr Alec Cramer, who was closely involved in getting medical relief into the prisoner-of-war camps, went as far as to say that in his opinion, the appeal as drafted was 'too feeble'. Edmond Boissier, one of the three honorary members, observed that after three years of war, the moment had come to publish a 'balance sheet', setting out all that the International Committee had been able to achieve against the articles of the Geneva Conventions that had not been respected. 'If we do not act now,' he said, 'our conscience will reproach us later for not having done so when we could.' The afternoon drifted on. There was talk of responsibility and prestige, of cowardice and courage, of issuing not a direct appeal but a stern letter. Wagnière observed that the world was left with just two moral forces — the Vatican and the International Committee of the Red Cross — and that, as the guardian of the Geneva Conventions, only the Committee was 'singled out to act'. But now the mood began to change. Heinrich Zangger, a world expert in medical law who had come from Zurich for the meeting, warned that to speak out would sound like pronouncing judgement and that in itself was incompatible with the Committee's neutrality. Frédéric Barbey, historian and diplomat, observed that the Committee must guard itself from 'political questions . . . as against fire'. The balance was shifting further. There were now thirteen in favour of an appeal; eight against. That left two people to speak.

One was Burckhardt, a tall, imposing and somewhat intimidating man who could look rather like General de Gaulle and who certainly knew more than anyone else in the room about what was happening to the Jews of Europe, though he did not always share what he knew with others. Burckhardt's stance was cautious, deceptively mild. He doubted, he began, whether the appeal in the form in which it was drafted could in fact be considered an act of bravery. Reminding the meeting that part of the world was actually opposed to the 'ideas out of which the Red Cross was born', was it really so wise, he speculated, to make public statements at such uncertain times? Would work behind the scenes, a few judicious letters and messages perhaps, not ultimately prove more effective?

It was left to Philippe Etter to speak last. He spoke at far the greatest length and what he said was decisive. His statement was clever, shrewdly thought out. He had come, he seemed to be saying, not to bury Caesar, but to praise him. Etter began smoothly; he congratulated the Committee for their 'noble inspiration'. But then he wondered how anyone could judge the effect of a public appeal? Whether it could be made to look entirely impartial, in keeping with the Committee's long respected neutrality? What, he asked, would happen if one of the major powers decided to use the appeal as propaganda? Surely, the good Samaritan was a man who broke his silence only by his actions?

Chapuisat handled the meeting very adroitly. When all had spoken, he asked the members to vote. Was he right in thinking, he asked, that no one was in favour of a *public* appeal? There were now no dissenting voices. Was it everyone's wish that in 'certain grave situations' there should be a private, discreet approach made to an offending state? Everyone agreed. Huber, consulted at home, expressed his approval.

Only Mme Frick-Cramer, who had by now agreed in principle to abandon the idea of a public condemnation, demurred. Her tone of outrage comes across even through the dry minutes. The Red Cross might very easily disappear altogether, she said, during the current international turmoil. But it should not do so as a result of abandoning the very moral and spiritual values on which it had been founded. She asked that an immediate intervention – albeit private – be made on behalf of hostages and deportees. The minutes make clear that Chapuisat considered the discussion closed. If she wanted to say more Mme Frick-Cramer was perfectly free, he said, as all members were, to bring up any suggestion before the executive board.

And there the meeting ended. It was five o'clock, as planned. The members did not meet again for two months and the minutes for the next plenary session on 15 December record no reference to the October decision to keep silent. It was almost as if nothing had ever been said. Behind the scenes, the International Committee went on nagging, urging, reminding, trying to cajole the major powers into behaving towards civilians in accordance with the principles laid down by the Geneva Conventions, and trying in every way they could to devise means of getting inside the concentration camps. And for the rest of the war, they continued to organize the delivery of food and medical parcels to prisoners-of-war, to visit the camps in which they were held to inspect conditions, to trace missing soldiers, transmit messages between families, broker exchanges of wounded soldiers and hostages and to monitor the many articles of the Geneva Conventions which all the countries at war in 1942, except for Russia and Japan, had ratified. But they did not and would not condemn out loud Germany's mass murder of the Jews, gypsies, homosexuals, political opponents, religious leaders or the mentally ill in the countries its armies had occupied.

In December 1942, a public appeal to Germany was at last made by Roosevelt, Eden and Churchill.

Would it have made any difference if the International Committee had spoken out? Opinions differ but the consensus, more than fifty years after that October afternoon, suggests that nothing would have stopped or even slowed down the deportation of the Jews. However, it also seems highly unlikely that, *had* they spoken out, their work on behalf of prisoners-of-war would have been affected: the Germans needed their services and their parcels for German prisoners in Allied hands, just as much as the Allies needed them. And very few people today believe that

Germany would have invaded Switzerland whatever the stand taken by the International Committee.

That leaves the question of a moral stand. By the outbreak of the Second World War, the International Committee in Geneva had spun a definite aura of moral leadership. In matters of war, its voice counted. Max Huber was a deeply religious man of extreme probity. His views carried weight. What made these twenty-six men and women of the Committee important was that, in the absence of any official and public stand by the churches, and with the Allies resisting belief in what they had been told, there was no other body to take a clear moral view, indeed no other gathering of civilians in the world who knew more about what was going on in every theatre of the war, than this collection of middle-aged, middle-class Swiss. Even if there was nothing in their mandate to say they were responsible for civilians and internees in wartime and even if the Jews, classified as 'detained civilians' did not fall under the Geneva Conventions, their sense of moral revulsion was needed. The fact that they failed to express it has caused the organization great and lasting damage, both immediately after the war and in recent years when the deeds of the Holocaust have been repeatedly raised.

It may seem curious to dwell on the minutes of a single two-hour meeting that took place over half a century ago, but when the 130-year history of a remarkable organization is considered, there is no episode more important to its sense of itself than the decision taken that day. Much of the work done or not done in the seventy years before 1942 was, in some way, leading up to that decision, a gradual shaping and understanding of the International Committee's ultimate power and responsibility in matters of war and peace. Many of its subsequent decisions and stands can also be seen in the light of what those men and women voted to do that day.

It is impossible, in the 1990s, to talk to anyone about the International Committee without that meeting and that decision being raised. It was a true moment of reckoning. The Committee's failure to speak out, to take the high moral ground in a way that is seldom offered to any one individual or any one organization, has haunted it ever since.

ONE

Tutti Fratelli

The year 1859 opened on a Europe briefly at peace. Alexander II had been on the throne of Russia for four years, pushing through liberal reforms that were about to bring an end to serfdom. In Prussia, Prince Wilhelm, soon to be King Wilhelm I and German Kaiser, had taken over as regent from his ailing brother Friedrich Wilhelm IV the previous year, and Bismarck, already the most powerful man in the German confederation, was busy putting together a strong and efficient army. France was rich and its major industries were expanding rapidly; Austria, though enfeebled by a succession of revolts, was still hanging on in both Italy and Hungary. Britain remained the largest colonial and naval power in the world.

The trouble started in Italy. Piedmont, under the leadership of the revolutionary patriots Garibaldi and Cavour, had been in the grip of growing nationalist fervour and now sought to liberate northern Italy from the Austrians. British attempts to broker peace collapsed. On 29 April 1859, Austrian troops crossed the River Tessino, the border between the kingdom of Sardinia and Austrian Lombardy. They met little resistance.

Napoleon III of France believed that, by supporting the liberation of Lombardy and the Veneto, he could gain a valuable ally in a united Italy. On 3 May, he joined forces with the Italians and declared war on Austria. The first battles, at Montebello and Palestro, went to the Allies. The Austrians fell back towards Milan. The battle of Magenta was fought on 4 June, another victory to the French and Italians. The retreating Austrians fell back again, 115 kilometres in fifteen days.

On the evening of 23 June, the Allied commanders learnt that the Austrians were camped on the edge of the vast plain that stretches from Brescia to Mantua, near a village called Solferino, whose eleventh-century tower, known to the soldiers as 'Italy's spy', could be seen for many miles in every direction.

The order to attack came at dawn on 24 June. Three hundred thousand soldiers, the Austrians under their yellow and black flags emblazoned with the Imperial Eagle, the French to the sound of drums and bugles, faced each other across a sixteen-kilometre front. The men were, for the most part, exhausted by many days of forced marches, hungry, thirsty and hot in their thick uniforms. They had had very little to eat. The two armies were on the whole evenly matched; the Austrians had fewer men, but more horses and cannon. Both had emperors at their head; Napoleon III as commander-in-chief of the Allied forces and the twenty-eight-year-old Franz Joseph leading the Austrians. It would be the last major European battle directed by reigning monarchs.

All day long, while the heat and the sunshine lasted, the soldiers advanced and retreated across the plain and up and down the hills, pushing their way through the rows of vines that had been strung between mulberry trees, with dust kicked up by the squadrons of cavalry and shells from the artillery on the heights raining down on them. The tower of Solferino, taken, lost, retaken, became the symbol of victory. At 4 o'clock a storm blew up, and the exhausted soldiers were drenched by heavy rain. Squalls of wind carried dust into their faces. Hail followed, then thunder and lightning. Visibility became extremely poor but when it cleared towards nightfall, it was obvious that the Austrians were in flight. Napoleon sent a telegram to Empress Eugénie: 'Great battle! Great victory!'

Among the vines, in the ditches, under the mulberry trees and around the battlements of Solferino lay more than 6,000 bodies. Well over 30,000 soldiers, equally divided between the Austrians and the Allies, had been wounded. One man in every five who had joined battle that morning was now either dead or injured. The living were agonizingly thirsty. The heavy rain had turned the few dusty tracks that criss-crossed the plain into impassable rivers of mud. There was little question of moving the wounded from where they lay to the surrounding villages. In any case, the retreating Austrians had taken every cart and horse they could find.

All battlefields have visitors; some come to loot, others to stare, a few to help the wounded. On the evening of 24 June a young Genevan businessman in a light tropical suit arrived at Solferino; later, people would talk of him as the 'man in white'. Henri Jean Dunant was thirty-one, a pious, sentimental, serious, somewhat stout young man, but full of energy. He had never seen a battlefield before. 'The stillness of the night was broken by groans, by stifled sighs of anguish and suffering,' he would later write. 'Heart-rending voices kept calling for help. Who could ever describe the agonies of that fearful night!' To another visitor, the cries were like the 'endless, sad creaking of a door'.

Tactically, the battle of Solferino had not been markedly different from those of Magenta and Montebello. It stood apart by a particular combination of circumstances. Neither side expected to fight that day, having found themselves face to face by chance. There had been very little food or water for the soldiers; the heat had been so overwhelming that many had been forced to shed their thick, protective clothing; the few roads and paths, blocked by the storm, made outside help very difficult, and there was a desperate shortage of stretchers, ambulance wagons, orderlies and all kinds of medical equipment. The French forces had four vets for every thousand horses, but only one doctor for every thousand men, and a week before the battle one surgeon had reported that he had no instruments for amputations. 'When the sun came up on the 25th,' Dunant was to write later,

it disclosed the most dreadful sights imaginable. Bodies of men and horses covered the battlefield; corpses were strewn over roads, ditches, ravines, thickets and fields; the approaches to Solferino were literally thick with dead. The fields were devastated, wheat and corn lying flat on the ground, fences broken, orchards ruined; here and there were pools of blood . . . All around Solferino, and especially in the village cemetery, the ground was littered with guns, knapsacks, cartridge boxes, mess tins, helmets, shakoes, fatigue caps, bells, equipment of every kind, remnants of blood-stained clothing and piles of broken weapons.

The poor wounded men . . . were ghostly pale and exhausted. Some, who had been the most badly hurt, had a stupefied look . . . Others were anxious and excited by nervous strain and shaken by spasmodic trembling. Some, who had gaping wounds already beginning to show infection, were almost crazed with suffering. They begged to be put out of their misery; and writhed

with faces distorted in the grip of the death struggle . . . Many
were disfigured . . . their limbs stiffened, their bodies blotched
with ghastly spots, their hands clawing at the ground, their eyes
staring wildly, their moustaches bristling . . .

As it grew light, the villagers, who had been sheltering in their cellars
for the past twenty hours, crept out to find their houses torn apart by
shells and rockets. It took three days to bury the dead, in vast pits, as
more and more bodies came to light in trenches, hidden under uprooted
trees, or buried under piles of earth. In the June heat, the stench from
the dead – horses and men – was overwhelming.

But it was the living who most preoccupied Dunant. As he wandered
among the wounded soldiers, who kept calling out to him for water,
surrounded by muddy pools filled with blood, he began to realize how
very little attention anyone was paying them. There was no one to carry
them away, and nowhere to carry them to. What doctors and orderlies
had been found were already operating in the few buildings that still
afforded shelter. In the hours that followed, as very slowly the wounded,
who vastly outnumbered the local inhabitants, were carried to the villages to lie in churches, convents and in the open roads, Dunant set to
work. He gathered together a group of local women, organizing them
into teams to take food and water to the wounded; he set them to wash
the 'bleeding, vermin-covered bodies', so that their wounds could be
treated; he collected whatever fresh lint and linen he could find; he
directed small boys to fetch water in buckets, 'canteens and waterpots'
for the thirsty. On Monday 27 June he despatched his coachman to
Brescia, to buy lemons, camomile, sugar, shirts, consommé, sponges,
cigars, pins and tobacco. Making his base in the nearby vast neo-classical
Chiesa Maggiore of Castiglione, where 500 men were by now laid out
along the aisles with another hundred on the terrace outside, he pressed
into service a retired naval officer, four English tourists, '3 or 4 travellers',
a Parisian journalist, a young French count and a chocolate manufacturer
from Neuchâtel called Philippe Suchard. Soon, these people were dressing
wounds, fetching water, writing farewell letters to the families of dying
men. By now, the village of Castiglione had over 10,000 casualties, many
with multiple wounds from bullet, bayonet and sabre, some of them
still awaiting attention even four days after the battle. Such was the

exhaustion of the few surgeons that two fainted, and one was able to continue operating only if two soldiers held up his arms. Four million surgical dressings, which had been sent from France, were found after the war sealed in cases and intact.

Dunant was pleased to observe that following his lead all the helpers, as he put it, had quite forgotten the nationality of the men they tended; they were, as he put it, 'tutti fratelli', all brothers now. That same day, 27 June, Dunant found time to write a slightly self-regarding but eloquent letter, describing how he had seen, every fifteen minutes over the past three days, 'the soul of a man leave this world in the grip of unimaginable agony,' and send it to the Comtesse Valérie de Gasparin in Geneva, a woman known for her public-spiritedness and who had launched an appeal for funds and medical equipment at the time of the Crimean war six years earlier. The Countess was so moved by his account that she turned a précis of his words into a call for clothes, tobacco and medicines, which appeared in the *Journal de Genève* on 9 July. A rich Genevan called Adrien Naville and four theological students volunteered to serve, and donations poured in.

In Castiglione the chaos continued. Efforts to impose order were interrupted when a rumour spread that the Austrians were returning; in the ensuing panic, horses bolted, stretchers were overturned, the wounded crushed. 'Oh the agony and suffering of those days,' Dunant would write.

> Wounds were infected by the heat and dust, by shortage of water and lack of proper care . . . The convoys brought a fresh contingent of wounded men into Castiglione every quarter of an hour, and the shortage of assistants, orderlies and helpers was cruelly felt . . . With faces black with the flies that swarmed around their wounds, men gazed around them, wild-eyed and helpless. Others were no more than a worm-ridden, inextricable compound of coal and shirt and flesh and blood.

Beyond the application of camomile, water and the donation of cigars, there was often very little to be done. In the middle of the nineteenth century, nothing was understood about the nature of germs and anti-septics. And though ether and chloroform had both been discovered, they were virtually unknown outside the main civilian hospitals. Surgery after a battle mostly came down to two very simple questions: whether or not to amputate, and how soon to do so.

On his rounds, Dunant came across a twenty-year-old corporal, Claudius Mazuet. The young man had a bullet lodged in his left side and understood perfectly that he was about to die. Dunant was to describe this scene with some care: 'When I had helped him to drink, he thanked me, and added with tears in his eyes: "Oh sir, if you could write to my father to comfort my mother!" I noted his parents' address, and a moment later he had ceased to live.' Some months went by before Dunant was able to trace them in Lyon, where he learnt that the young corporal had been their only son. 'The only news they received of him,' he recorded, 'was that which I gave them.' This gesture of Dunant's would prove important in the years to come.

By the evening of the 27th, Dunant had had enough. 'Worn out with fatigue, and unable to sleep a wink', he called his coachman and set off at 6 o'clock to 'breathe the fresh evening air in the open.' By 9 pm he was in the village of Cavriana, where Napoleon III had slept after his victory, occupying the bed that Franz Joseph had vacated that morning. That night, Dunant slept for a few hours at Borghetto, another village in the plain, returning next morning to Cavriana and then to Castiglione. By now, those whose limbs had been amputated too late were dead of gangrene. The survivors were being ferried by ox cart and a few private carriages to nearby towns, where private houses had been turned into temporary hospitals, and whose inhabitants had volunteered to help with the nursing. By 30 June, Dunant was in Brescia, where he distributed more tobacco and wrote letters to the families of the wounded men.

In later life, Dunant went to some lengths to muddy the record of his exact movements during the aftermath of battle of Solferino. Neither the timing nor the intent had been altogether as he would have wished them, even if he was to write a little defiantly in his memoirs many years later, 'Certainly, I was a tourist, but a tourist much concerned with questions about humanity.' For Dunant had come to Solferino not as a concerned citizen to help wounded soldiers, but as the president of an ailing industrial enterprise in search of Napoleon III who, he felt, could alone salvage what was left of his scheme to turn a stretch of

North Africa into a bread basket for Europe. That spring, the lack of water for his corn at Mons-Djémila in Algeria and his need for backing had become desperate and only powerful sponsors could now save him from ruin. Dunant had been told that the Emperor was to be found near the battlefield and there, in his white suit, he had gone to seek him bearing a handsomely printed book he had written called *The Empire of Charlemagne Restored*, a homage to the Emperor in which he described Napoleon III as the successor to Romulus and a 'new Cyrus'. Dunant came with good recommendations from well-placed French military men. Distracted for a while by a genuine sense of shock and pity at Solferino, he pressed on afterwards to Castiglione, Cavriana and Borghetta in pursuit of the Emperor, and though he had failed to obtain an audience he was able to leave with assurances from Charles Robert, Napoleon's civil attaché, that his book would be delivered. He also took the opportunity to tell the French Marshal MacMahon – made Duke of Magenta for his role in the campaign – of the terrible condition of the wounded and to obtain from the French promises that the captured Austrian doctors would be allowed to help their overwhelmed French colleagues.

Peace was settled rapidly between the Austrians and the Allies. The French were now being threatened by the Prussians on their exposed northern and eastern flanks and in any case the soldiers were exhausted by two months' campaigning in great heat. Both emperors expressed horror at the number of dead and the agony of the wounded. By the terms of the Armistice, drawn up in a school playground at Villafranca on 11 July, Franz Joseph accepted the loss of Lombardy and an end to Austrian hegemony in northern Italy, while Napoleon III agreed not to press on into the Veneto.

By this time, Dunant was back in Geneva attending to his muddled affairs. A note from Charles Robert informed him that Napoleon III did not wish to see the book dedicated to him, and his application for a concession for a second waterfall to irrigate his parched corn at Mons-Djémila was turned down. The livestock he had bought were dying of thirst. But because what he had seen had truly appalled him, and he continued to be haunted by the dying soldiers for whom so little had been done, he sat down in 1861, once his business had collapsed, to write about the battle of Solferino. Dunant was an inspired reporter and he held nothing back. His descriptions are vivid and memorable. Much of his book was an account of the horrors he had witnessed, the 'sheer butchery', the 'crushing of skulls, ripping bellies open with sabre and bayonet', the terrors of the dying, the moans of the wounded, amputations without anaesthetic, the dying words of countless brave men, the selflessness of his team of Lombardy women. But he also used his book to put into words the questions that had come to obsess him. The last few pages contain, almost in its entirety, an idea that was soon to sweep the capitals of Europe. Why, asked Dunant, could societies of volunteers not be set up in peacetime to be ready to help the wounded when wars broke out? And why not at the same time draw up 'some international principles, conventional and sacred, which once agreed and ratified would form the basis for these national societies to help the wounded in different countries of Europe?'

A Memory of Solferino was finished in October 1862. In his memoirs many years later Dunant would say that, while at work on his book, 'I was as it were lifted out of myself, dominated by a superior power, and inspired by the breath of God.' He oversaw the drawing of a map of the battle formations, then sent the manuscript to be printed at his own expense by Jules-Guillaume Fick, who charged him 2,407.50 francs, of which 256.50 were for the 342 hours he had spent on the numerous 'author's corrections'. The 1,600 copies he ordered, destined at first mainly for friends and acquaintances, were not for sale. But when favourable responses began to come in, he sent his remaining copies off to publishers in Paris, Turin, St Petersburg and Leipzig, asking them to be distributed first to the protagonists of Solferino then, as he grew bolder, to princes, ministers of war, generals and kings.

Dunant's instinct that his book was both shocking and timely was right. A Memory of Solferino was greeted everywhere with admiration, horror and guilt. People had written of battles before, of course, but not with such a sense of indignation and revulsion. Speeches were delivered, lectures given; from their pulpits, priests spoke of Dunant as a man whose name deserved to enter history. In France and Germany, throughout Holland and Prussia, Dunant was referred to as a poet, a philosopher, a literary genius, a man de coeur, of vision, of inspiration, of initiative. Generals, doctors, writers and statesmen all wrote to congratulate him. 'You have created the greatest work of the century,' wrote Ernest Renan, the French historian and writer, 'Europe maybe will stand in dire need of it.' Victor Hugo told him that he had performed a great deed for humanity. The Imperial Medical Society of the Caucasus – among many others – welcomed him as a new member. 'These pages are sublime,' announced the Goncourt brothers. 'It is better – a thousand times better – than Homer . . . After this book, the reader curses war.' And if a few recipients foolishly wrote before reading what Dunant had written – a banker called Etienne Rivoire assured him that the first pages 'provide a charming recreation for country evenings' – far more took Comtesse de Gasparin's line. She had wept, she said, while she read; Dunant's devotion to God had lit up 'the most sombre pages with a serene glow'.

And throughout the courts of Europe, the royal families were full of admiration. Dunant's first royal blessing came from the Queen Mother of the Netherlands, who praised him for a work so 'eminently philan-thropic and Christian'. After this came messages from Victor Emmanuel II of Italy, Franz Joseph of Austria, the Queen of Prussia, the King of Württemberg, and Queen Isabella of Spain. Dunant's book was indeed, as the *Journal de Genève* put it in February 1863 after the publication of a third edition, 'a great and beautiful idea'. That same month, Saint-Marc Girardin recounted Dunant's story in the prestigious *Journal des Débats*, read widely throughout European society; and his fame was assured.

When the contributor to *Baedeker* arrived in Geneva in the 1860s on one of his periodic tours of inspection, he was not altogether impressed. True, there were fine tree-lined quays along the lake front, a Jardin Anglais had just been opened, the gilded domes of the new Russian church, put up with contributions from the Russian imperial family, gleamed brightly over the town, and the old buildings and steep, crooked streets were being knocked down – in the approved Haussmann manner – to make way for imposing neo-classical hotels and specialized streets, one for bankers, another for lawyers. But anything of any note, the inspector observed in a somewhat disapproving tone, could easily be seen in less than a day. And though Geneva possessed what were reputed to be the best hotels in the world, the local wine served in them was a 'source of such vexation' that travellers were urged to sample more expensive vineyards. Better, said *Baedeker*, to pause only briefly in the city, glancing at the romanesque cathedral of St Pierre and at the Hôtel de Ville, built in the 'Florentine style', before setting off to walk in the mountains with a guide, though he conceded that a trip on one of the new steamboats along the lake provided excellent views of the well-to-do villas with their gardens leading down to the water. At Ferney, just over the border in France, omnibus passengers were advised to look up at Voltaire's villa and the church he had built with its impudent inscription – *Deo Execit Voltaire* – though here *Baedeker* became stern. Voltaire had been, the guide noted, a man 'whose stupendous talents exercised so great, though injurious, an influence over the age in which he lived'. Only the lake of Geneva itself came in for unreserved praise, with its water a unique shade of blue – ascribed by the British scientist Sir Humphry Davy to iodine, a speculation much contested by Swiss natural-ists – its twenty-one different species of fish, many of them delicious to eat, and the woods of sweet and wild chestnut, walnut and magnolia, vines and cedars of Lebanon, which covered its shores.

At the time Dunant settled down to write *A Memory of Solferino* the city of Calvin and Jean-Jacques Rousseau was expanding at great speed, though a quarter of its 60,000 or so inhabitants were 'aliens', as foreigners were known, many of them descended from families who had settled there when Geneva was one of the few cities to welcome free-thinkers and revolutionaries. Though it had never quite lost the stamp of Calvin's austere regime, Geneva in 1860 was a curious mixture of piety and fermenting social ideas. Home to Pastor Louis Gaussen of the fashionable *Reveil* movement, who preached according to the teachings of the Scottish evangelist Robert Haldane interpreting history in the light of scriptural prophecy, it remained both curiously ignorant of current intellectual movements in other parts of Europe and resolutely open to social reform. A strong spirit of humanitarianism was taking root among people who regarded themselves as enlightened conservatives. Pacifism, the abolition of slavery, the freeing of serfs, were all topics much discussed in the salons along the lake and in the old city, and much reported in the *Journal des Débats*. The city's many philanthropic institutions, orphanages, hospices, homes for former prisoners and refuges for repentant prosti-tutes were to quadruple from forty-five to over 200 during the nineteenth century. Dominated by an aristocracy of families dating back to the fifteenth and sixteenth centuries, a scholarly élite who took pride in the city's achievements in philosophy and theology, and particularly in the natural sciences, Geneva was prosperous, serious, hard-working and for the most part piously Christian. As were most of the towns in this mountainous landlocked country which acted as guardian to Europe's natural trans-Alpine routes. Switzerland's constitution, like its position, would prove crucial in the story of Dunant's dream. About half the size of Scotland, the Swiss Confederation of twenty-two cantons and almost 3,000 communes was traditionally neutral, its absolute neutrality sanctioned by the Treaty of Westphalia in 1648 and confirmed by the Treaty of Vienna in 1815, since when its borders had remained stable and its laws of asylum welcoming for people at times of unrest.

Dunant belonged to one of Geneva's prosperous old families. His father was Jean-Jacques Dunant, rising merchant, superintendent of an orphanage and supervisor of prisons. His mother, Anne-Antoinette, was the daughter of Henri Colladon, a city councillor and mayor of Avully in the Rhône valley. Jean-Henri, as he was christened, although he was always known as Henri, was sent at the age of ten to Geneva's most prestigious school, the Collège de Genève, founded by Calvin. He started well, but by the age of fourteen was so far behind in his studies that it was judged more sensible to move him to live with a pastor, whose wife was a teacher, before sending him as apprentice to the banking house of Lullin et Sautter. About his schooling Dunant was later to say that he did not care for boisterous games, but preferred to read books that transported his imagination to distant adventures. 'He kept a diary,' he was to write in his memoirs, referring to himself in the third person, 'which was remarkable, and demonstrated his early literary talents'. Not that he ever said very much about his childhood, beyond painting a lyrical picture of his many visits to his grandparents' house at Avully where they bred pigs and cows, kept poultry, and where wonderful picnics were had, with many strawberries and wild berries. 'At the age of ten,' he once said, 'I was a little aristocrat, and entirely respectful of aristocracy.'

The Dunants' own house was called La Monnaie in Petit Saconnex on the outskirts of Geneva, with views over the lake and to Mont Blanc, and cannot have been altogether disagreeable. Jean-Jacques loved rare trees and planted a great many in his garden, along with conifers and fruit trees of every variety, especially plums. From time to time Anne-

Antoinette would invite the girls from the orphanage to spend a 'few happy hours among its flowers and shrubs', under the supervision of their headmistress. From the windows of La Monnaie, the young Dunant could see the coach set out for Lausanne, laden down with cases, and hear the distant sound of the coachman's horn. Other children were born, two brothers and two sisters. At the age of eight, Dunant was taken by his father to inspect a number of Swiss prisoners held in Toulon in France, and well into old age he would describe his sense of horror at seeing the men shackled to one another as they broke up stones in the road. From childhood he had 'experienced a keen compassion for the unhappy, the humble, the weak and the oppressed,' he wrote later.

What Dunant lacked in scholarliness, he made up for in piety. The *Reveil* movement, urgent and prophetic, with its mission to revive the faith and the true spirit of the early church, was made for him. He loved the well-attended services at the new oratory in the rue Tabazon. By the time he was nineteen he was an enthusiastic member of what was shortly to become the Christian Association of Geneva, a group of young men in their late teens and early twenties who met every Thursday evening at the Evangelical Society to discuss the divine inspiration of the Holy Scriptures, or tramped the hills above the city repeating the teachings of Pastor Gaussen. The language of their conversation and their writings was eager, even fervent. By 1851, Dunant was on the committee of the Evangelical Alliance, a movement of Christians who preached religious commitment and tolerance. Soon, he was in touch with other Christian Associations in other countries, travelling to meet their members, and working towards the first World Conference that took place in Paris in 1855. Not surprising, then, to find him a keen admirer of Harriet Beecher Stowe, whose *Uncle Tom's Cabin* had made her world famous by the time he met her during her visit to Geneva in 1853. Dunant was by now the author of a first book, *Notes on the Regency of Tunisia*, a passionate attack on the American slave trade, full of colourful accounts of slave auctions and manhunts, culled from newspapers from the American South, interspersed with serious, somewhat plodding facts about the geography and ethnology of North Africa.

Though Dunant willingly gave his Sundays to reading travel stories to the prisoners in Geneva's gaol, he was not only serious-minded. He went to the occasional ball or reception, as he reported in the few letters to his grandparents that survive, and he evidently enjoyed picnics. Photographs of him in his early twenties show a well-dressed young man, with hair cut short and a small moustache; his face is open, agreeable, almost childlike, but not altogether joyful. He has the look of a mild schoolmaster.

In 1853, Dunant accepted an offer to replace Baron de Gingins-la-Sarraz as head of the Compagnie Genèvoise des Colonnes de Sétif in Algeria, which was associated with the banking firm of Lullin et Sauter and had received from the French government, by imperial decree, a concession of 50,000 acres with which to promote colonization. He left for North Africa at once. Reports reaching home soon suggested that he could be a little hasty in his judgements, making decisions based on little more than enthusiasm, a feeling echoed by one of his friends in the Christian Association, Max Perrot who, writing to his brother in Paris, commented: 'What a pity he has no judgement. With judgement he would be pure gold. His energy and zeal are astonishing.' Though Dunant kept up his missionary fervour, distributing copies of the Bible in Arabic on his travels, he was quickly entranced by the spectacle of North Africa, by this apparently pagan and primitive land, and as quickly seduced by the fortunes visibly being made around him. A first venture of his own, the purchase of a load of timber which he sold on at satisfactory profit, produced congratulations from Geneva. Dunant now fell in with a young man from Württemberg called Henri Nick. Nick was married to a niece of a rich Parisian banking family, the Lauronts, and was making his way in Sétif as a corn dealer and land agent. Eager to repeat his timber success, Dunant proposed to his employers that they lease him part of their concession; he intended to grow corn and build a mill. While they deliberated, he began to raise money in Geneva, extravagantly promising fortunes in shares, and although capital was forthcoming, the trust of his employers was not. In 1856, the Compagnie Genèvoise terminated his contract.

One of the people to whom Dunant had sent an early copy of *A Memory of Solferino* was General Guillaume Henri Dufour, hero of the Sønderbond when the secessionist Catholic cantons were defeated in 1847 and a man widely admired throughout Switzerland as military strategist, writer, politician and engineer. He was also a humane and thoughtful man, instructing his men before the battle:

> If a body of enemy troops is repulsed, give to the wounded the same care as you would give to your own men; treat them with all the forbearance due to one who is stricken ... After the battle, restrain the fury of your troops; spare the vanquished ... People should say of you: they fought courageously when they had to, but remained generous and humane throughout.

Dufour was now seventy-six, a scholarly, independent-minded figure with a somewhat pointed face and pleasingly mischievous eyes, known as a staunch supporter of asylum in Switzerland for political refugees, providing they renounce all political activities. In the years since the Sønderbund, he had overseen the building of the new Pont des Bergues in the middle of Geneva, brought gas lighting to the city, launched steamboats on the lake and drawn up a map of Switzerland. He was an expert on trains and a fervent Bonapartist, Louis-Napoleon having been his pupil at military college, and from a young age had been convinced that neutrality was the only possible position for Switzerland, but that to have its neutrality respected it needed a strong army. Dunant and Dufour were acquaintances from meetings of the Geographical Society to which both belonged and Dufour had evidently thought well enough of the younger man to write a letter of recommendation for him over the ill-fated Mons-Djemila project.

On receiving *A Memory of Solferino*, Dufour was impressed. On 19 October 1862, he sent Dunant a friendly note. 'It is most important that people read accounts like yours so that they can see what the glory of the battlefield costs in terms of pain and tears. We are all too ready to see only the brilliant side of war, and to shut our eyes to its sad consequences.' Dunant, enchanted by the support of so eminent a figure, hastened to Fick and had the General's words of praise printed as an afterword to his memoir. He did not, however, include the entire letter. For while agreeing with Dunant's overall idea that volunteers should and could be recruited to help the wounded at times of war, Dufour very much doubted that any such corps could be made permanent. 'You need a crisis,' his letter had gone on to say, 'to spark off such devotion.'

More importantly for future developments was the interest taken in

Dunant's words by a lawyer and philanthropist called Gustave Moynier. Descended from Geneva shoemakers, merchants and bankers and author of a life of the apostle Paul, Moynier was thirty-seven, two years older than Dunant; the two had met at receptions in their youth. He was austere, driven and possessed of considerable self-importance; he was to have a determining effect not just on Dunant's personal future but on the future of his ideas. A stocky figure, with a large moustache that wound around his chin and cheeks and a fixed stare, Moynier was seldom seen to laugh. He could be touchy and jealous, and expressed extreme dislike for those he branded mere 'humanitarian dreamers' and 'philan-thropic dilettantes'. But he was dogged, and in 1863 he was in search of a cause. In a rare and touching passage of self-revelation written many years later, he said that his legal studies in Geneva and Paris had left him with a narrow lawyer's mind devoid of all originality, extremely shy, and prone to doubt everything except the infallibility of the law. He had long been involved with Geneva's philanthropic institutions − his forty different interests ranged from prison to alcoholism and orphans − and he was currently president of the Geneva Society for Public Welfare, a private institution concerned with social reform, where his talents as an organizer had won him much admiration. In his writing, as in all else, he was precise, brief and cool. But he had no appetite for litigation, much preferring analysis and statistics and this, together with his failure to make an impact with a thesis on Roman law, had driven him away from the bar.

A few days after receiving his copy of *A Memory of Solferino*, Moynier went to call on Dunant. He carried with him an invitation to discuss his ideas before the next meeting of the Public Welfare Society, a place in which Geneva's philanthropic and utilitarian spirit found true expression. (Many of its 180 members had read Alexis de Tocqueville's *Democracy in America* and been educated in Paris and Heidelberg, and all shared a belief that it was possible, with sufficient hard work and Christian commitment, to improve education, reduce poverty and 'reclaim' erring citizens from alcoholism and prostitution.) Present would be General Dufour, a former president of the society, and another acquaintance of Dunant's, a forty-five-year-old doctor called Louis Appia, a taciturn and brooding man fascinated since his earliest days with medical surgery and war wounds. Appia, like Dunant, had visited the battlefields in Lombardy, but he had gone there to see for himself the terrible injuries caused by the new dum-dum bullets, and stayed on to attend the wounded, before returning to Geneva to write a paper on the treatment of fractures and talk about his belief that the physical healing of injured soldiers was influenced by their morale. Like Dunant, Appia had left the battlefield appalled at the inadequacy of the medical services and he too had appealed in Geneva for supplies. Like Dunant, Appia was pious and philanthropic but he was also wealthy, having married a rich wife.

The meeting of the Public Welfare Society on 9 February 1863 was held as usual on the ground floor of the Casino de Saint-Pierre, one of Geneva's cultural centres and home to many charitable societies. The agenda included one item on a popular new edition of French classics and another on the founding of an agricultural colony for delinquent children. In between came a proposal to discuss the provision of a 'corps of volunteer nurses for armies at war (conclusion of M. Henri Dunant's book, entitled *A Memory of Solferino*)'. Of the 160 or so members of the society, fourteen attended that day. After reading extracts from Dunant's book, Moynier suggested that the idea should be submitted to the International Charity Congress, due to take place in Berlin in October. Dunant sketched out his plans. What he had in mind, he told his audience, was not simply sending volunteer nurses to the battlefield, but the improvement of methods of transporting the wounded, as well as the care of soldiers in hospital. What was more, he dreamed of having a permanent committee, if possible under the patronage of Europe's crowned heads, working to make it easier to despatch relief in wartime without customs duties, a committee that would also be able to draw up a covenant, signed by all civilized powers, which would agree to adhere to some basic code of behaviour in wartime.

No one that February afternoon seemed particularly enthusiastic, though Dr Théodore Maunoir, a friend of Appia's and something of a mentor to him in Geneva's medical world, did comment that he had long felt the ambulance services to be defective. Descended from a family of doctors, Maunoir was neither an orator nor a writer but he had a quick, often caustic wit and he worked extremely hard. Unlike the others, he had never had any private money and there was mystery in his past: he had married the widow of a writer called Paul-Louis Commer, who had been murdered in unexplained circumstances for which his wife had been arrested, charged with the crime, then exonerated.

The meeting adjourned with an agreement that a working party be set up to investigate Dunant's idea further.

Moynier, at least, was intrigued. On 17 February the five designated working-party members — Moynier, Dunant, Dufour, Appia and Maunoir — met again. This time they decided to turn themselves into an International Committee for Relief to the Wounded, of which Dufour was to be president, Moynier vice-president and Dunant secretary. The background of the group was crucial. All five men belonged to Geneva's oldest, most prosperous families, active over many generations in the law, medicine, the army and politics, and three of them — Dufour, Moynier and Appia — were rich enough not to have to work. All were Protestant and practising Christians and shared Dunant's feelings about the ethics of war, 'the moral sense of the importance of human life, the humane desire to lighten a little the torments' of the wounded.

The five men had long been supporters, to a greater or lesser extent, of the conservative Council representing the cantons — Dunant's father and grandfather had both been members — and were out of sympathy with the radical new politics of Jean James Fazy, an ardent follower of Jean-Jacques Rousseau, and his call for a new constitution and elected government. They felt distanced from power, their political exile making their need and desire for a role all the greater. And though between them they spanned three generations, from Dufour at seventy-six to Dunant at thirty-five, they knew each other socially, having met in church, at social gatherings and at meetings. All would prove susceptible to flattery, with a definite taste for medals, decorations and honours. But while similar in background and outlook, they were very different in character. Moynier was cautious, shrewd and a superb organizer, an admirer of the Old Testament prophets and fascinated by St Paul, Dunant was impetuous and imprudent, Maunoir humorous and retiring and Appia gloomy, a little truculent and reputed to be a ladies' man. Over them presided the sensible and good-tempered General Dufour.

During the spring and early summer of 1863, the committee made rapid progress. Dufour's experience, as well as his innate generosity of spirit, coloured many of their deliberations. The fact that he had himself once been wounded and captured while fighting for France against the British, and then returned to France in a prisoner-of-war exchange, made his remarks all the more pertinent. Dufour, who had by now swung round to Dunant's idea of a permanent corps of voluntary helpers, proposed some kind of badge, uniform or armlet to distinguish the band of auxiliaries. Maunoir, asked to formulate specific proposals, outlined the idea of a corps of male nurses subject to the military authorities but not paid by them, to remain at the ready to help, but who would 'cause no embarrassment, create no hindrance'. Borrowing what he believed to be an English phrase, he suggested that the Committee should 'get up an agitation', in order to gain the support of 'the rulers of Europe as well as the masses'.

When, at their third meeting in August, news came that the Berlin Charities Conference had been cancelled, it was Moynier who suggested calling a conference of their own in October, asking states to send delegates to Geneva to consider this question of volunteer relief societies, and Dunant who proposed a tour of European capitals to drum up support among the military and the royal princes. Dunant had been further inspired by a letter from a Dutch military doctor called S. H. C. Basting, who had been so taken by *A Memory of Solferino* that he had already translated it into Dutch and now longed to meet its author. 'I really believe that in this cause you are carrying out God's work,' he had written to Dunant on 3 March, suggesting that they attend a second Berlin conference together, this time of statisticians, but relevant in that one session was to be devoted to the health and illness statistics among civilians and the military. Could they not meet in Berlin first?

The two men met at the Hotel Töpfer in Berlin early in September. Fired by each other's ideas, they talked far into the night about the necessity of removing casualties as fast as possible from the battlefield and of carrying out operations rapidly. But how were doctors and medical personnel, wearing the uniforms of their regiments and thus indistinguishable from fighting men, to be protected from attack? Their exact conversation is not recorded, but it seems that it was Dunant who now had one of those sudden and elusive ideas that in retelling seem so obvious. Why, he asked, should medical personnel not be made neutral? Why not get states to agree to return all doctors and nurses to their own armies after patching up the wounded, so that they could continue their work? The remainder of the night was spent drafting their speech for the statistical conference, in which they proposed a status of neutrality for all medical personnel and, when they delivered the speech the following day, their ideas for neutrality and for a voluntary corps of helpers were greeted with approval. After the meeting, with characteristic impetuousness, Dunant wrote a supplement on neutrality to add to the International Committee's original proposals, and sent it off to everyone who had been invited to the October meeting in Geneva.

Dunant's next few weeks were frantically busy. Using money borrowed from friends, and hiring secretaries to help him, he hurried from one European capital to another. Having canvassed the German minister for war, Albrecht von Roon, in Berlin, and won his approval, he moved on to Vienna to see the Archduke Rainer, head of the permanent imperial council, who told him his idea was 'magnificent', and to Munich, to persuade General Frankh, the Bavarian minister of war, to support him. Of all his royal audiences, he would retain the most pleasant memories of his meeting with the King of Saxony in Dresden who, as he rose to go, announced gravely: 'A nation which did not join this work of humanity would fall to the bottom of European public opinion.' Dunant returned home with a list of 'august protectors'.

Back in Geneva only a few days before the October meeting, he was momentarily troubled over his failure to consult his partners about the idea of neutrality. He asked Moynier for his opinion. Moynier's answer has been quoted often. 'We thought,' he is said to have replied, in a dry and somewhat chilly tone, 'that you were asking the impossible.' Dufour said nothing.

Their caution turned out to be misplaced. Europe's ministers of war had already expressed a desire to limit the evils of war in the Treaty of Paris of 1856, and shown sympathy for the idea of arbitration. They were now equally taken by Dunant's dream, bold as it was. They were being asked to endorse a proposal quite unlike any that had come their way before and agree to a covenant that rose above the right of nations to make war. There was nothing pacifist about these men; on the contrary, they all represented essentially war-loving nations. But Dunant had been right. Militaristic they might be, but in a particular way. Like Dufour, they wanted 'civilized' and 'humane' war, which could be invoked or set aside as a political instrument.

*   *   *

The day fixed for the meeting in Geneva — 23 October 1863 — dawned without anyone being entirely certain who would attend or what line they would take. In his memoirs, Moynier would describe the Committee's mood as one of apprehension and misgiving. Whether Dunant shared these feelings seems unlikely, though he was a timid, uncertain figure when faced with large gatherings. Mme Eynard-Lullin, a rich widow known in charitable circles as 'la belle Eynard', had offered them a salon in l'Athénée, a pretty new house built with a Renaissance façade near the botanical gardens, where she planned to put on exhibitions and open a library. The Committee need not have been so fearful. Sixteen states had sent delegates, and there were four more from Europe's main philanthropic institutions. Prince Heinrich XIII of Reuss, representing the Order of St John of Jerusalem, accepted the role of vice-president. Dufour, in black coat and wearing his rosette from the Légion d'Honneur, took the president's chair.

Moynier, who did this sort of thing very well, opened the first day with an outline of their proposals. They wanted, he told his audience, to create a committee in every European capital which would ensure that in the event of a war the services of a volunteer corps would be accepted by the armies; a corps which would follow the soldiers, close enough to bring instant help but not so close as to get in the way of their manoeuvres; a corps wearing some kind of distinctive uniform or badge which would distinguish them from the fighting men. After Moynier, Dunant read out some of the letters the International Committee had received from kings, military men and doctors, expressing interest in the deliberations. The kings of Belgium, Denmark and Portugal wrote to say that they would support the Committee, while Prince Demidoff, chamberlain to the Russian emperor, proposed that prisoners-of-war, 'taken into exile far from their homelands', be included in their discussions.

For the next four days the mood of the meeting swung backwards and forwards. There were moments when it seemed most likely that the venture would founder. Dr Rutherford, deputy inspector of hospitals, sent by the British government, dismissed the whole idea as unnecessary, proposing instead that other countries reorganize their medical military services, as the British army was in the process of doing. The French deputy intendent, Préval, said that he believed that mules would be far more useful than volunteers, in that they did not need so much food and care. However, the Spanish delegate, Dr Landa, spoke up about the 'disproportion between the development of the means of protection and the means of destruction' and described his own revulsion when having to mend the damage caused by the lethal dum-dum bullets, and the mood of the gathering turned more generous. Moynier, perhaps paying Dunant back for his cavalier behaviour in Berlin, now went to some lengths to leave the entire issue of neutrality to one side. Basting, who like Moynier was skilled at handling meetings, did not hide his irritation. The plan to make doctors and nurses neutral was deftly introduced and unanimously adopted, as was an idea proposed by Appia that the volunteers wear a white band around one arm, with a distinctive red cross in the middle. On Basting's urging, the full congress rose to honour Dunant who had earned, as he put it, 'the incontestable right to universal thanks'.

At the end of the four days, when the social gatherings were all over and the delegates had returned to their sixteen respective countries by train, the five men were able to conclude that it had all gone extremely well. Ten articles, endorsing almost all their ideas, had been adopted. They included the setting up of committees to assist the army medical services, which would spend the years of peace preparing for those of war; the sending of 'voluntary medical personnel' to the battlefield; the wearing of white armbands with a red cross by medical people and volunteers, and occasional meetings of committees to 'communicate the results of their experience'. These voluntary bodies would assist – this was made clear – but not displace the army medical authorities; and the International Committee in Geneva would act merely as a link between them.

A new movement had been born, in private, among private people and in a small, apparently powerless country, which would soon catch fire among the European rulers before spreading, country by country, throughout the world. Though the Red Cross would eventually spawn national societies and a federation to oversee them, draw in many millions of members and every kind of new activity, the International Committee in Geneva would remain faithful to Dunant and his dream, the keeper of a humanitarian code of conduct. Dunant's idea, greatly helped by the good fortune of right timing, was in tune with the pietist and utilitarian currents of the day, but also coincided with the interests of the states most likely to go to war. It was humane but it was not subversively pacifist. As Appia put it:

> To humanize war, if that is not a contradiction, is our mission
> ... But once we have voiced our undisguised rejection of war,
> we must take it as it is, unite our efforts to alienate suffering ...

It would have been hard to disagree.

Dufour evidently left the gathering with some doubts, expressed in a letter to a friend. The ideas were all good, he said, but could they be achieved? For now had to be found 'men of good will to set up these societies, who are going to need a great deal of money ...' Dunant, too, was uncertain, as he confessed many years later in his memoirs. Nothing, he felt, was going to be at all easy. This was a strange new idea and the public, faced with such a proposal, was unlikely to be anything other than 'sceptical, lazy, denigrating, jealous ... and prejudiced'.

TWO

Inhumanity Under Another Name

All their lives, Dunant and Moynier would insist that they knew very little of what was being said elsewhere when they came to draft their humanitarian proposals. Their protests were plausible for such ignorance was in keeping with the insular spirit of Geneva's philanthropists. It is clear, however, that similar ideas were on the brink of explosion in many other parts of the world, and could as easily have surfaced elsewhere. A terrible battle, a dreamer who was also an inspired reporter, a canny and efficient organizer and, in the air, a wind of change – together, these triggered a movement that others, working alone, had not managed to bring about. It was not surprising then that long before the delegates met in Geneva in October 1863 there was talk of theft of the ideas of others.

Though the Geneva proposals came to be seen as the first codified humanitarian principles, the laws of war had a long and honourable history, with their implication that an adversary was entitled to a certain respect, as did the medical treatment of enemy wounded, the protection of prisoners-of-war and army medical services. In the fourth century Saint Augustine of Hippo (354–430 AD) argued that war is a crime if it is waged 'with a malicious intent to destroy, a desire to dominate, with fierce hatred and furious vengeance'. On the other hand, it becomes a duty if fought in a 'just cause', with the intention of turning wrong into right and 'dissension into peace'. Throughout the Middle Ages, and particularly during the wars of religion, the 'soldiers of Christ', as Saint Bernard preached in the twelfth century, were afraid 'neither of doing wrong by killing the enemy nor of running any risk if they perish: for killing or being killed in the name of Christ is by no means a crime.' As for the enemy wounded, it was customary to kill them, unless they were likely to fetch a high ransom. Even so, rival generals could be generous: during the siege of Orleans in 1429 the Earl of Suffolk sent the French commander Dunois a present of figs, dates and raisins, receiving in return some fur trimming for his cloak.

In the sixteenth century, the distinguished Spaniard Francisco de Vittoria, adviser to Charles V, pointed out that as war could in fact be seen as 'just' by both sides, it was right to temper the demands of absolute justice by conceding that an 'infidel' was owed respect for his belief in his own cause. A 'law of nations' was emerging, in which many 'customs and habits of war' would be accepted. One of de Vittoria's followers, Francisco de Suarez, in his work *De Legibus ac Deo Legislatore*, went further, spelling out the difference between 'natural law' based on the Book of Revelations and the salvation of souls, and a 'law of nations', which he described as a 'human law and a positive law'. Peace treaties, he argued, should fall under the law of nations because 'it is the custom and the general consensus of States that have confirmed them'.

With the Reformation came a further split between the temporal and the spiritual. As Luther put it in his letter to the German princes of 1520: 'Let the Pope pray and leave the business of governing kingdoms to the Princes.' The day was coming when sovereignty would provide a justification for all kinds of war, just or unjust. With Hugo Grotius, the seventeenth-century Dutch Protestant jurist and theologian, the notion of war itself appeared to have come full circle, for Grotius believed that the law did not precede action, but was derived from it. 'Everything,' he wrote, 'which serves the cause of war is permitted.' All people on the opposing side were enemies, whether the old, children or the sick – as were all soldiers, whether able-bodied or wounded.

War, however, was gradually becoming a more humane affair, in which armies and soldiers, and not entire countries, went to war. As early as the beginning of the eighteenth century, a distinction began to be made by the French between soldiers and civilians; men such as chaplains and surgeons, for example, were spared when captured on the battlefield. There began to be talk of evacuating wounded prisoners, and of striking agreements as to their fate not after but before war broke out. During the Austrian war of independence of 1743, proposals made nine days before the battle of Dettingen on 27 June, in which the sick of either side were not to be taken prisoner, were later respected. The Duc de Noailles, commander of the French forces, even sent a message to the enemy to say that he had given orders to his troops not to harass the wounded. Though the word 'neutral' was never used, these were clear precursors of the proposals discussed by Moynier and Dunant over a hundred years later.

In *The Social Contract*, Jean-Jacques Rousseau left a description of the laws of war as he saw them in the eighteenth century. War, he wrote, 'is not a relationship between men, but rather a relationship between States, whereby the individuals involved only happen to be enemies, not as men or even as citizens, but as soldiers.' As soon as they lay down their arms, they cease to 'be enemies . . . and become once more private individuals over whom one no longer has the right of life and death'. Emmerich de Vattel, the Swiss jurist, adviser to Friedrich II of Prussia (Frederick the Great), said as much in his *Droit des Gens* in 1758: 'As soon as your enemy lays down his arms and surrenders, you no longer have any right over his life.' Rousseau's friend, the French philanthropist Piarron de Chamousset, went further, proposing the setting up of a special order of voluntary helpers, similar to that of the Knights of Malta, with members trained as 'administrators, quartermasters, clerks, bursars etc. and medical orderlies', and distinguished from soldiers by a special 'uniform, ribbon or cross'.

With the thirty-three-year war between France and the rest of Europe, however, humanity on the battlefield was forgotten. It was the Prussian general Clausewitz who, in 1833, laid the foundations of laws to govern modern warfare and who spelt out their philosophy. Clausewitz had little time for wars governed by philanthropic restraints. The sole aim of war, as he saw it, should be to overthrow the opponent: all acts arising out of a spirit of generosity were dangerous. Wars, he said, involved all able-bodied men, soldiers and civilians. 'We can never introduce a modifying principle into the philosophy of war without committing an absurdity.' The days of protected or 'neutralized' hospitals were, for the moment, over, despite the attempts by a number of remarkable doctors serving with Napoleon's Grande Armée (but who had trained under the ancien régime). Among these were Pierre-François Percy, who made many suggestions for the treatment of enemy wounded, for the most part ignored. Dr August Wasserführ of the Prussian army and Kaspar Lehmann, adviser to the Russian court, did no better with their proposals for international agreements on the treatment of the wounded, who continued to be regarded as enemies and made prisoners-of-war, just as enemy hospitals continued to be bombed. When Napoleon III freed forty Austrian surgeons, after the battle of Montebello, so that they could help look after their wounded compatriots, he was acting on an impulse that had little to do with contemporary customs.

The end of the eighteenth and the beginning of the nineteenth centuries saw others who found the inhumanity of the battlefield repugnant. Even as Dunant was writing *A Memory of Solferino*, Dr Ferdinando Palasciano was lecturing colleagues in Naples on the 'neutrality of the wounded at times of war', proposing that they be declared neutral for the duration of their treatment. Palasciano had served as a military surgeon under the Bourbons, narrowly escaping death by a firing squad for refusing *not* to treat wounded enemy soldiers. He was a controversial figure in Italy and had not made himself popular by taking a contrary view to all other surgeons over a wound to Garibaldi's foot at Aspromonte in 1862, only to be proved right. By the end of 1861, Palasciano had lectured on neutrality at the Academy in Naples, and been to Geneva, Paris and Turin to promote his ideas – to a largely indifferent reception. When he died not long afterwards, isolated and mentally ill, having at one point irritably dismissed Dunant's book as the 'travel impressions of a tourist', he was soon forgotten and his ideas never received the recognition they deserved.

And even as Palasciano was lecturing on neutrality, a French pharmacist supplying the French armies, Henri Arrault, published a pamphlet in which he proposed that the staff and equipment of military ambulances be declared inviolable. An 'alliance between sovereigns' should be formed, said Arrault, to do away with the 'causes which prevent surgeons from carrying out their holy mission'. At much the same time, the Russian philanthropist Anatoli Demidov, who had been in touch with Moynier and Dunant about the need to include prisoners-of-war in their deliberations, was setting up an organization in St Petersburg designed to collect information on prisoners-of-war, and to find ways of putting them in contact with their families.

Parallel to these fluctuating views on the laws of war, an evolution in military medicine had been taking place, coaxed along by a number of inspired military doctors. In the Middle Ages any help handed out to wounded soldiers was random, most of it provided by so-called surgeons who followed behind armies peddling their elixirs. France was at the forefront of military medicine for many years; the first army field hospital or a 'home to accommodate and dress the wounded' having been founded by Henri IV. A pioneering French doctor, Ambroise Paré, is now regarded as one of the fathers of military medicine. In 1563, Paré entered Milan with the French army. An old soldier, pointing to three men who had been badly burned by gunpowder, asked him whether anything could be done for them. 'I told him no,' Paré wrote later. 'At once he approached them and cut their throats gently, and, seeing this great cruelty, I shouted at him that he was a villain. He answered me that he prayed to God that when he should be in such a state he might find someone who would do the same for him.' Paré improved on the standard treatment for gunshot wounds − cauterization with burning oil − by using a mixture of egg yolk, rose oil and turpentine, and he preferred to tie the ends of the severed arteries in an amputation with cord, rather than apply a red hot iron to the stump from which patients regularly died of shock. Paré proposed and drew up a set of recommendations for military hospitals, the treatment of the wounded and their transport, some three hundred years before those that made their way into the Geneva deliberations. With each French reign, the care of the wounded improved. Richelieu, Louis XIV, Turenne, Colbert and Louis XV all introduced medical services into their armies better than those of their predecessors and, at the end of the eighteenth century, French army surgery reached its peak: 1,200 doctors for fewer than 300,000 troops. It was not to be as good again for many years.

Meanwhile, the steady development of weapons was altering the nature of wounds out of all recognition. The percussion cap and the revolver were followed by the bayonet flintlock and the smooth-bore cannon. With each new weapon came an increase in accuracy, range and volume of fire. By the 1850s, the exploding dum-dum bullet, invented to hunt tigers and elephants in India, had been adapted for use against men and was causing immense damage to tissue, bone and muscle on the battlefield. For every man killed by a bullet, sabre or cannon ball, seven or eight more were dying of carelessness and negligence. What Dunant had overlooked at Solferino was illness − during the eight-week

Italian campaign 120,000 men had contracted dysentery, scurvy, typhoid or typhus.

During the Italian war it was still not uncommon to amputate limbs from thirty or even forty per cent of the wounded, as septicaemia spread rapidly from the large wounds made by artillery projectiles and shrapnel balls which carried shreds of clothing into the wounds. Doctors on the battlefield often paid little attention to the sensibilities of their patients, wandering around in huge aprons covered in congealed blood, their hands and arms glistening as if they were wearing dark red gloves. The Russian military surgeons, in particular, had a reputation for simply summoning nearby soldiers to hold a patient down while an arm or a leg was chopped off, though it was a Russian, Nicolai Pirogov, who in the 1840s made a breakthrough in the use of anaesthetics and the treatment of sepsis. At much the same time two Boston dentists were proposing to replace opium, cannabis, alcohol, hypnosis and ether with anaesthaesia. Chloroform — powerful, cheap and easy to administer — did not reach the battlefields until towards the end of the nineteenth century.

It was only in the 1870s, soon after Solferino, when understanding of germs began to improve, that the number of amputations at last fell, as did the number of wounded dying of infections contracted during surgery. Until the British surgeon Joseph Lister published his findings on antiseptics in 1867, operating theatres contained surgeons in frock coats, sinks with brass taps, china basins, and buckets of sand with which to mop up the blood spilt on the floor. Mercury for syphilis, digitalis for the heart, iodine for goitres, all came later.

Some at least of all this was known to the International Committee as they debated their proposals, for Appia was keenly interested in medicine and a frequent visitor to the battlefield, and would in the years to come write and publish important contributions on war surgery. A great deal less, however, was known about the many contributions by lawyers and military men to the laws of war. Astonishingly, neither Moynier nor Dunant seems to have paid much attention to the work of either Arrault or Palasciano, their contemporaries, and still less to that of earlier jurists. Moreover, Moynier was determined to confine the debates in Geneva to the wounded and not to allow suggestions like Demidov's on prisoners-of-war to dilute the proceedings. It says much about the hermetic nature of Geneva life that the two men were able to proceed as if they were the first to try to introduce a humanitarian dimension into the conduct of war. Yet it was perhaps this very spirit of discovery, this slightly incredulous note, as well as the element of timing, that provided the spark needed to get the fire burning. And it is essential to remember that it was not important either to the founders of the Red Cross or to those who drew up the first Geneva Convention whether a war was just or unjust, right or wrong. Neither in the 1860s nor today are the causes of a war, or its legality, challenged by the International Committee. It is the way that war is conducted that matters, the way in which the men and women waging it behave towards their enemies, and the necessity of drawing up rules and codes that all those who adhere to the Conventions will respect themselves and monitor in others.

Palasciano, Arrault and Demidov were all solitary figures, pursuing their causes largely on their own. The 1850s and early 1860s had, however, seen two major conflicts — in the Crimea and in America — which could have acted as a strong influence on the workings of the International Committee. The fact that they did not, and that some of the most important conclusions that had been reached by soldiers as well as surgeons in the course of them were ignored, was to some extent responsible for the initial slowness with which Dunant's ideas were accepted in Europe. Both wars had thrown up powerful individuals, far more assertive and strong-willed than either Dunant or Moynier. Both were women.

In his *A Memory of Solferino*, Dunant had paid tribute to Florence Nightingale who, he wrote, 'had given up the pleasures of opulence in order to devote herself to doing good' and whose 'passionate devotion to suffering humanity' was well known. He frequently repeated that, along with Harriet Beecher Stowe, Florence Nightingale had been one of the people who had given him most inspiration. Yet they never met, and their relationship got off to an inauspicious start; Dunant appears to have been strangely oblivious to what this reliever of 'suffering humanity' had actually been doing and saying, while Florence Nightingale at first refused to take him seriously.

Having received and read Dunant's book, she sent him a definite snub.

> Miss Nightingale ... entertains no doubt with regard to Mr
> Dunant's proposal. She says it is objectionable because first, such
> a Society would take upon itself duties which ought to be per-
> formed by the Government of each country and so would relieve
> them of responsibilities which really belong to them and which
> they only can properly discharge and being relieved of would
> make war more easy. Secondly, it is proposed to establish in *time*
> *of war* the means which ought to exist *always* in order to be really
> efficacious.

She had failed, it seems, to understand Dunant's full message. Somewhat
embarrassed by the curtness of his sister-in-law's words, Sir Harry Vernon,
who was responsible for sending off the letter, added how sorry he was
'to convey to you a message which seems to damp the ardour of a good
and philanthropic man'. To Sir Thomas Longmore, Deputy Inspector
of Hospitals, Florence Nightingale spelt out her reservations about the
Committee more strongly. 'I need hardly say that I think its views most
absurd,' she wrote in the summer of 1864, 'just such as would originate
in a little state, like Geneva, which never can see war.'

That Florence Nightingale took such a vehement line was not surprising, for what Dunant was proposing – a volunteer corps – would obviate
many of the gains she had so painstakingly brought about in the Crimea
and after her return to London. Her experiences of the battlefield were
of a very different order from his. They had been no less dramatic.

In May 1853, the political differences between Russia and Turkey had
reached such a pitch that diplomatic relations between the two countries
were broken off. In October, after Russia had invaded the Danubian
Principalities, the Sultan declared war. A month later, the Turkish fleet,
caught in harbour by the Russians, was annihilated with the loss of 4,000
sailors. In March the following year, France and Britain, united in their
fears of Russian expansion, became allies for the first time in two centuries
and declared war on Russia.

Reports were soon reaching London, in the despatches of *The Times*'
correspondent, William Howard Russell, of atrocious conditions in the
British hospitals. Cholera, dysentery and gangrene spread among

wounded soldiers for whom there was a totally inadequate, inefficient and ill-prepared medical service. The team of men designated to carry the wounded from the battlefield were lazy, drunk and incompetent. The barracks hospital at Scutari, a former Turkish military hospital taken over by the British in May, was filthy, damp and infested with vermin. 'The manner in which the sick and wounded are treated is worthy only of the savages of Dahomey,' wrote Russell in one of his despatches home. The Inspector General of Hospitals, Dr John Hall, was not keen on anaesthetics, cautioning his medical officers against the use of chloroform in cases of severe gunshot wounds: 'however barbarous it may appear,' he told them, 'the smart of the knife is a powerful stimulant; and it is better to hear a man bawl lustily, than to see him sink silently into the grave'.

The French, Russell observed, were in fact coping rather better with their wounded and sick soldiers, and had already sent fifty admirable sisters of charity to help with the nursing. Sidney Herbert, Secretary at War, wrote to Florence Nightingale (who had run a sanatorium in London) asking her whether she might be willing to recruit and supervise a group of British nurses in the Crimea. Early in November, accompanied by twenty-four carefully selected women, she reached the barracks hospital.

Four miles of sick and wounded men lay on beds and palliasses down the wards and along the corridors. The smell, from dead rats under the floorboards and blocked and overflowing sewers, was overwhelming. There were no brooms or brushes to sweep up the dirt and rubbish, and very little water. Men, clothes and blankets were filthy and covered in blood, and the men themselves plagued by fleas, lice, bugs and maggots. There were no spoons, bowls, plates, scissors, knives or towels. It was, Florence Nightingale reported, a 'calamity unparalleled in the history of calamity'. She summoned a thousand mops, fifty quart bottles of disinfectant, three thousand tin plates and two thousand yards of towelling and put her nurses to work. She was not altogether popular. But within an amazingly short time, she had installed boilers with which to wash the filthy clothes and linen; introduced special diets that the wounded and sick men could actually eat; reorganized the kitchens; imposed order on chaos and misery. The hospital became clean, efficient and relatively comfortable.

From superintendent of female nurses, Florence Nightingale turned into a quartermaster for the army, using money raised by herself and through *The Times* Fund to buy clothes, food, clocks, operating tables, nightcaps, buckets, bedpans, candlesticks, shoebrushes and port wine. The wounded and sick were brought in dressed in rags; they left the hospital with clean clothes, drinking cups and knives and forks. By the time the war ended, the barracks hospital had two recreation rooms with maps, prints, newspapers and writing paper, and four schools in which convalescents could learn to read and write. And women nurses had been introduced into military hospitals. Florence Nightingale had ensured that there would be a future in nursing for respectable women, as long as they were, as she wrote, 'sober, honest, truthful, trustworthy, punctual, quiet and orderly, cleanly and neat'. She had no time for 'excellent gentlewomen more fit for Heaven than a hospital'. What was more, she had managed to reduce the deaths from sickness dramatically. During the second winter of the campaign, after the fall of Sebastopol, the French lost 21,191 men through sickness, the British only 606.

Florence Nightingale had seen a great deal more of the disorder, inertia and incompetence of the military medical services than Dunant had in Lombardy. Her conclusions, at this point at least, were totally different. What was needed, she believed, was not a team of volunteers and outsiders, though she recognized the value of the work of the Russian and French charitable sisters, but a total overhaul not only of the British army medical services, but to some extent of the entire administration of the army. And this is what she had returned to London to do. Dunant's book, which recommended the removal of at least some of the responsibility for sick and wounded men from the army by putting it into the hands of volunteers, was in direct contrast to Florence Nightingale's plans.

It was from the other side of the world, from the battlefields of the southern states during the American Civil War, that there emerged a second Dunant in the shape of a small, determined woman called Clara Barton – though her work, like that of Florence Nightingale, seems also to have been unknown to Dunant and Moynier.

By the time the Civil War broke out in April 1861, Dunant had already started to write his book. Though news from the United States took at least ten days to reach Geneva – there was no telegraph link with Europe until 1868 – interest in the fighting and the progress of the war was considerable. But there seems to have been no mention in any Geneva newspaper of the new American Sanitary Commission until the autumn of 1863, by which time *A Memory of Solferino* was not only published but a great success.

It had become clear to President Lincoln and the government in Washington that the number of troops required to beat the secessionist states would be very great indeed. Soon after the outbreak of fighting, the small standing army in the north issued a call for volunteers; some 75,000 men came forward. The casualties were immense: 22,000 men, Union and Confederate, were wounded at Gettysburg alone. Five days after the battle, they were still being collected from fields, woods and gardens.

The Medical Bureau of the Union army was in poor shape. Its long-serving head, Surgeon-General Thomas Lawson, was a parsimonious, unimaginative man, resistant to all new ideas. As the numbers of wounded grew, so his medical services struggled and failed to keep up. Soon, as at Solferino, they all but collapsed. After the battle of Shiloh in April 1862, the defeated Confederates withdrew, leaving their dead and wounded in Union hands – some 24,000 men needing attention, scattered over several square miles in impassable mud and rain. Government stocks were quickly exhausted; there was no chloroform, no bandages and no rags. Battle after battle left badly wounded men without water or food, many to die slowly of gangrene and untreated burns. Years later, W. M. Howell Reed described the horrors of transportation after the fighting in Virginia. The wounded men, he wrote,

> jolted, racked, thrown from side to side, holding on to extempor-ized straps suspended from the framework of the wagons, screaming, sometimes dying in agony . . . Stretching along the route from Fredericksburg to Belle Plain on the Potomac were fifteen miles of wilderness. All along the way . . . were poor individual remnants of these battlefields, half a dozen or a dozen men to every mile, who had died in the ambulances, and had one by one been removed from them, and left by the roadside.

In the north, from the start of the war, there had been stirrings of a volunteer spirit. In New York particularly, women began to talk of sending relief to the front, or of going themselves to help with the nursing. Much of this initiative came from Pastor Henry W. Bellows of the First Unitarian Church in New York City, a farsighted and energetic man. On 29 April 1861, a meeting was held in the hall of the Cooper Institute. 'Our gallant soldiers to be soothed in these hardships. And their wounds dressed by delicate hands,' read a headline in the *New York Herald* the following morning. Three thousand 'brave and philanthropic women,' it reported, had come forward and 'among these thousands of Spartan women were those whose delicacy of physique showed that they had been nurtured in the lap of luxury.' Soon, they were meeting 'in the churches, in the schools, in the salons of the rich' to prepare lint and bandages. Pastor Bellows realized that this vast surge in charitable instinct needed harnessing in a more effective way. On a train to Washington to discuss the co-ordination of relief work, he fell into conversation with two doctors, William van Buren and Jacob Halsen. They talked about Florence Nightingale's work with the wounded in the Crimea and the need for a national body to bring together the volunteers and to gather much-needed information about the army and wounded soldiers.

At first, Lincoln and the army were highly doubtful; there was talk of an unnecessary 'fifth wheel' to the coach of state. But Bellows was a persuasive figure and when he left Washington, he took with him permission to set up a Sanitary Commission.

Its first members were New Yorkers, professional men giving their services free. The Commission was extremely lucky in its choice of secretary: Frederick Law Olmsted was a man in Bellows's mould, a former scientist and farmer, architect-in-chief of New York's Central Park and someone accustomed to marshalling large numbers of helpers. It was just as well. Casualties at the front were growing rapidly, the medical services were overwhelmed, and men were dying in their hundreds. Olmsted recruited a mixture of doctors, professional men and clerks, and sent them off to inspect camps. Soon the Commission was producing papers on the diseases spreading round the camps, all of which warned, much as Florence Nightingale had warned, that only hygienic conditions and skilled doctors could lessen the rising numbers of dead, and included fierce criticisms of the food being given to the soldiers. In May 1861, a Dr Satterlee observed the way in which the cooking in the army, 'one of the principal gates through which sickness attacks', was simply handed over to two men in each company '*to guess how to do it*'. Beans, he said, 'kill more than bullets'.

The Sanitary Commission had never intended to go into relief work. Olmsted saw that they had no alternative. The Union soldiers were cold; they had too few clothes or blankets; they were being ill-fed and inadequately cared for. A mixture of incompetence, inertia and corruption was to blame. 'Timidity and caution,' noted a writer in the Commission's bulletin, was tying up 'even the boldest hands.' Supplies now came from New York, bought with money raised by the Women's Central Association, another society also born in Pastor Bellows's church.

Olmsted kept up steady pressure on the army; what it needed, he kept saying, was a major overhaul of its medical services. By the spring of 1862 he had managed to push through legislation for a complete reorganization, under a new Surgeon-General, William A. Hammond. Hammond was determined, open to change and honest. While the Army Medical Bureau embraced reform, the Sanitary Commission expanded its work to include floating hospitals – the Bureau having had 'no steamer of its own and was not disposed to try experiments' – a corps of stretcher-bearers, the setting up of convalescent homes, and the distribution of ever-growing quantities of relief. At Kingston, over a period of five weeks, it reported, 'Whole numbers of men refreshed, 9,820'; at a small station called Resaca, 'Refreshments served: 524 gals coffee; 120 gals. soup; 11 bottles spirits; 7 bottles milk punch; 808lbs crackers; 12 shirts; 12 prs drawers'. The Commission might have expanded further had it not been for the rivalrous Christian Commission whose desire to take God rather than hygiene to the battlefields, and whose members were gentle do-gooders rather than dry professional men, was soon winning followers throughout the Union army. Even Walt Whitman, who worked as a male nurse in Washington hospitals, took to calling the Sanitary Inspectors 'a set of foxes and wolves', who contrasted ill with the 'good fellows' of the Christian Commission.

Among the keenest admirers of the Sanitary Commission was Clara Barton, a slight, feisty, neurotic woman aged forty when the Civil War broke out and employed in the patent office in Washington. As soldiers gathered around the city and the first news of the terrible casualties trickled in, she hired a team of black servants, collected all the food and supplies she could coax out of friends and set off down Pennsylvania Avenue on her way to help the 'boys'. Supporters flocked, drawn by her sense of outrage, her determination and her competence. When her own house was swamped with parcels and boxes of supplies, she rented a warehouse; when that was full, she rented two more. Like Dunant at Solferino she soon realized that what the wounded men wanted above all was tobacco.

In many ways their experience of war was remarkably similar. The southern victory at Culpeper left two thousand northern casualties. Drawn by the 'groans of suffering men dying like dogs', Clara Barton saw young soldiers lying in blood and filth four days after the battle, suffering from acute thirst and shock. After the Unionist setback at Bull Run, she found three thousand men who had had no food or water for two days and, determined to keep as many alive as possible until doctors could be found, she began to cook a concoction of crushed army biscuits, wine, water and brown sugar, handing it out in any bowl or bottle she could lay her hands on. At Fredericksburg she crossed the Rappahannock with the troops, and had her clothes ripped by a bullet. At Antietam a man died in her arms. Like Florence Nightingale, Clara Barton soon became a figure of legends. 'Here comes the stormy petrel,' the soldiers are said to have called out as she passed.

Clara Barton was not the only woman to visit the battlefields of the Civil War. Nearly two thousand women served as nurses during the four years of fighting, and their work did as much to change the image of women on the battlefield in America as Florence Nightingale had in Britain. What was more, auxiliary societies had been formed to raise money for relief. But Clara Barton, like Dunant, was an emotive and lively writer, powerful at conveying disaster. In letters clearly aimed at publication, she described the 'golden ringlets of the fair-cheeked boy, the weeping, waiting, mother's idol . . . The bright stream that trickles . . . to the floor – is it wine? Ah, who shall count the value of the wine of life?'

Later, Dunant and Moynier would say that it was not until November 1863, a month after their meeting in Geneva and the drawing up of the first Red Cross articles, that they had read about the work of the Sanitary

Commission. If, for years to come, the Swiss would continue to regard the American organization as nothing but an off-shoot of the Red Cross, the Americans took the exact opposite view. Without *their* pioneering work, they argued, Dunant would not have known what to say. As for the Geneva meeting, that was nothing but a 'strange spectacle of a group of scientists meeting to discuss, at the heart of Europe', a system already running successfully in America. This rivalry would plague the movement for years to come.

The work of the Sanitary Commission was not the only aspect of the Civil War that Dunant and Moynier failed to absorb. From the start of the fighting Union generals had been concerned about the nature of the war itself and the rules that should apply to it. When it came to treatment of the enemy, the legitimacy of targets and looting, army regulations were widely regarded as woefully inadequate. How should the army treat civilians? What was the status of guerrilla fighters?

Francis Lieber was a university professor, a German writer, pamphleteer and popularizer of ideas who had been wounded at Waterloo and had later emigrated to the United States. He had a son called Hamilton, who lost an arm fighting for the north, and when Lieber went to see him in hospital he was struck by the very different experiences of capture and imprisonment – some excellent, some dreadful – reported to him by soldiers. Back at his university desk, he wrote a series of lectures on the laws of war and delivered them to Columbia University Law School in the winter of 1861. When General H.W. Halleck, who had attended his lectures, was made General-in-Chief of the Union armies, Lieber produced a sixteen-page paper of concise, sensible notes about the treatment of guerrilla forces, spies, brigands and what he called 'bushwhackers,' armed prowlers. Halleck ordered and distributed five thousand copies.

Lieber was now invited to propose amendments to the few existing army regulations. They were published in the spring of 1863 – six months before the Geneva meeting – as General Orders 100: *Instructions for the Government of Armies in the United States in the Field.* Like all of Lieber's work, they were a mixture of military severity and basic humanitarian principles. Written more in the style of an essay on ethics than as a rigid code of conduct, the paper was both compassionate and respectful of legal institutions. 'Men who take up arms against one another in public war,' he wrote, 'do not cease on this account to be moral beings, responsible to one another, and to God.' He judged the destruction of people and their property to be permissible — provided the damage was absolutely vital to ending the war. But he ruled firmly against cruelty towards prisoners-of-war, and against maiming, torture, use of poison or wanton destruction, as well as against 'any act of hostility which makes the return to peace unnecessarily difficult'. Lieber accepted the principle of retaliation, but called it the 'sternest feature of war', expressing his own sense of revulsion at racist behaviour by Confederate forces. In one widely reported massacre, southern troops had slaughtered dozens of black soldiers, and also their wives and children. 'The negro soldier must be protected,' Lieber wrote. 'He is a soldier, our flag is his flag. He wears our uniform.'

Though pleased with his work, Lieber was prone to dismiss it as a little pamphlet, 'short and pregnant and weighty like some stumpy Dutch woman when in the family way with coming twins'.

Lieber's rules did bring some order and conformity to the behaviour of the northern soldiers during the Civil War though they were of course never binding, since they were addressed to only one side. Another of Lieber's sons, Norman, taught them to several generations of West Point cadets. And though, like the work of the Sanitary Commission, they were barely mentioned during the Geneva meeting, Lieber's laws paved the way for a second strand in the rapidly emerging movement to bring standards to the conduct of war which would culminate in the Hague Conventions of 1899 and 1907. They continued to influence military conduct in one war after another, right up to and through the First World War.

When the Geneva meeting broke up at the end of October 1863, the International Committee was left with two tasks. They could have been designed specifically with the two most important executors in mind, for it was by now fast becoming clear that Dunant and Moynier were the driving forces behind the Red Cross. It was also apparent that Moynier did not greatly care for his more flamboyant partner.

To Moynier fell the kind of job he most enjoyed, that of drafting the text of a treaty along the lines agreed by the delegates, and asking the Swiss government whether it would be willing to convoke a diplomatic conference, the correct forum in which such treaties were debated. It was left to Dunant to persuade military and political leaders throughout Europe to set up their own societies for the wounded in wartime, and to agree to send representatives to the forthcoming diplomatic conference. In this he was helped by Basting, who was an excellent, self-taught linguist. As before, everything moved with gratifying speed.

Wisely, the conference had left open the exact form these national societies should assume. All over Europe, well-wishers, philanthropists in search of a cause, as well as existing charitable associations, set about interpreting Geneva's suggestions. Dunant hastened between them, cajoling, explaining, conciliating. The first society to come into existence was Württemberg's in December 1863 after the royal family was persuaded to support the cause. Early in January 1864, at the general assembly of the Rifle Association of the grand duchy of Oldenburg, a resolution was passed to launch a second society, which went under the name of 'aid for soldiers wounded on the battlefield'. The Grand Duke put himself forward as patron. Next, on 4 February, came a third, Belgium, with a society presided over by the king's aide-de-camp, Lieutenant-General Renard. Two days later, Prussia followed, with a committee set up in Berlin under Prince Heinrich XIII of Reuss, who had taken the chair in Geneva.

Then the International Committee had an extraordinary piece of luck. A small war was declared, confined, brief and very central to Europe's concerns. It was to provide an excellent test of all that had been debated in Geneva.

At the end of January 1864, Prussia and Austria attacked the duchies of Schleswig and Holstein, thereby invading Danish territory. Bismarck's Prussian policies had entered their next aggressive phase. The causes of this war lay in a complicated mix of history and legal altercations. Claims and counter-claims over the control of the two duchies had been going on for most of the past decade and many of the European powers had strong views about, if not stakes in, the outcome. The British were on the side of the Danish, the Prince of Wales having recently married the Danish Princess Alexandra. Russia supported Prussia. France declared itself neutral. The two sides were unevenly matched. Faced with the overwhelming force of the combined Austrians and Prussians, the Danes, with just 40,000 men, quickly fell back.

In Switzerland, as in other European countries, '*soirées de charpie*,' lint parties at which fashionable ladies prepared bandages for the battle-field, got under way. In Geneva, a meeting was hastily convened by the International Committee and a decision taken to send delegates to the war, one to each side, to monitor the conduct of soldiers and officers, to publicize the ideas reached at the Geneva meeting and to try to implement the concept of neutrality of medical services on the battlefield. General Dufour spoke up about the need at all times to uphold 'our stamp of impartiality and internationalism'. Dunant declared that he wished that he could have gone as one of the delegates, but since French support for the coming Diplomatic Conference was crucial and since the Emperor was proving hard to convince, he felt that he would be more usefully employed in Paris.

In the event, Appia volunteered to go to the Prussian side, and a Dutch former naval officer called Captain van de Velde offered to go to the Danes. Van de Velde, like Basting, has never really received his due in the early history of the Red Cross. A genial, whiskery man with a friendly expression, he was an artist with private means who had wandered around Palestine and the Dutch East Indies doing watercolours and drawing up maps. Van de Velde was both practical and modest. He was anxious, he told the Committee, that his mission should be seen as a 'simple enquiry, so as not to appear too pretentious in the eyes of the public'.

As soon as the war had broken out Appia had offered his services directly to the Prussians, only to receive a polite refusal. As official delegate, he was now in a far stronger position and if he made few efforts to disguise the fact that his sympathies lay with the Prussians, he was also a conscientious worker and a meticulous reporter. Much of what he saw and did became known to the Committee through letters Appia wrote to his wife, scratched out hastily in pencil on scraps of paper, which she passed on.

His mission started awkwardly. He arrived in Berlin to a distinctly cool reception, caused by a recent article in the *Journal de Genève*, apparently inspired by something Dunant had said about the Prussians nursing their wounded with poultices of straw and grass. However, Appia's evident enthusiasm soon opened doors and before long he was able to set off for the front with a letter from the commander-in-chief of the Prussian forces allowing him to wander where he wished. Brandishing his white armband with its pronounced red cross — the first ever worn in this way on a battlefield — and for much of the time up to his waist in mud, he reported home that he was being accepted as an authority on war surgery, that he was much impressed by the Order of St John of Jerusalem, and that the Prussians on the whole accepted the idea of having volunteers on the battlefield, even if they remained unsure about making doctors neutral. It would be a dishonour, the military surgeons assured him, to have to give up their swords.

Appia loved all things military. He was drawn to battlefields, and to the grandeur and solemnity of war which, he once said, was 'like all the other major trials of life, a step towards the perfection of man'. In his reports one senses admiration, sometimes even adulation, for the Prussian soldiers, 'martial figures, strong in body, of medium height, with a robust constitution, an expression of gay bravura, nothing exaggerated in it, nothing arrogant, and above all, nothing frivolous — a true and fitting military bearing . . . I will not forget the spectacle.' Though capable of shedding 'tears of pity over the many victims, of which many undoubtedly are innocent', he does not seem to have been unduly bothered by the sight of a great military machine crushing a small and almost defenceless country.

For all his admiration for Prussian militarism, however, Appia was very conscious of his role as the first true delegate and never forgot that one of his main duties was to spread the Geneva ideas. Sensing that too much brandishing of his armband could only irritate the soldiers, he gained an entrée among them by offering his skills as a surgeon. In the evenings, after the operations, sitting in tents or by the fire, he talked about Geneva and the idea of neutrality for doctors and about how the International Committee had plans to draw up a treaty to bind nations to a humane conduct of war. He was soon able to report that the red cross armband was becoming so well known that at the sight of it alone he was offered not only access to wherever he wished to go, but a bed for the night. He also kept his eye open for any ideas that he could pass on to the new national societies. In a depot in Rauhenhaus, Appia caught sight of a pile of needles, cotton and the 'wherewithall to write' and suggested that, wherever possible, volunteers should help those soldiers who could not write to send letters home. Gradually, idea by idea, the future tasks of Red Cross workers were taking shape.

Van de Velde did not prosper so well. The Danes, who already had volunteers raising money for relief, were wary of what they saw as foreign intervention. However, he pressed on towards the front, expressing admiration for these 'brave people overwhelmed by war', and appalled by the freezing wind and dank fog. Crossing the Baltic, the sails and ropes of his boat froze solid. Everywhere he went, he found the Danish officers suspicious of his motives, reluctant to hear what he had to say and absolutely determined to let him nowhere near the fighting. Soon he was reduced to inspecting ambulances, far to the rear. Danish newspapers, choosing to misunderstand his mission and his description of the new Red Cross movement, protested loudly that the International Committee was failing in its duty to condemn the brutality of the Prussian aggressors – refusing to listen to van de Velde's explanation that the point of the new movement was not to censure countries for their conduct of war, but to help its victims. As the war turned more strongly against the Danes and their casualties rose, van de Velde courageously offered to cross behind the Prussian lines to compile a list of Danish prisoners in enemy hands, thereby demonstrating another task proposed by Geneva. The Danes refused. But he did have the satisfaction before leaving of persuading an already existing charitable association to declare itself the Danish National Aid Society for the wounded. A fifth national society was born.

By the time the peace terms had been signed in August 1864, Appia and van de Velde were back in Geneva. Even if Appia's impartiality had been to some extent compromised by his blatant admiration for the Prussians, the two men had set standards for the delegates who followed them. They had been everywhere, seen everything and their red cross armbands had been respected; they had worked hard to communicate their message to hundreds of soldiers; and they had left people talking. Their experiences, though pleasing to the Committee, were not, however, unproblematic. The Danish protests that they had done nothing to complain about some of Prussia's more brutal attacks – the bombardment of Sønderborg was loudly condemned by several European powers – touched on what would become one of the trickiest of all Red Cross issues, and which would split the movement again and again. 'The duty of the International Committee,' Dunant wrote to Moynier on 26 April 1864, 'whose opinion has so much significance and influence, is to know and then to utter the whole truth, to publish this truth in all its good or evil, to set the facts straight and to stigmatize every kind of hateful occurrence.' Even then, the Committee was divided. Not everyone agreed. For most of the founders, the duty of the Committee lay in helping the wounded. No one could be both good Samaritan and arbiter at once.

The spring of 1864 had been marked by minor setbacks in Geneva. France in particular, crucial to the coming Diplomatic Conference, continued to stall, objecting principally to the idea of auxiliary forces. Military men like Marshal Vaillant could be heard to say that they regretted that the days had passed when entire cities were put to the torch. Just the same, Dunant pressed ahead with his contacts at the French court and in French society and soon had the pleasure of seeing Madame de Staël lay a white armband with a red cross on the table of her entrance hall. As Napoleon III's former instructor, General Dufour wrote to his old pupil to encourage him. On 21 May came the excellent news that Napoleon was finally prepared to cast his vote behind the Diplomatic Conference. Invitations, stressing the obvious links between Swiss neutrality and the aims of the new Red Cross, now went out to governments all over the world.

Dunant, however, at this most crucial moment of his life, was in trouble. His business affairs had taken a severe turn for the worse and he wrote unhappily to Moynier suggesting that he should now 'fade completely out of the picture'. Moynier's reply was brisk, fulsome and reassuring. 'We are simply your assistants . . . to abandon us is the surest way to jeopardize the success of our work at the very moment when it seems to be coming to fruition.' He would not feel this way for very much longer, but for the moment at least, Dunant returned to Geneva.

At one o'clock on 8 August 1864, the Diplomatic Conference opened at last in Geneva. A large conference room had been set aside in the Hôtel de Ville. Moynier's anxieties about rank and correct precedence for those attending had been solved at the last minute by a resourceful decorator called Derabours, who had come up with the suggestion of a round table. The Swiss federal government had named Moynier, Dufour and their chief medical officer for the army, Dr Lehmann, as its official delegates. Astonishingly, the man without whom the occasion would never have taken place was not invited to the round table. Dunant had been designated chairman of the entertainments committee, charged with organizing soirées and fireworks, though, as an official observer along with Appia, Maunoir and Captain van de Velde, he was allowed into the conference room. The slight was not lost on the satirical newspaper, the *Carillon de Saint-Gervais*, which printed an imaginary conversation between a certain Fouillet, and a doctor, clearly intended to be Dunant:

> *Fouillet*: Well then, Doctor, what was said at the Congress?
> *Doctor*: They forgot me at the first meeting. When they let me
> in, I was not allowed to speak.
> *Fouillet*: What, you, the instigator? . . . Now I understand why
> you sulk so . . .

Twenty-six delegates attended, representing sixteen states. The portrait painted to celebrate the occasion, by Charles-Edouard Armand-Dumaresque, shows a gathering of dark-suited men with beards, mutton-chop whiskers and lavish moustaches. No one is smiling. Moynier and Dufour figure prominently, as does Friedrich Löffler, an army surgeon who was attending as the senior Prussian delegate, the artist having perhaps glimpsed the importance of the Prussians to the birth of the Red Cross. If the men gathered in the Hôtel de Ville were clear about one thing, it was that they wished to 'limit, as far as possible, the evils inseparable from war, and to eliminate unnecessary suffering'. The emphasis was clearly on the 'unnecessary'. No one, at that moment, considered interfering in the business of war itself.

During the days that followed, the eminent delegates reached agreement over neutralizing hospitals, field stations and medical personnel. They accepted that captured doctors should be returned to their army. There was some reluctance at including nurses among the neutral, but no one demurred at including civilians who took in and cared for the wounded, whose houses were now declared inviolate. As for the wounded themselves, those deemed unfit to serve again would be allowed home.

However, not every session was totally harmonious. Some of the mutual distrust, diplomatic intrigue and bureaucratic ponderousness, set against a backdrop of sentimentality and confused internationalism, comes across in a long letter written by one of the two unofficial American delegates, Charles Bowles of the Sanitary Commission. Coming fresh from the battles of the Civil War, Bowles was somewhat affronted to find how very little the Europeans knew about the workings of the Sanitary Commission, frequently discussing ways of helping the wounded whose usefulness had already been proven on the battlefields of America. Describing the debates on the question of volunteer helpers, who had proved so successful in the Civil War, Bowles noted that the Europeans appeared too entrenched in their own national habits to be open to any such radical idea. 'The very idea of associations independent, even in a humanitarian way, of the government, is presumptuous, and too democratic for the limited comprehension of such persons,' he wrote scathingly. 'It is an idea wholly foreign to everything in their own education, and one which the traditions of their forefathers utterly ignore.'

Two weeks later, on 22 August, the first international legal instrument to regulate certain aspects of warfare was ready for signature. Formally known as the Convention for the Amelioration of the Condition of the Wounded in Armies in the Field, it covered care and respect for wounded soldiers regardless of their nationality (Article 6); and it enshrined the principle of neutrality for ambulances, military hospitals and hospital personnel (Articles 1 and 2). Anyone helping the wounded was to be 'respected and remain free' (Article 5). And since neutrality clearly depended on being able to recognize them, a red cross against a white background — conveniently the Swiss flag reversed — was to be accepted as the universal emblem for all medical people and places, whether on a flag or as an armband. From now on the words 'Red Cross' were increasingly used when referring to the new movement. The plenipotentiaries put on their full dress uniforms and, with only a little jibbing, twelve countries signed, the others saying that they needed to refer back to their governments first. The two countries with the most immediate experience of military medicine, Britain and the United States, both stood back. The American delegates, Mr Fogg and Mr Bowles, who had presented charts, pictures and plans showing the work of the Sanitary Commission to the Conference, were not empowered to sign and it was some years before the US consented to do so. Dr Rutherford had no seal with which to stamp his commitment on behalf of the British but General Dufour solved the problem by taking out a penknife and cutting a button off his tunic for him to use. Even so, it would be many years before the British ratified the Convention.

Nevertheless, the five founders were justified in feeling proud. Though governments still had to ratify, and nothing was binding until they did so, something remarkable had been achieved: sixteen bellicose nations had agreed to put their pen to a treaty that overrode the boundaries of national sovereignty, and had undertaken to respect a code of conduct in war. It was true that many of their ideas were not original and that many of their recommendations had been put to use at other times by other people. But Dunant and Moynier had brought together ideas floating in the air and turned them into international law. The organization they set up had solid foundations, in the shape of a legal convention on the one hand and national societies on the other. By August 1864, eight societies had been formed. Even Moynier had come round to recognize the immense significance of Dunant's concept of neutrality. Later, he would speak of the first Geneva Convention as a 'legal watershed with respect to efforts to reduce the suffering engendered by war' and a step towards 'the gradual disappearance of war'.

In his letter to the Sanitary Commission in America, Charles Bowles was no less admiring:

> The result of the Congress is a treaty which, althou' less than perfect, is far more than was really to have been expected ... Its grand test, future practicability, remains to be applied. To reconcile humanity with the exigencies of war, or inhumanity under another name, is a task of almost insurmountable difficulty. Its influence will be felt, and the justice of its principles acknowledged, and those who violate it will at least be morally accountable ... It will be marked by the future historian as a forward step in the civilization of the nineteenth century.

Dunant personally emerged from Bowles's report in a glowing light. 'With all his resources, mental, influential, and pecuniary, and with his courage and great energy, he has been at once the pioneer, prop and successful promoter of this work.'

The deliberations of the Diplomatic Conference had taken place in secret, behind closed doors. Cartoons circulating in Geneva made much of this spirit of secrecy, and this, too, would become a prickly issue in the decades to come. The Swiss papers, which had published countless articles in praise of Dunant's *A Memory of Solferino*, continued to champion his ideas, though during the conference itself they were driven to describing the many social events, receptions in country houses and banquets given by Swiss grandees, laid on for the delegates. The *Carillion de Saint-Gervais* chose to caricature the meetings as a series of sumptuous social gatherings:

> First meeting. Tuesday. Two thousand dead bottles lying on the floor, five hundred partridges, trout, pâtés, etc buried or tended. Second meeting. Wednesday. Even more meetings, a veritable *Solferino* . . .

Not all reporters shared in the mockery. The correspondent of the *New York Evening Post*, having dwelt at length on the elegance and style of the occasion, remarked favourably on the decision to turn the event into such a sociable event: 'perhaps their success in endeavouring to mitigate the horrors of war may be traced more or less to this hospitality and universal sympathy in their important mission.'

Not all the delegates went home to wholehearted applause. In her reply to a letter from Dr Longmore describing the meeting, Florence Nightingale sent one of her more acerbic notes. 'I agree with you,' she wrote on 31 August,

> that it would be quite harmless for our government to sign the Convention as it now stands. It amounts to nothing more than a declaration that humanity to the wounded is a good thing.
>
> It is like an opera chorus. And if the principal European characters sing,
>
>> We never will be cruel more,
>> I am sure, if England likes to sing too,
>> I never will be cruel more,
>> I see no objection.
>
> But it is like vows. People who keep a vow would do the thing without the vow. And if people will not do it *without* the vow, they will not do it *with*.

47

England and France will not be more humane to the enemy's wounded for having signed the Convention. And the Convention will not keep semi-barbarous nations, like Russia, from being *in*human.

Besides which, tho' I do not reckon myself an inhuman person, I can conceive circumstances of '*force majeure*' in war where the more people are killed the better.

Much of what she said would prove true. Dunant, Moynier and the International Committee were not in for an easy ride. And furthermore Dunant's personal finances were heading for a crisis.

To obtain a valuable concession of land was the ambition of all who went to Algeria in the middle of the nineteenth century. But by the time Dunant reached North Africa in 1853 colonial expansion was at its peak and the richest plots along the river and around the springs had already been taken. Dunant, overwhelmed by the exoticism and the smell of success, had failed to explore either the fertility of the remaining plots or the agonizing slowness of the bureaucracy involved, equally and confusingly split between military and civilian authorities, in both Paris and Algiers. Though in the end he had won his concession of a waterfall, some good land and many acres of forest, it came too late. He was in too deep to climb out.

By the time the Diplomatic Conference opened in Geneva in the autumn of 1864, Dunant was in desperate need of capital. And as calls for more money kept coming, so he entered ever deeper into debt. In 1865, together with his partner Henri Nick, Dunant bought a marble quarry at Felfela, between Philippeville and Bona. It was a speculative, desperate measure and to meet the costs he began to play the Paris stock market; he also became a director of the Crédit Genèvois, a bank already in a shaky state. As the severity of Dunant's financial position became clear, General Dufour wrote to Napoleon III on his behalf. Though that letter is missing, the emperor's reply is revealing. He had seen Dunant in Algeria, as his old teacher had asked him to, he said, but 'it does not seem to me that M. Dunant's projects are clear or precise. It is not enough to build castles in Spain . . . I will give him all reasonable support but . . . he must be clear about what he wants.' Two weeks later, the French government announced that it would be supporting a different venture.

On 17 October, the Crédit Genèvois went into liquidation. Its creditors appealed. The court of civil law ordered the directors to make good the losses, and Dunant took the blame, in the public eye, for the downfall of the bank. The inspectors sent in to examine the books discovered huge debts. Dunant was not the only director in default nor the one owing the most, but unlike the others he handled his own affairs very badly, failing to turn up for important meetings, and proving awkward at defending his interests when he did so. Preferring to immerse himself in Red Cross matters, he finally put everything into the hands of lawyers and took off for Paris.

Events now followed quickly. From Paris, Dunant wrote to Moynier offering to resign from his post as secretary of the International Committee. Under the organization's statutes, any member whose 'behaviour or comportment was dishonest or immoral' could be expelled and Moynier chose to interpret the rules with extreme severity. He replied that he accepted Dunant's resignation not just as secretary but as a member as well. No one appears to have intervened. Dufour, though clearly fond of Dunant, said nothing. Appia, whose piety and Christian zeal were unforgiving, stayed silent. Even Maunoir, who had lived through a scandal himself, did not lift a finger in his defence.

Dunant's disgrace became even more humiliating when the bankruptcy court's verdict declared that Dunant had 'knowingly swindled' his colleagues. This was the final blow. Dunant left Geneva for ever. Turning his back on former friends and rejecting the Calvinism of his youth as dour and uncompromising, he veered between bitterness and bouts of self-pity, though a letter to his mother, written not long afterwards, still contained a certain optimism:

> When I have paid all that I owe and have regained my former standing, public opinion in Geneva, which has turned against me, will certainly swing my way again. Surely the best proof that I never intended to deceive anyone is that I am penniless myself . . . Doubtless I made mistakes, serious mistakes, but I have been amply punished for them.

There is something very touching about Dunant, in triumph as in adversity, buffeted by enthusiasms and moods of extreme dejection. Though he left Geneva, he did not vanish altogether from sight but continued, like a wolf ejected from the pack, to haunt the fringes and corridors of the growing Red Cross movement, assisting at the birth of new societies, travelling from one end of Europe to the other to talk about his book and the Geneva Convention and to urge governments to sign.

As for Moynier, Dunant's departure must have been delicious. Repelled by behaviour he claimed to find morally repugnant, Moynier found it hard to disguise any longer the animosity and sense of rivalry he had always felt for the opportunistic Dunant. Moynier's self-righteous, moralistic soul must have found Dunant's lightness and sense of adventure maddening. And he was unbearably jealous of the way that Dunant was so continually fêted as the true architect of the Red Cross, when it was he who had made it all possible by his legal knowledge, his dedication and his many hours of hard work. With Dunant's departure, he would rewrite history, removing bit by bit every trace of his rival's name. He was even said to have invited a historian to write the history of the organization, and instructed that Dunant's name would not appear in the book. This story is hard to confirm, but the older Moynier got the more jealous he seemed to become, and the more intolerable he found the idea that a man as financially unscrupulous as Dunant could ever have had the inspiration for an idea that he had come to regard as his own. Moynier, people would say, was afraid of nothing – except for Dunant's shadow.

THREE

True Metal and Tinkling Brass

No philanthropic idea has ever caught on with the speed with which the Red Cross proposals now travelled across the continent of Europe. Though the founders were all practising Christians, the ideas had no religious overtones and clashed with no religious tenets. And the timing was excellent. Hastened by the revolution in communications, ever closer links between nations were on the way, as illustrated by the formation of the Telegraphic Union, the International Statistical Congress and the Postal Union. As Professor Longmore, the British inspector of hospitals, told a group of potential Red Cross supporters in Britain in March 1866, the 'machinery for the rapid diffusion of intelligence and personal observations', meant that nations could no longer get away with treating their soldiers with the callous indifference of past wars. The following year, Appia and Moynier collaborated on a book that was to become the Bible of the Red Cross movement, *La Guerre et la Charité*. They went further than Longmore in their appraisal of a changing world:

> The increasing rapidity, the very instantaneousness of communications, has favoured this awakening; for by this means we live much more in the intimacy of the army than we formerly did. Those who remain at their hearths follow, step by step, so to speak, those who are fighting against the enemy; day by day they receive intelligence of them, and when the blood has been flowing, they learn the news almost before it has been staunched, or has had time to become cold.

The increasingly lethal nature of weapons, they argued, made the humanizing of war all the more urgent. 'It would be a disgrace to humanity if its imagination were less fertile for good than for evil. Murderous refinements of war should have correlative refinements of mercy.' The Red Cross fitted naturally among mid-nineteenth-century concerns — the movement and congresses for peace, the struggle for the emancipation of workers, the sanitary reforms, and the discussions currently under way in Prussia and Russia about greater efficiency in the army. Dunant's eloquent cry, 'is it not a matter of urgency ... to press forward in a human and truly civilized spirit the attempt to prevent, or at least to alleviate, the horrors of war?' had a timely ring to it.

Dunant was also right to have sensed that the Red Cross idea was a perfect expression of the spirit of philanthropy and reform blowing through the corridors of Europe's royal palaces. It was safe, constructive and admirable, and the close-knit nature of Europe's royal families, enmeshed to an improbable degree by intermarriage, helped spread a cause that fitted easily with the belief that rank entailed duty as well as privilege.

Women were not regarded as significant in the early Red Cross. Dunant himself described them in *A Memory of Solferino* as 'lovely girls and kind women', devoted but essentially placid, weak and ignorant, beside whom were needed 'kindly and experienced men, capable, firm, already organized, and in sufficient numbers to get to work at once in an orderly fashion'. But these royal ladies were animals of another colour, 'of great merit, great heart and high rank', and Dunant put his faith in what they would achieve. He was right to do so, for everywhere from Bavaria to Spain, aristocratic ladies were soon enthusiastically at work. In Paris, the comtesse de Saint-Aulaire, widow of one of Louis-Philippe's ambassadors, was already promoting the Red Cross in the salons of the Faubourg Saint-Honoré, and soon other Parisian ladies, literary, aristo-cratic or fashionable, were talking of little else. And if women continued to be excluded from the serious deliberations in Geneva — it would be half a century before the International Committee appointed a woman to its board — it now fell largely to the ladies to coax their countries into setting up national committees.

Within three years of the Geneva Convention, as it was soon being called, twenty-one states, among them the Ottoman Empire, had ratified the treaty. Six of them were German kingdoms or duchies soon to fall under Prussian dominance. Of the great powers, both the French and the Russians baulked at the idea of civilian volunteers interfering in purely military matters, and there was considerable relief when they at last entered the fold. Without their support, the whole idea risked sinking into oblivion, as one of those passing enthusiasms of nineteenth-century philanthropy. Even if Dunant and Moynier did genuinely see themselves as natural heirs to the Enlightenment, and their work as proof that Europe was becoming more civilized, the backing of the major powers, however cynical and selfish their motives, was crucial.

But what did the signatures actually amount to? In January 1866 the International Committee sent out letters asking every country which had signed to say whether or not they were using the Red Cross emblem – flag and armband – in their armies and medical services, in order to be ready should war break out. The answer was extremely disappointing: only one, Sweden, replied that it was. The others gave as excuse the expense and the fact that they wanted to be certain first that others were doing the same.

A test was not long in coming. At the Congress of Vienna in 1815 a Germanic confederation had been formally set up which seemed to promise years of harmony between the various states. But the distribution of the recently conquered Danish lands between Austria and Prussia, both jostling for supremacy in the new Germany, led to a renewed burst of fighting and in June 1866 they went to war.

Prussia had been a strong promoter of all Red Cross affairs since the very first days and already had 120 local committees under a central one in Berlin, with vast stocks of supplies ready to send to the front. It had also been one of the first states to sign the Geneva Convention. Austria had not signed, and behaved as if no Convention had ever existed. Throughout this short war, no red cross was ever seen on the Austrian side. Just the same, Prussia announced that it would do exactly as if its enemy were obeying the same rules.

A first clash of troops left 1,500 men wounded. Within days, seventy trains left Berlin for the war zone loaded with Red Cross supplies and carrying a thousand doctors and nurses, many of whom were already operating on the battlefield before the arrival of the regular army medical services. The war lasted a little over a week. On 3 July, the determining battle took place on the plains between Sadowa and Königgrätz (now Hrádec Králové). It went on for nine hours. When the Austrians finally retreated, they left behind them 30,000 wounded and dead men, to 10,000 Prussian casualties, having proved no match for the Prussian Dreyse, pin-action, breech-loading rifles, which fired up to five shots a minute.

Care for the wounded of both sides fell entirely to the Prussians. By the time night fell, stretchers bearing the Red Cross emblem were transporting the wounded to field dressing stations, where Red Cross surgeons, using chloroform, began to operate. Along the railway lines which carried the casualties back from the front, volunteers had set up refreshment centres; in the main Prussian cities, the Berlin central committee arranged for hospitals, convalescent homes and the fitting of artificial limbs. Members collected and distributed books, games and writing paper and laid on interpreters for the Austrian soldiers who could not speak German.

For their part, the Austrians had been ill-prepared and uncoordinated. Their existing charitable societies had almost no contact with the military and therefore no access to the front. In a clearing in the forest of Hořice, five days after the battle of Sadowa, volunteers from the Prussian society found a primitive Austrian field hospital, with 300 badly wounded men barely alive. Eight hundred others had died from lack of treatment. As Moynier was later to remark, 'Charity should not be caught unprepared.' The battle for the Geneva Convention had been fought – and won – on a battlefield. Volunteers, not Préval's mules, had proved their usefulness. On 21 July, Austria signed the Convention.

Dunant was in Berlin when the victorious Prussian soldiers marched through streets decorated with flags and banners, the Prussian colours flying alongside the red and white of the Red Cross. Queen Augusta, granddaughter of Catherine of Russia and soon to become Empress of Germany, was an admirer of Dunant's book. Ever since first reading it she had been encouraging 'all classes', from royal princesses to 'actresses from the minor theatres', to join committees and set about implementing Red Cross suggestions. Now she invited Dunant to the palace for a gala dinner. Dunant loved royal families. He devotes fifteen pages of his memoirs to his reception, his usual staid tone giving way to flights of humbleness and pride. 'I passed by unnoticed,' he wrote, describing his arrival at the dinner, 'making myself as small as possible. I took my place at a distant table, at the very end of the furtherest room, little knowing that a place had been set for me in the main chamber, with the King and the princes . . .' The King, he said, though elderly, was courteous in the extreme, and 'gracious and frank in his simplicity'; the royal prince 'tall, straight, majestic, like a noble Knight of the Middle Ages, but filled with cordiality and simplicity'. Bismarck's 'thin face,' he noted, 'was as pale as that of a corpse'. Before he left, the Queen summoned him to her side, showed how she wore an armband and red cross on her bare arm, and presented him with an alabaster statue of the Archangel Michael, the cross sculpted on his breast picked out in bright red paint. There was nothing Dunant enjoyed more than life at court.

Even as Moynier and the International Committee worked frantically to bring all the states involved in the struggle now under way for German unity into the Red Cross fold, Austria was at war on another front. Seven years after the battle of Solferino, King Victor Emmanuel still had plans to wrest Venice from Austrian sovereignty. This time, fighting broke out at Custozza, a village not far from Solferino. The Italians were better prepared than they had been in 1859. The Milan committee of the Italian Red Cross society had been building up its medical stocks in preparation and, mindful of Article 5 of the Geneva Convention which spelt out that help could be sought from the committees of neutral countries, appealed, ahead of time, for ambulances. After some slight delay in Geneva, the Swiss and French despatched supplies.

The Italian forces were defeated at Custozza, but Garibaldi's calls for more soldiers had brought hundreds of volunteers to Lake Garda. Among them were Appia and his brother George, a Protestant pastor working in Florence. The two brothers joined Garibaldi's men and obtained permission to work as medical volunteers amongst his troops. Appia asked a local tailor to make up grey knapsacks with prominent red crosses and, having filled them with surgical instruments, bandages, vermouth and lemons, and with bread and cheese for themselves, the brothers worked for almost forty-eight hours without a break looking after the wounded from a battle near the village of Tiarno in the Adige valley. The Appias, together with two friends, called themselves the *Squadriglia dei Soccoriti voluntari delle Valli* (corps of volunteers from the valleys) and set up a makeshift surgery – Appia was in fact the only qualified doctor – in a church. He was soon writing home: 'Every minute, a little cart with 2 wheels would arrive, bringing two or three new victims. Our stretchers went without pause between church and carts, carts and church.' This new Italian campaign gave him a chance to see for himself what happened when the Geneva Convention was *not* respected. Since there were no provisions for making the church a neutral zone, when orders came to fall back there was no alternative but to evacuate the wounded along with the army. In the chaos of the retreat, many failed to survive. What made Appia such a fitting pioneer delegate, even if he was in Italy unofficially, was that he had a buccaneering side to his nature, something that has marked the best delegates to this day, an odd combination of morality and a love of adventure, like the heroes of John Buchan novels, concealed behind neat moustaches and sober, formal clothes.

The first Geneva Convention had said nothing specific about war at sea. On 20 July, a great naval battle took place near the island of Lissa, off the Dalmatian coast. It lasted four hours with vessels becoming inextricably tangled and booming clashes as the new steamships, or ironclads, crashed into each other, slicing through armour plate. When the *Re d'Italia*, pride of the Italian fleet, was pierced by the Austrian *Erzherzog Ferdinand-Maximilian* and a 140 foot-square hole opened, 600 men went down with her. Two hundred were drowned, the rest pulled out of the water to safety. The dead sailors, like Solferino's dead soldiers, would act as a spur for an addition to the Geneva Convention, to take in war at sea. This time it was the Empress Eugènie, who, hearing a description of the sinking of the *Re d'Italia* from Admiral von Tegetthoff, summoned Dunant to the Tuileries to tell him that she desired the Convention to be extended to wounded sailors.

Dunant seems to have seized this moment to publicize some of the recent developments in the Red Cross world. Though by now distanced from the movement he had inspired, Dunant continued to act, as its most ardent, roving, solitary ambassador.

He had much to say, for Red Cross affairs were continuing to advance at a remarkable pace. One after the other, new societies were springing into life – three in 1865, four in 1866, three in 1867 – shaped and guided by the Geneva Committee who, while at pains to inculcate basic principles, like the independence of the societies from the government in power, took care to leave room for individual interests. One of the questions that had perturbed the founders was how societies should occupy themselves in peacetime, and much thinking now went into the development of new equipment for transporting the wounded, and into building up sufficient and appropriate supplies in preparation for what might come. Imaginative, sometimes dotty, projects, with camels as stretcher-bearers, or odd surgical instruments, filled the pages of a magazine, known as the *Bulletin*, launched in the late 1860s by the International Committee, and illustrated by charming black-and-white drawings. There was an ice-making machine, a device which claimed to turn salt water into fresh, and a portable kitchen which folded into a knapsack containing a spirit lamp, a rubber pipe for men too weak to drink from a cup, nails, rope, pots, towels, candles, rum and cognac, mustard powder, tea, salt, pepper and meat extract – the only trouble being that it was too heavy to carry more than a few paces.

At the Universal Exhibition held in Paris between April and October 1867, 700 square feet were given over to a display of medical equipment, models of new ambulances and samples of the field dressings recently carried by Austrian troops, though Moynier was disconcerted to find the Red Cross stands set up not far from where Krupp was exhibiting the world's newest and most deadly cannons. Dunant had been living in Paris for the past months in considerable poverty, sleeping in station waiting rooms and often hungry. 'I struggled as best I could,' he wrote many years later in his memoirs. 'I had been left to drown without help and in the most atrocious agony.' He now haunted the corridors of the exhibition, where his bust, crowned with laurels, had been given a place of honour. Though several visiting monarchs asked to see him, not knowing of his fall from grace, and though the exhibition's gold medal was awarded to him, along with Dufour and Moynier, Dunant wrote to his mother, describing a painful encounter with his former colleague. 'I did not show that I had seen Monsieur Moynier,' he reported, 'and, as he made no move to come towards me, we neither saw nor met each other.' In fact, Moynier had written to various members of the French committee, warning them against Dunant, as well as to a senior organizer of the exhibition, putting him 'on his guard' and adding 'If he . . . offers to act on our behalf, I would be obliged to you to get rid of him . . .'

The Red Cross was ever rivalrous. There was much acrimonious talk during the exhibition when the gold medal went to the members of the

International Committee rather than to Count Sérurier, organizer of the Red Cross display.

On 26 August, the first International Red Cross Conference opened in Paris. It was a splendid occasion. There were delegates from sixteen countries, nine governments and two orders of knighthood. Various possible additions to the 1864 Convention were debated, for example the extension of the existing neutralization of medical personnel to cover the wounded themselves. This idea, favoured by Baron Percy of the Grande Armée as early as 1800 and repeated by Palasciano in 1861, was in fact preferred by most army medical officers, who felt that the sooner the wounded could be treated the better the chance of saving their lives, and that this way they would not have to be moved from the battlefield to receive medical help.

This proposal made its way on to the agenda for the meeting to debate the second Geneva Convention, which took place once again in the same room of the Hôtel de Ville in Geneva on 5 October 1868. Eleven of the twenty chief delegates were the same. Pressure to review the entire first Convention had been squashed by Moynier, who feared – as he would again and again – that this could easily lead to it being thrown out altogether and nothing put in its place, and a decision was taken instead to approve 'additional clauses'. Along with the neutrality of the wounded, the ban on plundering bodies and the need for identity tags for soldiers, new articles were drafted, largely at the instigation of a Dutch rear-admiral called von Karnebeeck, to cover hospital ships, merchant ships made neutral if they took on board wounded men and relief ships which were to be painted white with large red crosses. There was little doubt that the discussions at these gatherings had come to matter among European leaders. When the second International Red Cross Conference took place in Berlin in April 1869, seventeen governments sent representatives. The Prussians took it all very seriously. Bismarck attended, Queen Augusta made several appearances and prayers were said in Berlin's churches.

It had never been the founders' intention to create a permanent committee. In their early meetings they talked of phasing themselves out, once the idea of neutrality of medical personnel was accepted and new societies had been safely launched. Whether, having tasted fame and power, Moynier and the three remaining founders would actually have stepped down is doubtful, but in Paris their role had been suddenly and unexpectedly challenged and they fought back strongly.

Moynier had come up with a proposal to open up the International Committee to a wider membership and turn it into a Supreme Council. This suggestion was pushed briskly to one side by a French delegate, Count Breda, who suggested that it would be far better if the whole operation were now shifted from Geneva to Paris. The French had been meddling long before the conference opened, their Central Committee having hijacked what Moynier had envisaged as a restricted and influential gathering, and turned it into a major jamboree open to all for 10 francs a head, with a 'General Commission of Delegates'. (Moynier referred to this as a 'temporary and unstable formation'.) Words were exchanged. Count Breda offered to resign and the meeting ended with the International Committee still firmly in place, its various roles as go-between and monitor endorsed and its home to remain in Geneva. It would be neither the last, nor the most bitter of attempted coups.

The early days were not without other threats. In December 1868, Tsar Alexander II convened a conference in St Petersburg 'to mitigate as far as possible the calamities of war'. The acceptable goal of war, as he saw it, was to enfeeble the military strength of the enemy: to go further, to cause unnecessary death or suffering, was to go too far. This was a clear reference to the dum-dum bullet, the hollow bullet that exploded on contact, condemned by his minister for war, General Dmitri Miliutin, as 'barbarous'. On 11 December, the delegates in St Petersburg issued a declaration outlawing 'any projectile weighing less than 400 grammes that is either explosive or loaded with inflammable or fulminating material'. The St Petersburg Declaration, a foretaste of the later Hague Conventions, was concerned with defining the 'technical limits where the requirements of war should give way to the needs of humanity' – and was little short of revolutionary for it forbade, on humanitarian grounds, the use of a weapon developed as a result of advances in technology. Unlike the Geneva Convention, it came into play before, not after, battle, to 'prevent an evil being committed'. As Moynier, who had fought to combine the two aims and resisted a second front opening up elsewhere, put it somewhat dismissively once the debates were concluded, the Geneva Convention was a 'protest by the people', while the Declaration came from the top.

With Dunant's disgrace, Appia had taken over the job of secretary to the Committee, now ruled over with increasing lordliness by Moynier, who conducted all business from his desk at his house in the rue de l'Athénée, in which the files and documents were kept and to where he had taken to abruptly summoning his colleagues, sometimes at eight o'clock in the morning. The first paid employee, Ami Privat, was taken on to work ten hours a week. There had been talk of bringing in a Catholic as a new member, but this was soon rejected, and a colonel in the Swiss Federal Army, Edmond Favre, every bit as Protestant and Genevan as the founders, was invited to join to bring members up to five again. General Dufour was ageing and the Committee felt the need of a military presence. After the unexpected and early death of Dr Maunoir in April 1869, new calls for a Catholic member were made by the meddlesome French society but Moynier was unshakeable. Religion, he announced, had nothing to do with the Committee and once you let such considerations matter you would soon find yourself appointing representatives of every religion and minority. A Swiss politician − Genevan, Protestant − called Louis Micheli de la Rive, was brought in. A pattern was being established. No non-Genevan would make it on to the Committee for another fifty-three years; no Catholic for another fifty-four. A woman, Mlle Cramer, appointed in 1918, would just beat them to it.

On 15 July 1870, France declared war on Germany. Spain had announced on 3 July that it would be making Prince Leopold of Hohenzollern-Sigmaringen its new constitutional monarch, subject to the approval of the Cortes. Prince Leopold was a kinsman of King Wilhelm I, and Napoleon III was not prepared to tolerate a Prussian on the throne of Spain. Believing the French army to be invincible, he ordered his foreign minister, the duc de Gramont, to announce that while the French desired peace, they desired peace with honour.

For the first time in its seventeen-year history, the whole Red Cross jigsaw was in place. Both France and Germany had acceded to the 1864 Geneva Convention; both said that they would comply with its articles, as well as with those of 1868; both had formed their own Red Cross national societies. In Geneva, the International Committee was ready to carry out its role of liaising between the various committees and monitoring the course of the war and contacted the two warring governments immediately with a reminder of their commitments. The twenty-three other countries which had formed their own Red Cross societies were in a position to offer help. This war would be a proper test. New and increasingly lethal weapons would make greater demands than ever before on the skills of nurses and surgeons while trains could now both carry troops far greater distances and carry back the wounded to safety. The military diet had been revolutionized by tinned meat, dried milk powder and margarine (invented after Napoleon III offered a prize for an acceptable substitute for butter). But the real question that worried Moynier and his colleagues in Geneva was how far the states at war would obey what was in essence no more than a moral precept. It would be a test not just of the Convention, but of the power of public opinion.

Ever since July 1866, when it had defeated the Austrians at Sadowa, Prussia had enjoyed supremacy over the German confederation. The Prussian army was in excellent shape with a million well-trained and well equipped men under arms. Its medical services were superb with regimental companies of trained stretcher-bearers. Its soldiers had been briefed on matters of hygiene, food and clothing, and each had been issued with a first aid kit. Soon after the outbreak of war, the Prince of Pless was named 'Royal Commissioner and Military Inspector of Voluntary Treatment of the Sick' with supreme authority over all voluntary services. Bismarck had recognized that, for all the excellence of his army, there was much that could still be done by volunteers.

In 1869, at the time of the second International Red Cross Conference in Berlin, the various German aid societies had voted to unite under a central committee in Berlin in times of war. Queen Augusta and her daughter Princess Louise had then set about raising money and arranging supplies, and by the end of July, two weeks into the war, Prussia had 2,000 committees working on behalf of its soldiers. More than 6,000 men and women were ready to leave for the front as volunteer nurses. Queen Augusta, though described as sickly by her many biographers, was proving what could be done by Dunant's 'august protectors' to promote his dream. Twenty-one specially adapted trains had been prepared, in which the wounded could be transported on mattresses stuffed with straw, which reduced the jolting, the Prussian medical services having rejected the American model of suspending stretchers from the roof of the carriages on the grounds that German patients would feel uncomfortable hanging one above another. As for the Red Cross emblem, the Prussians had dutifully provided all the members of their medical services with white armbands with red crosses and had red crosses painted on to all their medical vehicles. They had also distributed 80,000 booklets with a summary of the Geneva Convention, helpfully written in both German and French. Count von Moltke, chief of the general staff, was constantly inveighing against cruelty towards civilians. 'It is bad enough that armies have sometimes to be set to butcher one another,' he wrote to his brother Adolph, 'there is no necessity for setting whole nations against each other – that is not progress but rather a return to barbarism.'

In contrast the French were in disarray. Despite Field Marshal Le Boeuf's boast that there was not a single button missing from a single soldier's gaiter, its men were ill-equipped and poorly trained while their officers continued to place foolish trust in guns that were no match for the Prussian Dreyse and Krupp cannons. The fighting began in torrential rain and the French soldiers, with only a few tents between them, found themselves sleeping in the open. Their shoes had papier mâché soles and their uniforms were made of thin, flimsy material, unscrupulous suppliers having skimped on quality. The medical services had virtually no stretcher-bearers and no white armbands with red crosses. Very few soldiers had ever heard of Geneva or its Convention. A senior French surgeon, Dr Beaunis, was soon writing from the front: 'As for equipment, nil. No means of transport. No instruments. No linen. No lint. No dressings.'

The French Red Cross society, cajoled into existence largely by Dunant in the spring of 1864, had two dukes, six barons, two *maréchals* and seventeen counts on its committee and was, for its part, ill-organized, penniless and interested chiefly in receptions. Aristocratic ladies were to be seen on the society pages of fashionable magazines wearing white aprons with red crosses over their ordinary clothes beneath the immense flowery and feathery hats of the day. There were barely ten committees, struggling into life under a resourceful lawyer from Lyon called Léonce de Cazenove, who had been calling on local priests for help.

The war opened with a series of Prussian victories. Battles were fought and lost by the French at Wissembourg, Wörth, Froeschwiller and Reichshoffen. The French army fell back and the Prussians crossed the border into France. Metz was surrounded and, despite apparently glorious victories for the French at Borny, Gravelotte and Saint-Privat, remained encircled, its inhabitants driven to eating horse and bread made from sawdust and straw. At Sedan Napoleon III was wounded and taken prisoner, and 80,000 French soldiers were captured. The rain kept falling and French losses mounted. The wounded were crammed into makeshift vehicles, alongside guns and supplies, and jolted their way back at a crawl along crowded and muddy roads. The Prussians, observing that the French military services were not wearing the Red Cross emblem, became increasingly suspicious and felt even less charitable when the French soldiers took to imprisoning Prussian doctors they captured on the field. Soon, French doctors and nurses were taken prisoner too, marching back towards the Prussian prisoner-of-war camps, with all their equipment confiscated. After one particularly ignominious defeat, when the French had retreated leaving their doctors to look after a church full of wounded soldiers, a German officer suggested to the French that they at least tie strips of white cloth round their arms, with red crosses drawn on them in the blood dripping from the injured.

In Geneva, as soon as the war broke out, the International Committee had met to discuss its programme. This war would see the shape of the future Red Cross emerging clearly, and much of the work and thinking that would dominate the movement for the next 120 years would be explored and developed on and around the battlefields of Wörth and Sedan. Identity tags for soldiers, visits to prisoners of war, the active involvement of foreign societies, concern about how to monitor the Geneva Convention and respect for the Red Cross, the repatriation of wounded soldiers, would all be subjects discussed and tested in the weeks and months to come. And it was during the Franco-Prussian war that one of the most important later ingredients of the Committee's work – arguably one of its best initiatives – would be pioneered, that of tracing missing soldiers and putting them back in touch with their families.

At the Berlin conference in 1869, there had been talk of setting up a bureau to transmit information about missing soldiers in times of war. In August, Moynier and the others debated opening an office in Luxemburg, not far from the fighting, but such was the anxiety of this already customarily anxious group that it was decided that Luxemburg was too far to allow close supervision by Geneva and that, as the minutes of the meeting for 26 August, put it, 'either it will be run by men who are too indolent, or by men who are too active'. Eventually, Basle was chosen as a suitable spot, nearer to the fighting but close enough to Geneva to be supervised, both to act as a warehouse for the goods now flooding into the International Committee and as a centre for information. Rooms were taken in the chapel belonging to the Knights of the Teutonic Order, a modest-looking building in a cobbled street and, having persuaded both sides to allow the severely wounded to go home through neutral Switzerland, a letter was put out, addressed to the fathers of sons fighting in the war. 'If your son is wounded in such a way that he will never again serve in the army,' it said, 'there is nothing to stop you taking him home.' Instructions were given about transport and travel. Moynier, who had gone to Basle to set up the new agency, also persuaded the French and the Prussians to allow wounded prisoners to write to their families, using the agency as their address. Soon more than a thousand letters a day were passing through Basle, the agency had overflowed into the Casino and volunteers worked day and night sorting and readdressing post, recording every letter in a ledger. With successive victories, the Prussians were taking enormous numbers of prisoners and the Prussian army now also agreed to draw up lists of the wounded men, which were printed and distributed throughout France. Though the exercise started only with the wounded, it soon extended to take in the sick and, not long after that, the healthy prisoners as well, though the agency decided that it would handle only letters and not parcels, which might be in breach of the treaty.

Once again, Dr Appia was restless and eager to get to the front. While Moynier was in Basle, he spent his days drawing up lists of things that his experience on the battlefield had taught him were essential, like very full flannel shirts, cotton vests, slippers, light dressing gowns, and 'sundries — cigars, soap, combs, brushes, pins, little boxes containing everything needed to sew on buttons'. When Moynier returned to Geneva, Appia proposed going to join the Prussians, but so worried were the Committee Members that this might in some way prejudice their neutrality that they told all who asked that Appia was going only in a private capacity. Just as before, however, he proved an excellent witness to Red Cross concerns.

Appia had a cousin, Frédéric Ferrière, a shy, somewhat delicate young man of twenty-two, just embarking on his medical studies. He was to become a crucial figure in the International Committee. Like Appia, he was enthusiastic, a hard worker and an excellent reporter. At the end of July the two joined the Prussians, where Appia hoped that his fluent German and his friendship with the Prussian medical services from his days in Schleswig would help. They were there in time for the battle of Wörth.

Ferrière kept a diary of his experiences. He wrote vividly, but clearly did not share his cousin's admiration for all things military. He described 'scraps of human corpses and dead horses'. The ground, he said, was 'sticky and blackish, there was blood everywhere and a suffocating stench'. And he was to have first-hand experience of the dangers of working for the Red Cross without suitable identification. Arrested in the first few days as a spy, he was only just able to persuade his captors not to put him before a firing squad.

From the towns, Appia was also soon writing to Geneva: 'You can hear the moans of the dying; with a single breath the wounded cry out for help, and God remains deaf to their pleas.' Using his wife once again to transmit his letters, Appia sent a telegram to the Committee: 'Help needed urgently. Need 10 proficient doctors and 20 volunteers.' It was all very like Solferino. 'A storm seems to have passed by here,' wrote another young relation of Appia's, Emmanuel Ferrière, who appears to have joined them. 'Farms are burnt or razed to the ground, many of the trees have been uprooted, the earth is covered in the remains of broken weapons, crushed helmets, tattered harnesses, cartwheels, fragments of baggage-wagons and cannons, bloody and torn military uniforms, the bodies of men and women.'

Appia had never worked harder. When not operating or patching up wounds, he talked ceaselessly about the Geneva Convention, worrying about how to improve the wording of the various articles, how to make them more precise and easier to follow. 'What will be the deciding factor when it comes to neutrality?' he speculated on 13 August. 'The degree of severity of the wound, of course. But who is to be the judge of that?'

Towards the middle of August, he witnessed the battles of Gravelotte and Saint-Privat. The casualties were terrible, but by now the French Red Cross was sending regular contingents of volunteers and Appia wrote home enthusiastically to say that the Prussians were respecting the neutrality of foreign doctors. Everywhere he went, he reported, he found approval for Red Cross work and it was clear that the time taken to attend to the wounded was falling at a satisfactory rate. Sometimes his letters had a mystical ring to them, as if he felt called upon by God to work with the casualties of war. He was haunted by the sight of the long lines of refugees, driven from their homes by the fighting, dragging themselves along roads clogged by deep mud, in the driving rain.

Dunant had been in Paris the day war was declared. 'At last', he wrote, 'I have a fine role to play.' Turning to his contacts at court and in the army, he set about reminding everyone who would see him of their commitments under the Geneva Convention. His early overtures were rebuffed. The Empress would not grant him an audience, while General Louis Jules Trochu, military governor of Paris, declined to discuss his proposals for making Versailles, Fontainebleau, Saint-Cloud and Provins into neutral zones, saying that he was too busy. When he did finally manage to get the question of the Red Cross emblem raised in the senate, the voice of the speaker, Baron Brenier, honorary vice-chairman of the French Red Cross, was drowned by the tapping of paper knives on desks, and the sound of voices, as the bored senators went on with their conversations. And his one apparent success, getting Jules Favre, minister of foreign affairs after the Third Republic was proclaimed on 4 September 1870, to agree to publicize Article 5 – the neutralizing of all buildings taking in wounded soldiers – met with too much success. Red Cross flags soon blossomed in the towns and villages lying in the path of the troops, streets and private homes were festooned with vast white banners and bright red crosses. At Dôle, the mayor handed out red crosses to the town's butchers and bakers. Soon, there was talk of spies, using the Red Cross as a means to reach the battlefields and pillage the dead. A Captain Fürstenberg of the 10th Prussian Hussars regained consciousness lying in a field after a battle to see, in the pale dawn light, shadowy figures bending over the dead and the wounded. Seeing one of them dressed as a chaplain, and detecting red cross armbands on the others, he was about to call out to them when he realized that 'they were cutting open the front of the uniforms on the dead men with scissors and knives'. The wounded were soon finished off. 'To get the rings,' Captain Fürstenberg wrote later, 'they cut the fingers off. The "priest" pocketed the jewellery.' When the gang noticed that Furstenberg was still alive they started towards him. Fortunately he still had his revolver and was lucky enough to hit and injure the man posing as a priest. The others ran off. Later, the men were caught and identified as an inn-keeper and three miners; in their bags were found eighty rings, some still on fingers, 300 watches and several purses full of gold and silver.

If the French Red Cross had faced the beginning of the war in total disarray, they had the good sense to quickly appoint an energetic and competent man, comte de Flavigny, as president. De Flavigny immediately embarked on a frenetic round of fundraising. He persuaded the empress to donate 500,000 francs to the society and to arrange for the vast Palais de l'Industrie to be turned over to it. In six weeks de Flavigny managed to raise over four million francs, as well as a great deal of supplies. Posters went up all over Paris, asking for money, linen, shirts and blankets. 'The needs are immense – Time is pressing – Give-oh-Give quickly!' De Flavigny's wife and the Maréchale Canrobert began to recruit nurses and were soon at work from six in the morning collecting and packing up clothes, food and wine. Within days there were 330 committees at work and 110 more about to start. Towards the end of August, a vast Red Cross display was held in the Champs Elysées, with Red Cross members in their distinctive blue uniforms with red cross badges, wandering through the crowds with bags on the end of long poles, rather like fishing nets, collecting money.

It was during the Franco-Prussian war that the term 'ambulance' was first used to describe anything from a single cart collecting the wounded, to field hospitals, first-aid stations, buildings given over to temporary hospitals and entire self-sufficient medical units, with surgeons, priests, nurses, carriages, horses and all food and medical supplies. They could move or stay still and consisted of buildings, vehicles or groups of people. From the day the Franco-Prussian war was declared, foreign Red Cross societies from all parts of Europe, recognizing in this conflict the perfect opportunity to test all that had been discussed during the many meetings held towards the end of the 1860s, began to organize their 'ambulances' for the wounded of both armies.

Many of the people who went to the war in the name of the Red
Cross, whether doctors, volunteer nurses or retired army officers, found
time to keep diaries and write letters home. Like Appia and van de Velde
in Schleswig, these men and women – intrepid, humane and adventurous
– give a remarkable sense not just of how this new relief operation
would work, but of war itself in the third quarter of the nineteenth
century and how it was viewed by ordinary people. It was as if they
believed that the nature of future conflicts might be rethought in the
light of their experiences. Received warmly by the military, though not
at first by the medical services who saw the very existence of the Red
Cross as a reproach to their own inefficiency, these volunteers and their
'ambulances' were soon accomplishing extraordinary things.

The Belgian Red Cross reached the war first; after it, in rapid succession, came volunteers from Luxemburg, Switzerland, Russia, Italy and
Scandinavia. One of the earliest Red Cross photographs shows a Dutch
unit at Mannheim sitting in the sun, the women in their full dresses,
the men standing around; they seem leisurely and confident. The Dutch
also sent a unit to Versailles under van de Velde, who wrote cheerfully
to Moynier: 'Here I am then in the middle of doing fine and important
work . . . It is said that the King will install himself at Versailles. It is
not likely to be in the palace, neutralized as it is by my ambulances and
contaminated by twenty cases of typhoid.' The Geneva Convention had
stipulated that all gifts were first to be shared equally by both sides at
war, and along with the doctors and nurses came supplies, collected in
vast depots in northern France and Belgium, of meat, potatoes, wine,
tobacco, shirts, sheets, blankets and medicine. When bread for the
armies grew scarce, villages and towns all over Luxemburg began to bake
and loaves were despatched to the front. Once the Prussians were seen
to be holding the larger number of prisoners and nursing more of
the wounded, then a greater part of the supplies were directed to
them.

No foreign aid society was to become more involved in the Franco-
Prussian war than the British and none has left so many memoirs. Until
the summer of 1870 there had been very little interest in England either
in Dunant or in the Geneva Convention, beyond a number of desultory
meetings among the backers of a provisional aid society in London, who
had been unable to rouse much enthusiasm for the idea in the public

at large, and some intermittent sniping from Florence Nightingale. The Franco-Prussian war changed all that. The British society went into it cautiously, full of doubt, with the War Office opposed to the idea; they emerged committed, organized and keen.

In July, when news reached London about the first battles of the war, John Furley, a young solicitor who had been responsible for pushing through the provisional committee and had translated the book by Moynier and Appia, *La Guerre et la Charité* into English, went to call on Colonel Loyd-Lindsay, hero of the Crimean War battles of Inkerman and Alma for which he had been awarded the Victoria Cross, was another supporter of the Geneva Convention. Furley proposed to him a further determined effort to launch a British society and send volunteers to the front.

On 22 July, a letter by Loyd-Lindsay appeared in *The Times*. 'The news which daily reaches us from abroad,' it stated, 'shows that nations can at times go mad as well as individuals.' Describing the 'pain and suffering of those who remain hours and days unattended to', he announced that he was placing £1,000 in the hands of Messrs Coutts and Co., to go towards a 'Society for Aiding and Ameliorating the Condition of the Sick and Wounded in Times of War'. If the money was not wanted, the letter continued, 'we shall all rejoice, but I fear that much more will be needed'. His words had an immediate effect. Support flowed in.

On 2 August, Florence Nightingale, overcoming her worst fears about untrained volunteers, herself wrote to *The Times* asking for people to come forward and her letter was read out at a public meeting. Money and offers poured in. On 4 August, John Furley — described dismissively by Florence Nightingale as a 'pert young solicitor . . . who . . . had some correspondence with me, the folly of which could only be equalled by its impertinence' — left for France. He spent six hours in Paris talking to Comte de Flavigny and admiring the energetic war work of the French ladies, went on to Geneva to see Moynier and returned via Berlin, where he met Baron von Sydow, President of the German Red Cross, and watched German ladies preparing *Liebergaben*, gifts of love, for the soldiers at the front. By the end of the war, 426,253 handkerchiefs and 2,039,195 pairs of woollen socks would have reached them.

He returned to London to find the new society launched. Queen Victoria had agreed to become its patroness and the Prince of Wales its president. The provisional committee had taken rooms at 7 St Martin's Place, just off Trafalgar Square. But by the summer of 1870, the new British society had already overflowed into two nearby houses. Furley discovered a ladies' committee at work, headed by Princess Christian of Schleswig-Holstein, Princess Louise and Princess Mary of Teck. Calls were being made for charpie (a kind of lint) coats, 'ice bags of Gutta Percha' (a form of rubber), smelling salts, concentrated meat essences and 'drawers'. A label from one of the incoming parcels, now in the archives of the British society, lists its contents as eighteen flannel bandages and six pillowcases from Queen Victoria, and eighteen flannel bandages, twelve pairs of socks and two invalid coats from Princess Louise. By the end of August, £30,000 had been donated in cash and, as more and more supplies kept arriving, so the British society flowed over into houses belonging to the Board of Works and then into St Martin's workhouse and the vaults of the church itself. Outside, the streets were full of porters and vehicles; inside, teams of women checked and ticked off the contents of every parcel, finding among the offerings pink silk petticoats and baby clothes. Men, lent by a nearby firm, packed bales for France. Upstairs, Princess Christian presided over her ladies' committee, answered letters, kept the books and supervised seventy-three women volunteers who washed old clothes and turned them into charpie. A gentleman's committee nearby interviewed surgeons and tested their French and German. By the middle of September, sixty-two surgeons, paid £1 a day, had been taken on for the duration of the war. Florence Nightingale was now chafing at the 'dilitoriness' of the society, writing scathingly of a rumour that Loyd-Lindsay was uncertain about what to do next: 'Have they really got no further than that? It makes me despair of Englishmen.' She had been asked to take charge of the volunteers, but felt too frail to do so and was anxious and agitated about the need to send responsible, trained women under which volunteers could serve, 'not sentimental enthusiasts but downright lovers of hard work,' as she wrote to Sir Harry Verney on 2 August. 'There are things to be done and things to be seen which at once separate the true metal from the tinkling brass.' On 7 August she wrote again. The volunteers should on no account be shipped off unprepared 'like cows or bottles of wine'.

One of the first people to volunteer for the British society was a young woman called Emma Thomson. Little is known about her, beyond the fact that she was well connected and had become intrigued by war during a visit to a battlefield of the Italian campaign of 1867. At much the same time, another young woman, Louise MacLaughlin, who had the benefit of 'long hospital training', came to St Martin's Place to volunteer. The two women were sent to join the first 'English Column', consisting of one surgeon, one paid nurse, one male secretary and themselves, and on 16 August they set out for Sedan. While they travelled they kept notes, and on their return to London eight months later, turned them into a book, *Our Adventures During the War of 1870*, a curious but evocative mixture of genuine sympathy, social etiquette, homespun philosophy and travel notes.

Emma Thomson and Louise MacLaughlin reached Dover with 'all the fresh enthusiasm of untried soldiers' and bought second-class tickets for the crossing to France, intending to save the society money. It was very rough and they sat on deck, which later earned them a reprimand for lowering the dignity of the society. Their first taste of war came when they saw trains bringing the casualties back from the front; in forty-eight hours they counted 2,000 wagons of wounded men. When the train taking them to Sedan halted, as it frequently did, the lines being almost continuously blocked, they strolled in the fields. From their carriage, as they neared Saarbrücken, they could see the fires from the German camps and hear the soldiers singing 'Vaterland'. Like Dunant and Appia before them, they were appalled at the injuries of the wounded. 'Darkness came on,' they wrote of their arrival at Rémilly. 'Moans of pain, and sudden sharp cries of agony added to its fearful effect. Crimson-stained rags and bits of torn clothing, dirty straw, blankets, caps and guns were strewn about, and the heat was stifling, whilst the smoke of the torches choked wounded and assistants alike.' Writing about starving men eating the entrails of dead horses, about looting and the desperate refugees, they observed: 'There was a low, distant grumble in the air, but no cloud in the blue sky. "They are fighting in front," we said, as we sipped our morning coffee; but we did not dream how an empire was being lost.'

It would be unfair to paint them as dreamers. At Sedan they got briskly down to work, nursing the French wounded and the Bavarian soldiers who fell ill after gorging huge amounts of unripe grapes, noting with horror the mutilated bodies, the smouldering ruins and the sense of utter desolation. Their book is a fine portrait of the war, with its chaos and shortages, its harshness and bursts of altruism. When they had free time, they went to listen to the Prussian band playing in the Place Turenne, and watched the faces of the French who stood about, 'half sulky, half admiring'. The two young women were true spirits of the Red Cross as Dunant had dreamed it would be, partly practical, partly crusading, and he would have admired their stern views on what the war was doing to the soldiers who fought it, filling them, they said, with a 'brand of licentiousness, brutality, dishonesty, untruthfulness and revenge'.

At the end of September, Thomson and MacLaughlin joined the Anglo-American ambulance at Sedan, a unit set up and funded by the foreign community in Paris, with eight American and eight British doctors. Sedan stood in the centre of a circle of fire from 600 Prussian field guns. During that terrible battle, William McCormack, one of the British surgeons, living on horseflesh soup, black bread and brandy, operated continuously for an entire day and most of the night: 'till the floor and everything about was saturated with blood, and the severed limbs were ghastly to behold'. When the city was captured, leaving 80,000 French prisoners and thousands of badly wounded men, the surgeons reported on the wonders of the new chloroform for amputations.

Later, the Anglo-American ambulance clashed with the French medical services over the question of whether or not the windows should be kept open in hospital wards, the foreign surgeons saying that the only way to prevent 'virulent infection' was to have the wind blowing through, while the French argued that the lives of the patients would be endangered by the draughts. The Americans, who won the day, also objected to the way the French troops left the area scattered with the 'offal of slaughtered beasts and dead horses', and complained bitterly that the seventeen French male nurses detailed to help them were 'ignorant, dirty, negligent, disobedient and insolent'. When the ambulance moved on to Orleans, they turned the railway station into a hospital, converting the first-class waiting room and the buffet into wards, the ticket office into a storeroom, and the telegraph office into an operating theatre. For a long time afterwards, wrote Charles Ryan, a twenty-one-year-old Irish medical student taken on by the ambulance as a dresser, 'I never entered a large terminus . . . without speculating on the number of wounded that it would accommodate'.

Their services no longer needed at the front, the unit, taking Thomson and MacLaughlin with them, set off back for Versailles, at one point loading wagons, horses, supplies and themselves on to trains, crossing through Prussian and French lines carrying Union Jacks, the Stars and Stripes, and huge red-and-white Red Cross flags. One of their drivers was 'Nigger Charlie', a black ex-slave who had followed his former master to the front and who was an excellent cook; as they rode, he entertained them with stories of slave life in Virginia. Reaching Versailles after many days on the road, they met Loyd-Lindsay who told them sharply that their uniform was far too similar to that of the French soldiers, and that they should change into the 'undress uniform of the Royal Artillery' and attach themselves to the German Field Hospital Service. They had to wait while the uniforms were sent for.

Loyd-Lindsay was now chairman of the new British society and early in October he had set off for France on a tour of inspection. He took with him £40,000, raised from the British public, to be divided equally between Prussian and French medical services. His manservant Mr Whittle went with him and later wrote a pamphlet about their travels. They carried one small knapsack and a water bottle each. At Le Havre they did a little sight seeing and watched the Gardes Mobiles goose-stepping, before catching a coach for Paris, peering anxiously out of the window for the 'dreaded Uhlans', while admiring the autumn country-side and the apple and pear trees laden down with ripe fruit. At Les Andelys, they spent the night in the Lion d'Or and Whittle grew increas-ingly nervous that, 'not having a Frenchified face,' he might be taken for a spy. Next day they saw magpies, pecking at the remains of a soldier's meal. The two men reached Versailles on 9 October, and were astonished to find the Prussians sightseeing. Whittle was pleased to note that though the palace had been turned into a hospital, great care was being taken not to harm the paintings.

The Comte de Flavigny had proposed to Loyd-Lindsay and Whittle a meeting with the Prince of Pless, the man in charge of the German volunteers, in order to discuss the 'victims of war'. Carrying a Red Cross flag, the three men were able to move backwards and forwards through Prussian and French lines, and in keeping with the niceties of Red Cross life lunched with the prince, Bismarck sitting on Loyd-Lindsay's right.

Once the money had been delivered, the Englishmen returned to London after a very rough crossing. Whittle's pamphlet, good-tempered and leisurely, reads like an amiable tourist's guide to war. For his part, Loyd-Lindsay was delighted with what he believed had been a triumphant success for the Red Cross. 'The fact of being thus escorted by a German officer through the Prussian front lines, in order to make my way into a town besieged by them, in order to take relief to their enemies' wounded and ill, is something that could be carried out only under the safe-keeping and the spirit of a treaty such as the Geneva Convention.'

Florence Nightingale was somewhat less impressed. A long letter written to Emily Verney, raising questions about the best form of help to be provided by foreign aid societies in wartime, and remarking that all would become clear once Loyd-Lindsay returned and reported on his mission, has a note in pencil, scribbled along the side. 'N.B. L.L. has made no inquiry. Cannot give the slightest information – visited no hospitals – knows nothing – or will tell nothing.' Her letters to her niece are fractious, irritable. Speed was needed, better organization, efficiency; the society's work, to date, was 'far from satisfactory'.

She was too harsh. By now British surgeons and nurses were scattered all over France, either serving with their own ambulances or attached to others, while retired British army officers, under the Red Cross flag, were handing out supplies that were leaving London at the rate of four tons a day. One load consisted of 250 iron bedsteads, sent at forty-eight hours' notice to a church converted into a hospital at Pont-à-Mousson. Major General Sir Vincent Eyre returned from a visit of inspection full of praise for the 'admirable services' of the British ambulances, whose equipment was turning out to be far superior to anything the French possessed, but full of horror at the numbers of dead horses floating down the river after the battle of Sedan and noting that he had come across Sir George Sinclair handing out two tons of biscuits and 4,000 cigars to 4,000 starving French prisoners. He himself had 'breakfasted at the Hôtel de la Croix d'Or, very bad and very dear; . . . beef (horse) steak, some cold mutton, fried potatoes and red wine'. At Balan, a Dr Frank had spent all night after a battle looking after 200 wounded men, removing bullets and staunching the bleeding from shell wounds, with just one large bottle of morphine and the help of the two daughters of a local dyer and a schoolmaster. Everywhere, up and down the lines, groups of British Red Cross volunteers were running soup kitchens in stations for the wounded trundling by on trains and doing their best to produce hot food as near the battlefield as possible.

John Furley, the most indefatigable of them all, whose account of the war reads as if he was permanently out of breath, hurried from battlefield to battlefield, supervising depots, handing out supplies, seeking wounded men who had been overlooked in the countryside or abandoned in ruined houses, struggling through mud that reached to his knees, bumping into other foreign ambulances, and protesting strongly that the French were 'wanting in punctuality, order and discipline'. The Dutch ambulance, he observed, had an amiable bulldog called Bismarck, on account of his 'highly developed faculty for annexation'. After the battle of Sedan, Furley removed his red cross armband, saying that the emblem was being so abused by commercial travellers doing business among the troops, and by spies, that he was ashamed to wear it. Furley is a sort of aesthetic Scarlet Pimpernel dashing backwards and forwards across the Channel, finding deserted châteaux to sleep in, ever in search of more wounded men in need of help, but also interested in furniture and tapestries, noting with pleasure some of the paintings he came across in abandoned houses. While based briefly in Versailles, he arranged a concert among the foreign correspondents, at which Beattie Kingston of the *Daily Telegraph* played the piano, and the notorious 'spiritualist' Daniel Dunglas Home, the subject of Browning's 'Mr Sludge, "The Medium"' recited poems, every now and then breaking off for 'spiritualistic manifestations'.

One of the first activities of the British society had been to open depots at convenient spots in northern France from where they could hand out supplies and provision their ambulances. Sir Vincent Eyre, calling on the help of expatriate 'English Ladies and Gentlemen', had set up a depot in Boulogne, with a sub-office in Amiens under a Colonel Cox and his wife Emma, a nurse in the Crimea. Cox, who ran a field kitchen on the battlefield of Querrieux, maintained that a cup of hot coffee could reduce the death rate among the wounded by up to thirty per cent. A long letter from Emma Cox, written to Sir Vincent and Lady Eyre on 7 November, is revealing of another, less attractive, side of Red Cross life. 'Yesterday,' she reported, was a busy day. After early morning prayers we set to work packing . . . This sort of hospital visiting is not fatiguing, as I have only to make myself pleasant to the sufferers and they are all so gentle and quiet, it is no great effort. I tell you only hospital news, as I never talk or think of anything else. One feels one can be of use, then one is proud of one's Queen and Country . . . Changed shirts of men who had never had their clothes off for three months! We had to cut them off their back . . . Such an afternoon's work it has been!

After the war was over, the Boulogne Committee published an account of its activities. The tone is distinctly self-satisfied, and there is much talk of 'kindliness of manners' and the handing out of 'Port wine jelly, four or five milk biscuits, a pot of calves foot jelly'. A tetchy note has been added on the fly-leaf, evidently written by someone in London. 'The Boulogne Committee no doubt did its work well enough but with more fun and self-assertion than were shown in St Martin's Place, where we had no time for anything but hard work and no thought of advertising ourselves.'

The siege of Paris provided the International Committee and the various national Red Cross societies with a further challenge. It was also one of Dunant's finest hours, perhaps his last really fine hour of active Red Cross life, away from the slights of his former colleagues, able to make decisions on his own and still held in esteem by the French aristocracy. And it gave rise to a fresh burst of memoirs and diaries, in which a most peculiar range of activities carried out in the name of the Red Cross were fully reported.

On 4 September 1870, following the disastrous battle of Sedan in which the French were hopelessly outclassed by superior Prussian artillery and better generals, and Napoleon III was captured, the French Second Empire toppled. A popular uprising established a provisional government of National Defence, under Léon Gambetta and Louis Jules Trochu, who called on all shades of political opinion except the Bonapartists to join them. Empress Eugènie slipped away from the palace, took refuge with an American dentist, Dr Thomas Evans, and then left Paris for England.

An army of 120,000 men, veterans, reservists, boys and older men, was recruited to help defend the city.

On 18 September, the Prussians reached Paris. The next day the city, completely surrounded by a ring of German troops, was cut off. But the Parisians had been preparing for the siege. Outlying forts had been abandoned once the decision had been taken to retrench within a fortified inner circle and houses which might have helped the enemy were burnt down. Morale was high. Provisions filled every warehouse and loft; 220,000 sheep, 40,000 cows and 12,000 pigs were put to graze in the parks of Luxemburg and Vincennes. The Parisians believed their city to be impregnable. The early days were spent perfecting ways of communicating with the outside world and balloons and pigeons were soon airborne, carrying letters over the Prussian troops and into French hands. Even when the food shortage became acute, pigeons were considered so sacred that, unlike dogs and cats, they were spared. The progress of the famine reached the Germans through intercepted balloons.

Barracks, makeshift hospitals and factories now filled the city. The Gare du Nord became a flour mill; the Gare de Lyon, a cannon factory, and the Gaîté theatre was given over to sewing uniforms. From the boulevards came the constant sound of marching and drilling. Whenever they could, men appeared in uniform; women abandoned their bustles for nurses' aprons.

The siege of Paris opened with three separate kinds of ambulances. There were the ones run by the army, which were inadequate and inefficient; those attached to the foreign community and the press; and private ones which acted independently, often set up by people keen to safeguard their property with prominent red crosses. Soon, Paris was garlanded with red cross banners and flags, hanging from windows, nailed on to doors and walls, draped over carriages and carts. Parisian women, eager to demonstrate their patriotism, had special dresses run up, and went about the city ostentatiously in their uniforms, rolling bandages busily in their carriages. In the rue de Courcelles, once home to Princess Mathilde, Mlle Hocquiny presided over the linen store of the French Red Cross, keeping the books and watching over the sixty local women who came twice a week from one of Paris's main laundries to pack bales of clothing.

By early October, the number of private ambulances was such that the military governor ordered that they should all be registered under a central office, and that the mobile ones should carry papers certifying that they had the right to leave the city to collect the wounded. Some 1,319 permits were issued. Though some of the moving ambulances returned to Paris at night piled high with vegetables rather than casualties, some sort of order was introduced. And as the numbers of the wounded grew, so medical services took over the Palais-Royale, the Théâtre Français, the Tuileries, the Bibliothèque Nationale, the Ecole des Mines and the Ministry of Foreign Affairs. Rivalry between private ambulances became bitter. 'The wounded soldier,' observed Edmond Goncourt in his diary, 'has become an object of fashion.' An Englishman called Felix Whitehurst was a visitor to Paris during the siege. 'As for respecting ambulance flags, why, they must "respect" all Paris,' he wrote in a memoir, 'it is one white wave over which ripples the "Red Cross".' Whitehurst made fun of the squabbles:

> There are ten times too many ambulances, and two hundred times too many ladies to manage them. At evening receptions – such as exist now – Deputy Bandage-Mistress taunts First Poultice with having less 'serious cases' than she has at her place. 'I don't know,' says First Poultice, 'we lost three last night, and we have had five "legs"' . . . A charming young girl said: 'Look in that basket, and you will see the most delightful little foot you ever saw, just cut off a drummer.'

The early optimism and delicacy of the Parisians began to fade. Soon there was a terrible smell of sewage – traditionally collected in the city by Germans, who had now fled – from the piles mounting in the streets, and Whitehurst complained that the Gardes Mobiles had a 'capacity of filth exceeding even that of Spanish soldiers'. In mid-November it rained; then it snowed. Typhus and smallpox broke out. Food started to run out, and a ferocious black market cornered the remaining eggs and butter. Foreigners, looked at with considerable hostility as so many mouths to feed, were readily taken for spies. The Paris zoo was mobbed, and the young elephant Pollux cut up into steaks, said to taste delicious. Crows and the roots of dahlias went into the pot and pet dogs were judged as good as mutton. Edmond Goncourt visited the English butcher, Roo's on the Boulevard Haussmann, to see what he still had to sell. 'In the midst of nameless meats and unusual horns,' he wrote, 'a boy was offering some camel's kidneys for sale.'

Conditions in the hospitals and fixed ambulances deteriorated as the numbers of sick and dying overwhelmed the few doctors and trained nurses, and people walking near the Palais de l'Industrie, which remained a hospital until acute cold drove patients away, were haunted by the cries of the wounded having their legs amputated. Nurses were described by Edmond Goncourt as 'old whores, fat, superannuated'. The killer infection was septicaemia, followed by gangrene. 'Death sheds' were erected into which men with septicaemia were moved and one surgeon confessed later that he had been unable to save a single amputation case during the entire siege. Of the Grand Hotel, the most fashionable of all the ambulances, with fifty-nine ladies, most of them titled, vying with each other to nurse the patients, it was soon being said that a man could not cut his finger in the wards and reach the door alive.

The best ambulance, in which a man could actually hope to survive the war, was that run by Dr Evans, the genial, round-faced American dentist, with a moustache so long and so wispy that it looked like two halves of a beard flowing down his cheeks. Dr Evans was much liked both by the Parisians and the large foreign community. He had come to Paris twenty-three years earlier to take up a partnership with a fellow American, and made his fortune after being named 'surgeon dentist' to Napoleon and buying up houses with advance information of Baron Haussmann's demolition plans. In 1867, after the Great Exhibition in Paris, Dr Evans had purchased the whole collection of up-to-date medical equipment from the Civil War shown by the Americans. After calling a meeting of all Americans resident in the city at the time of the siege, he presented his ambulance to the war effort and appointed a Dr Swinburne as chief surgeon. Like the doctors working with the Anglo-American ambulance at Sedan, Dr Swinburne was convinced that the only way to fight septicaemia was to have plenty of ventilation. His patients were laid out in draughty tents, which grew draughtier as the weather worsened, heated only by a small stove in a hole in the ground. Four out of five of his amputation cases survived. French officers were soon said to carry cards with them requesting that they should be sent to Dr Swinburne if anything befell them.

Although some of the foreign residents who had been unable to flee Paris continued to meet in clubs and stroll along the boulevards, Loyd-Lindsay described the city, during his visit in October, as dead and gloomy. He dined with the Comte de Flavigny, who gave him a 'very good dinner, tho' eked out with brains, foie gras etc'. John Furley, still in pursuit of needy wounded soldiers, arrived in Paris driving a wagon with a huge red cross flag, full of fresh meat and vegetables, destined for a house where some patients from Brittany were being nursed by a Mme Tronchu. He unloaded the supplies on to the marble floor of the War Ministry, before going off to dine on fresh sole with Baron Mundy. It is not clear where the sole came from. Others were eating ostrich from the zoo and mouse.

The siege found Dunant still in Paris, helping the French Red Cross Society run its ambulances, living in comfort in a room in the Hôtel de Ville, in exchange for hanging a red cross flag out of one window and the Swiss flag out of another. Towards the end of September, he set up the French Provident Association and issued primitive first aid kits, with bandages and gauze steeped in disinfectant, as well as identity tags for soldiers to tie around their necks with string. He wrote and had printed thousands of copies of a leaflet in which he spoke of the need 'to instruct, to instil morals into, and to humanize the young men who are being obliged to take up arms'. They should be awakened and everything done to develop their 'nobility of character'.

In December, when the temperature dropped to −17°C, the Seine iced over and what gas was left was being kept for the balloons to communicate with the outside word, Dunant set up a commission for warm clothing. A series of rooms in the armoury in the Rue de Rivoli were turned over to him, and here people came with any clothes they could spare for the soldiers in the trenches, most of whom had no socks and the thinnest of jackets and coats. Dunant was not greatly impressed by Parisian generosity. 'The French, and particularly the Parisians,' he wrote later to his mother, 'only got what they deserved; they were profoundly egotistical, before and during the siege. They need a tyrant, and I for one would be delighted to see one.' Dunant tried, but failed, to get access to the German prisoners in French hands. On 3 December, he was writing that he was in splendid health, 'and I eat neither cats nor rats, though they say that they . . . make excellent pâté'.

By Christmas Day, Paris was without hot water; furniture was being chopped up for firewood. The Parisians were freezing, starving, and smallpox and cholera were spreading rapidly among people already weakened by lack of food. On 27 December, the Prussians advanced their gun battalions and began to shell the city, adding further to the misery in the hospitals. When Paris capitulated a month later, Jules Favre, the Minister for Foreign Affairs, and Bismarck had just signed an armistice, ceding Alsace and north-west Lorraine to Germany and agreeing to pay $1 billion in indemnity. The siege was in its 131st day.

No sooner was it lifted than Comte de Flavigny asked Dunant to accompany him to Versailles, to intercede with the Prince of Pless on behalf of a group of wounded French irregular troops, who were scheduled to be shot as soon as they recovered from their wounds. The prince proved obliging and the men's lives were spared. Versailles was full of Prussian officers Dunant recognized from his earlier visits to Berlin. They invited him to dine, and his memoirs record his delight, for he had not eaten for some time. And it was in Versailles at the end of January, in the Hall of Mirrors, that Wilhelm was enthroned as kaiser of Germany.

On 18 March the French National Guard rose up, refusing to accept defeat, and set up a new government, the Commune, in the Hôtel de Ville. The old guard withdrew to Versailles, and a mob of well-armed and disaffected men took over the streets. By now, many of the representatives of the foreign Red Cross societies had gone home, but Dunant, who had stayed on in France, was there to witness the closing acts of the war, and to help the French Red Cross care for the wounded of both sides, Communards and old guard, to do what he could for the many hostages, and to plead with Bismarck, via his aide the Prince Baden, to allow the neutralization of certain areas. According to Dunant's memoirs, the prince replied that humanitarian concerns did not unduly burden Bismarck's mind. Taken to be a spy, first by one side, then the other, Dunant bravely lent his Swiss passport to someone in graver danger than himself. From time to time, he dropped in to see viscomtesses who had turned their homes into hospitals, commiserating with those who had seen them vandalized in spite of all the red flags hanging from the windows.

On Monday 23 May he watched the first government troops, in their distinctive red trousers, enter the city. Street by street, they cleared Paris of the Communards, killing 20,000 people in reprisals and despatching many more to penal colonies. Tricolours took the place of red cross flags, sprouting from every balcony and on every carriage. Soon, trains full of pale, thin French prisoners-of-war, returning from Germany, began arriving at the Gare du Nord. One of the last hostages of the war to die at the hands of the Communards was the Abbé Allard, a member of the French Red Cross Society, who went before the firing squad still wearing his red cross armband.

The war was over. It had lasted ten months, and 138,000 French soldiers were dead. In Paris, the Tuileries had been destroyed, the Hôtel de Ville burnt down, the Bois de Boulogne made treeless; the city looked, as one visitor put it, desecrated by a 'savage, barbarian massacre'. Throughout France, towns and villages were in ruins and broken weapons and the detritus of war lay scattered over the fields. But peace between Germany and France had been signed, and, as Edmond Goncourt wrote in his diary, the solution to the civil war had been 'brutal, imposed by sheer force of arms' but the 'bleeding' had been done thoroughly and France could look to 'twenty years of peace before it'.

For the International Committee in Geneva, the Franco-Prussian war was a victory, even if a flawed one. The Geneva Convention had been flouted, and the red cross emblem abused by all sides from one end of France to the other, particularly by the French army. A pamphlet which appeared in Berlin listing France's violations ran to forty pages. Moynier, bitterly accused of having done nothing to censure the French, was able only to keep repeating that it was not the job of the International Committee to act as judge and jury. Early in 1871, Bismarck had complained that the Convention was being so profoundly ignored by Germany's enemies that the whole question of German adherence to it would need reconsideration.

But its achievements had also been considerable. Answering his critics, Moynier was able to point to the post and information service in Basle which had put out ten reports in ten days, to the special committee to look after the needs of French prisoners in German camps, to the repatriation of several thousand disabled French, to the countless lives spared in the name of the Geneva Convention, to the enormous amount of relief that had been channelled through its offices in both Basle and

Geneva, and to the excellent work of the different national Red Cross societies. If there were army officers rejoicing at what they took to be the failure of Swiss jurists to draw up effective laws of war, there were also many voices congratulating the International Committee on the range of its achievements. For Moynier, Appia and the others, the Franco-Prussian war would provide not only an invaluable benchmark for future conflicts, but the occasion for a careful re-evaluation. 'The baptism of fire which it received,' Moynier wrote later about the Convention, 'far from shaking it, consolidated it, so much so that universal condemnation would strike any one of the signatories who dared denounce it, if ever, God forbid, one was tempted to do so!'

For the two Red Cross societies most closely involved, the war was perceived as a test that both had passed with glory. The Prussians, well equipped medically and militarily in 1870, had soon realized how essential their many volunteers had been when it came to looking after 400,000 French prisoners of war, most of them in need of medical care, food and warm clothes. By the end of the war, the German society comprised twenty-five main groups, and over a quarter of a million members. The French Society had even more reason to feel pleased. Starting from virtually nothing, it had raised over 18 million francs and another 4 million more of relief, and treated 340,000 casualties, at the cost of just eight of its members. Following the Basle agency's example, it had set up an information office employing fifty-six officers, dealing at its peak with 41,000 letters a day. As a French doctor, Dr Nandin, reporting on the work of the society, put it, 'If, on the one hand, we saw a war of savages, on the other we will always congratulate ourselves for having collaborated with a work of the most remarkable philanthropy.' Building on its experiences, the society now set about starting committees all over France, spawning two strong women's organizations, which would merge under the umbrella of the society in 1892.

In all, fourteen Red Cross societies had played a part. A total of 347 foreign doctors had served on the battlefields, of whom forty-six were dead. If individual foreigners had sometimes found the rules of impartiality irksome — a surprising number started the war pro-French and ended it pro-German — neutrality had been dutifully observed, and help given to both sides regardless of feelings. Something of the foreigners' irritation with the French is summed up in a report prepared by Sir

J. G. Tollemache Sinclair, one of the many adventurers who wrote about the work of the Red Cross societies and the effectiveness of the Geneva Convention. Tollemache Sinclair, in a number of pieces written for *The Times*, and in a booklet describing his experiences, accused the French soldiers of attacking ambulances, murdering wounded prisoners, mistreating enemy surgeons, using the banned explosive bullets during the battle of Wörth, incarcerating 300 Bavarians ill with typhus and dysentery in small cells on a diet of bread and water, and allowing the 'savage Turcos and Arabs' to mutilate the German wounded, decapitating them and cutting off their noses and ears. He criticized French generals for their sumptuous living, 'every day a dinner of eight courses, and dessert, with champagne and four or five other sorts of wine' and then for not paying their bills. He expressed revulsion at the 'obscene prints and books . . . in large quantities . . . found in captured French baggage', and horror at the destruction of the magnificent library in Strasbourg. The German troops, he said, left 'French poultry untouched' even when hungry.

The British society, born of this war, and from now on to play a major part in the entire Red Cross movement, returned to London to take stock of its achievements. They had been considerable. £294,445 had been raised, an enormous sum for the times, much of it in small individual contributions that even Florence Nightingale found touching. She wrote to Harriet Martineau in February 1871 that they were 'collected by half-pence from poor negro congregations in the West Indies, from Ragged Schools, National Schools, Factories — not the rich and comfortable but the whole mass of hard working honest frugal stupid people — who have contributed every penny they could so ill spare' in places she had never even heard of. Some 83,800 blankets had been collected and distributed, as well as 68,440 pairs of drawers, 156 bottles of opium, 100 nosebags, 65 tons of preserved meats, 60 bottles of ink, 49,706 cigars, 1,087 dozen port and 'large quantities' of pins, needles, pin cushions and buttons. Shipments of money or stores had been sent as far south as Lyons, east to Breslau and north-east to Stettin. The Loyd-Lindsays celebrated the end of the war with a banquet in Greenwich.

Discussing the war, Loyd-Lindsay and Furley agreed that entire ambulances run by the society with no more than four or five surgeons had worked the best, that fresh air and proper food could achieve miracles, that getting food and drink quickly to the wounded was crucial, and that the response to the 'sheer size and horror' of war, among people 'simply interested in doing good and with no special skills' had been overwhelming. 'It has been,' noted Loyd-Lindsay, 'a great step in the advance of international friendly feeling.' The consensus, among the British members who had served in France, was that the Geneva Convention had been of great value in drawing many more doctors to the battlefield, in pioneering new methods of treatment and prodding the professional military surgeons into action, and that the voluntary effort had transformed the life of the sick and wounded. The 'ideal man' to lead a Red Cross team, wrote Archibald Forbes of the *Daily News*, who had followed the war and the activities of the various doctors and nurses closely, should 'possess great command of temper, an entire absence of paltry self-esteem' and be a figure of 'promptitude and without fussiness . . . or bristles'. Give such a man the command, Forbes recommended, and 'make him a despot'.

Florence Nightingale's warning that there was a danger that too much activity by Red Cross societies would 'diminish the responsibility of each belligerent for its own sick and wounded' had proved unfounded. Florence Nightingale herself, who had worked much harder at rallying supporters than her carping words about the British society seem to suggest, had come round to saying that there was 'evidence that you have done more good than all the Orders acting under rules', though she held on tenaciously to her view that 'training, discipline and prompt obedience on the part of the agents' was absolutely essential. At the end of the war, she received the bronze cross of the French Red Cross society, and the Prussian Cross of Merit from the German emperor.

Not least of the many interesting aspects of the war was what it had done for women, who had been present on and near the battlefields in an official capacity in a way they never had before. Not all the reports on them were flattering, even if Maxime du Camp, in an appraisal of the Franco-Prussian war written in the 1890s, claimed that the wounded had turned with pleasure to one whose 'hand was gentle, heart compassionate and speech tender'.

When it was all over, a questionnaire went out to a number of carefully selected British surgeons, doctors and military men. In their replies they agreed that respect for the emblem would have to be enforced by 'stringent bye-laws' with John Furley observing that until a couple of men had been tried and shot for abusing the red cross, soldiers would go on doing so. But the question about women provided the most revealing replies. 'To what extent and with what results,' was the panel, exclusively male, asked, 'have female nurses been employed; and in what manner can female labour be best utilized during a campaign?' The answers expressed caution and mistrust: Florence Nightingale's highly trained women were just tolerated and almost total contempt was reserved for the lady volunteers.

Surgeon Manley, VC, talking about these 'inexperienced lady volunteers,' said that in his view 'amateurs fail by want of method; questioning orders; offering their own opinions'. All female labour, other than that provided by the Roman Catholic sisters, he considered 'superfluous, and, from the sentimentality connected with it . . . quite out of place'. A Captain Uniacke said that he objected to 'ladies, especially married, in the field'. Staff-Surgeon Wiles suggested that their employment, if strictly necessary, should be limited to the 'supply of nourishment'.

One suspects that, among these soldiers and doctors, there were few who did not agree with Dr Mayo, who felt that women nurses, though useful, 'ought always to be kept with the heavy baggage'. It would be some years before British ladies made their mark in the field.

FOUR

Stone Heaps Full of Snakes

Although the Red Cross movement was born in Europe, sparked by the vision of Dunant, a dreamer, and shaped by the organizational skills of Moynier, a bureaucrat, its logical development, to help the victims not just of war but of natural disasters in times of peace, took place in America through the frenetic lobbyings of another dreamer, Clara Barton. There too it owed its final form to the administrative talents of a less immediately likeable figure, a stern, upper-class spinster called Mabel Boardman, and the tensions between these two women were as palpable as those that soured the early days of the Committee in Geneva.

Where Clara Barton was a populist, a woman who craved admiration and relapsed into neurosis when seriously crossed, Mabel Boardman had little time for histrionics and still less for trying to please a crowd. Like Moynier, she had a taste for the minutiae of accounting and found financial casualness repugnant. Like Dunant, Clara Barton was a visionary, imprudent and lovable. The battlefields of the Civil War were her making. Older than Florence Nightingale at her first moment of triumph – Clara Barton was forty in the Civil War, Florence Nightingale thirty-six in the Crimea – she overcame her nervous illnesses to conduct a tireless campaign for an American Red Cross and for the United States to ratify the Geneva Convention. Between 1881 and 1904, years in which the American Red Cross *was* Clara Barton, she took help to twenty-one national disasters. All her life she was dogged by Florence Nightingale's reputation, complaining bitterly that while she was often referred to as the Florence Nightingale of America, no one ever spoke of the Lady of the Lamp as the Clara Barton of Britain. Yet the two women were in many ways alike, with their dogmatic certainties, their impatience with unnecessary bureaucracy, and the way they both used work to escape troubled minds, bouts of depression and, in Clara Barton's case, fears of insanity. The world saw both women as invincible; the Clara Barton who emerges from her diaries is insecure, touchy and obsessive about loyalty. Florence Nightingale and Clara Barton never met. They seem never to have wanted to meet: the one time they were in the same country they exchanged notes, then retired to their beds.

Clara Barton was born in New England on Christmas Day 1821 in a village of steepled churches and white clapboard houses called North Oxford. Her father was by temperament a democrat, a one-time soldier turned farmer and miller with interests in education and charity; her mother was a frugal and industrious woman with a keen temper. Their eldest daughter, Dolly, had been born mentally handicapped and Clara, their fifth child, was timid, overwhelmed by the forceful personalities of her parents, and quick to take refuge in obligingness and good works. At eleven she gave up most of her time to help nurse an invalid brother.

At a time when teaching, domestic service or factory work were the only possible jobs for women, she opted in her late twenties to teach a class of difficult and truculent boys, and her success with them prompted her to dream of opening a free school of her own, for the children who could not afford to pay New England fees. When the one she managed to start in 1850 proved so successful that it attracted the attention of rivalrous men teachers, she fled the bickering and went to Washington, where, in 1853, she found work in the Patent Office, transcribing entries and tracing the work of various scientific expeditions around the world. It was improbable work for a woman, but through it she perceived in herself a streak of competence and a definite appetite for leadership. When the going got too rough, she retired to bed. The Civil War found her at her desk, a by now solidly built woman, with rather small brown-black eyes, and heavy eyebrows. Her passport gave her height as 5ft 5 inches. 'Miss Barton is what we call a strong hearted woman, not "strong minded" in the invidious sense of the word,' wrote a journalist at around this time. 'She is noble in person, has a fine head and face, and is gifted with a rich voice which she modulates exquisitely.'

In the chaos and unpreparedness of the medical services of the army during the Civil War, Clara Barton discovered a new life. She was unthreatening, to the army and the Sanitary Commission alike, and forays to the front as the fighting came close to Washington won her the admiration she longed for. If she sometimes found it hard to fit in with other helpers, particularly women, her relations with ordinary soldiers were excellent. Like Dunant's, her accounts of war were stark and memorable: 'All blood and carnage . . . our wagon wheels within six feet of yet unburied dead. A mingled mass of stiffened, blackened men . . .'

But it was one particular vision that did the most to transform her future. Working among prisoners returning from captivity in the south convinced her that, as well as food, clothing and medical help, the men needed news about their families, just as the families were desperate to know what had happened to their sons and husbands. After some delicate negotiations with the military, and a personal endorsement by President Lincoln, Clara Barton drafted a letter. Addressed to 'The friends of missing persons,' it read: 'Miss Clara Barton has kindly offered to search for the missing prisoners-of-war. Please address her at Annapolis, giving name, regiment, and company of any missing prisoner.' The War Department was struggling to cope with returning prisoners and had kept no record of the dead or wounded. Clara Barton's appeal struck an immediate chord and, in the late spring of 1865, she was given a tent and a camp table and set up a centre for returning soldiers in Annapolis, Maryland.

The success of her scheme depended on the helpfulness of the returning Union veterans. 'They were enfeebled men,' one account described them, 'and the knowledge or facts now living in their memories would die with them.' With every enquiry she processed, Clara Barton added to her lists. Sub-divided into states, these lists were then published in newspapers and posted up in every government office and medical centre. The veterans were asked to check the lists and come up with any extra information they had. Letters arrived, first in tens, then in hundreds. By June, 20,000 names had been recorded and published. Clara Barton's 'office of correspondence with friends of the missing men of the United States Army' turned into a highly efficient headquarters, with clerks, ledgers and messengers, though she remained firmly in control. As favourable reports kept on appearing in the papers, the centre kept on growing, to take in not just missing prisoners but all 'missing men of the army'.

One of Clara Barton's problems was money, and in the weeks to come funds, begged and borrowed from friends, supporters and the government, were sunk into the venture with very few attempts at accountability. When peace was signed, and the missing men mostly accounted for, she petitioned the senate for the reimbursement of $15,000 she claimed had come out of her own purse. At the senate hearing, a Mr Nesmith, in a curious foretaste of a theme that would later haunt her life, inquired 'whether any voucher or evidence had been presented of the expenditure of the money?' Clara Barton was too famous and well loved for his words to matter. Mr Nesmith was silenced with a fulsome declaration that Clara Barton 'deserves well of Congress, and . . . has accomplished a most humane and excellent work'. She received her $15,000. Audiences were soon gathering, at $75 or $100 a lecture, to hear her talk of the 'work and incidents of army life', during which she often reduced her listeners to tears with her photographs of dying soldiers.

As so often, when things were going her way, Clara Barton now suffered one of her periodic bouts of crippling ill health. A doctor recommended a long visit to Europe, to convalesce in the Swiss mountains, and she booked a ticket on the *Caledonia*, bound for Glasgow. Portraits of the time show a sturdy matron in black silk; her brown hair is parted neatly in the middle and scooped up into a bun behind. Her eyes are watchful, and her skin looks sallow.

After the American south, Switzerland seemed to her cheerless, lonely and cold. She was thinking of moving on when she received a deputation one day from the International Committee led by Dr Appia. He had read of her work in the Civil War and had come to ask her why the United States continued to refuse to ratify the Geneva Convention. Clara Barton had never heard of the Red Cross. What surprised her most was to learn that the United States government had been approached three times, and each time refused to sign.

She was still convalescing in the mountains above Berne when the Franco-Prussian war broke out. After a few weeks, feeling isolated, she moved down to Geneva. Appia came to see her on his way to the front and she decided to set out for Basle, where she was soon marvelling at the warehouses filled with goods from Red Cross societies all over Europe. Moynier, who shared the prevailing dislike of having women on battlefields, was loth to encourage her desire to visit the war front. She got no further than Strasburg, where she helped refugees and was dismayed to find herself ridiculed by soldiers and in danger of being taken for a spy. She spoke very little French or German. What struck her particularly was the degree of civilian suffering, for the Civil War in America had not thrown up the same thousands of desperate and terrified women and children trying to escape the fighting. Summoned by a telegram from the Grand Duchess Louise, to help in the Red Cross hospitals in Baden, she toured the wards with her new royal patron commenting severely on the 'discord and dust'. By the end of the war she was looking after families whose lives had been destroyed by months of bombing, long sieges, and epidemics of smallpox and typhoid.

It was now that she was able to test a long-held theory that what was needed in a famine was not handouts but work, to revitalize the economy. With the help of the Grand Duchess and a court governess called Anna Zimmerman, she opened a number of local workshops to employ the refugee women to cut out and sew clothes which were then sold. Hearing of the desperate straits to which Parisians were reduced under the Commune, she moved on to Paris, walking the last seven miles when her train gave out, and she failed to find a horse that had not been eaten in the famine. She had with her a cheque given by a group of philanthropic Bostonians and spent the next two months distributing small sums of money and some 40,000 garments sent from her workshops in Baden. Her health, once again, was failing. She was worried about her eyesight. Returning at last to New York in the autumn of 1873, she found her sister Sally dying; she took instantly to her own bed with nervous exhaustion, saying that she could neither eat, sleep, walk nor talk. Her brown hair turned white.

Clara Barton was now fifty-two. This latest collapse could well have marked the end to a not unadventurous public life. As it was, she spent two years under the care of a fashionable New York doctor, who maintained that good food and 'cheeriness' were the best cures for nervous disorders, and she recovered, rising from her sickbed to announce that 'like the old war horse that has rested long in quiet waters' she was now ready for the 'bugle call' of a new war. She wrote to Appia and Moynier of her desire to further the cause of the Red Cross in America, 'to strike a blow on the great anvil of humanity'. Moynier was vague but fulsome in his reply, declaring himself delighted that someone so 'well qualified . . . should plead the cause that is so dear to us'. Appia was more precise. The International Committee, he assured her, saw her as the 'soul' of the Red Cross in America. What it needed now was a body, with an 'arm to write, to arrange methodically, to publish,' as well as feet 'for running, to go, to come, to collect, to buy'. The best method for introducing the Red Cross into America, he told her, was by four different paths: publicity, the setting up of a national organization, the collection of money and lobbying for government recognition. Clara Barton, delighted by their response but still some-what unsure of her own position, begged them to send her an official letter 'asking in your own name or that of the International Society that I do all in my power to aid you'. With this, she became their representative in Washington. They could not have asked for a better one; her new war was declared, not in the field, but in the offices of the capital.

The United States had spent fourteen years successfully resisting the Geneva Convention. Like the French, the Americans disliked the idea of having volunteers interfering in military matters. Efforts by Dr Henry Bellows, the New York clergyman behind the Sanitary Commission, to get the American government to 'join the civilized world' had failed to such an extent that an early version of an American Red Cross had simply died of neglect.

In the autumn of 1877, Clara Barton was ready to marshal her forces. Many of her influential old friends were retired or dead. America, at peace for over ten years, showed little appetite for talk of war. Wherever she went she found not just apathy but total ignorance of the whole idea of the Red Cross. Much of her time was spent in translating the International Committee's publications into English and holding soirées at which she would talk of Geneva's work. It was heavy going. The president and the secretary of state were polite but indifferent. 'Every civilized nation on earth *but ours,*' she wrote sadly to a friend, 'has signed that Convention or Treaty, we alone class with the barbarians.' About the many hours spent lobbying congressmen, she observed: 'I have talked and they have listened, but if I were to pipe I doubt if they would dance unless perchance it were to the jingle of "Silver".' With the terrible losses of the Civil War behind them, and an isolationist government fixing its sights against any 'entangling alliance', her cause seemed to her increasingly hopeless. No one read her pamphlet on *The Red Cross or the Geneva Conventions.* By the spring of 1878, she had made her mind up to 'let better persons run the world'.

One of Dunant's and Moynier's earliest concerns, expressed in the course of some of their earliest meetings, was how to occupy the new national Red Cross societies during peacetime. Clara Barton provided the solution, which would not simply galvanize support for the cause of the Red Cross in America at a moment when it seemed lost, but ensure that the United States would at last ratify the Geneva Convention. What she suggested in her pamphlet was an entirely new role adapting the wartime energies and strengths of the organization to help the victims of 'national or widespread calamities, such as plagues, cholera, yellow fever and the like, devastating fires or floods, railway disasters, mining catastrophes etc.'.

At first, the government remained indifferent. Finding strengths that seemed to desert her when things went well, Clara Barton turned her house in Dansville, a small town in Livingston County, New York, into an office, and called on a young protégé called Julian Hubbell, a chemistry teacher, to train as a doctor so that his medical skills could help in her campaigns. Playing on the sensitivities of the newly founded Associated Press, a loose union of telegraph operators sending out news over the wires, she decided to tap directly into the great American public. Making Appia's emphasis on publicity her priority – the Red Cross in America continued to remain 'a Mystery' – she courted the men of the Associated Press, sought out sympathetic journalists and took to lecturing. It worked. Something about her grit and plain speaking appealed to ordinary Americans. People began talking about Red Cross work. The new president, Garfield, and his secretary of state, James G. Blaine, shared her vision of a less isolationist America and the Geneva Convention fitted well into their plans. Even so, there were further falterings. Unlike the European aristocracy, America's leading families were only just waking up to the philanthropic tides sweeping across Europe. Then President Garfield was shot dead by an assassin. There were more delays, as a rival organization, the Women's National Relief Organization, moved in on territory that Clara Barton had thought her own. Still fighting, she pressed on and set up a first local Red Cross unit in Dansville.

Nature was clearly on her side. In the middle of September 1881, after several weeks of hot winds blowing from the south, a forest fire broke out in Michigan. Rumours reached Washington of 500 people dead and thousands more made homeless. Soon, Julian Hubbell was on his way with money, tools, bedding and clothes. Clara Barton followed close behind, raising the white flag with its red cross for the first time on American soil. Remembering the lessons of the refugees from the Franco-Prussian war, she kept her mind on the future, the need to provide work in the shape of seeds and plants rather than just handing out rations to those left homeless. Her efficiency was much praised and the fact that she had acted without consulting her supporters — the politicians, businessmen and journalists who had agreed to become supporters and founders of Red Cross 'chapters' now being set up across the country — was tactfully forgotten.

By the end of the year the new president, Chester Alan Arthur, having been lobbied by Clara Barton through his aides and political colleagues, was won round to the importance of the Geneva Convention. In December, in his annual message to Congress, he unconditionally supported the passage of 'that humane and commendable engagement . . . the Treaty of Geneva' through Congress. In March 1882, the United States became the thirty-second country to ratify the Treaty. With understandable pride, Clara Barton wrote to Moynier:

> In the ranks of the American Red Cross, I am by far the oldest
> soldier, and I believe my brave companions do not realize that
> I have ploughed a very stony furrow . . . during the five years
> I have walked alone as Red Cross pioneer.

She could at times be extremely smug.

In 1881, Clara Barton was sixty years old and about to embark on the most energetic and demanding period of her life. That summer she was awarded the International Committee's medal, their highest honour, a 'simple memorial' as Moynier somewhat pompously phrased it, 'to the more meritorious of our assistants'. Clara Barton did not see herself as an assistant. From her headquarters in Washington, a two-storey, ivy-covered house, she presided over the birth of one local Red Cross chapter after another. Though often exhausted, she did not look her age, her now white hair dyed back to its former brown and crimped according to the fashion of the day. The *New York Tribune*, while admiring her 'friendly' eyes and 'large and strong' features, commented somewhat unkindly that she could hardly 'even in her youth, have been considered a beautiful woman'. Power had made her harder and more censorious and few of her supporters now spoke of her, as they once had, as their 'precious angel'. She was not unaware of what was happening to her, writing one day: 'I am always afraid I am not as jolly as I was thirty years ago . . . I laugh when I don't forget it and have time.' More and more, she gave the impression that the Red Cross was the child she had never had, and that it was God who had placed it in her care.

She was right to have misgivings. Raising sufficient funds from government, business and private donors for her many enterprises would consume much of her coming years. Matters were complicated further by her lack of administrative skills. She found it impossible either to delegate or collaborate, and took offence when the new Red Cross chapters showed too much independence of spirit. She had decided, she confessed, that she had no choice but to 'learn to do all myself'. Her followers took to referring to her as 'the Queen'.

Clara Barton needed a disaster; it justified her existence, proved the worth of the child she was raising, and brought her the constant admiration on which she thrived. Once again, nature obliged. In the spring of both 1882 and 1883, heavy rains and melting ice caused the Mississippi river to flood and each time she hurried to the scene. In the spring of 1884, the Ohio river flooded, the waters sweeping entire towns away and leaving Cincinnati under seventy one feet of water. Clara Barton dealt with these emergencies in an increasingly intelligent and professional way. She had learnt the value of inspecting first and then providing for the actual needs of the victims rather than despatching goods at random. These were ideas far in advance of her times. 'This,' she wrote, 'is the original style and spirit of real Red Cross work.' During the Ohio flood she rented a steamer called the *J. V. Throop*, raised the Red Cross flag and set off downriver, bringing assistance through the mists and sleet to families waving frantically for help. The newspaper reporters loved it. Clara Barton had developed a keen understanding of the powers of the press and made much of the more poignant tales of hardship. A story she wrote on the 'little six', six children in Waterford who had put on a variety show to raise money for the Red Cross flood relief, was published all over the country. Crates and boxes of clothes, blankets and tools and handfuls of cheques flowed in. She rented a second steamer and, when that got stuck in mud, she put on long rubber boots and waded to shore with provisions. Sometimes, it all looked rather like a royal progress, with children presenting bouquets of flowers and passing gunboats sounding a salute.

With every disaster Clara Barton's fame grew. In September 1885, when the International Committee held its third conference in Geneva, she was told by Frederick T. Frelinghuysen, the secretary of state, that she was 'the only American who could really represent the United States'. Reluctant to make the long journey, she nevertheless went off to Switzerland, to be fêted and called the 'peer of the foremost members of the conference'. Reporters praised her 'unobtrusive yet dignified appearance'. She returned to America to raise more funds and preside over more disasters, though she was now beginning to wonder whether the American Red Cross, in its focus on disaster relief – what she called the 'knitting work' – was not moving too far from its early mandate to alleviate the miseries of war. Though she committed the American Red Cross to work during the yellow fever epidemic in Florida in 1888 and the Johnstown flood in Pennsylvania in 1889, she was becoming more conscious of the need to reserve the full weight of Red Cross intervention for the more serious disasters.

Then came an event that could not be ignored; what was more, it happened abroad, and the American Red Cross had not yet tackled a foreign disaster. Though Clara Barton wondered how wise it was to commit the society to such a vast and distant enterprise, once she saw others dither she entered the game with her customary zeal.

During the summer of 1891, rumours reached Washington of 18 million people 'without clothing, fuel or shelter' in the main harvest areas of Russia. 'In certain parts of some of the southern provinces,' reported a businessman returning from Moscow, 'most of the children are dead.' The immediate cause of the famine – which the Russian government insisted was no more than a 'bad harvest' – was the weather. The winter of 1890 had begun early and been unusually hard. Plants had frozen and died before they had time to root. Along the banks of the Volga, temperatures had fallen to −40°C. Spring had brought not rain but hot sun which scorched what crops there were and high winds which blew off the topsoil and turned the fields into dust bowls. By the early summer the landscape looked autumnal. Peasants used the thatch from their roofs to feed their dying animals.

On its own, the weather would have brought terrible hardship, but not catastrophe. But by the 1890s, the economic and financial policies of the tsarist government, emancipation, the parcelling out of plots of land too small to sustain a livelihood, as well as ferocious taxation, had already driven the peasants into an unbreakable cycle of poverty. When the crops failed across the 900,000 square miles of central European Russia, 36 million people were left destitute. 'The present famine,' wrote Charles Emory Smith, the American minister in St Petersburg, 'is one of those stupendous catastrophes which almost baffle description.'

Initial government reaction was slow and ill coordinated. There was no sense of urgency. Only in July 1891, after food riots and desperate appeals from the afflicted provinces, was a ban imposed on the shipment of rye abroad. By then, over 12 million people were starving. Slowly, a number of agencies were established to administer relief, while the Church and the Russian Red Cross society, set up among the ladies of the court and active in a fairly small way since the 1870s, were encouraged to form local branches in the famine areas. A Reuters correspondent, travelling through central Russia, sent *The Times* a revealing picture of small town Russian Red Cross life. He was taken to an estate in which the

> local branch of the Red Cross society was to be opened . . . The particular nobleman we came to see was young, handsome and intelligent, and had a remarkably pretty wife. The members . . . had assembled when we arrived. They consisted of two young, fat, and extremely stupid-looking priests. There was a Jew, who looked out of his element, a German estate agent, energetic and practical, and a Circassian Cossack in uniform . . . An old lady was also present. The country gentlemen in attendance were the Prince and his host . . .
>
> Then came the question of funds. The Circassian had given 100 roubles, a lady had sent 1,000 roubles, and this inadequate sum of 1,100 roubles for . . . a district having a population of 83,000 half-starved peasants was opened. Millions and millions

have fallen into the coffers of the central committees of the society at St Petersburg and Moscow, but where they go, nobody knows . . .

As the weeks passed, rumours spread of Russian Red Cross corruption and inefficiency and the richer merchants were soon reported to be refusing to contribute funds they doubted would ever reach the starving people.

In America, reactions to the famine were mixed, not least because there had been stories of the Russian government tolerating pogroms against the Jews and because several visitors had returned to paint a dark picture of repression. Was Russia a country that *should* be helped? On 13 November 1891, Clara Barton appealed for donations. A bare $200 was raised.

The most enterprising call for action in fact came not from the American Red Cross, but from a number of millers and editors in the Midwest, who now proposed that a bushel of corn be donated by every farmer. 'It seems like a grim, gaunt tale,' wrote the editor of the *Northwestern Miller*, 'the poorest dog which hangs about the city streets of America can pick up better food.' Slowly a bandwagon gathered speed. From the pulpit, preachers described the horrors of famine to their congregations, and by January 1892 one and a half million sacks of flour were ready and waiting in warehouses. While Congress continued to hesitate, Clara Barton kept urging speed, having agreed to involve the American Red Cross in the distribution of the flour. She was hard at work collecting more funds, arranging transport and preparing a team, under Julian Hubbell, to sail to Russia. A group of women from Iowa, who had banded together as a women's auxiliary of the Red Cross, proposed to accompany the mission and to sail up and down the Volga, nursing the sick, distributing leaflets in Russian with recipes for corn and teaching the 'hungry peasants how to prepare and cook palatable and nutritious dishes made from American grains'. Nationalistic fervour was seldom absent from early Red Cross life. Early in May, the *Tynehead*, costing the Red Cross $12,651.62 in charter fees, set sail from New York laden with Iowa corn, one of four shipments destined for the famine area. They were met in Riga by Russian military bands playing the 'Star Spangled Banner'. Tolstoy, who came to greet them, spoke of a 'dawning universal brotherhood'. From Geneva the International Committee, which had been observing the American Red Cross reaction closely, commented with satisfaction: 'The Red Cross Society is like a sentry on a tower, surveying the horizon to see from which quarter fire might break out.'

The famine appeal soon raised over $125,000 for the American Red Cross, the donors receiving notes to say that their money had been 'passed over to Miss Barton . . . who will be responsible for its judicious use', something that would later return to haunt her. She announced that the money had gone to feed 700,000 people for a month. Just the same, 650,000 people, many of them small children and elderly people, were dead and Russia's claims to be an efficient, modern state were proved hollow. If the Russian famine did something to awaken American interest in the needs of other countries – in a not altogether disinterested way, one American observer caught the mood of the country when he noted that 'philanthropy and business may properly walk hand in hand' – it had also served to bring the American Red Cross firmly into the field of foreign relief work.

While the Americans had doubts about succouring the Russians, they had none about going to the rescue of the Armenians. In August 1895 stories appeared in the *New York Tribune* about the massacre of Christian Armenians by the Turks. Over the next few weeks, the newspapers carried reports of pogroms and atrocities, of Armenian villages sacked and their inhabitants either burnt to death or left to starve, the Turks having confiscated their remaining food. Already aroused by the spectacle of Muslims killing Christians, public feeling was further incensed when they learnt that American missionaries and teachers, of whom there were over a hundred in Turkey, were being accused of sheltering the Armenians and were being persecuted as a result. On 12 November, Alexander W. Terrell, the American minister in Turkey, reported that 10,000 Armenians had been slaughtered in under a month and called for something to be done to protect foreign residents in the area. In America, friends and relations of the missionaries began to clamour for action.

The missionary organizations were not reluctant to come to the aid of their representatives, but knew that any overtly Christian intervention would only inflame Muslim passions further. A group of businessmen set up a national Armenian relief committee and began to call for donations, but once again the logistical problem of distributing the provisions had to be faced. The American Red Cross, its religious and political neutrality guaranteed by the Geneva Convention, seemed the obvious choice and, though Clara Barton again hesitated over the size of the problem and the immense distances that would have to be covered, she eventually agreed to mount an expedition for Turkey. She did stipulate, however, that the American people would have to demonstrate that they wished her to go by donating a sufficiently large sum of money: she asked for $500,000. Only $116,000 was eventually raised, she set off for Constantinople just the same, taking with her the faithful Dr Hubbell, as well as an 'Oriental linguist' called Ernest Mason, his mother, who was to act as stenographer, her financial secretary, George H. Pullman and an assistant called Lucy Graves. Miss Barton chose to ignore both the murmurings of disapproval about her age — she was now seventy-four — and the growing unease in Washington about her autocratic and impetuous methods. At a large farewell party held in her honour early in January, she announced: 'If I live to come back, judge me not harshly, nor praise me unjustly, for I shall only have done all that I could. I may not meet you again, and therefore bid you good-bye.' As she sailed, good American Christians prayed for her successful journey and the Reverend T. Dewitt Talmage led his Washington congregation:

> May the ships that carry her across the Atlantic and Mediterranean seas be guarded safely . . . the chariots of God are twenty thousand, and their charioteers are angels of deliverance, and they would all ride down at once to roll over and trample under the hoofs of their white horses any of her assailants.

As was becoming clear, the assailants now tended to be at home rather than in the field.

Clara Barton had been right to feel uneasy. She was entering hostile and difficult waters, full of political and religious currents of which she knew little. Philanthropy and relief work were becoming forces to be reckoned with, and she was no longer alone in the game. What was more, she had taken the decision to set out before getting permission from the Turks to carry out her mission. There were some troubling moments in Constantinople before the Sultan decided to accredit her, and even then his permissions covered not the American Red Cross as an organization but herself and her team personally. She was told that help had to go to Muslims as well as to Armenians. 'I shall never counsel nor permit a sly or underhand action with your government,' Clara Barton reassured the minister of foreign affairs, Tewfik Pasha, 'and, you will pardon me, Pasha, if I say that I shall expect the same treatment in return.' Tewfik Pasha agreed to let her send five expeditions into the interior and offered to have them escorted by Turkish soldiers. Then there was another pause, after a series of inflammatory anti-Turkish stories appeared in American newspapers, reporting in outraged tones that the Turks were about to insult Clara Barton and the American Red Cross by throwing them out of the country. Eventually, tempers were calmed and Clara Barton set to work.

Having established her headquarters in Pera, the European quarter of Constantinople, Clara Barton began buying up supplies and equipping her teams. They were to have travelled to the disaster area by steamer, through the Mediterranean to Alexandretta, but when word came from the British ambassador, Sir Philip Curie, that smallpox, typhus, dysentery and typhoid had broken out in the ransacked cities of Marash, Arabkir and Zeytoun, she changed her original plans. The five different missions assisted by locally recruited helpers set off by mule, on foot and occasionally by camel for what would be five months of living among families whose houses had been reduced to rubble, whose children were malnourished and in rags, and whose faith in any future had disappeared, since the Turks had taken away their sickles, pots, looms, water bags and animals. Towards the end of March, Clara Barton wrote one of her more purple letters to American supporters at home about 'Christian martyrs . . . alone, bereft, forsaken, sick and broken-hearted, without food, raiment or shelter, on the snow-piled mountain sides and along the smoking valleys they wander and linger and perish'. In itself contentious, given the strictly non-denominational character of the Red Cross, it went on to talk about the 'angel of disease' flapping 'his black wings' and 'camels heavy laden, not with ivory and jewels . . . but food and raiment for the starving, the sick and the dying'. Meanwhile the American Red Cross team set about rebuilding stocks, teaching hygiene and overcoming the Armenians' profound sense of mistrust. One of the greatest of the Red Cross contributions, one of the volunteer doctors observed, was the way it convinced people that they had not been 'left abandoned of all men' a theme that would recur again and again in wars to come. In Armenia, medical care rather than relief was what counted most. 'Never to my dying day,' wrote Dr Ira Harris, an American missionary from Zeytoun, 'will I be able to dismiss from my mind the horror of the pinched, haggard faces and forms that gathered about me . . .' Within a month, the death rate was dropping sharply.

Nothing in Constantinople was quite as straightforward or easy. Clara Barton's abrupt decision to alter her original plans was construed in America as incompetence. Mrs Mason, the stenographer, suddenly died. From America, the National Armenian Relief Committee plagued her with petty enquiries and tetchy reprimands. Catholics complained that she was issuing Protestant propaganda, and Protestants that she was favouring the Catholics. 'I learned,' wrote one sour critic, 'that this has been their policy, to take all the money they can, and never render any intelligible account. This, of course, is disquieting to the generous public.' Most of her time was spent grappling with Turkish officialdom, trying to come to grips with the currency and failing to understand the Turkish language. It took her six weeks to communicate with her teams in the interior. As criticisms mounted, she began to see more clearly the political minefields of charitable work and ponder how much strength she had left to cope with them. 'I doubt if I will ever feel the same in my country again,' she wrote. 'It will seem to me a fair, pleasant field, with every stone heap full of snakes.' Yet her mission was on the whole judged a success by the American press and a measure of peace returned to her mind after she decided to part company with the quarrelsome and nit-picking Armenian relief committee. Though conscious of the fact that her help had not been nearly enough – it was estimated that 50,000 more Armenians would die before the spring – she had spent her $116,000 well, giving homeless people not just care but the means to start their lives again; and she had walked the tightrope between Turkish politics and American charity without falling off.

Before she left for home, the Sultan, behaving as if he had no part in the Armenian massacres, awarded her 'the second class of my decorations', which turned out to be a medal covered in diamonds and precious stones, never before awarded to a woman. If her diary was full of agonized reflections on the nature and complications of her work – 'I must . . . withdraw within myself and close up the tangled web of a long jagged life' – she took care to paint an arcadian picture when she got back to America. The members of her expedition, she wrote later in *A Story of the Red Cross*, had come away with memories of 'those great valleys of golden grain, bending and falling before the harvesters, men and women, each with the new, sharp sickle or scythe, the crude threshing planks, the cattle trampling out the grain, and the gleaners in the rear as in the days of Abraham and Moab.' Of the massacres themselves, the genocidal policies of the Turks towards their Armenian citizens, she wisely said nothing.

She had not been back long before there was more foreign trouble, once again of a distinctly political nature, but this time closer to home. In 1895, Cuban revolutionaries had risen against Spanish colonial rule; as it became clear to the insurgents that they were losing, they launched a series of raids on Spanish military installations. In revenge, the Spaniards rounded up and put scores of local people into prison camps. The *reconcentrados*, as they were known, were left to rot in appalling conditions. Later, it was estimated that a third of them had died. Soon, there were calls for Red Cross help. As with the Armenians, there was a specifically American dimension, for a number of American citizens had been rounded up alongside the insurgents. What was at stake here was something that lay at the heart of the Red Cross message: not just the essential neutrality of the movement, but its duty to intervene in all disasters, whoever and whatever the cause. 'The Armenian venture,' observed the *New York Tribune* in January 1897, noting a principle that would be debated for generations to come, 'has established the precedent that it is not necessary that two countries should be at war in order to admit of the intervention of the Red Cross on behalf of the suffering'.

Clara Barton, even if she agreed, was becoming cautious, but she was about to pay dearly for her enormous success. Having persuaded the American public that the American Red Cross could, and would, help everywhere, there was now no disaster to which she was not summoned. As over Armenia, she demanded a clear mandate, telling President William McKinley at a private meeting in the White House that she saw the Cuban situation as war and needed his authorization to act. In the event, the president decided to set up a central Cuban relief committee to co-ordinate the work not just of the Red Cross, but of a varied collection of private donors. Soon the appeals were going out and money and supplies flooding in. Clara Barton, with a fulsome commendation by the president, set out for Havana.

Never had she seen such misery. 'The massacres of Armenia,' she wrote, 'seemed merciful in comparison.' She found the insurgents and their families crushed together in the camps behind barbed wire with too little space, too little food and no medical care. Pregnant women and small children were dying. There was no clean water and just as she was deploying her forces to deal with the misery, an American ship, the USS *Maine*, was blown up in Havana harbour. No one was certain who was responsible, but 260 American crew members died and war between Spain and America now looked certain. 'I am with the wounded,' Clara Barton cabled the president. There were, alas, almost none.

Sensibly avoiding all contact with the reporters who came flocking to Cuba, Clara Barton set off on a tour of the island, from which she returned genuinely shocked by what she found. Cuba was not her happiest hour. Louis Klopsch, editor of the *Christian Herald* and deeply involved with the fund-raising for Cuba in America, arrived to meddle and complain; he offended her by making disparaging remarks about the 'old fogeyism of certain members of the Red Cross'. (She managed to get him ousted from the president's Cuban relief committee.) Then on 25 April 1898 war was declared, leaving her stranded in Tampa for nearly two months at a cost of $400 a day while permissions were sorted out. Perhaps worst of all, the American government was now refusing to honour its commitments under the Geneva Convention, choosing to forget that after a declaration of war the American Red Cross should have been given an active role within the medical services. Many officers had never heard of either the Red Cross or the Convention. For Clara Barton, it began to seem as if twenty years of work had been in vain. When she protested, she was told that the medical services had no need of her, beyond, perhaps, providing a few delicacies for sick men. And though, after endless negotiations, the military did finally accept the presence of the American Red Cross, the bickering went on.

To make things worse, other independent aid societies, using the Red Cross emblem and often calling themselves offshoots of the national Red Cross, were suddenly proving extremely efficient at raising funds of their own and sending them off for the war effort. These groups showed very little interest indeed in taking orders from Washington and, even if they had, there would have been no one there to issue them, for Clara Barton was still in Tampa, leaving only Lucy Graves, her young helper, behind at headquarters. Her absence at this delicate stage proved disastrous.

The news, however, was not all bad, for in Cuba she did enter the war, not in the wake of the American forces, but in spite of them, finding herself suddenly and unexpectedly in the midst of heavy fighting at a time when there were no medical services in the area. She proved herself to be considerably better prepared than the US navy. But her feelings of triumph were brief and did her little good. She was soon reflecting sadly that none of the lessons of the past twenty years had been learned: the American medical services were little better than they had been during the Civil War, while the doctors were so dismissive of this band of neatly uniformed women that she was obliged to offer their services to the Cubans. At the end of the war, Surgeon General George M. Sternberg, echoing the words of some of the British doctors after the Franco-Prussian war, said that he had no time for women nurses, describing them as 'demanding, skittish and flighty'.

For Clara Barton herself the Cuban war brought one sweet moment of glory. Through a combination of good luck and good friends, the *State of Texas*, the relief ship she had been chartering when war broke out, led a victorious procession of naval vessels into Santiago harbour, with herself and her colleagues standing to attention on the deck singing 'My country 'tis of thee'. 'Miss Barton,' as one of those present later described the scene, 'stood queenly and majestic, one of the bravest of the brave, always going where suffering humanity most needed her.' The city was starving. In twenty-four hours, she fed 10,000 people, and in the next five weeks the American Red Cross set up soup kitchens, hospitals and orphanages.

Clara Barton was to make one last visit to Cuba in the late spring of 1899. The war was over, but not the misery. Cuba had been turned into a wasteland, and in some parts of the island, starvation and illness had reduced the survivors to little more than skeletons. For all the admiring publicity that surrounded this visit, these were not good days for her. She was nearly seventy-eight, a 'very tired old lady' as one aide described her, and critics, interlopers, rivals and even former protégés were gathering menacingly around.

Clara Barton had always wanted to move to the country, where she could keep animals and plant a garden. In the middle of the 1890s she had been living in a rented house on the corner of 17th and F streets in Washington, a few minutes' walk from the White House. The building was known locally as General Grant's house from the days of the Civil War, when he had kept his office there. She had furnished it more as a museum than a home, with flags, portraits, photographs and some leather bolsters donated by the Russian government, and kept a new kind of gramophone with a long trumpet for dictating letters. The mansion was perfect for the receptions she held for Washington society, when she would stand in a receiving line with the founder members of the American Red Cross, wearing pearl satin and pink brocade, her bosom covered in medals and jewels. Determined to hold on to her youthful looks and painfully aware of all references to her years, she took to cutting ten years off her age and padding her corsets with tissue paper to 'make a nice rounded bust'.

During the years of the Armenian and Cuban missions she at last made her move to the country, to a hamlet in Maryland called Glen Echo, where she had earlier put up a large wooden warehouse for her relief supplies out of the planks left over from one of her earlier operations. As the lure of a more peaceful existence grew ever more appealing, she added running water and converted the building into part-office, part-home, modelling it on a nineteenth-century hotel, with a gallery round every floor and a large hall with big cupboards in which blankets and linen for emergencies were stored. From Washington, in wagons, came her books, her relics of Red Cross life and some splendid carpets given to her by the Sultan of Turkey. She kept the house very simple, with walnut banisters, painted muslin covering the walls, a stained-glass window with a red cross and a wooden veranda; from the roof, she flew a large red cross flag. It is a charming place, surrounded by lawns and trees, with a faint and agreeable smell of wood, now run as a museum and kept precisely as she had it.

Clara Barton was to take the leading role in just one more major

American disaster. It had none of the political snares of the recent foreign ventures and none of the bad-tempered rivalries that had come to beset the charitable world.

On 8 September 1900, a hurricane hit Galveston in Texas, a town built on an island in the gulf and separated from the mainland by a bay. At 2 a.m. a high wind began to blow, coming sometimes from the north and sometimes from the south-east, its strength increasing steadily all day until the gale was scooping the water from both the bay and the gulf into tidal waves which crashed over the city. There had been warnings of the approaching hurricane, but few people had listened. In the hours that followed, wind and water destroyed over 3,000 homes, killing hundreds as the walls collapsed inwards, and drowning thousands more as they were swept away by the waves. All through the night, the waves pounded the city. When the winds dropped and dawn came, some 6,000 people, over a sixth of the population of Galveston, were dead. All the bridges were down and the public services including the telegraph system were wrecked. 'Roofs, cisterns, portions of buildings, telegraph poles and walls were falling, and the noise of the wind and the crashing of the buildings were terrifying in the extreme,' reported the *New York Tribune*. 'The people of Galveston were like rats in traps.'

No method had yet been devised to notify the Red Cross of a disaster. It was not until 10 September that Clara Barton heard of the hurricane and not until 15 September that she arrived in Galveston with three ladies, five gentlemen and relief and funds raised largely through the *New York World*. She found the waters receded and the survivors 'a dazed and tearless throng, such as Dante might have met in his passage through Inferno', while 'raving maniacs searched the debris for their loved ones'. A heavy cloud of smoke and mist hung over the wreckage of the city, rising from the huge piles of debris and bodies that were being hastily burnt to prevent epidemics. Corpses, dumped by barges in the gulf, came floating back to shore. For years afterwards the rescuers would remember the sickening smell of burning flesh. Clara Barton, orchestrating the relief work from a day-bed in her hotel, behaved with unaccustomed humility and tact, agreeing to supplement the work already set up by a hastily convened citizens' committee, rather than assuming total control, and forming a local chapter of the Red Cross, whose more efficient members she entrusted with different tasks. She asked engineers and architects to calculate precisely what was needed in the way of timber and building materials, then sent off for 4,000 door frames, and 'rough timber, spruce or pine' of various lengths. Clothes lists were precise: one order was for a 'white girl of medium size'. After three weeks, she boasted to a friend, 'There is not a discordant element in our entire force.'

Although most public attention went to the ruined city of Galveston, a thousand square miles of surrounding countryside, as well as sixty smaller towns and villages, had suffered severe damage. When the worst of Galveston's problems had been solved, shelters and temporary houses built, a soup kitchen and orphanages opened, Clara Barton transferred her work to the mainland, where local farmers had lost their entire crop of strawberry plants. Her by now established policy of restarting local work was repeated and a million strawberry plants brought in from other areas. The sensible and tactical application of relief work had come to seem crucial to her, and she fumed when an eager manufacturer sent her a gift of a million Mother Hubbard dresses 'of the sleaziest print and scrimpiest pattern' with no fastenings. There were 'wrappers enough', she commented crossly, 'to disfigure every female in Southern Texas'.

Not everyone was quite as satisfied with her handling of the Galveston hurricane as she claimed to be. Leaving Texas on a wave of grateful thanks, she returned to Washington to harsh criticisms over her handling of the funds raised for the hurricane victims. The moment was fast arriving when her enemies, grumbling now for several years, could no longer be silenced. Clara Barton's diaries from this period are agitated, full of inconsistencies in style, spelling and punctuation, and veer between bouts of self-congratulation and passages of anguished and defensive insecurity. 'There are so many grasping at us, that it is impossible to stand ... The vipers are so poisonous and sting so deep,' she wrote. For the next few years, as she engaged in an exhausting struggle to retain control of the American Red Cross, her enemies became increasingly bitter.

The trouble lay in one simple fact: she had always run the Red Cross as her personal fief. She had co-opted helpers, not always wisely, taking under her wing young men who were not always either efficient or totally honest, decided on policy, devised relief programmes, and handled money basically on her own. Her standard response to interference was paranoia and rage; her method of overcoming it dictatorial and unyielding, dealing with complaints by retiring ever more determinedly into her small band of close supporters and referring disdainfully to the 'pygmy tricks' of her enemies. She consulted no one and held no meetings. By 1900, even former supporters — of which there were many — were beginning to grow restive.

More damaging, however, was her attitude towards money. She kept the Red Cross accounts which, as the years went by, rose to vast sums, much as she coped with her own accounts, jotting down figures on scraps of paper or in notebooks, and then forgetting where she had put them. After the floods of Johnstown, she produced accounts that ranged between $40,000 and $250,000. The rumours about her financial irresponsibility only grew louder when one of her most loved protégés, a young man with a snub nose and dapper beard called George Pullman, who had accompanied her to Turkey, took off on drunken binges and was admitted to a New York hospital with suspected syphilis. She returned from Galveston to face mounting attacks over the scraps of paper she called accounts. There was also the unfortunate question of her involvement with an unscrupulous newspaper tycoon called William W. Howard, who seems to have pocketed Red Cross funds at will. For a shrewd woman, Clare Barton could be remarkably gullible.

At the Red Cross in Washington, a newly appointed board of control was waiting to question her closely over every cent spent in Galveston. Surely, she wrote in her diary sourly, 'a Board of Control is a most controlling thing'. She found the experience humiliating, particularly as she saw in all this scrutinizing plans to oust her from the Red Cross she still considered to be her child. 'I always had great respect for mighty forests and giant trees,' she complained, 'but I never until now learned the power of a single board.' In her diary, she confessed: 'It is a hard ugly day, a little more hatred and bitterness added but I can bear it.' As the board continued to query every postage stamp, she wrote: 'This wire-pulling and meeting are all so foreign to me, so distasteful that I can scarcely *live* in the atmosphere of them ... If *this* is "humanitarian work", one prays to be delivered from it.' Deliverance was at hand; but not in the form she wanted it.

It was at this point that Mabel Thorp Boardman entered her life, as antagonistic and unforgiving towards Barton as Moynier had been towards Dunant. Neither Clara Barton nor Dunant was a match for the self-righteous and moralistic spirit of the age. A financial committee had been set up to audit her accounts. Mabel Boardman was one of its three members, a tall, fashionably dressed, well-connected woman of forty-one, described in the *American Magazine* as 'rather slender, with a liking for modish gowns and the details of the business of the Red Cross'. She had been brought in as part of the new rules of incorporation, which had given the organization a new status and a new board, and was known to be an able and diligent administrator with friends in government – both William Howard Taft, the solicitor general and Theodore Roosevelt, governor of New York State, were old friends. At public meetings she spoke well and bracingly. She was said to resemble Queen Mary, her head held regally high, and a story circulated in Washington that when the Duke of Windsor caught a glimpse of her at a reception, he blurted out 'Good Lord! There's mother!'

Mabel Boardman's first encounters with Clara Barton were cordial. But as she settled down to make order of the chaos of the Red Cross finances, so her sense of disapproval grew. For quite some time, Clara Barton held firm. In the autumn of 1901, somewhat to her own surprise, she managed to fight off a move to get rid of her with a pre-emptive strike that at one blow abolished the board of control and had her elected president for the next three years. Though she had failed, as she put it, to rid herself of the 'bugs and the worms' eating away at the 'roots of our Red Cross tree', she had bought herself a little time. At the seventh International Red Cross conference, held in St Petersburg in May 1902, she was fêted and admired as never before and dined with the tsar at Tsarkoe. Praise for her grew when she was able to report that at last President McKinley had signed a bill incorporating the American Red Cross and giving some protection to the Red Cross insignia, which had at one point been widely abused in the United States by unscrupulous medical suppliers like Johnson and Johnson. That same spring, at a meeting of Spanish war veterans, the applause for her work 'was so great that all seemed to quiver with the might of human voices'.

But time was all it bought. In her absence, a coup had been plotted among the new members itching for a proper reorganization of the society. Though Clara Barton continued to ward off disaster with vigour, holding on to power by a narrow margin, Mabel Boardman was proving a formidable adversary. Her next move was to go over Clara Barton's head straight to Roosevelt, chairman of the American Red Cross – who had become president of the United States on McKinley's assassination in 1901 – it having been decided that all American presidents would automatically be chairmen of the society. Roosevelt never seems to have cared much for Clara Barton; he was perfectly willing, now, to write to tell her that he felt that she was guilty of 'loose and improper' financial dealings. While Clara Barton cowered and fumed, efforts were made to find ways of persuading her to step down. She was offered an annuity and the title of Honorary President. It was not an unreasonable request: she was now eighty-four, frail, with frequent attacks of bronchitis and not very good eyesight. 'The paths of charity are over roadways or ashes,' she had written not long before, 'and he who would tread them must be prepared to meet opposition, misconstruction, jealousy and calumny. Let his work be that of angels, still it will not satisfy all.' She was not ready to go quietly.

Open war was now declared. Mabel Boardman, who had started her attack on Clara Barton in the interests of a new, more professional organization, now turned it into a personal vendetta. She despatched spies to dig up old scandals, root around her property deals, pick over gossip. Clara Barton, she declared, had never been anything but 'an adventuress from the beginning and a clever one'. The battle lines were being drawn: on one side Mabel Boardman, a little haughty, clever, respected but not always loved, digging around past relief operations in search of financial peccadilloes, and on the other Clara Barton's old friends and supporters, figures like her nephew Steve, who announced that his aunt was still as 'smart as a whip, and fuller of energy than an egg is full of meat'. For her part, Clara Barton handled the attacks with outward dignity, confiding only to close friends and her diary her sense of anguish at the 'snapping' and 'barking' of her critics. They were, she said, a 'crowd of vultures and vampires', whose accusations were just a 'sack of wind and lies'. She wished, she added, that she were a rhinoceros, for she envied the animal his hide.

And so the months dragged on, in an atmosphere of enmity and sadness, while her detractors circulated rumours of her financial 'malfeasance' and extravagant lifestyle. At Glen Echo, Clara Barton continued to pursue the frugal existence she had always led, rising early, doing most of her own housework and living principally on apples and cheese. In March 1904, a hearing was held to unravel the last of the Galveston accounts. Mabel Boardman led the attack, with minute details of funds she claimed had been misused or squandered; Clara Barton replied crossly that, in the heat of the disaster, there had been no time for such small-minded considerations. The *New York Herald Tribune* entered the battle, accusing the American Red Cross of being a 'discredited and decaying institution'.

For an instant, fortune seemed to sweep back Clara Barton's way. A crucial witness for the prosecution, who had details of her apparent shenanigans at his fingertips, suddenly vanished just before giving his testimony. Senator Redfield Proctor, who had been put in charge of the hearing, ruled the accusations unproven, and closed the investigation. Clara Barton could probably have held on until her death. But she had lost her taste for confrontation; on 14 May 1904 she resigned. After twenty-three mostly triumphant years, her going was bitter. The Red Cross, she would say, had been her child, and she had never dreamt that it would need a stepmother.

Mabel Boardman and her friends swept to power in the weeks that followed and set about 'rejuvenating' the Red Cross. Proper accounting systems were set up, and steps taken to bring it firmly into line with the new professional standards being set for charities. She was seen to be successful and L. R. Root, the secretary of state, wrote to congratulate her on her service to the Red Cross 'which you are conducting so admirably and in which you have saved the good name of America from a most serious and threatening situation'. (Not everyone agreed. Mrs John Logan, later vice-president of the society, accused Roosevelt of driving the 'first nail of distrust and suspicion against Miss Barton.') Asked about Clara Barton, Mabel Boardman declared that 'her connection with the Red Cross is like a skeleton in the closet upon which the doors have been closed'.

Clara Barton, momentarily contemplating flight from the 'vultures' who continued to torment her, found a new and happier cause in the National First Aid Association and rejuvenation from supporters who were charmed by her energy and drive. She grew fruit in her orchard at Glen Echo and gardened in an old calico dress on to which she pinned her various medals and decorations. Though a little deaf and forgetful, she retained her love of new inventions and welcomed the gramophone, the telephone and even the car. Through a sympathetic medium, she got in touch with Abraham Lincoln and Kaiser Wilhelm I. She struggled on, with increasingly poor sight and bouts of pneumonia, but continued to insist on total independence and refused to let people help her carry luggage or get on or off trains, until the morning of 12 April 1912 when she woke and those around her heard her say, 'Let me go, let me go.' She died a few moments later.

Like Moynier, Mabel Boardman would be haunted all her life by her predecessor and, like him, jealousy made her mean-spirited. When, in 1917, a prominent women's organization proposed putting a bust of Clara Barton in a memorial to the women of the Civil War, she wrote hastily: 'You know so well what she was that I cannot imagine you could ever have thought to recommending such a thing. I should consider it an outrage upon the name of the other women that building com- memorates.'

Clara Barton was an extraordinary woman, who had managed not only to get a firmly isolationist government to ratify a treaty that bound it to an internationally accepted code, but had pioneered an entirely new programme of work for the Red Cross movement. The Red Cross role during peacetime had been defined; under her rule, disaster relief had been experienced and made to work. But Clara Barton's day was over. By the turn of the century, Americans expected business methods and efficiency. They wanted their organizations large, professionally run, accountable and highly visible. Under Clara Barton, the American Red Cross, with a handful of local chapters and a few thousand members at its peak, had assisted in twenty-one disasters, and received about $2.3 million in cash and supplies. Between 1905 and the outbreak of the First World War, years dominated by Mabel Boardman and her friends, just under one hundred disasters were handled, $12 million was raised and spent on disaster relief, and membership rose to over 22,000. By 1914, the American Red Cross would be the foremost relief organization of its time, cleverly treading a line between the old school of powerful and conservative societies which saw human needs as a physical problem to be solved by relief, and the new school of progressive, proselytizing societies, revolting against bureaucracy and materialism, committed not only to provide relief, but to address the root causes of poverty and misery. Mabel Boardman, daughter of a wealthy banking family, was the right figure to lead it but she would lead it from her desk and not in the field. The days when the head of the American Red Cross would wade ashore in waterproof boots to bring relief were over.

The new administration was concerned to set up a body whose officers were 'men of such prominence and standing . . . that the people [would] place perfect confidence in the organization and feel no hesitancy in placing funds and supplies at its disposal in time of great calamity'. Building on the Red Cross charter of 1900, a new charter was drawn up early in 1905, laying down precise and clear rules about management, local branches, membership and property; and about its relationship with the government. With Mabel Boardman in the office, and a former newspaper man called Ernest Bicknell, who had been secretary and director of various state charitable boards, in charge of disaster relief, the American Red Cross set out to tackle not only a spate of natural catastrophes but the themes that lay at the heart of the current debates – economic reform and helping people to get on their own feet financially. It was a question, as one charitable director put it, of seeking out and striking 'effectively at . . . organized forces of evil . . . at causes of dependence and intolerable living conditions'. It is worth looking ahead briefly at the fortunes of the American Red Cross until the First World War.

Under its new charter, authority lay with a central committee of eighteen members. But since these members represented different interests, and had careers of their own, they seldom came to meetings. A smaller executive committee was given the power to make decisions and its five or six members were normally appointed directly by the president. That is, all of them except for Mabel Boardman, who was an automatic member and, being always in the office, attended every meeting. Though Mabel Boardman herself took the view that 'the chairman must always be a man', and in theory at least deferred to George W. Davis, the retired general who held the post of chairman until 1917, in practice she ran the organization, recommending the names of people she approved of to the president, drawing up the agenda for meetings, formulating changes in policy, and keeping in touch with everything that was happening nationally. She had a very useful friend in William Taft, now secretary of war under Roosevelt.

Like Moynier, Mabel Boardman found it difficult to delegate responsibility. Ernest Bicknell has left a revealing portrait of the woman whose character would stamp the American Red Cross in every way as powerfully as had Clara Barton. Arriving to take up his job, he found her 'enthusiastic, dynamic, driving through or around all obstacles'. There was no question but that she was the 'chief'. Her mind, wrote Bicknell, in a memoir written many years later, 'flickered like lightning around and through any subject . . . and her opinion or decision came almost instantly'. Though receptive to new ideas,

> once her mind was made up it became virtually unchangeable. It used to be said, not in her hearing, that her mind was like concrete; it was plastic and responsive before it hardened, but once fixed it could not be changed. If shattered by an overwhelming blow, every resulting fragment would retain some fraction of the original mould.

Bicknell himself got on well under her 'benign dictatorship', though not everyone found it quite benign enough, and concluded that it was due to her skills that the American Red Cross found itself 'ready to leap into its full stride' when the major test of the First World War arrived. He was being over-modest. The emergence of the Red Cross as the main co-ordinating relief agency in America, with carefully thought-out disaster relief policies and a highly effective combination of branches, chapters and members, in fact owed as much to Bicknell's vision of Red Cross people 'swinging like soldiers into line and without excitement entering into the rapid organization of relief measures', as to Mabel Boardman's administrative skills. She called him a 'silver lining for many . . . a cloud'. The two made a formidable pair.

At 5.12 a.m. on 18 April 1906, one of the most violent earth tremors in history struck San Francisco. People woke to buildings swaying like cradles, to the sound of crashing and screaming, and in the case of Alfred Hertz, a conductor with the Metropolitan Opera Company, to the roars of terrified lions in the nearby zoo. Five minutes later came a second shock. Though not as strong, the streets were by now crowded and the buildings, weakened by the first tremor, began to collapse, crushing and trapping people underneath the falling masonry. Soon thousands of people, dressed only in their nightclothes, were combing desperately through the debris for survivors. Some of California's most prized modern buildings, the Merchants' Exchange, the Nevada Bank, and the Western Union and Postal Telegraph Office crumbled, as well as the magnificent Sutro library, with its unique collection of French and English newspapers.

No one quite took in the scale of the disaster until it was discovered that the earthquake had destroyed the water supplies, brought down electric light and power wires and cut off all communication with the outside world. By 9.45 a.m. the city was on fire. Explosions could be heard on all sides as gas tanks burst. At first there were rumours of tens of thousands killed. The final count was only a little under a thousand; but thousands of others were injured, and two-thirds of the city's 450,000 inhabitants were now homeless, for the most part with only the clothes they stood up in.

The mayor of San Francisco was an energetic and resourceful man called Schmitz. He soon had troops patrolling the streets, with orders to shoot looters and to destroy any large stocks of liquor, in order to prevent mob raids. In the Italian quarter, finding the water cut off, people rolled out barrels of red wine, soaked mattresses and sacks in it, and began to beat at the flames. By the time night fell, the roads leading out of San Francisco were blocked by a desperate collection of people dragging and carrying what little of their possessions they could salvage; the city behind them was lit up as brightly as by day. 'All racial distinctions were forgotten in the scramble for safety,' reported an observer — as it turned out inaccurately, for the Californians' natural antipathy to their large Chinese population led to clear discrimination when it came to relief and help.

Once the fire got hold, it proved virtually unstoppable. By midday on Wednesday it had eaten over a square mile of the city; by nightfall it had enveloped the downtown business district and was advancing rapidly westwards. It was still going next morning, consuming block after block. Dynamiting to check its advance was tried but achieved little, not least because no one had much experience of explosives. A car 'loaded with newspaper men' returned from a tour of the city to report that the fire now stretched twenty-six miles in circumference. It stopped only on Friday night, when the wind changed. Four square miles of buildings had been totally burnt down. Sewers had collapsed. The water that remained was not safe to drink. There was very little food. Everywhere lay rubble, with hundreds of people still trapped under the debris, or 'burnt alive, their moaning and crying for help . . . heard by many in the different localities but to no avail'.

When news of the disaster began to spread, doctors and nurses volunteered in such number that orders had to be issued to stop them descending on the city. But nothing could be done to prevent the hordes of anxious relations arriving, or the thousands more keen to marvel and stare, until Mayor Schmitz issued instructions that no one was to enter San Francisco without a permit. In Washington, Taft, also president of the American Red Cross, immediately despatched shelters for 100,000 people, a million dollars in relief and $150,000 more in medical supplies without waiting for the approval of Congress.

Though the American Red Cross was still in the throes of its reorganiz-ation and Clara Barton had never committed to paper all the skills and lessons she had learned from her own disaster experiences. Mabel Boardman swung into action. President Roosevelt announced that all relief funds would be channelled through the Red Cross, and two men, Ernest Bicknell and Dr Edward Devine, secretary general of the Charity Organization Society in New York and probably the best qualified director of relief in America, were sent off to San Francisco.

When they reached the city on 24 April they found a relief committee of fifty leading citizens in control. Though not best pleased at the sudden and arbitrary imposition of outsiders, the committee grudgingly let them in and agreed to allow them to co-ordinate the relief, leaving the job of actual distribution to the army. The task that faced the two men was daunting. It was not just a question of size – this would be one of the worst disasters and largest relief funds administered in twenty years – but of the fact that the Red Cross was now under close scrutiny. As President Roosevelt wrote anxiously to Mabel Boardman, 'We have to remember that when once the emergency is over there will be plenty of fools and plenty of knaves to make accusations against us, and plenty of good people who will believe them.'

He was right to sound cautious. Devine and Bicknell did an excellent job of marshalling and organizing the relief while remaining on harmonious terms with the army, the committee and other local aid societies. Some 1,850 railway wagons of relief were brought into the city and distributed; welfare workers were borrowed from local agencies and put to work; epidemics were kept at bay and 'honesty and faithfulness' were agreed to have been 'the rule among those charged with responsibility'. But when it was all over, the Red Cross was accused of hoarding supplies, treating the people they cared for as 'paupers', and of acting far too slowly. A Dr Margaret Mahoney, a local physician, led the attacks, saying that it had taken the Red Cross two months to floor the tents properly or supply sufficient mattresses, and that it seemed at times more obsessed by statistics than by trying to meet the dire needs of the San Franciscans. President Roosevelt was also criticized for putting so much into Red Cross hands.

But Devine and Bicknell set off home with the satisfaction of knowing their job to have been well done. A great deal of soul-searching went on about the nature of such relief operations, made all the harder since the effectiveness of the work was impossible to assess without the 'ultimate, tangible results which appear only with the lapse of a certain period of time'. But a number of crucial lessons had been learned, like the value of assessing needs before despatching relief – something that Clara Barton had instinctively known and acted on – and the importance of finding a reliable way of getting news of disasters as rapidly as possible to Red Cross headquarters. The newly reorganized society could afford to be pleased. If Dunant and Moynier had created a new movement for the relief of the victims of war, Clara Barton and Mabel Boardman had proved how adaptable it was to the years of peace.

FIVE

Rebels, Barbarians and Perjurers

The first magazine put out by the International Committee appeared in the autumn of 1869. Its earnest, quiet tone perfectly reflected Moynier's own cautious style and Moynier himself would effectively oversee and shape its quarterly volumes for nearly thirty years, commenting somewhat smugly in 1877 that it was doing an excellent job in upholding 'the permanent moral unity' of the movement. Nevertheless, the *Bulletin*, as it was named, provides a clear insight into the workings of the International Committee's mind, as well as into the hundreds of experiments, ideas, technological developments and fears of the age. It became a notice board on which national societies could air their worries or pass on useful tips. In these early issues, one gets a glimpse not only of what Europeans felt about the new Red Cross and the Geneva Convention, but also of what they felt about war itself. Dr Frédéric Ferrière, Appia's young nephew, voicing the apprehensions of many other people, repeatedly speculated in the *Bulletin*'s pages about the changing nature of war, as new and even more lethal weapons were invented to inflict wounds as yet untreatable by known medicine. Alongside the precise medical and technical details are genuine anxieties about what a world committed to war might bring.

But it was not all serious. In between protests about the Red Cross emblem being misused by chemists and editorials on the importance of not turning a battlefield into a necropolis, came reports of inventions of a decidedly Heath Robinson nature, often illustrated by charming and absurd drawings. There was the machine capable of producing 15 kilograms of ice, with a horse-drawn pump which emitted steam; there was the travelling box in which could be stored a mixture of cocoa, icing sugar, cognac and egg, which turned into a 'nutritious and stimulating drink with an exquisite taste'; and there were a great many proposals for stretchers, the Dutch suggesting that they be pulled by balloons and dirigibles, the British by four cyclists, the Finns by reindeer and the Russians by camel. What, one anxious reader wondered, would ladies do during wars, now that charpie was being replaced by lint which did not need doing over and washing? What, asked the Italians, was the best refreshment to send to troops in the field, adding that they tended to stick to marsala, cognac and chocolates? Through the brief descriptions of the many Red Cross receptions and soirées taking place throughout Europe in the closing years of the nineteenth century comes a picture of a band of men and women, enlightened though not radical, humane, essentially prosperous, committed to 'humanizing' war, but seeing no reason why they should not have fun in the process.

From time to time, the *Bulletin* published the diary or memoirs of individual delegates, for the most part doctors who, like Appia and van de Velde in Schleswig-Holstein, took off for distant wars, in countries they knew nothing about, where languages were spoken they had never thought to learn, enduring without complaint the most extreme privations, only to return to volunteer for more. The tale told in the *Bulletin* by a Monsieur Meledine, recruited by the Committee as a delegate, gives a flavour of their unboastful, buccaneering style.

In December 1885, Meledine was asked to take hospital provisions for 100 beds to the war that had broken out between the Serbs and the Bulgarians. He left Odessa on the last ship out that winter, in weather that worsened every day. Despite terrible storms in the Black Sea, he made it by sea and land to Galatz in Romania, only to be told that there was no ship or other transport to carry him and his supplies any further. He returned to Odessa, planning to take a steamer up the Danube. However, the river soon froze over, and his steamer, the *Charles Louis*, was forced to pause while floating ice and dense fog cleared. Then he was held up by a snowstorm. At last he reached his destination, but when he tried to hand over his supplies to a member of the Russian Red Cross, he was told that they were already overburdened with goods brought overland from St Petersburg. Meledine re-embarked with his supplies to go further up river.

The weather grew worse. The ice grew thicker. The captain warned that they would probably have to winter in the next town, and agreed to press on only in the face of Meledine's pleas. The water round the

Charles Louis froze solid. The passengers were so cold that they scrambled across the ice and cut wood from the frozen bushes along the banks. Then, after many days, came an unexpected break in the weather, the sun shone, and the ice melted sufficiently to move on. But Meledine's problems were only beginning. He still had to cross the Balkans to Sofia. There were no carts, no carriages and no horses. The local prefect offered him two bullocks, which he turned down, making his way instead to a nearby town where he hoped to find a house to rent. There were none. He retraced his steps, accepted the offer of the two bullocks and set off, through snow and sleet, very slowly. Remarkably, he did eventually reach Sofia, and did deliver his medical supplies; as would thousands of Red Cross delegates faced by similar obstacles in the decades to come.

With the end of the Franco-Prussian war some of the urgency left the International Committee's deliberations, not least because they did not immediately recognize that, far from causing people to admire the Convention, the war had prompted serious doubts about its usefulness. They met less often, and when they did a new member, a twenty-five-year-old lawyer called Gustave Ador, Moynier's nephew, often sat in for Appia as secretary. But Moynier continued to worry about how best to consolidate the Committee's position in the face of the widespread reorganization taking place in many of Europe's military medical services and amid growing talk that volunteers should be relegated to the background in future conflicts. For all Moynier's anxious urging, no one seemed at all keen on a new international gathering of Red Cross societies. Neither he nor Appia were in favour of militarizing the Red Cross and both men spent much of their time lecturing on the 'humanizing' of war and reminding newcomers of the Geneva Convention. The most important thing, Moynier urged, was to restore friendship and confidence between the countries and Red Cross societies involved in the war.

In 1874 the Committee moved into fine new rooms at 3 rue d l'Athenée in Geneva's most prosperous old quarter. A large drawing room was given to the movement's rapidly expanding library. For all Moynier's concerns, people across Europe were now talking about social conditions – the exploitation of children in mines and mills, deficiencies in the health services, negligence in military administration. The notion that the individual, be he soldier or civilian, needed defending was raised again and again, at the international gatherings of statisticians, doctors, pacifists and military men that seemed to occupy so much of Europe in the 1870s and 1880s, and at the vast exhibitions held to celebrate the inventions of the age. What was more, the movement to codify laws of war, to find ways of getting them respected, was intensifying all the time, with more and more people expressing themselves keen to find ways of ensuring good relations between countries, and a 'more stable and lasting peace between the belligerent nations'. Increasingly, the progress of civilization was seen to be bound up with economic development and free trade; leading economists like Frédéric Bastiat and Richard Cobden had long ago warned that excessive armament budgets would bankrupt societies. War, they argued, should be curbed, not only on the grounds of morality but of economic self-interest.

With twenty European countries now enrolled, America falling into line and ten imperial or royal families professed supporters of Red Cross matters, the question facing the Committee was how wise it would be to extend the fellowship further, how far it would be possible to inject this 'new blood' of Red Cross humanitarian ideas into the 'veins' of other 'civilized races'? 'Civilized' was the crucial word. Egypt, under an enlightened viceroy, was considered acceptable, but Moynier took the view that it would be 'puerile' to ask 'savages or barbarians' to follow the example set by the West and that only countries whose 'moral standards or philosophy' were compatible should be invited to do so, even if, like organizations working with alcoholics, the Red Cross could be likened to a 'spiritual and moral ambulance'. Like many other philanthropists of his time, he felt particularly strongly about the 'negro,' on the grounds that the 'black tribes of Africa are ... still too savage to take on this humanitarian thinking'. Blacks could perhaps, he would say later, co-operate, but only as 'subordinate nations'. At the European exhibitions attended by representatives from all over the world, it was noticeable that he and Appia treated those who came from China, India and Turkey with disdain, not least because their suggestions and exhibits seemed to them technologically backward and artistically unsophisticated.

When a Japanese mission arrived in Geneva to call on Moynier in the autumn of 1873, it was greeted with a mixture of gratified snobbery —

Japan had taken care to select diplomats from the imperial family – and contempt, on the grounds that a country like Japan was simply not ready for such a progressive idea. Moynier's natural prejudices were fuelled by the former Swiss ambassador to Japan, Aimé Humbert, who told him that the Japanese people believed it right to kill anyone who set foot on their sacred soil. The Japanese emissaries returned home, however, to set up a national society which briskly ratified the Geneva Convention, after which they acted decisively. When, some time afterwards, a questionnaire went out to all societies asking for the number of their members, the Italians and the French replied in hundreds; the Japanese put down over 150,000.

Moynier was now working towards the idea of having a 'league' of societies, to bind the 'sisters' who were showing such a 'true and touching' interdependence within a loose confederation, and to declare their formal solidarity during the 'misfortune' of wars. Moynier's league was not instituted until some years later, and not in the way he had planned. What he was able to do, however, was to solve a problem that had long been irking him. The various societies, as they formed, had taken different names, using words like 'Relief' and 'Aid' in their titles. Most were now at last persuaded to adopt the official name of Red Cross Society of . . . It was a mark of how little Moynier wanted to govern the movement, as opposed to guide it, that he had refrained from insisting on a single name before.

The sisters were encouragingly united in their support of the International Committee; governments less so. After the brutalities of the Franco-Prussian war, there was talk that if war broke out, it would be better to let it take as rapid a course as possible, unchecked by time-consuming humanitarian principles. The Geneva Convention, remarked one German paper contemptuously, was nothing but a 'humanitarian Bull'. The Germans in particular were furious about the French disregard for the Red Cross emblem. Von Holleben, the new president of the Berlin central committee of the German Red Cross, observed that in his view the Convention was actually harmful in that it had attracted 'into the theatre of war a number of dubious officials wearing a distinctive sign which was used to spy, incite desertion or disorderliness in the army, or to steal from corpses'. A move was made to write the articles of the Convention directly into the military regulations of individual countries and jurists now began work on ways to codify laws of war. The distinguished professor of constitutional law at Heidelberg, Johann Kaspar Bluntschli, drew up in legal form what had hitherto been merely accepted custom, and there was fresh talk of replacing the Geneva Convention by general regulations covering the whole law of war. From Geneva, Moynier and Appia fought back fiercely, arguing that what was wrong was not the Convention itself but the fact that it was not being used properly. Moral censure, they agreed, was not enough; what was needed now was a tribunal, with judges chosen from both neutral and belligerent countries. In a *Note on the Creation of an International Judicial Institution Designed to Prevent and Repress Infringements of the Geneva Convention*, which appeared in January 1872, foreshadowing much of what later made its way into the International Military Tribunal at Nuremberg, Moynier clearly modified his earlier stand on moral sanctions. What both men feared was that any revision of the texts of the Convention would threaten its very existence. As General Dufour put it, during one of the International Committee's regular meetings, 'the Convention is what it should be; it must not be changed'. After talks in Vienna, Appia wrote to Moynier: 'Geneva must stand firm . . . Some people would have been only too pleased to see us fade away.'

For all their protests, a move to replace the Convention gathered strength and in July 1874, a new conference, once again under the aegis of Tsar Alexander II and at the invitation of the imperial Russian government, opened in Brussels. It was well attended. Moynier's note on a tribunal had prompted considerable debate and the legal world had greeted the idea of an arbiter with interest, but remained doubtful about the wisdom of allowing any international authority actually to pass judgement on a nation-state. There was much discussion in Brussels about the various categories of combatants and the spread of war to civilians – it was apparent to everyone that the tacit understanding of the eighteenth century, that war was a matter for soldiers, not civilians, was no longer going to be respected – and the conference ended with a clear definition of a soldier as a man in uniform, bearing his arms openly, conforming to the customs and laws of war and under the orders of an officer.

Moynier, who had lobbied furiously to keep the Convention intact, emerged from the battle bruised but satisfied. The idea of having a tribunal had been dropped. But the Geneva Convention was to continue unchanged as the code of behaviour for the treatment of wounded soldiers and non-combatants.

What *had* changed was that the Convention would now be one chapter in a larger code, covering all the most important aspects of war. Between these two strands, the Geneva Convention and the *Brussels Declaration Concerning the Laws and Customs of War* — which did not have the force of law and was not ratified by any country — most matters relating to the conduct of war had now been sketched out, and would change little in the next seventy-five years, even if the International Committee still had many miles to cover before it established the exact nature and range of its duties, its priorities and the identity of the men and women it had set out to serve. Progress of a crucial kind had been made: an acceptable conduct of war was now taking shape. Geneva would concern itself with the victims of war; Brussels — later The Hague, as the parallel movement would become known — the means of limiting war itself.

A first test for Moynier was not long in coming. In 1875, the Christian communities in the Turkish provinces of Herzegovina, Bosnia, and Bulgaria rose up against their Muslim overlords. The Bashi-Bazouks, the most ferocious of the Turks' irregular forces, put down the rebellion with great brutality and rumours were soon reaching Geneva of 30,000 Christians tortured and massacred and thousands more pouring over the borders into Austria. Indignation grew throughout Europe and the International Committee pondered whether this crisis properly fell under its mandate. Moynier, who in 1870 had argued firmly that the Geneva Convention did not apply to civil wars, now changed his mind, and spoke of 'rebels, barbarians and perjurers' being entitled to humane treatment. It was a question of 'humanitarian faith', he announced, 'which cannot be compulsory in certain cases and optional in others'.

With a certain amount of confusion, disentangling who had ratified what and when, Moynier now redrafted a number of statutes to take in his new views, even if they were not formally recognized or endorsed for some years, and despatched a mission, consisting of a Serb-speaking naturalist, a chemist, and the young Dr Ferrière to organize help for the wounded, as well as for refugees (but only if these last were sick). The delegates struggled through heavy snow to reach Montenegro, while the war continued to spread, and while the Turks — old but lapsed signatories – continued to strip and mutilate prisoners, amputating feet, ears, hands, noses and genitals and showing their complete contempt for the Red Cross – a symbol they associated, with loathing, with the Crusaders – by chopping the arm off a man wearing a red cross armband. Desperate negotiations were now conducted about the introduction of a red crescent instead of a red cross on the battlefield.

The war, which is remembered principally for its brutality and for repeated abuses of the Red Cross emblem, was to leave three new ideas in place: a red crescent as an acceptable alternative to a red cross, the extension of Red Cross aid to all victims of conflicts and a new title for the International Committee in Geneva, which now also added the words 'Red Cross' officially to its name.

From the day of Dunant's financial downfall, the International Committee's attitude towards him had been implacable. Moynier missed no occasion to belittle him, to warn others of his dishonesty and to erase his name as far as possible from the annals of the Red Cross. He was not altogether successful, for Dunant was a man bursting with ideas and his Red Cross triumphs had unleashed in him not just a vision of humanitarian projects but a very real understanding of how they could be made to work. Cut off from the movement he had inspired and helped to found, Dunant roamed Europe, discussing new projects on peace, on slavery and above all on the fate of prisoners-of-war, infuriating Moynier each time his name was mentioned in connection with some new humanitarian cause. Even Dunant's continued success in bringing new countries into the Red Cross fold irked him almost beyond endurance. Learning that on his travels and acting on his own authority Dunant had even managed to persuade the Shah of Persia to sign the Geneva Convention, Moynier was unable to conceal his fury: 'For the honour of the Red Cross,' he announced, 'we ourselves feel very strongly that it should not be served by individuals with tarnished reputations.'

When exactly Dunant took up the cause of prisoners-of-war is not clear. During the 1863 Geneva conference, when giving the messages from people who could not attend, he had read out in full a long paper by Prince Demidov, the tsar's chamberlain, outlining a series of proposals for providing protection and help for captured enemy soldiers. Other messages, on subjects that interested him less, were put to one side. No article specifically on prisoners-of-war was in fact included in the first Geneva Convention, not least because Moynier was anxious not to broaden its mandate too far. But from that moment on, Dunant kept writing and talking about the need for a parallel convention to cover the rights of prisoners-of-war. He was not, of course, alone in doing so, for Demidov continued to push his suggestion and even Moynier, in the course of the Franco-Prussian war, had agreed, through the agency in Basle, to cover the needs of the French prisoners.

In 1871, penniless and living in Paris on the charity of friends, Dunant, introduced by the Comte de Flavigny to men who shared his vision of a fairer world – among them the pacifist Frédéric Passy and Ferdinand de Lesseps – founded a Universal Alliance for Order and Civilization. Concerned with slavery and labour conditions, the Alliance announced that it intended to fight 'ignorance, selfishness, mercenary motives, indifference to the common good, idleness and debauchery, weakness, isolation and abandonment' wherever it found them. Exactly where prisoners-of-war fitted into this is not obvious, but the Alliance held its first meeting in Paris in June 1872, at which it was decided to 'further social and political peace through arbitration and the codification of international law'. A Mme Kastner, widow of the musician Jean Georges, lent her house in the rue de Clichy as headquarters. Carrying his campaign across the Channel to London, Dunant was invited by Lord Elcho, a member of parliament and of the Social Science Association, to give a paper entitled 'A proposal for introducing uniformity into the condition of prisoners of war'. What he had in mind, he told his audience, was a 'special international treaty, which will uniformly fix the condition of prisoners of war in all civilized countries'. The meeting was well reported in the newspapers. With the Alliance as his base, and a new international conference as his platform, Dunant now set out to turn the cause of prisoners-of-war into another Solferino.

He might well have been successful. The British liked him, and even Florence Nightingale wrote to congratulate him on his 'noble work – work truly inspired by God'. (By now, Dunant had taken to spelling his Christian name with a 'y', but whether this was because, as he claimed, he had found a bootmaker in the Paris directory calling herself Mlle Henri Dunant, or because of the anglophile snobbery of the French-speaking world, no one knows.) What was more, Dunant had once again drawn around him a group of wealthy supporters, not only in France and Belgium, but in London, where the dukes of Wellington, Norfolk, Somerset and Sutherland agreed to become honorary patrons. Even Moynier's malicious decision to send a copy of the Geneva court verdict against him to the London society seems to have done him little harm.

But the indignation inspired by Solferino had evaporated, the mood of the hour was different and prisoners-of-war failed to conjure up the same degree of passion as the wounded. Despite Dunant's feverish comings and goings between London, Paris and Brussels, and despite a talk he gave to a large and appreciative audience in Brighton's Royal Pavilion, matters continued to move slowly. 'I am not losing hope,' he wrote to his sister Marie, on the subject of his new enterprise, 'but it's often very hard.' Though he was not yet fifty, friends found him aged; he had eczema, and some of his remarks spoke of a real – and understand-able – sense of persecution.

The British government decided to turn down Dunant's request that they convene, as the Swiss had in 1864, a diplomatic conference at which to discuss prisoners-of-war. A conference *was* called, in Paris, for the late spring of 1874, but it never took place. Even as it was being planned, the tsar of Russia, taking up Demidov's earlier proposals, announced that he was intending to include the treatment of prisoners of war in his forthcoming Brussels conference on the laws of war. Dunant was not altogether disappointed, particularly as the Russian proposal con-tained many of the same ideas as his own and referred to prisoners of war, as he did, 'not as criminals but legal, unarmed enemy soldiers.' But he was not invited to the conference and managed to get to Brussels only with the help of a grant from the London Anti-slavery Society. And though the question of prisoners-of-war was extensively debated, little was concluded, and it was not until 1929, fifty-five years later, that the subject was fully addressed in a new Geneva Convention.

For Dunant, the end of his labours for prisoners-of-war meant obscur-ity. Though he did champion other causes – slavery occupied him briefly – he was again destitute and without a home. Rumours and slanders put about by his creditors brought an end to what had been his agreeable friendship with Mme Kastner, whose inventor son Dunant had been helping in return for some modest fees. Whether there had been more to

The founders: *top* Gustave Moynier;
centre from left Théodore Maunoir, General Dufour, Louis Appia;
bottom Henri Dunant

Above left The attack on the tower of Solferino during the battle of 24 June 1859 by Gustave Doré

Above right Red Cross volunteers from Neuchâtel during the Franco-Prussian war, 1870-71

Below Dutch Red Cross medical team at Mannheim, Franco-Prussian war, 1870-71

The Hall of Mirrors in the Palace of Versailles was transformed into a Red Cross ward, 1871

One of the first Red Cross ambulances during the battle of Champigny, Franco-Prussian war

Hospital train No. 4. This was one of the specially designed British ambulance trains which first saw service during the Boer War, 1899-1902

Foreign Red Cross volunteers during the siege of Ladysmith during the Boer war. Ladysmith was relieved by Sir Redvers Buller after 121 days on 28 February 1900

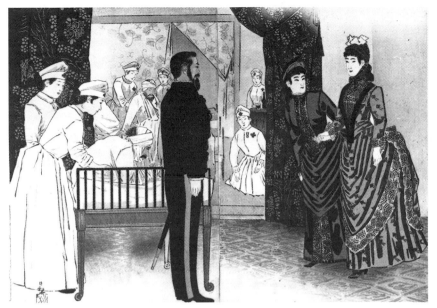

The Empress Shôken visits the wounded at Hiroshima during the Russo-Japanese war of 1904-5

By 1904, the Japanese Red Cross was the largest society in the world with nearly a million members

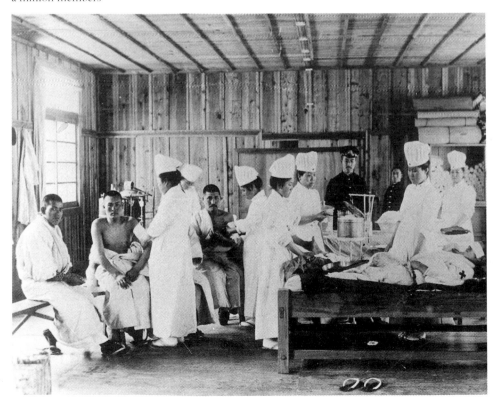

Clara Barton of the
American Red Cross,
'the precious angel' to
the soldiers in the
Civil War. This photo-
graph was taken in
1905 and dedicated to
Henri Dunant

Brought in to put the
American Red Cross
in order, Mabel
Boardman referred to
Clara Barton as the
'skeleton in the closet
upon which the doors
have been closed'. She
was to remain promi-
nent in the society for
nearly fifty years

Red Cross
Christmas
Roll Call
Dec. 16–23ʳᵈ

The GREATEST MOTHER in the WORLD

The best-known of all the American Red Cross
posters painted by A. E. Foringer in 1918

Right Shirley Temple, used for fund-raising for
the American Red Cross during the 1930s

Henri Dunant photographed by Princess Marie Thérèse de Bavière shortly before his death on 30 October 1910

their relationship than friendship has never been proved. In his memoirs, Dunant wrote that he had never been her lover. But in a note found among his papers, dated ten years after her death in 1888, he confessed that he would have gone through fire for her and that he still bore the stigmata of the pain she had caused him. He added that she too had loved him, but that, ruined and heavily in debt, he dared not approach her. Towards the end of 1876, Dunant took off for Stuttgart where he stayed with Pastor Wagner, president of a charitable society and translator of *Solferino* into German. For the next twenty years he disappeared from the public eye.

General Dufour died in July 1875 at the age of eighty-eight, his declining years marred by toothache, depression and acute boredom, fought off with bouts of frenetic activity. He had never enjoyed leisure, being interested neither in sports nor the theatre and had always been intimidated by women, despite having a wife he was attached to and four daughters. Sixty thousand people, from all over Switzerland, came to Geneva for his funeral.

For Moynier, the end of the 1870s and the 1880s were ever better days. It was a time of reflection of a most satisfactory kind. In 1884, Geneva was host to the third International Conference of the movement – the first to take the official name of Red Cross. Twenty national societies, and twenty governments sent representatives; the role and powers of the International Committee were debated at length, but with none of the rancour and quarrelsomeness that had marked earlier debates. 'The authority enjoyed by the International Committee in the work of the Red Cross,' read the minutes of a meeting held on 25 May 1885, 'is above all a moral authority.' In Geneva, as in Karlsrühe in 1887 at the next international gathering, there was no threat to its pre-eminence and no move to wrest its authority away into other hands, even if its two foremost members, the only survivors of the early days, had grown somewhat staid and complacent.

Moynier was still president, even if he protested from time to time, somewhat feebly, that his place should be taken by a younger and more energetic man. Appia, in his late sixties, continued to combine his medical practice with his work for the Committee and was still learning new languages – Japanese, Chinese and Amharic – with which to help the new societies develop. He looked older and more lined, but the years had made him a softer, more genial figure though no less principled: he continued to write and speak passionately on the need to protect the humanitarian inspiration of the Red Cross from military encroachment. As he grew older, he talked more and more about 'liberty', drawing up a model for an ideal state, in which social equality for all would be guaranteed by the constitution.

In 1888, the International Committee celebrated its twenty-fifth anniversary. To mark the occasion the street in Geneva in which the first conference had taken place was renamed rue de la Croix Rouge and a handsome monograph, with accounts of the thirty-nine existing national societies, was prepared. On Moynier's suggestion the motto *Inter arma caritas* was inscribed on the cover. The world conjured up in its pages was one of powerful committees made up of well-connected men and women, warmly supported by the various courts, aristocracies and medical services of the European powers. Some national societies, like the French, kept solvent on charitable balls, flamboyant and inventive occasions with pageants, floats and stands. The Russian was benignly ruled over by the tsarina and her daughters, in specially tailored Red Cross uniforms. Photographs from Japan showed a team of the new Red Cross nurses wearing long, pleated white dresses, dwarfed by enormous cotton hats, like those worn by chefs. Behind all these ladies were increasingly professional organizations, steadily founding one hospital after another, one local committee after another, moving in directions and into fields that neither Dunant nor Moynier had ever contemplated. Dunant's dream had acquired a life all of its own. Why had it all been so successful? Moynier was often asked the question. Surveying all that had been achieved, as he wrote in an introduction to the memorial monograph, he put it down to a combination of the Christian spirit of the age and the spread of the 'humanitarian impulse' by the newly discovered 'electric telegraph' which carried news of disasters and conflicts at great speed, and to the railways which 'gave wings to the vehicles bringing aid'. And, he would add, to the new science of statistics, which made it possible for the first time to evaluate what war meant in material and human terms.

On 26 October 1888, the surviving founders, the new committee members, many of Geneva's ruling families and a number of carefully selected foreign visitors assembled in Geneva's Hôtel des Bergues. A specially commissioned painting of a battlefield was unveiled. Soldiers and politicians gave speeches. Moynier, after a somewhat self-congratulatory speech about the 'fruit of Christian civilization', toasted the country in which the Red Cross had been born: 'Ladies and Gentlemen, to Switzerland! Let us drink to Switzerland! Long may she live!' Appia paid homage to General Dufour, and to Maunoir; Ador thanked the city of Geneva for all it had done. Telegrams of greetings from thirteen national societies were read out. Of all of them, the one from the American Red Cross most accurately caught the flavour of the occasion, a little sentimental, somewhat adulatory, decidedly fulsome. It had been delivered with an immense bouquet of red and white flowers. 'Affectionate greetings . . . from your daughter in America, present in spirit among you . . . and calling down blessings upon her parents.'

Throughout the entire evening, Dunant's name was scarcely mentioned.

In Tokyo, on the same day, Moynier's despised new recruit, the Japanese Red Cross, was busy celebrating the occasion in some style. A party for 1,700 guests was held in the Vyeno public gardens, attended by the imperial family. Medals were presented. It had been raining hard, but as the guests began to arrive the sun came out, lighting up an immense picture showing the work of different national Red Cross societies. Three bands played. When the emperor went home, the guests were joined by 30,000 Red Cross members. What Moynier would have said, had he witnessed these immense, lavish, and superbly orchestrated celebrations, one can only guess.

Of all the major powers, Britain seemed the most reluctant to press ahead with an active Red Cross society. As the Swiss remarked, the British were generous with their help, but only at 'moments of excitement'. The Aid Society – it had as yet refused to take the now accepted name of Red Cross Society – formed during the Franco-Prussian war appeared to take little interest in peacetime activities and during its infrequent meetings preferred to discuss ways of 'husbanding' its resources rather than prepare for future conflicts beyond financing the training of a number of military nurses. (Recruits, between the ages of twenty-five and thirty-five, had to be certified healthy by a doctor and pious by a clergyman.)

In all this, the position of the few enthusiasts, like Colonel Loyd-Lindsay or John Furley, was not helped by a very real spirit of wariness held by the Foreign Office towards the Geneva Convention and the International Committee, or by a strong feeling that the Red Cross idea of 'humanizing' war was in fact a very doubtful moral proposition. As Thomas Gibson Bowles, a prospective Conservative candidate for Dartington, expressed it during his selection interview in January 1875, 'It is a scheme for rendering war more easy, not less easy. I want to make war more difficult; that is the humane plan, it seems to me.' His main objection, he told his audience, referring to the now banned dum-dum bullet, was the absurdity of being allowed to blow your enemy to 'pieces with a large shell, but you must not do it with a small bullet'. Gibson Bowles was not the only member of parliament to mistrust what he saw as something that would only help people to slaughter each other with less guilt.

The 1880s and 1890s were marked by a series of skirmishes, rebellions and wars across Europe and Africa. The British Aid Society played a relatively small part as an organization, right up to the Boer War in 1899, but these years were remarkable for the number of exceptionally dedicated British figures who, following in the steps of the doctors and administrators who had gone to serve in the Franco-Prussian war, set themselves up in field ambulances and sailed for far-away conflicts. Because, like the earlier volunteers, they tended to be literate and articulate, they left a series of vivid accounts of their work. These are remarkable documents, testimonials to the philanthropic spirit of the age, long, detailed, full of medical notes, but also reflections on war and peace; nothing was too small or too speculative to be left out. By the later years of the nineteenth century, newspaper reporters had also taken to accompanying armies into the field, and they too came back with stories about these pioneering Red Cross adventurers. British volunteers who had set off for Belgrade to help the Serbians against the Turks in 1875 and 1876 had been funded by private organizations as well as by the British Aid Society.

In the spring of 1877, after the failure of the great powers to prevent the conflict from spreading across the Balkans, and after Russia's declaration of war on the Turks in order to free the Christians, the question of British Red Cross Society intervention was again raised, as stories of fresh atrocities and massacres filled the British papers. Though not in a very healthy condition, warding off criticisms about its lack of preparedness, inefficiency and bias – Loyd-Lindsay, veteran of the Franco-Prussian war, seemed to find the concept of neutrality as envisaged by Geneva hard to grasp and saw nothing wrong in remaining chairman of a Red Cross society while personally championing the Serbian cause – the British society again called for volunteer doctors. This time they were required to be able to speak enough of the languages of the countries at war to sustain a conversation. A small steamer, the *Belle of Dunkerque*, was chartered and set off for the Black Sea with five surgeons and supplies worth £7,000.

In the early months of the war, the Russian Red Cross and army medical services, fighting in the Caucasus as well as the Balkans, insisted that they were coping well on their own without help, at one point even causing a diplomatic incident by taking a number of the British society's doctors prisoner. But all through July and August 1877 the Russian troops fell back, through heat and dust, then under rain that turned their route into a never-ending river of mud. More than 20,000 horses died and were left to decompose by the roadside. Journalists travelling with the Russian soldiers reported a smell so terrible that they had to cover their faces with handkerchiefs covered in camphor, which left their noses bright red. Russian troops began to sicken. There were few doctors and almost no medical supplies. Dr Armand Leslie of the British society reported back from Shipka in Bulgaria at the end of August:

> I have, necessarily, witnessed many atrocities since my arrival at the front . . . On August the 4th I attended to a girl who had been violated by eighteen Cossacks . . . I have very frequently seen little children wandering, nobody would claim them. Large numbers die of hunger and thirst.

The wells, he added, were full of corpses; the sky was blue by day and 'livid at night from the incessant fire of flaming villages'. Leslie begged the society to send out more surgeons.

This war would be remembered by Red Cross doctors for the atrocities they were forced to witness. Both the Turks and the Russians decapitated, eviscerated and mutilated enemy soldiers, often chopping off their prisoners' heads and carrying them back to camp on the top of spikes. One British doctor left a terrible account of what he found in the remains of a Muslim village, where Cossacks had caught the women and children as they fled.

> The death of one young woman could only have occurred two or three days ago ... the flesh was still adhering to the almost skeletal remains and what had not been devoured by the dogs was quite fresh-looking ... We all stood round that awful sight without saying a word. Her face, which the dogs had respected and left intact, was most strikingly beautiful ... her hair was lying all round her head like a rich brown wavy halo. She was entirely nude, and her throat had been cut with one clean, deep, cut, which must have severed the jugular and windpipe immediately.

When Plevna fell to the Russians in December, 30,000 Turks were taken prisoner. As the Russians prepared to march them back to captivity, Dr Campbell Fraser of the British society recounted to Loyd-Lindsay the horrors that he and his Red Cross companions faced, working in appalling conditions, wearing white raincoats and hats with red crosses on them, amputating twenty hours at a stretch. Plevna, he wrote, had become 'one vast charnel house'. Along the route leading back towards Russia were black bundles half buried in snow, which turned out to be wounded men abandoned without medical help. 'Everywhere,' reported the correspondent for the *Daily News*, 'pale withered hands and feet stick out of the soil on all sides, and horrible dead mummified faces stare at one from every little hollow in the ground.' Nothing the volunteers from the British Red Cross Society had witnessed on the battlefields of the Franco-Prussian war had quite prepared them for this.

It snowed, thawed, then froze. The plain of the Danube turned into one vast sheet of ice. All landmarks disappeared in the whiteness. Men weakened by fighting, by typhoid, smallpox, frostbite and hunger were formed into convoys, 4,000 strong, and ordered to start marching. Behind them flew an escort of birds of prey and the growing numbers of corpses, stretching away to the horizon, were fought over by dogs and pigs. Dr Fraser did what he could. He travelled up and down the 'march of death' in a sledge, handing out food and clothing, much as the International

Committee delegates would do during the Nazi death marches in the closing months of the Second World War, and he set up depots of blankets in the villages through which the marching men passed. He scoured the countryside for honey and tobacco, the two items the captive Turks most craved. The cold grew more bitter, the Russian guards more brutal. Peasants looked on, appalled, as their land was stripped bare and left littered with sick soldiers and dead bodies. During the next few days, a quarter of the prisoners died.

The most badly wounded men were in fact the luckiest, for they were sent directly to Bucharest, where British surgeons from the Aid Society waited with medicine, food, clothes and beds. As the men trickled in, relief organizations, made up of private citizens, religious orders, the Romanian Red Cross and foreigners, set to work with unaccustomed harmony.

By the spring of 1878, the British had also set up their headquarters in Constantinople and thousands of refugees were now flocking desperately towards it. A reporter, observing a scene of panic as the enemy advanced on the fleeing refugees, wrote: 'Many women, almost mad with grief, horror and hunger, fling their children over the bridges as they pass along in the train. Some throw them over the bridges when they reach the coast.'

A committee of foreign ladies, gathering in the gardens of the British embassy at the request of the ambassadress, Mrs Layard, set about making sheets, pillowcases, bandages, mattresses and clothes, sitting in the garden in the cool of the evening, occasionally pausing to play tennis. The ladies did the cutting themselves; the actual sewing was passed on to refugee women already living in Constantinople.

In June 1878, a conference of the great powers opened in Berlin and the Ottoman Empire was dismembered. Romania, Serbia and Montenegro were pronounced independent states; a new Slav state, Bulgaria, was created; and Cyprus became British. The British Aid Society had entered this last war ill-prepared and not at all certain about its future. It emerged with a far clearer picture not only of its role but of what it could achieve, and was able to reflect, with some satisfaction, that it had, despite Loyd-Lindsay's difficulties with neutrality, upheld the International Committee's insistence on impartiality with considerable efficiency. Two thousand blankets had gone to the Turks, 1,924 to the

Russians; 576 ounces of quinine had been issued to Turkey, 588 to Russia. Red Cross volunteers, who had been exceptionally brave, operating in terrible conditions for days on end, had shown the need for doctors to be enterprising, in excellent health, adaptable, and above all to have strong stomachs.

The International Committee had not played a dominant part in this war though it had, in the summer of 1877, set up an agency in Trieste, modelled on the Basle agency of the Franco-Prussian war, which had kept the different societies – Russian, Turkish, Montenegrin, Serbian and Romanian – in touch with each other, and done its best to collate lists of prisoners-of-war. Where it had made its mark, however, was over civilians, later to become one of the most painful and contentious issues in the work of the Committee. The societies, both those whose countries were at war, and those of the neutral countries, called on by Moynier to help with funds and medical supplies, had responded generously. Civilians, in this war at least, had been recognized as victims of war, in just the same way as wounded soldiers were.

With every fresh war, the skills of the British Aid Society grew, even if it could do nothing – as was agreed under the Geneva Convention – without permission from the army. And the British government remained extremely wary of using its services when its own army was involved, stubbornly insisting that it had no need of help and declining all offers beyond the providing of a number of trained nurses for the first Egyptian expedition in 1882. It proved more receptive when trouble broke out again in Egypt and the Sudan in 1884. It was prompted to do so after suffering criticism and complaints about its own military medical services, which some said were no better than during the disastrous campaign in the Crimea. In January 1884, General Gordon left Cairo for Khartoum to evacuate the garrison. A few months later the Mahdi's followers besieged the town and Gordon was cut off. An expedition to relieve him set out, and in October, Major J. S. Young was appointed British Aid Society 'Commissioner to the Nile' with instructions to supply whatever help was needed. A launch, the *Queen Victoria*, was bought, and a patriotic Englishman, Sir Allen Younger, offered his yacht, the *Stella*, to evacuate the sick and wounded.

The British army, still sceptical about private volunteers, was not really ready for all that the Aid Society was capable of providing. After a slight delay, they announced that they would be happy to accept 'luxuries' and 'special medical comforts' but not much else. From Cairo, Young wrote to ask for soda water. By May 1885 a local ladies' branch had been set up to send visitors to the hospitals where the British soldiers were being nursed and to supply them with 'gifts' – screens, chairs, games and oranges bought out of Red Cross funds. Two of the ladies, the Misses Edwards and Durham, agreed to go as 'instructeresses in cooking' to the hospital in Suez, and were soon turning out chicken, custards, pancakes, 'baked tapioca pudding and calves' foot jelly made into shapes'. In the hospital at Abu Fatmeh, a Colonel J. Maurice began experimenting with growing fruit and vegetables. By April, he was able to report a 'splendid supply of melons', one weighing 9lbs 9oz, 27 inches tall and 24 inches wide, and a good crop of 'round or olive shaped' radishes. His spinach, he reported to the society in London, was proving popular with a Major Poe, a double amputee. Broccoli and cauliflower, he added, 'promise capitally'. The new soda water machine, Major Young wrote, was giving 'every satisfaction'.

In February 1885, the Princess of Wales and 'a few ladies' announced that they wished to use the British Aid Society to send out a number of 'small comforts' to the British troops in Egypt, 'to include of course the Indian and Australian contingents'. Three duchesses, two marchionesses, six countesses, as well as Mrs Gladstone and Florence Nightingale joined the committee, and all over England other countesses and duchesses began to form committees of their own. Lady Maud Wolmer decided to send insect powder, Queen Victoria cushions and tobacco, Messrs Barton & Co. champagne; the Hampton sub branch collected 8,329 pairs of pyjamas and 5,035 pillowcases. At the end of June the *Lancaster Guardian* carried a long piece about an amateur concert put on in St James's Hall by the American colony in London in order to raise money for the Aid Society. Two thousand people of 'means and position' turned out in their most elegant clothes; one, noted the reporter, wore 'scarlet tulle, with trimmings of scarlet chenille fringe (a band of which latter formed the only sleeve) and a flight of humming-birds on the skirt and round the right side of the bosom'. Some, no doubt, sported the new Order of the Red Cross, crimson enamel edged in gold, with a dark blue ribbon, 'red edged, tied in a bow and worn on the left shoulder'. Red and white, the colours of the Red Cross, were the theme of the day, red trimming splashed across countless white gowns, and the platform was decorated with a bank of scarlet geraniums and a lyre of white flowers. 'I never saw the dingy big room look half so gay,' commented the reporter, adding kindly: 'Lacking a little, perhaps, in refinement, but gracious, courteous, intelligent and most graceful are the many educated American men and women.' They gave generously, she admitted, but commented that it was a great pity the women had never learnt to curtsey gracefully.

The 'little comforts' and the money were despatched by the society to Egypt where Major Young, still acting as go-between, reported that the troops, embarking on long, hot, dusty journeys, were able to take grapes and melons with them and that the 7,000 limes and 11,000 oranges had arrived in excellent condition.

In its own way, the relative ease of the Egyptian campaign was as important for the British society as the harshness of the winter in the Balkans, for it caused the army to reflect on what it actually wanted of its Red Cross auxiliaries in wartime. It also brought to light the absurd rivalry felt by the military medical services towards the society and the shortsightedness of the military in turning down not just 'comforts' but necessary supplies. More importantly, perhaps, it made the society reconsider its own role. In the months following the occupation of Egypt, the British newspapers were full of articles about the British Aid Society's work, triggered by a piece written by John Furley for the November issue of the journal *Nineteenth Century*, in which he compared the aimlessness and apathy of the British society in peacetime with the zeal and activity of many of the Red Cross societies on the continent. An angry correspondence followed, with attacks on the society's inefficiency. There were accusations that the money raised from the public was handed over with no accountability – shades of the attacks on Clara Barton – that all good suggestions were just 'pigeon-holed in some dark corner' and that while the volunteers were excellent, the society itself was stagnant. From Geneva, the International Committee joined in the debate, pointing out in the *Bulletin* that very little indeed had been heard of the British society in recent years, a matter that had already been raised at the recent sixth International Conference in Vienna. Fifteen years had passed since the Franco-Prussian war, observed a writer in the *British Medical Journal,* and still nothing had been done to analyse the British society's role or plan for its future. Was it not time that the society took itself in hand?

And so the debates dragged on, through other skirmishes and other wars, until in January 1899 a permanent central Red Cross committee for the British Empire and its dependencies was finally officially reorganized and approved. Loyd-Lindsay, now Lord Wantage, was appointed chairman, and John, now Sir John, Furley, honorary secretary. An office was set up in the army medical department of the war office. At last, after nearly forty years, there was a strong society, spending the years of peace in preparation for times of war and ready to supplement the work of the army medical department.

The British society was barely in place when it was faced with a more severe test. On 11 October 1899, the long-running British dispute with the Boers in South Africa turned into a full-scale war. The next two years would challenge the resolve and resources of the British society, as well as the generosity and preparedness of other national societies, but it would also bring to light something of the ultimate powerlessness of the entire Red Cross movement when it came to the actual conduct of war. Despite the Geneva Convention, by now signed by forty-two countries, there was still nothing to be done if governments chose to disregard it. Moynier's increasing conviction that a tribunal was needed to pass judgement on those who failed to comply with the new rules, was turning out to be sound. For now, in a war in which a major and ostensibly civilized power decided to do little to prevent widespread violations, the 'moral authority' he had once thought sufficient to control the conduct of war would count for little.

Few people in England imagined the conflict in South Africa would involve a long military campaign. The British society, eager to show off its new efficiency, quickly issued an appeal to the public and did its best to prevent too many other private charitable organizations from invading its patch. Colonel Young was once again appointed chief commissioner and by the middle of November was already in Cape Town with orders to bring together the various local voluntary societies. Shortly after the Jameson raid of 1895, the International Committee had invited the governments of the Transvaal and the Orange Free State to ratify the

Geneva Convention. Despite British protests that neither was entitled to do so, both had ratified and when war broke out in 1899, Britain decided not to contest the applicability of the Convention. However, when the International Committee asked the Portuguese to open an agency in Lourenço Marques – now Maputo, capital of Mozambique – to handle enquiries, money and post for war victims, based on the earlier agencies in Basle and Trieste, and proposed to place it under the direction of a representative from the British Red Cross, one from the Afrikaner societies and one from the Portuguese, the British refused. They would not, they said, sit on a committee with Boers. No agency was set up.

Young reached South Africa to find that the 'loyal residents' of the Cape Colony had already formed a local committee to organize help for the sick and wounded. He cabled to London for two assistants, planning to station one in Cape Town and the other in Durban, and wisely decided to act as co-ordinator of the work already under way.

There was a great deal to do. Money and supplies, raised by the Red Cross in London as well as locally, now poured in; Young opened stores and depots, visited hospitals and inspected prisoners. Hospital trains, which would play a huge part in this war, were already bringing back British casualties from the front, to be met by volunteers with 'comforts'. On their return journey, they took with them special kits to hand out to wounded men. Known as 'lucky bags', they contained pyjamas, a towel, a hairbrush, socks and a toothbrush. Casualties began to mount. In the spring of 1900, Young was replaced by Sir John Furley, who had designed and commissioned a special train, which had been built in the record time of three months by the Birmingham Railway Carriage and Wagon Company, at a cost of £10,000, and shipped out to South Africa in sections. The *Princess Christian*, as she was called, set out immediately for the fighting, picking up casualties, dropping off surgeons, travelling through glorious countryside with a 'patch of lobelia, large as an English lawn and dazzlingly blue – a sapphire in a surrounding of emerald'.

Neither of the two British commissioners found their job easy. The fighting had brought thousands of civilians into Cape Town, which was now overcrowded and in a state of chaos with control equally divided between military and civilian authorities. Every ship brought more visi-

tors to the war and many of these were women, the wives of serving
soldiers or would-be nurses, in smart new uniforms who were soon, as
one journalist put it, 'pottering about the wards in flounces and furbe-
lows, hindering the nurses and irritating the patients'. A story was told
of one long-suffering wounded soldier hanging a notice at the end of
his bed: 'I am too ill to be nursed today.' Many had come principally
to have a good time and when they were not irritating the patients
they went off on picnics. The Mount Nelson Hotel was soon the most
fashionable place in town. Mortimer Menpes, a journalist who later
wrote an account of the war, noted that

> Cape Town at that time was loathsome, filled as it was with
> heartless society butterflies — ladies overdressed and not over
> pretty ... Middle aged women who in London would have
> seemed quite passable here in this glorious light appeared tawdry
> and artificial. It was the place only for hard workers — for the
> women whom the doctors call angels.

The trouble was that there were not enough angels and Furley was soon
reporting the appalling behaviour of 'ladies who think they have a right
to walk about the hospitals as they please' to Lord Wantage. A Mrs Dick
Chamberlain came in for particular comment after boasting that it was
'within her power to make or break the career of army officers', and
was busy inciting other lady volunteers to do the same. News of these
troublesome women reached Queen Victoria, who was apparently so
disapproving of the 'way in which ladies are jumping their way to the
front' that she prevailed on Joseph Chamberlain, the colonial secretary,
to send a telegram to the governor of the Cape, telling him to issue an
edict that these volunteers were not wanted. It achieved little. It took
the intervention of Kitchener, when he became chief of staff, who gave
the 'idling young staff officers' who were acting like a magnet for the
volunteer ladies, the choice between the war front or a speedy return
to England, to move them.

The war was going slowly. The occupation of Bloemfontein was followed by a typhoid epidemic which spread rapidly through British troops
already weakened by forced marches and insanitary camps. Soon more
than 4,000 sick soldiers had been put in makeshift hospitals around
Bloemfontein in appalling conditions with far too few beds or mattresses.

William Burdett-Coutts, sent by *The Times* to report on the war, came home with stories of hundreds of sick and wounded men, 'their faces covered with flies', lying on the bare ground, and of hospital wards 'full of vermin, badly equipped and badly tended'. Though the account shocked the British public, the war office refused to declare it a crisis, particularly when their two senior surgeons in South Africa, William MacCormac and Frederick Treves, the foremost surgeon of his day and best known as the doctor who befriended Joseph Merrick, the Elephant Man, continued to send back soothing reports. (On their return to London, Treves told a dinner at the Reform Club given in their honour that there had never been a campaign in which 'the horrors of war had been so mitigated, and the treatment of the wounded had been so complete'.)

On the outbreak of war, the International Committee in Geneva had, as was now customary, asked the Red Cross societies of the governments at war whether they would welcome help from other national Red Cross societies. The replies from both sides had been at best lukewarm, but the German Red Cross had nonetheless sent surgical dressings and money, the Italians their usual cognac, marsala and Sicilian wine, the Spanish cigars, the Greeks more cigars and wine. A number of foreign doctors and field hospitals arrived in South Africa and painstaking reports on wounds, diseases and the conduct of war were soon reaching Geneva, where Dr Ferrière conscientiously wrote them up into articles for the *Bulletin*. But among these reports were criticisms, particularly of British condescension towards the foreign societies. There were also attacks on the haughty Boers, whose poor manners were due, thought Ferrière, to the 'ruggedness' of their natures, and the fact that they were a proud, tenacious people 'evidently lacking in courtesy and agreeableness'.

For all the reassuring and complacent reports despatched home by MacCormac and Treves, a crisis was about to break. After the fall of Paardeberg early in 1900, 4,000 Boer prisoners were sent back to Cape Town and Simonstown, the terrible conditions in which they had first been held — in the open, for three wet days — having caused an outbreak of enteric fever. No hospital was ready to take them, but after Furley's stern intervention efforts were at last made to improve their lives. The Red Cross in London sent £500 to be spent on Boer tobacco, matches and books in Dutch. None of the prisoners-of-war, either Boer or British, were in fact faring very well and Dunant's dream of a special Convention for prisoners had never seemed more necessary.

After reports that the Boers were treating their British prisoners with harshness and criminal negligence, a court of inquiry opened in Pretoria in June 1900 at which evidence was heard from doctors, officers and former prisoners. Dr Rudolph von Gernet, a medical officer, told the court that when he had inspected the prison camp and hospital at Waterval, 'the streets were in an indescribably filthy condition, rotting animal and vegetable refuse and even human excrement lay freely all over them and the stench was awful.' Much of the blame for this was laid at the door of Dr Veale, head of the Transvaal Red Cross, who had been 'unwilling to risk trouble with the government and imperil his own position'.

On the British side, a scandal now broke out over Captain Ernest Kenworthy, a former trooper in B Squadron of Kitchener's Horse, who had been taken on by the Red Cross as assistant commissioner in Mafeking after being invalided out of the army. Kenworthy worked hard but, being still unwell, ran much of his work from his bed, telling hospital staff to send their servants to collect supplies directly from him. A fellow officer called Duhan seems to have had some terrible grudge against him. In September, Kenworthy was informed that three of the servants had sworn affidavits before Duhan to say that Kenworthy had sexually assaulted them, a William Baxter swearing that he had 'asked him into the room and commenced tickling his chin etc. He undid his coat, felt his chest and private parts, and asked if Baxter wore drawers.' Whatever the truth of the allegations, the matter was hushed up, and Kenworthy left South Africa, but not before the British Red Cross had complained officially that one of their members was being victimized.

Far worse trouble was to follow, in which neither the British Red Cross nor the International Committee would have a say. It provides a first glimpse of what was to prove one of the Red Cross movement's most enduring failures – the near impossibility of helping civilians in times of war, unless refugees, without value as military pawns.

Soon after the capture of Bloemfontein stories about the British destruction of Boer homes started to appear in the newspapers. These were ostensibly farms owned by insurgents, who were tearing up railway lines and destroying bridges in order to impede the progress of the British troops. As the burnings spread, so Boer women and children were made homeless. The guerrilla attacks continued and Lord Roberts, then commander-in-chief, ordered further burnings, spurred on, it was rumoured, by his dictatorial wife Nora, whose rage against the Afrikaners was said to have been sparked off by the death of her only son in the fighting. A Captain Phillips later described how the Boer women in the farms the soldiers had been ordered to burn, had brought out milk for them, not understanding what they were about to do. He and his men, he said, had set fire to between six and twelve farms every day, and their progress across the Orange Free State had been 'marked by pillars of smoke by day and fire by night'.

With the war dragging on indefinitely, Kitchener ordered a 'policy of punishment' to flush out the guerrillas in a series of 'drives' modelled on pheasant shoots, with a weekly 'bag' of those killed, wounded or captured. This clearance of the land, sweeping it bare of everything that could sustain the guerrillas, from their homes to their crops and herds, would dominate the last months of the war.

But what to do with the homeless Boer families? At first a few were sent back across Boer lines to join the Afrikaner men in open cattle trucks. But as the numbers kept growing, camps were opened, one of them reserved for the 'undesirables', women accused of having supplied the guerrillas with food. By the end of 1900 there were eight camps in the Transvaal and four in the Orange Free State. No meat was included in the diets of families whose men were known to be in the field. The women and children often received little more than vegetables. There was no fresh milk. Diseases began to break out.

Emily Hobhouse, a small, stout Englishwoman from Cornwall and a Quaker, was the honorary secretary of the South African Conciliation Committee, a body set up in London to counter the spreading jingoism triggered by the war. Early in 1901 she travelled out to South Africa on a mission to 'express sympathy with the women of the Transvaal and Orange Free State'. She was soon meeting refugees from the burnt farms. Receiving permission to take a load of 'comforts' to some of the camps, she set off in a wagon. What she found appalled her. Open railway trucks, full of women and children with no food or water, were being left for days at a time in sidings, exposed to the icy rain of the high veldt. In the camps, water was in very short supply, and there were no beds, very few mattresses and no soap; and there were many poisonous snakes. Clothes were so scarce that many of the children were half naked; everyone was barefoot. Worse, many of the children were ill. Measles, bronchitis, pneumonia, dysentery and typhoid were spreading rapidly. In one camp, among the dying children, she saw a four-year-old boy who had 'nothing left of him except his great brown eyes and white teeth, from which his lips were drawn back too thin to close'. What struck her were not only the appalling privations but a 'death rate such as had never been known except in the times of the Great Plague . . . the whole talk was of death – who died yesterday, who lay dying today, who would be dead tomorrow?'

Finding very little sympathy among the British officers in charge of the camps, Emily Hobhouse sent a report back to London. It was circulated among members of parliament and published in late June. A civil surgeon called Dr Alec Kay commented that it was simply 'agitation . . . raised by a few unsexed and hysterical women who are prepared to sacrifice everything for notoriety'. However, questions now began to be asked by the public, and other people went to visit the camps, returning to declare that unless something was done to halt the death rate, the Boer people in the camps would all be dead within three years. The deaths were now rising rapidly – 550 in May, 782 in June, 1,675 in July.

A commission headed by Millicent Fawcett, the suffragette and philanthropist, was sent out to Cape Town on a tour of inspection. Travelling on a special train, with a Portuguese cook and five other women, she visited thirty-three camps in four months and came back with a ferocious indictment of British behaviour. In parliament, there was talk of a 'policy of genocide'. 'When,' asked the Liberal leader Campbell-Bannerman, 'is a war not a war? When it is carried out by methods of barbarism' – a phrase soon picked up and repeated around the world. The term 'concentration camp', taken from the *reconcentrado* of the civil uprising in Cuba, began to be heard. Lloyd George declared that a 'banner of dead children's bodies will rise up between the British and the Boer races in South Africa', while the Afrikaners claimed that the British were intending to destroy their race. Across Europe, foreign newspapers accused Britain of waging a war of extermination, while a confidential report, drawn up and signed by representatives of Portugal, Austria, Hungary, Germany, Switzerland and Turkey spoke of women and children suffering as 'have never suffered before'. In America, the government came under pressure to issue a public protest, but the secretary of state John Hay refused, saying he saw no reason for the US government to take steps to 'stop a war in which it has less concern than any nation in the world'.

Despite attempts to play down these stories and notwithstanding Kitchener's complaints about Emily Hobhouse (he called her 'that bloody woman') and her meddling, conditions in the camps did improve and, bit by bit, the death rate dropped. But when, after two years and eight months, the Boers finally acknowledged defeat, 26,000 of them were found to have died in the camps, at least 20,000 of those being children under the age of sixteen. Counting the blacks as well, rounded up in great numbers after Kitchener's scorched-earth policy, more than 42,000 people had died as a direct result of concentration camp policy.

Neither the British Red Cross nor the International Committee in Geneva had been able to do anything about it. Civilians did not fall under their formal mandate and if one wonders why nothing was said, why no questions were raised in Geneva, no protests made by Furley, one can only conclude that the subject was felt to be too delicate. None of the codes of conduct so ardently upheld at conferences from one end of Europe to the other appeared as yet to apply to women and children.

The British Red Cross returned home to analyse its own performance. It had raised and spent £182,371 and despatched everything from fifty-five cruets to thirty doilies, along with games of draughts, halma and ludo, and innumerable copies of newspapers and magazines, found to be one of the most appreciated of all 'little comforts'. In one three-month period, 65,000 fresh eggs had been distributed. The *Princess Christian* had ferried 7,548 casualties in comfort and safety. There had been very little waste or duplication with other relief organizations, and the public had dutifully been kept informed about the society's work and expenditure through frequent articles in *The Times*.

The army medical service had rather less to be proud of. Despite the early, glossy accounts put out by Treves and MacCormack, investigations carried out by the British showed the service to have been seriously flawed, with a great deal of reform required before another war broke out. Treves later admitted to the Royal Commission on the War in South Africa that the medical services had indeed been inadequate, the standards of hygiene abysmal, the equipment antiquated and the army doctors poorly trained, adding somewhat flippantly that the typhoid crisis had partly been the result of a 'plague of flies and a plague of women'.

The American Red Cross had also suffered an embarrassing incident. 'With humility, mortification and indignation', it was forced to confess that it had somehow allowed fifty-six people, claiming to be 'physicians and their assistants', to travel to South Africa under the flag of the society, where they had instantly 'torn off their brassards and trampled them, and taken allegiance to the Boer commander and entered the army as "Irish American recruits".'

As for the International Committee, it was forced to conclude that proper attention had not always – or even very often – been paid to the Geneva Convention. The Red Cross had been fired on by both sides, and Dr Ramsbottom, president of the Orange Free State's Red Cross society, had been taken prisoner by the British and thrown into a cell full of fleas and bandits. What was more, one of the most important laws of war had been flouted in an incident at Elandslaagte when ninety Boers had been set upon by 300 men of the 5th Lancers, who had massacred them to cries of 'Kill the buggers' (delicately translated into French for the *Bulletin* as '*tuez cette vermine*'). Even Lord Kitchener had the haziest notion of what the Geneva Convention was actually about, having made a spirited attempt to attach his personal military carriage on to the back of a Red Cross train.

Faithful to its policy of non-intervention – Moynier's suggestion for a tribunal remained after all only a dream – the Committee simply allowed reports of atrocities and breaches of the Convention to appear in the pages of the *Bulletin*. There they were allowed to rumble on, in issue after issue, bald, polite in tone, without comment, almost as if the Committee had no view on the matter. A precedent was being set: faithful reporting but no criticism, which would, in years to come, be judged harshly. At the seventh conference of the Red Cross movement in 1902, a jamboree remembered more for the splendour of its receptions than any substantive discussions, the conduct of soldiers as witnessed during the Boer war found its way into a vague resolution about the need to study the question of 'aid to prisoners-of-war,' but it was so imprecise that it was far from clear to anyone what was meant. Nowhere, at any time, was anything actually said about the concentration camps.

SIX

American Angels of Mercy

Bit by bit, the different elements of the Red Cross movement were falling into place. Looked at from a distance of nearly a century, it is sometimes tempting to see all that happened before the First World War as a dress rehearsal for the chaos that was about to break over them all, the International Committee in Geneva and the Red Cross societies alike. There had been a number of international wars, brutal but contained, during which the Red Cross societies of the great powers had tried out their skills and resources. The Geneva Convention itself had been tested, and some of its rules seen to work while others were found wanting. The medical services of various armies had had a chance to observe their new Red Cross auxiliaries in the field and determine what, precisely, they wanted from them. And there had been many natural disasters, earthquakes, floods and famines, in which the increasingly vexed question of 'preparedness' had been challenged. It is as if pawns were being moved around a board, and certain positions and moves discussed. For the most part, as they moved into the twentieth century, Moynier and his colleagues could look around the world with an understandable sense of achievement.

Just two more major challenges now lay between the Red Cross movement and the First World War. One called for an unprecedented degree of international co-operation; the other showed how successful an individual powerful Red Cross society could be.

For as long as anyone could remember, relations between Japan and Russia had been uneasy. Soon after Commodore Perry's arrival in Yokohama in 1853 and the opening up of Japan after 200 years of isolation, the Russian navy had put in at Nagasaki, to make certain that Russia would have its share in the concessions negotiated by the major powers. Though Japan did sign trading agreements with the Russians in the

1850s, as she had with the other western powers, the two countries remained wary of each other. Eager to extend control itself over neighbouring Korea and Manchuria, or at least to prevent others from taking control, Japan watched Russian expansion in Manchuria with alarm. At the end of 1903, Japan demanded that Russia withdraw its troops from the left bank of the Yalu river. Russia agreed; but then failed to do so. In February 1904, without declaring war, Japan sent its fleet to take Port Arthur at the southern tip of Manchuria.

On 15 February 1904, the now familiar letter went out from the International Committee to the Red Cross societies of the countries at war, offering to act as intermediary in seeking assistance from sister societies. Both replied saying that their own resources were sufficient. Moynier sat back to wait and observe.

Japan, whose signature of the Geneva Convention in 1886 had caused the International Committee such incredulity – the first 'pagan nation' to sign – had a strong national Red Cross society in excellent shape. Since the Meiji restoration in the 1860s and the beginnings of a remarkably rapid programme of transformation, from the building of railways to the striking of coins, many powerful Japanese had been urging the adoption of a wide range of western ideas and institutions, not only because they believed them essential to survival – on the principle of knowing your enemy – but because they viewed at least some of them as civilized and enlightened. A number of missions were planned to establish good relations with western powers and to study ways in which Japan could be made stronger.

Japanese diplomats, court dignitaries and students had been despatched abroad, either on official visits or secretly, returning with descriptions of what they had seen. In the 1870s, Japanese doctors had come back so impressed by German medicine that Japanese medical students were sent off to Germany to pursue their studies. As Baron Kenchu told a conference of diplomats and politicians, describing the Japanese fashion for imitating western ideas, 'Take what is long in another, and amend it with what is short in yourself.' Into all this the Red Cross fitted perfectly. It was an obvious, unthreatening commitment, a perfect vehicle for closer relations with the West. But no matter how much it appeared on the surface to be an apparently conscientious and docile member of the sisterhood of societies, the Japanese Red

Cross was to become a very different animal; and not a pliant one.

Japan already had a charitable model to build on. When, in 1877, an insurrection had broken out in Satsuma Province, Count Tsunetami Sano, a member of the senate, had founded a largely aristocratic society, the *Hakuai-sha* or Philanthropic Society, to take care of the many wounded. As he told his audience at a lecture, good doctors were as important as good statesmen: 'Nothing annoys us more than sickness in this world.' Count Sano was one of the Japanese diplomats who visited the Universal Exhibition in Vienna in 1873 and went on to see the International Committee in Geneva. Back in Japan, he reported on the similarities between his society and the new European Red Cross Societies, and in 1886 the *Hakuai-sha* was rechristened the Japanese Red Cross Society.

Drawing inspiration from a special edict of the Emperor in 1890 entitled the 'Educational Imperial Rescript', which extolled filial piety, brotherly kindness, courage, loyalty and patriotism, and basing itself around the tightly structured nature of Japanese society, the new Red Cross set about building up a membership. It was greatly helped by the enthusiasm of the Empress Shoken. There was very little of the western volunteer spirit about it. The Meiji government, which was keen on universal conscription, saw in its Red Cross a possible role for the men and women who were not in the forces. A goal was set to recruit at least one in every 400 people. Numbers rose steadily, particularly after the Sino-Japanese war of 1894, and members were divided into regular, special and honorary classes, each with its own distinctive badge. When enthusiasm in the countryside seemed to lag behind that in the cities, a magic lantern show was sent on tour, with images of the Emperor by the bedside of wounded soldiers and the Empress overseeing the despatch of artificial legs to the wounded. The delicate question of how to draw women into the movement, an unthinkably public position for the times, was solved by involving the imperial princesses, who agreed to stand as 'moral guides'. They were added swiftly to the lantern show which now included slides of the princesses making bandages. By the outbreak of war with Russia, the Japanese Red Cross was the largest society in the world, with nearly a million members.

The Russian Red Cross did not share its purposefulness or efficiency. For one thing, the philanthropists who helped to organize its various committees were a mixture of Russians and foreigners – French, English,

Greeks and Portuguese. For another it was extremely social, dominated by the Empress, the Dowager Empress, the princesses and the grand duchesses, many of whom had instructed their dressmakers to run up some becoming nurses' uniforms in which they paid their visits to hospitals. Though very wealthy, raising its funds through special taxes on foreign visitors and theatre tickets, it was also corrupt, its riches not always accounted for. Founded in May 1867, one of the first societies to be created and inspired largely by the volunteer sisters of the Holy Cross who had served in the Crimea, it had spent the years of peace working for 'public calamities' – a train crash in 1896, a terrible hailstorm in 1898, an earthquake in the Caucasus in 1899, an outbreak of scurvy among fishermen in 1901 – and it had kept up a permanent campaign to prevent and cure syphilis, which had become widespread by the end of the nineteenth century. In a country in which aid for the poor and needy was a right but not an obligation, and where it was not begging that was seen to be shameful but the refusal to give alms, a vast, chaotic, charitable world had been born to provide help where it was most needed. It was fuelled by a growing sense of affinity with western cultures and guided by the Empress Maria Feodorovna, whose benevolent interests ranged from schools for impoverished girls to hospitals for soldiers.

When the war with Japan broke out, a competent and well-respected courtier, Count Voronzov-Dachkov, was appointed to run an executive committee of the Red Cross and he began to set up mobile field units. Maria Feodorovna opened a workshop in the Hermitage Palace, calling on the ladies of St Petersburg to come and sew linen, warm clothes and bandages for the Russian soldiers. Soon the hum of sewing machines filled the halls in which Catherine the Great had once held court and played cards. Tea was served by court footmen while the Empress did her rounds, preceded by a black page in eighteenth-century dress of wide red trousers, a short gold-laced coat and a white turban, who carried her furs and her workbag. Individual grand duchesses were detailed to take charge of the various sewing groups.

The first naval engagements went to the Japanese: other victories on land followed. At Mukden, the Russians lost 97,000 men to the Japanese 45,000. People observed with disbelief that it was the first time a non-European army had got the better of Europeans in modern times. Both armies had up-to-date weapons, the Japanese using the smallest bullets ever seen and which caused wounds that healed very quickly. Just before Christmas 1904, the Japanese took Port Arthur, which the Russians had believed impregnable. The numbers of Russian prisoners and Russian casualties started to rise, the Japanese noting disapprovingly that the Russian officers they captured were decked out in costumes more suitable for a ball than a war. Soon the Russian medical services proved totally inadequate for the needs of their wounded and the Russian Red Cross was stretched thinner and thinner. The grand duchesses did what they could and turned out to wave farewell to the troop trains as they left for the front.

Among the Japanese the mood was very different. As much as anything, it was all about regimentation, about the loyalty and obedience the Japanese Emperor rated so highly. It was also about money. The Japanese Red Cross was, by European standards, extremely rich, guided by the fiscal policies of the minister of finance, Count Masayoshi Matsukai. The two main tasks of the local branches were to recruit new members and collect subscriptions. Its headquarters in Tokyo consisted of a pleasant, large, single-storey house surrounded by gardens in which a special room was reserved, unused, for the Emperor and Empress. The style of the organization, formal, courteous and hierarchical, mirrored that of Japanese society itself. The presidency was firmly in the hands of the aristocracy, moustachioed men in sashes and epaulettes, and marchionesses in turbans and jewels, who stare out impassively from early portraits. Each rank of Red Cross helper had an equivalent military rank: stretcher-bearers were privates, 'chief lady nurses', non-commissioned officers.

Like the military medical services, the Japanese Red Cross Society had dutifully prepared for war. In 1890 the first training programme for nurses had been launched, and since then competition for places had been intense. Screening of young women recommended by a ladies' committee was thorough: they had to be aged between seventeen and thirty, no smaller than 4ft 6in in height, not in debt, nor married, nor 'bound to a family' and above all pure, not having once 'disgraced themselves morally'. They were to be gentle, humble and obedient, and to know something of mathematics. Training lasted three years and included many hours of coaching in morality, as well as lessons in 'how to handle dead patients . . . and dispose of their wills'. English language was optional. War widows were welcomed and later called 'Mothers of the Nation'.

When news of the Russo-Japanese war reached England, a nurse called Mrs Richardson, who had served in the Boer war, offered her services to the Japanese minister in London, saying that she was willing to pay her own expenses. She spoke French and German, and possessed her own starched uniform. Photographs show wispy hair and a kindly expression. Mrs Richardson was only one of a number of foreigners who travelled to Japan to observe or work with the Red Cross, and she came home extremely impressed. By the time she reached Tokyo, groups of lady volunteers had been hard at work producing bandages for two months, working eight-hour days and disinfecting their hands each time they entered the workroom. 'Tokyo,' she noted approvingly in her memoirs, 'is not a city of loafers.' Thirty thousand bandages had already been sent to the front. The ladies – even the princesses – wore unbecoming uniforms of a black alpaca bodice and skirt, with bonnets tied with bright blue ribbon. Working alongside them were groups of young girls who did nothing but sew knots in cross stitch on to handkerchiefs and towels destined for the front, each knot said to express a good wish. The Empress too took her hand at bandages and hers were considered sacred, with magical powers. Passed first ceremoniously to the grand chamberlain, they made their way down the hierarchy until they reached the divisional commanders, who gave them to wounded officers. Later, washed, rewashed, washed again, they were used on ordinary soldiers. The Red Cross surgeons Mrs Richardson met were all passionate patriots; they spoke at least one European language and were distinguished from other surgeons by a small red cross pinned to their kimonos. When the Empress came one day to visit the hospital, all the windows were closed and the blinds drawn as she drove up, as it was forbidden for anyone to look down on her.

The foreigners marvelled at the way small, delicate nurses did twenty-four-hour shifts without complaint and carried their patients to and from operations on their backs, all the while remaining 'silent and graceful' in their movements and attentive to the slightest needs of the men they looked after.

Ethel McCaul, a British Red Cross nurse who visited Japan after the war broke out, was shown around the Red Cross hospital with an interpreter by her side, who kept up a constant refrain of 'please bow' every time they came across a doctor. She observed that whenever a surgeon entered a ward the patients, if able to stand, leapt out of their beds and stood 'at attention'. Those too ill pulled themselves up into the Buddha position, at the bottom of their cots. The diet given to the patients was, she remarked, excellent and nutritious and she much admired the way that the operating theatres were kept clean by flooding them every few hours with a solution of bichloride. Meeting Marchioness Oyama and Baroness Sannomiya, both pillars of the Red Cross society, she noted that they were 'shining with a feverish anxiety and determination, in order that no part of the duties undertaken by the society's women members shall be found imperfect or wanting in this hour of need'. The Red Cross hospital, with its reserve of 3,000 trained nurses, ready at all times for immediate service, was the only one permitted to supply the army with nurses at times of war. When ten American trained nurses came to join them, they were greeted with banners that read: 'Welcome, American angels of mercy.'

The nurses were intensely busy. With the fall of Port Arthur, 41,000 Russians were taken prisoner, of whom 17,000 were sick or wounded and 9,000 suffering from scurvy. Stories started to reach Europe about the excellence of their treatment by their Japanese captors. Quickly evacuated from the front in a human chain of stretcher-bearers, they were screened for disease and isolated into groups – white tags for smallpox, red for dysentery, yellow for cholera – while enormous pains were taken to keep everything around them sterilized. (Every Japanese soldier bathed before going into battle, so as to be as clean as possible if he needed surgery.) Louis Livingstone Seaman was an American volunteer surgeon who was taken to see the Russian prisoners in Matsuyama hospital where the Japanese Red Cross was active. Probably, he wrote later, 'no prisoner of war has ever been so comfortable or so free.' Russian officers, who were each given their own personal servant, were kept in a magnificent Buddhist temple in a park near a lake, with irises, lotuses and goldfish, and once convalescent they were encouraged to stroll under the maples and cherry trees, the Japanese believing that beauty and tranquillity aided recovery. Those well enough were taken on expeditions to hot springs. If they needed artificial limbs, these were paid for by the Empress. Heavier and larger than their captors, the Russians were particularly delighted with the food — generous helpings of fish, soup, vegetables and white bread, instead of the meagre portions of black rye bread and broth they were used to. When news reached the hospital of further Russian defeats, the Japanese naval ministry sent the patients presents, as consolation. The Russian prisoners were reported to be extremely cheerful. Seaman came away full of praise.

After the fall of Port Arthur, Russian hopes had turned to their Baltic fleet, a motley collection of ships which left on a 20,000 mile trip, in terrible weather, to confront the Japanese navy and cut off communication between Japan and Manchuria. Many of the crew were peasants with no naval training. On 14 May 1905 — the anniversary of the coronation of Nicholas II — came a decisive and devastating battle at Tsushima. Japanese shells tore through the wooden Russian ships. By nightfall, practically the entire Russian fleet had been sunk and thousands of men drowned, a disaster from which Russia never fully recovered.

It had been a magnificent victory for the Japanese military, which had quickly adapted to western weapons, and for its medical services, but no less splendid for the Japanese Red Cross who had lost seventy-eight workers in the war. Its efficiency had been awesome. It had played a significant part in improving the care for the wounded and achieved a record in preventing deaths: in other contemporary conflicts it had become acceptable to lose four men to disease for every one lost from wounds, but here the figure had been reversed and stood at one death from disease to every five dead from wounds. (In the French campaign in Madagascar in 1894, of 14,000 men sent to the front, 7,000 had died from preventable diseases.) The Japanese had taken 60,000 Russian prisoners, many of whom were sick or wounded: of these only eighteen officers and 595 men were lost. The importance of clean water, good food and above all readiness had been demonstrated to the satisfaction of Japanese and foreigners alike. As in La Fontaine's fable, the Russian grasshopper's unpreparedness had proved fatal in the face of the triumphant Japanese ant. True there had been complaints, duly noted by the International Committee in the *Bulletin*: the Japanese had taken prisoner the two Red Cross ships accompanying the Russian fleet. But no one could deny that the Japanese had gone considerably beyond their commitments under the Geneva Convention. Not only had a prisoners' intelligence service been set up, with orders to treat the Russian prisoners with respect, but accurate lists had been drawn up of the dead and wounded and at every turn the Japanese had proved courteous and fair. The war, concluded Baron Suyematsuy writing about the victory, had shown Japan capable of 'great moral heroism in the cause of humanity and civilization'. What was more, he argued, it had dispelled the misconception that Japan was nothing but a 'petty, infantile, imitative, shallow, bellicose and aggressive nation'. In all this, the Japanese Red Cross had been invaluable, demonstrating to the rest of the world not just Japan's strength, but its humanity. 'This business-like organization,' wrote Sir Frederick Treves, after inspecting Japanese Red Cross hospitals, 'is the most remarkable and efficient of its kind in the world.' Moynier's deep mistrust of the movement's first 'pagan' member would need fundamental revision.

Shortly before dawn, on 28 December 1908, tremors were felt on both sides of the Messina straits between Sicily and the Italian mainland, over an area of about a thousand square miles. It was raining and very cold. The local houses were made, for the most part, from stones, bound together loosely with mortar, much of it old and crumbling, under heavy tiled roofs. As the tremors grew stronger, many houses collapsed. A tidal wave followed, levelling what few buildings remained standing. Within hours, news began to reach Rome and the northern Italian cities of a disaster quite unlike any experienced in modern times. More than fifty villages and towns had been destroyed; the city of Messina had disappeared; between 75,000 and a quarter of a million people were dead. Roman and Greek remains, splendid public buildings, Renaissance churches and the houses of up to a million people had been reduced to rubble.

In the days that followed, the Red Cross movement launched the largest relief operation ever known, in terms of money, volunteers, provisions and co-operation, though at times the work would be marked by bickering, rivalry, criticism and extreme chaos. Used as we are in the 1990s to immense and highly efficient relief operations, it is easy to forget that at the turn of the century the telegraph was in its infancy, the railway system still being developed, there were no stockpiles of emergency relief and no machinery for co-ordinating international action.

For all the disagreements, Dunant's much repeated phrase 'tutti fratelli' had never been more apt. The Messina earthquake would establish models — both to avoid and to follow — for relief work for decades to come. As the Bulletin said in its next issue, 'an immense cry of pity went up throughout the entire Red Cross'.

The first to reach the area were sailors from Italian, English and Russian ships anchored in the southern Italian ports. They were appalled by what they found. Messina, a fine city of vast, imposing buildings along its sea front, had been completely flattened. Nothing, beyond a few pillars, remained standing; fires flickered in different districts; among the ruins, in the faint winter dawn light, dazed survivors wandered calling out for lost relations, drenched by the heavy rain that continued to fall. As many as 100,000 people were thought to be buried somewhere under the rubble, and as the sailors began to sift through the stones and beams the cries and moans of those trapped beneath could be heard. From time to time, fresh tremors disturbed the work, dull, rumbling waves that toppled what little remained standing; and then, as one man later wrote, 'from all directions would rise a weird, high, thin wailing from the frightened populace.' There was no food, no water, and no light. Along a fifty-mile stretch of coast all that could be seen were ruins and fire.

The Italian Red Cross, which had originally been slow to organize, now moved with admirable speed. A central relief committee was set up, Messina was placed under martial law, trains and ships were commandeered and despatched south with supplies, while the Red Cross societies from France, Germany, Portugal, Holland, Switzerland, Britain, Denmark and Norway were allocated tracts of land outside the city on which to set up their headquarters and begin to build shelters. On paper, it all sounded excellent. It failed, however, to take into account that no one present had ever seen a calamity of these proportions. The president of the Italian Red Cross, Giovanni Ciraolo, who had lost two sisters and most of their many children in the earthquake, could be forgiven for being less than perfectly efficient. Soon, chaos spread. The French Red Cross train was blocked for many hours by heavy snowstorms and the volunteers on board survived on marrons glacés and chocolate. When they finally reached Messina and were allocated a hospital in a former girls' school they were revolted by Sicilian manners. Used to silent, orderly wards, they were dismayed to find the building awash with aristocratic ladies from nearby towns and country estates in thick furs and plumed hats, and with students, artists and passing tourists. Graduates from Italy's only nursing school in Milan, young girls with only a month's training and who had never attended an operation, keeled over when asked to hold on to a leg which was about to be amputated. Gangrene from wounds caused by the falling houses took life after life. Soon, confused survivors were to be found wandering from one relief station to the next, trying to understand what was going on.

The American Red Cross, veteran of the San Francisco earthquake, believed itself with some justification to be professionals in this field. Within hours of the news reaching Washington, President Roosevelt had cabled King Victor Emmanuel that help was on its way. Calls for funds were met generously by rich Americans who remembered with fondness the classical ruins and orange groves from their European tours, and the American vice-consul in Milan, W. Bayard Cutting, set off for the south with a first sum of $15,000. By 4 January, barely a week after the first tremors, Lloyd Griscom, the American ambassador, was able to hand over $320,000 to the Italian Red Cross. This would be one of Ernest Bicknell's finest hours. Already dominating the operations side of the American Red Cross, he moved with considerable efficiency. A German ship, the Bayern, standing idle in Genoa, was chartered and set off south loaded with medicines, food, mattresses, clothes, rope, shovels, saws, stoves, soap and matches, while Bicknell himself boarded the first liner for Italy. He reached Messina, called on various Italian dignitaries, contacted the heads of other national Red Cross societies camped around the countryside and was soon hard at work, putting in seventeen-hour days, overseeing the labours of various stray Americans who had happened to be on holiday when the earthquake struck, and supervising the building of 3,000 houses. Using oxen and 1,200 Italian workmen, an 'American village' began to take shape.

The confidential reports that he despatched to Mabel Boardman in Washington, however, were not altogether reassuring. Signor Taverna of the Italian Red Cross, he wrote, though 'an exceedingly honest and well meaning gentleman' was 'noted for being very slow to make up his mind'. In fact, the Italian relief programme was 'so painfully slow that it would never be tolerated for an instant in an Anglo-Saxon country'. Worse, there was talk that the first $100,000 raised in America and handed over to the Italian Red Cross had been embezzled and Mabel Boardman was terrified about how the American public would react if this became known. After Clara Barton's troubles, no one was in the mood for financial irregularities. Next came an angry rumour that the Americans were allowing non-Catholics to look after Catholic orphans, while Methodists in America complained that Italian Protestants were being discriminated against when it came to relief. Then came criticisms that the eight American carpenters who had arrived to design the new houses were drawing models more appropriate to the American suburbs than the hills of Sicily and Calabria.

Nevertheless, relief did arrive in huge quantities and was distributed, orphans were placed in homes run by local women who had lost their own children in the earthquake, rubble and debris was cleared, Greek nurses took over ambulances in Catania, French ships distributed 70,000 meals along the Calabrian coast, and the Duchess of Aosta took in lost children. The Viale Taft, Viale Roosevelt and Via Bicknell were laid out. Documents in the archives of the American Red Cross give a very clear picture of the conscientiousness with which Bicknell and his companions tackled the apparently endless task of putting a community back on to its feet. 'Rossetti: 200 lire', reads one entry in an accounts ledger. 'A little boy of 2, to allow the charitable people which [sic] have sheltered him to buy some clothing for him.' And: 'Ciraolo, Oreste: 500 lire. To buy a piano for his daughter which [sic] was a renowned piano teacher in Messina and would like to start again in giving lessons in Rome.' The same sort of work was taking place among all the foreign delegations. Huge sums of money had been raised throughout the world – the American Red Cross alone had collected and spent over a million dollars, more than they had ever raised for any disaster at home or abroad. Amid the welter of reproaches and criticisms, an extraordinary degree of co-operation had been reached. If the war between Russia and Japan had shown the importance of Red Cross societies being prepared at all times, the Messina earthquake proved the need for a proper system of international collaboration. It also demonstrated to a European public and to the International Committee, both equally unaware of it, the muscle and determination of the American Red Cross.

*   *   *

Not very much is known about Henri Dunant's movements in the years following his bankruptcy and the failure of his campaign for prisoners-of-war. From papers and letters concealed under old newspaper cuttings in the attics of the Dunant family house until sixty years after his death, it is just possible to follow his tracks through restless years of penury and bitterness, wandering from place to place, avoiding old friends. He never returned to Geneva. 'No power on earth will make me go there,' he wrote to a friend some years later. 'I don't want to. I hate them. I curse them.'

In July 1887 he arrived in Heiden, a pleasant, large spa village in the Appenzell above St Gallen, famous for its whey-cure of goats' milk, surrounded by orchards. He had bad eczema and was so poor that he had to stay in bed while his clothes were washed. Taking a room in the Pension Paradis, he found that it had a pleasant garden, clean rooms, good food and magnificent views over Lake Constance and the mountains. Its prices were reasonable. Lack of money dogged him, though it is clear from letters to nephews and nieces that his family, despite having themselves lost money in the Mons-Djémila project, did not desert him but sent him just enough to live on. Complaining bitterly that he had been forgotten by the world – with some justification, for the history of the Red Cross which fails to mention him had by now appeared – he spent long hours reading and re-reading biblical texts, talking of a forthcoming apocalypse and fretting against the Calvinism of his youth. Europe, he warned, was menaced by social revolution, by a future bloodbath provoked by the masculine negative forces of militarism, brute force and egotism, while women, more loving and more peaceable, watched on. For his few visitors, like Dr Altherr who came to tend his eczema or the young schoolmaster William Sonderegger, he drew diagrams linking the Creation to the various religious movements with which he had been involved, tracing the passage between the birth of the universe and the apocalypse, urging people to do something before it was too late. Writing about himself later in his memoirs, using the third person, he said that 'Dunant was not attracted to any confession, any church, any sect, any religious gathering or organization. He would say: I am a member of the invisible spiritual Church of Christ, and that is enough.' He had not, he told his visitors, lost his faith, but he had come to regard it simply as an individual 'Communion with God'. Increasingly, according to the later reports of Altherr and Sonderegger, he talked with respect about America and what he saw as an admirable combination of zeal and tolerance. Virtue, he would say, as defined by the New Testament, was all to do with energy, power and moral values.

Drawn to settle in the Appenzell by these new friends, and in particular Sonderegger and his family, Dunant's moods swung between sociable and energetic and lethargic and morose. Some days he would talk cheerfully of clearing his name and prepare plans for work on human rights, slavery or Zionism, and on others he would sit all day in front of the fire, unable to eat or to write, reliving his early glory, and railing against all those who had reduced him to poverty. 'I was deceived by those I employed in Algeria,' he wrote in his memoirs. 'That was my greatest crime . . . I was duped, fooled, above all by the infamous French administration. The clergy were against me.' Sometimes, he likened his fate to that of Captain Dreyfus. 'The world gives us nothing but deceptions and regrets,' he wrote to his niece Adrienne, 'while distancing one from God and from all true happiness on earth.'

The next few years were spent wandering Europe, returning from time to time to Heiden. At the end of 1892, he was admitted to a small residential hospital in the village, a handsome white house on the side of a hill. For the next eighteen years, a first floor room with a small terrace, an iron bedstead, a table and two chairs, would be his home. He paid 3 francs a day for it, and 10 francs a week for his expenses, most of it going on stamps and paper. When he had the energy, he spent the entire day writing, filling one blue exercise book after another with his memoirs, his warnings of the apocalypse – which appeared in a pamphlet entitled *L'avenir Sanglant* – and the wounded pride and fury he still felt about Moynier and his former colleagues.

As the years passed, his moods turned darker, and days were often lost to depression; feelings of persecution clouded his mind, when he was haunted by suspicions that his post was being opened, or that someone was putting poison in his food. Some days, the hospital cook had to take a mouthful in his presence to prove that it was safe for him to eat. His diaries grew increasingly accusatory, dates, names, attacks, betrayals jumbled together. The hospital, he wrote in a bleak, furious letter to his brother Pierre, was a sort of 'hell', and very noisy on account of a road being built just outside his window, 'without mentioning all the cries and lamentations'. He felt, he reported, perpetually irritable, made worse by troublemaking 'Protestant clerics' in Geneva 'who have turned the Jesuits against me, and now the Jesuits, in their turn, are turning a whole other collection of fools against me too'. In these moods, Dunant was obsessive, extreme and rancorous, refusing to see anyone and keeping his shutters closed for days on end. Dr Altherr, who treated him until his death, noted, alongside some minor intestinal problems, growing melancholia and persecution mania.

There are various accounts of the way in which Dunant was remembered and rediscovered. The most romantic has it that in 1895 a journalist called Georg Baumberger, from a St Gallen newspaper, passed one day through Heiden and, wandering into the public gardens to admire their view over Lake Constance, fell into conversation with an old man sitting on a bench, discovering to his astonishment that he was talking to the founder of the Red Cross. Whether or not this version is fanciful, an article did appear in Baumberger's paper, *Die Ostschweiz*, on 26 June 1895, calling for public recognition for the 'hermit of Heiden', and on 7 August he did pay a long visit to Dunant who, both excited and exhausted by the prospect of clearing his name and returning to the public eye, agreed to provide him with material for a longer piece. For the next week, fat envelopes left Heiden for St Gallen every day, filled with passages from Dunant's memoirs, copies of letters – from Florence Nightingale, Gladstone, Napoleon III – extracts from pamphlets, reminiscences, circulars and the accolades of Europe's royal families. Dunant had lost none of his taste for royalty. On 12 August a photographer called Otto Rietmann came to take his picture.

Baumberger's article appeared early in September. It was picked up by many of the main Swiss papers. Dunant was now sixty-eight. Everything that he had so longed for began to happen: flattering portraits in journals, visits from Swiss and foreign dignitaries, letters from former royal supporters. The Empress Maria Feodorovna awarded him a pension; the City of Moscow gave him a prize; Pope Leo XIII sent him a signed photograph. The money Dunant had long felt to be his due: in his memoirs he commented that Europe in its entirety owed 'me a universal debt for my work on the Red Cross and the Convention, which I alone have the task of promoting'. The fame pleased and soothed him. Some of the anguish of the last twenty years evaporated before telegrams like

the one he received at the time of the 1902 Red Cross conference in
St Petersburg:

> The members of the 7th International Conference of the Red
> Cross, at the end of their deliberations, send their best wishes
> to you, founder of the Red Cross, and promoter of Red Cross
> societies, expressing their feelings of profound recognition and
> most sincere veneration.

Did Dunant ever realize how profoundly he haunted Moynier's life?
During his years of exile, when no one knew where he was, Moynier
can have felt only relief. After Baumberger's article and apparently endless tributes to the hermit of Heiden, the minutes of the meetings of
the International Committee in Geneva record several, somewhat terse,
debates. When the minutes for all meetings held between 1863 and 1867
were suddenly found to be missing, Dunant was the chief suspect. When
requests came for photographs of Dunant, they were turned down.
When articles appeared describing Dunant as 'founder' of the Red Cross
and a question was raised about whether something should be done to
put this 'right', the Committee voted, on 10 October 1904, to do nothing,
on the grounds that it 'could only lose its dignity by attacking an old
man at the end of his life'. Still, Moynier worried away, anxious lest by
keeping quiet, as the minutes of 20 November 1905 record, the 'truth
about the birth of the Red Cross be lost'.

In February 1901 came a move guaranteed to torment Moynier. News
reached the International Committee that under the terms of the will
of Alfred Nobel, the Swedish industrialist and arms manufacturer, a
peace prize was to be set up. Candidates, whether individuals or organizations, were now being sought 'who have contributed the most to frater-
nity between nations, to abolishing or reducing permanent armies, and
to the organization of peace conferences'. Dunant's was one of the names
that had been put forward. The International Committee, at their next
meeting, debated whether to enter as an organization, or send in
Moynier's name alone.

The story of Dunant and the Nobel Peace Prize is revealing, for it
challenged the very nature of the Red Cross movement which, while

determined to mitigate the horrors of war, had never been very clear as to where it stood on pacifism.

Since the middle of the nineteenth century an active and well-organized peace movement, most developed in Britain and America and supported by outspoken public figures like Richard Cobden and the chairman of the US senate foreign affairs committee, Charles Sumner, had called for arbitration at times of war and for disarmament before colossal expenditure on new weapons caused economic ruin. Following Kant – who had prophesied that war would end once people understood where their real interests lay – peace societies, using both economic and financial arguments, had flourished on both sides of the Atlantic, while a series of universal peace congresses had attracted wide interest among the public. Most recently, Tsar Nicholas II had called for a conference in May 1899, held in The Hague, to unite 'in one powerful combination the efforts of all states which are sincerely seeking to make the great idea of universal peace triumphant'. By now Alfred Nobel had become an intimate friend of Bertha von Suttner, the founder, in 1891, of the Austrian Society of Friends of Peace. In her memoirs, von Suttner would say that Nobel had been steered towards offering a peace prize by her own pacifist views, though he himself was far from clear about the best way to secure lasting peace, sometimes saying, in words that presage the later debates about nuclear weapons, that he suspected his own factories achieved more than peace congresses, since once armies had the power to annihilate each other in a single second, they would recoil from war.

If there was something ironic about a peace prize being offered by a man whose financial empire was based on the manufacture of dynamite, cordite and gelignite, who arguably had done more than most to contribute to the frightfulness of war, there was also a distinct ambiguity in Dunant's position. What had actually inspired Dunant at Solferino was not so much a desire to bring about peace, as to create, as he wrote in *Charity on the Battlefield* in 1864, a charitable organization 'in the form of a relief society, to snatch from war all those victims whom weapons have wounded but whom Death has not yet scythed down'. At that stage Dunant wanted to protect victims, not abolish war itself. Like Moynier, however, he had gradually come to believe in the need for an international court of arbitration to 'judge all disputes grave enough to cause a war of extermination'. One of the avowed aims of his universal alliance of 1871 had been to further 'social justice' and in so doing remove the causes of conflict. As the years passed his sense of horror at war turned more vehement. 'War,' he wrote in *L'avenir Sanglant*, 'the science of disorder which proceeds from anarchy in high places, kills not only the body but also too often the soul. It humiliates, corrupts, withers, demeans.' Yet all this time he seems to have remained strangely ignorant about the vast peace movement taking shape throughout Europe and North America.

In June 1892, Dunant read a copy of Bertha von Suttner's book, *Down with Arms*, a novel about war, which contained flattering references to him. A correspondence began between them, with Dunant describing himself as a 'peace loving person, an enemy of war and militarism', and by 1896 he was outlining grandiose plans for a League of Peace, driven by the energy of women, similar to the Red Cross in that it would be led by Europe's aristocracy. Bertha von Suttner, herself a member of the Austro-Hungarian nobility, replied sharply that when it came to peace 'it is in the ranks of my cousins, male and female, where I find the greatest resistance.'

Bertha von Suttner attended Nicholas II's peace conference at The Hague in August 1898, carrying with her one of Dunant's more ebullient declamations: 'Rouse yourself from your lethargy, your culpable indifference, your futile, petty squabbles . . . Wake up before it is too late . . . War or peace. Choose. The future is in everyone's hands. Are you for peace?' She also took with her a statement from Frédéric Passy, one of the founders of the International Federation for Peace. 'One does not humanize slaughter,' Passy had written, 'one condemns it because one is in the process of becoming more humane.'

In these words lay the paradox that marks the Red Cross position on peace to this day. If its aim is to mitigate the effects of war without actually trying to abolish it, then it rightly must fall within the framework of war, along with the army medical services; if it is seen as questioning the inevitability of war, then it can be said to be campaigning for peace. Could the 'humanizing' of war really be said to be a pacifist gesture? Baroness von Suttner returned from The Hague perturbed by proposals to codify further laws of war, but at this stage Dunant appears to have been more interested in attacking what he called the 'new engines of death', the Krupp cannons, torpedoes, dynamite and 'other surprises in store, to our future sorrow'.

In December 1896, Alfred Nobel died. Under the terms of his will, the Norwegian Parliament was made responsible for administering the peace prize. Dunant had a friend in Stuttgart, a teacher called Rudolf Müller who, together with Dr Hans Daae, a captain in the Norwegian army medical services who had met Dunant almost forty years earlier at the statistical conference in Berlin, began to lobby on Dunant's behalf. They wrote to newspapers, talked to professors and academics, pleaded his case before disarmament groups. Dunant helped by supplying them with copies of his earlier letters and pamphlets and by continuing to assure everyone that what had drawn him to Solferino in 1859 had been a desire to so horrify the world by his descriptions of war 'in all its frightful reality' that they would have to act.

At this stage, Moynier's dismay can be forgiven. He too had worked hard at persuading the world to set up a tribunal to arbitrate at times of conflict and he, too, had spoken of destroying 'by all possible means, the spirit of rivalry and sometimes of hatred that divides different peoples'. More than Dunant, he seems to have worried about the contradictions inherent in the Red Cross position, though he remained firmly of the view that the Geneva Convention could only be beneficial while the world moved slowly towards the day when 'humanity will be spared the great evils from which it is still suffering'. Though somewhat pessimistic that this moment would ever come, he continued to speculate:

> Gradually, but inevitably, shall we not have to ask ourselves whether it is really necessary to massacre thousands of men to restore harmony between two States, and whether just causes could not triumph by gentler methods?

Early in 1901, Moynier drafted an article on peace for submission to the Nobel judges. It was debated at the meeting of the International Committee on 15 March and the suggestion was made that he rewrite part of it to stress the active international nature of the Red Cross as compared to the 'far more Utopian role played by the peace societies'. In the event, it was decided to put forward neither Moynier's name nor that of the full Committee, though the reasons for this do not appear in the minutes.

There were thirteen candidates, from Tolstoy — who had written to Bertha von Suttner 'the longer I live and the more I consider the question of war, the more I am convinced that the sole solution . . . is for citizens to refuse to be soldiers' — to the Permanent International Peace Bureau. Though seven Dutch and three Belgian professors, as well as countless organizations, supported Dunant, there continued to be doubts about his eligibility, not least from Bertha von Suttner, whose position was unambiguously pacifist and who wanted the prize to go to Passy, 'the oldest, the most deserving and the most highly regarded of all pacifists'. On 10 December, Dunant learnt that the Nobel Prize was to be divided equally between himself and Passy. He was delighted. This meant not just money with which to finance more ventures — a way was found to keep his share of the 104,000 francs out of the hands of his creditors — but vastly more public recognition. He wrote to thank his supporters, reassuring Bertha von Suttner all over again that his main desire had always been to 'awaken horror of war'. For her part, she seems to have understood matters very clearly. 'Highly as I regarded and still regard Dunant,' she was to write in her memoirs,

> persuaded as I was and am of his friendly attitude towards peace, nevertheless his services and his fame rested on a quite different field from that which Nobel had in mind. The granting of the prize to Dunant was once more a concession to that spirit which managed to force its way even into the Hague Conference, and which supports the dogma that the endeavours against war should be discreetly limited to its alleviation.

In honouring Dunant lay the tacit admission that one of the few things that could be done about war was to mitigate its horror. The Nobel Peace Prize went to the International Committee in 1917, 1944 and 1963.

Even as the Nobel judges were deliberating, the weapons industry was developing at great speed. Articles filled the pages of the *Bulletin* voicing fears of the powers of the new bullets and the new guns, and what challenges they would pose to the medical services and the Red Cross societies. An Austrian, Baron von Horst, contributed a long article on the rush 'to perfection' in the art of war by the invention of ever more murderous weapons, which ensured that no one any longer really knew what the future might hold in store. It was clear, he announced, 'that any future conflict will bring with it more wounded men, because armies are getting larger and weapons more destructive'. Colossal battles, he forecast, 'lasting several days, will replace the short, sharp skirmishes Europe has grown used to'. How would field hospitals, he wondered, 'get close to battlefields, when guns can now fire at a distance of over four kilometres?' Would those living near battlefields be willing to take in casualties – and in the case of officers, would they accept their servants as well? Would the new electricity that everyone was talking about be able to provide lights by which stretcher bearers could search for the wounded? The peace lobby, spurred on by Bertha von Suttner and Frédéric Passy, warned of the coming years of 'aviatic warfare', though General Baden-Powell, hero of Mafeking in the Boer War, chose to regard them in a positive light. 'When all the powers have airships,' he remarked, 'I give you my word that no war will be possible.' A cartoonist in the Berlin *Lustige Blätter* showed smiling plenipotentiaries at a peace conference, some of whom were stuffed pigeons; underneath the table lay a pile of bombs, cannons and revolvers. For most people, the spectre of war from the skies was haunting; a few of them, at least, would live to see their worst fears realized.

While talk continued in the capitals of Europe and amongst the military about ways in which the Geneva Convention should be revised and whether it should be extended to cover war at sea, Tsar Nicholas II had called his new conference on the laws of war. It opened in The Hague in May 1899, the Emperor declaring that he wished to put an end 'to this incessant production of armaments' and seek ways to 'prevent the calamities that threaten the entire world'. Attention now shifted away from Geneva and towards what would become a series of meetings at The Hague. For the peace-seeking Russian emperor this first Hague gathering proved something of a disappointment. Few of the ninety-four diplomats, representing twenty-six states, seemed to share his views on disarmament. Remarkably quickly, with very little opposition, they agreed that it would be futile to attempt to restrict the size of armies and absurd to ban submarines and explosives. They did, however, as a sop to the peacemakers, accept that some kind of veto should be imposed on 'the launching of projectiles from balloons', though one speaker pointed out that since no one had yet done so, balloon or aerial warfare was unlikely to pose much threat. There was also talk of banning gas shells, though again there was speculation about whether they really could be manufactured. Seventeen articles drafted at The Hague were devoted to prisoners-of-war. There was a nasty moment when the idea of scrapping the Geneva Convention and incorporating its provisions within The Hague's laws of war was raised but Edouard Odier, a round-faced, anxious-looking lawyer, now secretary of the International Committee, fought off the threat by agreeing to a proper revision; and then went on to fight off a second threat to replace the red cross as emblem with a crescent, a sun or a red flame. *The Hague Convention Respecting the Laws and Customs of War on Land*, as the final declaration was called, concluded with an obligation on all 'belligerents with regard to the sick and wounded' to be guided and governed, as before, by the Geneva Convention. During the conference the leading powers had also agreed to limit their freedom to go to war whenever they chose. If their concessions seem modest, they had at least appeared to accept the principle that belligerents might not inflict on their enemy 'harm disproportionate to the issue at stake'. 'Unnecessary suffering' was proscribed, as was the use of poison gas. Undefended towns were not to be bombed. The idea of 'fairness' in fighting dominated many of the discussions and resolutions were taken on everything from spies to declarations of war, flags of truce and conditions of capitulation.

During the promised conference to revise the Geneva Convention, a number of articles were drafted in a clearer form, though a long-held wish by the International Committee that states should agree to comply with the Convention whether or not the enemy was party to it was abandoned. Photographs of the occasion show 100 delegates in top hats, plumes, helmets, swords and tunics, moustaches and whiskers. There is one black face.

While the diplomats were debating the laws of war and the International Committee was tinkering with the Convention, the Red Cross societies spent the early years of the twentieth century exploring ways of expanding. Everywhere from Denmark to Venezuela, Hungary to Portugal, imposing buildings went up to house Red Cross society headquarters, nursing schools were opened, first aid classes started and new uniforms designed. In Spain, the paper *El Censor* poured scorn on uniforms they described as dull and austere. Wherever Red Cross nurses were sent, they tended to be chaperoned by the older ladies of the societies, who made sure that they were settled in the 'most satisfactory material and moral conditions'.

For the most part, the aristocracy remained in charge. No example gives a better flavour of a Red Cross fundraising event than one that took place on a Sunday in summer at the turn of the twentieth century at L'Isle-Adam near Paris. The hostess, Madame Desfosses, was a keen member of the French Red Cross. All day long, visitors arriving by train wandered through gardens decorated with garlands and flags, stopping to admire *tableaux vivants* and displays of gymnastics, or to take tickets for lotteries with chickens and ducks as prizes. There was a fishing competition on the lake, a parade of carriages drawn by mules dressed in flowers and a talking dog. When it got dark, the gardens were lit by illuminations designed by the fashionable electrician of the day, Henri Beau; after a ball came fireworks. Invited guests dined in the château.

In Britain, after the Boer war and the troubled years of reorganization, Queen Alexandra had agreed to become president and King Edward VII patron of a new British Red Cross Society, incorporating existing aid associations. However, fears were expressed at the cliquishness of the society, not just by John Furley, who refused to join the committee, but by Colonel Favre of the International Committee who travelled from Geneva to pay it a visit. Favre reported that the English were almost totally ignorant about the International Committee's work on the conduct of war over the last half-century and had a somewhat lofty attitude towards the strides made by other societies, dismissing them as 'insignificant'. There was something both patrician and hearty about the British Red Cross. During one summer, fifty young women, wearing short skirts and berets, and carrying knapsacks, assembled in Studland Bay in Dorset to spend eight days riding, cooking and learning 'practical skills', so as to be ready to form a 'Women's Corps' which in future conflicts would remain behind with the wounded too ill to be ferried back from the front.

Most of the founders of the Red Cross lived to a great age, and most continued to work until the very end of their lives. Louis Appia and Captain van de Velde, his fellow delegate during the war of Schleswig-

Holstein both died in 1898. Appia, a little stooped and troubled by rheumatism, spent his last days in his rather dark flat in Geneva, showing visitors the armband he had worn in Schleswig, the first red cross band ever worn. Lord Wantage, the former Colonel Loyd-Lindsay of the British Red Cross, died in June 1901. The summer of 1910 saw the deaths, within eight days of each other, of Gustave Moynier, who had reached the age of eighty-four as upright as ever, with his beaked nose and thin lips above a great white beard, and Florence Nightingale, who had started out so vehemently opposed to Dunant's dream. Moynier's obituary in the *Bulletin* was ringed in black and sang his praises as the true spirit behind the Red Cross. The minutes of the International Committee's meeting of 21 August report that: 'all the International Committee is today, and all that it has ever been, is due to him'. Eulogies and condolences poured in. Chile proclaimed an eight-day period of mourning.

In the wider world, Moynier's reputation has always been a little clouded by his animosity towards Dunant. But he was a remarkable if humourless and anxious man, greatly respected for his contributions to international law and for the tenacity with which he kept working on apparently intractable problems until some tolerable solution could be found for them. His interests extended far beyond the Red Cross: he had always been interested in Africa and the need for the 'white race' to make amends for its deplorable record among the blacks.

Though he remained shy until the end of his life, often appearing far stiffer than he really was, those close to him came near to hero-worshipping the moral certainty and incorruptibility which had, because of him, dominated the spirit of the Red Cross movement for almost half a century. Dunant had the dream, but without Moynier's scholarly and pedantic obsessiveness it would very probably never have gone further. Yet he was never lovable and could be very pompous. Towards the end of his life, he decided to create a shrine to his own past glories, giving a room of his house over to medals, portraits, diplomas, decorations – he had awards of one kind or another from twenty-four different countries – and copies of his many written works. He compiled a catalogue of them and had it printed.

Dunant outlived Moynier by nine weeks. Europe's newspapers were full of eulogies, yet his obituary in the *Bulletin* was brief and its tone chilly. Readers were reminded that it was Moynier who had been 'the true founder . . . the man who should be known as the architect of the Red Cross.' At the meeting of the International Committee held on 10 December, Ador observed that Dunant's death had provoked a public outburst of emotion out of all proportion to the role he had played.

The final years of Dunant's life had not gone badly. Princesses and duchesses had made the trek up the mountain to Heiden; one of his last callers was the crown princess of Bavaria who, as he wrote to a friend, 'stayed for half an hour at least, arranging the pillow of my arm-chair as I was very ill'. Dunant, too, could be vain and snobbish. His last act, according to the nurses who watched over him, was to send a book on the origins of the Red Cross, written by his friend Rudolf Müller, to the queen of Italy, with an admiring dedication. On Sunday, 30 October 1910, at ten o'clock in the evening, after exclaiming 'How dark it is!' Dunant died. He was eighty-two. He had left instructions that he was to be cremated in Zurich 'with no ceremony whatsoever'. After legacies to various recent friends, his books and papers going to his nephew Maurice, the rest of his money was divided between charities in Norway and Switzerland. In his will, Dunant referred to himself as 'the founder of the universal movement of the Red Cross'. Ungenerous even after his death, the International Committee, learning that the Dunant family planned to send a portrait of him to a forthcoming conference, said that unless it was withdrawn they would send portraits of Appia and Moynier as well.

Moynier and Dunant died at the right moment, looking out at a world apparently at peace, in which their ideas seemed to have played a part. The years of stability, with the great powers locked into some kind of political balance, were rapidly coming to an end. In 1911 came popular uprisings in Mexico and China, then the war between Turkey and Italy; that in turn led to two Balkan wars, generally regarded as heralding the outbreak of the First World War.

From Geneva, as fighting began in Tripoli, Gustave Ador, to whom Moynier had turned over the 'moral responsibility of the Red Cross movement', made the by now standard offers of help to the countries at war. On the Tripoli front, in the autumn of 1911, Italian pilots threw five-kilogram bombs from their cockpits on to the soldiers below. War, it suddenly seemed horribly clear, was no longer to be a clash of armies, but one of weapons, launched from considerable distances and with no way of distinguishing between combatants and civilians, or between military targets and protected buildings. The words spoken at The Hague might never have been uttered. A spirit of adventure still clung to the various Red Cross societies — the German Red Cross carried 48,000 kilograms of equipment and stores across the desert on 360 camels in the desert surrounding Tripoli — but it was beginning to have a rather old-fashioned ring to it.

In May 1912, in Washington, America played host to the ninth International Conference of Red Cross Societies. It lasted eleven days, the longest ever held. In the new Pan-American building lent by the city for the occasion, delegates from the Bavarian Red Cross described their new sanitary trains; the Prussians talked about their battle against contagious illnesses; the French spoke of ambulance dogs, the Mexicans about yellow fever. Representatives from China and Siam put in their first appearance. At the vast exhibition which accompanied the conference were seen stretchers of every design, wagons, glass syringes, campaign operating tables; the Japanese sent twenty-six exhibits, one of them a stretcher made of bamboo. Prizes went to a portable wash stand, to be carried on the back of a mule, and to a mobile radiology laboratory. There were discussions about how to spend the fund set up in memory of the Empress Augusta of Germany and the announcement, by the Japanese delegate, that the Empress Shoken proposed to endow a second fund. Her early opposition to the Red Cross forgotten, it was agreed to create a Florence Nightingale medal. On the last evening, President and Mrs Taft invited 3,000 people to dine at the White House.

The Washington conference broke up to cheers for the women who had done so much to promote the Red Cross, — the *élément féminin* as the *Bulletin* put it — and plans to meet again in five years' time. Ador and his colleagues set off back to Switzerland, to organize celebrations for the fiftieth anniversary of the Red Cross movement due to take place in 1914. But on 28 June 1914 Archduke Franz Ferdinand, heir to the throne of Austria-Hungary, and his wife, the Duchess of Hohenberg, were assassinated at Sarajevo. A month later, just a few weeks before the Red Cross turned fifty on 22 August, Austria-Hungary declared war on Serbia.

SEVEN

The Little Cushion of Europe

By the outbreak of the First World War, the International Committee, though extremely small – nine unpaid members, a minute secretariat, a few professional men willing to serve as delegates – was respected and listened to by governments and acknowledged by the military as a moral force in all matters concerning war. How far its humanitarian zeal would actually prove a determining factor in the conduct of a major war, however, had still to be seen: the laws and codes laid down in Geneva and The Hague remained at best fragile agreements. Wounded and sick soldiers, hospital ships, the shipwrecked, wounded and sick in war at sea, and prisoners-of-war were all guaranteed some kind of protection. There were rules to govern the 'internment of belligerent troops in neutral territory'. There were also codes of conduct laid down for the protection of civilians, but these were vague and for the most part indirect, such as specifying limitations on the bombardment of undefended towns and houses. Much of what would come had not been, and could never have been, foreseen by those who had drafted the laws. Forty-two nations had signed and ratified the Geneva Convention, and thirty-eight national Red Cross societies had been formed, some in countries as remote from Switzerland as China and Brazil. True, there had been challenges to the authority of the International Committee over the years; but the critics had now fallen silent. It was as if the world, drifting towards a war that already promised far to exceed in scope, military power and casualties anything ever seen or contemplated before, was relieved that some international influence, above the interests of nation states, existed, however imprecise its powers.

Yet the International Committee itself remained a curious animal. A code of warfare had been invented, drafted, nursed and coaxed into being through a series of conferences, and this had happened not just

in a very small and politically insignificant country, but by the efforts
of fewer than a dozen men, only one or two of whom had ever travelled
far outside Switzerland. In 1914 the International Committee was still
entirely Swiss – the 'International' in its name serving, then as now, to
confuse – and still a private organization, of little importance either to
Geneva or Switzerland. In the forty years of its existence there had been
just two presidents; for fourteen of them – 1899 to 1913 – no new
members had been appointed. Members continued to be selected from
a tight-knit, interrelated group of people, prosperous Genevans from
the city's oldest families. There were no women and no Catholics among
them.

Gustave Ador, who had taken on the mantle of guardian of the Red
Cross movement from his uncle, Gustave Moynier, only four years
earlier, was sixty-nine; he had been with the Committee for forty-four
years, ever since he had been asked to negotiate with the Swiss government for the loan of the Château de Chillon on Lake Geneva for
wounded French soldiers during the Franco-Prussian war. Ador, who
up until his appointment as president had combined service with the
International Committee with a busy political and financial career, would
later be called the 'ideal president' by his own nephew, Paul des Gouttes,
himself a secretary to the Committee. Photographs show a genial, even
jaunty figure, elegant in brightly coloured waistcoats, wearing a rose in
his buttonhole, his neat beard more pointed than those of many of his
contemporaries. He was lighter, more humorous than Moynier, and
much loved by his colleagues. His voice was rich and pleasing, and he
relished parliamentary debate. A lawyer by training, Ador was said to
take pains to curb a tendency he recognized in himself to impose his
own views on those around him, though he was always a ferocious critic
of Karl Marx, whose theories he rejected as destructive. All his life, he
would worry about how to enforce the Geneva Convention, how to
reconcile the essentially volunteer spirit of the movement with a sense
that its rules were to be obeyed. During the 1912 conference in Washington, he alone had been able to soothe the Russian and American delegates, threatening to walk out over a disagreement about civil war:
admirers would tell the story of how, when things grew tense, a search
party had been sent to collect him from the cemetery at Arlington,
where he had gone in search of a few hours' reflection. Some of the

International Committee's finest successes of the First World War would owe as much to Ador's tenacity as to his shrewdness at finding compromises during particularly sour disputes.

One of Ador's vice-presidents, on the outbreak of war, was an old friend called Edouard Naville, a distinguished Egyptologist in his late sixties; another was Frédéric Ferrière, the thin family doctor with the face of an aesthete and intense pale blue eyes, who would later be referred to by members of the Committee as the 'apostle' of the movement, and a 'perfect knight'. Ferrière was the son of a prison chaplain and grandson to Mme de Staël's tutor, as well as being related to Dr Appia, the movement's founding doctor. Like Ador, he had served the International Committee in various capacities for over forty years, having accompanied Appia to the Franco-Prussian front in 1870. He was a specialist in military medicine and engrossed by questions of public health. With these three decidedly elderly men were members of the Odier, d'Espine and Favre families, all Genevans, who look out, solid, bearded and unsmiling, from the portraits of the day. It would fall to these men to shepherd the Red Cross movement through a war that would draw in twenty-eight countries, see an average of 20,000 people die every day for the fifty-one months of conflict, and challenge fundamentally, repeatedly and with considerable brutality the very basis of the Geneva Convention, the Committee and the Red Cross movement.

Militarily and scientifically, it was to be a war of surprises, breakthroughs and logistical challenges which no one, and certainly not the Red Cross, could have envisaged. The armies lining up in 1914 were a mixture of ancient and modern. The actual killing power of the new Lee Enfields, Mausers, Spandaus and Hotchkisses was of a different dimension from that inflicted by soldiers when battles were decided by the numerical strengths and tactical abilities of each side. Field howitzers and heavy guns fired high explosive rounds fitted with Lyddite and a fuse which burned when they hit the ground. As the war became static, high explosives would prove murderous weapons.

Railways now carried soldiers rapidly to battle: the journey from Rome to Cologne, which took a Roman legionary sixty-seven days' marching, took less than 24 hours in 1914 in a train. But not everything had progressed. Once at the front, the men would find themselves barely more mobile than they would have been in the Middle Ages, and when generals wished to command battles in person they had little choice but to go forward themselves. Some seventy British generals would be killed or die of their wounds on the western front alone.

While it was known by 1914 that certain bacteria were to be found in the soil which, when introduced into the body, gave rise to diseases, no one had foreseen the extent to which those bacteria would prove deadly, spreading tetanus, typhoid and gangrene at a ferocious rate as bullets entered soldiers' bodies carrying shreds of uniform impregnated with soil. And no one, yet, had seen either the effects of continuous high explosive shelling on men kept too long in the trenches, or the fear and terrible injuries caused by gas.

On 28 July 1914, Austria-Hungary declared war on Serbia; orders went out throughout Russia for general mobilization in support of its threatened ally. On 1 August, violating the neutrality of Belgium, the German army entered France. In the days and weeks that followed, one country after another joined the war. On one side stood the Central Powers, Austria-Hungary, Imperial Germany and Ottoman Turkey; on the other, tsarist Russia, Great Britain, France, after 1915 Italy and later Japan and the United States. On 15 August, Gustave Ador sent out his 158th circular to the national Red Cross societies. It was short and stark. 'From today,' he said, 'the Red Cross is called to an intense labour of a kind never seen before . . . The needs will be immense, but the International Committee is firmly convinced that the charitable zeal of all our societies will rise to the necessary devotion.'

Ador was right. The Finnish Red Cross immediately began to put together two hospital units to be sent wherever they were most needed; the Portuguese offered beds for the wounded. The Japanese recruited doctors and nurses, clothed them in their distinctive chef's hats and sent them to Britain where they were installed in the Russell Hotel in London, taken to see Queen Alexandra and received a special message of welcome from Lord Kitchener, the secretary for war. From there they went on to Paris, where they ran a hospital in the Hotel Astoria, dressed their patients in white kimonos and soon became a tourist attraction for foreign visitors.

The outbreak of war found Mabel Boardman of the American Red

Cross on holiday with President and Mrs Taft in Canada. She hurried back to Washington and chartered what the newspapers called the 'Mercy Ship' to transport 170 doctors and nurses as well as hospital supplies to Europe. Ernest Bicknell who went with them, spent the early months of the war travelling around Europe, mopping up some of the 150,000 confused American tourists stranded by the fighting, terrified of being taken for spies and increasingly destitute when the banks stopped cashing their letters of credit. He carried $1.5m in gold coin with him. The departure of the mercy ship from New York stirred Mabel Boardman to a burst of grandiloquence. 'As the white ship passed the great statue in the harbour,' she declared, 'Liberty for the moment seemed to grasp in her uplifted hand the flag of the Red Cross flying from the foremast, and to hold it forth as a token of America's sympathy for suffering Europe.'

Everywhere from Berlin to Madrid, Tokyo to Washington, aristocratic ladies met to offer help and to form committees; empresses, queens and duchesses lent their names and their drawing rooms to their national Red Cross societies. In Russia, society ladies calling themselves 'Sister', flocked to join instant nursing courses, though as their duties as assistants to real nurses became both arduous and disgusting, a number fled. Soon, newspapers were full of photographs of Madame Poincaré, wife of the French president, sewing bandages in a stupendous hat crowned with a nest of feathers; of the Dowager Queen Margarita of Italy, a rather small woman swathed in a shawl; of the Empress of Germany on a platform, leaning down obligingly to shake the hands of curtseying nurses on their way to the front. Queen Eleonora of Bulgaria, serving tea to an early casualty on a stretcher, looked a little like Maid Marion in an orchard. She was a true Red Cross spirit, having led a convoy to Manchuria during the Russo-Japanese war and spent an entire winter on a train between Vladivostok, Harbin and Irkutsk. The intrepid Queen Marie of Romania, granddaughter of Queen Victoria, who never ceased travelling among the soldiers, was also a keen supporter, staring out quizzically from photographs in her nun-like Red Cross uniform and cowl and white shoes. 'Many a dying soldier whispered to me with his last breath that it was for me that he was fighting,' Queen Marie would write, 'for was I not his home, his mother, his belief and his hope?' The activities of the thousands of ordinary women — nurses,

Some of the experiments in the design of stretchers undertaken by various Red Cross societies and published in the pages of *Bulletin*

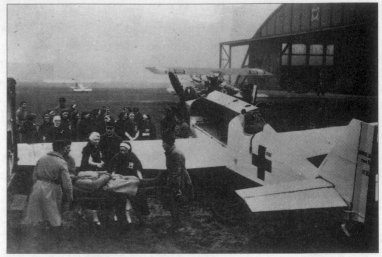

A French air-ambulance at Bourget, *c.* 1940

Transporting the wounded by mule, presented at the international conference on health in London in 1884

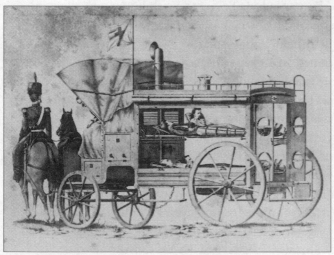

A horse-drawn ambulance from the end of the nineteenth century

Stretcher-bearing by bicycle as demonstrated by the German army, 1899

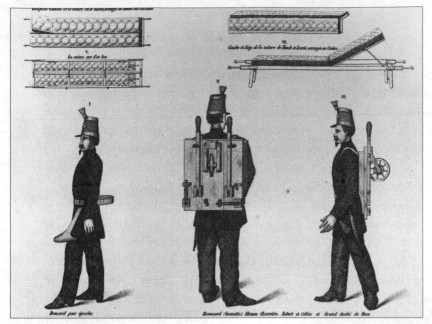

A folding stretcher design from 1867

A German motor
ambulance *c.* 1918

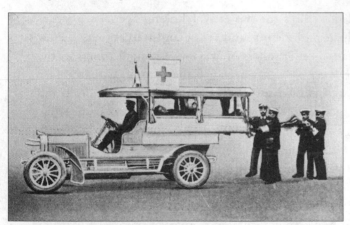

The interior design of an
ambulance train used to
transport wounded German
soldiers during the Franco-
Prussian war, 1870–71

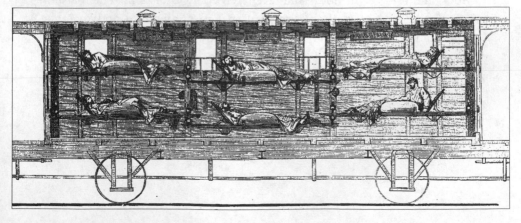

drivers, packers, despatchers — were seldom recorded, at least in those early days of war.

There is a sense of calm and order about the International Committee in the first days of the war, a feeling that a machine that has been serviced regularly and is in excellent working order is about to be tested to the full, and the first tests have shown how well it could perform. Depots were full of supplies; national Red Cross societies, some well trained by recent conflicts, were eager to show off their skills, and laws had been much rehearsed.

The Hague Convention of 1907 had laid down that, in time of war, information bureaux should be set up to care for prisoners-of-war. The battle of the Marne, in the second week of September, was fought along a front of 125 miles and checked the German advance on Paris, but several hundred thousand French, as well as many thousands of Germans, British and Belgians, were taken prisoner. All over Europe, families asked what had happened to their men: were they now dead? wounded? made prisoner?

Ador now decided to alter the pattern of linking agencies, such as the ones set up in Basle and Vienna, and create an International Agency for Aid and Information on Prisoners of War in two small rooms in the archives at number 3 rue de l'Athénée in Geneva itself, with the idea that it would act as go-between and forward lists of wounded, dead, and prisoners from either side to the proper authorities. It was manned by a rota of the nine current members of the International Committee, two boy scouts and a student. On 4 September it received its first list, with the names of twenty-nine wounded French prisoners. On the 26th, Ador, having put in his three statutory weeks' Swiss military service, left for Bordeaux, now the seat of the French government, a journey that took him forty-eight hours and seventeen changes of train. The marquis de Vogue, president of the French Red Cross, met him and together they called on the French minister for war, Millerand, who agreed to provide the International Committee with lists of German prisoners. While in Bordeaux, Ador dined with a number of the other French ministers, Delcassé, Viviani and Ribot, from whom he obtained agreements that they would promote the setting up of relief committees to send parcels to their soldiers in enemy hands. After this, he left for Berlin.

Returning to Geneva, Ador found that enormous numbers of students, married women, teachers, bankers, men of letters and travellers stranded by the fighting had descended on the Agency offering to help in any way they could. First a couple were taken on, the word being put about that the pressure could well become such that as many as sixteen might eventually be needed. Within weeks, several dozen were hard at work, then several hundred. By the end of September, they had burst out of the rue de l'Athénée and into the Palais Eynard, lent by the City of Geneva. However hard they worked still the letters of enquiry kept on growing – 3,000 a day by the end of the second month of the war – and they burst out again, this time to fly the Red Cross flag above the Musée Rath, the former Palais des Beaux Arts, where, looking out on to the statue of General Dufour, mounted on his stone horse in front of the building, they sat down to transcribe names on to cards.

The process was slow, nit-picking but efficient. Meticulous attention had to be paid to spellings – Schmidt, Shmitch and Schmit – and to details of birth, first name and regiment; a fine researcher, it was soon being said, was one who was able to work with the precision of a watchmaker. Every card was filed in a single index system. When the card with the request for information and the card with news of the man being sought met, there was said to be 'concordance'. News could then be sent off to his family of his condition and his whereabouts. As the months passed and the numbers of cards grew – there were to be seven million names by the end of the war – so the workers improvised. For the men whose names appeared on no lists, a tracing procedure was devised which included contacting every regimental comrade who might have news of the missing man. Special indexes were started for regiments, for the missing at sea, for airmen, for war graves. For French prisoners-of-war alone, the reports of missing men would fill 228 volumes, each of 400 pages, by the end of the war.

Among the volunteers who appeared at the doors of the Musée Rath were people who could speak Magyar, Slovene, Polish and Romanian. An *Entente* department was set up to deal with nationals of the countries at war, or those which had broken off relations with the Central Powers, and soon it became clear that a second agency would be needed to handle the north-eastern armies. The Danish Red Cross offered to act as the central clearing house for Russian prisoners in Germany and Germans in Russia. A department for parcels was started, to open, check and repack the many packages sent by anxious families, some addressed simply 'Genève, pour trouver mon fils', and a financial office, to handle gifts of money. One Saturday afternoon, Ador addressed his troops over tea. 'We have,' he declared, looking out across his volunteers, now 1,200 strong, 'as long as the war continues a great and noble mission to accomplish.' The troops worked in shifts and around the clock, replacing each other at the long tables, grappling in silence with the many variations in spelling and illegible handwriting; a photograph taken on Christmas Eve 1914 and sent off to the main European newspapers, showed banks of soberly dressed women in neat hats, standing on the steps of the Musée Rath in orderly lines. The agency was already, after just a few months of war, far more than an information office; almost instinctively, and certainly without planning, it had turned into an immense enterprise dealing in tracing, correspondence, translation, banking and research, like a vast radio network with outlying relay stations, watching over the different theatres of war. By 1918, 120,000 people would have come in person to the Musée Rath to ask for help in tracing lost relations.

From the basement of the museum, cliffs of wooden filing boxes rose up through the various floors. Occasionally, distinguished visitors like H. G. Wells came to view and admire the long rows of workers. Some, like the writer Romain Rolland, a mild figure who had published a stern article calling for an 'indictment against the criminal authors of this war', came and stayed, spending nine months silently and unobtrusively among the boxes, looking neat and frail in his starched high collar and donating 50,000 francs to the agency. Another who came, and in this case stayed for almost fifty years occupying many jobs and rising to a position of considerable influence, was the Swiss poet Jacques Chenevière, who appeared in Ador's office on the morning of 12 September and was put to work opening the post. 'Outside,' wrote Stefan Zweig after a visit to the Musée Rath, 'from one end to the other of our world, the crucified heart of Europe bleeds from innumerable wounds. But here, its heart still beats . . . For here . . . resounds another eternal feeling — human pity.'

One category of war victims not properly considered by those who shaped the Geneva Convention was civilians. The rapid spread of the war, the invasion and occupation of Belgium, Luxemburg and northern France, and the new weapons that made it possible to fire shells from great distances, were soon causing extreme civilian hardship. The anguish and chaos faced by refugees, by foreigners caught abroad by the outbreak of war, by men deported to forced labour, and by the growing numbers of those driven from their homes by fighting, brought new letters and new calls for help. There was some understandable hesitation about including them under Geneva's umbrella. But Dr Ferrière, contemplating the stories of the women and children fleeing the war zones, the lists of men of military age interned in ever greater number on all sides as enemy aliens, persuaded his colleagues to allow him to set up a civilian wing. Its demands and difficulties were immense. Ferrière, whose brisk, small steps could be heard pattering along the corridors of the Musée Rath at all hours of the day and night, was indefatigable. By the end of December, 60,000 civilian cards had been filed, though very few had yet achieved 'concordance'. Still, it was enough to give him an idea of the numbers of internees – 20,000 Germans and Austrians in Britain, 6,000 French and 2,000 Belgians in Germany, 2,000 Germans in France, 800 French, British and Belgians in Austria. As the conditions of civilians kept on worsening, so the *Bulletin* published a sad lament for those who were being reduced to '*le bétail humain*'. In his concern for civilians, Ferrière was prescient, voicing arguments that would continue to haunt the International Committee after over 20 million civilians had died in the Second World War. 'We find ourselves obliged to admit,' he wrote in the 1930s, while working on a draft convention for civilians, 'that modern warfare is no longer war between armies but a struggle between nations . . . War conducted in this way is inhuman, immoral, contrary to the law of nations and revolting to every decent human conscience.'

The question of repatriating these forlorn people, particularly children and the elderly, occupied many hours of the International Committee's time, as did the whole subject of repatriation for medical personnel, one of the cornerstones of the Geneva Convention, which had clearly laid down that once they were 'no longer indispensable', doctors and nurses were to be sent home. By the end of 1914, several hundred doctors and many thousands of Red Cross workers and medical orderlies were being held in prisoner-of-war camps, their captors arguing that they would be needed should epidemics break out. The International Committee reacted strongly, but it was not until the summer of 1916 that convoys of repatriated French and German medical people began to cross Switzerland on their way home. A number of bilateral agreements were eventually signed, in response to the new and unforeseen warfare with its unprecedented numbers of soldiers, the shortage of doctors, and the difficulty in coping with so many languages and so many races. Repatriation generally became part of Geneva's most important contribution to the war, as deals were brokered for the return of men too wounded to fight again, with internment in Switzerland offered for officers who might otherwise release men from their desks to join the war. To the numbers of doctors, the sick and the wounded and those suffering from 'captivity neurosis' who were repatriated would finally be added the fathers of very large families and men who had spent intolerably long periods of time in captivity. 'The war has piled up so many ruins, so many bereavements,' the *Bulletin* announced, 'and has caused so much blood to flow, that we must listen to the call of the heart, the voice of pity, and give back to their own countries all those who can still be saved.'

By the end of the first year of hostilities, there were eleven countries at war, the International Committee had sent out 234,734 letters to families, and Switzerland was being called by the *Bulletin* the *coussinet*, the little cushion, of Europe.

What no one had expected in the summer of 1914 was the sheer number of prisoners who would fall into enemy hands and need to be transported immense distances back to camps, then guarded, nursed, fed and kept warm. What was more, no country entering the war had any experience of looking after prisoners in the numbers and for the length of time that now faced them. Britain, which had taken 32,000 prisoners during the Boer war, was perhaps the only nation with a little recent understanding of what it would imply; and even that experience lay over a decade in the past.

With every battle the numbers of prisoners multiplied. By the end of 1914, the Germans were holding 8,120 Allied officers and 577,475 men — French, Russian, Belgian and British. By the summer of 1915, the number had risen to over two million, most of them Russian. By the end of

1915, Britain had 33,000 men in German hands, many captured during the retreat from Mons, and it was itself holding 13,500 prisoners. By Christmas Day 1915, there were no fewer than two and a half million men in captivity.

The International Committee had never been directly designated to act as mediator between countries at war in order to improve conditions for prisoners. But as the months passed it drifted into this new job, basing its activities on the Hague regulations of 1907, which had specified that accredited agents of the relief societies should visit places of internment to distribute supplies, and on the unanimous resolution of the Washington conference in 1912 that they should do so. In theory, the Hague regulations were not applicable, since two of the parties at war, Serbia and Montenegro, had not ratified them, and it needed both sides to bring them into force; but most governments gratifyingly quickly professed themselves prepared to regard the rules as customary law. How prisoners were in fact to be treated – fed, guarded, made to work and punished – had, as we have seen, by 1914 been enshrined in a number of agreements, and there was also an understanding that all conduct towards them would be 'humane'. Yet the treatment which would now befall the many men vanishing into detention throughout Europe would depend to a great extent on luck – the character of the camp commandant, the fortunes of war, the current feelings of the captors for their captives. The Germans, it was later said, had liked their Australian prisoners and treated them well but taken strongly against the Canadians, whom they treated harshly.

To visit detainees in order to deliver parcels to them, the International Committee needed to get into the camps, and for this they needed delegates. In Geneva, Ador set about recruiting volunteers, looking for men – Swiss as guarantee of their neutrality – who were robust, conscientious, intrepid, hard-working and who spoke as many languages as possible. Though members of the International Committee undertook a number of the missions themselves, a new kind of delegate was born with the First World War, and it was to some measure due to Ador's instinctive eye for suitable recruits, and to his willingness to leave a great deal of the initiative to the men he appointed, that the visits to the camps were so efficiently carried out. But it was more than just efficiency. In the face of the obfuscation and intransigence of some of the camp commandants on all sides, and the unscrupulousness of some of the military commanders, delegates had to be not just wily but authoritative. Courage, as much as perseverance and a diplomatic touch, was essential. The actual number of these men – forty-one at the height of the war – was ridiculously small compared to the distances they had to cover and the numbers of establishments that had to be visited, often several times, and the journeys they took became feats of organization and resilience. There is something very impressive about the way these former soldiers, lawyers, bankers and university teachers laboured on, from country to country, camp to camp, measuring rooms, inspecting lavatories, food, the delivery of mail, working conditions and sports facilities and investigating every complaint, however apparently trivial. Though their reports, published regularly in the *Bulletin*, reveal little about their characters and inner thoughts, an occasional aside manages to suggest humour, disgust, and even sometimes a greater sympathy for the captors than the captives. They were not complainers and did not greatly take to prisoners whose complaints they judged frivolous.

By the end of 1914, arrangements for camp visits for International Committee delegates – they were not the only visitors to camps, the Protecting Powers, neutral states appointed to protect the interests of 'enemy nationals' in the countries at war having their own – were in place, though every country they entered insisted on full reciprocity before committing itself. To ensure compliance with the Geneva Convention, Ador wrote to the central committees of the national Red Cross societies to put pressure on their governments for an agreement to provide identical treatment for all prisoners-of-war, wherever in the world they were held. Far more detailed than the broad outlines sketched in earlier documents, these went into precise numbers of blankets supplied, books and letters allowed, the frequency of religious services, the amount of soap and hot water per prisoner, details that became all the more important as months of captivity stretched into years and matters like food and baths began to assume enormous proportions in men's minds. From the documents drawn up in various countries, it is possible to see how the Germans tended to concentrate on preferential treatment for captured officers, while the Italians dwelt on food, the need to provide wine, beer and coffee. As time went on, the International Committee was able to broker bilateral agreements, like allowing captured officers to stroll about outside camps without guards. 'The word of an officer,' noted the *Bulletin* sanctimoniously, 'should be a better guarantee than the eye of a guard.'

It was not long before rumours of brutality towards prisoners started reaching Geneva, making the visits to camps all the more crucial. Though the foreign dignitaries at the Washington conference had all accepted the principle that prisoners-of-war were not so much 'criminal' as 'unlucky', it soon became clear that not all the parties at war agreed. The Germans, particularly in the early months of the war, seemed to treat their prisoners with disregard and neglect bordering on viciousness. A British ship's steward from Grimsby, taken prisoner in the North Sea and accused of being one of a mine-laying squad, reported being held in an open field for fourteen autumn days; on twelve of them it rained hard; on three he was given no food. A diary found on a German officer of the VIIth German corps contained passages that seemed to confirm the worst fears of German brutality. 'The sight of the . . . fury – not to say bestiality – of our men in beating to death the wounded English,' he had written on 19 December 1914, 'affected me so much that for the rest of the day I was fit for nothing.' Other British and French officers who managed to escape came home with tales of forced marches with untreated wounds, of being transported thousands of kilometres in cattle trucks full of manure, of being slapped and abused by guards. When their trains had stopped in German stations, women and children had turned out to spit and swear at them. One disquieting account described how German Red Cross nurses had declared themselves willing to provide refreshments for the German soldiers guarding the trains only on condition that none of it was passed on to the British prisoners.

Particularly gruesome reports came from one hospital in Germany, where a Canadian private called McPhail, blinded in one eye, was apparently put on to an operating table and held down by a nurse and three assistants. 'The sister asked a doctor a question,' McPhail told the *Daily Mail*, 'and he answered in English for me to hear: "No, I will not give an anaesthetic. Englishmen do not need any chloroform." He turned up my eyelid in the roughest fashion and cut my eye out. He used a pair of scissors, they told me afterwards, and cut too far down, destroying the nerve of the other eye.' McPhail never regained his sight.

Another report that reached the International Committee concerned a camp at Wittenberg. In the winter of 1914, some 17,000 prisoners were gathered in a ten-and-a-half-acre camp on a flat, sandy plain – giving them about three square yards each. The weather was bitter. There were not enough rooms, beds, clothes or blankets for all the men; some had no shoes or socks. The food was terrible. Vicious dogs were kept to terrorize the prisoners, who were often flogged by their guards for minor infractions.

Most of the prisoners were Russians and they arrived filthy and covered in lice, bringing typhus with them. Sleeping two and even three to every mattress, the infection soon spread to their comrades. When it threatened to engulf the entire camp, the German staff, including all doctors, left, drawing a tight cordon around the outside perimeter. Food and supplies were pushed over the wire.

Almost two months later, in February 1915, six British doctors, in contravention of the Geneva Convention, were sent as prisoners to Wittenberg. They wandered around the camp, through silent, darkened barracks, among dirty, apathetic, dying men in a state of semi-starvation. Some had toes and even entire feet eaten by gangrene. Major Priestly, one of the doctors, later reported that he had seen 'delirious men waving arms brown to the elbow with faecal matter. The patients were alive with vermin.' In the half-light he attempted to brush what he took to be an accumulation of dirt from the folds of a patient's clothes, and he discovered it to be a moving mass of lice.

Stories of this kind, reaching Allied headquarters, were rapidly conveyed to Geneva as the first Red Cross delegates set off on their early missions of inspection. Their findings were, for the most part, reassuring. Episodes of brutality were, given the logistical problems, relatively rare and, as the war entered its second year, dropping. M. A. Eugster, in ordinary life a member of the Swiss parliament, paid two visits to Germany, the second of them in February 1915, when he visited nineteen camps in three weeks. He was accompanied by two Spanish grandees, two members of the German Red Cross and a Baron Captain von Bonigk, who was representing the Prussian ministry of war. Eugster returned to report excellent sanitary conditions but an acute shortage of bread, not so surprising perhaps when prisoners alone were consuming 240,000 kilos of bread every day during a cereal blockade. Everywhere he went he met French prisoners who told him that the soup was too thin, but that they wouldn't mind so much if they could just have more bread. He professed himself satisfied that the floggings which had so upset him on his first visit had now been stopped. At times during his report a definite sense of irritation with the prisoners comes through, as does hurt pride that his reports on good German conditions were not always being believed among the Allied powers. The role of the delegate, he remarked, was indeed 'so difficult and so uneasy'. At the end of his long, detailed report, Eugster permitted himself a few reflections.

> What an atrocious thing is war! My heart bleeds and from this bleeding heart there rises a tremulous question delivered to the heart of the most noble of the two noble nations: 'How much longer will this frightful war go on?'

Eugster was one of the delegates who took most pains to reassure the world that prisoners-of-war were being treated adequately. Returning in May 1915 from a third tour of Germany, he announced that he believed that the German authorities were doing all in their power to improve the 'moral and material situation' of the prisoners, 'guided by the desire to fulfil most conscientiously the duties dictated to them by the laws of humanity'. By contrast, he noted that the French authorities were doing very little to make their officer prisoners in France as comfortable as the rules stipulated, and that the quality of food in French camps left a good deal to be desired. (Prisoners did, however, have access to food parcels and were sometimes considerably better fed than the civilians of the countries in which they were being held; until 1915, the diet of prisoners in Germany included frozen Australian rabbit.)

In November 1915, Professor Dr A. d'Espine, one of the International Committee's vice-presidents, went to Italy, where there had been complaints through the Austrian Red Cross of Austro-Hungarian prisoners being held in 'insalubrious conditions' in marshy malarial areas. He travelled around the north and then went down to Sicily. He tasted water drawn from artesian wells 200 metres deep, and pronounced it delicious; he found flowing rivers where critics had imagined marshes. In an old fortress in Finalmaima he came across what he called the 'model camp': nowhere, he wrote, had he seen such fine baths, showers and latrines, and nowhere had he tasted such excellent food. So he wandered on down Italy, noting the wine served to the men twice a

week at Baronissi, taking photographs of cheerful prisoners to send back
to their families at home.

The principle of reciprocity demanded that delegates be allowed to
visit both sides at war. Edouard Naville, Ador's Egyptologist friend, paid
several visits to England to check up on the treatment of the 10,000
German soldiers taken prisoner by the British by early 1915. In a former
cadet school in Hollyport near Bray he found German officers playing
croquet and was pleasantly surprised to see that no one objected to the
way that the senior German officer, Captain Pochkammer, insisted on
placing a German flag in front of him at meals. Asking a young officer
whether he had any complaints, he was told that there was only hot
water in which to wash in the mornings. Was this so very bad? 'For us
young people,' he was told, 'that is not healthy.' Another informed him
that the food had been revolting but that it had much improved since
German prisoners had been allowed to do the cooking. At a vast camp
in Dorchester, swollen from 930 prisoners to 3,408 between his first and
second visit in January 1916, Naville found a great deal of mud. Complaints here were about the monotony of the food, but he seems to
have felt little sympathy for the complainers when he discovered that
there was beef or mutton every day when what the young Germans
wanted was pork. 'Neither the German government, nor the prisoners'
families,' Naville reported to Geneva, 'should have any worries about
these prisoners in camps in Britain.'

In France, Dr de Marval toured Brittany, the Vendée and Touraine,
visiting seventeen places of detention. In the Château de Fougères in
Brittany he found 129 German officers and twelve men living in somewhat bare rooms, with food, wine and coffee delivered by nearby hotels.
In an old cavalry barracks at Dinan, he inspected 1,990 soldiers sleeping
on straw mattresses 'with a fair number of fleas' but eating good food
and drinking only filtered water. In the Château Chadrac at Le Puy, a
charming turreted castle with a magnificent view down a long valley,
he was told that the officers had been permitted to keep their sabres.
Asking one he met for any complaints he was told '*Gar eine*', not one.
'The life led by these men,' de Marval informed Geneva, 'is absolutely
tolerable, not to say relatively agreeable.' In Tunisia he discovered some
German prisoners in the Kasbah, suffering from fleas and lice, and tried
to ensure they were given more light; he encountered others sleeping

in tents in palm groves in the desert and still more working with a French archaeologist at the site of Monastir. In Austria-Hungary, Ador, Dr Ferrière and Dr de Schulten-Schindler came across men breakfasting on coffee with milk, lunching on cabbage soup, roast beef, roast potatoes, green beans, salad, bread and black coffee, and dining on roast mutton, potatoes, salad, tea and bread.

Portugal became the twelfth country to enter the war in March 1916. As the war spread so the journeys to reach the prisoners became long treks, necessitating many months away from Geneva, involving travel arrangements that tested the hardiest of the delegates. These Swiss men, for the most part highly educated and accustomed to the comforts of city life, criss-crossed Europe, Asia and North Africa, caught ships and trains, took cars and sledges, walked and rode hundreds of thousands of kilometres. They very seldom complained.

The accounts of these delegates are leisurely and confident. War, in their reports, comes across as a gentlemanly pursuit: nowhere is there any suggestion that attempts might be made to dupe them into thinking conditions better than they were. Only later would duping play an uneasy part in International Committee affairs.

But then, in the autumn of 1915, stories began reaching the West of terrible brutality by the Russians towards their enormous and ever-growing numbers of German, Austro-Hungarian and Turkish captives in camps far into the interior of Russia. The distances to reach them were so great and the journeys so complicated that few of the delegates from America, appointed by the Germans as Protecting Power, had actually been able to see for themselves what was happening. No one has left a more vivid and bleak picture of the conditions of these men – by 1915 there were some two million of them – than a young Swedish nurse called Elsa Brandström, the daughter of the Swedish ambassador to St Petersburg, who was to spend over five years trying to improve their lives. Having spent the first year of the war taking part in the exchanges of severely wounded men between Russia and Germany, she decided to travel to Siberia to see for herself whether there was any truth in the stories brought back by the emaciated and desperate men who had managed to escape. She was appalled by what she found. After the war she wrote her memoirs, in order, she said, that people should be warned, and never again allow such things to happen.

At the very beginning of the war, Russia's many German and Austro-Hungarian prisoners were relatively well treated. But as they were marched ever deeper into the interior, so their Cossack guards grew more brutal, rations were cut and men with wounds were left untreated to die of blood poisoning. When they were loaded on to trains, they found the carriages full of vermin and so cold that their clothes froze solid to the boards. The camps, Elsa Brandström discovered, were immense cities housing up to 35,000 men; often there was no lighting — and this was a land where winter brought total dark for many months each year. The barracks were cold, forlorn and bleak. There were very few bowls or plates; the prisoners were given scraps of food to eat with their fingers. When they were ill, guards threw the food on to their beds. There were beetles, lice, fleas and rats. In one camp alone, at Totzkoye, she heard that 1,700 of the 25,000 prisoners had died.

As the months of captivity turned into years, it was hard to know whether the enforced inactivity of some of the camps — no books, no paper, very little exercise, no permission to learn Russian, the commandants believing it would help the men to escape — was better or worse than being sent down mines, where the weaker men were repeatedly flogged, or to farms, where the peasants treated them as animals, inspecting their teeth and their muscles. All agreed, however, that the worst fate was to be sent off, as 70,000 men were, to build the Murmansk railway between Svanka and the Arctic Ocean. The line passed through hundreds of miles of swampy land, mosquito-infested in summer, in which the men laboured, in water up to their waists, for up to eighteen hours a day. Twenty-five thousand of these men died, Elsa Brandström reported; of the rest, 32,000 went down with scurvy, TB, rheumatism and diarrhoea.

The foreign prisoners-of-war were not the only victims of the fighting. In 1914, there had been 330,000 subjects of the Central Powers living in Russia, most of them Germans — businessmen, engineers and settlers. Fearing they might join the enemy, the authorities banished them also to the interior, herded into trucks and sent to provinces east of the Volga or to Siberia, where the local people, already overwhelmed by refugees, hounded them away. These civilians, too, began to die of disease and malnutrition.

As accounts of this brutality filtered through to the International

Committee and the Danish and Swedish Red Cross societies, pressure was put on the Russians, with the help of the Dowager Empress Maria Feodorovna, to allow delegates to visit the camps. A mission led by F. Thormeyer and Dr F. Ferrière, nephew of Frédéric, travelled over 25,000 kilometres to visit camps in Turkestan and Siberia in the autumn of 1915 and the spring of 1916. They found men rendered desperate and miserable by being moved around from camp to camp, by the unfamiliarity of the food – black rye bread, clear broth, no potatoes – and by being held with so many different nationalities, men whose languages they could not speak and whose customs were totally different. Austrians, Serbians, Czechs, Italians and Romanians, who had been transported thousands of miles from the small mountain villages of Germany or warm seaside towns of Italy to live in rugged barracks, in which temperatures regularly fell far below zero, squabbled to fill long, vacant hours. In a newly built camp not far from Samarkand, surrounded by flat plains with no vegetation and very little water, they found prisoners in states of extreme depression. Though the two Swiss delegates returned relieved to have found so little evidence of brutality, they noted that everywhere, as the war entered its third year, there was growing talk of boredom, of 'captivity neurosis' and of melancholia.

Elsa Brandstrom was impressed by their report. In Thormeyer and Ferrière's wake came other delegates, from the Swedish and Danish Red Cross societies, and by 1917, Sweden alone had forty-eight delegates working in Russia, Siberia and Turkestan. Germany was now allowed to send in parcels and trains left the northern German towns laden with '80,000 pairs of drawers', boots, blankets, medicine, food and disinfectants. With supplies coming in, the prisoners began to set up their own hospitals, baths, disinfecting stations and even shops in which cobblers and tailors worked. And even if local conditions often continued to depend on the energy of individuals who handled the incoming supplies – in Tientsin, a Frau Elsa von Hanneken, a German woman who had done relief work for European troops during the Boxer rebellion, distributed money and supplies sent in by the Americans – conditions did slowly improve. Books got through – two million by the end of the war; teachers started classes; musicians arranged orchestras. In the summer of 1917, Elsa Brandström reported, the 3,000 prisoners of war in Beresovka camp in Siberia grew 30,000 tomatoes, 15,000 lettuces and 1,000 lbs of peas, though the camp commandant refused to let them grow flowers.

Some of these men were destined to spend up to six years in captivity, and 'captivity neurosis' was increasingly reported by the delegates as they trudged from camp to camp. Nowhere was this more so than in Japan, where a tall, distinguished-looking Swiss resident called Dr Fritz Paravicini, doctor to the foreign legations, agreed to become delegate for the International Committee and visit the 4,000 or so German detainees, captured early in the war in China. The prisoners, reported Paravicini, were held in superb conditions – they were given work, books, sports, good food, music, and even taken on excursions to local beauty spots – but many were becoming anxious and homesick, and morale was sinking with every month in captivity.

These men were all prisoners-of-war, and as soldiers had expected captivity. The civilian internees of the First World War, however, had not; and as the war dragged on, their misery grew.

Few visits to camps for internees give a bleaker picture than that painted by the International Committee's vice-president Edouard Naville during his two visits to Britain, though he recognized, and repeated, that the British military authorities were doing all they could to make life in the camps tolerable. It was custody itself that seemed to those inside so unfair and, as the months turned into years, even small matters became insupportable.

At Queensferry, in an old factory six miles outside Chester, Naville met 2,000 wretched and ill-tempered Germans. They were all men of military age. They complained to him about the lack of soap, about being fed margarine even though it was called butter, about not being grouped according to social class and rank, about the presence among them of men with syphilis and fleas. When Naville left, he could only recommend weakly to the commandant that he improve the 'lamentable water-closets' and try to vary the diet of tea, bread and butter, doled out morning and evening.

In January 1916, Naville and a Swiss priest called Jacques Martin went to see a camp for 22,000 'interned aliens', all of them men and most of them German, who had been working as teachers, chefs and businessmen in Britain before the war. The site was a pleasant stretch of countryside on the Isle of Man. The delegates spent two and a half hours trudging around Knockaloe, a 'town made of wood'. The day was chiefly memorable for the mud. Squelching from barracks to barracks, they stared out across open fields where the men exercised, now turned into vast expanses of brown sludge. They gazed at the orderly buildings, but were prevented from reaching them to see inside by this 'veritable sea of mud'. Paths had been turned into mires. Knockaloe was run for the most part by the internees, the commandant fighting the boredom and discontent of the men with sports, orchestras and competitions. Though Naville and Martin came away admiring the orderliness, they felt depressed, reflecting that with such weather and such mud, it was perhaps inevitable. Of all the unhappy and bored inmates, they felt most pity for the men brought from the German colonies in Togo and Cameroon, who were suffering excruciatingly from the damp. 'They told me,' reported Martin to Geneva, 'that though not exactly ill, they never felt well.' The delegates recommended that these men be transferred to French care in North Africa.

The British internees in Germany fared no better. Some 4,000 were interned in the yards, stables and grandstand of a trotting track at Ruhleben near Berlin. There were complaints about the straw provided for bedding on the damp concrete floors becoming verminous, of cold, clammy lofts, of the total lack of sanitary arrangements. Many of Ruhleben's internees were elderly visitors to Germany who had been taking health cures when war broke out.

One of the more unexpected visits to civilians was paid by Dr Blanchot, M. Thormeyer and M. E. Schoch in Egypt. In January 1917, 229 Turkish women and their 207 children had been interned in the Bijou Palace in the old citadel of Cairo, having been arrested travelling home from Mecca. The so-called camp was run by a Miss Lewis, who evidently so impressed the delegates with her patience, tact, goodness of heart and intelligence, that they devoted an entire paragraph of their report to her qualities. Miss Lewis cannot have had an easy job. The ladies – some rich, some their servants – had been given forty rooms with marble floors, fine oriental carpets and magnificent views over the desert. They were allowed to send out for embroidered curtains and rugs. Doctors, speaking both Turkish and Arabic, called every day. Food was good and unlimited and there was a school for the children. Twelve rooms had been set aside for visiting husbands, who were allowed to come for three and four days at a time from their own internment camp nearby.

The delegates seem not to have taken to the Turkish ladies. Under 'intellectual distractions' in their report, usually filled with requests for books, Bibles, tools and musical instruments, they have noted: 'The women internees show no need, and no desire, for anything. Their day is passed gossiping and smoking.' Having gone on to visit the men's camp, the delegates were told by one man that his wife had complained to him that meat was only served three times a week in the citadel, and that the medical care was inadequate. They dutifully returned to the palace to investigate, and questioned the woman who had complained — they refer to her as Madame S. — closely. 'We received proof,' they wrote, somewhat dryly, 'that meat is served six times a week, a quarter of a pound per person ... After telling us that the cheese and olives were of poor quality, she finished by admitting that she found the cheese a little salty and the olives monotonous.' As for the bread, which Madame S. found inedible, 'it comes from the best baker in Cairo, and is served fresh twice a day ...' Evidently, Miss Lewis had come over as preferable to the spoilt Turkish ladies.

The next mission of these three delegates, to India and Japan, was rather more taxing. In a camp in Rajputan, they had to make sense of 3,366 male prisoners: Afghans and Persians, Hindus and Kurds, Turks from Anatolia, Syria and Adrianople, Arabs from Egypt and Arabia, Christians from Mesopotamia, Armenians, European Greeks and Jews from Kurdistan and Mesopotamia. Dr Blanchot and his two companions sampled the coffee in the various cafés the inmates had been allowed to open, inspected a bewildering array of shirts, jackets, robes, top coats, fezzes, turbans, berets and skull caps, and counted the implements given to each national cook (seven pans, four choppers, four ladles, two trays and five buckets); they noted disapprovingly that 'gin, vermouth and other spirits' were on sale in the canteen. In a hill station camp in Darjeeling, they found thirty-two Germans and four Austrians eating English puddings.

It would be wrong to give too contented a picture of the camps, whether for prisoners-of-war or civilians. The miracle was that, given the numbers and the immense difficulties of looking after them, there was any contentment at all. And there were many dreadful exceptions. Hard as they tried, the delegates seldom penetrated the camps of prisoners-of-war which had been set up, despite the Geneva Convention, inside military zones, particularly in Germany, Turkey, Bulgaria and in parts of Russia, from whence came persistent stories of hard treatment. By the spring of 1916, having perceived the value of prison labour, Germany was using French, Russian, Belgian, British and Serbian prisoners as agricultural workers, draining marshes, working in factories and down mines. The issue was particularly tricky, for The Hague regulations specifically forbade the use of prisoners-of-war to make weapons, munitions or anything connected with the war. At Krupps, by late 1916, there were 1,500 French prisoners at work. Those who refused to carry out orders were slowly starved. In March 1916, Dr Blanchot and Dr Speiser did manage to make a tour of some of these camps, though they were turned away from those the military authorities decreed lay behind military lines. Everywhere they went, the two men sought out the 'most mature and most reflective' among the prisoners in order to be able to put together a fuller picture. They watched men repairing typewriters, making railway lines, and working on military trucks; and they went down mines. They measured the height and width of underground galleries, they checked light and ventilation, they made notes about hours worked and money paid, they tasted bread and they ran water and measured its temperature. They came home with one major complaint: that for men of sedentary professions, the gruelling physical labour was proving not just tough but dangerous. Forty per cent had already had accidents, a few of them serious.

The matter of reprisals haunted the International Committee and the delegates all through the war. From the autumn of 1914, stories of hardship among prisoners on one side soon led to reprisals being exacted on the prisoners of the other. When Berlin received reports of Germans in Morocco, particularly the intellectuals, being kept by the French in 'inhuman conditions', guarded by blacks who insulted them and put them to hard manual labour, they immediately gathered all the French 'social and intellectual élite' prisoners and sent them to reclaim marshes near Hamburg. The era of reprisals was launched. Letters describing hardships poured into the agency in Geneva. The International Committee pleaded, pestered, agitated. On 12 July 1916 they issued a public appeal, condemning all reprisals as unjust and cruel. 'Surely such methods mark a relapse into barbarity.' They could not have chosen a worse moment. The battle of Verdun was at its height, a million men were advancing and retreating, a few feet at a time, along the hills by the Meuse, the British and French offensive on the Somme was just beginning, and there was fighting at Salonika, in the Near East, on the Russian front, and in Italy. After a long time, and many negotiations conducted by the International Committee with the countries at war, reprisals were to some extent checked, and in 1917 the French and the Germans agreed to withdraw prisoners thirty kilometres behind the firing line. Even then, not all agreements were kept, and when a medical mission from the International Committee managed to visit a prison hospital in Germany, one of the doctors, Dr Frédéric Guyot, reported seeing a 'disease hitherto unknown to me, I'm glad to say – famine oedema', the swelling that comes from severe malnutrition. The men he saw had been building a railway in the military zone for the past six months, and had received no food parcels in all that time.

There is no doubt at all that the delegates' visits were important, that conditions did improve as a result of their reports, and that physical brutality was curbed after their complaints. But right up until the end of the war, pockets of ill-treatment continued and there was little the International Committee could do. In February 1917, 500 British prisoners-of-war in Germany were told that they were to be sent to the Russian front in reprisal for the British having sent German prisoners to the front in France. The men spent the rest of the Russian winter, in thirty-five degrees of frost, in tents; their food was reduced to two meals a day of coffee, bread and thin soup. They were not allowed to smoke. Some had no blankets. Every day the men were marched to the German trenches where they spent ten hours working under Russian fire. By April, 200 were in hospital with severe frostbite. 'My hands are still too frozen to write well,' wrote one man to his family, 'but this is the first time they have been able to write at all.' Many of the men eventually died.

All his life, Gustave Ador would worry about how to make people respect the Geneva Convention. In the absence of a tribunal or enforcement procedures, how could countries be prevented from violating its Articles? His tone often had a desperate and weary ring to it. 'The war,' he wrote, after many months of fighting, 'has piled up so many ruins, so many bereavements, and has caused so much blood to flow, that we must listen to the call of the heart, the voice of pity, and give back to their own countries all those who can still be saved.' As the months passed and the war did not, as everyone had so confidently predicted, come to an early end, so violations followed fast in mounting spirals of reprisals and retaliations. By the time the fighting ended, over four years later, the International Committee had received eighty fully documented major breaches of the Convention — and they were only the tip of an iceberg that drew in all the armies, navies, air forces and countries at war.

On 21 September 1914, Ador sent out a first appeal to all the belligerents to show respect for the Convention that they had helped bring into force. 'The size of the battlefields,' he declared,

> and the magnitude of the armies engaged undoubtedly make it difficult at times to enforce observation of the provisions, but we are convinced that if specific instructions are given . . . the Geneva Convention will be respected everywhere and at all times.

He received pious noises of agreement.

However, protests quickly reached his office in Geneva. There was no formal undertaking that the International Committee would be responsible for monitoring the deal it had brokered but, as it had with the agency for prisoners-of-war, it now simply slipped into another new role. Soon the rate at which protests were arriving quickened. In October 1914 alone the Serbs reported that a Red Cross hospital in Belgrade, clearly marked with prominent flags and banners as specified by the Convention, was being bombed; the Germans complained that the French were locking up their doctors; the French that *their* doctors were being interned and that a hospital in Rheims had been shelled. Week after week, the accusations grew nastier. Russia claimed that the Austrians were using exploding bullets and that the Germans were shooting at their Red Cross nurses. Later, from the Germans, came fresh protests that the British and the French armies had recruited Pathan, Sikh, Spahi, Moroccan and Senegalese troops and that these men were introducing their own brutal customs into the war. There was talk of fingers cut from German corpses as trophies, of necklaces made of ears, of eyes gouged from the heads of wounded men. This, said the Germans, was a 'disgrace to twentieth-century armies'. (The International Committee agreed; these people were indeed barbaric; but then went on to ask Germany why it seemed to have done so little to control its allies, the Turks, in Armenia.)

As on land, there were growing breaches of the new rules of war at sea; as naval warfare spread, there were reports from all sides that hospital ships were being seized, bombed, attacked and torpedoed, and that they were being used to transport ammunition. A new chapter opened when the German admiralty decided to use its submarines as merchant raiders, aiming at both British vessels and neutral ships trading with Britain within what it declared to be a 'war zone' and giving no warning before firing their torpedoes. A torpedoed ship, it was soon found, could sink in a little more than a couple of minutes. Resentment reached new heights when a trawler called the *Acantha* from Yorkshire was fired on as its crew tried to reach the lifeboats. In retaliation, Britain announced that all captured German submarine crews would not be considered prisoners-of-war, but ordinary criminals. On 13 April 1915, Berlin responded that for every German sailor treated this way, a captured British officer would be moved from prisoner-of-war camp to jail. By June, the game had got out of hand. The British declared that they would stop playing; the Germans followed suit.

In such circumstances there was very little the International Committee could actually do beyond issuing stern rebukes and public appeals, or trying to negotiate agreements and hope that they held. Accusations continued; retaliations followed; all sides issued protests of their own and complaints that they were being falsely accused. 'The greatest danger that we run in this war,' the *Bulletin* quoted Lord Selborne as saying in Parliament after a British hospital ship called the *Dover Castle* was first torpedoed then shot at while its crew struggled for the lifeboats, 'is to fall to the level of the Germans.' Even the International Committee came in for attack, when the German Red Cross accused Geneva of jumping to conclusions without proof. Ador was unmoved. 'Our neutrality and our impartiality remain intact: they consist solely in having one single rule, immutable for everyone, and formulating our judgement . . . without considering for a single instant which side is the guilty one.' But the attacks went on.

Of all of Europe's small countries, Switzerland had the most reason to feel alarmed by the spreading conflict. Three of its borders were with countries which had entered the war at once; its fourth was with Italy, which joined the war in May 1915. True, its European neighbours had pledged to respect its neutrality by a treaty in 1815. But the Belgians were also neutral, and respect for their neutrality had also been promised in a treaty. It had not saved them from German invasion. In the first days of the war, the Swiss federal government had reaffirmed 'its neutrality and the inviolability of its territory' – though it was later known that it had somewhat hedged its bets in case of invasion by signing various secret pacts. When Swiss Germans and Swiss French each appeared to be becoming a little too outspoken in their support for their natural allies, the federal government issued a stern reminder that neutrality meant reserve and moderation. Just the same, the Swiss could not escape the war. They remained haunted by spectres of invasion and starvation, and, as the months passed, they became hosts to ever-growing numbers of refugees, as well as interned soldiers.

According to early terms of agreement reached with the French and German governments, Switzerland was to take in and intern sick prisoners-of-war. The first to arrive were tubercular cases. In January 1916, 100 French soldiers and 100 German soldiers captured by the opposing sides in France were admitted to hospitals, the Germans in Davos, the French in Leysin and Montana. Trains carrying these first men were greeted warmly: Red Cross ladies produced food and drink while hundreds of Swiss crowded the platforms, throwing flowers and passing out presents. Countries at war were now urged by the International Committee to send in the names of seriously ill and wounded men, with a view to recuperation or exchange: the *grands blessés* being designed for repatriation, those still capable of garrison or clerical duties for internment. The early agreements were meticulous about matching figures, but as the months passed the *Bulletin* was able to record that reciprocity had been dropped and 'for once, it seems, humanity prevails'.

Their hospitality was soon placing uneasy demands on the Swiss who had undertaken to provide not just medical facilities, but transport, housing, food, work and education, even if they were paid for their pains by the governments concerned. Between January 1916 and the end of the war 67,726 prisoners of war were admitted to hospitals in Switzerland,

and the agreements with governments were eventually expanded to include civilians, particularly children and the elderly.

The early spirit of welcome was soon somewhat dampened by complaints. Six hundred British soldiers billeted at Château d'Oex did not greatly care for what they found and soon wrote home about 'this miserable little saucer of a place, surrounded by hills, covered in slush at times and thoroughly unsuitable for wounded men'. In Vevey, rivalry broke out between English and French soldiers, the English claiming that the French were in 'a charming spot, working at their usual vocations, walking about with girls, leading perfectly normal and seemingly contented lives' while their own were far from satisfactory. From Montreux came a complaint from a British soldier who had lost a leg in the fighting. 'If I had been in Germany I could have purchased a Boche leg. Nice thing for a neutral country to see our men going about on crutches without artificial limbs and not one Frenchman.' From Piota, a 'dirty rotten old cow-shed' according to its new guests, another British soldier moaned that the house he was living in was overrun by rats and that the cheese he saw being carried along the streets was being sent to Germany. What the Swiss thought of their troublesome guests is not clear, but one reporter noted that while the British had immediately set about arranging sports, the 'French, who like to watch the crowds, feel uneasy in the high mountains'.

For the most part, the Swiss reacted tolerantly and with considerable generosity. They installed the recuperating soldiers in small hotels; they arranged for training programmes; they laid on recreations. Swiss hoteliers offered a three-week holiday to 1,800 Red Cross nurses: the British and the Italians refused, the French and the Germans accepted, the Germans making it a condition that their nurses did not mix with enemy nurses. A senior wounded British officer interned at Mürren requested and received a set of bagpipes. And, with time, the Swiss encouraged visits from wives, mothers and fiancées, who were escorted to Switzerland by Red Cross members. According to notes written at the time, wives were given stern instructions. 'Intercourse between the interned and their relatives,' they were told, 'is permitted.' However, they were ordered to make their own beds, pay for their own washing, refrain from discussing war or politics with the Swiss, avoid demonstrations both inside the hotel and out, and not consume alcoholic drinks in their bedrooms. Throughout the entire country, committees, associations and church centres flourished, run by Swiss women and by many of the foreigners who for years had made Switzerland their home. In Geneva alone, by the outbreak of war a lively city of over 100,000 people, its old fortifications cleared away to make room for new villas and immense public buildings and its lake given over to regattas and sailing yachts, there were no fewer than forty-six separate organizations. The Prisoner of War Bread Fund in Berne, presided over by Lady Grant Duff, wife of the British minister, despatched loaves to 19,000 British prisoners, the local ladies inspecting the bread regularly, and fielding complaints from camps when it arrived in dribs and drabs and 'green and mouldie'. Good continental loaves, with hard crusts and holes, were not, said one soldier, anything an 'average British Tommy would care for'.

When delegates from the Red Cross societies of Germany, Austria, Hungary and Russia met in Stockholm in December 1916, the Swiss chocolate firm Peter-Ciller-Kohler, sent every member a box of chocolates. As if to bring home more forcefully Switzerland's role in the war, they had asked a well-known Swiss painter, Burnard, to paint a symbolic picture for the cover. He drew a grateful mother receiving a letter from her prisoner-of-war son, which had reached her by way of the International Agency in Geneva.

In the spring of 1917, a political crisis led to a plea for Ador, whose diplomatic skills were now widely recognized, to join the federal government. He took leave of absence from the International Committee, installed Edouard Naville as acting president, and left for Berne. Ador had become something of a national hero. At Geneva station, he was seen off by an immense cortège, led by members of the International Committee bearing high one of the original silk Red Cross flags, followed by their daughters and granddaughters waving smaller flags. Flowers were strewn along the roads. Ador had good reason to feel proud. By 1917, although a million men were dead and the *Bulletin* greeted the New Year with sadness, saying that peace was now no more than a 'pale glimmer of hope on the distant horizon', the International Committee had made its mark on all the theatres of war. It was universally acknowledged to have transformed the lives of prisoners-of-war, pushing always for more and more concessions; it had transmitted two and a half million letters; it had reunited families scattered by the fighting; it had kept open communication between the different Red Cross societies; its prison visits were now accepted and respected and its repatriation schemes were working smoothly; and it continued to act, despite innumerable violations of the Geneva Convention, as a constant moral reminder of the atrocities of war. In 1917 it was awarded the Nobel Peace Prize.

EIGHT

One of Us, Heart and Soul

The man who would have been really pleased, had he lived just four years longer, was Henri Dunant. For while the International Committee in Geneva settled to its sober role of watchdog, monitor and upholder of the Geneva Convention, the national Red Cross societies all over the world burst into life. The seeds so anxiously sown by Dunant in the early 1860s now blossomed into a thousand endeavours. There was virtually no mile of the war front, whether in France, Serbia or Mesopotamia, not visited by the Red Cross in one shape or another. It was not merely that many of the societies had dutifully obeyed Dunant's plea that the years of peace should be spent preparing for those of war, so that many people were actually longing to prove what they could do. The whole idea behind his dream touched the mood of the times, the new spirit of philanthropy and the demand by women for involvement in the more serious concerns of life. The possibilities that were now open to them under the very broad umbrella of the Red Cross message, whether as nurses, doctors, administrators, caterers, fundraisers, drivers or quartermasters, were overwhelming; for many of them it meant a release from years of claustrophobia and boredom. 'I have not written for two days,' wrote Mabel Dearmer, a successful English playwright who abandoned a play in rehearsal to go to the front, to a friend, 'and that is because I am so happy. I am so much happier here than I could be anywhere else.'

The very nature of the Red Cross movement, its volunteers able to do as much or little as they felt like and belonging to affiliated groups and organizations under its umbrella, made possible every kind of enthusiasm and eccentricity. Beyond general guidelines, about fund-raising, responsibility towards wounded and sick soldiers, and supporting the army medical services, Geneva, once it had officially accredited a new member, was oddly detached from the work carried out in its name, reflecting Moynier's early determination not to interfere. Precise criteria, such as the degree of clear independence from the political bent of governments, were not spelt out until many years later, by which time the involvement of some national Red Cross societies in the totalitarian politics of their countries had caused immense harm to the movement. Like the International Committee's equivocal stand on pacifism, its relationship to the national Red Cross societies for most of the first century of its existence remained ill-defined and compliant.

From the Danish Red Cross soon came word that books were being sent to 20,000 prisoners-of-war, and that comic books were particularly sought after 'for otherwise the prisoners might well forget how to laugh'. From China came news that a Red Cross society had been launched, under the name of the *Tchoung-Kano-Loung-tsou-shitz-homi* society. From the German Red Cross, which celebrated its fiftieth birthday in November 1916 with a somewhat smug report that it had 75,000 stretcher-bearers on its books and ninety special trains, came an observation that patriotic ladies would be needed all the more urgently when the fighting ended, to act as 'moral deaconesses, inspiring courage in the invalid's entire family'. However, there were already intimations of how Germany would one day treat its Red Cross members: in April 1915, von Bissing, German governor in Belgium, instructed the Belgian Red Cross to do something about prostitution on the grounds that the state of the economy had driven many women on to the streets. The Belgian Red Cross refused. Von Bissing ordered the society to be closed and its assets transferred to an appointee of his own. The International Committee reacted sharply, furious protests were made by other societies and the Belgian Red Cross was reprieved; it continued to refuse to have anything to do with tackling prostitution.

All over the world, whether in belligerent or neutral countries, the national Red Cross societies now turned their efforts towards the war. Their stories — of recruitment and fund-raising, of hard work and acts of great courage — are similar, even if some societies were bolder, others more generous, others again richer or more autocratic. Nowhere more exuberantly and more imaginatively did Dunant's dream catch fire than in England, the major western power which had been the slowest to catch on to the whole Red Cross idea but which now took to the cause with flair and relish. The First World War would see a whole generation of women turn to war work, and when the Red Cross was unable to accept them because they were too young or too old or too unqualified, they went into the same kind of work just the same. And like their British predecessors in earlier Balkan wars, these men and women — mostly women — turned out to be diarists and letter writers, and many returned home in 1918 to write and publish accounts of their experiences. These give a remarkable view of the war. And because their records have been so carefully preserved, it is the story of the British Red Cross and those who worked in various capacities under it, that will stand for the others.

In July 1914, the British Red Cross Society, still prickly after years of rivalry with the St John Ambulance Association, the voluntary aid organization with which it had most in common, and preoccupied with the 'subtle and subterranean' forces at work behind the scenes, retained a modest appearance. Someone strolling down Victoria Street in London, on the shady side of the road, could have seen a small red cross, painted on a window blind. Inside, down a dark passage, they would have found three shabby rooms, a secretary, two clerks and an errand boy.

With the outbreak of war, all uncertainty vanished. Two days into the fighting, Queen Alexandra, as president, appealed for funds and herself donated £500. A trained matron was engaged to recruit suitable nurses. The Duke of Devonshire offered the ground floor of Devonshire House in Mayfair. And on 27 October, the British Red Cross Society and the St John Ambulance Association agreed to settle their differences, pool their reserves, and function for the duration of the war at least as a joint war committee of twenty-four people, twelve from each organization. Members included a heavy dose of aristocracy — the Marchioness of Lansdowne, Georgina, Countess of Dudley, the Earl of Plymouth and many more — as well as Sir Frederick Treves, the maverick surgeon of the Boer war, who had since removed Edward VII's appendix and been made a baronet and Knight Commander of the Victoria Order. Not long before the war, Treves had referred to the British Red Cross as a 'mother's meeting'; he was now made head of personnel and began to select doctors and dressers for the front. It was said of Treves that he loved money, fame and surgery, but royalty best of all. By Friday 30 October, when the joint war committee met for the second time, the Marchioness of Lansdowne's son had been killed. Soon members were crossing backwards and forwards to France to visit the front and report on most pressing needs.

Money was not a problem. *The Times* – 'If the sufferings of the wounded touch your hearts' – opened a fund on 31 August to supplement 'the aid provided by the state for our sick and wounded . . . and all the little luxuries and comforts which mean so much to the invalid on his bed of pain.' Donations flowed in. 'No newspaper,' it would be said, 'has ever performed a service of such magnitude to a like cause.' (Lord Northcliffe in fact played a valuable role in bringing the two societies together, announcing that he would refuse to publish in *The Times* or any other newspaper he owned advertisements from two separate societies appealing to the public for the same purposes.) The British society now made an excellent choice as chairman of the finance committee in Sir Robert Hudson, a churchgoing Yorkshireman from the Liberal Party, of whom friends said that he was 'far too human ever to be a true professional in that business'. Over money, Sir Robert was shrewd and persuasive; he also got on very well with Northcliffe, whose widow he was to marry. Sir Robert worked in bursts of great speed and energy. He was soon being referred to in London social circles as the 'most skilful beggar in London'.

It was Lady Northcliffe who thought up the great pearl necklace scheme. She called on rich and fashionable ladies throughout the British Empire to send their pearls, and with the 3,597 that arrived – Lady Wingate despatched 123 from Egypt – had forty-one necklaces made, which at auction fetched over £84,000. And it was not just pearls. Sales of donated 'articles of beauty' became the most glamorous social occasions of the season, every article given bearing a small red cross 'so that the value to purchasers may be enhanced in the future when history records the self-sacrificing and philanthropic aspect of the sale'; while the leading portrait painters of the day, like Augustus John and John Singer Sargent, sent in blank canvases on which the purchaser could have the sitter of his choice painted. Contributions to early sales included the first French exercise book used by Charlotte Brontë at the Pensionnat Héger in Brussels; Lady Jekyll sent an emerald and gold seal which had once belonged to Mary Queen of Scots; Balfour, an antique Chinese vase; Lady Wernher, a Spode writing set. The first auction, held on 12 April 1915, lasted twelve days and lots kept on arriving long after the bidding had started. The artists, in particular, were much praised for 'risking the arbitrariness of an auction' and in all £37,383 was raised. By the time the war ended, Christie's would have held seven such sales and raised £322,000.

The selection of volunteers was rather more complicated, though offers flooded in. Within a fortnight, some 3,000 fully qualified nurses had been recruited by the British society's new matron, who had the additional task, as the *Times History of the War* later coyly noted, of rejecting eager society ladies who 'gently but firmly . . . were restrained, and were told that only the best trained were good enough for the men who were giving up so much'. The first British Red Cross nurses were in France by the end of August, transferred by telephone and telegram according to where they were most wanted. What the *Times History* failed to add was that, despite the many discussions with the War Office and the Royal Army Medical Corps, the army remained wary of the British Red Cross offers until Viscount Esher, chairman of the Territorial Forces Association of the County of London, returned from an inspection of the front and convinced Lord Kitchener of the absurdity of leaving the Red Cross idle while the resources of the army medical services were clearly proving inadequate to meet the growing numbers of casualties. 'At the root of all the hospital trouble lies short-sightedness, obstinacy and professional jealousy,' wrote Esher in his journal on 30 September.

> What has been the result? A vast mess of unnecessary suffering; a quite unnecessary high rate of mortality; and a breakdown of organization that is a horror and a scandal! . . . The scandal is that . . . there are Red Cross hospitals fully equipped with surgeons, nurses and probationers waiting to come up, but refused leave by the Military Medical Authorities.

Kitchener, as Esher soon noted, 'made short work of the obstructionists'. And British Red Cross medical teams were soon being as overwhelmed by the ever-growing numbers of wounded and sick as everyone else.

There were, however, more than just nurses involved. In August 1909 the War Office, having studied the German and Japanese Red Cross societies closely, had issued a 'Scheme for the Organization of Voluntary Aid in England and Wales'. Its intention was to fill gaps in the territorial medical service. Male and female volunteers were to be taught basic medical skills and how to respond to calls for help, whether as drivers, pharmacists, or tea ladies along evacuation routes. The driving force behind what was soon known as the VAD scheme was not Surgeon General Sir Alfred Keogh, appointed the chief commissioner of the Red Cross overseas and soon to be director general of the medical service at the War Office (who had been known to talk of using the Red Cross as 'charwomen, maidservants, labourers *et hoc genus omne*'), but the British women themselves, who had begun to push hard for a proper role as medical auxiliaries. But, in case anyone was anxious, a St John Ambulance Brigade Officer hastily reassured the readers of *First Aid* that these ladies had not been influenced by the female suffrage movement, 'for the ladies of which I entertain a very strong measure of contempt, for the way in which they are lowering the prestige of women amongst all self-respecting classes of society'.

Women had, in fact, already been organizing on their own. In 1907 a Captain Butler, veteran of the Sudan campaign, a well-known 'advocate of physical culture and a thorough disciplinarian', who had earlier started a 'select club for girls', the Islington Drill Brigade Girls' Yeomanry, founded the First Aid Nursing Yeomanry Corps. Soon known as FANY, its members wore colourful uniforms — a 'crimson zouave, with the usual badges, crossed spurs etc. on the sleeve, blue riding skirt and riding boots, yellow sash, red and blue service caps, with chin straps, a natty riding whip completing the equipment'. One cannot help thinking that they must have looked somewhat like tropical parrots. By 1909, this 'busy band of aristocratic amazons' and 'gently-bred high spirited girls', as they were described in the society pages of magazines, aged between seventeen and thirty-five and over 5ft 3 inches tall, who had passed their 'course of horsemanship, veterinary work, signalling and camp cooking', were practising 'wounded rescue races' and chanting as the *Gazette* records:

> I wanted to be in Society once
> Danced and hunted and flirted once
> Had white hands and complexion once,
> Now I am a FANY.

Then there were the VADs, the Voluntary Aid Detachments, launched in 1909 to recruit volunteer men as stretcher-bearers and drivers, women as nurses and cooks. Formed by territorial associations, acting through local branches of the Red Cross, they proved so popular among young women that by 1914 50,000 had joined. If the nursing training was not particularly onerous, they also had to be able to march in single and double file, carry out stretcher drill, prepare invalid diets, do laundry, wash, mend, darn, sew and knit and be proficient in sanitation and 'housewifery'. Their uniforms of 'not too military a character' included a broad-brimmed hat, an apron and an outdoor coat almost reaching to the ground. It cost £1 19s. 2½d. There was a revolt against small white caps, so the women wore white headscarves instead.

The VADs brought together, as one observer noted, 'the duchess and the factory girl, the over-military-aged aristocrat and the under-military-aged errand boy'. When Guy du Maurier wrote a play called *The Englishman's Home*, about a family unable to cope with the enormous number of casualties after Britain had been occupied by a foreign power, thousands more young women volunteered. 'During the first six months of the war they were, in some respects, like shoals of fish trying to enter a main stream through some small culvert', a contributor to a magazine remarked, while Vera Brittain, the English writer who served as a nurse in the war, observing these recruits selling programmes at a charity performance, wrote in her diary, on 14 December 1914: 'It is an excellent thing for these idle people to have something as strenuous and useful to do as scrubbing floors and carrying dishes.' They would not be idle for long.

Nor were the duchesses idle, even if the *British Journal of Nursing* complained that 'when an untrained Lady of Title – backed by social influence – is placed in extreme authority in a military hospital, disorganization . . . is inevitable'. Adeline, Duchess of Bedford, joining forces with three dukes and an earl, started a British prisoners-of-war food parcels and clothing fund, to supplement rations being collected by the Red Cross. She had a highly emotional pamphlet printed, showing a group of prisoners behind barbed wire: one has only one leg, another is kneeling, his hands raised in supplication while a corpulent German guards them with a bayonet. Kippers, golden syrup and games soon flowed in.

In January 1914, the British Red Cross started a monthly magazine and nothing gives a better feel of the movement than its mixture of earnestness and snobbery, practicality and dottiness. In the first number, Sir Frederick Treves contributed a few useful hints drawn from his experiences in the Boer war. 'Among the luxuries much appreciated by the sick are hair brushes and tooth-brushes . . . Eau de Cologne, which was supplied to the amount of 272 gallons, fans and cushions.' Fans would not become popular in the trenches.

By the beginning of 1915, the magazine had become altogether more sober and less social; there was more black print and fewer illustrations. Among the cookery competitions and dates for bazaars there were items on frostbite in northern France; on the dwindling supply of leeches now that the European market had closed and the search for replacements had moved to India (where the leeches were larger but became very hungry during the long journey to England); about officers taking packs of hounds and beagles over to France for their periods of leave now that eighty Masters of Foxhounds were reported to be on active duty. Questions of behaviour and etiquette were debated, like whether a woman in uniform should be saluted, whether it was all right to pray for animals, and whether waders made out of mulberry leaves, worn by the Japanese during the Russo-Japanese war, would be suitable for the trenches. Food was always a popular topic and readers were urged to 'cultivate a taste for soup' and to make their meals more modest. A 'small family with 2 or 3 maids' was urged to content itself with an austere wartime menu of fish kedgeree for breakfast, 'braised silverside (fresh) and vegetables, potatoes, peas, rice mould, stewed fruit, cheese' for an early lunch, and 'clear vegetable soup, jelly pie, salad potatoes' and chocolate custard for supper.

The edition of October 1915 contained a picture of Chief Chee-poos-ta-tin, at 107 years old the oldest member of the Canadian Red Cross. Nearly every month, there were portraits of titled women, an early one being of Lady Constance Butler, a well-known figure in the hunting field, who was now putting in long hours in the general stores department, setting a fine 'example of unassuming application and quiet endurance'.

There were also fashion notes. The 'Paris modes' wrote a correspondent in March 1915, had become a little 'military in cut' and went by martial names. A 'Kitchener' was a neat blue serge dress with a black satin sash, while a 'Joffre' was made in the new French uniform blue and had short full skirts worn with very high boots with Wellington tops. The following month a little tiff broke out between a 'mother of two in Khaki' who wrote to say that this was no time for 'flimsy furbe-lows' and that 'this contemptible tyranny of fashion' should be abandoned for the war. 'We shall dress as we feel it appropriate to dress,' replied a 'Peeress', tartly. 'We shall certainly abstain, as far as we can, from accentuating the margin between rich and poor. But we shall do our best to save our tradesmen and tradeswomen from quite unnecessary distress. That is one of our contributions to the economics of the war.' With spirit of this kind, was it surprising that British women went to war with such gusto?

There were many jobs for British Red Cross volunteers in England in the hospitals and convalescent homes opening up around the country. But what the women really wanted to do was to pack up their regulation list of gumboots, garters, mackintosh, sou'wester, black cashmere stockings, folding bed, chair, table, washstand and bucket and go to France. When the official bodies, 'gently but firmly' turned them down, they went just the same. The day of independent-spirited adventuresses had firmly arrived, and these British women, especially those with private incomes, were not going to miss the action.

The war zone was soon full of a floating population of nurses and auxiliaries, who moved from place to place as they were needed, joining independent units or official military hospitals as directed with a remarkable lack of starchiness and an easy sense of fellowship between them. They were sometimes rather hearty and sentimental, interspersing their accounts of bombing raids and amputations with lyrical descriptions of the bluebells and cowslips of wartime France; but they were brave and they worked hard. Their stories are important, for they provide another step in Dunant's dream, even if their independent spirit did not always go down well, either with the army or with the British Red Cross Society itself. In a letter to *The Times* on 14 August 1914, Lord Rothschild, then chairman, warned of the 'evils of overlapping, of uncoordinated and disunited work'. Ladies, he observed reprovingly, were already 'starting individual base hospitals of their own'.

By the end of September, the British society had opened four hospitals in Paris, with thirty surgeons and 150 trained nurses. Wounded men were ferried from the front, while Sir Alfred Keogh hastened around the countryside, telegraphing back to London for stretcher-bearers for Le Havre, nurses for Rouen. Up and down the French coast, British volunteers joined forces with the three societies that made up the French Red Cross, with British and American residents and with the owners of châteaux, who turned over their salons to become hospital wards. They took over huts, tents, schools, hotels and casinos, and they navigated hospital and supply barges on the rivers and canals, travelling in flotillas of six pulled by steam barges, taking rugs and cushions up on deck to watch the countryside go by. At Le Touquet, the gaming tables were covered in sheets and drugs put to keep cool in the bar. The British women were sometimes a little in awe of their French counterparts, an article in *The Times* noting that while French women remained merely the 'power behind the throne in finance and politics' their influence was such that it would make very little difference 'in the existing state of things if women were accorded the vote because "*en France la femme est devenue presque omnipotente*"'. The rivalry counted for little, as the casualties mounted and the women fought to keep tetanus and gangrene at bay, and to find ways of helping young soldiers reduced to torpor by high explosive shells.

Before the war was four days old, Millicent, Dowager Duchess of Sutherland, one of the four duchesses to carry Queen Mary's canopy at the coronation, and who at forty-seven was still an exceptionally beautiful woman, arrived in France wearing a Red Cross nurse's uniform. The duchess was precisely the sort of woman Lord Rothschild had warned against. The least biddable of all the renegade society ladies, she planned to join the *Secours aux Blessés*, of which her friend the comtesse d'Haussonville was president. Pulling a few strings, she was soon wiring London for funds and on 16 August a young surgeon and nine nurses from Guy's hospital joined her unit, the Millicent Sutherland Ambulance for the Belgians. On her instructions, the surgeon had added to his provisions a generous supply of glycerine to keep the hands soft.

Their first quarters were a convent in the border town of Namur, which lay in the path of the invading Germans. On 22 August, Namur was bombed. 'A pause, and then came a perfect fusillade of rifle shots,' reads the 'vivaciously written' report that the duchess sent for publication in *The Times*. 'My door burst open, and Mr Winser, our stretcher bearer, rushed in calling out, "My God, Duchess, they have fired the town".'

Casualties began to arrive. 'In less than twenty minutes we had forty-five wounded on our hands,' the duchess noted in her diary. 'What I thought would be for me an impossible task became absolutely natural; to wash wounds, to drag off rags and cloathing soaked in blood, to hold basins equally full of blood, to soothe a soldier's groans.' She spoke excellent German, so she buried her revolver under an apple tree and went to call on General Karl von Bülow, commander of the German Second Army whom she had met at dinner before the war. Day after day she plagued him with complaints and demands, and when these failed, she quoted the Geneva Convention. The Germans, she observed, 'like well-known people'. With the General's help, she obtained papers to enable her to move her unit to Mauberge, which the French were about to surrender. The train carrying them stopped ten kilometres short of their destination, and the duchess, who had instructed her unit to address her as Sister Millicent, ordered them to walk the rest of the way, pointing out that 'one very nearly does that in a day's golfing'.

After a while, as she wrote later in her diary, 'we cut across country to shorten our walk, but we were perpetually tripped up by barbed wire or hindered by the deserted trenches.' The party spent the next few weeks crossing backwards and forwards between German and French lines, the duchess bullying her German social acquaintances into smoothing the path. In time, the Millicent Sutherland Ambulance became the Number 9 Red Cross Hospital at Calais — the Duchess of Westminster was running the Number 1 Hospital at Le Touquet and Lady Norman the Number 5 at Wimereux — near the dunes and by a marsh full of yellow irises the duchess picked to decorate the wards. Her nurses seem to have liked her for she put much energy into finding recreations for them in the lulls between the fighting, getting hold of a skiff for the lagoon and inviting officers over to dance. At Christmas, she gave each a handkerchief with black cats on it. Advancing with the Allies, recreation became walks among the ruins of destroyed villages, littered with helmets, bayonets and coats made all the more unnerving when the inmates of an enormous mental hospital near their base were released during a bombing raid. One day the duchess was told that her younger son, Alistair, had died of fever in East Africa.

The duchess had a sister called Angela, as intrepid and independent-minded as herself. Angela tried her hand at nursing in the Hotel Majestic in Paris, where the ballroom had been converted into a ward but, not much caring for it, she moved to Boulogne and opened a canteen. It was in the Gare Maritime; she had a few tin jugs, a pail to wash up in and an old tin boiler. Just before the Somme offensive of July 1916, alone on duty, she fried 800 eggs between four and seven in the morning.

And so the war went on, with the duchess wearing an overcoat over silk pyjamas and a tin hat on her head during night raids, continuing to bully and wheedle the military authorities, be they Allies or Central Powers, and doing what she could for her wounded, to whom she gave nicknames of 'Silly Billy' and 'Baby Boy'. She survived the war. 'We gave you rather a shifty and trying time,' said the letter she received from the HQ of the Second Army after the fighting ended; 'we felt that you were Outsiders pushing yourselves in, but really you were one of us, heart and soul.' Lord Rothschild's warning proved wrong: as the war went on, and the renegade ladies demonstrated tenacity, courage and a capacity for hard work, so they were absorbed informally into the system, working naturally both alongside the official Red Cross and within it.

Once women had trained with the British Red Cross Society or the St John Ambulance Association, they could apply to go wherever they wished. A number of the more sporting, who preferred to be out of doors and felt squeamish about operations, opted to become ambulance drivers, transport ranking only second to hospitals in the services provided by volunteers and the Red Cross. Ambulance cars, with no windscreens and no self-starters, driven by jaunty women in breeches and heavy coats, would soon become a familiar sight across the war front.

As soon as it became clear that there were not nearly enough vehicles to carry the vast and growing numbers of casualties in France, who were suffering agonies being bumped along in horse-drawn carts, *The Times* had appealed for cars. Offers of every shape, make, colour and horsepower poured in, the very best being touring cars; one was a converted Daimler which was soon clattering around Calais with a boiler and twelve collapsible baths. On 12 September, members of the Royal Automobile Club in London voted to offer themselves and their cars to the Red Cross and set off for Boulogne, where they fanned out to scour the fields for wounded men. By the summer of 1917, the joint committee had 1,100 motor ambulances in France and Belgium, and had commissioned the FANY to do much of the driving. The FANY ran the Calais convoy from January 1916 until the Armistice. At their peak, there were 450 of these energetic, stubborn young women, skidding and lurching their way determinedly among the potholes, battling it out against mud and ice to keep their vehicles serviceable. They came to regard themselves as an élite, in their khaki puttees or long brown boots, with their voluminous goatskin coats, though there were many complaints that they tended to be too casual about their uniforms. All but one survived the war. Nineteen received military medals, twenty-seven the Croix de Guerre and one the Légion d'Honneur. A Mrs Knocker was made Chevalier of the Order of Lèopold after setting up an advanced dressing post near the front where severely wounded men could recover from shock before undergoing the jolting journey to hospital.

The letters written by a Red Cross nurse called K. E. Luard to her parents from the front between 1914 and the end of the war give a good picture of the life these women led. She comes across as even-tempered, realistic and compassionate, her language and tone that of the middle-class girls of the day. She described shell shock to her parents, talked of paralysis, amputations and gangrene, and she told them how, when she had free time, she took her sandwiches into the sun or walked deep into the forest. 'I've never in my life seen so many aeroplanes or so many dead men or so many German prisoners,' she wrote on Saturday, 14 April 1916. The sisters she worked with were 'top-hole', bombing raids 'absolutely beastly', there was seldom butter for tea and the 'boys' were dying in droves, one of them a 'baby Lt. Colonel of twenty-four covered with crosses and bars'.

Miss Luard was at Ypres for the third battle of August 1917.

Bombardments still going on top-speed, bigger and longer than any in this war yet . . . Many die and their beds are filled instantly. One has got so used to their dying that it conveys no impression beyond a vague sense of medical failure. You forget entirely that

they were once civilians, that they were alive and well yesterday
. . . all you realize is that they are dead soldiers, and that there
are thousands like them . . . Pretty beastly, isn't it?

During the early years of the war, various sections of the British military
medical services remained sniffy about the Red Cross, preferring to ignore
its growing numbers of experienced surgeons and nurses, and dismissing
its admirably run stores and depots as no more than little luxuries.
But the British society persevered, its administrators travelled, wrote
clear-headed reports and continued to offer their services, and the depots
grew. By 1916, part of Devonshire House had been turned over to an
immense and highly efficient store house, despatching mosquito netting
for Mesopotamia, guinea pigs for medical experiments in France, dressing
gowns for internees in Switzerland, soda-water for convalescents in
Corfu. When Queen Marie of Romania called for condensed milk, it was
packed up and routed via Archangel and Odessa. There seemed to be
nothing that the energetic ladies in charge were unable or unwilling to
provide.

And, as the war spread and the forces were despatched to ever more
distant fronts, so the British Red Cross and its volunteers followed in
their wake, sending home diaries and letters that became more exotic
as the travellers moved east. In Gallipoli, an adventurer in the pure
Red Cross mould called Bimbashi McPherson reported helping a doctor
operate near a gully full of dead and wounded, holding arms and legs
'in position while they were being amputated. Sometimes there was not
much left to hang on to.' In Egypt, where Marguerite Fedden was sent
after offering to cook in a Red Cross hospital, she found herself pitching
the mess tent in a hurricane and deferring to a matron who had a small
marquee with a porch and a letter-bag in which the nurses put their
letters for her to censor. When it was hot, Marguerite Fedden wore a
long white dress and a sun helmet; when it rained, oilskins and gumboots.
Albumen water was in great demand, and it took her two hours to
break 400 eggs, separating whites from yolks in a haze of flies. To make
lemonade every day, three VADs and two helpers peeled and grated 300
lemons to distil into an essence. Junket was often requested, but it proved
impossible to 'junk' tinned milk. 'Later on,' she observed smugly, 'the

Canadian hospitals set up kitchens and those who ran them were called Dieticians, but we were proud to be known as Cooks.'

In Mesopotamia, where, after a good deal of ungracious resistance, the army finally succumbed to British Red Cross lobbying, a crucial convoy of fifty motor ambulances and thirty-five boats ferried wounded men and supplies, which included 1,500 gallons of pure lime juice a month and four to six tons of ice every day. Colonel Moens, joint war committee commissioner for the area, described transporting vegetable seeds for hospital gardens, baths for heat-stroke stations and musical instruments for bands, in temperatures that frequently reached 127°F in the shade. Colonel Moens's accounts of his tours of inspection, with tales of bivouacs and dawn climbs through the passes, read like the notes of an eighteenth-century explorer. Finding, one day, a 'wooded glade' by a stream he regretted only not having brought his fishing tackle to get a trout for his breakfast. Another day he decided to set up a forward depot in Hamadan and despatched a Major Stanley from Baghdad with a hundred camels, carrying 320lbs of supplies each in 'stout gunny covering' for a five-week journey through the desert. By the time the British Red Cross pulled out of Mesopotamia, it had brought in as well as medical supplies 151 badminton sets, 13,270 balaclavas, 24,431 bottles of Bovril, 1,417 cricket bats, 56,265 dusters, forty-six harmoniums, twenty one billiard tables and 7,706 bottles of calves' foot jelly, as well as 6,372 puggarees – scarves of muslin to protect the neck against the sun. Its motor ambulance convoy had driven a million miles.

'I doubt,' wrote George Trevelyan, who commanded the British ambu lance unit to Italy set up by Italophiles when Italy entered the war in May 1915, 'whether in the whole field of the European war there was such fierce fighting in scenery of such beauty and grandeur.' Wearing Red Cross uniforms his doctors, stretcher-bearers, VADs and nurses set off to start a hospital in the Villa Trento, near the village of Dolignano, a mile from the Austrian frontier. It was an eighteenth-century house, lent by the Italian government, with a formal garden of cypresses and statues; behind rose wooded hills, terraced vineyards and the high Alps; before lay the plain and fields covered in corn. In the months to come the Villa Trento would several times find itself completely surrounded by fighting.

One of the VADs who came to the Villa Trento was Freya Stark, who described in her letters to her mother how she would watch the convoys of military lorries in the plain below and the Austrian searchlights picking out the ambulances bringing casualties back to the hospital at night. 'It is the funniest sort of place here,' she wrote, in October 1917,

> every sort of person all jumbled up together, from the mechanics, who are paid, and not 'gentlemen', to the drivers, and Mr Trevelyan's set. The girls are all very nice, except two rather common ones who spoil things by flirting all the time . . . The only real trial was the one I worked with . . . a journalist and artist of uncertain age, kittenish manner, dyed hair, *fearful* snob and says clever and peculiarly ill-natured things.

The wards were called by names like 'Garibaldi'. In the evenings the unit met in the salon, which had a piano; they looked at the English papers, discussed Jack London and read aloud from the *Oxford Book of Italian Verse*. However fierce the fighting, the wards were kept tidy and tea was served on time.

Another volunteer at the Villa Trento was a fifteen-year-old Derbyshire boy called Kenneth Kennedy, the twelfth child in a Quaker family in which all able-bodied males joined either the Red Cross or the Friends ambulance unit. Among Kennedy's papers, found after his death in 1980, were letters from home and dozens of yellowing snapshots showing people squinting into the sun and wounded men in the gardens. His letters describe football matches with the Italians, Christmas Day with mince pies and plum pudding, swims in the river and the possibility of getting a pair of khaki trousers made in nearby Udine. One afternoon, he lit a fire of pine cones and invited one of the nurses to eat roast potatoes. 'You never see much of the kissing you would expect of foreigners,' he remarked, a little wistfully. For a while, Kennedy was put in charge of the obstinately English provisions – toast, porridge, cake – and in the summer of 1916 he produced a 'lovely Yorkshire pudding . . . cold blancmange or rice or semolina shapes' and a 'nice jam sandwich cake' which went a bit leathery. On Sunday, 28 October 1917, Kennedy was caught in the retreat from Gorizia as soldiers fled before machine gunners and mules and wagons overturned into the ditches. He was forced to abandon his car and run. 'I shall never forget,' he wrote home, 'the moving mass of men, carts, guns and lorries rushing as fast as possible utterly regardless of whom they trampled or crushed beneath them.'

In the retreat the unit lost twenty vehicles and was forced to abandon the Villa Trento. But the British party had proved a great success, rising to five units by the end of the war. Its members received twenty-eight *Croce al merito di Guerra* and eight silver medals for military valour. The unit had consisted of two cars with movable X-ray equipment run by two severe-looking women, Countess Helena Gleichen, daughter of Prince Victor of Hohenlohe-Langenburg, and Mrs Nina Hollings, who reported in August 1916 that they had X-rayed 'not only 49 heads, 58 thorax, 8 abdomen, 27 pelvises etc. but 2 horses and a mule.' 'We chose our zones deliberately and continually where the dangers of our work of rescue might be equal to the dangers undergone by the combatants,' wrote the poet and climber Geoffrey Winthrop Young, who came to the Villa Trento after serving at Ypres.

George Trevelyan, Kenneth Kennedy and Freya Stark all spoke of the closeness and intimacy between the members of the Italian unit. 'And so, after all, things came out at the end as nearly perfectly for us as human affairs ever do,' wrote Trevelyan later. 'It was a "Unit" indeed, with a soul of its own, not a mere aggregation of individuals. It left its impress on all of us . . . a fellowship which was an end in itself.'

In the late spring of 1919, the unit gathered once more at Paganini's restaurant in London. They ate salmon, chicken and asparagus, and signed a poem written by Young:

> But whate'ver our toil
> We'll know we grew together a long day,
> One small oasis, lifting, green and far,
> Merciful arms above the deserts of war.

The campaign in Serbia, with its military defeats and terrible diseases, struck a particular chord with the British. Of all the fronts on which the British Red Cross Society served, Serbia was possibly the toughest; it lasted for nearly four years, and not all the volunteers survived. But it was also the most free, far from the controlling hand of the British military. It drew in the rich and titled ladies, and also the new women doctors, VADs and nurses.

In the summer of 1914 the Austrians invaded Serbia with five army corps, advancing from the north and north-west. The European nations assumed that the Serbs, with an army only a third of the size of the Austrian army and far less powerful weapons, would be defeated swiftly. For a while, the Serbs fell back. But, strengthened by supplies of French ammunition and fighting with immense courage, they kept the Austro-Hungarian troops out of Belgrade for over four months and then began to push back. Town after town was recaptured, in a remarkable campaign that saw an Austrian retreat disintegrate into chaotic flight. By New Year's Day 1915 there was no Austrian soldier left on Serbian soil, except for 70,000 prisoners-of-war.

In October 1914 the joint committee in London, answering a desperate call for help from the Serbs, had decided to send a medical unit of six doctors and twelve orderlies to Serbia. In the weeks that followed other medical teams began to arrive, many of them consisting of women. There would be 500 British volunteers in Serbia by the summer of 1915. Though the Americans, the French and the Russians all sent medical teams, the work done by the British women stands out, not least because of the stir it caused in the British press — they were widely referred to as that 'noble band of women' — and because many were such good writers.

There was Lady Muriel Paget, wife of Sir Ralph Paget, a former British minister to Serbia and herself a veteran of the two Balkan wars of 1912 and 1913, who stares severely out of photographs in her starched Red Cross uniform, with her long face and disapproving mouth, sporting surprisingly frivolous earrings. She was a strange woman, generous, impulsive and a good golfer (though she was said to over-call at bridge) and the daughter of highly unconventional parents. Her father, Lord Winchilsea, was reputed to have the finest collection in Britain of eagles' eggs and hobbies that ranged from brick-laying to bell-ringing and digging dykes, while her mother was interested in the poor and the elderly and organized races for the over-80s in her village. Lady Paget set up her unit at Skopje.

Mrs Mabel St Clair Stobart was another veteran of the Balkan wars who, having taken an ambulance to Brussels on the outbreak of war had been arrested by the Germans and narrowly escaped being shot as a spy. Mrs St Clair Stobart was fifty, small, slight, fine-featured and sharp-boned, with a specially designed dark floppy hat and beautiful thick dark hair. A mystic, an authority on the Apocrypha and possessed of apparently limitless energy, she was a renowned horsewoman, a county tennis champion, a golfer and a fine angler. She had been a pioneer settler in the South African veldt. Not everyone found her easy: she was decidedly autocratic and her eyes seemed to stare disconcertingly towards a more interesting distant spot. Then there was Dr Elsie Inglis, devout, smiling and stubborn, one of the first British-trained women doctors and a strict authoritarian, her insistence on order redeemed by a good sense of humour. She wore a homburg with a wide tartan band. With these women, coming and going, setting up outlying dressing stations or driving ambulances, were Mabel Dearmer, who had said that although she had no skills, 'I am an ordinary, sensible woman and can learn quickly,' Dr Alice Hutchinson, who had bright red gold hair, and Mrs Harley, sister of Field Marshal Viscount French, who ran a flying column until killed by a shell in the spring of 1917.

In 1909 a French medical team had discovered that typhus, associated with dirt, overcrowding, famine and poverty, lived in the blood of rats, mice and humans, and was transmitted by lice in clothes and hair. The Serbian campaign was remarkable for the appalling conditions suffered by all, hundreds of sick and wounded men lying for days in open wagons or the filthy overcrowded corridors of hospitals. In January 1915 typhus became endemic, spreading rapidly through barracks and hospitals, among the Serbian army and the Austrian prisoners-of-war at the rate of 9,000 new cases every day. An anonymous dresser with the Serbian unit of the Scottish Women's Hospital left a diary which opened on 3 January 1915, at Skopje where Lady Paget was at work. It is, she wrote, 'like trying to drain the sea. More and more come in . . . They are put down anywhere, for the doctors to attend to or not, as they can; and ragged men lie in the fields, and huddle round the doors, with filthy suppurating wounds and die like flies.' From London, the British Red Cross appointed Sir Ralph Paget commissioner for the area and a battle against typhus was launched. A team of British doctors arrived to help the Serbs break the line of infection between the troops and the civilian population. A disinfection programme began with quarantine stations, the scrubbing and rescrubbing of cinemas, hotels and restaurants; train carriages were stripped of their upholstery back to bare wood. Some buildings were so badly infested the decision was taken to burn them. All new patients were washed thoroughly and completely shaved as the volunteer doctors and nurses took over wards full of men covered in bedsores and gangrenous wounds. 'Only a Zola,' wrote the unknown Scottish dresser, 'could have done justice to a description of the mingled smells of crowded human beings, foul wounds, tobacco . . . and greasy Serbian food.' The nurses had their own hair cropped and kept under a tight skull cap, masks covered their faces and they wore long cotton shifts with baggy trousers tucked into gumboots, their socks tightly bound at the ankle with bandages soaked in naphthalene. Lady Muriel caught typhus, but was nursed back to health.

Mrs St Clair Stobart arrived in Kragujevac with her third Serbian relief fund unit, nearly seventy strong, in April. The weather was fine, the typhus epidemic seemed at last to be waning and there were nightingales, larks and cuckoos. Within a few days a hospital village of tents, portable latrines, baths and disinfection areas had risen on the racecourse. Mrs St Clair Stobart ran a tight ship. Breakfast was at 6 a.m., lights out at 9 p.m. One of her most idiosyncratic doctors was Lilian Chesney, a gifted surgeon who did her rounds followed by a pet pig to which she fed squares of chocolate. Dr Chesney had a wig to put over her cropped skull, and loathed those she called 'socialites', the VADs who had come to Serbia to help. Mrs St Clair Stobart started a number of travelling roadside dispensaries, to which refugees now flocked with dysentery, diphtheria, TB and terrible skin infections. She arranged for two oxen, known as Derry and Toms after the London shop, to pull her ambulances.

Further south, two young women had just arrived to join the British Red Cross unit at Vranjska. Elsie Corbett was twenty-three, the only daughter of Lord Rowallan, and had played as a child with a toy Red Cross hospital with nurses and tents. The Corbetts were well connected and very social, and Elsie had done four London seasons by the time the war broke out. A family friend suggested she should volunteer for Serbia, being neither old enough nor well enough trained — she had done a short Red Cross course — to serve in France where, at the start of the war volunteers had to be at least twenty-five. She joined a party of twelve nurses, four VADs, and a doctor and four orderlies, with a matron to chaperone the younger women and set off for the front on board the *Erin*, whose owner, Sir Thomas Lipton, a fanatical yachtsman who dreamed of winning the Americas Cup, was ferrying Red Cross volunteers to the war. It was a highly enjoyable trip via Sardinia, Malta, Athens and the Corinth Canal, sitting on deck browsing through *Baedekers*, cheered by the crews of battleships and entertaining admirals for dinner under the kindly eye of the florid and genial Sir Thomas, who had an immense white moustache. On board, she met Kathleen Dillon, a renowned rider and the daughter of a distinguished Oxfordshire family, with whom she would spend the rest of her life. The last stage of the journey was by train from Salonika, past swamps with storks, orchards of pollarded mulberry trees and white opium poppies in fields of purple vetch.

Vranjska Banja had been a fashionable spa; it was here that a number of the foreign units congregated, setting up their hospitals in the casino and pump rooms or in villas with views over the forests and mountains. An Austrian prisoner-of-war called Karl, who had once been a head waiter in London, was detailed to help the third unit. The meadows around their base, wrote Elsie Corbett, were 'shimmering with wild flowers by day and all alight with the tiny spark of fireflies' at night. Sir Thomas and his party came to call and a blackberry and crayfish expedition was organized to entertain them. During the first few months, while the typhus continued to abate and there was a lull in the war, the various foreign units led a pleasurable and social existence. There were tea parties with members of the other units and excursions to pick wild strawberries; the red-haired Dr Hutchinson held regular 'at homes' with *tableaux vivants*, Serbian national music and even once a costume ball, at which nurses, sick of their cropped hair and ungainly shifts, appeared as queens and clowns. There was a fat nurse with huge lungs who blew the bugle. A shy brother and sister called Ellis arrived at the spa in their own lorry and spoke very little except to talk about grouse shooting and salmon fishing at home. In the afternoons Elsie Corbett looked after the hens, ducks and geese presented by grateful patients.

She was fortunate in having an easy-going matron in Miss Calwell, a friend of Yeats and Lady Gregory, who liked to read German poetry aloud. Miss Calwell had no time for germs but this scarcely mattered, noted Elsie, for 'under her compelling eye the most daring microbes fled'. In June, an epidemic of typhoid defied her, and two of the volunteers died. One was Mabel Dearmer, who had said not long before: 'I

227

am like a young lion – no, a middle-aged and cheerful lion – but I am feeling very fit indeed', the other a popular twenty-five-year-old nurse called Lorna Ferris who was about to leave for London to get married. They were given a funeral with full military honours, their silver coffins draped in the Union Jack and the King's Guard playing Beethoven's funeral march. A French officer said of Mabel Dearmer that '*elle est tombée avec la noblesse d'un soldat*'. The anonymous dresser decided to send her diary home with a departing nurse, saying that when men went home they never told the truth. 'Being a woman myself, I have no such feeling . . . No brain can realize the awful misery of war.' Dr Chesney attempted to lighten the mood by holding a gymkhana, without horses but with musical chairs and stretcher and crutch races instead.

Serbia was surrounded by enemies. In early October 1915 the Austro-German forces attacked; on the 8th they took Belgrade. Casualties began to pour into the hospitals, many of them with wounds already going septic. On 12 October Bulgaria attacked from the east. The British and French who had promised support – 'without qualifications and without reserve', as Sir Edward Grey, the foreign minister, had put it – did nothing. In Vranyska Banja there was much discussion and much anxiety about whether to go or stay. Lady Muriel declared that it was her intention to give help to 'all who were absolutely destitute and without resources, regardless of nationality' and to stay put. The Bulgarians arrived and famine spread, temperatures dropped and bands of boys, 'shoeless, destitute and covered in lice' came begging for help. She and Dr Hutchinson were both eventually taken prisoner, but Lady Paget managed to arrange with her friend Queen Eleonara of Bulgaria for her unit to be repatriated. By the spring of 1916 she was back in London, where she was severely criticized for accepting the help of the Bulgarian queen. Elsie Corbett, Kathleen Dillon and a number of other doctors and nurses decided to stay on and were able to go on working under the Austrians more or less normally, but with sentries posted outside their hospitals, until they too were repatriated.

Asking for eighteen volunteers from among her unit, Mrs St Clair Stobart decided to take her own flying field hospital and make for the coast where she hoped to find Allied ships to carry them to Corfu or Corsica. It was a terrible journey, across some of the most hazardous and inhospitable mountains of Montenegro and Albania. A final Serbian attempt at resistance failed when ammunition ran out and 200,000 men, in total chaos and lacking all provisions, joined the long trek over the mountains. The seventy-six-year-old King Peter, half paralysed with rheumatism, went with them. Mrs St Clair Stobart and her unit, as well as two groups from the Scottish women's hospital, were soon part of an immense sea of men, guns, horses, refugees and bullock wagons struggling up passes blocked by landslides and mud that grew deeper and more slippery every day. Caroline Tufnel, a British volunteer, died when her lorry went over a cliff; Ginger Clifton, a nurse, was wounded when a gun went off, but recovered. Oxen and wagons stuck fast in the mud and it snowed hard. Soon the only food left was raw flesh torn from the dead horses that lay by the roadside. All along the way they came across little huddles of forlorn boys, between the ages of twelve and sixteen, who had been forced to join the trek by the Serbian authorities who saw in them a future for a new Serbia. Few had ever been away from home before; they were hungry, terrified and miserable. At Prizren, once a fine medieval city and now crammed with wretched refugees, sixty members of various foreign units met up and agreed to make the rest, and as it turned out the worst, of the journey together. The women got rid of their cotton shifts and put on trousers made of army blankets.

Much of the track lay along a narrow shelf, just wide enough for two. Mrs – now known as 'Major' amongst Serbian soldiers – St Clair Stobart decided to push on with her unit, though some of her assistants rebelled and preferred to stay with the other volunteers. She had been given a black horse by the Serbians, so as to be more easily visible to her followers and she now made the running, plodding relentlessly ahead, spending anything up to eighty-one hours at a stretch in the saddle. She was helped by a twenty-four-year-old debutante called Cissy Benjamin who handled the extremely meagre supplies. The women seldom spoke; all that could be heard above what Mrs St Clair Stobart crossly called the 'silence of a funeral procession' was the squelching of mud. The journey took five weeks. When Mrs St Clair Stobart did eventually reach London, she was censured for her foolhardiness in pressing ahead, though she did not lose a single member of her unit. Angered and upset, she retired to a life of mysticism and the spirits. Out of the 200,000 Serbian soldiers who had set off on the walk to the coast, at least 40,000 died. Only 10,000 of the boys reached safety.

Elsie Corbett and Kathleen Dillon were two of a handful of volunteers who decided to return to Serbia. By August 1916 they had learnt how to drive and repair Fords, and they enrolled in the First Scottish Women's Hospital Motor Ambulance Column. They were back in Serbia for the next major offensive, when the Serbs regrouped to rid their country of the invaders. Elsie Corbett's account of their adventures, told many years later in *The Red Cross in Serbia*, is uncomplaining, humorous and totally unsentimental. It is a story of terrible roads, endless punctures, of freezing cold kept at bay with hot water bottles and good stews, of 'handsome air raids', suppers with Tubby, the unit doctor, and doing 'runs after tea' to collect the wounded. On 31 March 1916 she was caught in an air attack. 'My Serb officer patient became hysterical, of course, and wanted me to stop and let him get into a funk-hole.' She pushed on. Occasionally, the two young women took a few days' leave when they climbed the mountains, walked in the fir woods and watched the eagles circling in the valleys far below. After the war they received a letter from a Serbian officer they had met. Calling them by the strange name of 'fay', he told them that they would be 'for centuries the subject of the hero-tales and hero-poetry of our people. Proud they will be who could tell to have been driven as wounded or sick by these fays.'

On Armistice Day, Elsie Corbett was in Belgrade, severely ill with a mastoid abscess. She survived and returned to share Kathleen Dillon's home, Spelsbury House in Charlbury, Oxfordshire where she spent the next forty years hunting and becoming involved in local affairs. 'We seemed to be passing from the horrors and self-sacrifice of a noble war,' she wrote, 'to the horrors and selfishness of a most ignoble peace.'

NINE

The Greatest Mother in the World

Though the interest of the International Committee in civil wars and 'internal troubles' was as old as the Red Cross movement itself, the First World War broke out before there was time to draw up any coherent international agreement about them. True, the Committee had intervened in the second Carlist war of 1872 in Spain, and by the summer of 1914 had offered help in no fewer than nineteen civil wars. But the Boer war, among others, had brought to light the very real dilemma that faced the International Committee when a country – in this case Britain – simply refused to regard what was happening in South Africa as a civil war.

The whole subject of civil war and who, if anyone, should be responsible for its victims, had been tossed inconclusively from meeting to meeting, between Geneva and The Hague, for decades. Even President Ador had been able to do little more than soothe tempers when the Russian delegate to the Washington conference of 1912 had fallen out with the American representative, the one dismissing insurrectionists as criminals, the other welcoming them as soldiers. The conference had on the whole been little inclined to devote much time to civil wars, the mood towards them being, if anything, that they were things that happened to other people, far away. The Russian revolution of 1917 was to challenge this indifference.

There had been a Red Cross society in Imperial Russia since 1867, shaped largely by the aristocracy and under the extremely active patronage, as we have seen, of the Dowager Empress Maria Feodorovna and the ladies of her court. Having embarked on the war against Japan in 1904 complacently unprepared and emerged from it humiliated and battered, the Russian society had spent the years of peace that followed practising conscientiously on a series of natural calamities. By 1914 it was in good shape. With a magnificent headquarters in St Petersburg, it boasted over 500 hospitals and convalescent homes, some 8,000 trained doctors and nurses supported by 4,500 nuns and a large number of 'felcher', partially trained helpers, whose qualifications placed them somewhere between doctors and medical students. There were hospital trains with steam baths that had already impressed foreign visitors, as well as disinfection wagons, a post office, a shop and a rolling stable for horses. The Russian Red Cross nurses wore white overalls over their grey linen uniforms; they worked with their arms bare, their sleeves rolled high above their elbows. When it was cold, they put on leather jackets and boots with high tops, which was said to make them look rather like English bus conductors.

At the start of the war, the Russian army under Grand Duke Nikolai, first cousin of the tsar, had advanced rapidly and with little opposition until it crossed the German frontier to occupy Prussia. Then, as supplies of ammunition ran out, it faltered and turned. Its retreat began slowly, but grew faster and more disorganized as the Germans pushed the Russians steadily back towards Warsaw. The Polish dirt roads were churned into mud by heavy rains, transport wagons and field guns. The wounded men, one German wrote, turned the track into 'mud and blood'. They were joined by civilians fleeing the German advance from the plains of Lithuania, the ports of the Baltic, and the mountains of Galicia. Fields of grass and corn near stations and railway tracks were flattened as soldiers and civilians surged towards the few trains that could carry them towards safety. By the end of 1915, as the winter descended with a ferocity that had not been seen for years, St Petersburg (now renamed Petrograd) and Moscow had doubled in size, with more wounded and destitute arriving every day. Moscow alone now had 1,275 hospitals.

The Russian army medical services had been overwhelmed from the beginning. Within a week of the outbreak of the war, however, the Union of Zemstvos, unofficial local societies born at the time of the Russo-Japanese war to help the government with money and provisions, had come forward to offer to supply clothes, medicines and equipment to the army. Under the efficient and energetic Prince Georgi Lvov, the Union was, by the end of the first year of the war, not only running hospitals, ambulances, trains and canteens, as well as feeding some of the military units, but also working at the front, manning field hospitals and, where it could, helping the ever-growing number of homeless civilians. The Union had adopted the red cross as its emblem – another example of the way that Dunant's dream was permitted to take off in different directions, not always supervised too closely by Geneva – and between them, the two organizations, which had become facets of one single military-driven organization, were providing the bulk of the care for the sick and wounded. Bernard Pares, a British volunteer who worked in a forward hospital with the Third Army in Galicia – later professor of Russian history and literature at Liverpool University – described the Red Cross workers he served with admiringly: 'There was no drunkenness,' he wrote, 'everyone was at his best, and it was the simplest and noblest atmosphere in which I have ever lived.' The Red Cross general command had its own carriage, coupled to one of its 300 hospital trains, with a carpet, a hip bath and an upright piano.

Petrograd, by the time the retreat was in full spate, had become one vast hospital camp. Gone were the sumptuous banquets and receptions described by the last French ambassador to the Russian court, Maurice Paléologue, as a 'blaze of fire and flame', a 'fantastic shower of diamonds, pearls, rubies, sapphires, emeralds'. Many of the larger houses had been turned into hospitals, the electric trains doubled as ambulances and volunteers queued for hours in the streets to collect material from central depots to make into clothes and bandages for the army. Students and young women from good families waited at Petrograd's stations to greet the wounded as they came off the trains, though enemy prisoners-of-war were not always civilly received, the larger hospitals having what they called a 'menagerie' in which the prisoners were looked after. Inside their palaces, the dowager empress and the grand duchesses, in their Red Cross uniforms, directed women working as seamstresses. The imperial grand duke, the Duke of Oldenburg, had been put in charge of all relief work. The Winter Palace housed a royal hospital, in which the tsarina could be found preparing instruments for amputations, Russian doctors still being very much in favour of amputating. Society ladies joined in the rush for the front, receiving a blessing for their 'holy deeds' from the Metropolitan in the Hall of Catherine the Great as their units left for the war. They piled their hair severely under plain white handkerchiefs, left their maids behind and soon found themselves at

work in dressing stations where the floors were permanently slippery
with blood, and the smell of sweat, disinfectant and soiled bandages was
overwhelming. The ladies of Russia were proving no less dedicated to
war than their British counterparts.

Violetta Thurstan, a FANY whose chance meeting with Maria Feodorovna's nephew led her to volunteer for the Russian front, left a
detailed account of the Russian aristocracy at war in letters to her aunt
at home, scribbled in pencil. They are matter-of-fact in tone, the same
mixture of travel notes, sentimental high-spiritedness and gory descriptions as the many memoirs written from the French trenches. Attached
to Prince Volkonsky's Flying Ambulance, she was sent to train with
other would-be Red Cross sisters in the Smolny Convent, once a fashionable school for the daughters of the nobility. Here, she was able to
observe the royal princesses, Anastasia, Maria and Tatiana, when they
came to help bandage hospital patients. There was no difficulty with
language, as most of her fellow trainees had been cared for as children
by English nannies and governesses. Violetta Thurstan was amazed by
the size of Petrograd, describing it as a 'city for giants' made of 'blocks,
hewn by Titans'.

Within a few weeks, she was working under Princess Volkonsky in a
field dressing station in Lódź, which had been cut off by the Germans.
The unit was based in a school, which had no heating; blankets were
in very short supply. Her job was to sterilize instruments by boiling
them in water, but the pipes had frozen solid. Every patient and soon
every nurse was covered in insects, the 'red ones,' she noted, being far
'more ravenous' than the white ones. She longed for a hot water bottle.
The prince, 'grey faced' and as 'tall as a pine tree', and the princess, 'small,
fair and vivacious', were tireless, pausing sometimes only at midnight to
share a loaf of bread and a bottle of wine, before returning to spend the
rest of the night preparing the wounded for surgery the next morning.
After Lódź fell, Violetta Thurstan joined Grand Duchess Anastasia's
hospital, alternating long days of nursing with visits to aristocratic
families on their country estates.

In November 1915, the Anglo-Russian hospital, established by Lady Muriel
Paget when she heard from Bernard Pares of the huge numbers of

Russian casualties in the winter of 1914, funded by the British public and supported by the British Red Cross, arrived in Petrograd to set up a base hospital and organize three field hospitals for the eastern front. It was to be a gift from the British to the Russian people. Its emblem, a woodcut carved by Sir Richard Paget showing a British lion and a Russian double-headed eagle holding up a Red Cross, perfectly captured the ambivalent position of the hospital, expressing something between sympathy for the suffering of Russian soldiers and embarrassment that the British were not able to do more to meet Russia's military needs.

Lady Muriel, fresh from her triumphs in France, was in charge together with the daughter of another British earl, Lady Sybil Grey, who had joined the VADs. Lady Georgina Buchanan, wife of the British ambassador to Russia and also the daughter of an earl, was already running a separate establishment, the British Colony Hospital. The three ladies were formidable, brave, dutiful and decidedly rivalrous. They were supported by a number of British surgeons, doctors and radiologists, all resolute-looking figures in their military greatcoats and heavy moustaches. There were also sixty-four British nurses and VADs, interviewed and appointed by Lady Muriel and vetted by the Foreign Office, who were soon having trouble learning Russian, quarrelling over their inadequate quarters and the lack of Cross and Blackwell jam, and protesting when they were sent to make up bandages in the Winter Palace.

There was some trouble finding suitable premises for the hospital, but Grand Duke Dmitri Pavlovich offered the *piano nobile* of the palace belonging to his aunt, the tsar's sister, a magnificent baroque building with attics full of elderly retainers and very little plumbing at 41 Nevsky Prospect, opposite the pink palace of the dowager empress. The grand-duke would soon be Prince Yusupov's chief assistant in Rasputin's assassination. It took several months to cover the priceless parquet floors and engraved plaster walls with plywood. The opening ceremony was attended by the Russian court, 'strung all over' as Lady Sybil remarked, 'with medals and orders like an Xmas tree', and the imperial choir, 'in claret red and gold, singing the Graces'. Lady Sybil had wisely thought to bring her jewels to Russia. Crowds gathered on the Nevsky Prospect to watch a sailor climb to the roof to fly a Union Jack. The wards had been decorated for the occasion with pots of tulips and 'groves of palm trees', thoughtfully loaned by the Russian Red Cross.

Both Lady Sybil and Lady Muriel — who arrived at the end of April 1915, after a progress through Norway, Sweden and Finland — led field hospitals to the front after the Russian High Command, in order to relieve the pressure on Verdun, had opened an offensive in marshy country near Vilna, which left thousands of Russian casualties. Taking thirty-seven train carriages loaded with supplies, horses, mobile kitchens and medical staff, they roamed the countryside, picking up the wounded, suffering miseries in the seas of mud and icy gales, and pausing to picnic or play bridge when the sun shone. They were tormented by flies. Matron, who was being taught to ride, fell from her stationary horse and hit her head on a post. Lady Sybil noted that the Russian officers were 'v. exigeante & fussy, poor dears'. Lady Muriel was always keen to get 'closer to the enemy'. At the end of July 1916, the Anglo-Russian hospital was caught in the middle of a four-day battle along the banks of the River Stokhod; they nursed 538 wounded men, carried out seventy-four operations and lost only twenty-one patients. Later, Lady Muriel received a medal of St George, Second Class, for her part in it. At the end of December, following the assassination of Rasputin, Grand Duke Dmitri and Prince Yusupov took refuge in the palace on Nevsky Prospect that housed the hospital; amid rumours that both men were to be arrested and executed, Lady Sybil calmly oversaw the removal of a fishbone that had lodged in Prince Yusupov's throat.

The nurses of the Anglo-Russian hospital had an excellent view of the uprising in Petrograd in March 1917. They had been watching the lengthening queues of people waiting in the freezing cold with bread tickets and were not altogether surprised at rumours of possible bread riots. On the morning of Friday, 9 March, they stood at the windows overlooking the Nevsky Prospect to see striking mill hands and munitions workers gather below, jostled by Cossacks riding up and down among them. There were shots and they saw people fall. Thirty soldiers had been detailed to guard the hospital, but even so Lady Sybil thought it prudent to make up Red Cross flags out of sheets and an old Father Christmas costume and string them from the balcony. Casualties began to be carried into the wards and there were several unnerving moments when mobs threatened to search the building before being stopped by the loyal Russian orderlies. Troops of soldiers now joined the revolutionaries; the thirty hospital guards vanished. On 15 March, Tsar Nicholas

II abdicated and a provisional government was formed under Prince Georgi Lvov, the man behind the Zemstvos. He was soon replaced by Kerensky. One night, as Lady Sybil was doing her last rounds, students with revolvers burst in; she thought they were demanding wine, but finally understood that they had come to offer it, Kerensky having ordered that Petrograd's wine cellars be emptied to prevent drunkenness and their contents given to hospitals.

The Russian Red Cross, child of Russia's court and aristocracy, did not fare well in the months to follow. Orders were issued immediately that it was to be placed under a special committee of the Duma and that there was to be a 'purification of the central administration', a sweeping away of the old guard. The vast apparatus and network of the Red Cross, working efficiently alongside and with the union of Zemstvos, now rapidly fell apart, as new committees, sub-committees and delegations set themselves up to appoint new — and inexperienced — officers uncontaminated by aristocratic connections. Red Cross activities, whether at the front or in the supply depots, came to an almost complete stop.

Towards the end of June, a national conference of Red Cross employees opened in Petrograd. It was very unlike the staid and opulent gatherings of pre-war years. The first session was devoted to chasing out all 'reactionary elements'. At the second, a resolution was enthusiastically carried which denounced the Russian society for being run by favourites of the tsar who had furthered their own careers, recklessly spending money levied on the people, and for having been a refuge for rich and titled young men escaping military service. It was a tribute to the respect felt in Russia for the Geneva Convention and the whole apparatus of the Red Cross that it was not simply dismantled and left to die. When the final session came, delegates vowed to cleanse the society of all remaining aristocratic tendencies and to raise in its place a 'temple to international philanthropy . . . in the name of a new national Russian Red Cross', which would 'help our people in epidemics, in droughts and other national calamities'.

There were a few protests, soon silenced. Officers to run the new body were recruited among doctors, nurses and even drivers not tainted by the old regime. The Swiss businessman F. Thormeyer, who had lived and worked in Russia for some years and was to serve as a delegate, inspecting prison camps, wrote sadly to the International Committee about the loss of excellent and competent administrators whom he had come to know and admire, and on the rapid descent of the Russian Red Cross into incompetence and anarchy. The decision to bring it directly under the control of the ministry of war was, he added, a 'death sentence'. He was right. At the front, as the provisional government sank into confusion, chaos spread, with Red Cross nurses deserting their posts and the nuns appointed to help them fleeing back to their communities as the wounded and sick men they were caring for caught the committee bug and began to vote for their own nursing routines.

From Geneva, Ador and the International Committee viewed the disintegration of the Russian society with alarm: it was the first time a national society had been destroyed by its own government. They were also faced with an immediate problem. Under the Red Cross statutes, only one society per country could be formally recognized, even if other groups were welcomed as collaborators. The old Russian society, crushed at home, had gone underground where it continued to function and protest, helped by the many foreign branches which had flowered in various European capitals. Meanwhile, the new Russian Red Cross society was demanding recognition. After much debate, it was decided to do nothing at all while the war continued but to acknowledge both bodies, without comment, even if Thormeyer regarded the various turmoils with considerable foreboding. 'They bear a heavy responsibility,' he wrote about the society's new leaders. 'History will judge them, not by their theories, but by the results of their actions.' The October 1918 issue of the *Bulletin* contained a brief reference to the new Russian society, formed under a Dr Levsky; uncharacteristically it reproached the 'Russian revolutionaries' for their 'indescribable' behaviour.

Yet the Russian revolution had many interesting repercussions for the Red Cross men in Geneva, among them unsolved questions as to who did and who did not fall under the mandate of the International Committee, particularly those in an entirely new category: that of political prisoners.

Lenin reached Petrograd in April 1917. In October, after months of struggle, councils of workers, peasants and soldiers took power and set up a Congress of Soviets. By then, the Council of the People's Commissars had transferred all the assets of the old Red Cross to the state and confiscated much of its extremely valuable property.

The International Committee had no representative in Petrograd, but Edouard Odier, one of its vice-presidents, happened to be serving in Russia as Swiss minister. He now persuaded Geneva to let him appoint Edouard Frick, a Swiss national who had been working as a volunteer with the Russian Red Cross since 1914, as their delegate, and prevailed on the new Russian authorities to allow him to carry out routine International Committee tasks, as a mark of their commitment to the Geneva Convention.

On the outbreak of war, Russia had interned many thousands of foreign civilians; the revolution had seen the detention of many more, no longer simply 'enemy civilians' but internal 'political' dissidents. These fell under the military and the department dealing with prisoners-of-war. As the new Soviet regime descended further into lawlessness, shortages and social upheaval, so the conditions of these men and women began to deteriorate. Frick was an energetic and clear-sighted man, and he made the most of the constantly changing cast of new Red Cross figures, appointed only to be arrested and themselves investigated. Before waiting for confirmation of his new job he called on ministers to make certain that they understood the importance, to their own Russian soldiers and prisoners-of-war, of honouring their international commitments. Feeling his way into a role never before explored by the International Committee, he set about organizing the representatives of neutral foreign Red Cross societies into a badly needed co-ordinating body, tried to negotiate exchanges of hostages with the White Russians — those loyal to the imperial family — and sent off missions to the war front to report on conditions and epidemics. Everywhere he went, he spoke about the importance of a truly neutral, international, humanitarian body, to help not only prisoners-of-war, but 'unfortunate people in general'. In both Moscow and Petrograd, he managed to convince the authorities to let him set up special committees for the welfare of political prisoners and, in the process of taking in food and medicine, was able to determine the conditions in which they were being kept. It was the first time an International Committee delegate had been able to include political detainees among his constituents. The Soviets treated Frick courteously, at least on the surface, but let it be known that they frowned on too much help going to members of the former aristocracy. Comrade Frick was encouraged to turn his attentions to proper prisoners-of-war. When the International Committee seemed to be dragging its heels in giving full recognition to the new Russian society, some of Frick's plans were abruptly cancelled.

The new Soviet government signed an armistice with the Central Powers on 15 December 1917; under the terms of the Treaty of Brest-Litovsk, signed in March 1918, the Russians surrendered the Ukraine, Finland, the Baltic provinces, the Caucasus, White Russia and Poland. In Petrograd, the Anglo-Russian Hospital was handed over to the new Russian Red Cross, and Lady Muriel departed for Odessa, where the Bolsheviks were in control, with a number of the remaining British doctors and nurses. By now, conditions in the new Russia were bleak, and becoming bleaker all the time, creating what was to be an enormous task for the International Committee in the years to come.

*　　*　　*

There will be little of sleeping tonight;
There will be wailing and weeping tonight;
Death's red sickle is reaping tonight;
War! War! War!

So wrote an American Red Cross volunteer soon after the outbreak of war in 1914. His rousing and passionate tones, however, were not really matched by American commitment. Exhausted by giving to so many natural disasters, their minds turned inwards rather than towards a war 3,000 miles away in Europe. Americans responded sluggishly to early Red Cross appeals for help for the war: recruiting stands were set up on street corners, with banners saying 'Nurses, the call from No Man's Land is Come Across', but few chose to listen.

And some Americans, voicing the paradox that had long troubled its critics, continued to have real doubts about the moral basis of the Red Cross involvement in war itself. 'No Red Cross aid ought to be sent out in a war,' wrote a reporter called Miss Durham, who had covered the fighting in the Balkans, to a newspaper. 'To heal men's wounds and send them back to the front as soon as possible is to prolong war indefinitely.' What the American public really felt proud about was their highly developed peacetime programme, best exemplified perhaps by Commodore Wilbert E. Longfellow, known in the newspapers as the 'amiable whale', a huge, smiling man who travelled around America teaching swimming to Red Cross classes with an immense swimsuit stretched tight over his generous middle.

On 6 April 1917, the day that Congress voted for war, the mood changed. 'It is for you to decide whether the most prosperous nation in the world will allow its national relief organization to keep up with its work,' Woodrow Wilson addressed the nation, 'or withdraw from a field where there exists the greatest need ever recorded in history.' Now, the public rallied. President Wilson himself put sheep to graze on the White House lawn, later auctioning their wool. A war council was appointed within the American Red Cross; the country was divided into sectors; 'flying squadrons' of Red Cross leaders took off for the rich western states; quotas were set; chapters were fanned into life; meetings were held and fundraising lunches organized. 'She is an enthusiast of the tensely quiet sort,' one newspaper described Mabel Boardman, who was still at the helm of the American Red Cross, 'capable, clever and executive ... with ... a certain shrewdness, backed by dogged persistency.'

However, what the Americans wanted was not a dogged and quiet woman, but an energetic and outspoken man, with considerable powers of oratory. Mabel Boardman was pushed aside to make way for Henry P. Davison, a man who had risen from messenger boy to partner in J. Pierpont Morgan & Co., popular with his colleagues and good at catchy and quotable phrases. Davison was now appointed by the American Red Cross as chairman of the war council. He was fifty, good-tempered, selfless – his biographer would later complain that it was very difficult to write about a man who 'spoke little, and wrote nothing, about himself' – tolerant and decisive, and his crusading, homespun zeal with its particular blend of paternalism, whimsy and shrewdness touched some chord with the American public. 'The Red Cross never thanks people,' he announced. 'It congratulates them', perfectly capturing what was to be the American Red Cross mood of the war. 'Our job ... is to bind up the wounds of a bleeding world ... Think Red Cross! Talk Red Cross! Be Red Cross! Those people over there have been fighting for us; they have been bleeding for us,' he told a crowd of supporters. 'And we are going around those 3,000 miles of distress and death and we are going to say to those people: "We are late, but we are coming . . . We are today the richest people in the world, and the richest people in character and resources, the richest in money, and, I believe, as rich in sentiment as any people God ever made."' The powerful appeal of his message, the deliberate placing of America as the most generous of all international relief donors, would stamp not just the war years but the future of the entire Red Cross movement. How far Ador and his colleagues, few of whom spoke English or had ever travelled to America, recognized what would become a major threat to their position, is not known.

The first American Red Cross casualty of the war was its neutrality, though some had long argued that it had never given very much to the Germans. All national Red Cross societies of countries at war automatically become, as we have seen, auxiliaries to their armies, but in America, hitherto provider of aid to the Allies and Central Powers alike, the ties to the military would become exceptionally close. Despite an official statement by the war council that it would provide 'every aid and comfort', wherever it could, Davison was personally very clear. 'As to whether we help the Germans or not,' he told a Red Cross rally in New York, 'the answer is "No". But if a wounded German or a wounded Turk falls within our lines he is treated just as tenderly and carefully as an American boy.' The word 'neutrality' disappeared from the American Red Cross masthead. Its mission henceforth, as the US solicitor general phrased it, was to 'assist in winning the war'. Though precisely just what this would consist of took several months to establish – 'Forty different field directors consulted forty different generals,' reported one official later, 'and got forty different answers' – the American Red Cross now set out to take exclusive control of all relief for the sick and wounded in the army and to help the American soldiers in every way they could devise.

For this, and for the 'spiritual regeneration' that Davison had in mind, they needed money in vast amounts. While the marble hall of the new American Red Cross headquarters in Washington seethed with volunteers, many of them more willing than skilled, Davison turned his attention to fund-raising. He was brilliant at it. From among his Wall Street friends he drew in Grayson Murphy, vice-president of the Guaranty Trust Co., Harvey Gibson, president of the Liberty National Bank, and George F. Baker Jr., vice-president of the First National Bank. One banker gave him a million dollars; Henry Ford donated 5,000 Model Ts; clergymen were encouraged to pray for the success of the fund-raising campaign; the *Kansas City Star* was praised for running a headline 'Kansas City MUST have no slackers'; in Ohio, a woman gave a hen and a dozen eggs (auctioned for $2,002), and in New York, President Wilson was persuaded to lead a parade of 70,000 people down Fifth Avenue. Furthermore, the age of the Red Cross poster was born, which in years to come would see designers and artists all over the world produce exceptional art promoting the Red Cross message. Few, perhaps, are as memorable as Forsinger's saintly nurse, more Madonna than woman, cradling a wounded man over the caption: 'She's warming thousands, feeding thousands, healing thousands from her store: the greatest mother in the world: the Red Cross.' Later there was an acrimonious debate about Forsinger's model when Marguerite Fontrese, a mezzo-soprano from Cleveland, claimed that she had turned down a great operatic career to offer her services and Forsinger continued to insist that his model had been an artist called Miss Agnes Tait. There were also some protests from literal-minded military men, who objected that the poster was inaccurate as there were as yet no American Red Cross nurses at the front.

The fund-raising extravaganzas went on. Harry Gardner, the 'human fly', agreed to scale a New York skyscraper in a white suit with a large red cross painted on his back. Such was the response to the outdoor pageants, rallies, bazaars and 'Kick the Kaiser' parties that, according to Red Cross reports, vacuum cleaners were used to suck up the dollar bills. The first Red Cross war fund drive, in 1917, brought in over $100m and was reported to have involved more workers than any other single business venture in history.

In 1916, the American Red Cross had been dismayed to learn that while its membership stood at 31,000 members, Japan could count on 1.8 million and Germany on a million. A recruiting drive, brash, earnest and indiscriminate, was launched. Mabel Boardman, wearing a semi-uniform and what looked rather like a squashed top hat, now set about appealing to the volunteer spirit of American women. A knitting frenzy broke out and in what was later calculated to be two million hours at the needles, a pair of socks was soon being produced every twenty-five minutes. A tearful scandal in which it was said that these knitted garments were being thrown away — one woman claimed to have seen a marine 'actually cleaning the guns with a hand-knitted muffler because there was no other use for it' — was averted by soothing phrases from Davison that women were weaving a 'white magic . . . to shield their men from harm'. Red Cross chapters hastily issued instructions exhorting their members: 'DO NOT STOP KNITTING'. It was, wrote Davison later, 'the age of the wool: everybody was knitting'.

Children too were cleverly ensnared by vast junior drives that saw eight million of them join by 1918; they wore brassards and little red cross hats in school and scoured the countryside for tufts of wool scraped by sheep on to wire fences. The Junior Red Cross, Davison was to write, gave children a sense of 'responsibility, business management, thrift, co-operation, generosity, patriotism and altruism'. The number of members now grew dramatically, day after day. 'It was,' recalled one of the organizers, describing the first heady months of the war drive, 'a mess', like 'living in a cyclone'. And yet a contributor to the American Red Cross *Bulletin* was soon able to write, in one of the more fulsome of the many extravagant articles that now began appearing all across America:

> I am sustained by forty million souls. My mission is of mercy, kindness and charity . . . My reward is the gratitude of the widow and orphan, of the strong and the sick, of the unhappy and the bereaved . . . I lighten the horrors of the combat . . . I bury the dead. I help the halt. I cheer the sorrowful . . . I am the saviour of death. I am my brother's keeper. I am the Red Cross!

The American Red Cross, so went a saying that now did the rounds of Washington and New York, had been a toy balloon; overnight, it had become a Zeppelin.

The Red Cross girl, as described by the popular American journalist Richard Harding Davis, in a novel of that name written in 1912, had 'hair like a golden rod and eyes as blue as flax, and a complexion of such health and cleanliness and dewiness as blooms only on trained nurses'. When America at last entered the war, Belgium was crushed,

Russia disorganized and about to withdraw from the fight, France was ailing badly and Britain depleted of men, supplies, ammunition and energy. Europe had become an immense camp of the wounded, the dispossessed, the grieving and the sick. 'If you want to do something for me,' General Pershing, with the vanguard of what would become the American Expeditionary Force, told the American Red Cross, 'for God's sake buck up the French . . . They have been fighting for three years and are getting ready for their fourth winter.'

By the beginning of June 1917, Major Grayson M. P. Murphy, Davison's banker friend and a West Point man, was on his way to Europe; in his wake would flow legions of dewy nurses and blue-eyed Red Cross girls, vowing to turn the American soldier into the best fed, best cared for and most cherished fighting man in the world, and to bring supplies and solace to the suffering people of Europe. Their energy was boundless. The usefulness of the Red Cross message as propaganda was not lost on Davison. 'We must go over to our friends and "back them up",' read a statement issued by the headquarters in Washington, 'give them good cheer and sympathy as well as medicine and nurses and doctors and money and bread and meat. We must prepare at once to play a tremendous psychological part.' He regarded good planning as crucial. On board the *Lorraine*, bringing the first contingent of senior Red Cross men to Europe, Murphy told his volunteers that he would consider as extremely inefficient anyone who had not learnt French within three months. They started right away and were soon seen pacing up and down the decks with lists of vocabulary, coached by a young teacher from Smith College who happened to be on board.

From Bordeaux, the forward party caught a train to Paris, where a house in the rue François Ier had been the American relief clearing house since the beginning of the war. Murphy was in a hurry. Within weeks, missions had been despatched to draw up reports on needs throughout the country and the building was submerged under people and supplies, arriving by the ton every day. A second house, in the Place de la Concorde, was taken over; then several others; then the six-storey Hôtel Regina in the Place de Rivoli. The plan was to divide the work of the American Red Cross into a department of civil affairs, dealing with relief to civilians, and one of military affairs, to concentrate on the needs of the American soldiers soon to arrive in great numbers.

Paris, in the summer of 1917, was deserted and, apart from what they brought with them, empty of supplies, though an American ambulance was running in Neuilly, staffed by American expatriates who turned up in 'their own pretty blouses and their high-heeled slippers and their ear-rings, the rest being enveloped in the all-concealing apron'. There was no paper and no sign of a typewriter. It was here that Davison's business-minded appointees came in to their own: France was rapidly carved into nine different zones, and requisition slips sped off back to America with calls for everything that might possibly contribute to winning the war and caring for the soldiers — serum for gas gangrene, Christmas stockings, tapioca, croquet sets, candlesticks, galoshes, beans, folding beds and soup ladles, not to mention all the small items that Clara Barton had identified as necessary for the wounded, like writing paper, needles and tea strainers. The true Red Crosser, as the literature put it, not only had to be a 'good grocer, dry goodsman, apothecary, financier, doctor and linguist', but must have the 'strength of Samson, the patience of Job, and the cheerfulness of the morning lark'. He also had to be resourceful. By now, France alone had 600,000 disabled men, committing suicide at such a rate that one Red Cross man was detailed to set up a cemetery for them. To counter the horrors of disfigurement — trench warfare had left thousands of men with jaws and noses shot away — the American Red Cross set up a workshop to produce light, metal face masks, moulded to the wounded man's face with plasticine, with eyelashes in fine copper threads soldered on, and lips left slightly parted so that a cigarette could be smoked through them.

Two of the first American Red Cross arrivals in France were railway men. W. H. Atterbury was the vice-chairman of the Pennsylvania Railroad; named brigadier-general in charge of rail transport for the American service of supplies, he recruited a Major Osborne, an athlete and well-known expert on trains, and between them they set up what became known as the US Military Railroad in France. Seven other early arrivals were women, sent to write reports on canteen needs. They were soon followed by stenographers, schoolteachers, actresses, girls fresh from finishing school, all bearing trunks packed with sou'westers, black woollen tights and black hats in velour and straw. And if back home there were doubtful murmurs about the advisability of sending women to war, it was soon acknowledged that these women were keeping American troops 'clean in body and pure in spirit'. 'I think,' remarked a veteran later, 'that the presence of so many women is rather to be regarded as a real triumph for our Americanism.' As Davison saw it, they kept the soldier from the 'station-saloon and other temptations of the night, and went further than most people knew towards keeping him clean and straight and ready for his big job'.

The women seem to have had a lot of fun. Like their British counterparts, many had seized the chance of war to escape claustrophobic inactivity at home and they took to their new duties with considerable relish. The first American Red Cross canteen opened at Châlons-sur-Marne on 17 September 1917. It had a restaurant, several dormitories and bathrooms and a barber's shop. From one end of France to the other, American Red Cross ladies, most well born and none black, and many already friends before volunteering, were soon turning out the ubiquitous 'doughnuts for doughboys', looking after laundry, cooking hot meals and tending to stray casualties. A Mrs Belfont Tiffany personally dressed and bandaged the 'frozen feet of twenty-three Senegalese . . . great huge blacks, they were, whose feet were swollen three times the usual size'. These women wore uniforms, sometimes topped by improbable hats. Mrs Eleanor Roosevelt, asked to design a uniform, came up with a concoction in grey whipcord, its collar powder-blue, with a small brimmed hat and an immense cape modelled on that of Italian officers, so disliked by some of the women who had to wear it that they deeply offended her by covering it with lace collars, strings of beads and bright flowers. Few of the women who served in France were very young and a joke was soon being repeated among the soldiers about a man bidding his mother farewell as she left America for the war in Europe, saying to those around him: 'I'm too old to fight, but I'm sending my mother.'

For many of these American women, the war provided a first glimpse of Europe. They arrived a little uncertain about what to expect, having been told that, while British women were stalwart, French ladies tended to think only of clothes and intrigue. In the summer of 1916, Gertrude Atherton, an American widow and author of several novels, had been sent to France to draw up a realistic portrait of French ladies. She did most of her research in the Parisian shops and theatres, and amongst the pages of the fashionable and slightly *outré* novels of the day, producing a fascinating account; what they made of it back home is not known.

Mrs Atherton reached Paris decidedly sceptical. 'European women,' she noted briskly, 'tend to coarseness . . . their cheeks sag and broaden, and their stomachs contract a fatal and permanent entente with their busts.' She consented to become the American president of the *Le Bien-Être du Blessé*, run by the marquise d'Audigné, which provided delicacies to dietary kitchens. Fashionable France, she reported, had taken to 'oeuvres', good works, very seriously. Countesses and duchesses, better known for their political breakfasts and receptions in the red and gold salons of the rue Faubourg St Honoré, were running glass bead workshops, where convalescent soldiers were turning out necklaces so stylish that 'some of the best dressed . . . women were to be seen wearing them'. French ladies, she added, with a tone of surprise, were tough, wry, hard working and wholly admirable. What was more, they understood their station in life perfectly, for while the first division of the French Red Cross was run by a countess (Lady Muriel Paget's friend, the Comtesse d'Haussonville), its third division was 'composed of able and useful women whom fate has planted in a somewhat inferior social sphere'.

Gertrude Atherton was certainly snobbish, but she was not without insight. Soon dismissing the women of England as 'far more neurotic . . . as they have fewer natural outlets', she ended her book with a fiery warning. The new powers and freedoms offered to women by the war, she forecast, were likely to spell disaster for the post-war social world. Having found, for the first time, that life was full of interest *without* men — many men, she had decided, were really fit only to be servants — were they ever again going to be content with servitude? 'To be a nurse is no bed of roses,' she concluded darkly, 'but neither is anything else.'

By the autumn of 1917, there were Belgian refugees scattered across Europe, many of them categorized as 'old persons, not claimed', but it was the children in particular who were in terrible shape. The American Red Cross war council despatched a child specialist to Europe and a campaign, ranging from food to the 'adoption of war orphans' was launched, with American 'god-papas' among the soldiers, an idea that ran into momentary trouble when mothers and wives back home expressed horror at the prospect of their men returning after the war with a small French-speaking child.

Davison's plan had been to appoint commissioners for the different war zones, men 'boundlessly energetic, clear headed, decisive, good on organization, tactful and good in emergencies', who would respect the great 'sensitivity of the Latin races' and eschew all suggestion of condescension. The first commissioner went to France. He was followed by commissioners to Russia – where a man called Raymond Robins got on particularly well with Lenin and Trotsky – to Romania, Serbia, Italy, England and Belgium. Their reports, sober and humane, full of practical good sense, sent back to Davison week after week, make impressive reading. American Red Crossers, leading convoys of trucks with desperately needed medical supplies, made their way over the mountains to Caporetto where the Italians were suffering huge losses at the hands of the Austrians; they handed out thousands of tons of hot cocoa, and enough dressings to provide a five-and-three-quarter-inch girdle of gauze around the entire world; they sent 60,000lbs of blackberry jam to England; they set up networks of supplies that flowed smoothly, over enormous distances, against formidable odds; they trained dogs to search for wounded men lost on battlefields; they understood the need to return Europe to self-sufficiency, and restocked regions stripped bare by the Germans of all livestock; they coaxed soldiers back from despair with rousing musical evenings; they stunned Europeans with their lavishness, their insistence on soap and the inventiveness of their equipment; and they left diaries and letters which have a particular flavour of their own, an almost childlike mixture of naivety and shrewdness. They entered Vladivostok as the city became the last stronghold of Czechs and White Russians and they helped evacuate sick and desperate civilians; they covered 8,000 miles by sledge and fed 60,000 adults in and around Harbin in Manchuria and they did all they could, as Davison put it, to 'hold the Russians to the cause of right'. When they felt down, they sang:

> If you can sit up three whole nights of travel
> And smile with unwashed face at 9 a.m. . . .
> If you can bear to hear whole crowds of people
> Converse in tongues you do not understand . . .

By the end of the war, there were 6,000 American 'Red Crossers' in France alone. For the most part, they were welcomed, loved and applauded, even if there were inevitable lapses in tact and etiquette, and even if occasional misunderstandings led to narrowly averted scandals, like the sending of German-speaking nurses, fresh from work among the Germans and insisting on speaking German to each other, to help the destitute citizens of Petrograd. In the *Herald* back home in the United States, a Samuel Smiley complained that the ARC had become a 'sort of giant octopus' which threatened to 'monopolize the business of dispensing human charity'. Another of their critics was the novelist Edith Wharton, who had helped run the American ambulance in Paris before the arrival of the ARC – at first complaining to a friend that she didn't know 'anything ghastlier than doing hospitals *en touriste* like museums' – but then grew increasingly disenchanted with the ARC personnel whom she dismissed as 'incompetence and arrogance combined'. What anyone made of one American Red Cross mission to eastern Europe, celebrating the crossing of the Arctic Circle with a dinner of three turkeys, bagged on the shores of the frozen White Sea and fattened up by nurses who fed them sunflower seed, cooked by French chefs, carved by the leading American surgeon, washed down by six magnums of champagne, followed by ice cream made of snow, condensed milk and eggs, all lit up by the aurora borealis, no one ever found out.

And then the Americans became embroiled in one of the more extraordinary episodes of the Red Cross at war, that of the lost children of the Urals.

In the spring of 1918, alarmed by the increasing food shortages and uneasy political climate, a number of parents in Petrograd decided to send their children to safety, to colonies set up for them in the Urals. Their teachers agreed to go with them. In all there were about 4,000; the oldest was nineteen, the youngest barely walking. George Bakiroff, who was seven, was the son of an office clerk; thirteen-year-old Petro Boronin's father was listed as 'workman', and sixteen-year-old Maria Galikova was the daughter of a bank employee. For a while, the children were well looked after. But towards the middle of June, the Japanese chapter of the American Red Cross received a long cable from a YMCA field director in Siberia, Dr Russell Storey, saying that he kept hearing stories about bands of wild Russian children, living in the woods in the Urals, eating berries and leaves. Some were totally naked. His report was passed on to the American Red Cross in Washington, who cabled their own field directors in Siberia to keep a look out for wild children.

The rumours were soon confirmed. There were indeed some ragged, miserable children in the forests, deserted by their teachers and cut off from home by the civil war. Having arrived in the colonies with only summer clothes, many had nothing left to wear. They were begging at the farms and being chased away by furious villagers. The American Red Cross sent out search parties, having decided that the best thing to do was to gather up the children and take them to the relative safety of their base in Vladivostok. So began a political saga that would draw in not only the national Red Cross societies of America, Russia, Japan and France, but their respective governments. The wild children of the Urals made marvellous political mileage.

In Vladivostok, the 800 or so children who had finally been rounded up were put to live in an old stone barracks on a rocky promontory; the older boys were taught trades, the older girls basic nursing skills. A crude postal system was set up so that they could communicate with their parents in Petrograd, who expressed relief that their children were being fed and cared for.

Harmonious relations did not last. A Russian radio station soon began broadcasting messages that the children were being kept 'under the most disgraceful conditions, both physically and morally', a form of treatment only to be expected 'from the representatives of . . . imperialist governments'. Questions were asked in America. By now, however, Vladivostok was in chaos, and the Americans, evacuating their own forces, felt they had no alternative but to take the Russian children with them with a view to returning them as soon as possible to Petrograd. A journalist called Allen, serving with the American Red Cross, was put in charge. It was not an enviable task. On the *Yomei Maru*, the chartered Japanese ship that was to carry them to America, there were 428 boys and 352 girls; thirty-four were ill. Allocated to bunks, they roamed, reduced their sleeping areas to pigsties, and refused to do their lessons. The ship's lavatories blocked, backed up and began to spew sewage over the lower decks. The *Yomei Maru* was forced to put in to a port on Hokkaido for repairs where the recalcitrant teenagers were marched off to watch Japanese children doing gym and judo in orderly silence. Back on board, one boy became 'demented' and had to be isolated on the poop deck;

the emergency lifeboat rations were pilfered, and there was a riot over the food (a typical lunch was potatoes in their jackets and sago in milk). Some days, temperatures rose to 130°F below deck; on others, children had to be moved from the decks because of torrential rain. Scabies broke out. The Japanese stokers made passes at the girls – fifty of the children were adolescents. 'There were several complaints from the night policemen,' reads one rather laconic entry in the American Red Cross log of the journey, 'that they had difficulty in keeping the children in their sleeping hatches during the night.' A Mrs Mazoon, one of the Russian 'educators', spread a rumour that the older girls were destined for the white slave trade. Fights broke out between the Russian boys and the Japanese sailors.

The next port of call was San Francisco, where the children were bussed to a public ceremony in City Hall; the Russian newspapers published tirades about the exploitative behaviour of imperialist nations. In New York, the children were sent to see Staten Island; the Russians reported that they had been put in prison and were in danger of being shot and Soloviev, the president of the new Soviet Red Cross, muttered about national societies which failed in their 'elementary duties' when 'political or class interests come into consideration'. A boy was then indeed shot and wounded, in error, during a rally. Agents from the American justice department boarded the *Yomei Maru* and confiscated and then burnt books by Tolstoy and Dostoyevsky. One of the Russian teachers who had stood by her charges and who was much loved by the children, died.

By now the American Red Cross was divided over what to do with their profoundly unwanted charges, Allen arguing that they must be returned to Russia as soon as possible, others saying that their parents had to be consulted first. Thirty thousand lists of the children's names were printed and circulated throughout Europe and North America, in case any of the families had since emigrated. As Lieutenant Colonel Robert Olds, the newly appointed American Red Cross commissioner for Europe, noted, 'It does not require much imagination to see that whatever we do, we shall become the object of violent attack and bitter recrimination.' He was right.

From New York they sailed on to France; during the crossing, the boys mutinied, saying that they refused to go to a country 'thanks to which the population of Russia . . . is dying by the tens and hundreds of thousands'. At last, having spent weeks combing the Baltic in search of a country willing to take the children, tossed by storms that made them vomit all over the ship, the *Yomei Maru* berthed in the Finnish port of Koivisto (later Primorsk, Leningrad), where the children were taken to a Russian sanatorium by a lake. From here, in groups of a hundred, they were delivered over the border to Russia, the Estonian government acting as intermediary and members of the International Committee conducting the negotiations.

Only in January 1921 did the last child reach Petrograd, and only then was the American Red Cross commission to Siberia, for whom the children of the Urals had proved one of the worst nightmares of the war, finally liquidated. As for the children, they had been away from home for over two years, and sailed 14,600 miles. The venture had cost the American Red Cross $650,000.

It was absolutely inevitable, given the length of the war and the number of countries drawn into it, that there would be atrocities and breaches that the International Committee could never have imagined. From the very first, Dr Ferrière had watched, with growing despair, the way that the fighting had spread to engulf civilians. At a conference convened in Geneva for the national Red Cross societies of neutral countries in September 1917, he spoke passionately about the internees, a category of war victim unprotected under the Geneva Convention. Many, he pointed out, now faced their fourth winter in captivity. True, he told his listeners, there had been some successes, like the agreement signed between France, Britain and Germany in January 1916, mediated by the Red Cross, to repatriate women and children, and men who were ill or over fifty-five. But what of the 6,000 or so men and women held by the Germans for 'various acts of rebellion'?

The International Committee was cautious about its public appeals, anxious lest it devalue a currency that in any case had no power beyond that of morality and public embarrassment. Its messages, of censure or exhortation, were deliberated at great length and issued only with gravitas, like papal encyclicals. By no means all the many protests it received – about the sinking of hospital ships or the targeting of ambulances –

were translated into public statements. In February 1918 came its most grave and horrified public utterance.

Scientific progress, Ador and his fellow committee members declared, far from diminishing the evils of war, as the advances in aeronautics and chemistry had once seemed to promise, had in fact done the opposite; it had not only increased suffering, but spread it across the entire population in such a way that 'war will soon be a work of general destruction and without mercy'. What they were referring to was poison gas. They called it a 'more refined kind of cruelty'.

The Hague rules of 1907 had very clearly forbidden the use of poison or poisonous weapons, along with everything else that could cause 'unnecessary suffering'. The first major gas attack of the war came in April 1915, on the front at Ypres, between Langemarck and Bixcshoote, when the German army decided to launch waves of chlorine gas, pumped out of pressure cylinders and delivered by the wind across enemy lines. Its effect had been immediate and devastating. Five thousand men had been poisoned, gasping for breath, their eyes watering, writhing in spasms, their tongues blackened; many of them died. Two days later, two Canadian brigades were gassed.

After this, the tactic spread. It was not without its hazards, for the wind could change, returning the waves back over the heads of the men who were sending it. In July 1915, the Germans produced poison shells, filled with gas and fired more reliably far over enemy lines. All through 1916 and 1917, Allied forces and Central Powers alike poured money into research programmes, producing ever more effective poison projectiles. At Verdun in October 1916, the French used shells filled with phosgene, said to be so lethal that they silenced almost half the enemy batteries. On the Russian front, the 53rd Siberian regiment lost practically every man in a chloride and sulphur attack, in such numbers that they had to be hastily buried in 'fraternal' graves, one body piled beside another. In July 1917, the Germans used mustard gas, 'Yperite', for the first time. A doctor called to treat gas injuries left a description of seeing Australian soldiers caught by gas: 'It was a weird sight to see them led away through the camp in moonlight, in long single files, holding on to each other and guided by an orderly as leader.'

By early 1918, rumours were circulating that both sides were contemplating using aircraft and long range artillery to deliver gas more effectively far behind enemy lines. The losses, by this stage in the war, were enormous. In Geneva, the International Committee, seeking forecasts of probable use of gas, consulted a German chemist in Zurich. Professor Staudinger confirmed their worst fears. Poison gas was very easy to make, quickly and in great quantity.

On 6 February, Ador issued his most weighty message of the war. Addressed to sovereigns, the heads of governments and generals, and to 'all nations now pitted against each other', it seemed to step into new territory, to be closer to the language of judge and jury than ever before. Now that vast civilian populations were at risk, he said, he could no longer stay silent. Gas was barbaric; it violated all laws of war; it 'scattered death, and a most atrocious death at that'; and he who used it would be held responsible for turning the war in directions totally counter to all 'ideas of humanity'. What, he asked, would stop the world from descending into a conflict 'which will surpass in ferocity every barbaric act known to history'? He appealed to a 'spirit of humanity' he believed to be not quite dead in the hearts of men.

Three months later, in May, the Allies sent back their formal reply. Its tone was pious. The armies of Britain, Belgium, the United States, France, Greece, Italy, Japan, Portugal and Serbia shared the International Committee's feeling that gas was 'barbaric' and for their part they had assumed it to be a thing of the past among civilized nations – but what, given the behaviour of the Germans, were they to do? They would be delighted to discuss a total ban – providing the Germans produced guarantees that they would obey it.

A short article then appeared in the *Norddeutsche Allegemeine Zeitung*. The British, not the Germans, it said, were to blame for the gas. Had they not started it, well over a month *before* the German attack? Was their gas not the more barbaric, being made of white phosphorus? Then there was silence, though a courageous German deputy, Dr Oscar Cohn, rose in the Reichstag to deplore Germany's part in the affair.

At last, in September, came the German reply. It was not so much pious as lofty. Faced with outrages that recalled the most 'sombre and barbaric' days of history, of an 'atrocity and cruelty that defied the imagination', the German army had in fact behaved with great moderation. It, too, would be very happy to discuss a ban – though it doubted the word of the Allies.

The German reply arrived too late. Before the International Committee had time to draft an agreement over the use of gas, the war was over. But what would be remembered, in the years when the Committee would be severely criticized for its silence, was that, when faced by a practice it, together with the rest of the world, considered abhorrent and unacceptable, it had the courage and vision to speak out, to assume the role of public moral judge.

'*Elle est finie, la grande guerre!*' So began the first *Bulletin* of 1919, now rechristened the *International Review*. Though it would never be possible to know for certain how many casualties had been caused by a war that had lasted over four years and drawn in twenty-eight countries, a French army major soon produced a report saying that twenty million men had been wounded and thirteen million had died — a funereal army whose coffins, if laid end to end, would cover 10,000 kilometres, or the distance between Paris and Vladivostok. The money spent on the war, he added, was impossible to calculate, but it was certainly enough to give a home, furnished, and a garden to every member of the 'civilized' world, though just what counted as civilized, in the winter of 1918, was hard to say.

It was a time of statistics, some sad, some boastful, none very reliable. Of the 15 million men mobilized in Russia, over 1.5 million were dead, and the number taken prisoner was equal to three times the entire population of Switzerland. France had lost over 1.3 million men, dead or disappeared, but had seen deaths from wounds and illness in the army drop rapidly as more was understood about cleanliness, bacteria and vaccination. The American Red Cross, which had entered the war a poor relation to those of Japan and Germany, emerged from it in triumphant mood, with 28 million members, a quarter of the entire population of the United States. American Red Cross knitters, only momentarily slowed down by adverse publicity, had turned out well over 10 million garments. The British Red Cross had despatched 2.5 million separate parcels to prisoners-of-war from its stores in Thurloe Place. Everywhere, the Red Cross had opened doors for women and shown that they were stronger, braver, more independent and more resourceful than they had ever been allowed to think. Few would return willingly to their former lives.

The International Committee in Geneva could be forgiven a little complacency. It had carried the spirit of the Geneva Convention and the crucial Washington conference of 1912 in directions Dunant himself would never have dreamed possible. Forty-one delegates, all Swiss, all men, had visited 524 prisoner-of-war and labour camps across Europe, North Africa, Eastern Europe, Russia and Japan. Not only had it nursed, fed, transported, repatriated, traced and educated prisoners, ensuring that they were treated, as far as possible, according to a certain minimum code, but it had provided them with the wherewithal to 'tolerate their fate with dignity'. The International Committee had also played its part in some of the major medical and scientific discoveries of the war, the antiseptics, the inoculations, the disinfecting machines and the nursing of soldiers shocked by high explosives and terrorized by gas. And if there had been sadly little it could do for the *bétail humain* to which so many of Europe's battered civilians had been reduced, it had solemnly watched over the conduct of the war itself. A little known body of obscure Swiss businessmen and philanthropists in 1914, it came out of the war strong, prestigious and internationally respected, author and guarantor of standards of behaviour whose usefulness had been proved beyond all question. By the Armistice, it was hard to envisage a world without the Red Cross, and the International Committee had every intention, as it proclaimed in its newly named *Review*, of fighting 'without cease for the principles which are its *raison d'être*, for the triumph of right over force, of charity over egotism'.

It was as well that it felt so good, for the internal war about to split the Red Cross movement to its very foundations would prove extremely bitter; and very nearly fatal.

TEN

The Amiable Gentlemen of Geneva

Long before the fighting was over, while the Americans were still sending fresh troops to Europe and Germany had not yet abandoned its hopes of winning the war, Henry Davison had been thinking about the future. In the autumn of 1917 and throughout 1918, as he travelled between Washington and New York, he talked to friends and to business and political colleagues about what would happen to the Red Cross once peace returned. So much money had been raised, so many volunteers marshalled, such intensity of good will expressed; would it not be tragic to see it all evaporate? If his frenetic work as chairman of the war council of the American Red Cross had convinced him of anything, it was that the lives and aspirations of millions of Americans had been transformed by the service they had given during the war. Reports coming from Europe of famine and epidemics also told him that Red Cross help would continue to be vital. 'As the world now finds itself,' Davison announced in the autumn of 1918, 'the people of America are in a position to do the most, the people in America are looked to for the most, and in my opinion the people of America owe the most to suffering humanity.' The only question was: what shape should American charity assume?

Davison himself had few doubts. By the end of November he was outlining his ideas in a long letter to Harvey Gibson, American Red Cross commissioner for Europe. His immediate plan for post-war Europe, he said, was to organize a 'real international Red Cross', one of co-operation along humanitarian lines, somewhat on the model of the proposed League of Nations, with medical forces to fight disease and perhaps even a 'plan ... for treating the destitute where they are in masses resulting from the war'. Speed was crucial, to act while 'minds are more or less groping and pliable'. What he was thinking of doing, Davison told Gibson, was meeting the representatives of the French,

Italian and British Red Cross societies, some of whom were old friends like Sir Arthur Stanley, recently made chairman of the Joint Council of the Order of St John and the British Red Cross Society, and suggesting that the four of them set up such an organization. If they agreed – and possibly even if they did not – then they could go on to Geneva to discuss the idea with the International Committee. The Swiss, he added, could surely be persuaded to call a world conference of Red Cross societies to launch such a new scheme.

What Davison seemed to be proposing – essentially an extension of the vast labour of the Red Cross movement in the four years of war to peacetime work – was not new. Dunant and Moynier had talked about it repeatedly as early as the 1860s, and the idea of Red Cross societies working to relieve misery and natural calamities in peacetime had become such an accepted notion that it was no longer emphasized at the many international gatherings of pre-war years. But it was more complicated than that. Davison had in mind a strong, 'virile, effective' international organization that would focus on peacetime issues – public health, the eradication of disease, child welfare – and the kind of federation of Red Cross societies that Moynier and others had sketched out in the past was not exactly what he had in mind. Something of the mild contempt he and many Americans felt for the men of Geneva comes over very clearly in a letter written to President Wilson on 27 November 1918 by Stockton Axson, who had replaced Mabel Boardman as general secretary of the American Red Cross. Axson was the president's brother-in-law; he had taken on the task of convincing Wilson of the soundness of Davison's ideas. There was every reason for keeping the central committee in Geneva, he wrote,

> but it should be, in reality and not merely in name, an International Committee, a Committee on which there will be representatives from all countries, instead of, as at present, a committee consisting of amiable but somewhat ineffective Geneva gentlemen. That which calls itself 'international' has grown rather provincial ... New blood, new methods, a new and more comprehensive outlook, these things are necessary.

Harsh words; but were they fair? The International Committee was coming out of the war strong and united as never before in its fifty-five-year history. True, its members were old – Naville, Ferrière and Ador were all in their seventies; true, the picture they presented to the world was staid and exceedingly cautious, and they were only now on the verge of appointing to the Committee their first woman, a clever lawyer and historian called Marguerite Cramer. But they, too, had thought hard about the coming peace, and their almost identical programme for dealing with public health, child welfare and disease was launched sixteen days after the Armistice, on precisely the same day that Davison went to the White House to outline his plan to President Wilson. What they proposed was a meeting of all Red Cross societies to discuss post-war policy. Moynier and Ador had fought off earlier attempted coups. This one, against forces larger, richer, better organized and more determined, would prove considerably more dangerous. That the David of Geneva, a handful of elderly Swiss guarding what many considered an obsolete Convention, would prove a match for the Goliath of Wall Street businessmen, French politicians, Italian philanthropists, British military officers and Japanese entrepreneurs was indeed remarkable.

The Americans thought that they had God on their side. Axson assured the President that

> this same United States has in the Providence of God been able
> to take a foremost place during this war in carrying out the
> ideas of the Geneva Convention, and mitigating the sufferings
> of a world war, and that it should not cease from its good works
> simply because the war has ended.

America was not just bigger and richer than everyone else: it had a God-given duty to act, a notion of privilege and obligation that would be repeated again and again in the months to come. Wilson agreed. At a meeting at the White House on 2 December 1918, he supported Davison's proposals to sound out European backing for an organization 'under the not too obtrusive leadership of the American Red Cross', and said he would talk to Clemenceau, Orlando and Lloyd George, the other members of the 'Big Four', when he got to Paris. That the Americans, and Davison in particular, had no doubts at all that any such organization should be run and shaped by America comes across in a letter written by Robert Olds to Dr Livingstone Farrell, of the central committee of the American Red Cross in Washington. 'The dominant factor in the whole situation is the American Red Cross,' Olds wrote, describing a long meeting he had had with Davison. 'The League is the natural outgrowth of the worldwide activities of the American Red Cross, just as the League of Nations is the logical consequence of the entry of the United States into the war.' However, he went on, 'the impression that the Americans are doing it all must . . . be dispelled even if heroic measures are necessary.'

Davison, whose language could sound moralistic and even mystical, with exhortations reminiscent of the Boy Scouts, now moved at great speed. He went to Europe and met the leaders of the major Red Cross societies whose help he needed; he called on the International Committee in Geneva – finding them 'gladly co-operative' but more prone to talk loftily of 'raising eyes and spirits . . . towards a happier and better future' than to engage in concise plans; he drew up his proposals for a revised Geneva Convention ('as we are now proceeding upon the assumption that there shall be no more war'); he summoned medical experts to a conference among the potted palms of the Carlton Hotel in Cannes and heard them vow that the 'light of science and warmth of human sympathy' would be spread 'into every corner of the world'; he gave a flashy press conference to the representatives of 100 newspapers at the Hôtel du Palais d'Orsay in Paris; he drew in the Japanese Red Cross, whose Dr Arata Ninagawa would repeat again and again that he had had the same idea about a federation of societies but that no one had listened to him – Swierdoff, of the Russian Red Cross, would claim that he, too, had had the idea of 'transmitting the links formed by moral solidarity into legal ties', but he, too, was overtaken by the rapidly moving Americans; and 154 days after the evening of his discussion in the White House with President Wilson, Davison launched a League of Red Cross Societies.

The International Committee, for whom such speed and such cavalier methods were anathema, seems never to have stood a chance; it was as if they barely existed. Asked perfunctorily whether they would convene the necessary conference to launch a reshaped International Red Cross with clear peacetime goals, of which they could have remained at least titular master, they replied that their mandate forbade them to act other than with neutrality and universality, and that they could therefore do nothing until the peace terms were signed. Davison was not prepared to wait. 'The world is bleeding and needs help *now*,' he replied, and in any case the Allies and their Red Cross societies were 'set like steel' against including Germany and the German Red Cross in their deliberations, 'seeing that they have grossly violated the Geneva Convention and are beyond the pale' as one diplomat wrote to Davison. It was 'impracticable', announced Davison smoothly, for the International Committee to take on the new programme, but they had 'encouraged' him to 'proceed without delay'. Davison's letters to Geneva, unctuous in tone, verge on the offensive, the steel fist well padded in insincere flattery.

'Gentlemen,' he wrote on 3 May,

By sympathetic understanding of each other's positions we are now brought into such close and gratifying harmony that there is little left to explain and nothing left to agree . . . From the onset we had conceived our proposed plan as but another step in the development of that magnificent humanitarian movement which originated in the minds and hearts of that group of wise and benevolent Swiss gentlemen who in 1863 set in motion the Red Cross movement . . . The League is not a secession nor even a separation, but a convenient plan of operation for the immediate utilization of the spirit and resources of the Red Cross as developed during the war . . . The attitude in which you have met and negotiated with us is not only personally gratifying to us in the highest degree, but is also to us a sign and symbol of the vitality of the Red Cross spirit.

Mlle Cramer was sent to Paris on 5 May 1919 for the launch of the new League, which, as Geneva had begun to say, rather wistfully, was really nothing more than a 'transitory organism'. Davison saw nothing transitory in it at all. Mlle Cramer met Dr Ninogawa who told her that his efforts to get other societies to agree to a revised Geneva Convention, which would simply make peacetime work by national societies mandatory, had failed. A League born of the Covenant of the League of Nations and like it in spirit was, he asserted, inevitable. 'You shall do as you please,' Mlle Cramer is said to have replied. What the members of the Committee really felt was not recorded. They could be forgiven for being bitter. They had spent five years learning more about war than anyone alive and now felt in a position to formulate sensible policies for peace.

To be overtaken, suddenly and so bumptiously, must have been harsh indeed.

With this, the League of Red Cross Societies, with its headquarters at 9 Cour de Saint Pierre in Geneva and made up of five major societies, was born, with a mandate to do for peace what the International Committee had done for war — and would continue to do — thereby laying the seeds of a division and confusion that rumbles on to this day, with periods marked by rifts of considerable animosity between the two organizations. In phrases as woolly as they were absurd, relations between the two were pronounced to be 'intimate', but without 'statutory connection'; the League would 'supplement' the work of the International Committee, 'acting in harmony with it' but in no way would it 'supersede, absorb or conflict with the activities of national societies,' and it would certainly not become a 'Super Red Cross'.

Whatever passions and furies its members felt over the débâcle, concealed behind mild statements and old-fashioned manners, the International committee had survived though probably less on account of their abilities than because neutral, small, Switzerland did not provoke the same mixture of envy, fear and hostility as America, and because the Committee's pledge to Swissness guaranteed a neutral custodianship of the Geneva Convention that no other country could offer. Though it would be many years before some kind of workable partnership could be thrashed out — the debates soured the few remaining years of Ador's life; despite heart and prostate trouble he was in his tenth year as president — a joint committee was now set up to meet every fortnight and agree on common programmes, a forum made all the trickier as Davison spoke no French and only one member of the International Committee, William Rappard, spoke good English.

The first general secretary of the League was an Englishman, Sir David Henderson, a distinguished wartime director of aircraft production and former hero of the Boer war, with a bristly moustache and a reputation for unfailing charm, the British having deftly sidelined the American candidate, the secretary of the interior, Franklin Lane. Davison himself was to be chairman. Together, they set about putting into action schemes and promises there had been very little time to formulate before. A new magazine, *The World's Health*, its first issue appearing in January 1919, gives a good picture of the planned peacetime Red Cross world, one in which the horrors of war are resolutely forgotten and the social, medical and educational advances of peace take their place. Early articles were devoted to rickets, garden cities, venereal disease, alcoholism, insanity, playgrounds, the 'Deadly Automobile' (calling for laws to keep anyone with 'functional paralysis of mind and body in moments of stress' off the roads) and 'puericulture', how to save children and replace the huge fall in population. Competitions for posters proclaiming healthy habits were launched, with directions that the artists must avoid horror ('Fear is not a healthy emotion'). There were to be no 'delirious alcoholics with staring eyeballs' and certainly no 'louse gathering up a whole country into his hairy clutches', but rather two 'brother sprites playing ball with the most luscious-looking apples'. Children were made the target of 'health circuses' and 'health games', one child shown as lavishly praised for helping her small brother finish his soup, another for giving a strange small dog a bath in a public fountain. *The World's Health*, brighter, more optimistic, more gossipy, better illustrated than the International Committee's *Review*, entered the 1920s on a note of good cheer, as eager to spread the 'civilizing process' as the pre-war Red Cross movement had been to counter war, determined to put across the message that the world could be made into a healthy and peaceable place, providing its inhabitants could be coaxed into opening their windows, standing up straight, brushing their teeth and refraining from too such sex. War was a thing of the past, as Davison had made clear; reform of society itself, no less, was the goal now.

With the League, new players were to rise to prominence in the Red Cross, not so much replacing the men in Geneva as stamping their own national Red Cross societies with strong internal characteristics, while bringing new ideas to the international debates that continued, whether in the League or the International Committee or, to the continuing confusion of many, in both. One was Giovanni Ciraolo, the luxuriantly moustachioed new president of the Italian Red Cross, whose recruiting drive had taken Italian membership from 30,000 to 300,000 during the war; Ciraolo, who had lost his family in the Messina earthquake of 1908, was interested in disaster relief and wanted to set up an effective international force, ready at all times to intervene anywhere in the world. In America, Mabel Boardman, of the 'feminine wing of the old guard' with the end of the war had reclaimed some of her former power;

she was ousted yet again, in favour of Robert Olds in the frenzied rush to catch the 'Golden Moment'. In Sweden, there was Prince Charles, president of his national society, who had campaigned passionately on behalf of medical personnel held prisoner in defiance of the Geneva Convention; he would emerge as a strong political and moral force in the years to come.

In March 1920 came the first conference of the League, held in Geneva. Ador and Davison both gave long speeches, Ador remarking somewhat sourly, when he saw that the question of prisoners-of-war in Serbia was on the agenda, that in his opinion the League would do well to stick to their peacetime activities. Hundreds of reporters thronged the upper galleries. A letter from Arthur Balfour, former British Prime Minister and chairman of the Council of the League of Nations, was read out in which he begged the League to help avert a 'calamity' of economic destitution and illness in Europe 'which, following hard on war, seems almost worse than war itself'. At the dinner afterwards, the menu had been designed with the spirit of the occasion in mind. Guests started with perch from the Swiss lakes and *sauce genevoise*; then came Strasbourg foie gras, French *contre-filet*, Italian salad; pudding was American ice-cream, English cakes and Brazilian coffee. Even if no one was very clear about just what this new League would actually do, and how it fitted in with the International Committee, there seemed in the spring of 1920, a delicious promise that this two-headed Red Cross animal would solve all the ills of mankind.

There was a great deal for everyone to do, even if no one had yet worked out the rules. As Ador and Davison deliberated, Europe was sinking under hunger, sickness and misery. A third of Poland's 38 million people were seriously ill, four million of them with tuberculosis. Typhus and influenza were decimating the Ukraine. In Vienna, there were said to be 100,000 starving children. Whether from Hungary or Czechoslovakia, Serbia or Montenegro, the stories brought back by delegates from the International Committee or the new League were all the same: unless something was done, and done at once, deaths in the months to come would far exceed those of the war just coming to a close.

Under the Armistice concluded in November 1918 between the Allies and the Central Powers, prisoners-of-war were entitled to immediate repatriation, and prisoners, under the loose terms agreed by Ador and Davison, fell under war, and were therefore a matter for the International Committee. As early as 1917, the International Committee had warned of the problems of repatriating some three million men, scattered from one end of Europe to the other end of Russia, many of them sick and enfeebled by years of hardship, homesickness and bad food, some in camps, some down mines, some on farms and all intent on getting home as quickly as possible. The Armistice caught the Allies unprepared. The prisoner-of-war camp gates opened and Europe was soon awash with British returning from Turkey, French from Romania, Serbs from Monastir, Belgians, Portuguese, Italians, French and British from Germany, Germans and Austrians from Britain. A lucky few reached home rapidly, benefiting from efficient military arrangements; more, not prepared to wait even the few weeks it would take to arrange transport, left their camps and began to make their own way home, stripping countryside already laid waste by four years of war, begging and stealing from peasants so desperately poor that their own children were dying of hunger. Many others, too feeble to make the journey unaided, were persuaded to remain in the camps, where rations were often reduced to starvation level and morale sank lower with every week of waiting.

The actual position of prisoners varied enormously, depending on whether they were soldiers of the Central Powers, the Russians or the Allied forces. The Russians, though prisoners of the Central Powers, were after the Treaty of Brest-Litovsk no longer considered by the Allies as their responsibility. Much depended on the decisions made at the peace conferences, on the availability of transport, and on the emergence of new nations under the Treaty of Versailles. Moreover, the nationality of individual prisoners was not always clear, even to themselves, as Russians and Germans found that they were now Polish, and Austro-Hungarians found that they had turned Czech or Yugoslav.

The largest and most vulnerable group was the nearly two million Russian prisoners-of-war found in Germany and Austria in the autumn of 1918. Edouard Frick, the International Committee's energetic and determined delegate in Russia, threw himself with increasing desperation into the cause of the returning prisoners and wrote that these men had been 'literally abandoned by everybody and in a state of physical and psychological misery that defies description'. With the collapse of the German administration, the Russian prisoners surged towards home, carrying with them, as Frick was soon warning, not only disease but Bolshevism. As the men wandered north, they found almost nothing to eat. By December, trainloads of Russians were crossing Germany, where the Hungarians were not only refusing to feed them but were stripping them of everything they had left, including their heavy coats. The trains that did reach Stanislawów, reported Frick, disgorged hundreds of dead bodies, many frozen stiff. Three thousand men, he said, had already been buried. The living had been taken to local hospitals. A nun had told him that she had entered a vast waiting room, apparently full of sleeping people; only one was alive. A Czech returning from Poland and Galicia added that he had seen 'thousands of bodies, lying by the roadside and around stations. Trains carrying prisoners-of-war have been successively fired on by the Poles, the Ukrainians and the Germans who want to take them over in order to get home themselves.'

It was not of course only Frick who now reacted to a drama that threatened to submerge much of Europe. Red Cross societies from all over the world rallied with food and medicine, but it was often too late and always too little, and the authorities seemed curiously reluctant to take the reports seriously. But there was something about Frick's remarkable optimism and good spirits, as he hastened around Europe, tall, thin and very fit, his wide-brimmed hat worn at a jaunty angle and wearing clothes that, like those of an adolescent, seemed too short for his arms and legs, that sparked off energy in others. Frick was soon at the heart of a handful of International Committee delegates, most of them already exhausted by four years of missions, and yet who now set off willingly for distant parts of central Europe, to regions in a state of anarchy and famine, disappearing for weeks and months on end and sending back conscientious, minutely detailed reports of numbers of sick and wounded, of proposals for possible routes of evacuation, of accounts of money spent and money needed. Only very rarely did these men allow themselves personal comments, though they must frequently have observed sights that nothing in their past, including the years of war, can have prepared them for. Usually they travelled on their own or in pairs. Geneva was encouraging but often impossible to contact, and in any case all through the winters of 1918 and 1919, the senior men at the International Committee were distracted by other things, such as the setting up of the League. They were absolutely clear, however, that it was the job of delegates to gather reliable, regular and detailed information, and to make sure that it reached Geneva as quickly as possible, via couriers specially engaged for the purpose. And once relief did start getting through and plans for transporting the prisoners were drawn up, the delegates were instructed to check, co-ordinate and monitor the operations. 'Information, control, protection', was how Mlle Cramer, overseeing it all as best she could from Geneva, put it.

And so the reports began to flow in, some neatly typed, some scrawled in pencil or pen, some in French or German, some in Italian and occasionally English, page after page with asides, brackets, figures, recounting lack of trains and carriages, falling stocks of coal and medicine, suggesting alternative routes for the evacuees – down rivers, by train, by road – where prisoners could be fed, and where they would neither catch new diseases nor be infected by dangerous political indoctrination. Delegates, who had been teachers, lawyers and businessmen in their pre-war lives, found themselves becoming experts overnight on mining, nutrition, European politics, disease and transport. And even if their reports sometimes read as essays they needed to write to exorcise the horrors they witnessed, many managed to continue to sound affable and even unhurried, with the leisure to comment on the kindness of certain officials. Nothing has left a clearer or more poignant picture than these letters and reports, written in the same dispassionate tone – long, repetitive, full of figures and lists, occasionally lit up by details of individual people, like the story of Ziprian Stefan. According to a report sent by Charles Piaget and Rodolphe Haccius, Stefan was an eighteen-year-old Polish boy from Krasny, caught by the Germans in 1914 and sent to work down the mines in Essen, where he spent four years looking after the horses and acting as a loader. He lived on bread and soup. Freed by the French, he had wandered through Germany and was now, in the winter of 1918, in a camp outside Warsaw, 'pale, thin, without a shirt, his light coat in tatters, with no socks and only wooden clogs'. What happened to Ziprian Stefan? The delegates did not know. Endless figures like him, homeless and destitute but alive, disappeared and were never mentioned again.

Day by day, as the returning masses of freed men dispersed in all directions, as epidemics died out in one place, only to burst out in another, as political alignments shifted and fresh fighting broke out among factions, so the picture kept changing. Should the prisoners go home via the Ukraine? Travel by the Vistula or the Don? By sledge or by train? Via Bohemia or Hungary? Which country was poorer, more lawless, harder hit by disease? Much of the planning had to be done in the dark, as contact between one country and another broke down, as delegates were delayed, rerouted, fell ill or encountered new and unforeseen disasters. Frick's letters and reports read like despatches from the front, as he described the packed trains crossing Europe, full of men shivering with exhaustion and apprehension at what they would find, with cold and malnutrition or from the onset of a disease, which they would conceal for as long as they could, hoping to reach home before they were detected and taken off the train. Those who decided to get off the trains themselves spread infection around the civilian population and were soon robbed by bandits or other desperate roaming prisoners, and left to die, often naked, by the roadside. There were villages in Poland, reported Frick, through which had passed, in rapid succession, Russians, Germans, Austrians, Turks, Bolsheviks, Ukrainians, then Bolsheviks again.

So impressive were these sad reports that Frick was eventually sent to Paris to try to interest the Allies – who seemed not to have shared his sense of urgency – in the fate of the prisoners. He must have been persuasive, for the Inter-Allied Armistice Commission finally voted to take responsibility for feeding the Russian prisoners and instructed the Allied generals to liaise with the International Committee over the question of prisoner repatriation. Frick's plan to send missions and delegates everywhere that Russian prisoners were to be found, to report not only on numbers and the state that they were in but on the economic and social condition of the countries through which they might pass on their route home, was accepted by the military authorities, as were his proposals that ways must be found of avoiding areas already devastated by the war. It was a huge and daunting task. Everywhere they went, the delegates discovered that there was no coal, no food, no soap and no transport. In Munich, two Russian doctors warned the delegates that they should avoid entering any of the former camps – the prisoners were now known as 'internees' and the camp commandants as 'directors'

– unless they had immediate orders for repatriation. It was too dangerous otherwise. Frick and his colleagues fanned out across Europe, setting up feeding centres in camps, disinfection centres at stations and borders, overseeing the handing out of warm clothes and identification papers, the 'protection papers' pioneered by the Committee and adopted for refugees in years to come.

It was not only a question of food and transport. Disease, particularly typhus and influenza, began to spread rapidly through the prisoners-of-war, finding excellent ground in men weakened by privation and living in filth. Prisoners refused to listen to entreaties for them to wait for relief and proper transport, and disappeared into the countryside to flee the epidemics, where they died in the fields of hunger, cold and illness. The flu, which had struck Germany in July and August 1918, struck again between October and December bringing in its wake pneumonia and bronchitis. A quarter of the remaining prisoners died. Thirty doctors, with thirty kilograms of medicines, set out from Geneva, a response so small as to be absurd, and in any case useless, for there was no known cure other than rest, warm food, blankets and good nursing, and none of that had been available in Europe for many months. The influenza, known as the 'Spanish lady' in many parts of Europe after rumours that it had travelled up from the south, struck in many parts of the world simultaneously, killing some 30 million people by the time it burned itself out. Nothing else, no war, no infection and no famine has ever killed so many people so quickly.

By now, Frick had set up his headquarters in Warsaw where he acted as focal point for the delegates scattered around eastern Europe and where exanthematic typhus was rife. Every day, reports reached him of new outbreaks, rising numbers of dead, and every week he passed on increasingly frantic reports to Geneva. On 30 January 1919, 'Typhus reigns here, in the most appalling conditions'; on 22 February, 'the hospital in Kowel has a hundred cases'; and on 26 February, 'in the district of Kowel . . . deaths are rising terrifyingly, but there is nothing I can do without means.' The Germans, Frick reported, had drawn a *cordon sanitaire* the whole way from Dvinsk to the Austrian frontiers, where all prisoners were disinfected. It did not hold; the typhus swept past. Frick begged for soap, for bathing stations, for clean clothes. Dirt, he wrote, had to be attacked. By March, he was writing that the few doctors and nuns still nursing were dying faster than their patients, and that typhus was now travelling at such a speed that there was a real possibility that it would engulf the whole of Europe. In some areas, he warned, syphilis was also taking hold; ninety per cent of some Red Army units had been infected.

On 11 March 1919, medical experts from Austria, Poland, Czechoslovakia, the Ukraine, Romania, Yugoslavia and Hungary met in Budapest to discuss the epidemics. They were gloomy. A Ukrainian doctor described how his country was overrun by typhus, syphilis, scorbutia, measles and dysentery; there was no soap; and the wandering prisoners-of-war had clothes so worn that if taken away from them to disinfect they disintegrated, leaving the men naked. From Warsaw, there was a report that 800 new cases of typhus were appearing every week. But these countries were bankrupt and had very little to offer, although Austria pledged four mobile disinfection units. The medical experts went home agreeing to pool what little they had and to set up a central office in Budapest. Frick arranged for a delegate to run it, the neutrality of the International Committee once again ensuring impartiality.

It was not only physical disease that alarmed the delegates and doctors. It was also a question of politics. If Russia had turned Bolshevik, was it wise to return 'healthy' men to catch a political disease?' Equally, given that a number of the prisoners-of-war were already Bolshevik, why send them back to spread the infection in areas of Russia still 'healthy' and uncontaminated? There was talk, among the delegates and in their letters to Geneva, of 'moral quarantine' centres. For some of them their neutrality now felt uncomfortable. Charles Piaget, sent on a mission to Budapest, reported irritably that the Russian prisoners were extremely stubborn, even when he told them that the International Committee could not take responsibility for sending them 'into the Bolshevik hell'. There was very little point, Piaget argued, in trying to keep these men back any longer, 'for it would be dangerous to hold on to a nest of bubbling revolutionaries in a city already impregnated by Bolshevism'.

*　　*　　*

There was yet another group of prisoners-of-war, and these were perhaps the most unlucky of all. When the Soviet government came to power in November 1917, all the prisoners-of-war that they were holding – mainly Germans, Austrians and Hungarians scattered throughout Siberia, European Russia and Turkestan – and all the foreign civilian detainees had been declared 'free citizens'. Some immediately left their camps and wandered west. A few joined the Bolsheviks. By the summer of 1918 at least 800,000 had satisfactorily been repatriated from European Russia. Anna Reutinger, one of three American nurses attached to a Red Cross mission in Kazan, later gave an account of helping with the evacuation of 11,271 soldiers and 1,734 officers by sledge and train, many of them almost naked, some blind, many crippled and ill, all of whom had had no contact with their families for many months. 'We often wondered if twentieth-century civilization was but a mere mockery,' she wrote later, defending the American Red Cross against attacks of interfering where they were not needed, 'or if it had only endowed the barbarian with more efficient and ruthless weapons and methods of slaughter.'

With those from European Russia gone, a further 400,000 prisoners-of-war remained in Siberia and the Urals, and 35,000 in Turkestan. But these men were trapped once the Czechs rose up against the Bolsheviks as their route home through central Russia was now closed. In eastern Siberia, General Semenov organized an army of fugitive White Russians, Mongolian mercenaries and Japanese troops, which had landed at Vladivostok to protect Japanese interests. In Omsk, Admiral Kolchak set up what became known as the 'Siberian government', supported by Czech fighters and the Allies. The former prisoners-of-war became embroiled in the changing political fortunes of the region, buffeted first by one side then by the other, imprisoned, tortured and shot as spies and traitors, used as hostages and in exchanges. Corpses, horribly mutilated, with their arms pinioned to their sides, were found floating in the Volga. In July 1918 Elsa Brandström, the Swedish Red Cross delegate, tried to cross Red and White army lines to take money to those remaining in camps. She was arrested by the Czechs, accused of being a spy, sentenced to be shot and reprieved only at the last minute. Not long afterwards another Swedish delegate in Khabarosh called Hedbloom and his Norwegian secretary were not so fortunate: arrested by the Cossacks, they were robbed and then hanged from a wagon.

By the time Germany fell, despair had settled on the remaining prisoners-of-war. They had no food, no money and could see no way of returning home. The more energetic and optimistic organized themselves into work groups and began to make furniture, shoes, saddles, toys and even hammers and tongs, fashioned out of iron bedsteads. By the summer of 1919 camp industry reached its peak, the engineers, architects and chemists among the former prisoners contributing actively to Siberian industry and trade. In October the White Russians and Czechs, overwhelmed by superior Red Army forces, began to fall back and the prisoners fell back with them, a long, slow march of death through the Siberian winter. Thousands, too weak to continue, lay down by the roadside and in railway stations, where they froze to death.

In Moscow, the Soviets now agreed to repatriate the survivors; but instructed the foreigners to leave the matter in their hands. Elsa Brandström was one of the few permitted to witness what she called the 'Siberian tragedy'. Recognizing how efficient their prisoners-of-war had been, the Soviets had little interest in seeing them return home before the local economy had been put back on its feet. The months passed and, with every change in the political situation, the prisoners-of-war were the first to be taken as traitors. There was very little the International Committee could do beyond negotiating with the changing powers and continue to distribute what relief they could. In Kiev, one delegate was reduced to collecting the bodies of those shot by the Bolsheviks for burial.

On 19 December 1919 two other delegates, de Muller and Simonett, arrived in Rostov on the Don after an interminable journey via Bucharest and Constantinople. The Red Army was advancing and the city was in a state of chaos. Representatives from various Red Cross societies had reported that the remaining Austrian and Hungarian prisoners were being held in atrocious conditions and de Muller set about negotiating their release. It took several months, thousands of meetings, appalling journeys and vast sums of money in constantly tottering currencies. First de Muller, then Simonett came down with typhus. At this point the prisoners were again in the hands of the White Russian army and Simonett delayed several weeks trying to see General Denikin. 'The current state of mind and political situation of Russia,' he wrote to Geneva, 'are deplorable. I could never have believed that corruption, speculation and cruelty could have taken hold of the entire Russian population.' This turned out to be one of the International Committee's more successful missions. The White Russians were longing to get rid of the prisoners and by the spring of 1920 most of them were at last on their way home.

On 11 April 1920, the League of Nations appointed the Norwegian polar explorer, Fridtjof Nansen special commissioner to deal with the repatriation of all remaining prisoners-of-war. He worked closely with the International Committee delegates and a coherent, properly organized plan was finally worked out. By the spring of 1922 — almost eight years after the outbreak of war — there was no prisoner-of-war left in a concentration camp. It had been an extraordinary saga, and one in which the International Committee could justifiably feel pride. Its delegates, without a specific mandate, acting on their own responsibility, often in circumstances of considerable danger, had altered the lives of many hundreds of thousands of trapped prisoners-of-war. This was another new activity, never specified in the Geneva Convention, which the International Committee had somehow tacitly assumed. It also proved the enormous value of neutrality, at the very moment when the Committee most needed accolades.

The League, meanwhile, was entering dangerous political waters. The devastation left by the end of the war offered the very scenario that Davison had envisaged when he talked about providing for the 'welfare of humanity' in a world crippled by famine, disease and poverty. It was all waiting for him in eastern and central Europe, for the returning prisoners-of-war were only one small part of the misery that had settled on the civilians who had lived through the great war.

In November 1918, the Austrian Red Cross reported that the children of Vienna were starving. The continuing Allied blockade imposed in order to force more disadvantageous peace terms on the Germans and Austro-Hungarians, was effectively reducing supplies of food and medicine to below the level of possible survival. Many of these children were now orphans, and they were wandering the streets of the capital barefoot. Frédéric Ferrière, who had spent most of the war working for civilian relief and protection, left hastily for Vienna, taking with him a young relation, Louis, for blockades belonged to war, and war to the International Committee; and in any case the League was far from organized. The report sent back by the two doctors was horrifying. Infant mortality had risen by forty-five per cent and was still rising; seven-year-olds looked like three-year-olds, gaunt, skinny, their heads shaved, their ages written on to school slates and hung around their necks to be photographed. Only the rich, who could afford black market prices, were eating, the poor having sunk into a state of profound apathy. How long, asked Ferrière, would it be before desperation led to revolt and looting? Switzerland rallied round and by the end of December a convoy of seventy wagons of food was on its way to Austria.

This was only the beginning. In January 1919, de Muller wrote from Warsaw to report that thousands of Polish seasonal workers, cut off in Germany for the duration of the war, were now returning destitute, what little they had left taken from them by the Germans at the frontier. So far, he said, thirty-two children had been found frozen to death on arrival. These refugees had nothing to eat, and in any case the Poles themselves were running out of food. 'Send milk with utmost urgency,' de Muller cabled, 'to check terrifying mortality, particularly of new-born babies.' Frick, now chief delegate for eastern Europe, added further warnings:

> Morality complete collapse. No schools. Parents of very low standards sending children to steal and beg . . . Dozens of little girls aged 12 to 14 turning to open prostitution . . . To address all these problems is not a simple question of food. You need workers. There are no men! It's a labour of Sisyphus. We do a great deal but it's always too little!

From the Hungarian Red Cross came a statement that of 18,000 newborn infants, 7,000 were unlikely to reach their first birthday.

The League, however, also had its eye on Poland. Its first mission, in the summer of 1919, was to Warsaw and its four high-ranking medical military men – one English, one French, one American and one Italian – had been appalled to see 'women and children barefooted, in all stages of raggedness' queueing piteously for bread. By day, the delegates travelled around the country by train, unloading their car from time to time to make tours of inspection; in the evenings, parked in a siding, they dictated their notes. One of their last visits was to a camp north-east of Warsaw; here they found refugees eating 'grass, bark, berries, wild apples and nettle soup.' Railway stations had become rallying points for the refugees. Those who managed to board trains died of cold when the trains stopped and the snow kept falling. Józef Jakobkiewicz, a Polish Red Cross delegate, described finding small children frozen to death on the naked bodies of their mothers, who had wrapped them in their own clothes in an attempt to keep them warm. Some had frozen tears down their cheeks. One refugee told him that he had been given the task of tracing forty Polish children known to have been sent east before the advancing Red Army.

> I searched for the children across the whole of Siberia . . . I went as far as Baikal asking for news . . . No one had seen them. When I came across the bodies of children frozen to death, I asked myself if this were them? . . . I don't know. To this day I don't know. I prefer not to know. It's better that I don't know.

But a far more ominous famine was about to break. If the League was already having some trouble sorting out its priorities and political position, as well as its duties and its relations with the International Committee, a considerably greater challenge was on its way.

By 1920, the people of Russia had been through six years of disastrous warfare, political upheaval and civil conflict. Twenty-five million people were dead; many others were crippled and sick. When eventually the Bolsheviks and the Red Army under Leon Trotsky were able to oust the remaining pockets of White Russian forces and set about rebuilding their country, they found industrial production reduced to a quarter of what it had been in 1914. Agriculture had collapsed. Despite their pledge of Land, Peace and Bread the Bolshevik leaders had been unable to solve the huge food problems of Russia's cities, which were now darkened and cold, the electricity and gas having been cut off and all oil and wax used up.

It might, slowly, have sorted itself out. But the summer of 1919 had yielded a terrible harvest, even in the most fertile regions of the Volga basin and southern Ukraine; this crop failure was repeated in 1920. Along the valley of the Volga, home to some twenty million people, the average rainfall of fourteen inches shrank to three. The earth turned black.

Livestock was slaughtered. Half of Russia's thirty-three million horses disappeared; in their place came a few camels, better able to survive on cactus and thistles, but disgusting to eat. Starving peasants started to converge on the cities.

When the representatives of the western countries had left Russia at the end of 1918, it was as if an immense mist had descended. What little news got out was tentative and uncertain and though there had been talk of food shortages, few people in the West understood that they pointed to an impending catastrophe. Then suddenly, in the summer of 1921, came a passionate public appeal by the author Maxim Gorky, who had been put at the head of a committee whose members had no obvious political affiliations to approach the West for help. His message, said Gorky, was addressed to 'all honest people' everywhere in the world. The failure of the harvest 'menaces death by hunger of the Russian population'. The newspaper *Pravda* was more specific. Famine, it said, was already affecting twenty-five million people.

There had been terrible famines in Russia before. But this was different. The first visitors to the famine areas — the Volga basin, the Crimea, Georgia and the Ukraine — came back with appalling stories. A young Quaker woman called Anna Haines was taken to see the House of Motherhood and Infancy in Buzuluk. It had been renamed, she wrote in her report, the 'Home of Death'.

> In three rooms ... was gathered the saddest group of babies that have ever lived or died. Deserted or left orphans by their parents, often taken from the arms of dead mothers fallen along the streets, most of them merely pass through this house on the way to the graveyard ... Those able to sit up or to walk were in the yard, huddled on a blanket, all of them wailing and holding out their hands to anyone who came in sight for food.

A rough iron garbage cart, she wrote, came every other day to take away the corpses.

If the famine in Russia handed the Red Cross national societies and the new League a wonderful opportunity to profess their humanitarianism, it also became a time of squabbles. By the end of September 1921, Serbia, Croatia and Slovenia were abstaining from voting in the League of Nations, saying that they wished to have it put on record that they deplored the economic and political regime of the Soviets who were responsible for this catastrophe. They added that it should provide a warning that the Soviets might do the same elsewhere if not checked. Lafontaine, a Belgian delegate, rose to the occasion.

> We have returned 350,000 prisoners of war to their families. We shall pull out of cesspits where they languish hundreds of thousands of women given over to the worst turpitudes . . . And this is the very moment that we shall take a resolution to wash our hands like Pontius Pilate, leaving to die of hunger twenty to thirty million mothers, old people and children . . . We cannot consent to be accomplices to such a crime.

As part of their appeal to the West for food, the Soviets had agreed to accept Voldemar Wehrlin as the International Committee delegate in Moscow, saying that they felt sure that the famine 'offered them a vast and fertile field of work in common'. By October, Wehrlin was notifying Geneva of 200,000 refugees starving in South Russia, and of 80,000 children in the Republic of the Bashkirs, now in desperate need of food. He added that there was talk of cannibalism. He passed on a cable from a children's organization:

> The starving people have eaten all the cats, dogs, corpses of animals and are now beginning to eat human corpses. During the night the sheds in which the bodies are put before burial are broken into and the bodies eaten . . . We buried in all 681 of which 509 are children . . . We cry to you for help, come to help us, otherwise this entire district will become nothing but a desert.

Soon, Wehrlin was reporting that

> cannibalism has ceased to surprise anyone . . . mothers no longer let their children out after nightfall because there have been many cases of theft of children . . . I do not know what other terrible forms the famine can assume, because already it goes beyond the limits of the imagination.

The delegate to the Ukraine, Georges Dessonnaz, reporting that there were 187,000 starving children in the province of Odessa, sent a series of cables: 'Mirskoe village, in the district of Mariupole: father and mother, together with their entire family, have eaten a 17-day-old baby. During investigations, severed head of baby found,' and 'In the village of Novo-chatilka ... a wife has eaten her husband's corpse.' The delegate as witness had never seemed so important − nor so silent, for his reports were seldom read by many people outside the International Committee before being stored in closed archives, a state of affairs so contradictory as to become, in an age of increasing barbarity and cruelty, intolerable to individual delegates and perplexing to the rest of the world.

Georges Dessonnaz returned to Geneva with a message that would ring out in Europe in the decades to come.

> I believe that the reason for our inertia comes from the fact that all these horrors are taking place somewhere else, somewhere far away, and that the cries and tears of the starving do not reach the ears of Europeans ... I have heard them; they ring in my ears.

In theory at least, these stories were precisely the kind to appeal to the new League of Red Cross Societies. Davison, who quickly rallied to the call, clearly had in mind taking over the vast stocks of supplies and equipment left over from the war, much of it in American military hands, and setting up an emergency relief programme in eastern Europe, to be run by the League and its mainly American administrators. There were problems. The public was far from keen to help the Bolsheviks when there were so many worthy victims of the war in Allied countries; the London *Morning Post* on 16 April 1919 branded the whole idea a 'scheme which would countenance crime, betray good friends, and be the beginning of commitments which might lead to universal anarchy'. Some of the national Red Cross societies protested that if they gave all their supplies to the League, this would leave them totally impotent in foreign affairs. More important, perhaps, Herbert Hoover, future presi-dent of the United States and director of the ARA, the American Relief Administration − by now a veteran of feeding operations in China, occupied Europe and Poland − was interested in running the operation himself. Hoover was not so much philanthropic as pragmatic: he thought that relief to Russia would provide a 'breathing space to build up some stability' and had long been arguing that the best weapon against Bolshevism was food.

On 15 April 1921, representatives from western governments, the Vatican and most of the major charities, as well as the International Committee, the new League and twenty-one national Red Cross societies, met in Geneva to decide a common policy. All agreed that the price of relief would have to be peace.

The League might still just have emerged as the full-blown 'international relief organization' that both Davison and President Wilson had dreamed of, but it was now hampered by lack of firm commitment, not only from most national Red Cross societies, but from the American Red Cross, which professed itself daunted by the 'limitlessness' of Russia's needs. When questioned, Henderson was clear: the League was simply not in a position to act.

In the event, an International Committee for Russian Relief was set up to co-ordinate all relief work, Fridtjof Nansen was invited to be its high commissioner and the League offered support and technical advisers. Nansen set off to see Chicherin, the People's Commissar for Foreign Affairs, in Moscow and they drew up an agreement to include International Committee delegates as overseers of the relief operation. Edouard Frick was named Associate High Commissioner, based in Berlin. Soon afterwards, Hoover's ARA, with a mixture of congressional funds and private donations, started moving stocks into Russia, operating not so much under Nansen's programme as alongside it, and despatched food to the worst hit areas. For all their grandiloquent speeches, most nations had responded sluggishly to the appeal, earning strong criticism in the pages of the *Review*. For the International Committee, the League's defeat must have seemed sweet indeed.

One of Hoover's ideas was to concentrate on children, and he sent an early mission to the Volga basin to find out how they had been hit by the famine. Its members reported that the cities had been turned into places of nightmare, with rubbish strewn around the streets, sewage overflowing, running water cut off; they saw children 'their bodies deformed by starvation, covered with vermin-infested rags, huddled together on the floor like blind kittens, the sick, the starving and the dead indiscriminately'. In Simbirsk, they had been told, 'sometimes the corpses remain among the living for more than five days . . . There is no way to stop this great wave of starving peasants who come to the city to die.'

Bit by bit, supplies were collected, money was raised, and a vast relief operation got under way, largely sustained by Hoover and the ARA. Buildings were cleared, disinfected and turned into warehouses and feeding centres; bakers were supplied with flour and bread was baked. Realizing how important it was to keep people in their own villages, the relief workers went out to the countryside, where they found hamlets silent and deserted but for dead bodies, children with distorted arms and legs and bloated stomachs, and where they heard terrible tales of butchery and cannibalism. The young American workers were appalled by such misery and by the fatalism of the Russians towards it. By the beginning of December, just seventy days after drawing up their agreement, the ARA was able to announce that over half a million people were already receiving balanced diets in towns and villages stretching all the way from Petrograd on the Baltic to Astrakhan on the Caspian. Beyond a few fixed rules – relief to all, regardless of politics, strict accounting – the ARA proved flexible, adapting to local demands.

The Save the Children Fund had been started in England in the summer of 1919, after two sisters, Eglantyne Jebb and Dorothy Buxton, had published accounts of children starving to death in post-war Europe on account of the Allied blockade. While a Fight the Famine Council was set up to lobby politicians, the Save the Children Fund was launched at a public meeting in the Albert Hall to raise money specifically to start feeding children in Vienna, Eglantyne Jebb having been influenced by Frédéric Ferrière's reports from Austria. Ferrière's niece Suzanne, who had been working with him since 1914, was a friend of Eglantyne Jebb's and together the two women pushed for an international union for children, finally launched under the auspices of the International Committee in January 1920 in the Athénée in Geneva, in the very rooms that had seen the birth of the Red Cross over half a century before. It was given the name *Union Internationale de Secours aux Enfants*; Ador was on the board; Etienne Clouzot, a member of the International Committee, became its first general secretary; its logo was one of the Andrea della Robbia plaques which decorate the hospital for abandoned children in Florence.

As the famine in Russia unfolded, Nansen asked the Save the Children Fund to undertake a feeding programme in the province of Saratov, one of the hardest hit areas. Eglantyne Jebb, whose position on the politics of relief was clear – 'all wars,' she would say, 'just or unjust, disastrous or victorious, are waged against the child' – now faced open disapproval from her supporters and a rabid attack from the press, in particular the *Daily Express*. 'Feeling runs very high,' she wrote to Suzanne Ferrière on 11 May, 'in regard to the relief of Bolshevik children, almost higher than in the case of German children. On our Committee I think the majority are anti-Bolshevik.' Just the same, by the summer of 1922, when the famine reached its peak, the SCF was feeding more than 300,000 children and had extended its programme to take in some 375,000 starving adults, with money donated from other sources. That summer the ARA was reaching over ten million people, Nansen's office 1.4 million. By August it was clear that the harvest would be, if not good, adequate, and slowly the relief operations shrank, then closed.

All this had shown, more clearly perhaps than anyone could have imagined, that international help was crucial in major calamities and that, if properly managed, it could work with impressive smoothness and efficiency. Delicate political feuds, appalling weather, the collapse of the railway system had all been overcome, immense problems of logistics had been solved and for the most part money and supplies had been raised and distributed quickly and well. What the famine had also revealed, however, was that the relief world was underpinned by bitter rivalries. An extraordinary amount had been achieved – perhaps as many as fifteen million people saved – but Davison's vision of a League harmoniously united to bring universal contentment to the world was in tatters.

It was partly a question of jealousy and bickering, of which there had been a great deal, with not only the League and the International Committee sniping at one another, but the British Red Cross fighting an inglorious campaign against the Save the Children Fund; and, everywhere from Washington to Paris, there had been accusations of fiddling and corruption, laziness and incompetence. The world, it seemed, was too rivalrous a place for Davison's dream and the national Red Cross societies, which seemed prepared to tolerate the sovereignty of an International Committee which was in reality Swiss, were not so happy to relinquish control to an American-dominated League. But it was also to do with the nature of the work. Relief was a highly political matter, as Davison had known when he envisaged America as the League's not too conspicuous driving force. It was also fraught with misunderstanding and constantly under threat from manipulative outsiders.

Something of the quarrels already besetting this odd philanthropic world, in which sentimentality ran side by side with the need for ruthless efficiency, comes across very vividly from the reports sent in to the International Committee from two of its delegates stationed in faraway outposts. In 1920 a doctor called Georges Montadon was sent on a mission to Siberia. He found misery and chaos and tried to impose some kind of order. Within weeks, the Austrian, Hungarian and German Red Cross societies were all filing complaints to Geneva. Montadon, they said, was an autocrat. He was 'all used up, exhausted and utterly incapable of continuing with his job'; what was more, did Geneva realize that one of his relief trains had been 'organized by a Jew of the most despicable kind'? Bernard Rouvier, sent to Constantinople in October 1921, described to the Committee the Russian Red Cross, already active in the city; it was, he said, a 'nest of enemies . . . Babenko, a creature as false as Judas and a consummate liar, Tatitcheff (Count) a vague, colourless nonentity, and Senator Glinka, a feeble, idiotic old man, the senile tool of the other two'.

Two of the League's pillars, men who at least shared the same vision of united international relief, were now dying. By the summer of 1922, both Henderson and Davison were dead, Davison failing to survive brain surgery for a tumour. 'Temperamentally,' he is quoted as saying, not long before his death, 'I have never been able to accept failure, or indeed moderate success.' The men who replaced them − Judge John Barton Payne of the American Red Cross succeeding Davison, William Pearce, an American railwayman becoming director general and Sir Claude Hill his deputy − were resolute and impressive figures, but something of Davison's wider vision had been lost. What was more, America's initial contribution to the League of $2.5 million was fast disappearing and it was clear that, with America's growing isolationism, not a great deal more would be forthcoming. Recent struggles within the American Red Cross had again given Mabel Boardman some of her former power and she was pushing hard for the society to return to its earlier domestic concerns, a 'drowsy giant to be aroused only by fire, sword, storm and flood – acts of God, war and pestilence'.

The early months of the League's existence had been marked, some said marred, by continuous bickering – little rows that echoed in the pages of the rival magazines – with the International Committee now delighted to observe that the interloper was in fact weaker and more vulnerable than it had first appeared. The League's bid to be the co-ordinating body for all international relief had failed; so did its wish to take responsibility for international health work: the League of Nations now announced that it was setting up its own health section.

The decision was taken to abolish some of the League's more grandiose plans, while waiting for a more propitious day, and to move to Paris, which was cheaper, more agreeable to the many Americans who con-tinued to fill the League and far from the International Committee's meddlesome and disdainful glance.

Plans to hold the tenth International Red Cross Conference had been deferred at the end of the war by the prevailing mood of hostility between national societies, by the ill-tempered birth of the League and by the famine and diseases plaguing so much of Europe. In March 1921, almost ten years after the last memorable gathering in Washington, the Red Cross world met again, this time fittingly in the Palais de l'Athénée in Geneva, which had seen so many of the movement's most significant moments. Delegates from forty Red Cross societies attended, but not those of France or Belgium, who announced that they were not prepared to sit down at a table with the German Red Cross unless Germany apologized for its behaviour during the war. (There was no apology.) There was an exhibition, with stands reflecting the new interests of the various societies in first aid, nursing, social work, nutrition and disease. Everywhere, artists and designers had been turning their skills to Red Cross art and dazzlingly illustrated *telegrammes de luxe*, stamps and posters appeared on every stall. It was becoming increasingly clear from articles appearing in the *Bulletin* and *Worlds Health* that the war had made people far more conscious of social welfare and those areas which had once been in the hands of individual philanthropists were now moving into the mainstream. An almost tangible desire to talk no more of war – for to talk of it was to prepare for it and so bring it about — hung over the meeting.

The delegates were in mixed spirits. The war was at last over and the national societies had much to feel pleased about — their wartime performance had been, for the most part, excellent — so the mood of the occasion was optimistic, one of new suggestions and good resolutions. For the first time, the role of the Red Cross in civil wars was properly debated, the meeting agreeing that help should be offered to both sides, and that the International Committee should intervene if the national society in question was unable or 'unwilling' to call for assistance — a resolution that would have many repercussions. Senator Ciraolo's call to all nations and all societies to combat the spirit of war was widely applauded by men and women who had come to see that war itself, in becoming capable of causing widespread destruction, had also become a threat to the future of the human race. It was no longer enough to deplore war, then hope as Dunant and Moynier had hoped, to 'humanize' it. As Ciraolo saw it, peace had left the victorious intransigent, the losers truculent, newspaper editors bellicose, financiers rivalrous. 'Every man,' he declared, 'as far as lies in his power, must contribute to make peace permanent.' He was loudly cheered. A resolution called on both the International Committee and the League to address an appeal to 'all peoples to combat the spirit of war which is still rife throughout the world'. It went out on 19 July 1921 and, in urging the movement to work 'towards making war itself disappear' represented a major change from the former stand that war was inevitable.

But if the First World War had provided the societies with the opportunity to demonstrate their worth, it had also shown up the impotence of the International Committee when it came to enforcing the Geneva Convention and opened a Pandora's box of terrifying possibilities of what the future might have in store. Calls for a tribunal to introduce a 'rigorous justice to the world', Moynier's proposal, continued to come to nothing. Civil war, the fate of civilians, the needs of the huge numbers of refugees still being buffeted around the world, stateless and in an ever more pitiful condition, chemical warfare — these were all questions discussed and argued over, with varying degrees of urgency, in the years that followed. What would happen, as Senator Ciraolo kept asking, when countries at war chose as their targets 'unarmed populations incapable of action, composed of old men, women and children?' Ciraolo was echoing Frédéric Ferrière's words. The 1920s were a decade of talks, of international meetings, of taking stock, of formulating articles and trying to codify laws of war to cope with the new forms of warfare that all could see were on their way. No weapon was more keenly and anxiously debated than gas, Maxim Gorky warning in an article quoted in the *Review* that any new war would be a 'war of extermination by gas, a war which will cause millions and millions of dead, mad, mutilated and idiots'. The International Committee devoted considerable energy and time to drawing up a new protocol prohibiting 'asphyxiating, poisonous or other gases and of bacteriological methods of warfare'. It was ready for ratification on 17 June 1925.

And, as peace returned to Europe, the national societies began exploring where they could go next. Children, identified as the main sufferers in the post-war famine, now came in for widespread attention. In Geneva, Eglantyne Jebb was working to produce a first Declaration of the Rights of the Child, a precursor to later human rights legislation, with a ten-point plan to provide certain minimum standards in the treatment of children. Its tone, one of duty, responsibility and optimism, struck a chord. George Werner of the International Committee, which had remained a close supporter of Eglantyne Jebb's work, greeted the declaration with an unaccustomed burst of praise. 'May its pure and dazzling flame,' he announced, 'reach the very ends of the earth!' Soon, Eglantyne Jebb, extremely thin, her pale blue eyes shining with great intensity, a heavy silver crucifix hanging round the neck of her severe brown dress and veil – 'all in brown, before the Brownshirts made brown proscribed' as one friend put it – became a familiar figure at conferences, rising to her feet to put her case for children. She seemed, as the *Journal de Genève* wrote on the day of her funeral in December 1938, 'humanity's conscience'.

New charitable organizations for children were set up from one end of Europe to the other, with magazines running articles both practical and dotty, like one in *La Revue de L'Enfance* which insisted that babies should be given only red or yellow rattles, these being most soothing to the eye and more liable to induce physical and moral calm. When the first International Assembly of Red Cross Youth met in Prague in April 1923, with delegates as young as eight apparently thinking nothing of sitting through five-hour sessions without a break, vegetarians, pacifists and boy scouts all flocked to hear a young Czech speaker appeal for an undertaking to 'replace hatred and laziness by love and joyful toil'. At a boy scout jamboree the following year, 100,000 boys from thirty-five countries gathered round immense camp fires: the Scottish boy scouts reeled, the Japanese wrestled and the Hungarians mimed. This hearty, sentimental tone was echoed across countless Red Cross gatherings, though nowhere more so than in America, where the Red Cross celebrated its annual convention in 1921 in Ohio with a 'monster' spectacle of children dancing, horsemen in armour, a stage covered with nurses, kings, monks and philosophers, a choir of 1,000 singers and a *tableau vivant* showing Dunant standing alone amid the chaos of war. At conference after conference, distinguished medical men preached the 'gospel of soap and water' and spoke of their conviction that the true foundation of happiness and national power lay in good health. When, on 1 September 1923, the last day of the eleventh International Red Cross Conference, news came of a major earthquake in Tokyo and Yokohama, after which raging fires consumed the two cities, leaving 200,000 dead, and tidal waves pounded the shore, thirty-five national societies demonstrated their new energy, vying with each other to provide more assistance, more competently and at greater speed.

In 1927, after nearly a decade of lobbying, Ciraolo, the genial Italian who had been ousted from the presidency of the Italian Red Cross by a Fascist appointee, was able to push through his 'International Relief Union', for 'relief and assistance to disaster-stricken populations'. Though always better on paper than in action, the Relief Union provided a constant reminder of Davison's view on international obligations; one of Ciraolo's ideas had been to draw up a world map, showing where calamities appeared, so as to be always better prepared. Because Ciraolo was a good friend of the International Committee, seeing his plan as another arm of the Geneva-led movement, there was none of the rivalry that dominated relations with the League.

The 1920s also saw a new canny spirit enter the movement. During the war the American Red Cross had had the idea of setting up an office of 'Conferenciers' to recruit a corps of speakers, and judges, writers, businessmen and university presidents had obligingly trudged the country on lecture tours, extolling the virtues of the Red Cross movement. In 1921, Eglantyne Jebb had gone further, employing a professional publicity agent to advise her how best to tap into the pockets of the rich for the famine children of Europe. The Save the Children headlines, about children 'naked and starving' had brought in huge sums, as had a clever campaign reminding readers of the 'little children in Russia . . . passing beyond the border — going to meet Him whose birth you celebrate' while they sat down to their Christmas turkeys. Though none was as successful as a picture showing Britannia, standing at the door of a fashionable London shop with a well-dressed woman wearing a cloche hat. Britannia's arms are stretched out in supplication and she wears an expression both despairing and pleading; the caption reads: 'They are dying like flies.' It is important to find out, said Eglantyne Jebb, 'how to touch the imagination of the world'. Publicity, the fund-raising potential in starving children, was a lesson soon learnt by the Red Cross societies.

Meanwhile, as the national societies forged ahead, the International Committee and the League continued to bicker. 'There is nothing people will more readily fight about than doing good,' commented Colonel Guy Carleton Jones, delegate to the 1912 Washington conference. Negotiations between the two organizations were constantly brought to a halt by bad-tempered stalemates, by nitpicking, by wounded feelings, by disagreements over boundaries, duplication, membership and power. Talks were interrupted by long delays, as everything was translated and retranslated. The League complained about leaving so much power in the hands of 'worthy sons of this noble capital'. The Committee replied that its close-knit character was the key to its success. Tetchy notes went backwards and forwards across the Atlantic. 'Apparently,' wrote the chairman of the American Red Cross to Sir Claude Hill, the International Committee

> have decided to rule or ruin. The question is, how much strength it can exert. If our Board is lukewarm or hesitant, the future of the League is in peril . . . If any member of the League can patiently accept this situation and fall in with the plans of this selfish group, they of course have no real interest in the League.

Some of those involved called for an amalgamation of the two bodies; others insisted on simple co-operation; some wanted a single international voice, others favoured each society going its own way. Most

Right Gustave Ador, described by his nephew as the 'ideal president'. He was president of the International Committee from 1910 to 1928

Centre Dr Frédéric Ferrière. He served the International Committee in various capacities for over forty years

Bottom Mlle Margarite Cramer. She was the first woman appointed to the Committee and served from 1918

Seated third from left Madame Poincaré, wife of the President of France, led French women in war work, c. 1916

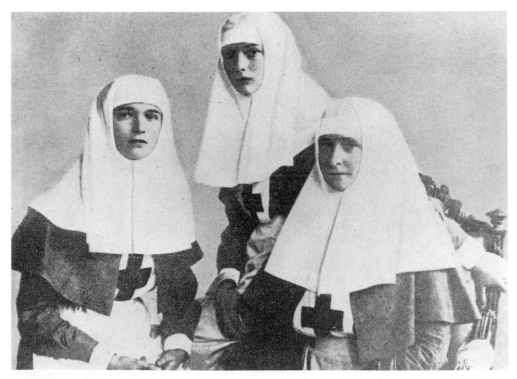

The Tsarina of Russia *right*, with her daughters the Grand Duchesses Olga and Tatiana, dressed in the uniform of the Russian Red Cross, c. 1916

FANYs in action during the First World War. By 1917 there were 450 driving ambulances in France and Belgium

The FANY drivers regarded themselves as an elite. All but one survived the war and forty-seven were decorated

An International Committee delegate visits German prisoners-of-war in a camp in Morocco in January 1916

Gustave Ador is greeted by Red Cross supporters in Geneva on 27 June 1917

Left A Red Cross postcard commemorating the execution of Edith Cavell

Centre A disinfection station in Poland. The International Committee played a major role in efforts to prevent the spread of famine and disease in post-war Europe

Bottom American Red Cross volunteers on their way to Europe, 1917

The tracing service at work in the Musée Rath, Geneva. By Christmas 1915, there were two and a half million men in captivity throughout Europe. 'The crucified heart of Europe bleeds from innumerable wounds,' wrote Stefan Zweig, 'but here its heart still beats.'

Top left Dr Elsie Inglis, one of the first British-trained women doctors. She was a strict authoritarian with a good sense of humour

Above Mrs St Clair Stobbart, known as 'the Major' during the Serbian campaign of the First World War

Left Two British Red Cross drivers, Baroness Serclass and Miss Mairi Chisholm in Pervyse, 30 July 1917

Overleaf German prisoners-of-war at a clearing depot in Abbeville, 2 October 1918

dreaded a schism. New proposals, whether from Prince Charles in Sweden or Sir Arthur Stanley in London, were drafted, discussed then rejected. A special conference was convened, to be held in the federal parliament building in Berne in the autumn of 1926. Twenty-seven societies turned up. It, too, ended in failure.

It may have been exhaustion that finally drove the two organizations to make peace of a kind; or it may have been the great good fortune of having a new president of the International Committee, a widely respected judge from Zurich called Max Huber who replaced Ador in 1928 and happened to get on well with the League's new vice-president, a German called Colonel Draudt. Together the two men were at last able to map out an intricate and not too hostile partnership, with statutes stipulating an international conference to be held every four years and a standing committee to provide continuity, the two bodies remaining separate but linked by various articles. The International Committee took war as its area of responsibility, the League peace, John Barton Payne writing wearily to Col. Draudt, 'We want of all things simplicity, and clearness, an absence of provisions leading to disputes . . . leaving both the League and the CICR [ICRC] fundamentally equal and governed by their own statutes.' It wasn't exactly what he got, but for the time being, it was agreed, it would have to do. Gustave Ador just had time to praise a pact that would endure, if uneasily, for some years to come (and to ponder whether the Committee had not been a little harsh on Henri Dunant's memory) before he died on 30 March 1928, at the age of eighty-two. He had served the Committee, in one capacity or another, for fifty-seven years, the last eighteen of them as president, from the Franco-Prussian war to the First World War and beyond, watching the power of modern weapons grow beyond all recognition and constantly trying to keep abreast of their destructive properties with ever more precise articles on the conduct of war. The sanctions Ador had longed for — what he called a *tribunal de pitié* — had never come about, but he had earned a reputation far beyond Switzerland for his honesty, his hatred of all forms of extremism and his good temper. His last meeting at the International Committee took place the day before his death.

The International Committee now began to prepare for its future, discussing how best to remain ready for war. The League, from their magnificent offices on the Avenue Velasquez in Paris, settled down to preside over a vast range of nationalities and interests — snake farms in Siam, opium addiction in the Far East — and turned increasingly to primary health care and preventive medicine. From Shanghai came a report from an imaginative Red Cross doctor describing how he was putting across a message about clean water in the shape of a travelling pageant, moving from city to city with a band playing 'Yankee Doodle' and actors dressed as Giant Flies, Mister Cholera and Mister Health mingling with the crowds, as students chanted, 'Firewood is cheap! Coffin wood is dear! Boil your water! Or buy your coffin!'

Max Huber would be a crucial figure in the next stage of the Red Cross history. In 1928, the year he began his seventeen-year presidency, he was fifty-four, descended from one of Zurich's oldest and most respected families, rich, a director of a number of industrial companies, widely travelled — a world tour at the turn of the century had taken in East Asia, Australia, Japan, China and the United States — and known for his strong advocacy of Swiss neutrality. In 1922 he had been appointed first judge, then president, of the International Court of Justice at the Hague and was widely regarded as Switzerland's foremost jurist holding, at one time or another, every important legal position. Pious, cautious, internationally acclaimed for his expertise in the legal world of concili- ation and arbitration, he would take his new job, as he took all his occupations, extremely seriously. 'The magistrate's office,' he had written, 'always carries with it something of priesthood, since the justice it rep- resents is moral in character and therefore related to the divine and hence the absolute.' For Huber, the International Committee would become a ministry where he would face moral questions as difficult as any in the church. He wished, he said, to live up to the goals of the founders, to keep faith with their historical roots and to introduce, in times of war, 'the recognition of the existence of a moral principle'.

Huber would be much tested in the years of his leadership, which would coincide with the hardest in the organization's history; an invariable expression of anxiety, as if he dreaded the responsibility of his position and felt powerless in the face of the world's barbaric ways, stamps every photograph of him. He would carry the moral debate into areas never mentioned and perhaps never dreamed of by Dunant and Moynier, just as his intensely cautious and legalistic spirit would influence most strongly nearly every International Committee decision in the years to come. He had, recalls a delegate, 'the purety of a dove and the watchfulness of a snake'.

The year 1928 was not a bad one for peace. With the Briand-Kellogg pact, forty-six nations had condemned the waging of all war and called for settlement of disputes only by peaceful means. Two new Geneva Conventions, one for the sick on the battlefield, the other for prisoners of war, attempts to address the many *lacunae* revealed by the First World War and resolutions to ensure that men would be given the 'right to have their personality and honour respected' were drafted. They were important, because they did away with the *Si omne* clause which had held that, in order to be binding, all the parties at war and those not just involved at that moment, had to have ratified – which, given the numbers of countries soon to be sucked into conflict would give the International Committee a little more leverage.

'The Red Cross path,' announced Huber, as he took up office that year, was one 'filled with grandeur and tribulation'. But the age, he added, was 'apocalyptic'.

ELEVEN

The Feet of Little Angels

On Tuesday 16 October 1934, delegates from fifty-seven national Red Cross societies gathered in Tokyo's Constitution Memorial Hall for the opening of the fifteenth International Red Cross Conference. It was a splendid affair. The decision to hold the event in Japan was both a mark of recognition for the second largest national society in the world — the American was now the largest — and a wish to affirm the Red Cross 'presence in every continent'. The Japanese were determined to make the most of it. The 252 foreign delegates, joined by 13,000 Japanese members who had come to hold their annual general meeting as a start to the international forum, were welcomed by the Empress, surrounded by the princes and princesses of the Imperial Court and by dignitaries from the army and the navy. She spoke, as the newspapers later remarked, in a 'soft clear' voice; and she wore western dress, to honour her foreign guests.

The delegates, too, had resolved to do Japan proud. It was, apart from anything else, good diplomacy and the Americans, more perhaps than any other national society, had a keen appreciation of the political power of the now immense and prestigious Red Cross movement. As Judge John Barton Payne of the American Red Cross society wrote to his friend John Merrill, president of All American Cables, 'All things of this kind have an effect on the relationship between the two countries and we do not want to leave anything undone which will show that the attitude of the US towards Japan is of the most friendly sort.' Notes to the delegates accompanying him to Tokyo included points of etiquette and instructions to the men to pack 'a cut-away, Prince Albert, Tuxedo and full-dress'.

The visiting delegates had been preceded to Japan by Lewis Gielgud of the League, who had been asked to help with the preparations. Gielgud, (a diplomat and playwright, elder brother of the distinguished actor) was greatly impressed by the organizational skills and courtesy of his Japanese hosts – he called them 'punctilious with the punctiliousness of *grands seigneurs*'. He returned to Europe marvelling at the banquets, the trains on which passengers were offered books to read and the blend of the traditional and the modern at the imperial court. He described the day when a Japanese official apologized for 'cockroaching' on his time. Perhaps, Gielgud had asked carefully, his visitor had meant 'encroaching'? 'Ah' said the Japanese, 'encroaching, of course, I had forgotten that the bird was feminine.' Little of the Japanese Red Cross efficiency, however, had been lost on Gielgud, who noted the nearly three million adult members, 'permeated by a spirit of self-sacrifice', the thirty immaculate hospitals and the eagerness of the junior members who filled their spare time hunting locusts, both to keep down the insect population and to raise funds by selling them by the thousand as culinary delicacies.

Welcoming the foreigners in the pages of the League's magazine in the months leading up to the conference, Prince Nakagawa, vice-president of the Japanese Red Cross, had spoken of the pleasures of a Japanese October with unclouded skies and pure air, the chrysanthemums in full bloom and 'mountains and meadows . . . steeped in the rich scarlet tints of autumn. Thus, Nature herself will join us in welcoming our overseas guests to Japan.' The Emperor spoke of 'Red Cross weather', neither raining nor too hot.

The first ship bearing the delegates, the *Asama Maru*, reached Yokohama harbour on the evening of 14 October flying the Red Cross flag. Outside the breakwater, the ship was boarded by a distinguished welcoming party; thousands of Red Cross members, waving lanterns decorated with red crosses, waited on the quayside. On board the *Asama Maru* were Judge Payne and most of his sixty-seven-strong delegation – Mabel Boardman, delayed by speaking engagements, was following on the *President Coolidge* – as well as the Duke of Saxe-Coburg, grandson of Queen Victoria, the new president of the German Red Cross and a personal friend of Hitler. The duke was travelling, as the newspapers put it, 'incognito, simply as chief delegate of the German Red Cross'. With him came Colonel Draudt, the well-liked vice-president of the League. In the days that followed, whether by ship on the *President Harding*, *President Grant* or the *Empress of Russia* or on the Trans-Siberian railway via Manchuria, came Lady Muriel Paget, one of the six British delegates, Miss Adelaide Mohr from Norway, who brought just one small suitcase, saying that she never wore anything but her Red Cross uniform or climbing clothes, and Miss Norah Hill, organizing secretary of the Indian Red Cross and veteran of the famine relief missions to Russia, a sensible-looking woman with a formidable jaw. 'From the Antipodes' arrived a Mrs Carlyle Sythe, who spoke warmly of getting junior Red Cross members to knit quilts for hospital beds. Among the International Committee's delegates was Mlle Lucie Odier, a thin, somewhat mouse-like former nurse, who had worked with military internees and civilian refugees in the First World War, recently appointed the Committee's second woman member, and whose gentle manner concealed a steeliness of purpose and considerable intelligence; Mlle Cramer — now married to Edouard Frick and calling herself Mme Frick-Cramer — and Dr Paravicini, the Swiss society doctor from Tokyo who had worked on behalf of the International Committee during the First World War. Max Huber, who had been unable to come because of ill health, sent fulsome messages about 'internationalism, denuded of all political colouring'. The Marquise de Noailles, the only woman among the French delegates, an 'aviation enthusiast,' had decided to fly herself out to Tokyo, to demonstrate the potential of air ambulances; the marquise had recently caused a stir in Paris by suggesting that working women should be allowed two weeks' rest before and after confinement.

Never had the Japanese, whose thirty-eight delegates were all men, seen or even imagined so many women in positions of importance. Alerted in advance, they had chosen the wives and daughters of 'Distinguished Notables' to take the ladies shopping and sight-seeing and the pressures of the conference were frequently broken up by excursions, banquets, tea parties, Noh and Kabuki theatre and concerts. The Imperial palace orchestra had been practising western tunes for the past year. Many presents were exchanged. For their part, the foreign visitors found their Japanese hosts charming, distinguished and very small. Baron Hirayama, the president of the Japanese Red Cross, who spoke excellent French, was under 5 feet tall. The foreign ladies were told that the Japanese Red Cross had been making enormous strides in getting Japanese women to abandon the constricting obi worn tightly bound around the chest in favour of 'comfortable coats and loose knickerbockers', and to sit on stools rather than crouch or squat.

It was not all pleasure. Five commissions were set up, to discuss membership, relief work, health, nursing and junior members. The International Committee and the League had judged the moment right to welcome the Red Crescent societies of the Soviet Union – the Soviet successor to the pre-war Russian Red Cross – formally into the fold, there having been strong opposition all through the 1920s from the emigré Russian world. There was an embarrassing moment when Christian Rakovsky, the leader of the Soviet delegation, made an impassioned appeal for the Red Cross movement to throw itself wholeheartedly into campaigning for peace which was anathema to the French and British contingents.

Far more crucial, however, and of lasting importance to the whole Red Cross movement, was the debate on civilians, a long-running saga hampered ever since the end of the First World War by the impossibility of finding workable common ground for a category of war victim that ranged from refugees to deportees, stateless people to nationals persecuted in their own countries. The 1920s had been marked by intense lobbying on behalf of civilians, first by Frédéric Ferrière, who had devoted his life to securing some kind of international protection for them, then, after his death, by his niece Suzanne, and Edmond Bouvier, who had both given a great deal of time to drafting and redrafting possible conventions to bring protection to civilians in the event of another world war. Though they had eventually been forced to restrict their draft to two categories only – civilians resident in enemy territory and civilians in occupied territory – they had still found themselves in a legal quagmire. In Tokyo, after much debate and a certain amount of watering down, their draft convention was accepted, though not officially approved, which meant that more lobbying and work would have to go on. Though disappointing, this at least gave the International Committee a mandate to push ahead, with a view to asking the Swiss government to convene a diplomatic conference to examine the draft – only governments, as we have seen, could do this. The Tokyo Draft, as it was soon known, would prove crucial in the years to come.

After a week of many resolutions on members, nursing and new developments, more banquets, more tea parties and more courtesy, the meeting broke up. The delegates set off home impressed, even if the members of the International Committee complained to one another that many of those present seemed to have had very little understanding of what the Committee actually did, and that several had confused it with the Swiss Red Cross. At their regular monthly meeting in January 1935, Mlle Odier reported that she had decided not to attend Mabel Boardman's special session on female social work, on the grounds that feminism had not seemed appropriate in the circumstances. For the Japanese, the Tokyo conference had been an overwhelming success. It was the first international gathering of this size ever held in Japan and a publicity coup that had served not only to demonstrate to their citizens that their country was indeed a world power, but to the foreigners that Japan was a progressive, highly efficient nation, committed to humanitarianism.

The trouble was, it was all something of a sham.

The Red Cross was good at shams. Decades of delicate negotiations over sensitive issues, of pushing endlessly for concessions it had no mandate or power to demand, had made its leaders skilled at the art of displaying apparent public harmony. The chrysanthemums and tea parties in Tokyo belied a Red Cross world already heavily implicated in political realities which were growing more sensitive and dangerous every day.

Even the timing of the Tokyo conference was ironic. Using the pretext of defending the lives and property of its subjects, Japan had invaded Manchuria in the autumn of 1931, then gone on to set up the 'independent' state of Manchukuo in March 1932. For reasons of tact, none of this was mentioned at the conference, nor was the fact that, alarmed by reports of atrocities and the bombing of cities and responding to an appeal from China, the League of Nations had sent in a commission whose report had resulted in the prompt withdrawal of Japan from the organization, thereby seriously weakening the whole idea of collective security. At the time the delegates were arriving in Tokyo to talk about peace, Japan was actively rearming. What was more, Japan was not even a proper member of the Red Cross movement, in that it had failed to ratify the Geneva Conventions of 1929 with their increased protection for prisoners-of-war. And though it did finally agree, in the wake of the Tokyo conference, to ratify the Convention relating to the sick of the armed forces, it refused to do the same for the Convention dealing with the treatment of prisoners-of-war — a refusal that would have immense repercussions later. By 1934, the peacetime spirit of the early Japanese Red Cross was rapidly evaporating in favour of ever closer ties with the army and navy. Looking after soldiers, not reaching for humanitarian ideals, was its main concern.

None of this was unknown to the foreign delegates as they sipped their mint tea. In February 1932, the International Committee, alerted by telegram to the worsening conflict in the Far East and to the repeated violations of the Geneva Conventions, had despatched Sidney Brown to Shanghai. Brown, who would soon become one of its most controversial and interesting delegates, was in China for a month. His report, published in the *Review*, is an extraordinary mixture of hard-nosed reporting and diplomatic niceties – Brown evidently relished the exquisitely courteous manners of both his Chinese and Japanese hosts. He returned praising the helpfulness and civility of the officers, but comparing the devastation caused by the Japanese to what he had witnessed on the battlefields of France in 1918. Some of the Chinese dead, he remarked, had been bayoneted to death in their beds or while they ate. Travelling around the area occupied by the Japanese forces – a spectator to the horrors of war in the way Henri Dunant had been at Solferino – Brown had found that while the Japanese had cremated their own dead, they had left the Chinese where they fell, scattered around the fields, in ditches and canals, partly concealed by fresh snowfalls, some hacked to pieces or blown apart by shells. Together with the Chinese Red Cross, Brown had succeeded in collecting the remains in order to give them a proper burial and had even persuaded the Japanese to lower the water level in some of the canals, in order to fish out bodies 'in a state of advanced putrefaction, and revolting to look at'. In some places, Brown went on, he had come across Japanese tourists who had brought their wives and children to be photographed holding the Japanese flag, surrounded by the corpses of Chinese soldiers. Despite appeals, the Japanese authorities refused to allow foreign missionary doctors from Shanghai on to the battlefields to attend to the wounds of Chinese casualties. This was all quite clearly counter to everything being discussed in Tokyo.

The most peculiar thing about Brown's report is his description of both atrocities and social gatherings in the same flat, dispassionate tone. It was all a little as if none of it were quite real, an impression that comes across strongly in many of the reports of early delegates, from

Appia on, suggesting that, like the organization they represented, they were far from clear about the precise nature of their role, whether they were meant to be observers, commentators, jurors or judges.

The Chinese, though satisfied with the Commission's report, had been taken aback by the passivity of the European response. As Dr V. K. Wellington Koo, Chinese representative at the League of Nations, asked the Council, was such an attitude 'of a great Power like Japan ... consonant or compatible with the sentiments and ideals of the post-war world? Has the Great War been fought in vain?'

It was a question everyone in the Red Cross was beginning to ask. The jovial mood in Tokyo concealed more than Japanese aggression. By the middle of the 1930s, the optimism and energy that had characterized the Red Cross world in the wake of the First World War – expansion throughout Africa and South America, vast international relief operations, imaginative programmes like the sending of VADs or 'fisher lassies' to Scottish ports to tend to the cuts of returning herring fishermen – were fading fast. Davison's dream of a happy and united Red Cross brotherhood, able to cure all the ills of mankind, had been extremely short-lived. What had seemed so clear in the heady gatherings of the 1920s now, in the increasingly bellicose spirit of the mid-1930s, looked naive and absurd. The crash of the American stock market in the autumn of 1929, growing American isolationism, the rise of fascism in Europe, the bleak realization among pacifists that the world peace they had preached and so truly believed attainable was little more than a dream, had all served to dampen spirits and cut budgets.

The International Committee neither could, nor wanted to engage in politics. Under its mandate, enshrined at successive international meetings of the entire Red Cross movement, it could protest against the horrors of war, do all in its power to mitigate its most murderous aspects, but it could not lobby actively against war itself, even if some of the national societies that made up its membership were actively in favour of pacifism. Discreet negotiation, and where that failed public denunciation, remained its principal tools.

The awkward exchange in Tokyo over peace had been revealing, as had been the passing of a resolution that national societies should do all they could to promote peace short of asking their governments to draw up new rules to prevent war breaking out. Not all the delegates had of course gone along with the watered-down agreement. James Feisel, a member of the American delegation had visited Judge Payne privately to urge him to 'say something that would make the world sit up and take notice about the drift to war'. But Payne, who was a realist and a true exponent of neutrality for the Red Cross, had been adamant: such a statement, he had told Feisel, would have been both 'unwise and inappropriate', since the role of the Red Cross remained what it had always been, a mitigator of the horrors of war and not a pacifist organ-ization.

Never, in fact, was the International Committee's fundamentally para-doxical position on war and its own power clearer than in the 1930s, and never was a shrewd and steady leadership more necessary, to hold the Red Cross to a limited but crucial set of objectives — primarily obedience to the Geneva Conventions — while allowing national societies to develop their own enthusiasms. The Red Cross movement, as Payne and Huber well knew, owed its immense prestige to its success in helping the victims of wars and natural disasters, and to its moral voice, used to keep the conduct of war within tolerable boundaries. Its power, measured against that of governments and armies was, after all, based on nothing but intellectual consent.

But Feisel was right: the world *was* drifting towards war, and though there was little the International Committee could do about it, the several million men and women who now made up its membership were excellently placed to observe it and clearly few had doubts that it was coming, as their letters and contributions to their national societies' publications showed. Everywhere, peacetime Red Cross activities were giving way to reviews of kit, uniforms and supplies, and to the checking of registers of volunteers. In the pages of the *Review*, which, month by month, continued to monitor the activities and interests of the Red Cross world — which made it such an excellent mirror of the times — the talk was all of readiness.

Read carefully, however, the *Review* could also be seen as a warning of things to come. From across Europe now appeared reports of youth work with decidedly ugly overtones.

In Switzerland, a children's organization called *Pro Juventute*, was reported in the *Review* as having announced that 'difficult children, and above all the feeble-minded, cannot be brought up at home'. One *Pro*

Juventute drawing showed a group of provocatively dressed young people, with a vast, menacing, devil hovering above the signs to a cinema and a café. 'Who,' read the caption, 'will help them to keep off the streets and point the way to real joy and the foundations of true family happiness?' *Pro Juventute* was also known to have its eye on gypsies.

In Italy, the Fascists were building swimming pools and sports stadiums to 'promote the harmonious development of young Italians'. In Germany, so the *Review* noted, medical magazines were running campaigns about hygiene and the need to provide society with 'healthy, normal and active individuals'. At a conference on hygiene and sport, held in Berne in the summer of 1931, there had been much talk about the importance of removing small children from 'noxious influences'. Across the Red Cross world, the battle for the hearts and minds of children seemed to be taking on an almost desperate note, as people began to realize that the Junior Red Cross movement – standing at over 12 million members in 48 countries in 1930 – could go well beyond imparting a simple code of health to shaping a whole new generation. As Walter S. Gard, acting national director of the American Red Cross, wrote in the early 1930s: 'Anything that will tend to restore world order, encourage international understanding, appreciation and friendship' needed promoting. But even as American Red Cross junior members despatched little gifts to their pen pals abroad, Red Cross youth societies in Europe were increasingly marching not to the tune of clean teeth and dead locusts, but to the bands of Fascist, Nazi and Komsomol youth organizations, all of whom had perceived the vast success of the Red Cross junior membership drive and courted the young members. How far this was seen as dangerous is nowhere reflected in Red Cross publications. The tone of the *Review* itself, however, was altering; gone were the ebullient, self-congratulatory reports of post-war years; in their place had come bald, tight-lipped warnings – about chemical warfare, about uncontrollable new weapons, about the need to protect civilians – that seemed to grow more urgent year by year.

Max Huber was an intensely pious and moral man; but as the disarmament talks failed, unemployment spread, and national rivalries sharpened, so his repeated likening of the Red Cross to the Good Samaritan began to sound increasingly hollow. Gustave Ador's hopes for an international tribunal of arbitration had long since been rejected as unworkable. Huber's appeal to morality, as well as the preparedness of national societies rendered bureaucratic by fifteen years of world peace, would now be severely tested by three events – the Italian invasion of Abyssinia, later known as Ethiopia, the Spanish civil war, and the Japanese occupation of China.

The middle and late 1930s were to be a time when the professional Red Cross delegate was moulded, and it was in the hands of these new International Committee representatives – bold, romantic, with clear views about right and wrong and a certain arrogance born of their standing and their scarcity – that the identity of the Committee itself would be clarified. With its role so imprecisely defined, it would be up to its delegates – and their controllers in Geneva – to carry their powers and responsibilities as far as they could go, feeling their way forward, endlessly adapting and re-adapting in the search for the best ways in which to protect the victims of war.

Sidney Brown's middle name was Hamlet. He was tall, lanky and good looking. The second son in a family of anglophiles from Baden outside Zurich – his mother was always known as Jenny, his brother as Harry – Brown spoke not only French and German but perfect English, the result of an English governess and an English grandfather, founder of the Brown-Boveri engineering firm. He was gregarious, made friends easily and had a passion for sunbathing.

Sidney, his parents agreed, was not cut out for industry. He was sent to study law instead in Geneva, Zurich and Berne, went to the Sorbonne to take a course in legal history, then on to a final degree at The Hague. It was here that he met Max Huber, then president of the International Court of Justice, though it is probable that the Huber and Brown families already knew each other well in Zurich. After Huber was made president of the International Committee, it was only natural that he should call on a fellow Zuricher – efforts were now being made to escape the purely Genevan character of the organization – and former pupil, particularly as he wanted a young lawyer to help him investigate the possible humanitarian dimensions to the treaties of the League of Nations. What was more, the lack of English speakers had become a source of some embarrassment at international Red Cross gatherings, dominated nowadays by the Americans and the British. As for Brown, the International Committee was fast becoming a natural home for talented second sons of good Swiss families.

In 1929, at the age of thirty-one, Sidney Brown entered the organization as secretary. When not acting as Huber's intermediary — for the first years of his appointment Huber continued to live in Zurich, coming to Geneva only when needed, and Brown travelled between the two, keeping him informed of all developments — he used his legal skills to draw up a long and detailed report on current humanitarian law. Like Ferrière and Ciraolo, he was concerned at the way so very little had actually been achieved to protect civilians in the event of another war. As representative of the International Committee in Shanghai in March 1932 and, more importantly, as secretary of the International Committee at the Tokyo conference of 1934, he had been well placed to follow the apparently unsolvable debates on the vulnerability of civilians in wars where they too seemed to have become legitimate targets.

On 4 October 1935, Italy, using a clash over waterholes on a disputed frontier as a pretext, went to war against Ethiopia. There had been no major conflict for sixteen years and the International Committee was a little rusty. Just the same, it followed its usual path and sent telegrams to the Italians and Ethiopians offering help. In Geneva, the Committee met to discuss the war. Huber and Mme Frick-Cramer were there, as was Mlle Odier, whose quiet, serious voice was now often heard raising questions about the moral duties of the Red Cross, and Jacques Chenevière, the acerbic poet and writer. Among the newcomers was a distinguished soldier, Colonel Guillaume Favre, carrying on a tradition of family service to the International Committee — he was the fourth Favre to serve on it.

There was also Carl Jacob Burckhardt, son of a professor of law and politician, and author of a much admired first volume of biography of Cardinal Richelieu. Burckhardt was as steeped in German culture and tradition as Chenevière was in the French, clever, vain, ambitious, beautifully dressed, a little like de Gaulle to look at, with a small, neat moustache. He is one of the most interesting of all the people who joined the International Committee and one of the most influential. According to his biographer, Paul Stauffer, his ambition was to enter world history and when that seemed to be failing, at least to enter the record of history by writing about it.

Descended from one of the great Basle families and related to the historian Jacob Burckhardt — his Burckhardts spelt their name with both the 'ck' and the 'dt' to distinguish themselves from the more lowly Bourcarts — he provoked strong feelings both for and against in all who met him. 'For the world he was a demi-God,' says Stauffer, explaining why he chose him as a subject for biography, 'I thought he was a fake.' Burckhardt took himself very seriously and had little time either for the English — he never learnt to speak the language — or for the art of understatement. He could, friends said, be witty but he had no sense of self-irony. A former diplomat, serving at the Swiss legation in Vienna after the First World War, Burckhardt had come to Geneva in 1932, not long after his marriage to Elizabeth de Reynold, daughter of Cronach de Reynold, writer and arch Catholic historian and an admirer of Mussolini and Salazar, to teach history at the Institut Universaire de Hautes Etudes Internationales. This became a meeting place for prominent European jurists and, in the 1930s, was seen as a bastion of liberal thinking and internationalism, home to young refugee lawyers from Nazi Germany, in direct contrast to the law faculty of Geneva University, where fascists were said to be welcome. Burckhardt's own view on history was bleak. 'We are moving into a period of vulgarity and cruelty,' he wrote in a letter in 1927,

> one above all of lies. Many things are going to vanish; this fine and noble 19th-century spirit of humanism will fall into ruin ... We will find ourselves fighting for principles in a way that we have never fought for anything; in the service of sectarian fanaticism we will see hatred ... torture, murder ... Yes, that is the nightmare that comes to haunt me.

On the International Committee, Burckhardt's voice was that of high diplomacy, of German and Austrian culture, of intellectual clarity. Younger members, according to Jean Pictet, the lawyer who joined the organization in the 1930s, were intimidated by his steely glare and disconcerted when he wrote letters during meetings without ever losing track of the discussions.

The war in Ethiopia was to be a delegates' war: it was here, in the highlands and among the diplomats and missionaries in Addis Ababa that the modern delegate would be born, one who, unlike his predecessors, saw his role as that of humanitarian actor, one able to influence events. War, whatever the barbarity with which it was waged, had always been viewed by the leaders of the International Committee as a military matter, even if they spoke up over breaches of the Geneva Conventions and talked wistfully, from time to time, about peace. As Brown's report from Shanghai in 1932 suggests, the delegate still at that time saw himself as a witness and a bystander — which partly explains the dispassionate tone of the despatches.

Ethiopia was to change all this and would bring to the fore men who were obstinate, adventurous, dutiful, but who also had strong views on the conduct of war itself. Because the distance from Geneva was so great, and communications so slow, there was no choice but to give them independence and power, and it was one of Huber's strengths that he was now willing to let the men he appointed run on very long leashes. Later, Huber would contribute an introduction to one of the bibles of the International Committee, a book called *Le Troisième Combattant*, written by a young doctor called Marcel Junod. The ideal delegate, Huber wrote, worked for both sides and was interested only in the suffering of defenceless human beings, irrespective of their nationality, convictions or past; he was brave, morally and physically tough, decisive, tactful, firm, able to stand his ground even when those he sought to defend were being abused, and was ever faithful to the Red Cross principles of neutrality and impartiality.

For the most part, Huber's trust paid off. Even if the selection process was extraordinarily casual — a friend of a friend, a distant cousin, a few brief conversations, then sent off, untested and untrained, into challenging situations often of considerable danger — the Swiss men who set out from Geneva tended to be steady, modest and irreproachable; occasionally they were also brilliant. However, not surprisingly perhaps, some were also prima donnas, who hated interference and balked at authority. For the delegates, being selected by the International Committee was often the fulfilment of John Buchan-ish boyhood dreams — adventure, risk, man pitted against the forces of evil.

Something of this spirit clings to the delegates to this day: you see it in their walk and gestures as they stalk around the headquarters of the International Committee in Geneva, a little arrogant, a little swaggering. Even the women give out a feeling of being different. They have, after all, exercised enormous power, and the fact that it is all so secret only adds to the lustre. It can, of course, go wrong. Delegates can and do become too involved: and it is then that they lose their neutrality and with it their usefulness to the organization. Sidney Brown was one of these.

On 5 October a telegram from Addis Ababa reached the International Committee in Geneva, which had hastily set up a special commission for Ethiopia, with Colonel Favre as president and Mlle Odier, Burckhardt and Chenevière among its members. It came from the Ethiopian Red Cross and it requested, with some urgency, ambulances, doctors and medical supplies: the Ethiopian medical services, it said, lacked everything from catgut to ether, anti-malaria tablets to milk powder. From Italy came a short reply to the International Committee's offers of help. It was signed by Senator Filippo Cremonesi, who had replaced Ciraolo as president of the Italian Red Cross and who was known to the readers of the *Review* as a keen supporter of the Fascists, under whom he claimed he had been able at last to bring the Red Cross to its full glory. The Italians thanked Geneva, but lacked, he said, for nothing. A number of Italy's allies, and in particular Portugal, now expressed their regret at not being able to demonstrate their 'admiration and esteem' for the excellent Italian Red Cross.

On 24 October Sidney Brown left for Ethiopia, boarding the *Chantilly* at Marseilles with thirty-two cases of medical supplies, including morphine, quinine and syringes. He had with him as second-in-command Dr Junod, the future author of *Le Troisième Combattant*, head of surgery for Mulhouse's civilian hospitals. Junod, like Brown, was tall for a Swiss, with straight dark brown hair worn rather long, a slightly pointed, egg-shaped face and a humorous mouth. He spoke broken English, with a marked Swiss German accent. They made a good pair, Brown with his lawyer's mind and wider perspective and Junod resolutely practical, though later it would be said that the two men had not got on very well. The third member of their party was Dr Hylander, head doctor of the Swedish

Red Cross, who had lived for six years in Ethiopia and spoke Amharic. No nurses accompanied them, the Ethiopians having cabled 'Female personnel impossible.'

Thirteen national Red Cross societies had reacted with speed – in all twenty-six would send help – and by the time the three men reached Addis Ababa, money was flowing in. Norway, Denmark and Sweden had gone further and were setting up their own field ambulances, and two British doctors, Dr Melly and Dr Macfie, were on their way from London to Dessie in the north, where the emperor had set up his headquarters. Before boarding the S.S. *Rampura* with sixteen Bedford lorries, the two men had been given an emotional send-off by Sir Arthur Stanley, chairman of the British Red Cross Society, and the archbishop of Canterbury, who turned up to bless the flag. The president of the International Aeronautical Federation, Prince Bibesco, was known to be contacting the members of the various new flying clubs, telling them, as he reported to Huber, that this war was 'a remarkable opportunity to demonstrate what private aviation can do for the Red Cross', in terms of ferrying doctors and medical supplies.

Even as they left Marseilles harbour, Junod and Brown were sitting down to write their reports. How they found the time to produce these long letters, page after page of remembered conversations, changes of plans, character vignettes and suggestions for action, is not clear. Junod was the more purposeful, Brown the more discursive, but the flow never stopped. As they left, Mme Frick-Cramer remarked to Huber that the lesson to be learned from earlier conflicts was that, given the increasingly competitive nature of charitable organizations – was she referring to Davison and the American Red Cross? – it was absolutely essential that the International Committee delegates be 'very practical' and possessed of a 'great deal of tact, *infinite discretion*, but also of firmness and authority'.

The two men were to need all the tact they could summon up. As soon as the war broke out various foreign missionaries and doctors, presided over by a handful of aristocratic Ethiopians, had hastily set up an Ethiopian Red Cross society in a small hut. On 16 November from Addis Ababa, Brown reported irritably that Sir Sydney Barton, the British minister, and his wife were determined to run matters their own way, and that what he called the 'occult influences' of the British Mission were making everyone miserable, while the Emperor, very disappointed to learn that he and Junod came not from the League of Nations but from the Red Cross, vacillated and took advice from everyone. While Junod devoted most of his time to helping set up the foreign ambulances and getting them to the front, trying to co-ordinate some of the independent Red Cross help that had not waited for directions from Geneva, Brown grappled with diplomatic minefields, writing to Geneva that he was having considerable difficulty in having Red Cross signs removed from brothels.

The foreign ambulances, using lorries backed up by 500 mules under a variety of foreign doctors, had fanned out across 125 miles of the front to the north. They were not finding their work altogether easy, not least because, as Macfie later wrote, the Ethiopians were not much impressed by the 'benefits of civilization'. They refused to be hurried. The British Red Cross had pitched camp in a grassy valley, full of yellow flowers, surrounded by high mountains, displaying, as the Geneva Conventions laid down, a prominent red cross on top of their tents. As the fighting intensified, patients began to arrive; many brought with them attendants and slaves. Macfie found them charmless, bad-tempered and sullen; he complained that they had fleas and lice.

On 30 December, the Italian air force bombed the Swedish ambulance serving on the southern front, at Melka Dida on the Ganale river. News came that Major Hylander had been wounded. Junod cabled the International Committee and, with Brown's agreement, flew off to investigate in a plane piloted by a twenty-four-year-old Swedish Red Cross volunteer, Count Carl Gustav von Rosen. They found Hylander badly injured in both legs and down one side; his driver, a young man called Lundström, had been shot in the jaw and killed. Twenty-eight casualties recovering in the field hospital had been killed and another fifty wounded. In his report, Junod noted that the ambulance had been clearly marked with the Red Cross emblem, that it was placed seven kilometres back from the front, and that the Italian planes had come in low and spent twenty minutes flying backwards and forwards, dropping bombs on the tents. In a short address delivered by Brown at Lundström's funeral in Addis Ababa – a 'brilliant' turn-out, he later noted, spoilt only by the unfortunate habit of the Ethiopian royal family of taking their many dogs everywhere, even up to the altar – he said that the young man had given his life for the 'idea of absolute charity

. . . the supreme sense of mercy that lies at the heart of the Red Cross'.

The war was taking a new turn. The Italians, in the minutes before bombing the Swedish tents, had dropped leaflets in Amharic accusing the Ethiopians of decapitating a captured Italian pilot. Protests, accusations of atrocities, reports of the Red Cross flag being repeatedly ignored and even made the target of bombing attacks, now began to pour in. Telegrams were exchanged. The Italians sent a supposed eye-witness report of the mutilation of an Italian prisoner whose body had been spiked through with a long metal bar, while Ethiopian soldiers danced around it. A cable was forwarded to the International Committee from Major Bourgogne, of the Ethiopian Medical Service:

> Woldia heavily bombed for 1 hour and 10 minutes this morning many killed and wounded native town was a target during bombardment . . . my tent and my aide's tent with all my medical supplies and other stuff blown up though bearing large Red Cross markings . . . Wake up Geneva as is evident Italians making special target any red cross.

The attacks went on. The British ambulance was now bombed, while Dr Melly was in the middle of an amputation; forty high explosive and incendiary bombs destroyed tents, equipment and wards. An American doctor called Hockmann was killed by an unexploded shell. Soon after, doctors taking shelter in caves watched as the Italian planes bombed and destroyed von Rosen's plane. By now, half the foreign medical teams were in tatters. On 23 January 1936, Huber wrote directly to Mussolini, strongly protesting against the repeated violations of the Geneva Conventions. Mussolini's reply was fulsome and evasive. The Italians, he wrote, felt a deep respect for the Conventions. They would not dream of violating them. On the contrary, it was the Ethiopians who were committing 'terrible atrocities' on wounded Italians. From the Italian Red Cross came a ten-page letter signed by Cremonesi describing how the Ethiopians were chopping the arms and legs from Italian soldiers and how a military chaplain had been murdered as he prayed by the side of a dying man. He added that the Ethiopians were using dum-dum bullets. *The Times*, not long afterwards, carried a speech by Count Ciano, Italy's minister of foreign affairs. The bitter 'memory of an effeminate peace that followed a heroic combat had now been cancelled' by the courage of the Italian soldiers, said the count, who were today 'aiming at the very heart of the Abyssinian barbarian'.

Brown's reports had been factual, if increasingly hostile to the Italians. On 21 February he sent a thirteen-page closely typed letter to Geneva; it was tense, heated — and accurate.

> It is now very clear that this little colonial affair has become a war of extermination and that if we do not manage to have the Red Cross emblem respected by a country calling itself civilized, we will never be able to do so later if we are ever faced by a war in Europe.

Saying that the Italian air force was 'becoming more and more murderous', he urged the International Committee to take seriously rumours circulating around Addis Ababa that in Geneva no one cared much what happened to the Ethiopian wounded, since their sympathies were largely with the Italians. By now, four ambulance units had been bombed by the Italian planes.

Then came rumours of another kind, which had long haunted the International Committee: gas. All through the 1920s and 1930s, while at the conference tables the Committee pleaded, urged, bullied nations to take seriously the implications of uncontrolled chemical warfare, the *Review* had devoted article after article to describing the different properties of gas and the harm that it could do, to soldiers and civilians alike. Sidney Brown himself had written a long article warning of the devastation that could be caused once chemicals and airplanes were harnessed together. The whole debate had intensified in May 1928 when a tank of phosgene gas exploded in a chemical factory in Hamburg and eight tonnes of gas escaped, to be spread widely by the wind, killing ten people and wounding many more. The German Red Cross had even proposed the banning of all bomber aircraft, as a way of coping with the threat of gas. There was something about gas, uncontrollable, unmeasurable, causing horror, panic and blindness, that made it the most hated and feared of all modern weapons.

Now, towards the end of March 1936, *The Times* published a telegram sent by the daughter of the Ethiopian Emperor to the British government.

For seven days without break enemy have been bombing armies
and people of my country including women and children with
terrible gases . . . The suffering and torture is beyond description,
hundreds of countrymen screaming and moaning with pain.
Many of them are unrecognizable since the skin has burned off
their faces . . .

There was no doubt that it was true. Junod, who with von Rosen
had been to investigate the rumours, burnt his hands touching a bush
that had been drenched in the gas. 'The vast plain of Kworam,' he
wrote,

is a veritable hell over which from 7 in the morning until 5 in
the afternoon the Italian air force is dropping bombs and toxic
gases without cease . . . Every hundred metres, you come across
a dead mule, killed by a bomb, a bullet or by grass impregnated
with mustard gas . . . I have seen for myself many wounded
crying out for help before the Emperor's shelter . . . 'Abiet! Abiet!'
– have pity . . . They are without help, without doctors, and
they are dying like flies.

Approaching to examine more closely the strange substance that stuck
to everything, the Ethiopians were burning their bare feet. From the
British field hospital, Dr Macfie, who later provided a memorandum on
the Italian use of gas in the war, described a man who 'looked as if
someone had tried to skin him, clumsily' as well as women and children
who had been disfigured, blinded and burnt by gas sticking to their faces,
backs and arms, and who had been left with 'blurred crimson apologies
for eyes'. Junod's report had been relatively muted. For Brown, there
was no turning back. The Italians, he declared, were clearly now using
the Red Cross as a target. 'There is no possibility of "caritas inter arma",
it's all-out war, pure and simple, with no distinction whatsoever between
soldiers and civilians, and as for the poor Red Cross, it's hardly surprising
that it has been swallowed up along the way.'
    The Ethiopian Red Cross appealed to Geneva for gas masks with
which to protect its citizens. Even as the rumours about the gas gathered
strength, as Junod began to collect photographs of the wounds caused
by the phosgene and as the Norwegian doctors prepared a sample to

send to Switzerland, a deputation was on its way from the International Committee in Geneva to Mussolini in Rome, to discuss the setting up of a special commission of inquiry into violations of the Geneva Conventions, by both sides. Huber, Burckhardt and Chenevière were all part of the mission, making it the highest ranking summit the Committee had ever conducted.

What happened in Rome has never really been explained. Most of those present, including Count Aloisi, Mussolini's *chef-de-cabinet*, left accounts of the meeting between the International Committee and Mussolini, but they all say something slightly different. Aloisi noted in his diary for 25 March, some days before the meeting, that he had strongly advised Huber to keep off the topic of gas, lest it prejudice the whole idea of an inquiry and that 'as for any conclusions reached by a commission of inquiry, I told him that we would consider them a purely arbitrary verdict'. Chenevière, who described the encounter which took place on 30 March at some length in his memoirs, *Retours et images*, said the subject was barely mentioned, beyond the words 'mustard gas' dropped once by Huber into a list of violations of the Conventions and then never brought up again. Burckhardt, who was at this point something of a defender of the Fascists, seeing them as a bulwark against Bolshevism, simply accepted, according to Stauffer, that Italy would agree to abide by the Conventions if the question of gas was dropped. It does seem clear that Mussolini was determined that gas would not be discussed – Italy had ratified the 1925 protocol on gas on 3 April 1928, Ethiopia on 18 September 1935 – not least because it was fast becoming plain that Italy was about to win the war. In any case, as Aloisi indicates in his diary, the Italians were not greatly bothered by the International Committee's visit and were currently far more preoccupied about what line the British would take. The communiqué to the press, noted Aloisi, saying that Italy had reassured the Committee that it had every intention of respecting the Red Cross emblem, 'greatly pleased the delegates'. In private, Mussolini told Aloisi to put it about that gas had only been used in reprisal against atrocities and that the gas itself was not lethal, only knocking people out of action for a few hours. Discreet negotiation, in which the Committee placed such faith, had achieved nothing.

And so there was no public condemnation by Huber, no rebuke that the Italians had totally disregarded the Conventions they had ratified.

Yet gas and chemical warfare was, together with protection for civilians, the most debated subject of the inter-war years and its use by Italy, in defiance of the protocol, was a blatant example of contempt for the Conventions and all they stood for. Did Huber's caution carry the day? Did Burckhardt's difficulty in believing the Italians capable of so arrogant a violation sway the others? Was a deal made that was never put down on paper? The International Committee's immense archives are silent on this. As Huber had said, in a meeting of the Committee early in March before setting off for Rome, there were things that 'one can say to the Italians . . . that one cannot publish'.

Whatever the truth, Huber's silence left its mark. Many of the national societies were bitterly disappointed and said so, even if their protests were boiled down later that year to a woolly statement by thirty-nine of them that the International Committee should be asked to ensure that means he found to make the Geneva Conventions stick 'even during an armed conflict in which all means available to modern technology are deployed'. The passivity of the Committee, even when handed such an exceptional opportunity to speak out on a question of which there was no doubt about right and wrong, was seen by many as an extension of the policy of non-interference which was to grow – some say fatally – in the years to come. Brown's agonized point, questioning how if the Italians were allowed to get away with gas now could other violations be prevented in a full blown European war, was pertinent. Anthony Eden was Britain's representative at a League of Nations' committee on the war in Ethiopia – to which Huber refused to submit Brown and Junod's reports on grounds of confidentiality. 'If a Convention such as this,' Eden said, 'can be torn up, will not our peoples . . . ask with reason . . . how can we have confidence that our own folk, despite all solemnly signed Protocols, will not be burned, blinded, done to death in agony hereafter?' The war in Ethiopia had shown up all too clearly the weakness of the International Committee, even if the Red Cross movement itself emerged glorious. As Junod was to put it: 'The best thing in Ethiopia was our ambulances'; whether his tone was ironic or not is not clear from the minutes.

Huber, for his part, insisted that he had been right to refuse the League of Nations the information they asked for. The International Committee, he wrote in the *Review* of May 1936, was not a judge. If he had been obliged to 'observe great caution and reserve', it was not because of indifference or lack of courage, but because the Committee's conduct had to be 'free from any suspicion of political or other partiality'. The Swedish Red Cross, who had lost much in the war, were not prepared to stay quiet. Prince Charles of Sweden, one of the movement's most outspoken figures, declared that he believed it to be the duty of the Red Cross to make its voice heard and called for a meeting at which to discuss not only the attacks on the Red Cross emblem, but whether or not the Geneva Conventions needed modifying.

The whole subject of gas, as it happened, now went away for Italy soon won the war, and the proposed inquiry was never held. But even as the meeting in Rome was taking place, anxious discussions were going on in Geneva about whether or not to send the Ethiopian Red Cross the gas masks they had asked for. On Wednesday 8 April, a meeting was held to discuss possible action and there was a debate on gas. According to the minutes, there was talk about the stand taken by the International Committee over gas in 1918; about modern wars in which civilians were indistinguishable from soldiers; about the need for irrefutable proof that gas had been dropped. Colonel Favre wondered what the world and the national societies would say if, when they asked why nothing had been done to protect civilians from gas, all the Committee could answer was that they had no legal basis from which to act. Paul des Gouttes rehearsed the distinction between healthy, fit enemies and the sick, for whom the original Geneva Convention had been drawn up.

Huber returned from Rome observing somewhat defensively that it had become clear to him that the Conventions definitely had holes when it came to modern warfare. Yet it had not been so very long since he had produced an important paper on neutrality. The work of the Red Cross, he had written, was crucial in that it testified to a

> feeling of human solidarity even when the orderly life of nations is shattered . . . it is of primary importance then that this last bridge connecting the warring nations, the bridge formed by the Red Cross, should not collapse, should not be materially subjected to violence and that its buttresses – neutrality and impartiality – should never give way under the pressure of passion.

313

Passion, for Huber, was a distortion; wherever it arose, it had to be checked.

It was left to Mlle Odier to put into words, not long afterwards, a dilemma that would increasingly trouble the members as they gathered for their regular meetings in the months of slow drift towards the Second World War: 'How,' she asked, 'do you reconcile our commitment to silence or at least to discretion with that of the voice of human conscience? That is the dilemma.'

Junod was in Addis Ababa for the end. As the Italian troops advanced on the capital, the Ethiopian soldiers deserted their posts and the city filled with frantic refugees. On 1 May, the Emperor abandoned the capital. Junod took refuge in an attic flat from where he watched the looters clearing the city of anything valuable or moveable while fires took hold and consumed most of the buildings. At one point he was discovered, chased by a mob and saved only when a soldier he had treated recognized him. When it became known that he was a doctor, the wounded gathered in a stable where he set up a rudimentary surgery. Later he went out to see the damage, finding bodies scattered in the roads, not only of Ethiopians but of Greeks and Armenians whose shops had been plundered. The building that had housed the Ethiopian Red Cross for the last seven months had been gutted and all its supplies looted; the Ethiopian society itself now disappeared altogether, having had, as the *Review* noted, 'but an ephemeral existence'.

On the second day of the rioting the British Red Cross unit, which had stayed on in Addis Ababa with ten helpers, decided to pull out. Dr Melly stopped his car to examine a wounded man lying in the road. He was shot in the chest by looters and killed. He was buried in the grounds of the British Legation; a wreath, with a cross in red roses against a background of white daisies and arum lilies, was laid on the grave.

After four days of confusion the Italian troops arrived. The war was over. Junod's final report to the International Committee was long, full of detail and strongly critical of Sir Sydney Barton, the man so disliked by Brown earlier. In a last half-page of confidential conclusions Junod wrote:

If today Addis Ababa has been ransacked and destroyed and hundreds of people, shopkeepers, dentists, doctors, craftsmen are 100 percent ruined, the most crushing responsibility for this must fall on the shoulders of Sir Sydney Barton, the British Minister.

Describing Barton as autocratic, small-minded and cowardly, he said that much could have been saved if Barton's small band of soldiers had stood up to the looters. Junod, like Brown, had become personally involved in the war, even if he remained curiously tolerant of the Italians. Some years later, in a revealing note to the Committee, he said that he felt that the League of Nations had made a fundamental mistake in allowing the Ethiopians among its members, a people so 'primitive, divided, uncultivated, cruel and barbaric'.

As for Brown, he had been recalled early from Ethiopia. There is no doubt that his outspoken fury towards the Italians had done him little good in Geneva and that even his friend and protector Huber was unable to save him in the face of mounting criticism, especially from Favre and Chenevière, for whom neutrality, even in the case of clear violations, was sacred.

But there was more to what happened next than an excess of irresponsible passion. Exceptionally, the letter of resignation that Brown is known to have signed, probably dictated by Burckhardt and signed in his presence, has not turned up in the archives of the International Committee. What does exist, however, in the Italian state archives in Rome, is a letter from the Italian delegate general of the Italian Red Cross in Geneva, Count Guido Vinci, founder member of a group of Fascist supporters in Geneva. It is addressed to Senator Cremonesi in Rome and concerns a certain Walter Bosshard, who had written to Brown while he was in Addis Ababa.

Bosshard, according to Vinci, was a director of a factory turning out uniforms, a known centre for freemasonry. 'He was a very good friend of B.,' Vinci wrote, 'and they were seen together after his return from Abyssinia.

'As for B. I should add that it has been confirmed that he was a homosexual and that it is probable that his friend had the same habits. Meanwhile the ICRC has sent him on leave to Zurich and I am told that this leave will last indefinitely.'

Brown never returned to the Red Cross. He joined Brown-Boveri and spent the rest of his working life on its diplomatic and public relations side. There was a rumour, never substantiated, of blackmail by the Italians and another that Huber had been given a letter during his stay in Rome portraying Brown in some light that even he could not defend. What is certain is that Mussolini would have taken strong exception to Brown's criticisms; and that, in 1936, homosexuality was no more acceptable within the International Committee in Geneva than business failure had been in Dunant's day.

There was very little time to take stock. Even as the International Committee was conducting the last of its post-mortems on the war in Ethiopia, a new commission to deal with another war was being set up in the Villa Moynier on Lake Geneva, which the Committee had now made its headquarters. Once again, Burckhardt, Chenevière, Mlle Odier and Col. Favre were among its members; they were joined by Suzanne Ferrière. Like the two other women on the Committee, Mlle Ferrière was soft-spoken and 'came from the rue des Granges', as Genevans like to describe the best families of their city. Like them she was hard-working, could be formidable and was outspoken on questions of morality.

On 18 July 1936, Francisco Franco, governor of the Canary Islands, who with the help of General Orgaz had taken control of Las Palmas, broadcast a radio call to his Catholic, monarchist and fascist Falange followers on the mainland to rise up. Seville, Cadiz, Burgos, Algeciras and Cordoba fell to the insurgents. The war which followed in Spain would provide the International Committee with the chance not only to explore new roles, but for it to move into the untested area of civil war, judged to fall within its remit since the tenth International Conference of 1921. This time, perhaps mindful of what happened when delegates became too independent, the commission for Spain sitting in Geneva kept an extremely close eye on the seventeen men they put into the field, helped by good telephone connections with parts of the country. On 24 August, Chenevière proposed a code to be used in telegrams – Junod became 'Neuchâtel', Franco, 'facteur', the Spanish Red Cross, 'santé'. Between the summer of 1936 and the early spring of 1937 the Commission met virtually every day. Between them and the work of the delegates, an extremely effective procedure was put into place: it would prove an invaluable dry run for the Second World War.

By the end of the first week of fighting, Franco's rebel nationalists controlled a strip of land in the north, Cordoba and Seville in the south, as well as Majorca, the Canary Islands, and Spanish Morocco. Valencia, Toledo, Madrid and Barcelona remained in the republican government's hands. Huber sent his first telegram to the Spanish Red Cross: 'Do you require aid sister societies, especially equipment?' The Spanish society was in a state of considerable turmoil, cars having been spotted driving around flying the Red Cross flag while men inside fired from the windows. But on 31 July, Dr Aurelio Romeo was placed at the head of a new central committee in Madrid. The answer he sent to Huber was clear: the society was desperately short of syringes, needles, rubber gloves, gauze, tweezers, quinine, thermometers, microscopes and ambulances — but more than that it needed help in finding and returning thousands of children from both sides, surprised by the war in summer camps in the mountains and by the sea and now trapped on the wrong side of the front.

The response from other national Red Cross societies to the conflict in Spain was for the most part speedy and willing, though the American Red Cross director, Ernest Swift, sent an apologetic letter to Huber explaining that the 'whole sentiment of the country is for keeping out of Europe and in official and private circles the feeling is that we should not expose ourselves in any way that might involve us.' The Latin American countries, however, proved generous and Huber was soon remarking, with some satisfaction, that the donors had accepted that the aid they sent should not be earmarked, but distributed equally where needs were greatest. Information bureaux were set up in Madrid, Barcelona and Burgos.

With surprising speed and ease, it was agreed that the International Committee would send delegates to both sides. Marcel Junod, not long back from Addis Ababa and eager to return to his hospital duties, was prevailed on by Huber to go to Spain for three weeks to explore just what the Committee should be doing. Junod was now thirty-one, Dunant's age at the battle of Solferino. He flew to Barcelona to negotiate with the legal government, was briefed by Dr Romeo, managed to persuade the republicans to agree to respect the Geneva Conventions and the Red Cross emblem, then set off for Madrid. It was already a war of great brutality. As if to confirm the worst fears of the 1920s and early 1930s, war was indeed turning into an event in which no one was neutral and no distinctions made between soldier and civilian. Everywhere Junod went, he heard stories of atrocities; everyone talked about hostages and reprisals. Hoping to win agreement on exchanges and the safety of hostages, he needed to see Franco's generals. Since neither side recognized him as a neutral intermediary or would provide him with a safe conduct, he was forced to retrace his steps to Barcelona, fly to France, travel by land to St Jean de Luz and re-enter Spain in search of Franco at Salamanca. The journey was nearly a thousand miles; it involved crossing 148 road blocks and removing countless bodies, freshly executed by one side or the other, from the road.

Franco's rebels had set up their own Red Cross society. The members, Junod remarked, were very different from the republicans, 'authentic caballeros, tight-mouthed and lantern-jawed', stout aristocratic ladies and 'condescending counts', who, assuming the Swiss and Protestant Junod to be French and Catholic, took him to call on a bishop. In Burgos, he met two of Franco's top aides, General Cabanellas and General Mola.

Both sides were friendly, if mistrustful. The nationalists had no intention, it seemed, of exchanging a 'caballero for a red dog', and there was no question of swapping prisoners-of-war, who were in any case an extraordinary mixture of people, now that Germany, Italy and Portugal were supporting the rebels, and the USSR and the International Brigade the republicans, from Italian blackshirts to Messerschmitt fighter pilots, from Russian tank crews to Falangists. However, both sides appeared willing to discuss the exchange of women and children, and Junod set to work with lists and descriptions, on what would prove the trickiest and most rewarding work of the war. Met with suspicion, obfuscation and subterfuge at every turn, he wheedled, bullied, negotiated a few women here, a few children there. Don Esteban Bilbao, a nationalist who later became Franco's minister for justice, was swapped for the socialist mayor of Bilbao, Señor Ercoreca. After that, 130 nationalist women held by the republicans in a convent outside Bilbao were exchanged for 130 republican women, some awaiting execution. Then a troop of nationalist boy scouts, caught by the war camping in the Pyrenees, were allowed home, as were a company of singers and actors from Barcelona who had been on tour. From the first the British navy had agreed to ferry the hostages up and down the Spanish coast, so that the exchanges could take place in neutral French territory.

Hostage exchanges were crucial to Junod's work, though no pattern was ever established and nothing could ever be taken for granted. 'If I let people go,' one general said to him, 'people would take me for a traitor.' 'We are at war,' declared a mayor on the other side. 'We have already sacrificed our own families.' Some captives were executed just as he was on the verge of success — he failed to save a hundred men shot as a reprisal for the bombing of Bilbao; others 'disappeared' as he turned up to collect them, and their gaolers claimed no knowledge of their whereabouts. Both nationalists and republicans frequently reneged on their promises and though Junod devoted hours to drawing up written agreements, they were not always honoured. As time went by a few crude rules were, however, established. A hostage came to be accepted by both sides as a 'person who has been arrested without having a weapon in his hand and without being guilty of a grave offence such as treason or espionage'. Then it was agreed that a Falangist could not be exchanged for a militiaman or for a Basque policeman, nor a soldier for a civilian. Mediation, at its best, involved small numbers of individuals — four Russians and two Spanish republican airmen for four German and two nationalist Spaniards; fourteen Italian volunteers for fourteen American militiamen. All Junod could really do was to keep talking and keep repeating that the laws of war laid down the inviolate nature of doctors, priests and civilians. 'The balance sheet of living and dead,' André Durand, author of the Committee's official history, *From Sarajevo to Hiroshima*, noted later, 'was drawn up like a business report.'

After his first three-week mission was up, Junod telephoned Huber to ask whether he might now return to his hospital work in Mulhouse. Huber begged him to stay in Spain a little longer; it would be seven years before Junod finally got away. In the spring of 1937 he moved his base to Valencia, now in republican hands, and the International Committee sent other delegates to northern Spain. After these came still more, until ten separate delegations, helped by 100 Spaniards, were running a primitive form of tracing agency, exchanging information about families and prisoners. Since neither side would agree to provide lists, it was a slow and frustrating task made more poignant by the long queues that gathered from dawn before the doors of the Roja Cruz Internacional.

Junod spent days at a time in various police stations and in the ministry for war, conscious that it was far easier dealing with prisoners already sentenced, even if awaiting execution, than those being held in secret as spies, about whom it was sometimes too dangerous even to ask. The particular secrecy and silence of this civil war, with its endless executions and disappearances, made it unbearably hard for families. Name by name, Junod's lists grew. Having in his hand a piece of paper with 2,000 names, he wrote later in *Warrior Without Weapons*, made him feel 'We were holding these 2,000 names by a single thread, all that stood between the sentence which condemned them and the open grave which awaited them.'

With one republican sympathizer, Junod scored a particular success. Calling to see José Giral, nationalist minister for foreign affairs, he was asked to organize an exchange for a 'friend of the republic' called Koestler. Junod had never heard of the man, who had been sentenced to death by Franco for his reports to English newspapers. It took a while to sort out but eventually an aristocratic lady from Seville, held captive in the relative comfort of the Hotel Inglés in Valencia, was transferred to a British destroyer and conveyed behind nationalist lines. Arthur Koestler was freed.

As the months passed and the bombing of cities took ever more civilian lives, talks began in the International Committee and at the League of Nations about the need for open cities, for neutral zones where non-combatants could find safety. All that Professor Louis Demolis – writing month after month in the *Review* since the late 1920s about civilians and the ever more deadly power of weapons – had warned against seemed now to be happening:

> the inhabitants of cities fleeing from fire or massacre, forced to leave their homes because of the devastating invasion of motorized troops; civilians . . . caught between two shifting tides of warring armies, swirling among and around military units . . . trying to find somewhere safe.

The war in Spain, he observed, 'may be interpreted as a forecast of a tragic future, as the smaller image of events which may occur elsewhere and with greater and more destructive force.' The daily contemplation of war and a historical perspective that by now stretched back nearly eighty years sometimes seemed to lend the men of the International Committee a sort of horrible prescience.

Both sides, who protested strongly to the International Committee about civilian casualties, indicated that they were willing to attend discussions. A team of inspectors from Britain visited Alicante and were mystified when shown five heavily bombed sites which seemed to have no military value: the nationalists told them that the guns they had been targeting had been rapidly removed by the republicans after the raids. A groundswell of public protest was building up, and the International Committee, quoting the Tokyo draft, appealed to both sides to cease the 'terrible ravages' of innocent people. Even as it went out, Philippe Hahn, delegate in Barcelona, watched a bombing raid. Entire blocks of houses collapsed into the street, cars were on fire and the roads were littered with the dead and dying. 'Trams, trucks and cars were hurled far away and set on fire . . . the houses, though tall, were nothing but a heap of ruins and a tangle of steel girders . . . It was just at the nicest time of day, at a time when the spring sun was shining.'

No activity was more urgently conducted or more rewarding than the search for the scattered children. There were several thousand of these holidaying children from nationalist as well as republican homes. Rumours that they had been eaten by 'cannibal Moors' fed the hysteria. When Junod, early in the war, failed to produce forty Basque children who had been trapped by the fighting not far from Burgos he was greeted with despairing cries of 'los niños? los niños?' and almost lynched. As the nationalists continued to renege on their promises to return hostages, Junod found himself branded in a San Sebastian newspaper as a 'renegade and a miserable idiot'.

Children played a part of their own in the Spanish Civil War. As the fighting intensified, not only the Red Cross but dozens of different organizations from other parts of Europe joined in the work, either to restore children to parents from whom they had been separated, or to take them abroad to places of safety. Some were spirited over the border into France; others went to Mexico; 2,000 to the Soviet Union. One group of 3,861, with ninety-five women teachers, 120 young helpers and fifteen priests, made their way to Southampton.

On 26 April 1937, the village of Guernica, not far from Bilbao in the north, was reduced to rubble by nationalist bombers. Fear spread that the raids would be repeated over Bilbao. The Basque government appealed to the Red Cross and to the French and British governments to evacuate women and children. France agreed. Air raids over the city were stepped up and the parents of Bilbao's children begged the British to come to their rescue.

Southampton was picked as the city to take in the children and a team of doctors and nurses was sent across to Bilbao to select 4,000. The inspections were not made easier by the continuous air raids; on the day of embarkation eleven of those who had been selected died in the bombing.

The children, accompanied by their teachers and priests, crossed to Southampton on a Spanish ship, the *Habaña*. It was late May and the sea was rough. When the British launches approached bearing supplies of glucose, milk and meat extract, they found the children sick, confused, longing for home and truculent, the young nationalists already at odds with the young republicans, since the *Habaña* had delivered a mixed political bunch. A few of the older boys were perched mutinously up in the masts.

First inspections on board the pitching ship revealed, as Dr Maurice Williams, medical officer of health for Southampton, wrote, 'an alert, intelligent group of children who compared favourably in physique with our own children'. The refugees were, however, covered in fleas and lice: 712 of them had to be deloused by barbers. Before disembarking, the children had coloured tapes tied to their left wrists, white for 'clean', red for 'verminous' and blue for 'infectious or contagious'. Journalists, photographers and Southampton's citizens waited on the dock to inspect the arrivals. Some of the children took the cameras for machine guns and threw themselves to the ground.

Camps had been prepared, the local Round Table volunteered to run a car service, hairdressers appeared to cut hair and scouts and guides were drafted in to help. The republican children fled from the scouts, taking them for a fascist youth organization. The distinguished painter Augustus John arrived with a tent and started to do drawings of the children. The cost of the whole enterprise, Southampton noted gloomily, would come to £1,000 a week.

It had been raining for some time; and it went on raining. The first few days were not a success. The children spoke no English, took violently against English food, refused to drink the milk and shocked the locals by hanging presents of teddy bears from posts, having cut their legs off first and stuffed them into their mouths. 'Camp in chaos,' reported Dr Garrett from the medical services. 'Latrines, approaches, ditches, tentlines and tents fouled with excreta — indescribable . . . Food tent with mud floor — not ventilated . . . particles of food, onion skins and potato peelings strewn about — stink.' A visit to the cookhouse revealed a bathful of meat bones covered with flies. When reprimanded, the cook obligingly laid over the top 'a woman's vest showing perspiration under armpits'. Instructed to cover a 'bath of sugar with a film of soot', she fetched a 'blood-stained cloth'. There were fears typhus might break out.

The people of Southampton had been amazed at the strong political feelings expressed by their young visitors. Though the rain stopped and the children came reluctantly to accept the English food, political allegiances, if anything, grew stronger. One evening a group of children chose to go without supper rather than wear a yellow armband to distinguish them from those who had already eaten — yellow was the colour of Franco's Moroccan troops. The day Bilbao fell to the nationalists and the camp director was foolish enough to relay the news over a loudspeaker, his words were soon 'drowned in a heart-rending wail of grief and mounting tide of hysteria'. Three hundred children broke out and ran away. Others 'went slowly to their tents and there lay sobbing until the early hours of the morning'.

The Southampton project ended much as it had begun, in considerable muddle. With the nationalists in control of northern Spain, parents began agitating for the return of their children. By now, however, battle lines had been drawn by the organizers in England — a Basque children's committee for the republicans, the Spanish Children's Repatriation Committee, chaired by the Duke of Wellington, for the nationalists — and a frosty exchange of letters broke out in *The Times*. A priest, Father Gabaria, was appointed by the Vatican to make arrangements. It did not prove easy to trace all parents but bit by bit 'Spain's Red Children', as the newspapers described them, were returned to Bilbao, though some of the smaller ones now spoke better English than Spanish and some of the older did not care for life under Franco.

The 2,000 Basque and Catalan children taken to be cared for in the Soviet Union seemed to have disappeared without trace for a while. Then, in July and August 1939, they were located and the International Committee began arranging for their return to Spain. It was too late. The Second World War broke out before a single child arrived home. It would be six years before any of them saw their families again.

The request for permission to visit prisoners, one of the fundamental tasks of Red Cross delegates, was at first met in Spain with total refusal on both sides. As weeks passed and Junod nagged, a number of concessions were made: delegate by delegate, area by area, prison visiting began. More than in previous wars, there was a vast difference in how captives were treated even by the same side, depending on the mood of the governor, the degree of overcrowding and the intensity of local passions.

Early in the war, Dr Roland Marti arrived to join Junod. He was a genial, old-fashioned man, with courteous manners and the instinctive belief in neutrality that the International Committee most admired. 'Do not choose,' he would tell younger delegates. 'Take only a clinical point of view.' One of Marti's first visits was to a prison in Almeria. The detainees, he reported, were 'piled into a few old rooms, about twelve to each, lying half-naked on old mattresses or sacks in total disorder or filth. Everywhere a disgusting stench of sweat and rancid oil.' Marti's reports ranged from the terse − 'Hygiene: deplorable, no soap, insects everywhere' − to long, almost sentimental disquisitions on the nature of detention itself, reminiscent of some of Appia's early writings. On 14 February 1937 at 4 p.m. he made his way up a steep track to the castle at Alicante.

'Night falls,' he later reported to Geneva.

> The 362 prisoners are summoned to the courtyard by a blast of trumpet. The calm is profound. A strange sensation of distance, of being forgotten. I inspect the prisoners, drawn up before me in two rows: blank faces, absent thoughts, no expressions . . . The silence is broken only by a rhythmic slippery sound of espadrilles on stony ground . . . In the dusk, you glimpse bearded faces which tell you nothing.

Taken to see twelve convicted 'anti-fascists', Marti asked them if they wanted anything. The men leapt to their feet and raised their closed fists in a salute. 'Nothing. All you can do for us is get us out of here and back in the trenches as soon as possible, so that we can fight fascism.'

Reporting to Junod, who had been made head of the delegation to Spain, the newly recruited delegates set off on long, hazardous journeys across the plains and into the mountains. Their reports, since the International Committee remains as silent about the characters and lives of its delegates as it does about most things, are all that is left today to make them come alive. Then, as now, the Committee gave the barest biographical details about the men and women it employed, and the 'personal' files of its early delegates are virtually the only papers in the now open archives to remain closed. There was Raymond Courvoisier, from an old Geneva family of bankers and priests who set up his headquarters in an old casino in San Sebastian. At the end of December 1937, he reported on a number of visits he had made in and around Bilbao. In an old convent, surrounded by a magnificent park, he found

> held in a room on their own . . . 40 priests who are prisoners. Discipline is the same for them as for all the others. They obey whistles and drum beats . . . When I entered their room, I found them lined up, standing absolutely still, each holding a Bible in his hand. I don't think I have ever been as moved as by the sight of these priests. They wear their soutanes, which they keep very clean, and, despite everything, they are very dignified . . .

He added that the discipline in this convent prison was 'of iron', but that there did not appear to be any brutality. Courvoisier reached Guernica soon after it had been flattened by incendiary bombs and machine guns on market day. He saw no people, no animals and no birds. Suddenly noticing one house still standing, though without a roof, he approached and found inside a makeshift hospital and men and women lying in rubble covered in blood. A single doctor had been operating without a pause for forty hours. Courvoisier returned to San Sebastian, contacted Geneva and next day turned a nearby village into a Red Cross hospital, complete with beds, kitchens and an operating theatre, to which he began ferrying the survivors. Guernica became a symbol of what civilians could suffer. Like the gas attacks in Ethiopia, it represented all that the International Committee feared most, demonstrating what could happen if warfare was not regulated by international agreements, and if civilians were not protected under them.

Georges Graz was in Bilbao when Franco's bombers arrived. 'I visited Durange, completely destroyed,' he wrote in a report summarizing days of negotiation and visits.

> I saw Guernica still in flames and its houses collapsing one after the other . . . The morale of the prisoners is good, except that they are all hungry. It would be pointless to try to negotiate an exchange of hostages . . . with the incessant bombing, tempers are strained.

By the autumn of 1938, Junod and Marti were living in Barcelona, in a flat at 95 Calle Lauria. Everyone was hungry. All the delegates had left in the way of stores was a little condensed milk and some chocolate. Marti reported to Geneva towards the end of September.

> Misery is approaching, with giant strides . . . From morning to evening in our neighbourhood there is a long procession of desperate people . . . they come to us in the hopes of receiving help, however small . . . Women, whose husbands have disappeared, either at the front, or because they have been shot, or because they are ill, most often bringing with them pale and thin children, begging us to give them, or sell them, at any price, a tin of condensed milk.

Send something, begged Marti, 'so that we can at least save the most desperate cases'. When a bomb fell on to a school nearby and the building collapsed, burying a hundred small children, Junod wrote: 'We managed to extricate only ten complete bodies. All the others had been blown to pieces. It was atrocious. I saw one of the attendants recover a small blond head. Others picked up what might have been the feet of little angels.'

On 26 January 1939, Barcelona fell to the nationalists. Marti had a code with Geneva using the weather. He just had time to ring the Committee. 'What is the weather like?' he was asked. 'Just a minute,' he replied, 'I'll open the window.' He did so and the men in Geneva heard the cheers greeting Franco's arrival. The governor of Las Cortès women's prison rang to tell Junod that the gaol was being mobbed by the families of those inside, terrified that there might be last-minute transfers. The fear, now, was that the republican gaolers would be lynched. Junod, negotiating roadblocks, mistrustful and frightened soldiers and exploding bombs, reached the prison to find the young, fair-haired governor and her 'awkward and dirty' guards locked up in her office. He called for the keys, opened the cells, ordered the prisoners to hurry away as fast as they could, arranged for the sick to be ferried by healthier friends and relations and, as the first shells broke overhead, managed to get away himself.

His job was not quite over. The republicans fell back towards the French border, taking hostages with them, and Junod and Marti joined the exodus, moving with the long column of refugees, trudging through the snow over the Pyrenees towards refugee camps in France, a 'flood of pitiful people, barrows, carts, riders on mules, people in cars and trucks'. As he left, he went to collect papers of safe conduct from the police. Colonel Ugria, chief of the nationalist police, handed him a slip of paper which had been found among the republican files, and which, said Ugria, had followed Junod wherever he went around Spain. It contained his name and a single word, underlined twice in red ink: 'Ojo' – keep an eye on this man.

The Spanish civil war, for the International Committee, did much to redeem some of the doubts left by the Ethiopian campaign. In Geneva, the commission for Spain had met nearly every day for well over two years, and virtually the entire Villa Moynier had by the end been turned over to monitoring the war. The message and news service for divided families which had proved its worth in the First World War, had shown itself to be as valuable in a civil war, despite enormous problems of logistics and communications. Staffed by Spaniards, there were by the end of the war bureaux in Santander, Bilbao, San Sebastian and Majorca, as well as those in Madrid, Barcelona and Burgos. Five million messages had been exchanged between the two Spains. 'The message service alone,' wrote Marti later, 'was enough to justify our action in Spain.' Fifty different countries had been induced to provide money and aid.

The war had been a conflict of hostages and reprisals, secret detention centres and executions. Yet seventeen delegates had visited more than 75,000 prisoners, and no one had been either compromised or wounded, though they had been vilified on the radio and in the newspapers and exposed to enormous dangers. Given the frequent changes in political leadership, the large numbers of autonomous units, the sheer barbarity of the war, it was almost miraculous that so much had been achieved. Junod had returned from Ethiopia convinced that the personal authority of the delegate was of more value than the Geneva Conventions. He emerged from Spain with a view of delegates as witnesses and monitors, with unique powers as protectors. As Sidney Brown had remarked, during his first meeting with Junod in the Villa Moynier shortly before setting off for Ethiopia: 'There are the official Red Cross texts, of course. But above all, there is the spirit of the thing.' Given what the delegates had been through, and what many of them were about to go through, it is remarkable how well they coped; it is also remarkable how very little they have ever been either recognized or praised.

TWELVE

Where a Savage Inquisition is Master

The Spanish civil war had established once and for all the right of the International Committee to intervene in civil conflicts. Its position towards political detainees, however, was still unclear. For all its reluctance and fear of politics, the International Committee could not but be drawn into the political turmoils of the 1920s and 1930s. These years would prove crucial in shaping its power and political future, as well as in developing the tactic of discreet negotiation. But while they would have some success with political prisoners, they remained powerless in the face of the increasingly strong political directions taken by some of the national Red Cross societies, and could do little more than watch from the sidelines, as the dictatorial edicts of the new totalitarian leaders in Italy, Russia, Germany and elsewhere engulfed their own Red Cross societies.

The actual 'droit d'ingérence', or right of initiative is one of the most subtle and most interesting of all Red Cross ideas. Dunant, who acted from an instinctive assumption that he was entitled to intervene on the battlefield of Solferino, had never foreseen the necessity for a permanent International Committee, believing that once nations had started their own societies and bound themselves to codes of conduct in war, there would be no need for an independent monitoring body. Not only had his rather naive assumption been proved wrong, but successive generations of Red Cross leaders had extended the Committee's powers further and further, action preceding law, rather like a game of grandmother's footsteps in which the players advance, alternating caution with cunning, hoping that no one will turn and order them back. No issue better illustrates this process than the Committee's sometimes bold, sometimes devious entry into the field of political prisoners. No actual *right* to act on behalf of these prisoners was formally voiced until 1930 and even then almost casually, as if no one could think otherwise. But to understand the Committee's position one has to go back to the spring of 1919, when, as part of the programme to repatriate the Russian prisoners-of-war, a delegate called Rodolphe Haccius was sent to Budapest.

He had not been there long when Béla Kun and the communists took power in the parts of Hungary not already controlled by Romania, Serbia and Czechoslovakia. Dozens of people were arrested. Haccius, together with a member of the Hungarian society called Louis Leopold, called on Béla Kun and obtained the revolutionary government's recognition of the Red Cross and permission to carry out its usual functions, providing it observed 'the strictest political neutrality'. However, the situation in Budapest deteriorated rapidly and the number of arrests rose sharply. On 23 April, Haccius wrote to Geneva: 'Hostages: I am getting urgent appeals to visit the prisons and enquire into their fate. I need . . . a telegram from the International Committee. There are apparently more than a thousand leading citizens, all Hungarians, of whom there is no news.' As Leopold observed, the delicate question facing the Red Cross was that of extending 'the principles of the Geneva Convention, hitherto applicable only to war between nations, to apply to the class struggle.'

There was no reply from the Committee, which received the letter only on 1 May. Haccius decided that he could wait no longer, applied directly for permission to enter the prisons, and received it − in the process becoming the first delegate to act on behalf of prisoners who were purely political. Haccius was both shrewd and imaginative. He hastened to reassure the new leaders that there was nothing odd in his request to visit the prisoners, since these bourgeois men and women behind bars were no less enemies than prisoners-of-war were enemies, and as such they were entitled to humanitarian guarantees under the Geneva Convention. The first official visit paid by an International Committee delegate to a political prisoner took place on 28 April 1919, in the gaol of Gyüjtöfogház, where 131 hostages and forty-eight political prisoners were being held. Haccius reported that they appeared to be treated well, but their food was insufficient. He did not, he wrote to Geneva, question the prisoners for the reasons for their arrest, 'to avoid reprisals after my departure'. On 3 May, he managed to obtain the release of the sick and those over sixty. Deciding 'at all costs to concern myself with hostages and political detainees', he visited two more prisons. From Geneva, on 17 May, came a telegram: 'Approve your activities. Hope you can visit prisons with full support competent authorities to accomplish this part your humanitarian work.' In the days that followed Haccius created a Red Cross correspondence card system for prisoners to write to their families, arranged for the release and repatriation of foreign hostages and, for the 134 days that Béla Kun was in power, helped the civilian population and kept open contact with neighbouring countries.

On 4 August the Romanian army occupied Budapest, and Béla Kun's regime fell. The revolutionaries themselves were now in need of International Committee help. Haccius and his successor Georges Burnier, kept up their work during the confusion and reprisals that followed, constantly adapting themselves to the changes around them, proving the point later made by Junod that the authority of individual delegates can often count for more than the Geneva Conventions themselves. Both men were calm and authoritative. On 1 October Haccius requested and obtained permission to visit the new political prisoners and 'report on the treatment to which they are subjected'. Discovering that two communist detainees had been violently beaten by prison employees, he protested vigorously and, gradually ill treatment stopped. By the spring Burnier was able to inform Geneva that there was 'no complaint to be made'. A women's prison run by the sisters of St Vincent de Paul was reported to be 'in perfect order . . . best possible spirit'. As the weeks passed their work spread to hospitals, TB patients, children, the repatriation of invalids. Writing later about the work in Hungary the Committee noted that it seemed to prove that 'in the event of civil war it is possible to persuade new governments . . . of the supranational value' of the Red Cross.

Something of this victory was reflected in the all-important International Conference of 1921, which recognized the idea that there was little distinction to be made between civil war and internal trouble when it came to victims and that it was enough for blood to be shed for political reasons for the Committee to be allowed to intervene. As the Italian delegate remarked, 'the Red Cross acts to help individual people, regardless of their political, civil or religious views, their race, class, social rank, culture – everything, remembering only their humanity'. It was with this recognition in mind, and a new mandate to 'intervene to bring relief in the case of civil war' that delegates were able to enter prisons in Ireland and Poland in the early 1920s and bring about some measure of improvement for political inmates.

In the Soviet Union the position was rather more difficult. The campaign on behalf of political prisoners waged by Voldemar Wehrlin in Moscow from 1921 to 1938 is one of the most tenacious and most frustrating in the history of the Red Cross.

Maria Kikava was a seamstress, living in Tiflis, in Georgia. Arrested by the Cheka secret police in 1922 for supposed political dissidence, she was locked up, naked, in a cell where a broken window let in rain and snow. In a letter which reached the International Committee she begged for clothes. Only after she had repeatedly lost consciousness was she at last moved. Mikhail Nodia, also from Georgia, was kept in the dark for twenty-eight days, several of them without food. For a week, buckets of cold water were thrown over his naked body morning and night. All through the 1920s stories like these reached Geneva, of people arrested by the Soviet secret police and held naked in basements, in cells kept so cold that prisoners fainted, or crammed into holes carved out of the rock; of starvation, beatings and torture, and, often, of executions.

Events from 1918 to 1922 – revolution, drought, famine, epidemics – had left five million dead from starvation; three million more from typhus, typhoid and cholera; three million children orphaned. Many hundreds of thousands of people had fled abroad, including members of the old Russian Red Cross who, in 1921, set up headquarters in Paris. From here they pestered and begged the International Committee to intervene on behalf of those left behind and now reported to be in concentration camps or prison. Voldemar Wehrlin, soon after his appointment as delegate to Moscow in August 1921, confirmed their stories. There were probably, he told Geneva, at least 900,000 of these people in detention, intellectuals, professors, journalists and teachers, banished to distant camps in the Urals and Siberia.

Wehrlin was the perfect delegate for the new Soviet Union. He had been born in Moscow in 1888. His father was a Swiss industrialist and his mother was Russian. He had studied law in Moscow and Kiev, become legal adviser to the Swiss mission to Petrograd in 1918 and later president of the short-lived association of Swiss in Russia, where he played a crucial role in organizing the repatriation of Swiss nationals in the summer of 1920, travelling at the head of the last train out. It was clear that Wehrlin loved Russia; but he was a humane man, appalled by the persecution he saw around him, and possessed of considerable diplomatic skills. He was to need them. 'We firmly believe,' the Soviet authorities informed Geneva as Wehrlin took up his appointment, 'that he will restrict himself exclusively to matters of interest to the Red Cross.' The question was what these matters were, and what he would be able to do about them.

Within weeks of his appointment Wehrlin was deeply entrenched in political matters. The Soviet Union needed recognition by the West as well as food for its enduring famine. It wished to make use of Swiss financial institutions and the Soviet Red Cross eagerly sought acceptance both by the International Committee and by the League. In return, the Soviets were prepared to make a few concessions, but how many and of what kind was up to Wehrlin to discover. The game which followed was played, for the most part, between just two actors: Wehrlin himself in distant contact with Geneva, and Zenoby Petrovich Soloviev, twelve years his senior, president of the new Soviet Red Cross since 1918 and a doctor by training, who had been deported several times in his youth and risen to take charge of public health after the revolution. Soloviev was reputed to work excessively hard, to possess admirable organizational skills and to wield a will of iron. Wehrlin does not seem to have been a match for him.

On paper, the Swiss delegate's brief was perfectly straightforward. Together with half a dozen Swiss and Soviet helpers, he was to provide Geneva with a general picture of what was happening in the Soviet Union, act as co-ordinator for any famine or relief programmes and keep open the lines of communication between the International Committee in Geneva and the Soviet Red Cross, which was finally formally recognized on 15 October 1921. In practice, it was considerably more complicated. There were dozens of destitute Swiss in Moscow alone, who had run out of money since the revolution and now longed to return to Switzerland; there were some 1,200 terrified foreigners — English, Polish, Dutch and German engineers, merchants and teachers — locked up as suspected spies in Moscow's gaols, their governments begging the International Committee to help; and then there were the unknown thousands of political prisoners held throughout the country, whose fate could in theory be influenced by Wehrlin – providing the new Soviet authorities proved as amenable as Béla Kun and his followers in Hungary and chose to respect the agreements about political detainees reached at the tenth International Conference.

Wehrlin's mission opened calmly, so calmly in fact that impatient letters asking for progress reports began reaching him from Geneva where the International Committee was being drowned by the Russian émigrés in stories of atrocities and put under considerable pressure to act by Senator Ciraolo and Prince Charles of Sweden. The fact was that Wehrlin was already in some difficulty. Discussions with Ekaterina Peshkova, first wife of Maxim Gorky, who was running an organization called the Political Red Cross mainly to help imprisoned Polish nationals, were broken off after Solovieff instructed him tersely to deal only with the Soviet Red Cross and warned him that any further meetings with Peshkova could lead to 'unfortunate complications'. To all his many requests for access to political prisoners and news of their whereabouts, Solovieff merely replied that there were no political prisoners in the Soviet Union and that what had indeed once been a civil war was now a 'civil peace'. The few detainees who remained, Soloviev added, were in no need at all of 'a special campaign on their behalf'. The International Committee in Geneva resolved to take the matter higher. Setting up codes in which Wehrlin became Vladimir – there was always something slightly comic in the Committee's choice of codes – Litvinov became Gaston, President Ador, Celeste and Soviet political detainees 'anxiété', they lobbied Guiseppe Motta, head of the Swiss federal political department, who at first agreed to discuss the subject with Lloyd George, but then, after further deliberations, said that present circumstances were 'not propitious to any intervention in favour of "anxiété".' The Committee decided to contact Soloviev directly, reminding him of the Soviet Union's commitments under the Geneva Convention and the Hague laws. Were the Soviets to allow 'a purely humanitarian intervention', they wrote in a flowery and delicately worded letter, it would 'do much to reassure the civilized world.' The churches also entered the debate, with the archbishop of Canterbury appealing to Lenin, 'in the name of Christian communities'.

None of this had any effect. News from the Soviet Union grew, if anything, worse. Heart-rending letters describing conditions in the camps reached Wehrlin at a steady rate and he forwarded them to Geneva. 'Enemies of the people,' he wrote, former professors, priests, judges and merchants were being sent to hard labour, while the secret police were resorting to ever greater terror and brutality. There was talk, he said, of a White Russian being crucified and skinned and of women having their breasts cut off. In July 1926, four women managed to escape from a camp in Solovki in the north. They told how they had been deported, ostensibly for prostitution, but really because they were the wives and sisters of Cossacks shot by the Reds; they described rape and harems set up for the guards and the spread of syphilis throughout the camps.

Wehrlin wrote, pleaded, used every power of persuasion; all he wanted, he told Soloviev, was to take medicine, food and clothes into prisons. Soloviev replied that only a formal request from Geneva would be considered. When that came, Wehrlin was summoned and informed that the Soviet Union was 'not in favour of any enquiry into the fate of political prisoners'. Ador, still president, wrote sternly to Chicherin, Commisar of the People at the Foreign Office, about the possible repercussions if the Soviets continued to refuse. There was no answer. He wrote again: no reply. Then news came of worsening conditions in camps in Tiflis and Moscow, and of 20,000 people held on a remote penal island. He wrote again. This time a reply came saying that the island held only criminals and that Soviet law permitted no contact between prisoners and foreigners. Ador was a persistent man. He repeated how painful an impression continuing refusal was making on the public. There was silence.

There was very little that Wehrlin could do. As the file on his time in Moscow shows, he worked extremely hard, pushing where he could, retreating where he felt he might do harm, replying to the many desperate letters that reached him with apologies and assurances that he would do whatever he could to help. In a letter written on 22 December 1930 he reported that he had been able to send a small sum of money to nineteen detained Catholics. 'The number of detained and deported political prisoners,' he added, 'is reaching truly fantastic figures.' Sitting at his desk in Moscow, he was putting together, piece by piece, a map of the camps. In March 1931, he said that he had heard of 32,000 women who had refused collectivization and been sent in cattle trucks without food or warm clothes to unknown destinations. A month later, he reported that thirty-seven political detainees, with frostbite and gangrene, had been moved to a hospital at Yaroslavl. In June, he described what was happening to the 5,000 or so Lutherans, Mennonites and Baptists of German origin deported to the Crimea:

> The percentage of deaths, principally among children, is terrify-
> ing and the number of suicides alarming. Recently, to give you
> an example, an entire family, Edouard Zohnes, aged fifty-two,
> from the village of Djankoi, his wife, fifty, and their two daugh-
> ters, aged twenty and eighteen, hanged themselves.

As famine spread once again throughout the Ukraine in 1932, he notified Geneva that starvation was reaching terrible proportions in the concentration camps. Wehrlin's reports provided some of the rare news coming out of a country now almost wholly cut off by political repression and secrecy; Arthur Koestler, travelling by train, would later write of seeing starving children from the window, looking 'like embryos out of alcohol bottles'.

From Moscow, all Wehrlin could do was to pursue the odd corners of work that were allowed him, tracing missing foreigners, providing passports for Yugoslavs and Hungarians caught by the war, forwarding money to destitute Swiss watchmakers whose families had emigrated in the middle of the nineteenth century from Switzerland, and acting as go-between for the occasional gifts that still managed to get through – children's shoes from the British Save the Children Fund, cod liver oil from the Danish Red Cross. 'The USSR is a huge world in itself,' he wrote, 'and never in history has a country been so cut off.' Conscious of the extreme precariousness of his position, Wehrlin became a master of evasion, of the imaginative deal, of conciliatory gestures and stealthy interventions, going to immense pains to remain on good terms with all around him.

In Geneva, when Huber became president of the International Committee in 1928, a mood of caution gradually settled over the question of the Soviet Union. As he put it early in 1935, 'The International Committee must handle these matters . . . with a great deal of discretion.' Not everyone on the Committee shared his desire not to offend. At meetings of the new Commission for Political Prisoners, set up on 1 May 1935, there was much talk of the need to be firm and to take the initiative. 'Inactivity and exaggerated prudence are what will harm . . . [our] authority,' Edmond Boissier said to the Committee. 'Wherever there is a civil war, a revolution, a coup d'état, a dictatorship, wherever there are political prisoners, we must remember that these people are often worse off than prisoners-of-war and deserve our attention and help.'

In June 1937, the Committee voted to close the Moscow delegation and wrote to inform Wehrlin that he had a year in which to pack up the office and leave. As Huber wrote to Motta — the Swiss government were paying part of the Moscow costs — it was becoming increasingly difficult to justify the expense and Wehrlin's job had really become almost entirely consular. In Moscow, as in Geneva and Berne, there were immediate protests from the foreign representatives, who had come to see that Wehrlin was able to accomplish things, however small, that they themselves could not. Why Huber refused to change his mind is not clear, except that Wehrlin himself had come to feel increasingly powerless as, year by year, all scope for manoeuvre seemed to shrink.

On 30 June 1938, he left Moscow. He remained a delegate for another seven years, when he retired to concentrate on the fine collection of icons and early ceramics he had managed to build up during his many years in the Soviet Union. He was not altogether downcast about his work, saying that given the climate of acute mistrust it had been little short of miraculous that he had been able to help anyone at all; he put it down to a certain respect for the neutrality of the International Committee among the Soviets, born of its performance in the Spanish civil war during which the League was branded in *Izvestia* as having been manipulated by 'forces of the great imperialist states', and to his own care to do nothing too public to offend the authorities. Over the years, he would say, he had been able to save the destitute Swiss residents from starving, secured the release and repatriation of a number of foreigners held as spies and distributed aid and relief as widely and generously as possible. They were not inconsiderable achievements.

But for the millions of men and women held in Stalin's gulags, he had been able to do nothing at all. It was not his fault. In the face of determined opposition, the right to intervene where a national society was unable or unwilling to act, granted to the Committee by successive conferences, was turning out to be frail indeed.

The International Committee had never felt very hopeful about the Soviet Union. The country itself was far away, enormous, prey to political turmoils of an alien nature and frequently devastated by famines on a scale scarcely imaginable by Geneva's prosperous citizens. What was more, its people not only spoke a whole collection of unfamiliar languages but came from a different culture, religion and historical tradition. Their feelings about Germany were very different. The Germans were friends. Back in the 1860s they had been among the first to promote the International Committee and the Geneva Convention. Many members of the Committee spoke excellent German – some, like Burckhardt, were bilingual in French and German – had been brought up on German literature and had even received part of their education in German schools and universities. The International Committee's relationship, in the 1920s and 1930s, first with the German authorities then with the German Red Cross would prove one of the most painful, confusing and controversial in its history.

In January 1923, the German Red Cross put out a pamphlet with a stark title: *Brauchen, (Want)*. It was about food shortages, dwindling supplies of clothes and coal, and hungry children. Privately, in letters written both to the Committee and to the League, it described climbing inflation, rising numbers of dead and fears of bread riots. Soon, these letters warned, Germany might easily go the way of the Soviet Union. The Committee and the League met and agreed to set up a mixed commission, the 'Commixte', and to issue an appeal to the national societies, though in the event unease about Germany itself so coloured the deliberations that the appeal was much watered down. The Dutch in particular judged it so cool, and so late, that they sent the Committee a highly critical cable: 'Appeal seems to us insufficiently eloquent to inspire international sympathy given critical situation German population seems to us that the Commixte could express itself in warmer and more positive terms.'

The Committee was in a tricky position. All but bankrupted by the immense demands from the starving Russians, undecided about its role in peacetime, at odds with the League and seeing its work continually pre-empted by the Americans, it was not sure how to act. It dithered. When offered competent reports on the famine by the German Red Cross it failed even to reply to the letter. (When the League got to hear of them, it immediately asked for copies.) At last, on 8 December 1923, it sent Colonel Edouard Wildboz as a delegate to Berlin to report on conditions.

Wildboz was appalled by what he found. A loaf of bread worth 480 million marks on 15 October had cost 1,000 million on 20 October and 440 billion by the middle of November. In some parts of Berlin, two in every five children were coming to school without breakfast and fainting during lessons, and many thousands were now going barefoot. Particularly badly hit, he noted, were those who had all their savings in devalued silver or paper money. The city's orphanages were overflowing. Like others, he now urged the importance of demonstrating a real will to help, to dispel the increasing feeling among Germans that 'their country at the end of the war was a land forsaken and despised by other nations'. Hurrying from school to school, soup kitchen to soup kitchen, Wildboz did his best to convince Geneva of the seriousness of the situation. 'The misery is overwhelming . . . Unemployment is very high and rising . . . Without help from the rest of the world, the Germans will drown.' He added that the Germans themselves were making heroic efforts to help themselves, and that he judged it essential to restore morale before Germany's cultural and professional tradition vanished altogether.

National societies and the International Committee did at last rouse themselves and aid, particularly from the Americans, started reaching Germany despite crises everywhere that year: the Greeks reported struggles to feed and house over a million refugees, the Ecuadoreans had to cope with a major earthquake and the Turks with a particularly savage winter. But this moment of German need has a wider interest in Red Cross history, for it prompted some of the more farsighted of the Red Cross thinkers to deliberate on the nature of the International Committee itself, and the need for it to adopt a clear moral voice and sense of leadership. For all its purported political innocence, the Red Cross movement was – and always has been – full of people with considerable political acumen. Prince Charles of Sweden, a rising player in the Red Cross world, was one of the first to send help to the Germans in the shape of 20,000 food parcels. But he used the occasion to urge the Committee to assert itself, to show proof 'of a spirit of initiative and total political independence in humanitarian affairs' that would demonstrate its intention of drawing up an effective peacetime programme. From Colonel Draudt came a long appraisal of the Committee's position within the shifting sands of post-war relief work. It was, said Draudt, another keen commentator on Red Cross matters, 'of decisive importance that the will of the Committee makes itself felt . . . with regard to relief for Germany. If this does not happen, we will see the American claim gain credence, that this whole enterprise in Geneva is nothing more than romantic idealism.'

As it happened, there was probably little that the International Committee could have said or done. Wildboz had been right in pointing out that the Germans were taking a strong hand in their own recovery. Nowhere does this determination to fight back against hardship came across more clearly than in the activities of the German Red Cross, which acted as a mirror both to the spirit of the times and to the growing prestige of German professional bodies. The rise of the German Red Cross throughout the 1920s and the 1930s is one of the most fascinating events in all Red Cross history, not least because it revealed a flaw in the movement for which, it turned out, there was no cure.

The German Red Cross was the oldest national society in the world. In 1863, the year in which Dunant, Moynier, Appia and Maunoir met in Geneva to found the International Committee, the Medical Association of Stuttgart, fired by Dunant's dream, decided to rechristen itself the Württemburg Red Cross society. It was soon copied by other associations in the new federal Germany. As with other early societies in Russia and France, Dunant's message had struck a chord among well-born, clever and energetic women for whom a patriotic humanitarian occupation seemed an uncontentious counterpart to the political interests of their fathers, husbands and brothers. The Franco-Prussian war provided these highly organized committees, with many remarkable women in charge, with the test they needed and its impetus carried them through the chaos of the First World War.

If the German Red Cross, by now long united into a single body, emerged from German defeat and the Treaty of Versailles subdued, ostracized by the American-dominated League of Red Cross Societies, it was rapidly regaining its sense of order and efficiency. Year by year throughout the 1920s membership grew: the 418 regional committees of 1924 had become 1,472 four years later. On Red Cross Day, 7 October 1928, it distributed 744,687 badges – it was keen on figures – and the Munich committee alone raised money from the sale of 85,000 flowers. In every town and village across the country, the Red Cross had become a natural home for the wives and daughters of landowning and aristocratic families, who attended a few hours of classes before supervising the ever-growing army of volunteers.

In 1925 the German Youth Red Cross was formed: the following year it started bringing out its own magazine, *Deutsche Jugend*. The articles written for its pages, and for those of the German Red Cross paper, convey a message of regimentation, healthy habits and unquestioning obedience, though perhaps it is only hindsight that gives the many references to 'regeneration', to fighting 'physical and moral decadence' and to a 'powerful' youth programme a slightly grim note.

In July 1933, with over six million unemployed in Germany and constant street fighting between Nazi stormtroopers and communists in the big cities, the National Socialists won 37.8 per cent of the votes in the Reichstag election, thereby becoming the largest political party. Six months later, President Hindenburg appointed Hitler as chancellor of Germany. Within weeks, the Reichstag was closed and, not long after, burned, triggering a wave of repression that swept first hundreds, then thousands of protesters, political opponents, socialists and Jews into detention. That same year – 1933 – Duke Carl-Edouard von Saxe-Coburg und Gotha, the fifty-nine-year-old son of Queen Victoria's youngest son Leopold and as such related to most of Europe's reigning families, was made president of the German Red Cross. It was a shrewd appointment. The duke had been educated in England – he retained a slight English accent in German all his life – had become heir to the dukedom only on the death of two more direct heirs, had seen an honourable war as a general in the German army and was now president of a number of prestigious but politically insignificant organizations like the Automobile Club. Blonde, almost white-haired, with a faint moustache, a bullish head and unexpectedly heavy eyebrows, he was good-natured, humane, but weak, a 'perfect gentleman', as Anton Schöling, a later secretary-general of the German Red Cross, would call him, who embodied the best of earlier German ideals. Though unable to stand up to the increasingly dictatorial directives coming from the Nazis, his mildness and geniality would bestow an air of legality and charitableness to Red Cross matters long after they had actually vanished. In May 1934 the duke paid his first visit to Geneva. It was a great success. Fêted lavishly by both the League and the International Committee, he sent a telegram of thanks to Huber. 'Please always count on me, and on the German Red Cross.'

The Red Cross movement, as had been clear from the ostrich-like behaviour of the delegates at the Tokyo conference, was extremely skilled at pretending nothing unpleasant was happening. In fact, as the files in the archives in Geneva show, reports of growing persecution Jews and political dissidents from one end of Germany to the other, had been reaching the Committee for some time. One of the first signs that not all was totally well within the German Red Cross itself was the strange story of a man called Heinrich Bürger. Bürger had been left a cripple by the First World War and he used a crutch. On the evening of 17 June 1931, during a training session for the Hamburg branch of the German Red Cross, he was standing talking to friends when another volunteer called Sevenheck dashed over unexpectedly and called him a 'pathetic cripple'. There was a brief scuffle, in which Sevenheck was hit by Bürger's crutch. Sevenheck filed a complaint; Bürger was sacked. All this was related to the Committee by a Herr Schlossmacher, who wrote in some agitation to say that he, too, had been sacked by the German Red Cross after supporting Bürger's plea for reinstatement. There was little that the International Committee could do beyond passing the letter on to Colonel Draudt, vice-president of the German Red Cross as well as the League, and hope that this incident was less a reflection of the growing contempt for any handicap in the new Nazi Germany than an unfortunate brawl between angry men.

What was not so easy to ignore were the letters that now began to arrive from Europe's many workers' and social organizations, from Jewish associations and refugees, from the Quakers and various religious and pacifist groups – and from individuals, whose desperate pleas form some of the most haunting material in the entire Red Cross archives. The stories they told were of random arrests, extreme brutality, humiliation and terror.

On 11 May 1933, Emile Kahn, secretary of the French League for the Rights of Man, an early human rights organization, wrote to Ernest Swift, secretary-general of the League of Red Cross Societies, about the 'terrifying misery' being inflicted on 'over 60,000 people' held in concentration camps in Germany. Swift, regretting that it was not within his mandate, which remained confined to peacetime relief work, to take the matter up, passed it to Clouzot at the International Committee. (Swift was not the only League member who worried about the lack of accountability of national societies; but there was nothing in the League's mandate to allow it to interfere.) There it joined a file that grew fatter every day. There was a long letter from a German called Friedrich Kahn, describing political prisoners who had been divided into four groups in a prison, held 'in solitary confinement in chains in the dark and kept for weeks on end on bread and water'. 'Please come yourself,' begged Kahn. 'It's no good leaving it to the German Red Cross, it is powerless ... Come quickly because these maltreated prisoners are shipped to another prison. I beg you once again, in the name of the prisoners: Help! Help!'

There was the note from Kurt Grossmann, head of the Democratic Refugee Care Association in Prague, saying that he had evidence of 160,000 people, 'a conservative estimate', already 'put to death in German prisons and concentration camps'. There was the long article in the British *New Statesman and Nation* of 26 August 1933, reprinting a letter written by a 'group of intellectuals from a large German city'. This described life in 'the present fascist Germany, where a savage Inquisition is master'. There were, said the authors, about a thousand internees in one camp, eighty percent of them communists and the rest socialists, some well over seventy and others disabled ex-soldiers, all kept lying on filthy straw with water dripping from the ceiling, at the mercy of sadistic guards who forced them to sing nationalist songs, and released only after signing forms saying that they would never reveal what they had been through. 'This banditry,' warned the writers, 'based upon incitement to war, may well plunge the whole world once more into fire and blood.'

The *New Statesman* article had been sent to the International Committee by Prince Charles of Sweden, who had already been agitating to the German Red Cross on behalf of political prisoners in German camps, but had managed to elicit only answers claiming that conditions in the camps were fine and that for the 'inmates who come from the working classes the standard of living is actually higher' than they enjoyed at home. Prince Charles's point was that if Germany had nothing to hide, why didn't the German Red Cross criticize the camps? Were they to do so, he claimed, it would 'undoubtedly help Germany's cause'. With the International Committee itself, the Prince was considerably more forthright. 'The decisions of our conferences,' he wrote sternly to the German Red Cross, sending a copy to Huber, 'must not be treated as worthless scraps of paper at the very moment when they are needed and where they ought to be applied.' From several national societies came indications that they felt the International Committee was being far too 'reserved' and failing to take a lead.

The Committee was once again in political difficulty. For several months now, the members had been meeting to discuss how far the existence of concentration camps could be said to be indicative of 'civil war, perhaps without weapons'. These were not, after all, the first such camps, the British having invented them to deal with the Boer women and children in 1900, and then the International Committee had done and said nothing. There was much talk of reliable reporting, of unclear legal positions, of a need to fall back on Resolution XIV of the 1921 conference, which had plainly laid primary responsibility to intervene in such affairs at the door of the national Red Cross society concerned – in this case the German Red Cross. Only if that failed would the International Committee really be in a position to intervene directly.

Huber, ever cautious, reported to Clouzot: 'the question of whether the International Committee should intervene on behalf of political detainees in Germany is a very delicate one.' On 26 September, Huber replied to Prince Charles's letter with a burst of diplomatic mumbo jumbo. Colonel Draudt, he wrote, who had recently been in Geneva, had been asked to carry a message back to the German Red Cross asking them to take up with the German government the matter of detainees in camps.

Somewhere in all this, it occurred to the International Committee that there had been a major flaw in the 1921 conference. What would happen if one of the national Red Cross societies really was taken over by a despotic government? What would it, or could it, do? And what, in such an eventuality, was the International Committee to do?

On 29 November 1933, new statutes were passed in Germany decreeing that the German Red Cross and all its activities were to be made directly responsible to the German government. Government ministers were to be allowed to attend all meetings and overrule all decisions. The president of Germany was to have the right to appoint and dismiss any German Red Cross president. The society became, overnight, just another part of the German state machinery, effectively violating all the principles of Red Cross independence.

Taking refuge in the teachings of the Gospel, particularly the parable of the Good Samaritan, and in high evangelical ideals, Huber fled from specific examples and returned to the safety of textual analyses, however contradictory they sometimes seemed. It would be both wrong and impossible, he argued, for a national society to go into battle against the regime in power in its country: it could not become a 'foreign body' within a state. At the same time, there was no question of abandoning the hallowed Red Cross tradition of offering 'disinterested assistance to all who suffered'. Fine words: but already at odds with the views of Himmler and Heydrich, both of whom were now busy describing charity as defeat and unselfishness as weakness. Faced with these conflicting currents, the Committee informed the German Red Cross that it would be forwarding on to them the many letters of enquiry about missing and maltreated German citizens — of which there were now dozens — and settled down to watch developments.

It did not have long to wait. With the rise of the Nazis in Germany, and the spread of violence by Nazi followers into Austria, the Austrian government decided, early in 1934, to arrest a number of 'troublemakers', both communist and National Socialist, and hold them in a camp at Wöllersdorf, forty kilometres outside Vienna. At the request of the Czech Red Cross, the International Committee asked Chancellor Dollfüss to delay the executions of a number of condemned men implicated in the worst of the violence. But on 24 July the chancellor was assassinated. Mass arrests followed. Soon Wöllersdorf was full and new detainees were sent to prisons in Vienna and Salzburg. A message expressing concern reached Geneva via the German Red Cross from Hitler, who had met the Duke of Saxe-Coburg at the Bayreuth Festival and asked him to intervene.

It seemed to the Committee the perfect opportunity to act. Here was a somewhat vague report about political detainees and a concentration camp: if the Committee obtained permission to visit them it would create a precedent on which they would later be able to fall back if needed. As Jacques Chenevière pointed out at a meeting on 3 October, 'It will prove a strong advantage for the International Committee to have acted in the present circumstances.'

Suzanne Ferrière's brother Louis, already known to the Austrians for his work during the epidemics of the early 1920s, lived in Vienna. He agreed to visit the camp and the prisons to report on the 'material and moral state of the detainees, their accommodation, food, clothes and hygiene, as well as the facilities for corresponding with their families and receiving money and parcels'. Though he was on no account to ask the reason for anyone's arrest, any 'flagrant error' he detected was to be reported. The Austrian Red Cross, setting up the visit, fired a warning shot. Huber was informed by Baron Max von Beck, the mayor of Wöllensdorf, that food, medical care, sanitary conditions 'do not only correspond to what is fair and just, but deserve fulsome praise'. Visiting the camp, he himself had witnessed 'hundreds of detainees . . . grouped around the camp commandant like children'. The authorities, von Beck assured Huber, profoundly regretted this temporary imprisonment but were certain that when the men were released they would take home stories of humane treatment.

Dr Ferrière visited Wöllensdorf and wrote to say that every word of von Beck's letter seemed correct. The detainees, for the most part 'good Austrians momentarily led astray by deadly propaganda', were in excellent form. The camp commandant was a man so naturally good-hearted that he had cut short one of his very rare holidays to make certain all was well. Ferrière had been shown intercepted letters, written in invisible ink, in which the prisoners praised the food and comfort. Asked why they had chosen to make them invisible, they replied that they thought that otherwise no one would believe them. Ferrière, in true Red Cross delegate style, tasted the meat and sausages and pronounced them good; the bread, he said, was particularly delicious. The only fault he could find was the poverty of the families of the detained men and he had already been in touch with the Union Internationale de Secours aux Enfants about helping them.

What Ferrière had not been allowed to see, however, were the prisons.

Clouzot, fearing that this might lay the Committee open to charges of incomplete inspections, asked Ferrière to try again. The answer came back to say that while prison conditions had indeed once been poor, almost all the prisoners had now either been transferred to Wöllensdorf, given proper trials, or sent out on work schemes.

The Committee decided that they could do no more. At least, they agreed, they now had a precedent to work on.

There was no way, now, that the International Committee could claim ignorance about what was taking place in Germany itself. As the letters, reports and cuttings from newspapers in the Geneva archives show, they were receiving regular, reliable information that Nazi bullying and repression was increasing in intensity every day. The first six months of 1933 alone saw the opening of Dachau, in the suburbs of Munich, the passing of one law excluding all 'non-Aryans' and 'enemies of the state' from the civil service and another allowing for compulsory sterilization of patients with a family history of epilepsy, schizophrenia, manic depression and alcoholism, the purging of Jewish and socialist doctors from state hospitals and the dissolution of the trade unions. None of this was lost on Geneva: any doubts that remained must have been dispelled when, in September 1935, the Nuremberg Laws, one of the most barbaric pieces of legislation ever known in European history, laid down criteria for defining Jews, limiting their civil rights and prohibiting marriages between Jews and Aryans. There were now two categories of humanity. 'The Jewish problem,' said a correspondent for *Das schwarze Korps*, the official SS paper, 'will be solved when these parasites in our body politic have been deprived of every opportunity of profiting from the lives of Germans.'

'There are things going on in Germany,' Suzanne Ferrière, in words as cautious as those of Huber, remarked to the Committee, 'as least as grave as those in Austria.'

It was impossible for the German Red Cross not to be drawn in. As a medical and social association and, after 1934, under the direct control of the Nazis, it simply turned into one aspect of the Nazification of the entire German medical profession, which would go, in just a few years, from sterilization to direct medical killing. Nazi ideas claimed that medicine had been 'despiritualized' by the 'mechanically oriented' teachings of Jewish doctors. What was needed, the party announced not long after Hitler came to power, was a 'return to the ethics and high moral status' of earlier times, a 'spiritual and mental regeneration'. Illness became a 'disgrace to be managed by health control'. A doctor was no longer to be a mere caretaker of the sick, but a 'cultivator of the genes', an 'alert biological soldier' and evangelist, inspired not by exaggerated Christian compassion for the weak, but totally dedicated to the health of the 'Volk', the people. Hostels for nomad or gypsy children were being set up, reported the League's *Bulletin* in 1937, without comment, so that they could be moved from 'unspeakable conditions of filth and promiscuity' to a 'healthy, well-ordered life and learn the value of discipline and honest toil'. Eugenicists like Alfred Grotjahn, Eugen Fischer and Fritz Lenz, appointed to chairs in social hygiene to promote the extermination of 'burdens to the community' in the interests of economy and racial fitness, pushed ahead with policies that not only gave people the 'right to die', but doctors the right to kill.

Nor was it all only a question of destruction. Himmler had a plan to breed his SS into a biological elite, a 'racial nucleus from which Germany could replenish an Aryan inheritance now dangerously diluted through generations of race mixing'. The *Lebensborn*, or 'fountain of life', the producing of biologically valuable children that extended to the kidnapping of good Aryan species, was launched. 'I really intend,' announced Himmler, 'to take German blood from wherever it is to be found in the world, to rob it and steal it wherever I can.' A photograph that appeared in the German Red Cross magazine showed four Red Cross nurses standing at a table covered in babies: Germany needed, said the caption, as many 'new, small, blonde, blue-eyed German babies' as possible to boost the German Reich.

This new Nazi medical ethos became the starting point for an entire reorganization of the profession — and the Red Cross. Known as 'Gleichschaltung' — co-ordination or, more ominously, bringing into line — it placed the control of institutions in the hands of trusted Nazis, who set about eliminating all opposition through a stranglehold on doctors' panels, health insurance schemes and professional bodies. The persecution of Jewish doctors was a part of the Nazi vision: within a month of Hitler becoming chancellor, Nazi doctors began ousting their Jewish colleagues. Medical students were even discouraged from referring to scientific papers written by Jews. Soon, German doctors were able to boast that they had one of the highest ratios of party members – nearly half – of any profession. A few doctors and nurses did resist and many felt little sympathy for Hitler, but as a profession medicine gave itself up readily to the Nazis. After the war, at the Nuremberg trials, 350 doctors were judged to have 'committed medical crimes': and these did not include the persecution of their Jewish colleagues. Did Colonel Draudt discuss these matters on his many visits to Geneva during the 1930s? One can only assume that he did, even if such discussions are nowhere to be found in the minutes of the meetings or in the files of correspondence. There are, on the other hand, many references to discussions that were 'better held orally'.

By 1935, the German Red Cross had almost a million and a half members. All of them, whether doctors, nurses, auxiliaries or volunteers, were in close, regular contact with the medical profession. There was no area of medicine or welfare, from first aid in mines to baby care, in which the German Red Cross was not active. From the mid-1930s, the *Deutsche Rôtes Kreuz*, the German Red Cross magazine, frequently published photographs of swastikas and Red Cross flags hanging side by side; of Hitler inspecting rows of Red Cross nurses; of young Red Cross workers marching under swastikas. Articles in the magazine quoted from *Mein Kampf*.

It soon became clear to Geneva that the German Red Cross, even if it had wanted to, was not in a position to intervene in Nazi repression. Minutes of meetings suggest a longing so great on the part of the Committee for things to improve on their own that every positive rumour that came their way was repeated and savoured. Huber wanted to believe Draudt when he said that Hitler was 'concerned over the fate' of those who had been arrested and wished to help them. He wanted to listen to von Cleve, another member of the German Red Cross, who assured the Committee that he had personally 'been deeply impressed by the faultless organization of these camps'. He wanted to trust statistics that suggested that the numbers of detainees were dropping not growing. He wanted to think, as he told the Committee towards the end of September 1933, that the camps held 'communists suspected of high treason', former civil servants 'guilty of corruption' and politically unre liable people taken into custody to save them from the 'many members of the public who wanted to lynch them'. As he put it, in words that have an almost desperate note to them, the International Committee was not in a position to follow up all these different political excesses. 'It is only in exceptional situations,' he declared, 'involving a very large number of people', that the Committee could act. The question was: how large did a 'very large number of people' need to be?

On 27 November 1933, Camille Drevet, secretary of the International League for Peace and Freedom, wrote to urge Huber to send a delegate to see 'what is really happening in police stations, in prisons and in concentration camps in Germany'. Huber stalled. It still seemed to him that the best course of action was to support the German Red Cross, taking care not to make things worse by precipitate action.

Not everyone on the Committee shared his views. Chenevière kept calling for better and more reliable reports; Suzanne Ferrière pushed for decisive intervention; and Burckhardt, whose authoritative voice rings out, even through brief minutes of meetings, vacillated, some days expressing his anxiety at what seemed to be happening, others dwelling on the many possible political pitfalls of interfering. Colonel Favre observed that 'as long as the German Red Cross shows no sign of ill-will or powerlessness, we cannot do much.' There was endless debate about whether or not a civil war could be said to have broken out in Germany and whether the moment had come to invoke Article 5 of the Geneva Conventions, which gave the Committee the power to act on behalf of political detainees.

In the autumn of 1935 matters came to a head. The Duke of Saxe-Coburg, in response to repeated, scrupulously polite pressure from Geneva and many reminders about the precedent established by the visit to Wöllersdorf in Austria, wrote to say that permission had at last been granted for a delegation to visit a couple of German concentration camps. Burckhardt was the obvious man to lead it. His account of the visit was published only in 1961.

On reaching Berlin, Burckhardt was told that he had been allocated four specific camps. He refused to see them. A proper visit, he said, one that would convince the world that no atrocities were being carried out, had to be on his terms, to camps of his choice, paid without warning and with permission to speak to the prisoners alone. The Duke of

Saxe-Coburg was appalled and Reinhard Heydrich, then in charge of the camps, angry. A dinner with Heydrich was arranged. When the Gestapo deputy chief arrived, Burckhardt noticed that he was wearing the first all-black uniform that he had seen, and observed that his hands were 'lily white, Pre-Raphaelite, made for slow strangulations'. After dinner, the two men discussed the camp visits. Heydrich conceded that Burckhardt would be allowed to see anything he wanted but would not agree to let him speak to anyone without advance notice or in private. Burckhardt remained adamant: either the visit would take place on usual International Committee terms or it would not take place at all; he would return to Geneva and say that he had been refused entry to the camps.

It was a good move; the Nazis were at this stage still reluctant to be thought to be concealing something. Next day, Burckhardt was summoned to Gestapo headquarters and told that Himmler himself had given permission for him to conduct his visits as he wished. He was flown to his first choice of camp, Esterwegen, with its 'modern and hygienic installations', near the Dutch border. Here 'prominent politicians and intellectuals whose former activities are known to be particularly harmful to the state and to the people' had been held for well over a year, without charge or trial. Asking the prisoners how they were treated, he was told 'like dogs'. 'To be tolerant,' said the camp rules, 'is to be weak.'

In the afternoon, Burckhardt asked to see Carl von Ossietzky, the Hamburg pacifist and recent winner of the Nobel Peace Prize, condemned for high treason after opposing German rearmament. The commandant of the camp, a First World War veteran called Loritz, said that he had no knowledge of such a prisoner. Burckhardt insisted. Ten minutes later, two SS men appeared, dragging behind them a small, pale figure with swollen eyes, chipped teeth and a badly mended broken leg. When Burckhardt greeted him, Ossietzky, 'a man barely still alive', stayed silent. Burckhardt noticed that he was trembling. At last, in a barely audible voice, the forty-six-year-old pacifist asked Burckhardt to tell his friends that he was very near the end; he gave a small bow and turned away. All the prisoners Burckhardt spoke to at Esterwegen appeared to him frightened and ill at ease; their answers were evasive. He watched as a work detachment stumbled back into the camp, thirty men in much the same state as Ossietzky, shivering and weak.

Burckhardt made a brief visit to Lichtenberg, a seventeenth-century castle in Thorgau, where he noted that there were six hundred political prisoners and two hundred homosexuals, and to Dachau, but knowing that he was expected he realized that there was little to be gained by talking to prisoners. He returned to Geneva to report that the mood of Esterwegen was 'military, rugged, pointlessly harsh – even brutal'. The physical conditions, however, seemed less important to him than the fact that the camp commandant Loritz was himself brutal and that the prisoners were begging to be brought to trial so that they would at least know how long a sentence to expect. He observed that criminals and political prisoners were held together. Ossietzky's position was, he said, 'desperate'. These criticisms were sent off to Heydrich and to the German Red Cross, and the International Committee decided that the best thing to do was to follow Burckhardt's advice and press to have a more humane commandant appointed – another way of 'humanizing' war. A second report via a secret intermediary, an 'eminent doctor' whose name Burckhardt did not reveal, went directly to Hitler, for it was still being said that the Führer knew little of the brutalities inflicted in his name.

According to Burckhardt, writing twenty-six years later, news reached Geneva that Loritz had been transferred, some said as a prisoner, to another concentration camp, and that Ossietzky had been placed in the infirmary, where he died not long afterwards. The Committee was informed that criminals would be separated from political prisoners as soon as possible. However, there was no question of any of the political detainees appearing before an ordinary court since what they had done was to 'deliberately threaten security and public order by their conduct as enemies of the state'. Their cases would, however, be periodically reviewed.

In the spring of 1936, Burckhardt returned to Germany. This time he was taken to see children's homes, asylums and labour camps. He met Heydrich, Reichsarbeitsführer Hirl and von Ribbentrop. He came back saying there he had detected real improvements. Programmes to 'convert' communists to the new regime were working well, though they were said to be more successful with workers than intellectuals. Having asked whether anti-Semitism was not making life very hard for families of Jewish detainees, he had been told that they were treated exactly the same as were the families of Aryan prisoners. In one of the labour camps he visited, where the men were building roads, bridges and canals, he met a number of former concentration camp inmates; they seemed to him 'sincerely content'. He had not, however, been to any of the camps themselves on this visit and Burckhardt admitted that he had met with considerable reluctance whenever he raised the subject. He also reported to the Committee that he had been led to understand that, as long as demonstrations on behalf of political prisoners and against the Nazis continued abroad, the treatment of political detainees would never be improved.

This account of what was to be the International Committee's only real investigation into Germany's spreading network of concentration camps – a short visit to Dachau in 1938 was even more shaming – comes from Burckhardt's book and from various official reports. More interesting are the letters in the archives relating to his two visits to Germany; and the true story of what happened to Loritz, the commandant of Esterwegen.

A few days after Burckhardt's first trip, Huber wrote to the Duke of Saxe-Coburg. The letter is warm and somewhat ingratiating. Thanking him for 'upholding in so fine a way the close co-operation of our two institutions', he drew particular attention to the help given to him by Heydrich, 'who arranged a private, individual talk with those in protective custody, thus enabling him to produce an objective report'. (The glib use of the term 'protective custody' is worthy of note.) Burckhardt wrote to Saxe-Coburg as well, to convey his admiration for the good work done for both criminal and political prisoners by such an excellent system; he repeated how important it was that the camp commandant should be a man of stature, for he alone could inspire 'the example of maturity and outstanding superiority which are the strongest qualities of the German way of life'. Saxe-Coburg's reply spoke of both Heydrich's and Hitler's interest in his report and conveyed Hitler's personal invitation to Burckhardt to visit 'several areas of constructive activity in Germany', and in particular 'National Socialist arrangements for the people's welfare, and the construction sites of the motorways'.

Early in 1936, the duke forwarded to Burckhardt a copy of Heydrich's reactions to his report. It spoke of separating 'those judged improvable from the unteachable' in the camps and remarked that 'protective custody' was reserved for those who 'while not guilty of punishable acts, have through their attitude of opposition to the State demonstrated their open disturbance of order and security'.

When Burckhardt returned from his second visit in 1936, he wrote to thank each of the people who had accompanied him on his travels; the letters are friendly, even excessively so; they include wishes not to be forgotten and hopes that they will meet again. To Hirl, the Reichsarbeitsführer, he spoke of the 'great and lasting impression' the labour service had made on him. 'The transformation of a great military tradition into productive, educational, value-creating aims seems to me one of the greatest and most promising achievements of our time.' That same day, 23 June 1936, he wrote personally to Hitler.

> Through the kind offices of the President of the German Red Cross I received the invitation which you, Herr Reichschancellor, had the great goodness to send me. Magnificent hospitality and outstanding organization made it possible for me to learn of the truly magical achievements of the motorways and National Labour Service in one short week spent crossing Germany.
>
> What specially and permanently impressed itself on me was the joyous spirit of co-operation that informed everything. These constructive achievements, the generous, concerned, social thoughtfulness, all added vividly to those impressions I had received on my other journey to Germany on behalf of the International Committee last October. I cannot sufficiently praise the willingness to oblige of the various gentlemen whose arrangements opened a whole new vista and understanding for me.
>
> Your deeply devoted, deeply grateful and deeply respectful
> C. J. Burckhardt.

Was he being honest? Had he been duped? Did he really approve of Hitler's Germany? Or did he instinctively share the anti-Semitism that had been endemic in Germany since long before the Weimar Republic? Burckhardt is never easy to read. At meetings, he showed himself keen to act and quick to voice his fears about what was going on. But there is no doubt that he admired Germany and, perhaps even more strongly than Huber, he did not wish to believe the Germans capable of atrocities. Or was he simply a mirror to the feelings of the International Committee?

By 1936, the gypsies in Germany had already been labelled 'asocial half-castes', the sick and disabled targeted for euthanasia and Jews sacked from all government jobs, libraries, museums, newspaper offices, concert platforms and even their own businesses. On 27 September 1935 the *Manchester Guardian Weekly* published an unsigned article about Dachau. It spoke at length about men held for years in unheated barracks on insufficient rations. It described excessively hard labour and punishments. It went on:

> Prisoners are sent to the 'cells' (known as bunkers) for the slightest misdemeanour and sometimes for no reason at all. The cells are narrow and in semi-darkness – some are completely dark. They are unheated. Several prisoners have suffered from frostbite in winter, and last winter two . . . were frozen to death . . . Life in the 'cells' is so terrible and the continual floggings and other ill-treatment so inhuman that many have died of the effects. The survivors have returned to camp as hardly recognizable human wrecks with festering sores and bruises . . . The treatment of the Jewish prisoners at Dachau is particularly terrible . . . nine have been done to death. Some of the prisoners were murdered in such a brutal fashion that it was impossible to allow the relatives to see the dead bodies . . .

Burckhardt was in Dachau three weeks after the article appeared.

Loritz, the commandant of Esterwegen, was indeed transferred not long after Burckhardt's visit – and to another concentration camp – but not as a prisoner. He was promoted to run Dachau. Why did Burckhardt lie? Because, say the historians Jean-Claude Favez and Paul Stauffer, Burckhardt needed to present himself and the Committee as effective and when he came to write his memoirs, *Ma mission à Danzig*, in 1960, he was already correcting his image for history.

It was at this moment, in the middle and late 1930s and not later as commonly accepted, that the International Committee took the next decisive step down the path of silence. With their failure to confront Mussolini over the use of gas in Ethiopia and their extreme reluctance to challenge the Nazis over the Jews and political prisoners – to the extent of not even daring to record conversations and meetings on paper – the Committee, led by an excessively cautious Huber and an ambivalent

Burckhardt, now began to store up problems that would later come to haunt them.

In 1936 Himmler appointed Dr Ernst Grawitz head of the health services of the SS and the police, and acting-president of the German Red Cross. The Duke of Saxe-Coburg's position was now purely nominal. Grawitz was ambitious, amoral and vicious. Peremptory with his subordinates, he fawned on superior officers and particularly on Himmler, whose orders he carried out devotedly. At Nuremberg in 1947, Dr Poppendick, who became his chief administrator, described him as polite on the surface but liable to turn suddenly offensive. 'He behaved,' said Poppendick, 'quite differently with those he judged influential . . . and acted as if he himself were . . . very important.' Grawitz came to wield enormous power.

One of his first jobs was to reorganize the German Red Cross and oversee its smooth absorption into the Nazi Party. He set about it willingly and was soon selecting doctors for senior jobs from among those known to be close to the regime and to support euthanasia. Gauleiters were made heads of local nursing associations. Though some of his worst excesses were curbed by the continuing reluctance of figures like the Duke of Saxe-Coburg and Generaloberin Luise von Oertzen, head of the nursing association, to co-operate, the society as a whole put up little resistance. Indeed, it was Saxe-Coburg who announced in May 1936 that the 'transformation of the German Red Cross according to National-Socialist principles has been carried out successfully'.

No occasion gives a better flavour of the close ties that now existed between the Nazis and the German Red Cross than the seventieth anniversary of the National Women's Association of the Red Cross, held in Berlin on 12 November 1936. There was an immense turnout. Many thousands of nurses and auxiliaries, in impeccable white uniforms and red cross badges, filled the hall where banners with swastikas hung side by side with red cross flags. The Duke of Saxe-Coburg and the new head of all the German women's associations, Reichsfrauenführerin Gertrud Scholtz-Klink, a beady-eyed patrician matron with a severe hat, took the parade. The occasion was marked by an orgy of praise for the new streamlined German Red Cross and for its highly 'reliable attitudes'. A

Dr Löffler spoke at length about the importance of racial policy and health. By now more than ten thousand trained Red Cross nurses were living in fifty-seven *Mutterhäuser*, nurses' homes, across the country. 'It is their duty,' said a Red Cross paper, 'to assist day and night in the well-being of the German people . . . Every leader within the German Red Cross knows that it is his duty to serve society and to follow Adolf Hitler . . . and that faithful service alongside the National Socialist movement is one of the conditions of leadership.'

From Geneva, Huber sent a telegram wishing the German society a smooth translation of its 'high aims and ideals' into practice; from Paris, the League wished it a 'successful and blessed future'. The December issue of the *Deutsche Rotes Kreuz* gave several pages to the event. The cover consists of a photograph of Hitler, 'Protector of the German Red Cross', greeting a line of nurses: inside are pictures of nurses lined up under swastikas, giving the Hitler salute: everywhere, swastikas and Red Cross flags flutter together in the wind.

On 9 December 1937, very nearly the last shred of German Red Cross independence disappeared in new laws that dissolved all associated organizations and brought them under one national body. The existing nurses' associations vanished; their property was taken over; their duties were redefined in such a way that they were now to work alongside the medical military corps of the army, navy and air force. There was to be no more social work. The distinctive German Red Cross official decoration – a white cross with a black eagle – was replaced by a red cross in a white circle. In the centre stood an eagle and in its talons a golden wreath with a swastika. 'The German Red Cross greets its leader,' Grawitz cabled Hitler on his birthday, 'with loyalty and obedience. The men and women of the German Red Cross stand ready for the highest and fullest duty.' Colonel Draudt retired, apparently for reasons of health. The Duke of Saxe-Coburg stayed on, despite a back injury and failing sight.

Grawitz had very little to do with Geneva. He spoke poor French. That autumn, Etienne Clouzot had been to see him in Berlin, reporting back to Huber that Grawitz had been cordial and had told him at length of the German Red Cross reorganization, intended, as he explained, to return the society to its former duties as an auxiliary to the army. In the case of war, Grawitz had added, the Red Cross would go to 'wherever there was a front'. When, in March 1938, the German army occupied

Austria and a union between the two countries was proclaimed, Grawitz wrote a terse note to the International Committee informing them that the Austrian Red Cross had now been incorporated within the German Red Cross and that all its international dealings, above all with members of the International Committee, had already been transferred. There was no comment from Geneva. Even the League, ostensibly the umbrella of all the societies, kept silent.

All through that spring, letters came reporting the atrocities to which Austrian Jews were being subjected. Huber's reply was to remark that there was as yet 'insufficient information' to justify 'an intervention on the part of the International Committee to Berlin'. He reminded members of the Committee that there was nothing in their statutes saying that action could be taken over arrests — only over unmistakable 'inhuman treatment' of detainees. 'If new information were to reach the International Committee,' he added, 'it should be judged with extreme prudence.'

In Germany, Jews were now being forced to sell their businesses to Aryans; they were banned from swimming pools, restaurants, hotels and shops. Jewish members of the German Red Cross were now among the ever growing population of the concentration camps, together with gypsies, communists, socialists and every kind of suspected dissident. Buchenwald, according to reports sent by British consuls to London and published by the HMSO, now held over 8,000 prisoners — Jews, intellectuals, Bible students, criminals and gypsies — living in filth and mud up to their knees, constantly flogged and hung by their arms for minor infractions of arbitrary rules, watched over by specially trained SS seventeen-year-olds. In the archives in Geneva are several drafts of a letter to Grawitz, drawn up by Suzanne Ferrière for Huber, proposing a new International Committee delegation to the camps. 'The favourable report [made by Burckhardt] ... allows me to think that a new visit would give rise to no unfavourable comments.' The draft has two possible endings: one that such a visit would reassure the relatives of those held prisoner, the other that the International Committee itself would like to be kept fully informed. In the event, neither was sent. Mlle Ferrière and Huber decided instead to use the sixteenth International Red Cross Conference, which opened in London on 20 June 1938, as an occasion on which to approach Grawitz directly.

It was the seventy-fifth anniversary year of the birth of the Red Cross. The conference was sumptuous, attended by 300 delegates from fifty governments and fifty-four national societies. It looked magnificent. Some of the sessions were held in St James's Palace; a garden party was given by the king at Buckingham Palace; and a final service in St Paul's Cathedral. The mood, however, was one of extreme apprehension. After the singing of the Magnificat the filing past of nurses, auxiliaries, volunteers, guides, scouts and royalty, the archbishop of Canterbury gave an address. Talking of the growing menace of nationalism, of the terrifying new weapons of war, he warned that 'death will descend from the skies like a terrifying rain'.

The United States had sent a team of four to London, one of them being Mabel Boardman, now in her seventy-seventh year; India sent Nora Hill, secretary of the Indian Red Cross and a formidable presence at Tokyo, and ten delegates; Czechoslovakia sent the daughter of Jan Masaryk, Dr Masarykova, first president of the Czech Red Cross. From Geneva had come Huber, Paul des Gouttes, Lucie Odier, Guillaume Favre and Edouard Chapuisat, who spoke in a flowery way of a 'new Crusade of Good against Evil, Life against Death'. The talk was all of neutrality and civil war, but above all of civilians and the continuing failure to pass proper articles to protect them. Norman Davis, chairman of the board of governors of the League, expressed his apprehension about a 'revolting and needless slaughter and maiming of helpless women and children'. Fears were also expressed that the International Committee might well find itself 'overtaken by events . . . and, faced by new tasks, will have to turn more and more frequently to the right of initiative'. There was only one sour note, when the Committee claimed that governments were sending ever less funding to Geneva. As the conference ended, Huber was praised for his efficiency and 'high moral authority', which had assured, so the delegates insisted, the International Committee its rightful high place in the world. It was agreed that the seventeenth conference would be in 1942 in Stockholm.

Grawitz received Huber's personal request about a visit to the concentration camps calmly. In a surprisingly short time word reached Geneva that a mission would be acceptable – but only to one camp, Dachau. Burckhardt was no longer free to lead the delegation, having been appointed the League of Nations High Commissioner for the disputed enclave of Danzig and taken leave from the International Committee, so Colonel Favre went instead.

On 19 August, taking with him Dr Chessex, a delegate who spoke excellent German, having like all pre-war Swiss military instructors served with the German army, Favre left for Germany. There had been talk of Mlle Odier going with them, but Huber vetoed the idea on the grounds that, since most of the detainees were men it might be a most disagreeable experience.

Favre and Chessex were told that they might talk to the prisoners, providing they spoke German. There was no question of seeing them in private, and Favre appears to have decided not to make a fuss. He returned to Geneva to report that his 'impressions were not unfavourable'. a phrase he repeated in a letter to Himmler on 31 August.

'Everywhere,' he told the committee, 'reigns order, cleanliness, even a certain elegance.' The delegates had seen a great deal of building going on and were told that new showers were being installed for the prisoners and a new sports field opened. They were taken to see ground being prepared 'for a large garden in which flowers were to be grown to decorate the camp and its buildings'. Dachau held, reported Favre, some 6,000 prisoners, half of them political. Though there were Jews, who wore their yellow stars, very few were there simply because they were Jewish: most had been a 'nuisance to the community'. Favre assured his fellow committee members that he was convinced that he had not been duped, or things hidden from him, but that what he and Chessex saw 'corresponds with reality'.

Dr Chessex asked whether he might give a personal opinion. He said that though the prisoners' faces had indeed given an 'impression of constraint and sadness, painful to witness', he had seen no signs of exhaustion, physical debility or ill-treatment. On the contrary, the men had looked to him vigorous and healthy. 'The camp of Dachau,' he concluded, 'is a model of its kind from the point of view of installations and administration. The regime inflicted on the prisoners, undoubtedly severe, cannot be described as inhuman. The sick, in particular, are treated with kindness, understanding and conscientiousness.

It is hard to know what to say. Were the two men duped? Or did they, like Burckhardt, simply not want to acknowledge evidence made easy for them to ignore? A report written by the British consul in Munich and sent to the British government in London a few months later, said that there were well over 14,000 Jews in Dachau, herded like cattle in a stockyard, with little clothing, sleeping on bare boards or on straw, buffeted, kicked and 'bastinadoed'. There were many deaths. The Jews were receiving half the food given to the Aryan prisoners.

That summer there were attacks on Jews in virtually every town in Germany. On the night of 9 November, *Kristallnacht*, 7,500 Jewish shops were looted and destroyed, synagogues burnt down and an unknown number of Jews died — apparently in spontaneous retaliation for the killing of a German diplomat in Paris by a Polish Jew whose family had been deported from the Reich.

In July, representatives from thirty-two nations had been invited by President Roosevelt to a meeting at Evian in France to discuss emigration from Austria and Germany. Germany was not invited: Italy refused to attend. One after the other, governments gave their reasons for not taking in any refugees; one delegate came away comparing the conference to a 'modern wailing wall'.

Within the League, anxiety about the 'darkening of the political horizon' prompted dozens of letters between various members of the board and some of the senior Red Cross figures in various countries. These were men and women of the same type, the same background and speaking a common language. Perhaps even more so than the International Committee, the League, as a federation of different societies, was in a very difficult position when it came to criticizing one of its members. In its *Bulletin*, the notice about the new German Red Cross emblem with its swastika was buried deep among articles about Swedish aviators, leprosy in Africa, and the number of tins of condensed milk distributed by the ladies' committee of the Iraqi Red Crescent: the *Bulletin* invariably favoured pieces on 'good feeding and sleeping habits'.

At a League meeting in Paris, fifteen days after *Kristallnacht*, there was a revealing exchange, a clash thinly veiled by diplomatic courtesies which gives some idea of how very strongly some of its members felt about their powerlessness. Norman Davis, who had taken over as chairman in February 1938, had sent a message saying that he was keen, given the worsening 'Jewish-refugee situation', to set up a study 'on the character of the emergency'. It was read out by Ernest Swift, the vice-chairman of the League, who shared Davis's fears and welcomed his intervention, reporting later: 'I held on like grim death until we had gained our point.'

Walther Hartmann, representing the German Red Cross and evidently under great pressure from home, replied curtly that such a study would be 'premature'. What was more, he warned, it could have serious repercussions in Germany. News of German disasters, he pointed out, had not always led to generous offers of help and no one in the German Red Cross had detected much concern over the famine that 'provoked suicides on a scale which the world had never before witnessed'.

Red Cross societies, continued Hartmann on a slightly threatening note, had no choice but to co-operate with their governments and play their 'merciful role in full accord with them'. In a letter describing the exchange to Davis, Ernest Swift remarked that Hartmann was not the only person present to want to 'suppress the subject' and that it was clear to him that he had received orders from Germany to 'try to prevent any discussion of the Jewish question . . . His presentation gave the impression that Germany had decided to punish the Jews and would do all in its power to prevent any other nation from comforting them.' He added: 'We all felt very sorry for Hartmann who really is a very decent person.'

The exchange represented barely a ruffle in the day's harmonious meetings. The summing up that evening by the marquis de Lillers was a model of soothing Red Cross sentiments. 'Political events are what they are,' the marquis declared, and it was not for the executive committee to judge or condemn them. The marquis and his wife then played host to the delegates at a tea-party.

Huber continued to sit like an oracle in his house in Zurich while members of the International Committee came and went, repeating to everyone that it was essential for the International Committee not to be drawn into political action, or make commitments that it would not be in a position to honour. When a group of Swiss German pastors asked him to intercede over Martin Niemöller, the Lutheran pastor from Berlin-Dahlem who had preached against the Nazis and was now in prison and very ill, he wrote to ask Burckhardt what action he favoured. As high commissioner for Danzig, Burckhardt was excellently placed to know precisely how the Nazis were treating the Jews. During a conversation on the Jewish question, Burckhardt wrote in *Ma mission à Danzig* Himmler had described the Jews as 'too ugly and too troublesome'.

The question was 'very prickly', he told Huber. Better to 'abstain from action'. He recommended telling the anxious pastors that a preliminary enquiry had been made and that the Committee as a result felt that it would be best to do nothing, particularly as Niemöller's health had now improved. (Another lie: no enquiry had in fact been made.) Surveying the worsening picture, Huber noted on 16 November, a week after *Kristallnacht*: 'In this undoubtedly anguishing moment we must keep our sang-froid.'

In January 1939 a letter arrived from Grawitz in reply to a question about whether the German Red Cross was doing anything about the destitute Jewish families. The society had done nothing at all, Grawitz stated, 'and sees no possibility and no necessity to associate itself with any action taken'.

There was to be one more conflict before 1939, but this time – unlike in Spain and Ethiopia – the International Committee almost totally failed to influence events. The war between the Chinese and the Japanese provided two lessons: it gave a glimpse of the immense difficulties the Committee, and the Red Cross movement as a whole, would face in the Far East in the war to come; and it suggested one possible way of protecting civilians during bombing raids. The idea of having 'safety zones' in which civilians could shelter had often been discussed in Geneva, but never until now properly tested.

At 11 p.m. on the night of 7 July 1937, the Japanese carried out an unannounced military exercise on the Marco Polo bridge at Lakouch'iao, ten miles south-west of Peking. Disputes had rumbled on between the Chinese and Japanese for the last five years, but the trigger for war came when a Japanese soldier was reported missing after Chinese soldiers fired on a Japanese unit. It was to be extremely bloody.

By August, the Japanese had 100,000 soldiers in China and had taken Peking: in September they landed at Shanghai with thirty warships; in December they advanced on Nanking. Eighteen million Chinese fled from their homes in and around Shanghai, Soochow and Wuxi. News of heavy bombing reached Geneva and Paris from Dr F. C. Yen, head of the Chinese Red Cross, who claimed that he had lost seven of his thirty ambulances to Japanese bombers, which had chased the well-marked vehicles along the streets. On 23 August at Lotien, an ambulance corps of forty-three were rescuing the wounded when they were surrounded by Japanese troops, had their Red Cross insignia ripped from their uniforms, were made to kneel down and were then shot.

Every day, the Japanese bombers returned to the cities. They aimed at hospitals, missions, refugee camps, bus stations and junks. They set fire to schools and colleges. The Shanghai *Evening Post and Mercury* called it 'murder. Murder beyond doubt, first degree, premeditated, with no extenuating circumstance.' In Paris the League was eager to act, Colonel Gielgud urging the ever reluctant Huber to initiate a decisive and swift response so as not to lose face in the east. After some deliberation, an appeal went out to the national societies and a new delegate, Charles de Watteville, former representative of the League of Nations in the Middle East, left for Shanghai. He reached the city at the end of September.

Shanghai, a city of 3.5 million inhabitants, had been split into an International Settlement, a French concession and an enormous Chinese quarter, which was now filled to overflowing with what some claimed to be nearly half a million refugees, fleeing before the Japanese advance. De Watteville does not appear to have thought much of the Chinese Red Cross, saying that, though charming and polite, its members were unaware 'of even the simplest rules of hygiene', but he was impressed by the various foreign relief committees already set up by diplomats and missionaries in the city. As for respecting the Red Cross emblem, he wrote, 'the question is extremely thorny. Both sides reproach each other.' What was needed, he thought, was a permanent delegation to China, a 'kind of technical counsellor, who would monitor violations.' Though de Watteville managed to get the Japanese to agree to abide by the Geneva Conventions – despite the fact that they had still not ratified them – he seemed more interested in the strange spectacle of the East than in the war itself. It was hard, he kept repeating in his reports, 'for the Oriental mind to see the question from our angle'. He noted with surprise that while the Japanese were bombing not a mile from his hotel, the streets below his windows were full of people playing football and golf. There was no point, he added, in trying to get figures for dead and missing: the Chinese soldiers did not wear tags and the Japanese were forbidden to identify themselves for fear of giving away secrets.

When at the end of 1937 he was recalled to Geneva, he proposed to the International Committee a replacement, in the shape of a Dr Louis Calame who had lived in Shanghai for the past eight years, having taken over a medical practice from a departing French doctor. Calame, said de Watteville, was a 'grand politicien' in local affairs. But it is possible that de Watteville did not stay long enough to make the acquaintance of the new delegate, for Calame turned out to be a delegate in the Sidney Brown mould, outspoken, somewhat romantic and very impatient with bureaucracy. Discursive and opinionated, he would come to annoy Huber profoundly.

In December 1937, Calame set about gaining access to the prisoner-of-war camps. It was almost impossible to do so. Neither Japanese nor Chinese were taking many prisoners, preferring to execute captives as quickly as possible, and weeks of badgering yielded only eight Chinese prisoners whom he was allowed to meet briefly in the press room of the Japanese consul. Two Japanese colonels were present and two interpreters of 'doubtful competence'. Calame was able to report that the prisoners looked healthy, clean and well cared for, with smart uniforms and 'brand new European style shoes'.

Early in the New Year, he received orders to visit Nanking – a town which would become a symbol of Japanese brutality – from where rumours were coming about Japanese atrocities, mass executions and rape. While waiting for permission, Calame sent to Geneva a report written on Christmas Eve by one of a group of twenty-seven foreign missionaries, doctors, diplomats and teachers living in Nanking, which had been occupied by the Japanese on 12 December. Calling themselves the 'International Red Cross Committee of Nanking', they were running three Red Cross hospitals and feeding and housing over 100,000 refugees in what they referred to as their 'Safety Zone'. The report ran to thirteen pages and was, in the words of its anonymous author, the 'story of a horde of degraded criminals of incredible bestiality'. What the writer described was indeed awful. He had been, he said, 'to see fifty corpses in some ponds a quarter of a mile east of headquarters. All obviously civilians, hands bound behind backs, one with top of head cut off completely ... A boy of 13, taken by the Japanese nearly two weeks ago, beaten with an iron rod, and then bayoneted ... Women and old men come kneeling and crying, begging our help in getting back their husbands and sons.'

It was clear, from this and several other accounts smuggled out to Shanghai and later reprinted as a book by the Australian correspondent for the *Manchester Guardian*, H. J. Timperley, that the Japanese were extremely brutal and that in their four-week occupation of Nanking they raped many thousands of girls and women between the ages of nine and seventy-five and killed tens of thousands more – the Chinese later said 300,000 in all – apart from setting fire to the city and looting everything of value it contained. It was clear too that a handful of foreigners, with nothing but their moral authority and their position as neutral witnesses to fall back on, had actually been able to curb at least some of the atrocities. (The anonymous writer, who kept a diary, was a Red Cross man in spirit noting, at the very height of the massacres, that he had sat down to a 'good dinner . . . with roast beef and potatoes', and that they had sung 'Christmas songs with Wilson at the piano'.)

Day after day, Calame pressed the Japanese authorities to be allowed to visit Nanking. Day after day, they blocked his visit. One day they said that it was too dangerous, the next that there was no transport. He was told that there were no longer any prisoners, that his predecessor de Watteville had caused offence, that it was all too delicate. Calame's persistence was impressive. One day he asked what kind of transport he would be offered; another he remarked that it would look very bad if he were not allowed in. He pestered the Japanese intelligence service; called on the military police; requested interviews with all the generals. Yet it was for nothing. 'We are faced here with an Asiatic war,' he wrote to Geneva, touching on an attitude towards the Committee and the Geneva Conventions which would shortly defeat them in a far more important and profound way. 'All the problems are still to be solved, the questions yet to be raised, the structures set up.' Calame never got to Nanking.

He did, however, do better with the refugees, for he was able to report to Geneva on the remarkable success of a Jesuit priest called Père Jacquinot de Besange from St Peter's Church in Shanghai in protecting civilians. Sidney Brown, during his visit to Shanghai in 1932 had already remarked on Père Jacquinot's 'day of truce'.

By the autumn of 1937, Shanghai had turned into an immense refugee camp, in which impetigo, trachoma and eczema were rife. Calame's reports read like emotional newspaper articles and, for all his love of China, he could he highly critical. This was, he wrote

the oriental laziness in all its horror ... this crouching mass of people, squatting on the pavement and covered in vermin, fleas, lice, crabs ... the feeling of horror grows and becomes unbearable and you sense the crowd itself turning into a gigantic vermin ... this symphony of smells is the real, the superb, the pure symphony of all the horrors of mankind.

Calling on the privileged of the world to step in and come to the aid of these unhappy people, he asked: 'We have refugee camps, are they to become famine camps?' It was not the kind of style to which Huber warmed.

When the Japanese reached Shanghai, they began their bombing campaign. Casualties, for whom very little could be done, mounted steadily in the vastly overcrowded districts. From Geneva, the International Committee issued one of its rare public appeals, calling on both sides to bring an end to the 'fatal ravages ... which cause so many innocent victims, especially among women and children'. There was no reply from either the Chinese or the Japanese.

It was now that Père Jacquinot, working on behalf of what he called the Shanghai International Red Cross Committee on Refugee Problems and wearing a Red Cross badge, negotiated with both the Japanese and the Chinese authorities to create a demilitarized zone in the Nantuo area. He seems to have acted entirely on his own initiative with no formal authority from anyone. The Chinese agreed to remove all their defences and soldiers; the Japanese pledged not to bomb an area out of which no one would be allowed to leave. Red Cross flags were hung at the entrances to the 'safety' zone.

Calame went to see Père Jacquinot. He found him sitting on a rickety chair surrounded by ringing telephones and he compared him to one of the portraits painted during the Deuxième Empire, a 'fine figure of a soldier'. The priest had been a captain in a cavalry regiment and had lost a hand. Together, in freezing rain and wind, the two men toured the demilitarized zone. 'All the alleyways, all the narrow passages, every corner, all are filled with refugees,' Calame wrote to Geneva later. As they walked, figures crouching on the ground called out to Père

Jacquinot, 'Thank you, Great Mandarin', while the priest replied, 'Be patient, wait, things will get better.' You can understand why Huber mistrusted Calame. 'Ah cruel Providence,' Calame continued, 'without following in Dante's footsteps, I have seen your Hell on this earth, and I no longer fear the Beyond. It could never be worse than this . . ! 'The reflections on history and philosophy . . . are banal and superfluous', noted Huber, who felt that Calame had failed 'to keep himself a bit above the crowd.'

Though Calame was to fall out of favour with the International Committee after he wandered off to visit parts of China devastated when the Yellow River burst its banks, and was eventually asked to leave by the Chinese Red Cross, he produced a shrewd and prescient observation on the question of safety zones, having greatly admired what Père Jacquinot had achieved. 'At this moment,' he concluded, 'as modern armies are becoming more and more murderous, as bombing raids are taking a more sinister and horrible form, as the build-up of arms is accelerating at an appalling rate, as the threat of war grows ever nearer, it seems to me that the International Committee should consider this matter with the utmost urgency.'

In Geneva, at some point, someone has drawn two pencil lines down the margin beside this passage.

The 1930s had not gone well for the International Committee. No amount of mediation had succeeded in ending, or even moderating, wars in Ethiopia, Spain or China. No amount of reminding governments of their obligations under international treaties or appealing to their higher moral duty, had won the Committee a toehold in the concentration camps of the Soviet Union or Germany. No lobbying for the protocol on chemical warfare and certainly no passionate articles about the horrors of gas had prevented the Italians dropping mustard gas on Ethiopians. No letters to Mussolini had stopped him reducing political deportees to the islands of Lipari, Tremili and Ponza to starvation and disease. Moynier and Ador had both fought hard for the setting up of a world tribunal of arbitration, arguing that all the International Committee itself could do under its mandate was advise, monitor and appeal. But their proposals had come to nothing and these three functions were now looking extremely weak. Worse, they appeared confused, for successive International Committee members had avoided precise definitions of where Geneva's power lay, believing, correctly, that it could sometimes achieve far more if nothing too precise was spelt out. It was this lack of clarity in the way the world perceived the organization that would now bring it such criticism and attack – much of it unfair.

As the frail bonds of the League of Nations dissolved, as Hitler annexed the Sudetenland and made a pact with Stalin, as nations everywhere rearmed, few people doubted that the war about to burst over them would bring terrors of mass destruction in a way that could as yet only be imagined. Not only was war becoming nastier: it was now seen to be so. For the first time in history, people were able to watch on newsreels the terror on the faces of women and children as they ran for shelter from aerial bombing.

Nor was the Red Cross movement itself in particularly good shape, even if visitors to Geneva continued to regard the city as an oasis of calm, prosperity and sanity. As the fiasco with the German Red Cross had shown, there was no system or machinery for bringing an errant society back into line. The essentially collegiate character of the movement, which had served so well in earlier, more gentlemanly times, now looked decidedly irrelevant. From America, watching the steady alienation of the German Red Cross, Norman Davis wrote to Bonabes de Rougé, the new secretary general of the League, in July 1939:

> I am becoming rather concerned about what is happening and may happen to the Red Cross societies in the totalitarian countries. It raises a very delicate question . . . because if those societies cease to function in accordance with the Geneva Convention we may sometime be confronted with the problem of determining whether or not they are eligible for membership.

Time had also run out for the most pressing of all International Committee concerns: protection for civilians. It had been the subject of repeated drafts, memoranda, letters and meetings for well over a decade, but no formal agreement had yet been signed between countries. Britain, replying to one draft, had said that it was not 'sufficiently prepared'; France returned another with 'a firm and definite refusal'. Jean Pictet, the young lawyer now involved in desperate last minute attempts to get at least some undertaking through, calling the danger posed to civilians in any future war a problem that 'becomes day by day more anguishing', begged governments at least to fall back on 'customs established between civilized nations, laws of humanity and the public conscience'. As the spring and summer of 1939 passed, so communications between the headquarters of the national societies and Geneva and Paris became ever more plaintive and urgent.

It was too late. By the end of August, despite five separate texts doing the rounds of governments, only fourteen national societies had even formulated coherent views on the protection of civilians or the question of safety zones. Social reforms, political alliances, new technology, had all altered the scope and nature of humanitarian intervention, and Huber's extreme caution, unchallenged in an organization that had come to regard him as infallible, had not helped. The Tokyo Draft, with its hesitant suggestions and watered-down commitments, was now all that stood between civilians and war. The events of the 1930s had simply been too speedy for the slow progress of humanitarian laws. 'Unhappily,' Colonel Favre concluded, reviewing the work of the past five years, 'the problem is so vast and so complex that a solution will probably need much more time to reach.' And, he might have added, many more atrocities. The race was now about to begin – between weapons, violence and the force of arms on one side, and peace, international treaties and the force of law on the other. Norman Davis's eloquent appeal in 1938 to governments to protect civilians 'with the spirit of chivalry and humane conduct for which the Red Cross stands' had a decidedly wistful ring to it.

THIRTEEN

New and Old Instruments
of Destruction

On 1 September 1939, at dawn, fifty Wehrmacht divisions crossed the German border into Poland. Later that morning, President Roosevelt appealed to the countries about to declare war to remember civilians and at least refrain from bombing undefended cities. On 2 September the French and British ambassadors in Berlin called on von Ribbentrop, the German foreign minister, to tell him that unless Germany withdrew from Poland within twenty-four hours, their countries would be forced to honour their promises to Poland. Europe was going to war.

In Geneva, the International Committee had been watching the political manoeuvrings, using the months of diplomatic activity to prepare for what it confidently felt it did best: to co-ordinate the world's humanitarian response to war and try to mitigate some of its horrors. In the elegant Villa Moynier by the lake, surrounded by its grounds and flying the Red Cross flag, the thirty or so employees – a few paid but most of them volunteers – had for many months now been conscious that their small and intimate world was about to be broken apart. 'Right up until the end of the war in Spain we were a family,' recalled Jean Pictet. 'We met as friends, we listened to music together in the evenings, we sang, we played games, we discussed legal texts. It was very quiet and there were seldom visitors. It was spartan, but fun.' Had Moynier returned to his villa, he would not have felt out of place. Overnight, added Pictet, 'the war plunged us into chaos. Suddenly, we worked late at night, all through weekends. To start with, no one was very good at administration on such a scale; but we learnt. And we quickly realized that it was crucial for the International Committee to retain its image as a circle of wise men, wise and infallible.' Pictet would later admit that the

Committee did make a fundamental error in bothering too little about the national societies, an oversight that would later come to haunt them.

It was nearly a year since a commission for war had been set up in the Villa Moynier to put the Committee on to a proper war footing, and *anciens délégués* — men like Edouard Frick who had fought so hard on behalf of the returning prisoners-of-war from the Soviet Union in 1919, Rodolphe Haccius, the engineer who had paid the first visit to political prisoners in Béla Kun's jails in 1925, and Horace de Pourtalès, the Spanish Civil War delegate who spoke perfect English — were discreetly sounded out to see whether they would be prepared to act as delegates again. Not one refused. They would set the tone for the new recruits — hard-working, sober, serious, apparently unemotional and with extraordinary reserves of energy — but with something extra too. They brought an idealism and a sense of the romanticism of the young Dunant or Junod, the feeling that the world could be a better place if men were made to behave humanely in wartime. Soon the Villa Moynier became the centre of an operation that before long was obliged to do something that it had never done before: recruit total strangers as delegates in distant places, usually from the local Swiss community, businessmen who themselves knew nothing about the Red Cross but who proved willing and for the most part extremely brave. The Committee made mistakes, but not often.

The Committee itself, now standing at twenty-five members, was made up for the most part of men beyond the age of call-up, or women. Having met once a month in peacetime, they would now often meet every day. Soon, Huber, who donated his entire salary to the Red Cross, would move from Zurich to Geneva, to be in daily touch with the war. All the most crucial members of the Committee had been in place ten years and several of them, including Chenevière, Mme Frick-Cramer and Mlle Ferrière, since the end of the First World War. Already there were clear distinctions between those who had ambitions for themselves as well as for the organization and who soon carved out and ran their own fiefs — like Burckhardt, whose post as high commissioner for Danzig had disappeared with the outbreak of war, and Chenevière — and those Committee members who had trouble translating the cosiness of the pre-war organization into a vast, international operation. Mlle Odier, who was now made second to Burckhardt in the department handling relief despite her work for Spain, was a good example of the latter. They were known not to get on well, Burckhardt dismissing Mlle Odier as lacking sufficient breadth of vision, though her modest and calm manner concealed a tough and extremely efficient business sense.

Chenevière had been asked to make plans for a new central prisoner-of-war agency, and had been offered by the City of Geneva the vast, currently empty Electoral Building, nicknamed *la boîte à gifles* from the political disputes that had taken place there at the turn of the century. He was driven, sometimes choleric and quick to voice doubts whenever a new role for the Committee was proposed. The younger members called him the 'brake' behind his back. He was also, says Pictet, witty and tyrannical. Knowing the younger man to be shy and retiring, he whispered one day in his ear: QOEMOEF. Asked what it meant, he replied, '*Quand on est modeste, on est foutu.*'* Mme Frick-Cramer was turning out to be an excellent and clear writer and was producing authoritative papers for the *Review*. The fiefs, Pictet observes, were soon working competently, but not without a few early absurdities: in the opening weeks of the war, the French bureau for prisoners-of-war received three separate, contradictory letters from three separate offices in the Villa Moynier. In Geneva, it was widely felt that while Burckhardt was skilled at foreign policy, Huber had influence because he insisted on legality.

The Swiss government let it be known that it was once again delighted to lend its support to an organization that reflected its own neutrality, endorsed yet again shortly before the war by the Federation. And amongst those most committed to a neutral Switzerland was Huber, for thirty years now a close adviser to the government on matters of international law: it was he who proposed that Switzerland take what he called an 'active neutral' role *vis-à-vis* prisoners-of-war in the coming conflict. Huber would return to the subject of neutrality – a neutral Switzerland, a neutral Red Cross – again and again, repeating the words of one of his most famous papers, *The Red Cross and Neutrality*, written in 1936. Its aim, he had said then, 'is to abolish or alleviate human suffering', to testify 'to the feeling of human solidarity even when the orderly life of nations is shattered ... It is of primary importance that this last bridge connecting the warring nations ... should not collapse ... and that its

* 'When one is modest, one is done for.'

buttresses — neutrality and impartiality — should never give way under the pressure of passion.'

On 2 September, the day of the British and French ultimatum, a letter went out from Huber to the European countries lining up against each other. The International Committee was once again ready, he said, to do whatever it could to 'remedy the evils engendered by war'. As in the past, it intended to run its agency from Geneva to gather information on prisoners-of-war and transmit letters between them and their families. It also planned to continue to study the feasibility of safety zones. In return, Huber asked that countries at war should set up their own information bureaux, as specified by the Geneva Conventions, and, most urgently, that they should respect the Tokyo draft when it came to civilians — even though the document was still in unfinished form. From Hitler, surprisingly quickly, came a reply that Germany intended to restrict its attacks to military objectives.

On 5 September, the League of Red Cross Societies packed up its fine offices in Paris and eighteen of its staff caught a train to Geneva to spend the war in the safety of 6 rue de l'Athénée. 'We have hoped to the end that war would be avoided,' wrote Ernest Swift, the League's vice-chairman, to the marquis de Lillers, the president of the French Red Cross, as he left Paris, 'but now the tragedy has come . . . We think of you constantly and wish to be helpful in any way we can.'

On 6 September, Cracow fell to the Germans; by the end of the second week of the war, Germany had taken a third of Poland's territory and eight countries were at war. As if to prove how right the Committee had been in its urgent insistence throughout the 1930s on the need for countries to reach agreement over protection of civilians and aerial bombing, Germany now announced that, as the Poles were showing resistance, measures would have to be taken to silence them. Bombs began to fall on the remaining free Polish cities. On 28 September, after three weeks of siege and heavy bombing, Warsaw capitulated. By the end of the first month of the war, Poland had been occupied and its government had fled into exile in France. The style of the Second World War — the bombing of cities into extinction, air-raids, civilians made refugees, governments-in-exile, and mutual accusations — had been set.

*   *   *

More than many, the International Committee had been ready for war; but not for this kind of war, nor for the abruptness with which countries abandoned so many of their earlier commitments. In Geneva, a call went out from Huber for sanctuaries for civilians, 'notably children, old people, women and all other categories of people needing protection'. The party held at the end of October for the seventieth birthday of Paul des Gouttes, the lawyer who had spent forty-six years working for the International Committee, was a muted affair.

The Swiss were proud of their Red Cross. Within hours of the declaration of war, volunteers were to be seen climbing the steps of the Villa Moynier, carrying their portable typewriters. The first four departments of the war – German, French, British and Polish – opened in the echoing halls of the Electoral Palace. Once again, the filing system of name cards seeking 'concordance' was started. The League of Nations sent round typewriters with Russian, Greek and Serbian keyboards and some extra chairs for the typists. (Later, the Central Prisoner-of-War Agency and the League would exchange a polyglot dictionary of communicable diseases.) Photographs taken for the newspapers in October 1939 show rows of serious-looking Genevans, in their neat hats and suits, sitting at trestle tables sorting out letters. Only the style of their clothes suggests that it is no longer 1914. Though new inventions, like the photocopier and the radio, would simplify the Agency's work, there would soon be 28,500 French prisoners called Martin, 2,400 of them with the Christian name Jean.

The American Red Cross was the first national society of a country not at war to offer its services. It was quickly followed by others. (In 1939 the Red Cross movement had sixty-two national societies and twenty million adult members.) In the pages of the *Review*, three contrasting reports appeared, each giving a very different flavour: a bombastic, self-congratulatory offering from the German Red Cross, Hitler reaffirming his commitment to the 'principles of chivalry and humanity in the conduct of the war'; a brief message from the French Red Cross, outlining practical details about hospitals and postal systems; and a somewhat gung-ho statement from Sir Arthur Stanley, chairman of the executive committee of the British Red Cross, on what he called a period of 'exceptional activity'.

Much would now depend on the imagination and persistence of the delegates of the International Committee. If the events of the 1930s had left the institution bruised, even compromised, it had done nothing but good for the men who had come to see themselves as its ambassadors. These had emerged from a decade in which they had witnessed horrors they could never have imagined – Sidney Brown and the mustard gas, Marcel Junod and the headless children in Spain – sharper, with a clearer sense of themselves and what they could do.

More important, they had come to agree that what they achieved lay less in the words of the Geneva Conventions than in their own personal authority. They understood that they had to be calm, cunning and resourceful, and they had to know instinctively – for there was no one to teach them – when to concede and when to stand firm. With very little to protect them, other than Dunant's emblem, these schoolteachers, historians, businessmen and lawyers, all Swiss, all but a few in their thirties, now signed pledges which bound them to 'observe the strictest neutrality at all times and in all places, to abstain from all activity of a political, confessional or commercial character', and to obey the strictest discretion, giving no interviews, anywhere, to anyone, at any time. What the letters, reports and telegrams in the archives in Geneva demonstrate is that during the six years' fighting which followed this small number of men – never more than 340 – achieved, in terms of miles travelled, camps visited and standards improved or maintained, a remarkable amount. They went into the war almost totally unacknowledged and came out of it anonymous, even perhaps a little tainted by some of the criticisms that would be levelled at the Committee at the end of it. Eleven were to die. And it was probably the last time that delegates would ever be so free, so able to act for themselves and so little bound to Geneva by the umbilical cord of modern communications, or so indignant and passionate in their reports. No delegate, after 1945, was ever again as emotional.

While the sometimes choleric but hardworking Jacques Chenevière began expanding the Central Prisoner-of-War Agency to keep up with the different nationalities joining the war, the International Committee delegates started out on their missions. They were soon confirming Pictet's worst fears. From Poland, Marcel Junod described Warsaw as a 'city bombed as no city has ever been bombed before in history'.

The 1929 Geneva Convention on the treatment of prisoners, more often called the Prisoner-of-War Code, had laid down an extremely precise set of instructions as to housing, temperature, food, hygiene, work, complaints and officer status. Under it, representatives from the Protecting Powers — neutral countries appointed to safeguard the interests of foreign citizens in countries at war — as well as delegates from the International Committee, were allowed to visit all places in which prisoners were held, talk openly to prisoners, privately to senior officers, with no limit on time, a rule which would not be contested in the Second World War except by Japan and Russia, neither of whom had ratified the Convention. Their failure to do so would condemn hundreds of thousands of prisoners to misery and death.

On 10 May 1940, 136 German divisions, supported by motorized units, crossed into Holland, Belgium and Luxemburg. Civilians escaping the fighting that spread throughout Belgium and into northern France were dive-bombed as they inched their way along crowded roads full, as Junod noted, of 'lost children and distraught parents'. On 15 May, the Netherlands fell; on 28 May King Leopold ordered the Belgian army to surrender. By 5 June, after Dunkirk, the number of prisoners in German hands was multiplying at a terrifying rate; with the fall of France there were nearly two million men in captivity and German domination extended from the far north of Norway to the Atlantic coast of France. Fifty thousand letters a day were now reaching the Agency, which set up branches in twenty Swiss towns to help with the index cards. By the end of September 1940, there were nearly four million names in its files. Hitler accused Britain of indiscriminate bombing, and retaliated with the fifty-six-day Blitz on London. As the archbishop of Canterbury had warned the Red Cross delegates in London just two years earlier, death was indeed now descending 'as a terrible rain from the skies'. That month, September 1940, Japan, Germany and Italy signed the Axis pact, soon to be joined by Hungary and Bulgaria.

The delegates were hard at work. Day after day their letters, cables and reports reached Geneva, with details of names and numbers of prisoners-of-war, of the food they were being given to eat, of guards who were humane and others who were not, of bunks that were too close together and barracks that let in rain. Dr Roland Marti, veteran of the Spanish civil war, crossed from one end of Germany to the other and back again, reporting that, for the most part, he found the authorities 'full of fine feelings', though the interned civilians he visited in Zweilager X111A, 972 men from various countries, told him that they were very bored. Their 'man of confidence,' (the First World War term still in use despite its associations with the Mafia), asked for food parcels and books for the French, soap and better bread for the Belgians, meat paste and olives for the Egyptians and cheese for the Greeks. Treatment of prisoners in Germany was turning out to be strict but fair, and in some camps the men were allowed four bottles of wine a week. In August 1940, Dr Marti and Dr Pierre Descoeudres travelled 2,000 kilometres in five days, inspecting camp after camp, some by now the size of small towns, with streets, chapels, libraries, sports fields and cemeteries, feeling the beds, tasting the food, measuring the size of the rooms, checking the temperature of the water, like housekeepers in some great pre-war hotel. They came away on the whole 'satisfied', saying that the German guards treated the prisoners with 'perfect courtesy' and that the sanitary arrangements were for the most part excellent, but that the men were sometimes hungry, sometimes rather cold and that they longed for more letters from home.

While Marti covered Germany, Junod went to France. In Depot 602, thirty-seven kilometres west of Toulouse, before the fall of France, he found 103 captive German officers living in a magnificent villa surrounded by a park. It was very hot and some of the men were sunbathing; others played football. Breakfast, which took place at 9 a.m., consisted of bread, jam and coffee. The other meals were chosen and cooked by the officers themselves, who could order what they wanted from the nearby village. Relations between the prisoners and their guards were, Junod reported, excellent. The 'man of confidence' had no complaints; on the contrary, he professed himself enchanted with their treatment. (In England, on hearing Hore-Belisha, the secretary of war, tell the House of Commons that it was costing £50 a day to keep twenty-one German prisoners in what became known as the 'U-Boat Hotel' — a former stately home with stained glass windows and panelled reception rooms — Colonel Josiah Wedgwood asked whether it would not be cheaper to put them up at the Ritz.)

Rodolphe Haccius was also on the road. Even as Junod was tasting the French bread, he was sampling the porridge provided for the breakfast of 2,870 Italian internees on the Isle of Man, living in requisitioned hotels and pensions on the sea front. Haccius noted that before the war the rooms had cost 8s 6d a day, that lunch consisted of kippers, boiled potatoes and salad, and that he had managed to persuade the camp commandant to replace, at least sometimes, potatoes with spaghetti.

In Italy, Horace de Pourtalès found British officers building a rock garden in Sulmona and going on long walks in the mountains accompanied by Italian officers. Their one complaint was that they were forbidden sheet music on the grounds that it might contain a secretly coded message. At Christmas that year, the Italian Red Cross sent all foreign prisoners-of-war parcels of biscuits, cake and wine, the Italian airforce presented them with beer and in some places the local chief of police came by for a festive drink. Later, when the war was over, men who had been held prisoner in Italy would remember the light and the mountain scenery; those in Germany the oppression of gloomy pine woods.

Dr Hans Wolf de Salis was appointed the permanent International Committee delegate to Rome for the duration of the war. Madame Denise Werner happened to be visiting her aunt in Rome when the war broke out. Many years before, her father had been a vice-president of the International Committee and she had once helped them produce a children's book on the work of the Red Cross. She decided to stay on in Rome and offer her services to de Salis. The two of them recruited a number of refugees to help with office work, providing in return not wages but protection. After the arrival of the Germans in Rome, Mme Werner would take the lists of people needing help – Jews in hiding, refugees without papers – home with her every night, in case of Gestapo raids. One evening she was stopped by a German patrol and only avoided being searched after persuading the soldiers that she was really Swiss German. She remembers the evening particularly well, for it was next morning that she heard of the massacre of 330 hostages at the Fosse Argentina, and that Gestapo officers came to see de Salis to ask him to confirm that all the men who had been shot were in fact wanted criminals. De Salis refused to do so. 'He was,' says Mme Werner of her employer, 'very clear, very firm and very open.' De Salis was haunted by how little he could do for people hunted down and deported by the

Gestapo. 'Our work is more and more a test of our nerves,' he wrote to Geneva. 'Every day they arrest people who we were doing our best to look after, or a neighbour, or one of our collaborators as he was leaving our office ... illegality is everywhere, and people turn to us from all sides in the hope of good advice.' For safety, de Salis and Mme Werner constantly moved office between the Belgian Embassy and the Swiss library in the Piazza di Spagna.

De Salis spent much of his time on the road, covering the immense distances from the heel of Italy to its far north in the company of Dr Morra of the Italian Red Cross. Visiting a house in Civitella del Tronto, in the summer of 1942, where thirty-eight Jews who had fled from Germany and the occupied territories were being held, he sent back to Geneva a request for a guitar, gardening tools and special knives for carpentry. Asked by the International Committee to comment on the effects of inactivity on the physical and psychological condition of the prisoners, he produced a long and careful report.

The British, he said, tolerated captivity far better than the men from the Balkans. 'Their race is physically much healthier ... their mental state, their education, their religious beliefs, everything predisposes them to take things as they find them and try to see something positive in everything.' The British regarded escape, he added, as a duty 'of a sporting nature'. The Greeks, on the other hand, were expansive, loquacious, tending to dramatize events, and were passionately argumentative. Though physically less robust than the British, with a high number of cases of syphilis and very bad teeth, they still stood up well to captivity. In their case, rebellion took the shape not of escape attempts, but hunger strikes. The Yugoslavs were taciturn, brooding, weighed down by captivity; one had already committed suicide. Though often fed better than the Greeks, they looked permanently malnourished which, together with the fact that they complained endlessly about minor ailments, made them seem profoundly depressed.

All through the war, month after month, year after year, the delegates kept travelling, asking questions, noting irregularities, ticking off, one by one, the long lists on their questionnaires, always on the lookout for signs of concealment or trickery. Were the men actually hungry, or simply missing meat? Was it boredom or real hardship that was causing so many complaints? If the reports occasionally sound bland, as if the camps were peaceful and well-regulated places, a little like modest hotels, it soon became a question of reading between the lines, understanding a series of adjectives that with time became a code in themselves. Delegates, Junod told a seminar not long before the end of the war, 'learn to remain totally objective whatever they encounter. They have to know how to limit their activities to take in only what is immediately possible and realizable', in order never to compromise the 'fragile edifice in which so many victims have found refuge'.

It is worth giving an account of another delegate's slightly different mission. Alfred Zollinger worked for the Relief Section run by Burckhardt and Mlle Odier. More clearly than those of most of the delegates, his reports read as if they were written by a cross between a travel writer, a head matron and a military historian. In January 1944 he was sent to America to report on internment and prisoner-of-war camps. 'Le Yankee,' he noted in his first report, was a good organizer, enterprising and bold, but he was interested only in projects that seemed to him full of promise and potential. Le Yankee was not a sentimental man but keen only on success, and 'because the whole world, so to say, turns to the Americans for salvation, this has convinced them that they are right.'

Zollinger evidently did not care for America and he took violently against the American Red Cross, bigger, more powerful, brasher than any national society that he had dealt with before, and whose logo, he protested to Geneva, was used more as an advertising gimmick than as the symbol of charity as conceived by Dunant. American Red Cross members, he added, regarded it as their principal duty to entertain off-duty soldiers with le dancing, and to distribute douceurs, sweeteners, in the form of 'le peanut' and 'les doughnuts'. No one brings out better than Zollinger the vast gap that lay between the professional puritan Swiss monitors and the great sprawling world of the Red Cross national societies.

Zollinger then set off to visit Germans held in two camps in the south who were complaining of the heat and the humidity. He came away irritable, saying that it had all seemed fine to him except that he thought that an hour off for lunch was too little and that it was a great pity that the Americans 'content themselves with such a light lunch'. He filed a request on the prisoners' behalf for more potatoes and came away saying that since the German prisoners seemed to be doing such a brisk trade selling their possessions and handiwork in exchange for consumer goods to take back to Europe at the end of the war, he feared there might well be a problem with excess baggage.

By the time the war ended, the 340 International Committee delegates had visited 11,170 camps, whose fortunes ebbed and flowed with the war and whose conditions, as food became scarce or numbers grew, tended to reflect the war itself. Their reports are endlessly fascinating for the light they throw not just on captors and captives, but on the whole nature of the Red Cross movement itself, on how its leaders viewed war and how the monitoring of it became almost a profession, from which it was possible to remain somehow detached.

No document gives a better flavour of this spirit and the ability of delegates to focus on the little things of life than the entries in the diaries kept by the Red Cross delegation to Berlin during the Russian advance on the city in 1945. Earlier entries, written in a dozen different hands, sometimes in French, sometimes in German but all unsigned, describe the first wild strawberries of the year, excursions and picnics in the forest, buffets at the Swiss legation – along with visits to camps, endless problems with visas and petrol, the distribution of relief, occasional glimpses of Grawitz of the German Red Cross and Frau Goering, who was involved with one of the nursing associations. When the Russians arrived, they took over the building where the delegation was housed, looted the flat, made off with their tins of sardines, got drunk on the stocks of wine and emptied the first-aid supplies. Mr Lehner, the diary keeper that day wrote: 'caught a slight cold'.

If inspection of conditions in the prisoner-of-war camps was one of the delegate's main activities, the other, the real pretext for being there in the first place, was relief. The First World War had seen relatively little relief, the stability of the fronts having enabled countries at war to keep most of their railways and postal systems intact. But the Spanish civil war had proved that a well-run relief operation could be crucial – the purchasing section of the International Committee for Spain was never disbanded in 1939, but simply became the nucleus of the relief committee of the Second World War – and that national societies had an enormous role to play in obtaining goods and packing and sending parcels. The needs of the Second World War were to become bottomless and alarming. The relief operation of the International Committee, which became the largest on the Continent, drawing on governments for funds, turning to individual donors when desperate, balancing books that grew more complicated with every month of war, reached its peak in 1943 and 1944. At one point 2,000 goods wagons were leaving and returning to Geneva every month.

Soon after the capture of half a million Polish soldiers in twenty-two days in September 1939, the Committee's delegates were reporting that parcels were in urgent demand, large numbers of the captives having lost all their belongings. They lacked, in particular, underclothes. Under the terms of the Cairo Postal Convention of 1935, the Swiss Post Office was to carry free all parcels originating in, or on transit through, Switzerland intended for prisoners-of-war. After the first flurry of packages — of every size, shape, wrapping, weight and content — a pattern was established: national Red Cross societies and families of prisoners prepared parcels of a specified weight and size — five kilograms became the standard — and sent them via Geneva to named prisoners. Anything that could lead to escape or sabotage was banned, resulting in an Alice in Wonderland mixture of forbidden items — coins, civilian clothes, tracing paper, compasses, torches and spare parts, acids and chemical products, books with maps. Alcohol was out. So, rather more confusingly, was fruit juice (lemon made effective invisible ink), toothpaste (tubes were good containers for messages), tin-openers (handy escape tools), salt and pepper (said to be useful in blinding guards), chocolates with soft centres (?) and black shirts. When a number of allied doctors were repatriated early in the war, they helpfully reported that the food provided by the Germans in the camps was too little and of very poor quality and that the prisoners were asking for less meat loaf in their parcels, that they didn't care for the fish balls, and that they would like less lemon curd and blackcurrant purée and more jam.

In the first weeks of the war, families provided the bulk of the parcels. But by December 1939 it had become clear that few of the 250,000 Polish prisoners in Germany could expect any parcels of their own, since their families were either dead or destitute. Collective relief consignments were started, with charitable organizations and businesses sending supplies to Switzerland, or money with which to buy them. In theory, all prisoners were to be treated the same. In practice a hierarchy of privilege was quickly established, with the British and Americans doing best, the Norwegians not too badly (because though not in a position to offer reciprocity they were at least of Teutonic race), and the Greeks, Poles and Yugoslavs at the bottom of the pile.

Nothing gives a better picture of the immense relief programme to prisoners than the workings of the British Red Cross, which both fed into the International Committee system with its parcels and provided its own comforts to British soldiers, the 'non-essentials of life' perceived by Dunant to 'transform a soldier's outlook'. Speed became a matter of intense pride to the society, its ability to anticipate needs or respond to them faster than any other society, particularly the Americans.

The British Red Cross began its relief operations in London, with depots in houses in Park Lane and Carlton House Terrace. These spread swiftly to the town hall in Birmingham and the Foresters' Hall in Edinburgh. Items despatched ranged from lime juice for ambulance convoys in Cairo to picture papers for prisoners who could not read, tinned turkey for troops spending Christmas in Greece, scenery for camp music-hall entertainments, seeds and bulbs for hospital gardens and, when football mania reached a peak, outfits to clothe entire teams — anything and everything that might keep at bay fear, boredom and anxiety. Given rationing, censorship and the blockade, the society, with its co-ordinating committees, its welfare officers, dieticians, filers, labellers, checkers, interviewers, its coupon and chocolate sections, and its file on every British prisoner-of-war, became a model of good tempered organization. When, at the end of the war, a number of parcels were returned to London because the prisoners they were addressed to had already been released, the packers noted with pride how very well they had stood up to several thousands of miles of travel and rough handling, even if rats had managed to force their way into those delivered to Casablanca.

John Hilton, who travelled to North Africa on behalf of the British Red Cross in the early summer of 1943, much as John Furley had gone to France during the Franco-Prussian war, left a diary of his travels which perfectly captures the Red Cross spirit, something between an agony aunt and quartermaster, moral tutor and senior officer in the Women's Institute. At Sétif, he learned that there was an acute shortage of bootlaces, radio sets and musical instruments, and he dined in the local mess where he discussed the Beveridge Report and the hideousness of the army boots, socks and gaiters worn by the staff. Afterwards, he visited Field Hospital No. 2, to find the nurses longing for 'some decent fine stockings, fully fashioned ones for choice'. The patients were sick of boiled potatoes and wanted them sautéed or chipped.

At Bougie, he reported calls for shaving soap, toothpaste and current copies of *Lilliput* and *Men Only*, and tennis balls, but no racquets, since there seemed to be plenty of them. He passed on a message from the local padre that it would be better if British newspapers printed fewer photographs of 'bevvies of pretty French girls greeting our soldiers', for though this 'showed the right sort of spirit . . . wives at home were apt to take it amiss'.

As the various national Red Cross societies got into their stride, the nature and amount of relief expanded in all directions. After food came spectacles, as malnutrition in the camps resulted in ever worsening sight. A campaign launched by the Swiss Women's Civilian Service invited people to look into their cupboards at home for unwanted pairs – 60,000 were delivered and questionnaires, in four languages, went off to the prisoner-of-war camps. Then there were medicines, masterminded in Geneva by a young chemist called Dr Pierre Calpini who had just completed his Ph.D. Dr Calpini responded to appeals from delegates and was soon making up remedies for diabetes, vitamin deficiency and malaria. With time, requests arrived directly from the 'men of confidence' in the camps, while advice on the movements of epidemics was sent across from the League of Nations. 'I was a novice,' recalls Dr Calpini today. 'We all were. It was a question of learning, sorting things out, establishing a system.'

As the months of captivity turned into years and the prisoners began suffering from acute boredom, so the delegates and the 'men of confidence' became more imaginative in their requests. Ping-pong tables were called for, harmonicas, Bibles in Polish and above all books. From Geneva Mlle Odier set up and ran an 'intellectual service' which was soon so overwhelmed with orders that a number of charitable organizations joined forces, formed a consultative committee and battled with dozens of different languages, styles and censors, with an early bias towards religion. By January 1942, it had sent off 50,000 books; by the end of the war over a million and a half.

Camp universities had been started in the First World War. The first of the Second World War opened in Stalag 1A in East Prussia in the spring of 1941. Soon, in virtually every large camp which held Allied or Axis prisoners, there were students in everything from physics to medicine, medieval French literature to advanced technology, taught both by correspondence courses — London University was one of the places which offered these courses free — and by teachers who were prisoners themselves. To various laboratories in camps across Europe, the International Committee sent skeletons, microscopes and live frogs. The first 450 undergraduates took their degrees early in 1942, the first successful examinee being a British accountant. In Geneva, the International Committee saw to the safekeeping of manuscripts and to the protection of copyrights and patents. For the captive musicians instruments were in constant demand, particularly banjos and recorders, the easiest to play, and by the time the hostilities ended, the Committee had supplied a number of complete fourteen-instrument orchestras.

Maître Lalive is a stocky, mild-looking and courteous lawyer with an office in Geneva's old town, in the building in the rue de L'Athénée that once housed the League of Red Cross Societies. In 1941 he was twenty-six and preparing for his *brevet d'avocat*, not long back from an exchange fellowship at Harvard and Columbia law schools. He spoke good English. One day, after a seminar on the Danzig corridor at the Institut Universitaire des Hautes Etudes Internationales, Burckhardt called him over and told him that he was thinking of setting up a joint committee between the International Committee and the League to handle relief to the occupied countries, particularly to civilians; and that he needed a young lawyer to help him. The League, Burckhardt explained, seemed to have succumbed to a certain sterility during its months in Geneva. Bonabes de Rougé, the League's well-liked general secretary, had just lost his son in the war and was eager to do more for the war effort, as was his assistant Georges Milson. The question was to find a formula which would enable the two organizations to harness their resources.

Burckhardt, Lalive recalls, that '*grand politicien*', had his eye on the prestige of the Committee rather than that of the League, but he was also genuinely concerned about civilians across Europe, who were benefiting neither from the League's peacetime mandate of relief, nor from the International Committee's wartime programmes. The important thing, Burckhardt stressed to him, was to make this relief a separate organization, away from the old guard – people like Jacques Chenevière and Mlle Odier – who both felt that relief to prisoners-of-war was already overstretching their resources and feared that by extending it to civilians they might jeopardize their mandate and antagonize donors. Chenevière, who dismissed the whole idea as *'la politique du morceau de sucre'*, had never made any secret of his hostility towards the League, to friends referring to it as *'l'alligator'* – *la Ligue a tort* ('the League is wrong'). Burckhardt had done as little to conceal his own impatience with the *'panier de crabes'*, his description of the good souls of Geneva devoted to charitable causes. A new organization seemed to him the only way to escape the obfuscation, prevarication and amateurism that had come to irritate him so.

The legal position between the International Committee and the League was soon straightened out, Lalive discovering among the Committee's articles a clever and satisfying formula allowing for co-operation under certain circumstances, and what became known as the Commission Mixte was formally launched. Lalive himself was asked to act as its secretary and to recruit helpers. He knew exactly who was needed. He wanted businessmen with long experience of buying and shipping provisions on an enormous scale, men who could locate and bring home cereals from Hungary and chickpeas from the Balkans. It was not a question of parcels to prisoners-of-war – these were being processed smoothly through Mlle Odier, Chenevière and the various national Red Cross societies around the world via a network of trains painted white with red crosses on top. (The trains brought the goods to fixed depots where they were loaded on to lorries for the final convoys to the camps.) The aim was to provide food, clothing and medicine for Europe's increasingly hungry and destitute civilian population, such as the Polish refugees now filling some 100 separate camps in Hungary; they were facing a winter when temperatures could drop to −34°C without coal, thick clothes or enough to eat.

Lalive took on a young diplomat, Olivier Long, later made an ambassador, a retired Nestlé employee called Rohner who had represented his firm in Morocco and knew all about buying in bulk, and a German of the old school, a slightly querulous but entertaining man called Robert

Boehringer, highly educated and a good manager, who was the literary executor of the poet Stefan George. There was also Jean de Schwarzenberg, an Austrian who had been able to take Swiss citizenship after tracing his ancestry to a bourgeois Zurich family. Burckhardt, Lalive noticed, enjoyed the company of men like Boehringer and Schwarzenberg: they represented German and Austro-Hungarian high culture, all he most admired. Lalive himself was different; his interests and background were more Anglo-Saxon. Soon, a central office for the Commission Mixte was opened at 4 Cour des Bastions. Rivalries simmered, with Chenevière barely keeping the acidity from his profoundly courteous voice and various members of the International Committee relishing their supremacy over de Rougé and Milson of the League, avenging themselves for the many toads they had been forced to eat in the days when the League had lorded it over them with its internationalism.

Food, bought with money raised from the national societies, began to arrive. Lisbon was the only port on the continent still open and through this increasingly tight bottleneck came supplies of flour, corn, medicines, dried fruit, condensed milk and sugar, which were then loaded on to the Red Cross trains for Geneva. By 1941, Lisbon was crowded and full of intrigues. The Portuguese Red Cross was criticized for being 'bloody minded and narrow', the British Red Cross for being cumbersome and obstructive. Colonel Frédéric Islin, the International Committee delegate in Lisbon, was constantly accused of being 'extremely rude' and 'unprepossessing in appearance'. His job cannot have been easy. The only vessels protected under the Hague Convention of 1907 were hospital ships and there had been talk, before the war, of setting up a Red Cross fleet. Now, with urgent need of more boats, the Committee and Islin chartered a number of ships, marked them with the red cross and furnished them with transport authorization known as navicerts, while begging and bullying the countries at war to respect their neutrality.

The system worked well during the European campaign, with 'free ports' established at Biel, Vallorbe and Geneva to avoid customs duty. Later, an entirely new foundation was formed to run what would be called Red Cross transport and the International Committee bought up a number of ships made idle by the war, named them *Caritas 1*, *Caritas 2* and the *Henry Dunant* (using the Anglicized version of Dunant's name), and recruited a new kind of marine delegate, a convoy agent who by the war's end had accompanied some 383 voyages of delivery. In Geneva, the vast Palais des Expositions was given over as a depot; here 500 packers and 300 clerks sorted and forwarded supplies.

In theory, Burckhardt's plan was excellent. Europe by now was a vast battlefield which trapped soldiers and civilians alike. As the months passed, as abandoned or unfertilized fields produced less and less food, as cities were obliterated by bombs and refugees took to the roads, so supplies dwindled and costs rose. Undernourishment and the diseases that come from dirt and poverty, tuberculosis and typhus, spread. The tone of the delegates' reports, as they travelled across Europe, became increasingly despairing. The misery caused by food blockades during the First World War had been the subject of many discussions in the International Committee. It now became plain that there was to be a new blockade, and that the British considered the control of food as central to their strategy as bombing and propaganda. The failure of the humanitarian movement to alter the British attitude was a further blow to the International Committee's authority.

In the first months of the war the British government took the position that food was conditional contraband, a commodity that could be seized by a blockading power if it was destined for the use of the enemy's armed forces. As the German army intensified its grip on Europe, the British decided that, since modern warfare no longer seemed to distinguish between soldiers and civilians, and since Germany wielded total control over all commodities in its territories, food had to be included in the blockade. However, the extension of the blockade to cover the whole of occupied Europe meant its victims would include not only Germans, but hundreds of thousands of people who were British allies. Protests were made by the public, by the churches, by the humanitarian organizations, by the Americans – who announced that the lingering death by starvation to which the British were condemning Europe's civilians was iniquitous – and by the International Committee.

The British were determined to resist. In the summer of 1940, the joint director of the Ministry of Economic Warfare was the Earl of Drogheda and he was far from certain about the wisdom of incurring the hatred of a 'continent where pestilence would be bred by famine'. His successor in the National Government, Hugh Dalton, had no such qualms. 'It is utterly pedantic,' he noted in his diary on 14 August 1940, 'to talk of "law" until Hitler's neck has been broken.' Churchill shared his belief in economic warfare. The British government's replies to the International Committee's appeals were that an effective blockade was an essential weapon for winning the war, that to relax it would be nothing more than 'fake humanity', and that relief would be stockpiled ready to pour into liberated Europe once the fighting was over.

It is unlikely that the International Committee could have done or said anything to influence the British government but the exchanges between the two are revealing of the way the British viewed the Geneva-based organization. At least part of British hostility seems to have come from Burckhardt's time as high commissioner to Danzig, the British sensing a definite warmth in his attitude towards Germany; some came from the British perception of Switzerland itself as distinctly pro-German. There was also the fact that few of the International Committee members spoke English, and that Rodolphe Haccius, delegate to London at the start of the war, was not considered to be, according to a brief note in Foreign Office files, 'a very live wire'. Because the delegates remained so anonymous, no one knew about his past successes in Hungary and elsewhere. More important, perhaps, the British government seems to have been unaware of precisely what the International Committee did. Notes written in the Foreign Office in the early years of the war suggest confusion, ignorance and fundamental differences of opinion. One memorandum, written in 1939, speaks of the International Committee's 'general attributes . . . most of which we disagreed with'. Just what these were thought to be is not spelt out. But British wariness was due as much as anything to the fact that the International Committee had never taken any pains to explain its purpose and ambitions to the British.

In April 1941, a first visit to London was paid by Marcel Junod and Mlle Odier. They called on the British Red Cross and various government departments. Junod later wrote that the appearance of his now elderly companion, frail, thin and soft-spoken after a throat operation, dressed invariably in a nurse-like blue costume, was extremely deceptive for she spoke out passionately and persuasively in excellent English about infant mortality and the suffering of British allies under the blockade. The Foreign Office remained unmoved. Notes suggest that they were suspicious that Junod might have come to England to make some kind of trouble over the British prisoner-of-war camps.

More interesting, however, is the reaction to Burckhardt's visit four months later. It occasioned dozens of anxious interdepartmental memos and many consultations with the British Red Cross. The British minister to Berne, Kelly, was in favour of the visit, saying that it could have 'important propaganda value', and that Burckhardt was 'master of vivid and impressive style of talk. He will notice every point of contrast between conditions at home and in Germany and spread the news.' Burckhardt, he added, was 'deeply sensitive to personal attentions'. Sir John Kennedy at the British Red Cross warned that refusing to allow the visit 'might have an unfortunate effect'. More messages arrived from Berne, describing Burckhardt as having a 'tendency to see himself as an international figure (rather than an historian and philosopher which he really is) and would deeply resent what he would certainly consider a rebuff. He has great personal influence in all important circles in Switzerland.' Anthony Eden, the foreign secretary had, it seems, 'considerable misgivings. . . in view of his political ambitions and the possibility that he might put peace feelers on behalf of the Germans, whether in official or unofficial circles. Whether he did or not, the Poles and Russians might have suspicions.' Long after the war, there would be some support for this view: Paul Stauffer and Jean-Claude Favez, the two Swiss historians who have studied Burckhardt's papers in greatest depth, both suggest that he may well have regarded himself as a possible broker for peace, a role that would have left him well placed whatever the outcome of the war. In the summer of 1942, Kelly was instructed to make it clear to Burckhardt that his visit to Britain was 'solely to discuss Red Cross questions and matters connected with them'.

It was not all politics, however. Burckhardt, whose English remained poor, was clearly regarded as a potentially awkward guest. Word came from Berne that he was 'very fond of shooting and good living' and plans were made to get French-speaking hosts to invite him for a few days' pheasant shooting.

Burckhardt did come to London but he was preceded by still more memos. 'The nearest way to his heart,' noted a Foreign Office member, 'is an occasional cigar, which he cannot get in Switzerland.' He was made an honorary member of the Athenaeum, and had long talks with the Foreign Office and the British Red Cross; but he was not received either by the prime minister or by the secretary of state. The verdict on the visit was one of both relief and satisfaction, all conversations having confined themselves to 'Red Cross questions'. Walter Roberts from the prisoner-of-war department wrote to Kelly that Burckhardt had been 'most sensible and helpful', on matters to do with prisoners and the way they were treated.

The blockade, however, remained in force. No one in England seemed much concerned when reminded by the Commission Mixte that it had made commitments to humanitarian relief under the terms of Red Cross agreements. The special requests for condensed milk for Belgian children and for milk products as Christmas presents to hungry children throughout Europe all came to nothing. Winning the war as rapidly as possible remained the priority whatever the circumstances, a situation foreseen by Churchill when, in December 1939, he observed, 'We have a right, indeed are bound in duty, to abrogate for a space some of the conventions of the very laws we seek to consolidate and reaffirm'. The main achievement of Burckhardt's visit to London was to illuminate how little the British actually knew about the Committee and its work, and how dismissive it was of its powers. Like the Americans, particularly in the early years of the war, they were suspicious of these dedicated and insistent Swiss in their neat suits interfering in matters that many of the military instinctively felt had nothing to do with them. This attitude was only brought fully into the open in 1996 when formerly classified American secret service papers revealed that some of the International Committee delegates, suspected of being spies, were watched and followed by the Americans.

At the height of the winter of 1941, during a particularly bitter cold spell, a telegram arrived in Geneva from Robert Brunel, delegate in Athens. 'Food situation in Greece extremely grave. Mortality increased sixfold in last two months. Catastrophe inevitable unless outside help arrives quickly.' Brunel was a Red Cross man of the old school, loquacious and full of passion; like Brown and Junod before him, he sat down to write a long, emotional report.

This land which nature has endowed with such beauty, this land blessed by the Gods, this Attica bathed in light ... is today a pure hell, a valley where reigns the harshest grief and the blackest misery, in the midst of which death reaps without mercy innocent lives . . . It is impossible, even for the keenest imagination, to grasp the depth of this misery . . . You would have to see for yourself the people falling dead to the pavements from hunger, the trucks and refuse carts carrying their piles of corpses to the cemeteries, you would have to visit for yourself the parts of the city where those near death sleep side by side with the bodies of those who have not yet been borne away

Brunel's report ran to eighteen pages. It talked of the streets of Athens filled with people sitting silently, their hands held out; it described children so skeletal that they could no longer move; it spoke of the many fresh bodies found on the pavements in the dawn. There was, said Brunel, nothing left for people to eat and no means to find any food: no milk, no cattle, no petrol, no fishing boats, no corn or seed, no medicines, no chemicals with which to spray the crops and no quinine with which to cure the malaria now spreading through the population.

Brunel had been expecting this. Greece, over the past year, had been moving steadily towards starvation. Having withstood the Italians in 1940, the country had fallen to the Germans in the spring of 1941. The Germans needed provisions for their armies in North Africa and requisitioned food, medical supplies and coal. The summer of 1941 yielded a very small harvest. The richer parts of the country in the north were occupied by the Bulgarians. Even in normal years, Greece imported well over half its food. Now, with the blockade preventing deliveries of supplies and the Germans seizing what there was, the country collapsed into total famine. In Athens and Piraeus alone, said Brunel, there were almost 2,000 deaths a day. One in every two infants failed to survive. And no one was quite sure what was happening on the islands since most were in German hands. 'Send bread or coffins,' came a message from one.

Greece had always been important to the British: Byron, the nineteenth-century classicists and the philhellenes had profoundly influenced the way they viewed the past. Among pacifists and churchmen a huge wave of protest now developed – which was to lead among other things to the birth of Oxfam – and a national famine relief committee, headed by the bishop of Chichester, George Bell, and Edith Pye of the Society of Friends, was set up. Sub-committees were formed all over the country. They too protested. From Oliver Lyttelton, British minister of state in Cairo, came a telegram saying that he was facing extreme hostility from the Greeks in Egypt. The effects of 'this ghastly suffering', Lyttelton said, 'will not be forgotten for generations, and however much the enemy is to blame, history will I believe, pronounce a stern judgement on our policy. I appeal not only to mercy but to expediency.'

The International Committee used Brunel's reports for all they were worth. It is difficult to determine how much Burckhardt's pleas to London counted but now, in the spring of 1942, the British government, pushed one way by pressure at home and pulled the other by the International Committee's intense lobbying, capitulated. The blockade was lifted. One ship, the *Kuntulus*, had already made five precarious journeys to Athens before Christmas — it was to sink on its sixth — under the aegis of the Turkish Red Crescent. Many more were now planned. The International Committee, with Brunel in charge and Junod despatched to help him, commandeered a number of ships, had them painted white with red crosses loaded with supplies from all over the world and despatched to the port of Piraeus, the food to be sent on throughout the mainland by convoys of lorries and to the islands on caiques. The Swedish Mission and the Swedish Red Cross poured in additional help. For a while, the death rate did not abate. In July 1942 alone, half a million cases of malaria were reported. Junod took back to Geneva photographs of starving children and babies, over a hundred different images of death from hunger. More relief was agreed and, bit by bit, other countries sent what contributions they could spare; Switzerland condensed milk, Italy corned beef and cheese, Turkey and the Balkans dried vegetables and fruit, even Germany a few potatoes and some sugar. Four hundred and fifty feeding centres for children were opened and, very slowly, stick-like dying children were seen to be walking again.

The *Stureborg*, a Swedish ship, had been taken over to bring British wheat from Egypt. On its way back to Alexandria, it disappeared. After some days a solitary survivor, a Portuguese sailor, was washed up on the coast of Palestine. It was from this man that the International Committee learned that, one day out of Piraeus, the *Stureborg*, despite the two large red crosses painted on its white sides, had been dive-bombed by Italian planes. The ship went down immediately. Nineteen men managed to scramble on board one of the lifeboats; Richard Heider, the new young Swiss International Committee delegate accompanying it, was not among them. One by one, as the boat drifted in intense heat, the survivors had died. Those who had tried to keep cool by covering themselves with sea water died first from sunstroke and burns. For the International Committee, it was another blow in a war which was capable of complete indifference to the very conventions many of the countries now fighting had supported so passionately.

The Committee had long known of the existence of camps in Greece, which were said to hold both prisoners-of-war and hostages but where they were and who precisely they contained no one would say. Bit by bit, word reached the Committee of three camps, in Salonika, Thebes and Larissa, holding a number of British prisoners-of-war who had escaped and been recaptured by the Germans, as well as Greeks found on the streets after the curfew and every kind of civilian detainee the three occupying powers – Germany, Bulgaria and Italy – wished to be rid of. A local Swiss resident called Gredinger, who had been in charge of the Nestlé factory in Athens for many years, offered to help the Committee trace the exact whereabouts of the camps, as did a Mme Zafari, a member of the Greek Red Cross and wife of an Athenian banker, who had friends among the communists in the resistance.

Since the majority of prisoners in these camps were civilians the International Committee had nothing in its mandate to invoke. But some of the camp commandants were prepared to listen to argument and the delegates in Athens pestered and begged until they were allowed in. The men they found inside were filthy, emaciated and dressed in rags. Many were ill. Most had had no contact with the outside world for a long time. In Greece, as it was to become clear across occupied Europe, it was up to the individual delegate to negotiate his own agreements, and those who pushed the hardest were often those who won the most concessions. André Lambert was a tall, gangling man with a moustache. He was an adventurer and a fine climber who had climbed Mont Blanc with his father before the war and liked to play his violin in the mountains. In September 1942 he put his career in films to one side and offered his services to the International Committee. They sent him to Greece as delegate.

Lambert was probably too independent-minded and flamboyant for their taste, for a distinct odour of unease hangs over their various exchanges with him. He was, however, dogged. In 1943, hearing rumours of a camp at Hardari said to be the headquarters of Gestapo interrogators, he set out with a truck and supplies and banged on its high gates. He was refused entry. People who lived nearby told him that they had heard that there were prisoners-of-war inside and that they were being tortured. Lambert decided to hang around the gates.

One day, he noticed that they had not been properly locked. There was no one about and he slipped inside, but was caught before he had time to explore and thrown out into the road again. The next thing he heard was that the Germans were planning to deport a number of the prisoners from Hardari. He loaded more trucks with supplies and, together with the Greek Red Cross, hastened to the railway station. There he saw cattle trucks with people inside; he backed his lorries as close as possible and began handing the supplies through the still open doors. When they were closed, he pushed food through the cracks and air vents. Orders were given for the train to leave. Lambert and his helpers drove their trucks along the side of the railway until the train stopped again and they went on pushing food through the vents. At last, several stops later, the supplies were finished. He watched the train disappear from sight. From his hurried conversations with them Lambert learned that the deportees were Jews; but he had no idea where they were going.

Much of the International Committee's success in Greece came down to courage and determination. Brunel was a pusher and the men who followed him to Greece copied his behaviour. When, in late 1942, the Germans issued orders forbidding any more deliveries to the islands, Brunel decided to ignore the ban and sent a delegate to the Cyclades just the same.

It was a cloak and dagger operation, of the kind the delegates thrived on. After negotiations with the Turkish government and the embassies of Greece, Britain, the United States and Italy, Raymond Courvoisier, the former delegate in Spain who had joined the team in Greece, set sail with four caiques for the islands. He reached German-held Chios to find that the island's archbishop was also the president of the local Red Cross. 70,000 inhabitants had no bread, rice, pasta, cereals, sugar, coffee, tea, milk, cheese or butter. They were forbidden by the Germans to net fish. Courvoisier wrote to Geneva, describing 'small children whose parents have died of hunger, wandering from door to door begging for food . . . Their skin is straw coloured, their eyes wild and shining, their bodies swollen . . .' In the monasteries, he found all the monks had died. Courvoisier unloaded 200 tons of food, and pressed on to Samos, where he distributed thirty-nine tons of oil, salted fish, olives and beans. On Mytilene, where he went next, even the soup kitchens had closed for there was no longer anything left to cook.

Britain had lifted the blockade on Greece, but those who hoped that this would be followed by greater lenience for other nations were to be disappointed. A little relief did enter Vichy France. Otherwise the Greek experience marked one of the high points of the International Committee's war. It had been a rescue operation, conducted with imagination and efficiency, and thousands of lives had been saved. When Brunel fell ill and returned to Geneva to die young, the Greek government ordered the Red Cross flag to be flown at half mast in all the places left under its control. In Athens a requiem mass was said for him, and a road was named after him.

At dawn on 22 June 1941, the Germans attacked the Soviet Union. By December they had laid siege to Leningrad and reached the outskirts of Moscow. In the first two months of their campaign alone, they took two million Soviet prisoners. In this vast, distant theatre of war, Geneva's humanitarian concerns did not count for very much.

The Soviet Union had never signed the 1929 Geneva Convention relating to prisoners. For a while, with Junod in Ankara trying to broker agreements on reciprocal treatment for captives, it looked as if both sides might honour some of the more basic undertakings. The Central Agency in Geneva felt optimistic enough to open a Soviet Service.

Winter and snow came. Dr Marti, watching the arrival of Russian prisoners in a camp in Pomerania in October 1941, commented on their 'pitiable state . . . many in rags . . . just like walking corpses', dragging their dying comrades behind them, the seventeen- and eighteen-year-olds emaciated and wizened like old men, 'whole lines' holding on 'to each other's shoulders so as not to fall', the living helping along the dying.

All in all, wrote Marti, 'the Russians are appallingly treated. They are not even regarded as livestock, but as savage beasts left to die without anyone taking any notice . . . I am profoundly moved by these columns of prisoners, hordes without names.'

Negotiations with both the Russians and Germans went on, the British and American governments joining the International Committee in its attempts to bring about some kind of humanitarian agreement. In 1941, believing that they would reach a deal of some kind over reciprocal treatment, the Germans encouraged the International Committee to start making lists of names of prisoners and to prepare to carry out camp visits. But as the months passed and the Russians said nothing, the German position hardened. In the camps, the rations handed out to Russian prisoners were cut, then cut again; their blankets were taken away; they were not given water with which to wash. Bodies, buried by night, were said to weigh no more than thirty-five kilos. In the files in Geneva, which grew smaller and smaller as the war went on and there was nothing to report, are scraps of paper, with odd rumours and bits of information. One is about Stalin's son, a lieutenant captured by the Germans. He was objecting, according to one story, to being held in a camp together with Jews.

But the International Committee went on trying; the letters in the archives bear witness to how very hard they persisted. It all came to nothing. To the end of the war, relief either to the Soviet prisoners in German hands or the German prisoners of the Soviets, remained meagre and haphazard. The Russians simply failed to reply to foreign overtures, while the Germans went on saying that there would be no lists of prisoners, no parcels and no visits by International Committee delegates without commitments from the Russians that they would do the same. For the prisoners – millions of men – this meant growing hunger, disease and despair.

In the summer of 1942, the Germans crossed the River Don and reached Stalingrad, where they soon found themselves cut off by a Soviet counter-offensive. When the twenty-three weeks of fighting for the city, in icy temperatures, at last ended, 200,000 people were dead. The Russian army regrouped and took 91,000 German prisoners to join the other Germans, Italians, Finns and Hungarians barely surviving in appalling prisoner-of-war camps. Voldemar Wehrlin, the former delegate to Moscow, was now despatched to Teheran to set up a base from which it was hoped that he would conduct more successful negotiations between Russians and Germans. Wehrlin was used to delays. It took him eighteen months to concede defeat, the Russian consul general in Teheran remarking to him in private that any 'limits on war-like action' should have been agreed long before. The fighting would be over before the International Committee would be allowed to take relief to German prisoners. It was only when they began their long trek home from the distant, freezing, destitute Soviet camps that the delegates had confirmation of all that they had feared. The archives in Geneva contain letters and reports written after the war, describing forced labour in temperatures of −75°F, of living off 400 grams of bread and three litres of soup a day, of hunger so acute that men were killed so their veins could be cut and their blood sucked. On 5 May 1950, the Soviet Union told the International Committee that they had repatriated 1,939,063 men, but were still holding on to 9,717 for serious war crimes.

The Russians, however, fared far worse. Three out of the five million Russians taken prisoner by the Wehrmacht died in captivity, most of them in the first two years. Stories reached Geneva of German guards stripping their Russian prisoners of their thick coats and warm boots, forcing them to build their own shelters before they froze to death, handing out rations too small to survive on. In Zamość in western Poland villagers later reported having heard the cries of Russian prisoners, slowly falling silent as they were overtaken by cold and starvation. The Poles were treated no better. After the occupation of Poland there were believed to be some 60,000 Polish soldiers in German hands. As early as May 1940, Hartmann of the German Red Cross, who spent the war unhappily and uneasily liaising with the International Committee, informed Mme Frick-Cramer that the 'Poles are perhaps no longer considered *prisoners* by the German government.' What this meant was that they had no Protecting Power and would not benefit from the Geneva Conventions. Despite repeated protests from Mme Frick-Cramer and the Committee, only one concession was ever won: while Russian prisoners could not be visited, Poles could be seen, but not spoken to. It did not help them. In the spring of 1941 a report reached the delegates stationed in Germany about Polish prisoners in Stalag V111C, on the west bank of the Oder. It is among the files in Geneva. The report describes '180–200 prisoners-of-war per tent in temperatures of −25°. Those too cold to rise in the morning are marched out by guards, slapped and hit, leaving broken ribs and black eyes . . . 50 percent are ill. 10 percent have frozen limbs. About 200 are wounded. A few have hanged themselves. Others have gone mad . . . Those who have tried to escape have for the most part been shot.'

It was unrealistic to imagine that so many countries would go to war and abide by the Geneva Conventions. As it was, the Conventions were violated by all sides, daily, casually, contemptuously, even if the violations committed by the Allies over prisoners-of-war, reciprocal agreements and respect for the Red Cross emblem, were minor compared to those of the Axis powers. The International Committee was appalled but, as with the Soviet prisoners, there was very little they could do. It is to their credit that they never stopped trying, Huber issuing appeals at strategic moments and trying to bring pressure to bear on those who most blatantly violated their own promises; and he did score a few successes.

By the spring of 1940 there had been dozens of complaints from the governments of countries at war about the treatment of captives, the bombing of hospitals, the arbitrary execution of hostages, the abuse of prisoners as forced labour and the siting of prisoner-of-war camps too close to the front. Some were genuine, some fabricated, all sides having understood that one way to strengthen morale at home was to depict the enemy as devoid of all human feelings. The correspondence with the International Committee on violations of the Geneva Conventions runs to many files in many languages. When, on 23 April 1940, an American Red Cross man in Finland reported to Norman Davis in Washington that there had been 1,800 aerial attacks by German bombers on Finnish towns and that 640 civilians had died in the raids, Davis wrote off to Huber complaining of 'systematic and barbarous' behaviour against which the 'moral force of the International Committee should be exercised to the fullest extent . . . even in the absence of precise conventions the Red Cross should mobilize the full strength of public opinion, the great force of condemnation' against 'hardships of war caused by new and old instruments of destruction'. Yet Davis knew better than anyone the weakness of Huber's position and cannot have felt greatly surprised by the somewhat vacillating letter he received back, written in Huber's absence by a new member of the secretariat, Charles Burckhardt, a distant relation of Carl-Jacob, outlining the difficulty of acting 'without positive proof' and repeating that the International Committee continued to believe that its most effective role lay in 'practical work'. At times, bombarded by requests, complaints and appeals, the International Committee gives the appearance of a weak headmaster, struggling to keep order in a school in which most of the pupils are destructive, bullying and wily.

Reciprocity was one of the few weapons at its disposal. But in mid-1940 the saga of the prisoners-of-war at sea shows how very weak even that could be. Until then, the numbers of prisoners transported by sea were very small. The Germans had taken most of their prisoners captive in Poland and France and sent them to camps by train. The British had captured only a few, and these were for the most part Luftwaffe shot down over Britain or crews of German U-boats rescued and taken back to Britain by warship. By the middle of 1940, however, British camps were full of interned Italians and Germans, resident in the United Kingdom when the war began, and there was growing unease about what this potential fifth column might do if the Germans followed up the capture of France with an invasion of Britain. It was decided to deport them by sea to distant parts of the Commonwealth. Almost immediately, there was a disaster: the *Arandora Star*, carrying 1,280 Germans and Italians, was attacked by a German U-boat and sank, drowning over half the detainees on board.

For years, the International Committee had been urging governments to make provision for the protection at sea of prisoners-of-war. It used the sinking of the *Arandora Star* to bring pressure on the British — who pointed out that the ship had been sunk by the Germans. The dispute rumbled on until 1945, with endless accusations by both sides and very little agreement, neither Allied nor Axis powers apparently willing to commit themselves to the Committee's proposal to neutralize ships carrying prisoners of war. The International Committee kept up a solid campaign, writing a series of letters to both sides, many of which went unanswered for months at a time. By the time the war was over, 15,000 prisoners had died at sea, bombed or torpedoed by their own countries, while the major powers continued to offer minor concessions only to withdraw them, endlessly citing distrust of the enemy and fear of losing strategic advantage as reasons for doing nothing. How much, if any, of this stemmed from mistrust of the International Committee's powers is hard to say, but a number of letters written by members of the British Foreign Office on the subject of violations of the Geneva Conventions are revealing. 'We should not forget,' wrote Walter Roberts of the prisoner-of-war department in the winter of 1942–43, 'that this Convention was drawn up some years ago in peacetime. It is perhaps natural that the conditions in which total war is now waged were not then foreseen.' 'From the legal point of view,' added Patrick Dean, assistant legal adviser to the Foreign Office, 'it seems to me most important to do all we can to keep the Convention in force, since although it has broken down badly during this war in one or two matters . . . it does provide a standard . . . If the Convention vanishes, there is nothing left.'

Nowhere, perhaps, was the issue of reciprocity and monitoring more important than over reprisals – banned under the prisoner-of-war code in 1929 – and here the International Committee did have some success.

Dieppe was raided on 19 August 1942 by a Canadian division, supported by the British. Germans captured by the troops as they came ashore were immediately handcuffed – a violation of the treaty. The Germans protested and announced that though the British had not intended to leave the handcuffs on they would handcuff 1,376 British and Canadian prisoners. The British replied that they would do the same to 1,376 German prisoners, arguing that what had happened at Dieppe had been due to 'exceptional circumstances'. Both sides removed the handcuffs during meals. The International Committee, drawn into the dispute, sent telegrams to both sides, reminding them of their guarantees over 'humane and chivalrous treatment' of prisoners. Negotiations continued. Dr Grawitz of the German Red Cross, appealed to by Huber, said that he could do nothing. In the meantime, delegates visiting the handcuffed prisoners in Germany reported that the chains had been lengthened, and that the commandant of the camp in which the prisoners were held disliked the measure intensely. No one would back down. It was now that the International Committee's preferred weapon of discreet negotiation came into play. In the middle of November 1943, Burckhardt went to Berlin to see the German foreign minister, von Ribbentrop. Together they formed a plan. The handcuffs would be removed from the prisoners held in Germany and reports saying that this had happened would be delivered − in confidence and not for publication − to the British and the Canadians. On 21 November all handcuffs were formally removed for good. A face-saving formula had been found.

The incident of the chains seems to have taken the Germans to an edge. There had long been rumours that if the British proved too intransigent Germany would declare itself freed from all further obligations under the Geneva Conventions and resort to methods 'which would carry with them a heavy aggravation of war methods for which Britain alone would then bear the responsibility'. There had even been warnings that the Germans might decide to abolish food parcels. In the event, both countries did step back, not least presumably because each held vast numbers of prisoners hostage. Once again, the British verdict on the affair seems unduly harsh on the International Committee. 'I feel fairly sure,' wrote Walter Roberts early in 1943, 'that the difference of view with Germany over the Convention goes deep, and no proposal . . . would have any chance of acceptance if it does not take this into account . . . I am afraid the reason for the present practice is that Switzerland is a weak state and that the Swiss are afraid to endorse in any way the representations which one side makes to the other.'

If 'comforts' was a key word for the British Red Cross, 'doughnuts' filled the equivalent American Red Cross niche. At the height of the war, American Red Cross women in Europe would serve doughnuts at the rate of 400 every minute.

The events of 1939 had found the United States at the end of a decade of depression. The isolationist feelings of the government were mirrored by the behaviour of the American Red Cross, particularly in the Midwest where there was much talk of 'charity begins at home'. Neither the Spanish civil war nor the Japanese invasion of China had seen much generosity. When news of the war in Europe reached America, donations were slow to come, although on 22 June 1940, the American senate passed a bill authorizing $50 million towards relief work for war victims in Europe. On 12 July a train, paid for by the Americans and organized by the League, left Switzerland for northern France, laden with chocolate, cheese, condensed milk and ham. By the middle of August, medicines were arriving regularly by air clipper.

With Pearl Harbor, however, came an immediate, dramatic change. Since 1934, farsighted figures within the American Red Cross had been meeting representatives of the army and navy to persuade them to let the American Red Cross be the 'sole non-militant organization to operate with the expeditionary force' if and when America should go to war. By the early winter of 1941 they were fully prepared. The sheer volume of relief that they poured into Europe, as well as the number of American Red Cross staff, was awesome.

At first, there was some anxiety that their overseas role would be curtailed by the American army itself, whose services for its men extended far beyond those of other countries and included every aspect of moral, physical and spiritual well-being. They need not have worried, particularly as, unlike the British Red Cross, their mandate allowed them to work not only with the sick and wounded but with the 'hale and hearty' as well. It was here that they would make their mark. American generals were in no doubt that the morale of soldiers would be crucial in the months to come: the American Red Cross was to be an essential contributor to that morale. Fifteen thousand Red Cross workers were despatched to Europe to set up clubs and what became known as a 'hotel chain' – the society boasted that it was the largest hotel in the world, able to sleep over 60,000 people in any one week – to act as welfare officers, to travel with the troops and provide a feeling of home. The Red Cross was there to take America to the battlefields of Europe, to surround the soldier with American accents, American cooking and American camaraderie so that he did not feel quite so lost.

While artists like Norman Rockwell and Lawrence Wilbur turned their hand to Red Cross posters and American Red Cross volunteers collected, packed and despatched food parcels to some 1.3 million allied prisoners-of-war, a huge, highly professional publicity and fundraising campaign engulfed America. A single month saw forty feature articles in national magazines, ten of them with Red Cross covers, 55,800 local broadcasts based on Red Cross material, speeches made by twenty-four 'public figures', 259 by Red Cross field directors and thirty-one by senior ranks from the army and navy. At the same time, recruitment got under way for the women who would lead the American Red Cross welfare effort. Volunteers had to be aged between twenty-five and thirty, have completed at least two years in college or its equivalent, come from good moral backgrounds, have excellent health and 'social graces'. Barbara Pathe was an early Second World War recruit. '1939 came at the end of the "noblesse oblige" time,' she says. 'The first volunteers were debutantes, plain folk came later. You were told you had to be strong, physically and morally, because you were likely to get two proposals and eight propositions a week.' A certain resentment was voiced by ordinary American soldiers when they discovered that Red Cross girls would be allowed to go out only with officers or civilians; there was talk of 'snooty dames'. Asked what made a good Red Cross woman, Mabel Boardman replied firmly: 'The three Ds – Drill, which is her training, Dependability and Discipline, the latter being the most important, particularly for Americans.'

Three million American servicemen visited Britain between Pearl Harbor and the end of the war. The first two Red Cross clubs to cater for them opened on 6 May 1942, one in London, the other in Londonderry. At the peak of the American presence, there were 252 of these clubs, many with bedrooms and all with a cafeteria, a shoe-shine kiosk, a barber's shop and chefs trained to turn out waffles and maple syrup. Someone had the inspired idea of hanging a large map of the United States in every entrance. Little flags with names and addresses were pinned to it to show where current club guests came from. It was all, as Zollinger, the International Committee delegate to America, had noted disapprovingly, bigger, richer, more intense, than its European cousins among the Allies, a huge exercise in American 'political and material power', even if it was said to remain extremely careful with its funds – perhaps a legacy of Clara Barton's early spending days.

The plans for Operation 'Overlord,' the Allied invasion of Europe, had specified that American Red Cross forces would go into France with the American army units. They were to get a view of war denied even to war correspondents, a freedom to come and go near the front almost at whim. Barbara Pathe went with them. Out of the service clubs in Britain had come the idea of Clubmobiles, sleek, grey vehicles built over the chassis of two-and-a-half ton General Motors trucks, staffed and driven by three Red Cross women and laden down with wooden barrels of doughnut mixture from the Mayflower Doughnut Company and fat in which to fry them. They travelled in groups of eight. Within days of the Normandy landings the Clubmobiles were hard at work, the women making doughnuts in the morning by adding water to the mixture in huge vats and distributing them in the afternoon, two to a soldier together with one cup of coffee, two cigarettes, three and a half Life Savers and one and a half packets of chewing gum. Watching the women frying, using the automated Mayflower Doughnut machines which pushed the raw doughnuts into the fat under air pressure then turned them over as they cooked, became a form of entertainment for the GIs, particularly as not all the young women were very deft with the prongs used to extract the cooked doughnuts from the fat.

Each Clubmobile, which could if necessary be transformed into an ambulance, was equipped with a portable victrola, records, a public address system, stationery, books and razors. The first 206 Clubmobile women and 105 men were observed closely for their 'physical and mental health, reliability' and grasp of foreign languages. Gregariousness was admired, as was the art of good listening, the army ranking a friendly ear high in the morale register, and even if not every girl could pass for a 'soldier's sister or mother' as one manual put it (one wonders why not) 'at least,' says Barbara Pathe, 'they were women, were civilians, were Americans.' The Clubmobile uniform consisted of a short jacket and trousers; the hat could be peaked or shaped like a turban, which made saluting rather peculiar. The women were told not to seem shy, to wear their collars open and put flowers in their hair. When they took baths, guards were posted. Those who became pregnant, in spite of all the moral scrutiny, were treated kindly.

There had been considerable doubts about the value of Clubmobiles in the first place, sceptics warning that it was not easy to churn out doughnuts on the run, but as Harvey D. Gibson, who had been Commissioner for Europe in 1919 and was again Commissioner in 1941, saw it, doughnuts were ammunition, ammunition for the spirit as for the heart. And after the doughnuts had been eaten, a lonely soldier or two could be invited to help with the drying up: while the 'girls' sang a 'song or two', the 'boys' helped with the dishes. At the end of the day, any food left over was handed out to local children. Supplies taken across the Channel on D-Day, intended to last ten Clubmobiles fifteen days, consisted of 2.5 million Life Savers, 140 gross of toothbrushes and 1.34 million cigarettes.

What the International Committee made of all this is not recorded.

But the Committee remained in close touch with the American Red Cross, using its services to broadcast a long, reassuring message by a delegate about the health and generally good conditions of American prisoners-of-war in Axis camps.

The American Red Cross did not escape the Second World War unscathed, returning home to accusations that soldiers were charged unnecessarily for their doughnuts, that there had been too few black women recruits and that officers had been better cared for than men. The Clubmobiles were only one small part in a highly efficient organization that undoubtedly did improve life for America's soldiers immeasurably, providing one of the more exuberant outposts of Dunant's dream. One suspects that, once he had got over his misgivings about using women, Dunant himself would have admired them hugely.

By the spring of 1942 there were delegates at work in all five continents. In Britain, Italian prisoners-of-war were asking for more books; in the military prison in Ravenna, Greeks and Yugoslavs were putting on plays and watching films; in Egypt, Italian and German captives had just received a consignment of pullovers, oranges and sweets; in Surinam, a delegate was agreeably surprised by the good conditions of a camp in Copieweg. The war had spread to the Pacific and telegrams from Huber had gone out to the new countries sucked into the war – Japan, the United States, Cuba, Costa Rica, the Dominican Republic, Guatemala, Haiti, Honduras, Nicaragua and El Salvador. In the Middle East, delegates wore white jackets and solar topees for their prison visits.

Geneva had been little changed by the war. People still went boating on the lake and climbing in the mountains, even though Switzerland was surrounded on three sides by the armies of Germany, Vichy France and Italy, and it would not be long before German units would set up bases just over the French border in the Jura and Saleve mountains high above the city itself. The League of Nations buildings, once full of busy and optimistic international civil servants, were now largely deserted.

The International Committee had never worked harder. Some 3,300 people filled five buildings – the Villa Moynier, the Electoral Palace, the Musée Rath, a house belonging to the Société de Banques Suisses, and a rented house – and would soon spill over into the Métropole Hotel, an imposing mansion on the shores of the lake overlooking the Jardin Anglais, whose 119 bedrooms and bathrooms would be stripped to make way for wooden partitions, kitchen tables covered in white paper and regiments of volunteers. Madame Schumacher, who joined the tiny archives section during the war, remembers the way everyone used bicycles to get from one building to another, the volunteer ladies in their hats riding majestically along Geneva's empty streets.

There were now information bureaux everywhere from Moscow to Cairo. In the central prisoners-of-war agency — the 'great notice board of stricken Europe' — which was about to send out its ten millionth civilian message, retired civil servants, professors and linguists were working round the clock in shifts, in silence, in fifteen languages and four scripts — Latin, Gothic, Cyrillic and Greek. Soon they would add Japanese. The agency now had seven main services, the French alone occupying the centre of the main hall of the Electoral Palace, four ground floor rooms, several tables in the gallery and a number of annexes. Something of the sheer complexity of the logistical problems, and the imagination it took to come up with answers, can be seen in the path taken by a civilian message destined for a part of Italy in German hands: from Geneva, it went by truck to Marseilles where it was put on board a Red Cross ship to Lisbon; it was then flown by military aircraft to Algiers, and from there forwarded to the International Committee delegate in Naples.

A personal effects section had also been formed to handle requests from next of kin. Searchers, some of them chemists, sifted through the personal belongings of dead soldiers to find documents, many of which had lain for days in mud and rain and were tattered, torn and covered in bloodstains and needed treatment with alcohol, solvents and ultra-violet rays, to find traces of names and addresses.

The Committee itself now met continuously. Seventy-one thousand people had paid personal visits to the Villa Moynier since the outbreak of war. Since all phone calls were recorded and typed up, since every meeting produced notes and every report memos, it is still possible, fifty years later, to get an extraordinary picture of the vast tapestry of the war that the Committee members held in their heads — the broken-down postal system with Denmark, the ban on German sports-wear in British camps, the request for musical instruments from a 'man of confidence' in a Stalag near Stuttgart, the search for the body of the comte de Moustiers by four members of the Belgian Red Cross near Aix-la-Chapelle – an immense, constantly changing jumble of requests and problems, ranging in size and difficulty from the very personal to the theoretical, in several dozen different languages, all of it requiring understanding, checking and acting on.

Huber, never in very good health, was often away. Power lay with half a dozen people, particularly Burckhardt and Chenevière. A newcomer working in the tracing service of the agency, Melchior Borsinger, who would soon take over from Junod the mantle of much loved and admired delegate, recalls that one day, not long after his arrival in 1942, Boehringer stopped him in the corridor. 'How are the men on the Committee doing?' he asked, for Borsinger was also attached to the central office. 'Do you mean Huber and Burckhardt?' 'No,' replied Boehringer, 'I mean the men on the Committee, Mlle Odier and Mlle Ferrière.'

For all the current worries of the war – ceaseless aerial bombardments, uncontrolled submarine warfare, the failure to negotiate agreements on the treatment of guerrillas and partisans, who were playing an increasing role in the hostilities – the Committee was riding quite high. Relief operations were being carried out efficiently, and 6,500 tons of food, medicine and clothes had been distributed to civilians by the Commission Mixte. Prisoners-of-war, in countries signatory to the Geneva Conventions, were for the most part treated adequately under the constant supervision of delegates, even if the length of the war, now in its third year, was taking its toll in boredom and despair. The tracing and message systems were altering the lives of millions of anxious families. Relations with a number of countries, like Britain, were improving as their governments came to appreciate not only the scope of the Committee's interests but the tenacity and dedication with which the delegates carried out their missions. Contacts with the Vatican, the churches, governments, the League and national Red Cross societies, of which five – those of Norway, Holland, Poland, Czechoslovakia and Yugoslavia – were now in exile in Britain, were regular and amicable.

Huber, the pensive and gentle figure in a dark suit and tie, whose view of states was that they had been ordained and were not to be criticized, was still in control, his cautious spirit hanging over the organization. Borsinger has a revealing memory of him at work. For him, Huber remains one of the most impressive of all Red Cross leaders, for both his spirituality and his intelligence, with 'something of Curzon about him, without the arrogance'. One of Borsinger's jobs was to draft letters for him. One day he took a number of letters in for him to read. He had signed them 'Your humble and obedient servant'. Huber, says Borsinger, was furious. 'I won't have this,' he told the astonished young man, who had used the words only as a standard courtesy, 'I am no one's humble servant.'

Just visible on the horizon, but now to grow menacingly, were difficulties of a nature to dwarf most of what had gone before. Huber, by early 1942, must have sensed them coming. Not long before, he had written a long, poignant, agonized paper setting out the limits, as he saw them, to Red Cross power. It comes across as a warning to those who were tempted to meddle in world politics, by a man of 'total realism, with regard for the phenomena of this life, and sublime devotion to those of the next,' as Jean Pictet would describe him. It was important, wrote Huber, reaffirming his faith in neutrality, that the Red Cross should resist all desire to stray beyond its appointed tasks, however noble its intentions. The only way for it to accomplish its mission was to remain universal and impartial. 'Its abnegation . . .' he concluded, 'is the source of its grandeur and its strength. It is thanks to them that the Red Cross can survive a series of catastrophes and, as the last link between men, can become the point of departure for future reconstruction.' Somewhere behind these self-justifying words stood a very apprehensive man.

FOURTEEN

Keep the Fires Burning
Under Those Old Gentlemen

Right up until the autumn of 1944 there was no reference to concentration camps in the International Committee's *Review*. The magazine continued to report month after month on all Red Cross activities, relief work, missions by delegates, violations of the Geneva Conventions, international gatherings, conditions in which prisoners-of-war were kept, new medical and military developments and newcomers to the Red Cross world. But beyond a few passing mentions of deportees and a veiled sentence or two about Jewish organizations, it was as if the camps and the atrocities inside them played no part in the International Committee's war. Yet eleven million Jews, gypsies, political dissidents, Jehovah's Witnesses and disabled people died in them, and of all its preoccupations, the concentration and extermination camps of occupied Europe were perhaps the most discussed by the Committee, and certainly the most painful. They were also its greatest failure.

There was nothing surprising about the weak legal position regarding civilians in which the International Committee found itself in 1939. They had watched it coming. Ever since the end of the First World War they had fought hard to get governments to agree to a code for civilians, much like the one for prisoners-of-war. And as the spectre of total war in which there would no longer be a distinction between soldier and civilian grew ever more real, so they had fought all the harder to define categories of civilian, earmark places of safety for children and put limits on aerial bombardments. But their efforts achieved little. Governments prevaricated, refused to comply with some proposals whilst insisting on others. Even Mlle Ferrière, architect of some of the best work concerning civilians, worried about the fact that any new Convention would be bound to base itself on the very different experiences of the First World War. No one had even contemplated putting civilians on to any list before, believing no war could seriously affect them. For the French, who objected again and again to the idea of a formal treaty, it was all a question of sovereignty, a reluctance to let the International Committee or anyone else meddle in what they still insisted were 'internal affairs'. Faced with such a negative response the Committee abandoned its attempts to convene a diplomatic conference. Mlle Ferrière and Mme Frick-Cramer, both of whom had worried throughout the 1930s about what could be done for civilians deported from countries which had been invaded, agreed that the early 1920s had been the optimal time to have pushed through a tough Convention. Now it was too late.

In September 1939, as the world contemplated the destruction of Polish cities by Hitler's bombers and listened to Huber's appeals for a civilized and humane war, the only protection for civilians lay in the Tokyo draft and all that dealt with was a class of 'enemy civilian', people caught in enemy territory by war.

One of the difficulties, and one of the reasons why agreement had been so hard to reach, lay in the very definition of a civilian. There were civilians who were nationals of enemy countries when war broke out; there were refugees, evacuees and political detainees; there were stateless people and nationals in their own country who were viewed with suspicion by their own governments; and there were non-combatants in occupied or annexed territories. Each of these groups was subjected to different interpretations by different countries.

Nor were they all equally vulnerable. As war was declared, the International Committee, falling back on the many oral commitments made at the Tokyo conference, managed to squeeze undertakings out of the countries going to war that foreign nationals found in enemy territory when war broke out, the so-called 'enemy civilians', would be treated in much the same way as prisoners-of-war, according to a code of rules. Over 160,000 civilians from fifty nations would benefit from this agreement by the time the war ended.

More problematic was the question of the treatment of civilians in occupied or annexed territories and of nationals or stateless people — and, ironically Germany at first professed itself willing to discuss the matter. Berlin notified the International Committee at the end of September 1939 that it was perfectly prepared to discuss visits to civilian internment camps.

But long before the war actually broke out, the Jews already knew only too clearly what could happen to unprotected civilians. With the Nuremberg laws had come a new purified German citizenship from which Jews had been excluded. This applied not only to Jews of German nationality, but to all Jews in satellite countries, in allied countries and, soon, in occupied countries. Falling outside the special agreements of 1939, which recognized only 'enemy civilians', they were now labelled 'detained civilians', which effectively placed them beyond the International Committee's jurisdiction. The Committee was now left with just one possibility for action, that of invoking the right to humanitarian initiative. This was perhaps the most interesting and fragile of all the weapons in its armoury, not only because it was open to so many interpretations but also because it was by nature subject to the agreement of the governments concerned.

In Edmond Boissier's paper on the droit d'ingérence (the right to interfere, usually rendered as the 'right of initiative'), drawn up when the Commission on Political Detainees was formed in 1935 – the most prestigious of all the sub-committees with the most powerful figures as its members – he stated that the 'ICRC's prestige is not harmed if, having done all it can to defend a humanitarian cause, it suffers a defeat; on the contrary, the authority is damaged by inaction and excessive caution.' In the years to come Boissier's words would be remembered and repeated again and again. Here was the heart of the International Committee's many paradoxes. Some members supported Boissier, saying that the worst regret would come from not having done enough; others argued that the International Committee was only a small institution, with a small budget, in a country soon to be surrounded by nations at war, and that it should restrict its operations to things it knew it could achieve; others again held that strict neutrality, to which Huber clung so passionately, had been and remained the Committee's strongest card.

It was in this mood – confused, uncertain, with no overall agreement – that the International Committee went to war on behalf of the Jews.

* * *

The precariousness of the Jewish position under the Nazis was not, after all, unknown to the International Committee. Information about Nazi repression and the concentration camps had been reaching Geneva in one form or another since the early 1930s. It came from the anxious letters sent by church and liberal organizations, Jewish bodies, individuals calling for help; it came in phone calls, newspaper articles, reports and in personal visits; it came from the delegates of both the International Committee and the League as they travelled around Europe and from members of the Committee, like Burckhardt whose years in Danzig had been filled by meetings with high-ranking Nazis. Himmler, Burckhardt would later note in his memoirs, made no attempt to conceal his party's anti-Semitism. And it came from the more humane members of the German Red Cross, like Walter Hartmann, its foreign director, who would visit Geneva eighteen times in the course of the war, and Colonel Draudt, who was also vice-president of the League. Neither of these men was a Nazi. The fact that they clung to their posts during the war was evidence of the need felt by the Germans for delegates from the International Committee to monitor the Allied prisoner-of-war camps and report on the conditions in which German prisoners were held. What Hartmann actually discussed on his visits to Switzerland, however, is not recorded owing to the Committee's practice of not committing to paper debates on many of the more sensitive issues.

The 'Final Solution of the Jewish Problem' was the name given to Hitler's plan to exterminate the Jews of Europe. With the conquest of Poland, the Nazis set about ridding Germany and the countries it occupied not only of Jews, but of gypsies, homosexuals, the disabled and all 'undesirables'. In January 1940, the killing of mental patients using gas began in a number of selected hospitals under a euthanasia programme. Squads of special assessors, members of a unit called Aktion T-4, registered, selected, transported and murdered those considered too unproductive for the German Reich. Among Nazi documents found in a hidden cache in the German town of Hartheim at the end of the war were the monthly graphs of the euthanasia programme showing the numbers of those killed, with projections indicating that if the same death rate was kept up until 1951, 5,902,920 kilos of marmalade would be saved – assuming that those sent to their deaths were eating an average of 700 grams a year. In occupied Poland, mental patients were shot.

As the German army advanced into new territory in the east, the Gestapo and the SS, the elite security force of the Nazi Party, with the help of the native population and *Einsatzgruppen*, killing squads formed by men too old or unfit to serve with fighting units, began to massacre Jews in their villages. Those not killed in the invasion of Poland were rounded up and moved into ghettos, while twenty main concentration camps and 2,000 branch camps were built in Germany and the occupied territories.

Article 19 of the Tokyo draft – so often and so passionately discussed, but never signed or ratified – had expressly forbidden deportation of civilians from occupied territories. But deportations began from all the twelve European countries occupied by the Germans by April 1941. Some civilians went to labour camps, where they were used as forced labour for the German war machine; those from the east in particular died at a rate which itself had to be made part of the design of the production process. Others were sent to transit camps where they were held until the concentration and extermination camps were ready. In all the camps, people died, from malnutrition, overwork, lack of medical care and extreme brutality. After June 1941 and the German attack on the Soviet Union, Soviet prisoners were murdered alongside Jews, gypsies, homosexuals and beggars.

At first Germany made very little effort to conceal what was going on. The detention of political opponents for so-called security reasons – *Schutzhaft* – and, after 1937, of people considered to be 'anti-social', like vagrants, homosexuals and 'marginals', had declared as one of its goals the education of German citizens. But with the *Nacht und Nebel* ('Night and Fog') decree of December 1941, a certain sense of mystery spread over the Nazi methods of repression. Suspected opponents of the Nazi regime were now secretly shipped away to concentration camps without notification so that families and communities would effectively cease to resist lest they endanger the lives of the missing. The Wannsee conference of 20 January 1942, at which Reinhard Heydrich outlined details of the Final Solution to representatives of all the relevant German authorities, was not made public, nor was the existence of the extermination camps whose aim was to realize Hitler's dream of a Third Reich 'Judenfrei', free of Jews. After the conference, deportation to Chelmno, Auschwitz-Birkenau, Belzec, Sobibor, Treblinka and Majdanek, and the killing of those sent on the 'transports', helped by the men of Aktion T-4 who were now experienced in the use of gas, was speeded up; and the first medical experiments on the prisoners in Dachau began.

How much of all this was known to the International Committee? Establishing exactly who knew what and when in which countries has become a question of endless fascination and the object of detailed research in recent years – numerous historians have sifted minutely through the archives of the allied foreign offices, those of the Vatican and of the different churches. The conclusion that seems to emerge from their work, the archives of the International Committee itself, and the memories of people active in the Red Cross during the war suggest that a very great deal was known at every stage of the war. How the Committee responded to the information, and why, is rather more complicated.

In 1939, Geneva lay at the cross roads of international life. Home to many humanitarian, non-governmental and religious organizations, from the World Council of Churches and the Jewish World Congress to the International Save the Children Fund, it was also a magnet for Germans who opposed the Nazi regime, for journalists and diplomats, and for refugees passing through on their way to America and Israel. Rosswell MacLelland, later President Roosevelt's representative on the War Refugee Board, was director of the Quaker office in the city. These groups and people in Geneva constantly received information from the occupied territories which was combined with information from its own delegates.

Nor should it be forgotten that Burckhardt, by now playing the role of foreign minister to the organization, taking over when Huber was ill, had many influential friends and contacts throughout Europe and particularly in Germany; Ernst von Weiszäcker, the German under-secretary for foreign affairs was a boyhood friend. It would later be said that Weizsäcker had known from very early on of the existence of the camps from Admiral Canaris, head of military intelligence, executed in the purge that followed the generals' plot to kill Hitler in July 1944. In December 1941, Fritz Gebhardt von Hahn, a junior official in the German Foreign Ministry, was asked to provide a statistical summary of Jewish deaths. He calculated that seventy to eighty thousand Jews had already been murdered by each unit of *Einsatzgruppe*; the report was sent to the various desks in the political section and initialled by twenty-two different people. This information was almost certainly available to Burckhardt, in part if not all. Then there were the reports sent in by the Red Cross delegates, especially from the Berlin office which had eight people by the summer of 1942, who paid visits to prisoner-of-war camps throughout Germany, Poland, France, Belgium, Holland and Norway. These delegates were, of course, forbidden to enter the concentration camps but their routes took them past the gates and fences and they heard and passed on accounts of hearing of men and women living and dying beyond the barbed wire in misery and squalor.

Marcel Junod, during his first visit to Poland in the autumn of 1939, had reported that 'between 20 October and 2 November . . . eighty-two Jews, among them thirty-six women, committed suicide.' Dr Marti, head of the delegation in Berlin, was allowed into Buchenwald, the camp in the forest above Weimar, but only to see 212 Dutch hostages and, on 14 August 1940, reported the presence of 7,000 detainees, from political prisoners and Jews to 'unsociables', and 'young people to be re-educated'. Conditions, he noted, were physically good, modern and very clean, with flower beds and 'gaily coloured' flowers, a large vegetable garden and a zoo with four bears, though he reminded Geneva that his visit had been prepared well in advance and much could have been concealed from him. Also, 'discipline is of iron and we were struck by the automatism, the rigidity and almost terror with which the smallest order is carried out. We cannot forget the stupefied and distant air of all the detainees.' Ordered to play some music, a group of detainees presented 'a poignant and unforgettable spectacle . . . steeped in profound sadness'.

There are far too many instances of knowledge of the camps circulating freely throughout Europe by early 1942 to give all but a few examples. The archives of the International Committee in Geneva are full of accounts of deportations, transports, round-ups. There was the article in the *Neue Zürcher Zeitung* of 19 February 1940 giving an eyewitness description of the deportation of 300 Jews who died of hunger and sickness on a transport out of Stettin. (The article is filed in the archives not far from a cable from Tel Aviv, asking 'whether Jewish congregation Stettin deported', to which the International Committee replied: 'Sorry unable answer such questions being outside scope of our activity.') There were reports of Jews stripped of all their belongings and put on to to trains 3,000 at a time from Berlin, bound for the east. In November 1941, René de Weck, the Swiss minister to Bucharest, wrote to Jacques Chenevière describing the atrocities to which Jews in Romania were being subjected, adding that the 'Armenian massacres which had shaken the European conscience at the beginning of the century were a mere child's play in comparison.' W. Rohner, president of the Commission Mixte, visited Hungary and Romania in March 1942. On his return, he sent a long memorandum to Burckhardt in which he referred to 'the most atrocious massacres', adding that he had been informed that in the Ukraine some 100,000 Jews had been slaughtered. There were mentions of Auschwitz, by the head of the Slovak Red Cross, Skotnicky (9 June 1942), and by a member of the French Red Cross, Colonel Garteiser (2 June 1942), who said that those deported to what he called 'Hauswitz' were never heard of again. Dr Marti reported that Dr Sethe of the German Red Cross had told him that these deportees were 'criminals' and that nothing could be done for them, and that he continued to hear news of SS units exterminating civilians in occupied Russian territories (20 May 1942). In January that year, when Marti had told Sethe that people were saying that German camps were worse than the Inquisition, Sethe had replied, 'Let them talk.'

In the late autumn of 1941, Pastor Visser't Hooft, the secretary general of the Ecumenical Council of Churches in Geneva, wrote to Huber and Burckhardt; he spoke of famine and typhus in the Warsaw ghetto and of the deportations. 'The Jewish question touches at the heart of the Christian message. If the Church fails to protect and to warn, if she fails to do all she can to bring relief, then she disobeys the Lord.' What can Huber, the devout Christian, have felt?

By the summer of 1942 the picture was becoming extremely clear. Details of the train transports and the extermination camps were now regularly reaching London, the other allied governments, the Jewish organizations, the Vatican and the United Nations via the Polish underground. The Allies themselves were proving extremely backward at acknowledging the possible truth of these reports. Nicholas Burckhardt, a distant relation of C.J. Burkhardt who was sent to London as a delegate for the International Committee early in the war, remembers giving a report on the camps to his contact in the British government. 'Day after day, I kept going back and asking what had happened to it? What was going to be done? I went on asking and asking. No one seemed very interested.' Gerhart Riegner was the young secretary of the World Jewish Congress in Geneva in 1942, and a central figure in the gathering of information. In August 1942, he believed that he had enough reliable proof of the Final Solution to convince the Allies to act. Looking back now at the files he put together day after day, Riegner says he is amazed to discover just how much material he received from Germany and the occupied territories. From his studies at the Institut Universitaire des Hautes Etudes Internationales – the meeting place of many people crucial to the International Committee – he knew Burckhardt well. At the end of August 1942, armed with a secret report about plans for the extermination of the Jews put together by a high-ranking German industrialist called Edouard Schulter, who had access to Hitler's headquarters and who had asked business contacts in Zurich to get the report to the Jewish community, Riegner went to see Burckhardt, Mlle Ferrière and Mlle Odier. He now had, he told them, irrefutable evidence of Hitler's plans to exterminate the entire Jewish population of Europe, using gas. They heard him out but said little, according to Riegner. Later he heard from Paul Guggenheim, a mutual Jewish friend from the Institut Universitaire de Hautes Etudes Internationale, that Burckhardt was already well informed about what was going on, but had chosen not to pass on what he knew to his colleagues on the Committee, though just why not continues to this day to puzzle Riegner. 'Burckhardt,' he says, 'remains one of the strangest figures in this whole affair.'

As all this information filtered through the intelligence networks, the churches, the underground and the various liberal and Jewish organizations in the allied countries, so pressure mounted for some kind of action to be taken and people turned to the International Committee for guidance. The various national Red Cross societies all wanted news, verification of the reports – and a public protest about what was going on. Their letters and telegrams, reaching Geneva day after day, became more urgent. To all of them, the International Committee replied one of two things: that it did not 'currently possess enough certain information on the fate of the Jews deported to Poland' (to the American State Department on 2 November 1942), or that it was a 'very tragic situation and we cannot do anything about it' (to the British Red Cross on 19 November 1941).

The crucial meeting of the International Committee on 14 October 1942, with which this book opens, has therefore to be seen in this light: the Committee knew, even as the Allies, the Vatican and anyone who read the European newspapers knew, that a wholesale massacre of the Jews was under way. In any case, by the autumn the State Department had its own information that Jews were being slaughtered in great numbers. In May, Jean Pictet had been put to work on a document designed to remind governments of their commitments under the Geneva Conventions, and on 16 September, Huber and Pictet had drawn up a first seven-page paper which was drafted, then redrafted. In essence, it was an appeal on behalf of the deportees, but an appeal so buried within a great web of humanitarian principles and undertakings as to be scarcely perceptible: no names were mentioned, no countries identified and no reference made to a Final Solution. At the end of September, twenty-one members of the Committee had indicated that they were in favour of some kind of public pronouncement, a fact that so impressed the upper ranks that the decision was taken to hold the plenary session of 14 October. Why then did the full Committee vote for what was effectively silence? The decision made that autumn afternoon in the Hôtel Métropole has left its shadow over much of what has happened to the organization since.

At least some of the explanation must lie in the very Swissness of the International Committee. Huber himself was the most revered and patrician of all Protestant Swiss, and his Committee was still largely Genevan and made up of cautious, careful people given to reasoned debate rather than precipitate action. In the autumn of 1942, the organization had 3,500 Swiss nationals working for it and over half – 55 per cent – of its budget of 33.5 million Swiss francs came from the federal government. Switzerland itself, as a neutral country, could not be seen to take any action that might be construed as unfriendly to Germany and the Axis powers. By 1942 it was virtually surrounded by Axis armies and countless people to this day testify to the very real fear of German invasion had the Swiss government been seen to step out ofline.

There was also the question of refugees. After the Wannsee Conference and the launch of the Final Solution, a flood of Jewish refugees began to beg for asylum at Switzerland's western borders. Nearly all were turned back; Switzerland's terror of overpopulation was fed by the head of the Swiss police, Heinrich Rothmund, who had been speaking out forcibly since the middle of the 1930s on the 'menace to our spiritual identity if too many foreigners live here'. Rothmund would later speak of his twenty-year battle against the *enjuivement* — the Jewification — of Switzerland.

Until 1937, the permeable nature of Switzerland's many frontiers and a somewhat lackadaisical attitude towards policing them had allowed a number of Jewish refugees through. The Anschluss of March 1938, however, and the German occupation of the Sudetenland, prompted the Swiss to tighten up their frontiers and to pass a series of increasingly discriminatory rules. A decision was taken to insist on a visa for all German visitors, but when Germans protested furiously that this would hamper their trips to Switzerland it was agreed that only German Jews would need a visa, their Jewish origins indicated by the letter J, printed inside a small circle, stamped in their passports. Anyone with a J would be denied entry, unless they already possessed a visa of entry into another country and a ticket to go there. With *Kristallnacht* came fresh demands to allow Jewish refugees entry into Switzerland. The federal government remained immovable, even over family reunions, making an exception only in the case of the very rich or those over the age of sixty with private means. They also increased the number of border guards. It was all, it would be argued, a matter of 'friendly anti-Semitism', not allowing so many Jews into the country that real anti-Semitism would have a chance to develop.

In the summer of 1942, Jezler, head of the Swiss Government Office for Refugees, produced a report. The Jews still inside occupied Europe, he wrote, 'have no idea from one moment to the next whether they will suddenly be deported, imprisoned as hostages, or even executed on one pretext or another'. It was likely, he warned, that there would be enormous waves of Jewish refugees begging at Switzerland's borders to be allowed entry. The debates within the Swiss government, the police and the border forces intensified. There was much talk of the 'boat being full' — a phrase used by both Jezler and Rothmund — and a decision was now taken to keep the frontiers closed. On 4 August the Swiss president Philippe Etter, personally ratified the vote. On 13 August, instructions went out to border police to accept no one but deserters, escaped prisoners, Alsatians on their way across to the Free Zone and political refugees. 'Those who flee only on account of their race,' Rothmund directed, 'the Jews for example, must not be considered political refugees.' Anyone trying to enter a second time was to be warned that they would be turned over to the German or French police. With this, the fundamental principle of political asylum — that the risk of death over-rides all other considerations — a principle long upheld by the Swiss, was effectively abandoned.

There had been public protests before in the Swiss papers and among members of the public against the harsh policies adopted towards the refugees, and the federal government was not in the mood for more. There were fears that they might reach unmanageable proportions, par-ticularly if the International Committee were seen to come out with a public appeal on behalf of the persecuted Jews. And so it was that Philippe Etter went from Berne to Geneva to attend the 14 October meeting of the International Committee in order to put the government's view that the best thing for everyone, at the moment, was silence. The small boat was already dangerously full.

Switzerland itself was therefore one reason for the Committee's silence. Another was a very real fear that a public appeal would so anger the Germans that all the work done for prisoners-of-war in Axis camps would be jeopardized. Another again was Huber's stated position that the job of the International Committee was not to denounce or judge, but to help victims in a world more and more divided ideologically and in which humanitarian principles were being lost. In 1939, Huber had said that the Committee intended to refrain from all public denuncia-tions, and that it would not carry out its own enquiries into violations of the Geneva Conventions.

A further reason, often overlooked, lay in the nature of the Inter-national Committee itself, both in its size and in the way that it was run. All through the early months of the war, the organization had grown and splintered into different sections and departments, its day-to-day running in the hands of full-time professional people while policy was made by the Committee members, who had little to do with the actual work and came together infrequently. The Villa Moynier, once an intimate club of people who knew each other well, was now full of strangers pursuing their own tasks. In the rushed early days of war, when the fighting spread far more quickly than Huber and his colleagues had imagined possible, there had been no time to do more than set up a number of separate departments to handle the different theatres of war and variety of tasks. Each had clear sounding titles but in reality there was little co-ordination between them. Neither Huber nor Burckhardt appear to have been good organizers. A revealing document from the Berlin delegation on 13 July 1942 contains complaints that reports and requests were being sent on to Geneva as into the dark and that weeks passed before answers came back. Roland Marti, who signed the report, concluded that 'we attribute these deficiencies to the lack of liaison between the secretariat and the different branches of the agency. This co-ordination body was clearly failing in its job.' It is now clear that there was remarkably poor collaboration between the side of the International Committee that dealt with relief and that dealing with information and the monitoring of the Geneva Conventions, and it was only in the late spring of 1942 that a special commission for Prisoners and Civilian internees was formed. As Jacques Chenevière wrote irritably to Huber that summer, 'Within the International Committee there is a deplorable lack of liaison, of discipline, or discipline among helpers and also certain members of the International Committee as well'. His point was that the Committee of Co-ordination, the body that should have ensured the smooth running of what is always referred to as 'La Maison,' was in fact often bypassed or left in ignorance.

Nor was any of this helped by tensions between members – Mlle Odier and Burckhardt were known not to get on very well – and by Huber's now permanent bad health. He was away for the crucial months between August and November 1942 thus missing the meeting of 14 October. And, despite its growth and the skills of its newcomers, the International Committee was, and remained, a 'club of the well-known and the amateur'. In theory, its flexibility allowed for rapid decisions; in practice it permitted rivalries to run riot and essential decisions were postponed or abandoned through failure to delegate responsibility. The result was the creation of three centres of command: the Committee, which theoretically ran the organization and made every major decision; the ordinary workers, who did not really know what was going on; and Burckhardt, who often, as the dealings with Riegner show, knew things the others did not and did not bother to inform them and who, without having a say in the day-to-day administration, sometimes took decisions of an arbitrary and personal nature.

In October, after the meeting in the Métropole, Burckhardt contacted his old friend, Professor Paul Guggenheim, a legal expert for the US Congress, and Paul Squire, the American consul in Geneva. He told the two men what he knew of the Final Solution and Hitler's plans, 'from two German sources, one foreign office, one military'. Squire apparently asked him whether he had seen the word 'extermination' used in any document and Burckhardt, according to Riegner to whom Guggenheim described the meeting, replied that the word he had seen was *Judenfrei*, and that its meaning seemed to him obvious. 'There's no question,' Burckhardt apparently said 'they are killing them.' To both these men, and to Riegner who met Burckhardt again at the end of November, he explained that the International Committee had taken a decision not to launch an appeal — hence the use of the words *non-appel* ever since to describe the whole event — on the grounds that it would jeopardize the work done for prisoners-of-war which, he reminded them, was the real job of the organization. (Interestingly, Burckhardt told the two Americans that he personally had been in favour of a public appeal, lying, so his biographer Paul Stauffer believes, because he wanted to be viewed well in America. To Riegner, he said that he had been against it, 'but the ladies spoke up for your position'.)

By November, Riegner had in fact changed his position on what the International Committee should do. Talking in 1995, he explained that in August 1942 when he had first gone to see Burckhardt,

> I really felt that nothing and no one was going to help the Jews and that the International Committee, as the only neutral organization of high moral standing, had a duty to make public the facts. But by November, things had changed. Montgomery was breaking through against Rommel, and the battle for Stalingrad proved that there was still real resistance to the Germans in Russia. My advice to Burckhardt, that day in November, was simple: when you can act, act, and don't protest. When you can't act, protest. But don't not act and not protest.

In Geneva, the decision had been taken to say nothing publicly about the deportations, but to make fresh attempts to get relief through to the concentration camps — no protest, but action — though this left a number of members and delegates far from content. Referring to the deportation of the Jews of Salonika, Schwarzenberg noted bitterly, 'Sadly, we have no way of preventing these deportations, or rather the Committee does not wish to make a fuss over this matter.' Attempts to put pressure on the German Red Cross continued, with countless letters travelling between Geneva and Berlin reminding the Germans of their obligations and hinting that the principle of 'reciprocity' might lead to reprisals against German internees in Allied hands. They came to nothing. Relations between the German Red Cross and the International Committee deteriorated still further after a terse letter from Berlin dated 20 August 1942 saying that they were unable to obtain any information about 'non-Aryans'. 'The German Red Cross therefore asks that no further questions should be addressed to them either regarding procedure or places of detention . . . in order to spare all the officers involved unnecessary work.'

And yet Burckhardt's words to Squire and Guggenheim were not without outcome. All through the autumn of 1942 pressure mounted on the Allies to make some sort of statement about what was happening in Germany, and Riegner would later say that Burckhardt's confirmation of his own reports about the extermination camps was influential in overcoming enormous American reluctance to believe in the truth of what they were hearing. Together with the mounting evidence from all sides, and in particular the eye-witness description of the extermination camp of Belzec brought to London in November 1942 by a Polish courier, Jan Karski, Burckhardt's statements carried weight. Early in December the State Department in Washington published figures indicating that the number of Jews deported or perished since 1939 in Axis-controlled Europe stood at two million, and that five million more were in danger of extermination. As if to confirm their words, Dr Ley, the German labour minister, speaking to armaments workers at Essen, declared that it was the Nazi intention to 'go on waging this war until the Jews have been wiped off the face of this earth'.

On 17 December 1942, the Allies signed a joint denunciation of the 'bestial policy of cold-blooded extermination directed mainly against the Jews' being carried out by Germany. It concealed none of the facts.

In Poland, which has been made the principal Nazi slaughter-house, the ghettos established by the German invaders are being systematically emptied ... None of those taken away are ever heard of again ... The infirm are left to die of exposure and starvation or are deliberately massacred in mass executions. The number of victims of these bloody cruelties is reckoned in many hundreds of thousands of entirely innocent men, women and children.

When Anthony Eden, as foreign secretary, finished his statement to the House of Commons in London, the whole chamber rose and stood in silence. Amongst the Allies and in Geneva there were ever more agitated discussions about what could – and should – be done.

Of all the countries under German occupation, Poland was perhaps the most comprehensively and devastatingly crushed: by the time the war was over, 6,028,000 of its people, Catholic Poles as well as Jews, had been murdered in concentration and extermination camps; hundreds of thousands more were tortured to death in Gestapo prisons; half a million Jews had lost their lives in the ghettos; 2,487,000 Poles had been deported as forced labour to the Reich, many never to return. One million eight hundred thousand of the dead were children; nearly a million Soviet prisoners-of-war had also perished on Polish soil. Until the very end there was extremely little that the International Committee was able to do for any of them. But even in the face of such horror, Poland under the Nazis provides another example of Dunant's dream, a case in which a few individuals, in the name of the Red Cross but not for the most part members of the organization, used the emblem as a symbol of authority and were able to do things that no one else could.

In 1939, Poland had a very active national Red Cross society. Over a million and a half members gave support, money and time to a series of hospitals, first aid courses, medical centres, asylums and blood donation programmes. Warsaw had a nursing school where trainees learned to fly and parachute before graduating. That summer, anticipating trouble, the society called for volunteers for basic training: from dawn, the streets around its headquarters in Warsaw were filled with people queuing to put themselves forward. When the Germans invaded, some of the more prominent leaders accompanied the Polish government into exile in Paris and then London to avoid arrest. In Warsaw, the former treasurer, Waclaw Lachert, a scrupulous and upright man, became acting president and embarked on a long war of attrition with the German authorities, seeking to preserve, in a way that the German Red Cross society never had, a certain autonomy. Though all Polish Red Cross medical supplies were soon seized by the German forces and German officers were appointed to oversee any activities run from its headquarters, Lachert kept links open with the underground and consistently refused to be bullied by German commands or to allow the Polish society to be subsumed by the German Red Cross. When challenged, he quoted the Geneva Conventions. Eugeniusz Sztomberek, a slight, wiry man in his seventies who joined the Polish Red Cross in the summer of 1939 at the age of eighteen, remembers Lachert as a man 'who would not lend what the Germans were doing any legitimacy'; offered a visit to what he dismissed as an 'exemplary' concentration camp at Murna, he replied only that he preferred to see Dachau or Auschwitz. (His request was treated no more sympathetically than those made by the International Committee.)

With the planning of the German invasion of the Soviet Union, everything changed. 'The Polish Red Cross,' announced Hans Frank, the German governor of occupied Poland, soon after his arrival, 'remains a symbol of independence, and we do not intend to tolerate it.' Dozens of Red Cross workers were arrested, among them Maria Borinowska, the head of the information department in Warsaw, and though no one was ever told why she was taken first to Berlin and then to Ravensbrück, it was seen as a warning not to meddle in German affairs for she had been destroying the files of people she suspected were vulnerable to Nazi arrest. On the third day of the Warsaw uprising in July 1944, the Polish Red Cross headquarters were set on fire by the Germans and those inside taken away. All Polish Red Cross activities were put in the hands of the RGO, *Rada Glowna Opiekuncza*, the General Welfare Council, an organization run by the Germans to carry out many of the same functions. Into it, however, crept many former Red Cross members, and if certain parts of the country now slipped entirely under German domination, others remained remarkably independent, and it was here that former Red Cross people were able to act.

The district of Zamość is in the east of Poland, along the modern border with the Ukraine. At its northern end where Lublin, the regional capital, lies is a landscape of farms, with black soil, excellent for wheat and sugar beet; in the south, the earth is sandy, with immense forests that stretch away into the distance, crossed by long, straight, dirt roads, with occasional villages scarcely touched by modern times. The town of Zamość was built in the sixteenth century by an Italian called Bernardo Morando, who modelled it on his native city of Padua.

Himmler came to Zamość in 1940. He liked it so much that he wanted its name changed to Himmlerstadt. A third of the local people were Jewish; by November 1942, the Jews had disappeared, rounded up by the SS and police commandos, some massacred in their villages, others sent off to Auschwitz and Majdanek, the concentration camp built in the eastern suburbs of Lublin. That winter the SS, bringing with them Ukrainian killers to whom they had promised land, came back for the Poles. The area had been designated for resettlement for Germans from Poznań, the authorities having found an excellent legal pretext in the fact that there had been German settlers in Zamość since the middle of the nineteenth century. Future plans included colonization by settlers from Bessarabia, Serbia and even the Baltic states, with a view to creating a bastion of the Third Reich in the east. A first experiment, a trial run to test the logistics of the enterprise, had convinced the Germans that the best way to do it was to surround each village with tanks and troops before dawn, order the villagers to congregate by 11 a.m. in the village square with no more than ten kilograms of personal belongings each, then start bringing in the Germans settlers at noon, giving them the time to occupy their new homes by nightfall. Arriving with no luggage, the settlers found homes, furniture, food, livestock, crops waiting for them. The beds were still unmade from the previous night. From the village squares, the Polish families listened as the soldiers went into their houses, shooting those too old or infirm to leave their beds, and searching for any who might have tried to hide in cellars or down wells.

When the whole village had been assembled, the Germans ordered them to start walking in the direction of the nearest station, down the long sandy roads between the trees. In the reception camp of Zamość, lines of barracks surrounded by barbed wire, they were told to undress so that they could be properly examined: weight, teeth, hair, muscle tone all measured, noted and recorded. The fit were sent one way, for eventual deportation to slave labour in Germany (after 1943, the criterion stretched to include fit and strong ten-year-olds); the sickly and old another, to what the Germans called 'rest camps'. For the children, the inspection was particularly thorough; those who passed an Aryan test − those whose hair was blond and eyes were blue − were gathered together for the 'Germanization' programme. Of the 110,000 Poles thrown out of their homes by the resettlement programme in Zamość, 35,000 were children. In 1945, just 10,000 came home. Six hundred, when found to be very small for their age, are believed to have been sent immediately to the gas chambers. Babies were the first to die.

In 1991, nearly fifty years later, these children, the ones who survived Nazi labour or were able to recover their Polish identities − who had met over the years from time to time but surreptitiously, afraid of the consequences of too much history in Soviet-dominated post-war Poland − came together to form an association. They were growing old and wanted some way to mark the past. Membership was reserved to all those who had been taken away before their fourteenth birthday. As news of the group spread, more and more of Zamość's survivors came forward. Today they meet formally to discuss the past and talk about how to make the young recognize and remember what happened. In the villages along the forest, they have erected monuments to the dead, crosses of white marble in clearings in the trees, as well as in the meadows where Poles and Jews were shot down.

Each has a story to tell, a whole family massacred, a brother disappeared, three sisters dead of typhus in the camps, aunts, fathers, mothers, picked up and never seen again. Outside the village of Bulginai, where the Gestapo had its headquarters in a small pink stucco house, there is a cross at the top of a flight of steep stone steps in an opening in the forest. It was here that sixty-three local men, arrested as partisans, were tied up in groups of four with barbed wire, herded into the forest and shot with machine guns. One man survived. He lived to tell those who came home later from the camps how one woman, an eighteen-year-old girl who worked for the underground and was arrested with the men, was so badly tortured that she tried to commit suicide by jumping from the window of the pink stucco house. She didn't die. The Gestapo tied her to a horse and drove it from village to village, along the dirt roads, to show what happened to people who resisted.

Bolesław Szymanik, one of the founders of the association, was five when the Nazis arrived for the Jews. He watched them being herded to the little cemetery outside Tarnogród where he lives today; the cemetery stands on a slope, up a hill between a row of trees, and is now a memorial to the dead. His uncle told him later what happened next. 'Deep pits, like trenches, had been dug. The Jews were put into groups and as each group came up they were ordered to take their clothes off. On one side of the trench they put the adults; on the other the children. They wanted the parents to see their children die.' He points to an uneven mound in the grass.

> Twelve hundred were shot that first day. Before they stopped for lunch, the Germans shot each Jew in the forehead with a pistol. By the time lunch was over, they were bored. So in the afternoon they put two machine guns in front of the trenches and shot the Jews in waves. The corpses of those who escaped were brought here later, after they had been hunted down with dogs. My uncle had to help carry the bodies. This is my first memory.

Tarnogot, overnight, became a silent village; 3,500 of its 5,300 inhabitants had been Jews.

During the night of 30 June 1943, Tarnogot was again surrounded by German troops. The resettlement phase was now underway. At dawn, the villagers were herded into the main square. 'It was a hot summer,' says Szymanik,

> but that day it rained hard. The day before, hearing of the approaching Germans, my mother had baked bread. She gave a loaf to me and a loaf to my sister and made us wear warm clothes. We walked thirty kilometres through the forest to the railway. The transit camp at Zamość was full, so we were sent to Majdanek. We were lucky. We were selected to go as labourers to a farmer in Bavaria. There were already three other Polish families there, a French woman and two politically suspect German families. The farmer was unusually cruel, a retired army officer from the first war, but we were all alive when the British arrived.

Bolesław Szymanik has no memory of any Red Cross contact or intervention. The International Committee meant nothing to him, beyond the work done for compensation for the Poles after the war. But the story of Zamość shows just what could, and could not, be done in the name of the Red Cross. Most of the others who returned and who now take part in association meetings have odd incidents to relate, pictures that stick in their minds of red crosses pinned on to white dresses, or hearing the words 'red cross' pronounced.

Marianna Blazynska comes from Aleksandrów, the longest village in Zamość. Small houses and barns, with long gaps between them, line fourteen kilometres of dusty track. She was ten years old and in the fields looking after the cows, when German soldiers appeared. Her eighteen-year-old sister escaped by hiding down a well that had been prepared months before, but with her parents and seven-year-old brother Marianna was taken by train to Majdanek.

> Every day we were called out to be counted. I remember a small boy leaving his row to pick something up. A guard in one of the towers shot him dead. If anyone did anything wrong, he was hanged. The man who carried out the executions wore red trousers and we were made to watch: long after the war I went on associating the colour red with death. My aunt had a nine-month-old baby. She died and my father was told to take the baby to be counted. Then he was ordered to throw it into the furnace.
>
> We were always hungry. One day, because we were strong and fit, we were taken from Majdanek to a transit camp nearby. The Polish Red Cross had managed to put people there. They gave my mother a large piece of bread and a pot of marmalade. Because we were starving it made us sick. That was what the Red Cross wanted, to make us so sick the Germans couldn't put us on the trains. It saved our lives. We never went.

She remembers people with Red Cross badges walking up and down outside the fence, throwing food over the wire. Permitted deliveries of medical supplies – what the Germans referred to as 'goodwill gestures' – became the pretext for sending in food. Records show that over the next few years the Lublin Red Cross managed to get vaccines, straw, cigarettes, shoes, spoons and blankets into the local camps. Ludwik Christians, chairman of the Lublin district, is remembered as one of the men with courage mentioned by Eugeniusz Sztomberek, who fought against German insistence that the camps, and particularly their Jewish inmates, were totally outside his jurisdiction.

Majdanek, which in time became a death camp and where common cruelty and sadism were replaced by systematic shootings and gassings, was one of the camps in which members of the Polish Red Cross and other voluntary groups were most active. Never formally accepted, they hovered on its fringes, searching for ways of getting food past the more humane guards, of carrying in the occasional cauldron of soup and bringing back with them information and lists later transmitted to families and to the underground. Jan Mwoczek was nine when he and his grandmother, together with a sister of six and a brother of a year and a half, were sent to Majdanek, his parents having been selected for deportation to forced labour. He has a memory of an occasion that does not appear in the archives in Geneva.

> There were rumours that a delegate of the International Com-
> mittee was coming. The camp was overflowing and filthy with
> a fresh arrival of Soviet prisoners-of-war. Some of these were
> murdered. Some of the Poles were sent away to other camps.
> Speakers were nailed to the trees so that music could be played.
> The roads were patched up, and the pavements cleaned and
> painted. The grass was cut. This is what I remember. I don't
> know if a delegate came.

There is no corresponding record in Geneva, where the files on the Polish camps are thin; as for the Polish Red Cross headquarters in Warsaw, their wartime archives were lost.

Zamość became the centre for one of the most extraordinary of all Nazi experiments; the Germanizing of foreign children to increase the dwindling master race. Based on pseudo-scientific theories about racial purity and the popular myth that the Aryan race, descended from an ancient Teutonic kingdom, was superior to all others, it held that the Germans had a duty to produce a purified people through extermination on the one hand and planned breeding on the other. Himmler, who was made Reich Commander for the Strengthening of German Folkdom in 1939, sincerely believed that it should be possible to eliminate all traces of impure blood within a few generations, and spoke in 1940 of creating an 'order of good blood that can save Germany', and 'so spread the idea that we shall attract to us all the Nordic blood in the world.' What Himmler had in mind, heeding the teachings of the party theorist, Hans Günther, was a 'tall, long head, narrow face, well defined chin, narrow nose with very high root, soft-fair hair (golden blond), receding light (blue or grey) eyes, pink-white colour'.

What he did *not* want was spelt out in a pamphlet, of which nearly four million copies were printed in German alone. He called these others 'sub-humans', 'completely different, dreadful' creatures, 'only a rough copy of a human being, with human-like facial traits but nonetheless morally and mentally lower than any animal'. Racial 'usefulness' was drawn up to include eleven racial types and two categories, positive and negative, and sixty-two specific points, from size and shape of eyes to colour of hair. A child's expression, seen as a particularly good guide to character, was given points for bearing a 'calm and frank look'. Much, thought Himmler, could be achieved by breeding and to this end a whole movement, extolling mothers and rewarding high birth rates, was put into effect in Germany. When Aryan children could not be bred, they would have to be stolen. The tracing of these missing kidnapped children from the occupied territories – said to be 200,000 in Poland alone – would pose the International Committee with one of its hardest and most poignant post-war challenges.

With the conquest of Denmark and Norway, Himmler found wonderful potential in the fair, blue-eyed Scandinavian children. In Poland, it was not quite so easy, but directives soon went out to the SS and their 'Brown Sisters', Nazi welfare workers recognizable by their brown habit-like long gowns, to start looking for children aged between two and six 'capable of Germanization'. Those from the resettlement programme of the eastern provinces were to be known as 'German orphans from the regained eastern territories', transported to the Reich, given new names and birthdays, forbidden to speak Polish, forced to join the Hitler Youth and march and sing, for marching, as one document put it, 'kills thought and destroys individuality'. No one, today, knows precisely how many of the 30,000 or so children taken to Zamość's reception centre were sent for Germanization, but the Association believes that the figure is probably around 4,500. Virtually none came back.

For the children, whatever their fate, the selection process was terrifying. Separated from the adults, they were held in dark, cramped barracks. Marianna Margol, who is now a Felician nun, remembers the noise, the constant sound of crying. It reminds her now of Old Testament stories. 'The children whose mothers had given them bowls,' she says, 'had soup. The others grew hungrier and hungrier. The crying went on all night and all day, the children calling for their parents.'

The village of Rozanec lies in rich farming country. It is a charming and peaceful place, with tall trees shading ponds on which ducks and geese swim. The farmhouses are trim, their barns ancient and made of wood. Rozanec does not seem to have been touched by the twentieth century.

There had been several round-ups for the resettlement programme before the Germans arrived, early in 1943, and set light to part of the village. A dozen houses burned and people trying to hide were smoked out of cellars and haylofts. Maria Katarzyna, a smiling woman in her late fifties with curly hair and the neat clean clothes of a farmer's wife, was only nine when she was taken away for racial selection. 'There were seven of us, told to stand in a line, naked. The man doing the measuring seemed to become interested in me. He said: "She is small but nice." He told an assistant to shave my head so that he could measure it properly. He opened my mouth, looked at my teeth and eyes. I wasn't taken in the end for Germanization, because they decided that I would do better as a worker and sent me to a farm in Germany.' Her neighbour in Rozanec, another farmer's wife, is Helena Pelc. She was ten in 1942, the youngest in a large family taken before the selection board. She too remembers the way that they were told to stand naked in a line while men in uniforms and white coats prodded and measured. 'Though I was a child, I could sense they didn't think much of us as human beings. I felt we were goods.' By the time the Pelc family's inspection came round they had already spent many weeks in a transit camp. The adults, who had given their food to the children, were starving. Helena remembers the horror of losing her mother in the crowd. 'When I looked round, there was this row of naked women. They looked like skeletons. Without her clothes, I couldn't see which one was my mother.' Only one woman from Rozanec was eventually chosen for Germanization. She is now seventy and returned to the village after the war. Helena, and the other survivors, sound a little scornful when they describe her. 'She follows us around saying "It wasn't my fault." We know she never committed a crime towards us, but she feels guilty.' They talk of other children, taken at the same time, who have never returned. 'We think they are Germans now.' So effective was Himmler's Germanization programme that many of the stolen children grew up unaware of their Polish origins.

Zamość had another, smaller, transit camp, Zwierzyniec, in a pretty village in the forest with wooden houses overlooking a lake. Built by forced labour, it became a camp for Poles, Russians and Jews destined for Majdanek. Zwierzyniec was the seat of an ancient Polish family called Zamoyski. After the RGO was set up in Warsaw, Count Zamoyski was asked by the Germans to be the president for the Zamość area, and his wife president of her local branch. It suited their plans perfectly. They hatched a plan to save children, and since they had no other emblem to work under, they used a red cross.

There had been an orphanage in Zwierzyniec for many years. As the resettlement programme began to empty the area of Poles, Count Zamoyski approached the German authorities, with whom he took pains to remain on excellent terms, and suggested that he might be able to take some of the surplus children and keep them in the orphanage, since the camp was collapsing under the rising number of detainees. The Germans, at first doubtful, agreed, telling him that it would be up to him to sell the scheme to the families held in the camp.

Wanda Cebrykow is now in her eighties and almost blind, living alone in a dark, musty house on the edge of the woods. In 1942 she was a kindergarten teacher when the count asked her to run a new, enlarged orphanage. 'On 25 July 1943 we heard that among the most recent arrivals to the camp were four hundred small children.' The count went to see the commandant while she waited outside with carts. 'He was,' she says,

> in a very difficult position. How could he convince parents to
> part with their children, without telling them what was about

to happen to them? The Germans were listening carefully. He went into the camp and starting speaking. No one said anything. Then two local women among the prisoners recognized him, and they whispered to the others that he was a good man. First one woman handed over her child; then another. We started taking them away in horse-drawn carts, and soon we had nearly four hundred of them. They were desolate, crying for their parents. Neighbours started arriving with food, medicines, clothes. There was no room for beds so we spread straw all over the floor and covered it with blankets. For the first few days they never slept, just cried all the time.

News of what was happening spread far from Zwierzyniec. A secret 'Save the children of Zamość' campaign was started, as the trains carrying the Polish children towards the German frontier set out. The Polish Red Cross was drawn in, sending people to the main stations through which the trains passed to see whether they could give the children food or even grab some of them and make off into the forest. All along the tracks in the forest, says Wanda, as the trains travelled slowly north, people came and stood by the line offering to buy the children from the guards. No one kept records, but dozens, perhaps hundreds, of Zamość's children were saved from Germanization, forced labour or the extermination camps in this way.

Towards the end of June 1945, the German settlers packed their belongings on to carts and set off back towards the west. Zamość was liberated by the Russians on 26 July. The Poles who had survived returned to find their barns and houses burnt down, their livestock eaten, their possessions looted. The cats and dogs they had left behind had gone wild; the fields had been abandoned and their gardens were full of weeds.

At the beginning of April 1943, the German authorities in Warsaw summoned Waclaw Lachert. They told him that mass graves had been found in the forest of Katyn, ten miles west of Smolensk, in territory formerly under the Soviets and now occupied by German troops. The order had come from Germany for the Polish Red Cross, alongside an international commission of scholars and specialists in forensic medicine, to take charge of exhumations. President Lachert hesitated, seeing in the order a ploy that could later be used to German advantage, but eventually a team of Polish Red Cross doctors and volunteers set off for Katyń and the digging began. It lasted five weeks. The task was overwhelming. Together with the bodies of what they estimated to be 4,000 men, all of fighting age, they found identity tags, photographs, letters and diaries. In one, the last entry read: 'We have seen pits being dug in the forest. They are probably for us.' The skeletal remains were dressed in high leather boots, with leather belts across what had been their chests, many with medals; they had been gagged and blinded by greatcoats tied round their necks. Many showed signs of struggle and the bodies of the cadets and younger men in particular had their arms tied behind their backs. Two were generals. With the military officers were lawyers, teachers, doctors, journalists and a priest. These corpses confirmed rumours that had long been haunting the Polish Red Cross headquarters in Warsaw ever since the families of 15,000 men held in Soviet camps in Kozelsk, Ostashkov and Starobelsk had reported a sudden halt to all communications with the men in the spring of 1940. All enquiries by the Polish Red Cross, the International Committee in Geneva, and by the various allied forces, had yielded no answers.

For the Germans, eager to rouse Polish anger against the Russians, the find was opportune. Lachert was ordered to issue a statement confirming that the Soviets had been responsible for the killings. There was little doubt in his mind that this was so, since the doctors and forensic specialists had been able to establish that death had occurred in the spring of 1940 when the area was still in Soviet hands. But he refused, unwilling to provide ammunition for the Germans against a country that was by now an ally; he quoted the Geneva Conventions, which stipulated that to issue the kind of statement about guilt that they demanded he would need two independent witnesses to each murder. To allay the painful uncertainty of the families, Lachert agreed only to issue death certificates, certifying that on some unknown date, the men had died in the forest of Katyń. The International Committee, asked by the Germans to send someone to Katyń, took the same line, falling back on the fact that not all those involved in the incident – meaning the Russians – were party to inviting their collaboration. The Germans were furious, but there was little they could do. A few weeks later, a member of the Polish Red Cross team, a former Polish officer himself, was shot dead in a Warsaw street. The Germans now offered Lachert the proceeds from the sale of a book of gruesome photographs taken at Katyń; he refused.

The dead of Katyń's forests would remain officially mysterious for many years. After the war, the Polish Red Cross made considerable efforts to identify those responsible. All requests for information on individual missing officers came back with the same reply: 'Not found in the Soviet Union.' It was not until the early summer of 1991 that a Polish and Russian team of public prosecutors joined forces to oversee further exhumations. For two weeks, diggings took place. Because of the chemical composition of the soil in one of the areas chosen, bodies of the missing Polish officers came out of the ground almost perfectly preserved.

Full details of Katyń have only recently become clear: how Germany and the Soviet government had planned the dismemberment of Poland. Evidence suggests that the Soviets took up to a quarter of a million Polish prisoners of war, including the 8,400 officers who were amongst the 15,000 murdered in the forest. The killers were Russian; the bullets turned out to be German.

For Eugeniusz Sztomberek, the fate of the Polish officers while the war was still on became eclipsed by his own experiences. After almost five years in what remained of the Polish Red Cross headquarters in Warsaw, pursuing a shadowy life as messenger, issuer of Red Cross identity cards to volunteers so that they could avoid deportation to labour camps, clerk in the token information office and organizer of the 'Godmothers', the women who sent food parcels to men they had adopted in the prisoner-of-war camps, he was arrested in February 1944 and taken to the Gestapo headquarters. Interrogated and tortured for three days, he was accused of belonging to the resistance: a neighbour had informed the Germans that he held strange gatherings in his flat. For the remaining fifteen months of the war, Sztomberek survived four concentration camps — Gross-Rosen, Sachsenhausen, Oranienberg and Buchenwald. 'By 25 August 1945, I was back in my old office in Warsaw. The Polish Red Cross had nothing to reproach itself for the war years. Directly and indirectly, helped by Lachert's clarity and the courage of now forgotten individuals, it did a great deal of good.'

*　　*　　*

By the spring of 1944, Hungary was the only country occupied by the Germans where the Jews were still free. The pre-war anti-Semitism of Admiral Horthy's increasingly fascist regime had given way in the early years of the war to a series of ever more restrictive edicts, including the deportation of 20,000 Jews without Hungarian nationality to the Ukraine; but for the most part, Jews benefiting from Horthy's ambivalence were still living in their own houses and working, though some of the professions were closed to them. Hungary became the country where a number of people and institutions – among them the Catholic, Protestant and Baptist churches, the foreign missions and, in its own way, the International Committee – behaved with a degree of imagination and courage towards the Jews, helped by the fact that the Russian army was advancing, the war was clearly drawing to a close, and Hungarians and Germans alike were becoming anxious about post-war accountability.

In an almost spontaneous movement of protection, a handful of men and women put into play a bold, at times even inspired, series of measures, encouraging each other to ever more audacious gestures. Some at least paid off with the result that Hungary which, after Poland, had the highest proportion of Jews among its people, lost fewest to the Nazis. And part of this salvage operation was due to the efforts first of a mild and agitated man called Jean de Bavier, and after him of Friedrich Born, one of the International Committee's more independent-minded delegates, a figure in the Brown and Junod mould. Born would not have much of a career with the International Committee, but for the few months that he acted as their delegate in Budapest he was able to prove Junod's point that more could often be achieved by the men in the field than by all the articles of the Geneva Conventions. The story of the Red Cross and the Jews of Hungary – when looked at beside Huber's paralysing caution, Burckhardt's realpolitik, Switzerland's obsessive terrors about neutrality and the curious way in which delegates, even when disagreed with, were given their head – does not put the International Committee in a particularly good light. But it is the best light in which we see them in their conduct towards the Jews during the Second World War.

In 1941, having regained through his alliance with Hitler and Mussolini parts of Hungary's territories that had gone to Czechoslovakia and Romania, Admiral Horthy entered the war as an ally of the Third Reich.

That year, waves of Jews fleeing Bukovina, Slovakia and Poland sought safety within Hungarian borders and Mary Dobransky, a member of the Hungarian Red Cross, travelled to Geneva to draw Huber's attention to the refugees being deported in appalling circumstances and to almost certain death. It was one of the Hungarian society's last moves, before being silenced. Huber was wary; it was a question, as always, of whether or not it was permissible to interfere in the internal affairs of a nation. And the resources of the International Committee, he pointed out, were already being stretched very thin. Suzanne Ferrière, constant crusader on behalf of civilians, was able to convince the Committee that something could be done through the Commission Mixte and, after a journey through the region in the spring of 1943, Chapuisat and de Traz recommended sending a delegate to Budapest. (Only one sentence in their report touched on the Jews: 'Some of the Hungarian Jews,' they wrote, 'have been taken from the towns to work out in the country, where they are well treated.') They chose de Bavier, the fifty-one-year-old brother of the Swiss chargé d'affaires in Athens and a businessman from Vevey, who had been helpful to the Committee during an earthquake in Japan many years before.

The International Committee's reputation in Hungary stood high, Haccius and Burnier having left good memories of impartiality and determination during the White Terror of 1923. De Bavier and his wife reached Budapest at the end of October 1943 and were pleasantly received by Miklós Kállay, president of the council, who advised them to wait until the winter, when the ice had formed, to make their trips since the roads were so appalling. Having been briefed by a number of Jewish organizations in Geneva, de Bavier set out to visit camps and move among the Jewish community. It was soon apparent to him that worse trouble was on the way, but that the Hungarians themselves were still open to negotiations over the emigration of their Jewish citizens. But Geneva, often slow to respond to suggestions, appeared deaf to all his letters. When answers did come, they were evasive.

One of the main dangers for the Jews in Hungary was the speed and ease with which official policy towards them shifted. De Bavier had been right to be apprehensive. On 19 March 1944, Germany invaded Hungary and installed a puppet government under the pro-Nazi General Döme Sztójay. Horthy remained regent. De Bavier now deluged Geneva with his fears for Hungary's 800,000 Jews. 'It is most disappointing not to be able to help the very large numbers of people who appeal to your delegate for aid,' he wrote on 15 April. On the 22nd he wrote again, 'I am continually being asked to take under your protection Jews . . . Their plight is tragic . . . Almost all possibilities of working have been withdrawn so when they have nothing left to live on they will be in utter poverty.' On 23 May came another letter: '. . . a tremendous duty stands plain: to save the lives of the Jewish children.' Huber temporized. Those of Hungarian nationality, he reminded his fretting delegate, were under the protection of their own government; for those of other nationalities, 'Race is subordinate to nationality, and they must be considered as civilian internees' – a poignant and ironic rejoinder, given what had already happened to civilian internees elsewhere. Close behind the invaders came Adolf Eichmann with his special forces, *Einsatzgruppen*, eager to use their now practised methods as wholesale executioners on what was still virgin territory. Appalled as he was by the Germans, de Bavier was now horrified to discover that the Nazi plans met with almost no opposition: 'the number of denunciations made among the Hungarians themselves,' he wrote to Geneva, 'astonished even the Germans, who said they had experienced nothing like it in any other country.'

De Bavier spoke no German. How much this weighed in the decision to replace him – his outcries were clearly not popular in Geneva – is not known, but on 24 March he was recalled to Switzerland. He had worked hard on behalf of the Jews: written a long report on their treatment at the hands of the Hungarian authorities, visited camps of internees, and even caused some forms of harsh treatment to be modified. Later it would be said that the International Committee had found him too extravagant (he had in fact paid for much of his work on behalf of the Jews out of his own pocket), that he was a fantasist and that his 'man-about-town' manner, appropriate enough for the gregarious Hungarians, did not go down well with the Germans. De Bavier's parting plea was a cable suggesting that Huber should personally contact Hitler to see whether some agreement over the Jews could not be reached. It was met with governessy firmness. De Bavier was instructed to 'desist . . . from taking any action and to maintain an attitude of the greatest reticence' and to leave Budapest 'without saying goodbye'. In fact, he stayed until May, working furiously to find ways of protecting the Jews, despairing at the high number of Jewish suicides and trying without success to trace Jews already snatched into Nazi hands. His last letters to the International Committee have a truly forsaken note. 'Surely,' he asked, 'an urgent solution is needed?' The Jews, he added a week later, were feeling 'that your protection would be a means of salvation'. Arieh Ben-Tov, author of a book on the Hungarian Jews and the Red Cross, would write admiringly of de Bavier as an excellent delegate 'and human being'. To recall him to Geneva at this stage was, he suggested, 'like recalling a fireman when a fire breaks out'. Huber wrote to Harrison, the US minister in Berne, clearly trying to divert rising antagonism at International Committee dilatoriness and obfuscation, that everything was being done to help 'wholeheartedly . . . all categories of war victims'.

The new International Committee fireman was no less bold than de Bavier and, as matters for the Jews entered a new and terrifying phase, just as determined to act. In 1944, Friedrich Born was in his early forties, a square, stocky, round-faced man with straight, receding hair and mild, protruding eyes; he spoke some Hungarian from four years working in textiles in Hungary before the war, as well as German and French, and he was a keen hunter, who had made good friends among Hungarian aristocratic families. These were to serve him well. Born also had contacts among the many Swiss who lived in Hungary and had been president of the lively Swiss Hungarian Chamber of Commerce; and he loved, says Géza Kiss, a young Hungarian reserve officer who drove for him during the war, to drink very cold champagne. While de Bavier now returned to Geneva to report at length and in detail on the trains with their 'up-to-date installations for putting people to death', on the taking of Jewish hostages, the requisition of Jewish homes and the setting up of ghettos, Born examined his position.

It was not an easy one. Eichmann had come to Hungary with clear orders and he set about them with customary relish at his headquarters, in Habsburg-style luxury, in the Hotel Majestic. The Jews were to be liquidated, beginning with those in the provinces furthest from Budapest, leaving those in the capital until last. Horthy, whose anti-Semitic plans for the Jews had not included extermination, was coerced into accepting that many were needed in Germany to fill the gaps in the labour force and into agreeing that it was foolish to leave them in the border areas. By the middle of April, Veesenmayer, Hitler's ambassador and plenipotentiary in Budapest, was able to report that the deportation of Jews from Transylvania and Carpatho-Russia was proceeding at an efficient rate and that they were being driven to the synagogues in villages and towns to give up their valuables, while trains loaded with furniture marked 'Gifts from the Hungarian nation to Germans bombed out of their homes' were ready to leave for the Reich. On 24 April 1944, the first transport of Hungarian Jews left for Austria.

Through a letter intercepted in error, the Swiss Federal government delegate on matters of international relief, Edouard de Haller learned details of the German plans for the Hungarian Jews. He sent them to Huber. 'It would seem,' he wrote on 6 June, that '170,000 of them have been deported to Auschwitz ... while 130,000 are being deported now ... Hungary is to be entirely disencumbered of Jews by the end of June.' (De Haller, whose brother-in-law was Pierre Bonna, head of the foreign affairs division of the Departement Politique, was also a crucial wartime member of the Committee.) Born, writing to confirm these rumours, described sealed cattle wagons carrying the Jews north and west by rail, plans to congregate all Jews in ghettos and concentration camps, and raids on Jewish homes. 'The idea of looking on impotent and without weapons at these dreadful events,' he wrote, 'is almost intolerable.' In Geneva, the reaction was muted: relief, not protest − Riegner's 'action' − had become the order of the day and, apart from urging Born to be discreet a letter went to him on 10 June asking whether he couldn't 'make personal representations to the Hungarian government, with a view to achieving a gentler execution of the said laws'. If Born replied, his answer does not seem to have survived.

Events now began to move at a quicker pace. The Russians were drawing closer, and it was obvious to everyone that when they reached Budapest they were likely to settle scores. One of the most famous of the accounts of what was happening to Jews in German occupied territory, the report carried from Auschwitz by Rudolf Wrba in April, had included mention that the camp authorities were making preparations to exterminate a million Hungarian Jews. The Allies and the churches now stirred. Public announcements were made; appeals went out; within the space of eighteen days, reports of what was happening appeared in newspapers throughout the world. On 25 June the Pope sent an open letter to Horthy, appealing to his 'noble feelings' to do all that he could to save 'many unfortunate people from further pain and sorrow'. On the 26th, President Roosevelt wrote to say that he would hold Horthy personally responsible for further Jewish massacres: 'I rely,' he added, 'not only on humanity, but also upon the force of weapons.' On the 30th, King Gustav of Sweden added his own personal appeal. The BBC broadcast a warning that 'every day the Red Army gets nearer to the heart of Hungary and retaliation will be certain'. Since May, according to a report by Veesenmayer, 437,402 Jews had been deported on 148 trains. At last, a reply came from Horthy: the deportations would stop. (Eichmann's reaction is said to have been one of fury: 'Such a thing has never happened to me before . . . It cannot be tolerated.')

Only at this point did the International Committee speak. On 7 July, Huber wrote to Horthy. Pressure had been mounting in Switzerland and an open letter to the Swiss government calling on the world to save Hungary's Jews had been signed by half a million Swiss citizens, while Professor Guggenheim, Burckhardt's old friend, informed him that there was considerable dissatisfaction among the Allies with the Committee's failure to speak out. Huber now invited Horthy to discuss emigration for Hungary's Jews in return for financial rewards for Hungary. The experienced Robert Schirmer, delegate from the Berlin office, was sent to Budapest bearing a handwritten personal letter to Horthy. Whilst the Americans went on stressing that everything had to be done to, 'keep the fires burning under these old gentlement in the Hotel Métropole', discussions went ahead on taking relief to the Jewish population, suspending the transports for ever, evacuating all Jewish children with visas and arranging for Jews with visas for Palestine to leave. On 18 July, the International Committee put out a formal statement that the Hungarians had stopped 'the deportations of the Israelites'. Horthy, the old-fashioned anti-Semite, had been wooed by talk — from both Huber and the Pope — of the Hungarians whose 'minds and hearts are filled with charity'. He summoned the Hungarian cavalry back from the Russian front, where they had been sent to support the German forces, and made efforts to purge the more extreme fascists from his entourage. 'Despite this news,' Riegner cabled gloomily to the World Jewish Congress headquarters in New York, 'do not count on any effective result by Red Cross always acting slowly prudently.' All over the world, frantic efforts were now made to raise money, arrange for visas, organize emigration and find safety for the Hungarian Jews. For a moment, while the Allies watched and temporized, the Germans hesitated.

But not for long. As the Russians advanced and Horthy struggled to keep some kind of political stability in a situation that grew more menacing every day, the Germans hardened. When the Soviet troops reached 100 kilometres from Budapest, he asked the Allies for an armistice for Hungary. On 15 October, the Arrow Cross Party, the most extreme of Hungary's fascists, staged a coup. Horthy was arrested and a known pro-Nazi called Ferenc Szálasi was made prime minister. The Gestapo were now effectively in control.

Within hours, Hungary's remaining Jews were under attack, confined to Budapest, ordered to give up their bicycles, cars, radios and telephones, to turn their shops, factories and offices over to Aryans, and herded into ghettos. Fifteen-year-old Arrow Cross supporters were seen driving Jewish families towards the Danube, where they tied them up and threw them into the river.

The neutral diplomatic missions in Budapest in the late summer of 1944 included those of Portugal, Spain, Sweden, Switzerland, Turkey and a number of Latin American states; the Vatican had a papal nuncio. These different organizations now set about increasing what little protection they could offer, guided by a handful of determined individuals. Among them was the papal nuncio Angelo Rotta, doyen of the diplomatic corps, and Gennaro Verolino, a young Neapolitan priest; Raoul Wallenberg, the thirty-one-year-old emissary from King Gustav of Sweden, who had stipulated that he be given an entirely free hand to use whatever methods he saw fit, including bribery, to save Jews, and Carl Ivar Danielsson, the Swedish minister; Carl Lutz, the acting Swiss honorary consul, who represented British and American interests, his wife Gertrude, and his assistant Peter Zürcher, a young lawyer who had been running a textile mill, as well as two other Swiss diplomats, the minister Jaegger and Harold Feller, the first secretary at the legation. There was Gaber Sztehlo, an evangelical priest, and Albert Bereczky, a pastor from the Lutheran Reform Church. And there was Friedrich Born, with a brave assistant called Otto Komoly. (Schirmer left Budapest on 29 October and continued his efforts from abroad.) Together, acting for the most part entirely on their own initiative, without orders from home or even much support, and in a city in the grip of total anarchy, with mobs of Arrow Cross teenagers on a rampage of looting and murder, in which the Jewish position seemed almost totally hopeless, this small group of people embarked on a race against time and the Gestapo to save the Jews. The truth about the Final Solution was a secret no longer.

The foreigners had not been idle during the summer months. While the Allies prevaricated over emigration, the Germans allowing them to believe that there were still possibilities of letting the Jews leave, Lutz, Wallenberg, Rotta and Born set about drawing up letters of protection, impressive-looking documents bearing the triple crown of Sweden in yellow and blue or the dignified stamp of the Vatican. These papers, matching certificates for emigration to Palestine and elsewhere, would, in theory at least, protect those who had them from immediate deportation.

In Geneva, Burckhardt consulted Riegner about the scheme. 'Give as many as you can,' Riegner told him. 'This is not Switzerland. This is a country governed by gangsters.' Without waiting for full endorsement from Geneva, Born was already at work. Lutz had had the idea of protecting individuals by giving them papers, but Born took the idea further. If you gave protection to entire buildings, then you could cram them with hundreds of people whom the Arrow Cross would not be able to touch. In Geneva, after much talk about whether this unorthodox use of the Red Cross emblem might not devalue its currency, Schwarzenberg and Burckhardt agreed to back his plans and started to send money collected on behalf of the Jews of Hungary. Increasing his office to nearly 500 helpers, paying them in food, money or protection papers, visiting the fascist authorities to threaten those who still had fear of International Committee displeasure with terrible reprisals if they did not accede to his demands, and aided by the Chalutzim, young Zionist pioneers who sped about Budapest as messengers on their bicycles, Born took over 1,840 buildings in the city – flats, clinics, hospitals and soup kitchens. Declaring them under the protection of the International Committee, he had them covered in red crosses and large messages spelling out what protection meant, written in German, Hungarian and French. Most of all he wanted to protect the children, and specialhouses now opened to take in some 6,000 children under fourteen whose parents had already been deported to slave labour and Auschwitz.

Born was obsessed with time running out. Of Hungary's 800,000 pre-war Jews, there were already fewer than 250,000 left. On 8 November 1944, Eichmann ordered the deportations to start again, to take able-bodied Jewish men and women to work on the 'east wall' ordered by Hitler as fortifications against the Russians; he called them *Leihjuden*, Jews on loan. Terrified Jewish families, escaping from the round-ups in the eastern provinces, had descended on the city. From among these, and the Jews of Budapest, people were now selected for deportation to Austria, ordered to report to the brickworks at Obuda, on the outskirts of the city, or dragged there by Arrow Cross thugs, who tore up any letters of protection they might be carrying. From Obuda, the Jews were to walk towards the Austrian border, 200 kilometres away, daily Allied bombing raids having disrupted rail links with the west.

Today Obuda is still a brickworks, a dusty, dispiriting place of open-sided sheds and derelict buildings. In 1944 it marked the start of what was then Hungary's Number One road, running alongside the Danube to Hegyeshalom on the Austrian border, sometimes following close to its meandering path, sometimes turning deep into the open countryside. It was here, during the summer months, that the people of Budapest brought their picnics, to eat under the poplars, acacias and willow trees. November 1944 was cold and particularly wet. The brickworks were filthy, with no sanitary facilities and no medical help. Among the so-called *Leihjuden* destined for forced labour were men in their eighties and small children. One of Born's helpers, who asked what was happening to a group of twelve-year-old children he saw being led away, was told by an Arrow Cross youth that they were 'going to be turned into soap'.

At dawn on 6 November, the first walkers set out, men, women and children struggling under heavy suitcases, the women sometimes wearing the high-heeled shoes in which they had been arrested. Marches that could have led to life, even if a life of forced labour, became marches of death. The journey took between eight and nine days with stops at night in barracks, village squares or open fields, where a very little food was handed out. Those who fell back or gave up were clubbed by Arrow Cross guards, then thrown into the Danube. Soon, road Number One was littered with the bodies of the dead and dying, and with suitcases abandoned along the way and looted by the Arrow Cross. Born and his helpers left an account of what they saw when they arrived at Obuda:

The deportees marched in endless lines, ragged, starved, exhausted people, among them the aged, who could hardly drag themselves along. The gendarmes drove them on with rifle-butts, truncheons and whips . . . We saw, after the so-called rest, when the marchers were driven on in the morning, how many dead remained on the frozen soil . . .

At Gonyu we also saw that some of the deportees were quartered in barges on the Danube for the night. Many of the people in this dreadful situation committed suicide. Scream after scream pierced the night: people resigned to death threw themselves into the freezing waters . . . We also saw that the gendarmes deliberately drove the Jews in the pitch darkness across the narrow plank leading to the barge with their rifle-butts and whips in such a way that they . . . lost their footing on the icy plank, many of them falling into the water among the broken slabs of ice.

Born and the other foreigners became frantic. Borrowing cars and light trucks, working continuously with very few pauses for sleep, they drove up and down the lines of marchers, much as Dr Fraser of the British society had during the Russo–Turkish war of 1877, handing out blankets, medicines, water and food, constantly invoking their papers of protection to draw individuals out of the lines and send them back to Budapest.

In one of the children's homes in the city, a rich young Hungarian Jew, a property man called Laszlo Szamosi, hit on the idea of questioning the children about the names of deportees, which he then printed on to a form using a typewriter with the same typeface as Lutz's protection papers, hastening off to the brickworks to distribute them. (Later, it would be said that of all the letters of protection, those issued by the Vatican worked best, those by Switzerland and the International Committee the worst, because of the high numbers of forgeries.) Wearing armlets describing them as 'delegates of the International Committee of the Red Cross', doctors went with him to liberate the 'sick'. Born's lists would be called the 'book of life', on account of the names of those he was able to save. Géza Kiss, whose father-in-law was a good friend of Born's and who acted as his driver, remembers a night of drizzle and fog when Born and Rotta joined forces to rescue deportees from barges

The British ambulance at Waldia during the Italian campaign in Ethiopia 1935-36. Despite the clear markings on the tents, it was later bombed by Italian aircraft whilst doctors performed an amputation

Right Count Carl Gustav von Rosen, the twenty-four-year-old Swedish Red Cross volunteer who worked closely with Junod and Brown

One of the photographs of the wounds caused by phosgene gas collected by Junod as proof of the Italian violations

Right International Committee delegates in Ethiopia. Sidney Brown is second from left and Marcel Junod is on the far right

One of the International Committee offices in Madrid during the Spanish Civil War 1936-39

An ambulance carrying refugees blown up during the Spanish Civil War

A fund-raising poster of the German Red Cross which was absorbed into the Nazi party in May 1936

Cover of the German Red Cross magazine for May 1940

One of the many gatherings of Red Cross nurses and auxiliaries in which swastikas and Red Cross flags hung side by side

Max Huber, president of the International Committee from 1928 to 1946. He presided over its most troubled years

Mlle Suzanne Ferrière, one of the three women on the Committee during the Second World War and a softening influence during the Committee's deliberations. She was the niece of Dr Frédéric Ferrière

The historian Carl-Jacob Burckhardt, arguably the strongest force in the International Committee during the Second World War. He is photographed with Mlle Lucie Odier, a former nurse and the third woman on the committee. Burckhardt did not rate her skills highly.

Left Dr Fritz Paravicini, the long-standing delegate to Japan who fought but failed to bring about improvements for Allied prisoners in Japanese hands

Left The delegate Dr Maurer at the time of the liberation of Dachau, 29 April 1945. Two members of the SS are confronted by bodies in a train

Below Red Cross lorries carry relief into devastated German cities

Bottom An International Committee delegate at Buchenwald shortly after liberation

Children dying of hunger during
the famine in Greece in 1942. This
is one of the photographs sent by
Junod to Geneva

Right Dr Junod shortly after
his arrival in Japan, in the
autumn of 1945

Relief leaving a Red Cross
depot in Geneva for the
prisoner-of-war camps
during the Second World
War

Dr Ernst Grawitz, acting president of the German Red Cross from 1936 until the end of the Second World War. He supervised medical experiments on humans in the concentration camps and committed suicide in the spring of 1945

British and Canadian prisoners-of-war examine their Red Cross parcels at the camp of Stalag VIIb (Lamsdorf). This clandestine photograph was taken by Warrant Officer William Lawrence, a fellow prisoner at the camp.

and rafts in which they had been put to spend the night. 'Everybody knew Born,' Kiss says, 'that was part of his success.' At Hegyesyhalom itself, Wallenberg set up a small relief centre, with medicines and a mobile kitchen, and went up and down the lines of marchers as they neared the frontier with cigarettes, food and rum. Wallenberg, it would be said, was particularly good at high-handed bluffing, ordering some of the younger and more impressionable guards to release marchers. Enough were pulled out by him and Born to fill several truckloads, Born distracting the Arrow Cross with gifts of medicines for long enough to get the convoy of those saved on the road back to Budapest.

To document what was happening, Born shot 4,000 metres of narrow gauge film for Rotta, which was used to bring pressure on the world to do something to halt the deportations. The sight of these death marches would haunt him all his life, 'the elderly, men and women, adolescents . . . children prodded like cattle, headed stumbling towards their Calvary . . . The ancient Wiener Landstrasse became the road to terror, and will remain a symbol of human barbarity and hatred . . .' Just occasionally, an echo of his anguish comes through his obediently dry reports.

The death marches lasted fifteen days. Every day, three to four parties, each of up to 2,000 people who had shivered through the bitter, wet night in the open sided hangars of the brickyard, set out in the rain and half-light of a November dawn for Austria. But on 23 November the order went out that the deportations were to stop. To this day no one is quite sure why, though Dr Laszlo Karsai, a historian at the Hungarian Academy of Sciences who has collected over 800 documents relating to Hungary and the Jews, believes that a meeting held by Born with Szálasi on 17 November, in which he told him that the behaviour of the Hungarians towards the Jews would be taken into account when the Allies arrived, played some part. Another reason seems to have been the fact that when the survivors stumbled into Hegyeshalom they were found to be not the able-bodied workers the Germans had in mind but pitiful and broken men and women, many too old or too young to have been any use in the first place, Eichmann having simply ordered that 70,000 Jews be provided for the earthworks, regardless of age, sickness – or protection papers.

Lutz and members of the Swiss legation have left their own description of those who made it as far as the Austrian border.

At Hegyeshalom we found the deportees in the worst condition imaginable. The endless ordeal of the marches, the almost complete lack of nourishment, intensified by the constant dread that in Germany they were to be taken to the annihilation gas chambers, have brought about such a condition among the unfortunate detainees that they no longer possess human shape and lack all human dignity . . . all the results of civilization and progress cease to exist . . .

Sixty thousand people had set out to walk to Hegyeshalom; later, it would be said that 20,000 never got there, either because they had escaped, been rescued by Born and the others, or been shot or drowned along the way. Of those who did reach the border, only 2,000 were ultimately considered fit enough by the Germans for the earthworks.

Though the marches were now stopped, the Germans had one more card to play. Seventeen thousand so-called 'protected' men in Budapest, who held papers issued by Born, Wallenberg, Lutz and Rotta, and who had been used in the city for clearing away rubble, were now bludgeoned on to trains by Arrow Cross men and despatched to Germany.

Fewer than 150,000 Jews were left in Budapest. As the autumn progressed Eichmann decided that the time had come to wind up his Hungarian campaign. His first targets were the elderly, the disabled, women, children and the sick who had been left out of the deportations.

A first ghetto had been set up in Budapest at the beginning of November, a 'protected' or 'international' ghetto in the grand old houses lining the Danube, where foreign countries had once had their embassies. Later in the month, a second ghetto was established near the Portuguese synagogue, and 11,935 non-Jews were cleared out to make way for 63,000 Jews. Heavy palisades, three to four metres high, were built around the perimeter, Eichmann having decided to model the Budapest ghetto on the one in Warsaw. 'There must be only one gate at each of the four cardinal points,' he directed, 'to admit the Jews, but never to let them out again.' All remaining Jews in the city were now rounded up and forced into the ghetto where overcrowding was soon such that people were living thirty to a room. Born, whose activities were making Szálasi increasingly suspicious, set up an office inside what now became known as the 'great ghetto', from where he did all that he could to bring in food and medicines and to protect the Jews from bands of marauding Arrow Cross men. He was now acting entirely on his own initiative, all communications with Geneva having become impossible.

Conditions worsened rapidly. More and more people were brought in until the staircases, corridors and cellars were crammed; at one point five days went by without a delivery of food. Electricity supplies failed as a result of overloading. Lutz, who visited the ghetto on 26 November, wrote:

> In several places there are also many consumptives and even people with lice. It is to be feared that dangerous epidemics will break out. In the house at 32 Kalona Jozsef Street there are five raging lunatics among the inhabitants.

On 8 December, Soviet forces began to bomb the city; several hit the ghetto, leaving heavy casualties. On the 10th, the ghetto was entirely sealed off, and rations set at 690 calories a day — a fraction of the nourishment needed to sustain life. Cheese and eggs sent in by Born were turned away by Arrow Cross guards. On the 14th, the Hungarian government left the city and Arrow Cross men began to confiscate Red Cross vehicles, arrest staff, close down protected buildings, while Born struggled on, tolerated at least in part because of his good contacts in Budapest. Soon only the Swedes and the Swiss were left, the other foreign missions having pulled out of the city.

Born had fought frantically to keep his orphans out of the ghetto, fearing that they would not long survive the malnutrition, or the diphtheria and typhus now breaking out. Christmas Day had been set as the last day on which the children would have to enter the ghetto. As it happened, chaos of another kind settled over the children's homes, for the heavy bombing of Budapest had scared away most of those looking after the children, who were now left to starve or roam the streets. An International Committee report described children of two to fourteen years, 'famished, ragged, emaciated to mere skeletons, frightened to death by the droning and detonation of bombs . . . their bodies eaten by filth and scabies, their rags . . . infested by lice.' Born had already moved a thousand of them to the Abbey of Panonalma, a Benedictine monastery placed under his jurisdiction by the bishop of Gyōr, which was eventually respected both by the departing Germans and the arriving Russians.

Eichmann's plan had been to massacre the remaining Jews in the ghettos, much as had been done in Warsaw. As it was, the Soviet advance proved more rapid than expected and he fled, leaving the ghettos totally prey to roaming Arrow Cross boys and men, who entered them to plunder and slaughter, sometimes dragging their victims into the streets beyond the palisade, to hang or shoot them. The Danube filled with corpses bearing signs of torture. Eichmann's plans, and carnage at the hands of the Hungarians, were forestalled by the arrival of the Soviet army, which entered the ghetto on the night of 16 January 1945. Budapest was to be the only ghetto in Europe to escape annihilation. Sixty-nine thousand Jews had survived in the great ghetto; 25,000 more in the international ghetto. As the rest of the city was liberated, 25,000 others crept out of their hiding places in convents, cellars, monasteries and the homes of Catholics who had hidden them.

Geneva, it seems, had not particularly liked Born's independent behaviour, nor the sprawling, anarchic organization he had put together, nor the bribery and forgery to which he had resorted. Dr Karsai adds that he believes that there were a number of things Born had never reported to Geneva but that news of these may have reached the Committee. Born's own closing report to Geneva, written in the summer of 1945, had an almost apologetic note to it. Because the situation in Hungary had been so particular, 'the delegation turned into a sort of autonomous organization inspired by the spirit of the International Committee'. He listed twenty collaborators by name, 164 by groups and added that he had handed out seven hundred papers of accreditation to 'occasional collaborators'. These papers, passed on to people over whom the Committee had no control, were soon turning up, according to papers in the archives, in the hands of 'some shady characters . . . harming the International Committee's good reputation'. In the closing months of the war a stern letter went out from Frédéric Siordet in Geneva, the man now heading the Commission of Delegates: 'It is absolutely beyond the competence of any delegate to issue any kind of "letters of protection" invoking the help of military or civilian authorities.' Later, these letters would come to haunt the Committee, adding to the Russians' growing suspicion that the International Committee was a cover for spies, and that they hoped, with such papers, to save the lives of some of the fascists hunted down by the Allies.

In December, a new delegate, Hans Weyerman, a former representative of CIBA in Hungary, arrived. When Buda, the southern side of the city, was cut off from Pest during the Soviet advance, Born stayed on in Buda and Weyerman in Pest. After the Russians had taken full control of the city, Born was forced to leave, partly because Russia had broken off relations with Switzerland on account of its continuing trade with Germany during the war and partly because he was compromised by his good contacts with the Hungarian foreign office. Weyerman stayed on and was able to negotiate and supervise a major relief programme for the starving city and for the deportees who had survived the camps and now made their way home after liberation by the Russians. When the tally was made of casualties among those who had mounted the rescue operation, a number were found to have been killed in the bombing. Otto Komoly, Born's assistant, had been murdered by the Arrow Cross on 1 January. A hundred of the young Zionist pioneers were dead. And Wallenberg, who had acted with such bravery, now vanished into Soviet hands.

Burckhardt was one of those who had pushed hard for emigration for the Hungarian Jews, saying that it would be a 'very good thing for Switzerland that at last something positive could be done for the Jews. This would produce a good impression abroad and at the same time dispel the resentment that could spread against our country from the stories of the refugees and the internees.' As it turned out, Switzerland accomplished little. Through a combination of German intransigence, Hungarian connivance and Allied and Swiss procrastination, fewer than 2,000 Jews were eventually given asylum in Switzerland, only forty-four of them children.

Born returned to anonymity in Geneva and died, appropriately enough, while shooting bears in Transylvania in 1963, having never even told his children about the Hungarian chapter of his life. He was just sixty. Like Lutz, who died a sad man in Switzerland, he was not recognized for his work until declared a Righteous Gentile in Israel in 1987, when a tree was planted in his name in the Avenue of the Righteous in Jerusalem. The delegate who had taken on over 500 local helpers, obtained and distributed 15,000 documents of protection, turned hospitals, schools and soup kitchens into safe zones whilst in Geneva they talked of the dangers of watering down the potency of the Red Cross emblem, was never even congratulated for his work. But the rescue operation in which he had played such a large part showed what could be done — and might have been done elsewhere — when the churches, foreign missions and the International Committee chose to combine and act bravely. Born's contribution had been to realize that it was ultimately a question of keeping Jews alive a little longer, while the Russians advanced, and that to do so one had to forget all the careful rules of the International Committee and play every imaginable card — contacts, bribes, threats, forgery and deals with violent and murderous people. None of this could have worked without the ambivalence of the Hungarians towards the Jews, nor without Born's ability to make the most of their greed, fear and ambitions, his own energy and his extraordinary courage.

In July 1943, after many deliberations, Huber had sent one of his weightier bulls to the governments of the countries at war, and to the national Red Cross societies. Once again, he urged them to respect 'the right of all men to be treated fairly, without arbitrariness, and without imputing to them responsibility for actions they had not committed'. Like all of the International Committee's edicts, it implied more than it said. Behind the schoolmasterly innuendos was a simple message: civilians, who had long since overtaken soldiers as the casualties of this war, were in a critical condition, and none more so than the Jews, dying in their thousands in the gas chambers of the extermination camps. No one, at this stage, felt anything but despair when faced with the intransigence of the Germans over access to the camps. As Marti, in the Berlin office, had put it in a confidential note to the Committee on 4 November 1942, after yet more talks with the legal department of the Ministry for Foreign Affairs: 'As for the Jews, Dr Sethe is absolutely immovable: the International Committee is forbidden to have a say over their fate . . . a visit to any of the camps is categorically refused. No hope is left.'

Marti was wrong. Suddenly, and for no immediately apparent reason, the German authorities opened a very small window on to the camps, informing the Berlin office that the International Committee would be allowed to send parcels to those interned there. There was, of course, a catch: the parcels could go only to named individuals. Given the very nature of the camps, and Hitler's *Nacht und Nebel* decree, which demanded that no one knew who was in them, it looked, for a moment, hopeless. But just a very few names were known to the Committee, and it was now that one of the organization's greatest strengths – its tenacity – paid off.

The widow of a former detainee in the concentration camp at Oranienburg had managed to discover the names of a couple of other prisoners held at the same time as her husband. She sent the information to the International Committee. From Geneva, a first run of fifty parcels went out. Since the entire parcel scheme relied on receipts, the Committee could do no more than sit back and wait. It proved far more successful than they had dared hope: within six weeks, two-thirds of the people they had addressed parcels to sent back receipts. For Suzanne Ferrière, Mlle Odier and Schwarzenberg, who was now asked to run a new department known as 'CCC' – *Colis aux camps de concentration* – this represented a unique opportunity. As news of what was happening spread, so more names reached the Committee, sent from all over the world. From the camps themselves, the receipts returned covered in names. Some arrived scribbled on little bits of paper, thrown from the windows of trains and picked up by railway workers. The Committee called them 'echoes'. Every name yielded more names. By the time the war was over, the Committee had more than a hundred thousand names of concentration camp detainees, to whom they sent regular parcels.

But the Committee now needed food to put into the parcels and once again it was faced with the obduracy of the Allies against lifting the blockade. Four months passed before the British even replied to a letter from the Committee. Meanwhile delegates had turned to begging around the rest of Europe and small stocks of food began to arrive from Romania, Slovakia and Hungary. There was a fortunate incident when an American ship, the *Christina*, went down in the Mediterranean and the 73,000 kilos of food recovered from her holds was donated to the Committee for use in the camps. The Committee began negotiations with the Germans not to bomb Marseilles and Genoa, two ports used to ship in food, and to keep the Saint-Gothard and Simplon tunnels open. After President Roosevelt set up the War Refugee Board on 22 January 1944, one of its directors, a thirty-four-year-old lawyer called John Pehle, managed not only to have $20 million transferred to Switzerland, but to get permission from the Germans for it all to go to the camps. There were, of course, thefts along the way. But at the end of the war it was found that almost half the packages sent out by the Committee to Buchenwald had reached those to whom they had been sent, as had almost all those sent to Ravensbrück and Dachau.

This was a definite breakthrough: and the Committee pressed on. Delegates were now instructed to go to any lengths they saw fit to gain entry to the camps. Marti, writing on possible tactics to the Committee, spoke of tobacco as the most valuable currency. 'We beg the International Committee to send us, in Berlin, as well as to the various sub-delegations, tobacco in the form of cheap cigarettes, in great quantities . . . More and more of the officials we have to deal with ask us for Swiss tobacco.' As they did their rounds and caught sight of work patrols staggering back to the camps, skeletal and apathetic, the delegates began to see for themselves the enormity of the Nazis' crimes. Louder and louder calls for action went back to Geneva. Schwarzenberg responded by persuading the Committee to increase the number of delegates in Berlin to forty. At the same time, in response to a suggestion of Marti's, eight new delegates were earmarked as 'specialists for the concentration camps'. When Allied bombing paralysed the railway networks and the British refused to release extra petrol, continuing to give prisoner-of-war camps priority, the Americans stepped in with petrol and the French and Swiss with vehicles. By April 1945, the International Committee would have 300 lorries, painted in white with red crosses.

A sense of urgency had at last descended on Geneva, particularly as there were fears that the Germans might suddenly decide to exterminate all remaining concentration camp inmates in a final orgy of killing, a policy known to be favoured by Hitler. After nearly four nears of futile requests on the part of the International Committee, the concept of repatriation and exchange finally entered the vocabulary of the war. On 12 January 1945, a former president of the Swiss Confederation, Jean-Marie Musy, had a meeting with Himmler in a train stopped for safety in a tunnel between Vienna and Breslau. Talks ended with an agreement that, in exchange for five million Swiss francs, the Germans would release into Swiss hands some 1,200 to 1,800 Jews, particularly those with relations in America, which had pledged itself to cover the costs. A first train, bringing 1,200 survivors from Theresienstadt, reached Switzerland on 8 February.

For many, things were still happening too slowly. Sweden had long favoured more decisive action. At the end of January 1945, the Swedish consul-general to Paris, Paul Nordling, travelled to Geneva to tell Burckhardt that the Swedes had decided that matters were now so desperate that it was too late to 'negotiate in a moral manner . . . from now on we must act very boldly'. These were tricky times, especially when the Germans protested vigorously at the amount of publicity given to the famished and broken survivors of Theresienstadt who reached Geneva. What Nordling was suggesting was that extreme measures should be taken to get doctors and medical services into the camps.

While the Committee again retired to deliberate, Count Folke Bernadotte, vice-president of the Swedish Red Cross and nephew of the King, embarked on a cloak-and-dagger rescue mission to collect all Scandinavians in Germany's concentration camps. At Yalta, Roosevelt, Churchill and Stalin had agreed to launch a simultaneous attack on Germany from all sides and Bernadotte sensed that there was little time to lose. In Berlin, he met *Obergruppenführer* Ernst Kaltenbrunner, who had been made head of the Gestapo after Heydrich's assassination by the Czechs. He found him, he later wrote, 'courteous, cold and wary'. Then came meetings with Walter Schellenberg, head of intelligence, who, he wrote later, struck him as willing to negotiate, von Ribbentrop, who harangued him, and finally Himmler, whose hands impressed him as delicate and manicured (much as Heydrich's hands had struck Burckhardt). All four had their minds on the end of the war and retribution. When he left, Bernadotte took with him an agreement that 200 Swedes, in Red Cross uniform, taking with them ambulances, lorries and mobile kitchens, would be allowed into Germany to collect 2,200 Scandinavians from Sachsenhausen, 1,600 from Dachau, 1,600 others from various camps north-west of Dresden. Bernadotte now masterminded a delicate rescue operation, constantly threatened by changes of mind among the German leaders. Reaching Neuengamme, the camp where the Scandinavians were supposed to have been congregated, he noted, 'It was with feelings of great emotion that I prepared to see these revolting creations of the Third Reich.' The Swedes were told about inmates being starved to death, gassed, hanged, shot, given lethal injections. Children of six, they learned, had been used for medical experiments on tuberculosis. During transfer of inmates to another camp by sea, a vastly overcrowded ship had gone down: 7,000 died, either drowned, burned to death or shot as they tried to escape.

Time was indeed running out for the inmates of the camps, as the Germans began evacuating survivors away from the advancing Allied troops to camps further inside German territory, in conditions that grew more pitiful day by day, while Himmler continued to think in terms of a sale of detainees to the Allies in return for immunity, and Hitler, enraged by reports of these negotiations, instructed commandants in the camps 'to let no camp inmate in the southern half of Germany fall into enemy hands alive'. Sinister news came that there were plans to segregate the Jews. Writing to Geneva, Marti reported that an SS officer had told him that 'there is a hundred per cent chance that all the inmates will be executed'. Burckhardt made repeated efforts to contact the German High Command. With every day, news came from the delegates of more atrocities as the concentration camps collapsed before the allied advance, but International Committee delegates were still not allowed inside. 'For the love of God,' Madame Frick-Cramer, in tones of rare emotion, had written earlier to Burckhardt, 'let us act as soon as possible.' She, together with Marti and Schwarzenberg, had been among those arguing all along for a direct approach to the more amenable Himmler. 'Even if it ends in failure,' Mme Frick-Cramer told Burckhardt, 'I believe it essential to try, because the International Committee cannot, morally, fail to do all it can.' All that winter, Riegner, the members of various churches, the many Jewish organizations and national Red Cross societies, kept putting pressure on Burckhardt, who had taken over from Huber as president on 1 January 1945, to act. But Burckhardt, like Huber before him, prevaricated.

There are many accounts of the remarkable meeting which at last took place on 12 March 1945. It seems that Burckhardt and an assistant called Hans Bachmann crossed the border into Germany at Feldkirch and were driven to a small inn on the road leading to Bludenz. Between 2.30 p.m. and 6.30 p.m. they and Kaltenbrunner covered a range of subjects, agreeing on the exchange of French civilians for German civilians, the provision of rations to concentration camp inmates equal to that of prisoners-of-war, the right of deportees to send and receive letters, the drawing up of lists of names of deportees, and the sending to hospital in Switzerland of women and young people from the army of Warsaw. The relief operation was to be intensified, and a number of delegates instructed to stand by ready to enter the camps as 'voluntary hostages' just before the arrival of the Allies – hostages in the sense that, in order not to betray the secrets of the war industry in which the detainees were working, they had to agree to remain inside the camps until the end of the war, preparing for the closure of the camps and trying to make sense of the identities and the needs of the thousands of people held. In return, the Germans would receive some kind of 'compensatory gesture'. Burckhardt, who had postponed his new appointment as Swiss Federal government envoy and minister plenipotentiary to France in order to follow up negotiations with the Germans, evidently returned to Geneva pleased. Even Riegner admitted to the World Jewish Congress that this was 'an enormous step forward'. What might have been achieved had this meeting taken place in 1942?

There is another version of the Kaltenbrunner meeting, unearthed not long ago by the historian Jean-Claude Favez. The International Committee had always let it be understood that the encounter had been brought about on the initiative of the Committee itself; in fact, as Favez discovered, the request for the meeting came from Himmler, who was anxious to strike a bargain for his own safety. Burckhardt, it seems, took a week to reply to Himmler's letter.

Favez also came across a curious letter in Burckhardt's papers from an aide to Himmler, saying that he was sad that he would not be in Berlin to receive Burckhardt on the occasion of his forthcoming visit. The date was September 1942 – a little over a fortnight before the 14 October meeting in Geneva. Was it possible that Burckhardt was himself planning to appeal to the German High Command on behalf of the Jews? Favez dug deeper into the papers. He failed to find Burckhardt's original letter, but since someone had scrawled in pencil 'Matter of Lanskoranska', on the reply from Himmler's office, he asked Polish friends to try and trace the name. It did not take them long to track her down. Karoline von Lanskoranska was a Polish countess, still alive and living in the Vatican. In 1942 she had been arrested by the Gestapo and sent to Ravensbrück. According to Hans Bachmann, the man who had accompanied Burckhardt to meet Kaltenbrunner, the countess had been one of the loves of Burckhardt's life and he had known her well during his years in Vienna. What Burckhardt had been planning to do in Berlin, in September 1942, was to appeal for her release — possibly then hoping to resort to the old International Committee tactic of trying to set a precedent for an individual which could later be extended. Why was Burckhardt's letter missing? Because Burckhardt did secure the countess's release — but not until his meeting with Kaltenbrunner two and a half years later. And this time he asked for the liberation of all the women from Ravensbrück, the countess among them. Favez believes that Burckhardt returned to the International Committee archives from time to time after the war, and removed documents 'correcting his image for history'.

After the meeting with Kaltenbrunner it became a matter of pushing as hard as possible for still more concessions. Delegates across Europe set about interpreting instructions in their own way, as the chaos around them grew. Georges Dunand, leaving for Slovakia, was told by Burckhardt: 'We can hardly give you precise instructions apart from our immutable principles. The watchword is: "Go straight ahead," but be careful that the Committee does not have to disown you.' To camp commandants all delegates pointed out that they would be held personally responsible for further deaths.

What the delegates and the teams of Red Cross people following them found, when they at last entered the camps, would haunt them all their lives.

On 15 April, Anglo-American forces entered Belsen, the first camp to be properly liberated by the Allies; Auschwitz, Treblinka and Sobibor had all been emptied of inmates by the Germans before the arrival of troops. They were closely followed by British and American Red Cross teams. On a blackboard, they found a list of thirteen 'types' locked up in Belsen: they ranged from Spanish communists to 'Clergymen, Anti-socials, Gypsies and Homosexuals'. A man called Ashton, who was among those who discussed surrender with the German commandant of Belsen, wrote home:

> This is going to be a horrid letter. I am almost unconscious
> with fatigue and impotent rage . . . It is beyond the powers of

description. In one camp there are 15,000 starving Europeans. In another there are 45,000 . . . There were 3,000 dead bodies in a heap and another 500 in a naked heap . . . Some were trying to crawl on their hands and knees – being too weak to walk – to a pile of rotten potatoes and were being potted at by the S.S. Emaciated skeletons weeping and moaning with joy and clinging to us.

They have become animals – starving, dying animals . . . Typhus and typhoid are raging . . .

There is little one can do just now but be as kind as possible and shed tears of impotent rage and swear to God that this shall never happen again as far as one's power goes and that the guilty shall be punished. Even my clothes smell of death . . .

As photographs of Belsen, published all over the world, at last gave confirmation of Riegner's testimony, the British Red Cross put out an urgent appeal and an International Committee medical mission on its way to Holland was re-routed. A hundred British and American medical students joined them. On 24 April, a fully equipped hospital was running, feeding the survivors with drips and carrying out blood transfusions. Colonel Johnston, the British officer in charge, ordered that respect and consideration should take precedence even over medical care. Families and friends, reported Amy Pfister, a member of the International Committee mission, were to be kept together 'surrounded by an atmosphere of affection and kindness'.

Twelve thousand corpses had been found lying around Belsen. Thirteen thousand more people died after liberation. Two miles away, in a Panzer training school, were nearly 800 tons of food and a bakery capable of producing 60,000 loaves a day. Ten thousand of the survivors, unwilling to wait, slipped away, taking with them their temperature and diet charts, the only documents they possessed that gave their names and a military stamp. In one barracks the Red Cross team found 500 children alive among piles of rags and bodies; some were even playing among the dead, lying four to five deep. Many, taken into hospital, lay still and quiet. 'Two little boys side by side,' noted Amy Pfister, 'whimpering softly, their wizened faces a queer brownish colour.' The white skin of the few babies found alive looked like tissue paper.

The Red Cross nurses had to learn how to cope with people who found it easier to remain naked, with those who continued to soil their beds and the clothes they had been provided with, and those who wandered around, screaming and laughing, their faces contorted and twisted. It brought to mind, said Amy Pfister, the 'men possessed of devils, delivered by Christ, spoken of in the Gospels'. One woman told her, pointing to a number tattooed on her arm, 'I am only a dog ... how I wish I were like you – a human being.' Another, whose baby died in the hospital, stole a baby belonging to someone else and vanished. Efforts were made to keep the sick inside the camp perimeter, but hundreds crept out of their beds at night to pilfer. In the mornings, the nurses would find chickens, and even parts of the carcass of a calf, under the sheets. As they recovered, the Red Cross turned to the overwhelming task of recording and tracing. Before leaving, the Nazis had destroyed all records. Enid Fernandez, of the British Red Cross, was asked to accompany fifty-one orphans who had been offered homes by the Swedish Red Cross. 'The Belsen mothers and children,' she wrote later, 'were very homesick. They found the rather severe manner of the Swedes very different to the British Tommies' easy humour and to the freedom allowed them by the British Red Cross.'

These experiences were being repeated all over Europe. Often the International Committee delegates were the first on the scene, desperate to ensure that no more massacres should take place, hanging around the gates of camps, for they were still forbidden entry by the German commandants. Victor Maurer reached Dachau, to learn that 2,700 of the 5,000 people recently transferred from Buchenwald had been dead on arrival. He was waiting at the gates with his white flag when the American soldiers arrived. A kilometre outside Dachau, Marti and a delegate called Jean Briquet came across a stationary train, some of its wagons open and covered in wire mesh. They contained only bodies. Harry Pires of the American Red Cross, assigned to Dachau by the Seventh Army, reached the camp next day. 'Dachau is a vile place,' he wrote. 'There were about two thousand bodies piled up in and outside the crematorium ... Especially among the political prisoners are many brilliant men. Doctor's degrees are plentiful ... Forty-three nationalities are represented. Many have been in Dachau or other camps for as long as ten years.' If he was right, if they really had survived a decade of semi-starvation and ill treatment, these men had been there at the time of Burckhardt's visit in 1936. Among the survivors were eight members of the Polish Red Cross. Pires brought with him doctors, food, civilian relief workers, medical supplies. Barbara Pathe whose Clubmobile was close behind the American troops, remembers that the decision was taken to park at the gates rather than inside the camp. 'We wanted to be there for those who wanted to come to us. They had been so badly treated. We didn't feel that they always wanted us.'

Just before liberation Dr Jean-Maurice Rubli arrived at Mauthausen, near Linz in Austria, with trucks in which to take away a number of detainees whose release had been negotiated. The German commandant in charge was Colonel Franz Ziereis, who was reputed to have executed thirty to forty inmates personally every morning with a bullet to the neck. Rubli arranged for the release of the 818 inmates and set off back for the Swiss border. Six died on the journey and were buried in the village cemetery at Schutz in the lower Engadine. Charles Steffen, another delegate, arrived with a second convoy, bringing in supplies; he took away 183 French detainees, remarking that there was 'something mysterious and horrible in the air' and that the crematoria seemed to be working at full pitch. Neither he nor Rubli was allowed past the gates. Then came a forty-one-year-old bank employee called Louis Haefliger. While Rubli hastened back to Geneva to ask Burckhardt to put pressure on Ziereis to let a delegate in, Haefliger camped at the gates. Burckhardt apparently overcame International Committee misgivings over such unorthodox procedure, and gave Rubli a letter for Ziereis threatening that he would be held personally responsible for all further deaths. 'There are also crimes which are not customary,' Burckhardt is reported as saying. 'Against an exceptional crime, exceptional measures.' His words must have struck some of his listeners as painfully ironic.

On 5 May, having persuaded Ziereis not to blow up the barracks with its 40,000 inmates, labourers in the underground Messerschmitt factory beneath the camp, as he had threatened to, Haefliger negotiated a surrender and white flags with red crosses were flown. (Haefliger turned out to be one of the Committee's mistakes; or it may have been that the sense of bravura and omnipotence went to his head. His reports became self-aggrandizing.)

With camps being liberated one fast upon the other, the International

Committee delegates concentrated on finding ways of getting convoys of food through, and doing all they could to prevent the inmates leaving the camps where they could be fed and looked after, rather than scattering out across the countryside, where they died in their hundreds from sickness and exhaustion. The German commandants for the most part neither knew nor cared about any deal that the International Committee might have struck with Kaltenbrunner and were simply intent on saving their own skins. The telephones were not working. There was no petrol. As the delegates pushed and fought their way into the camps, those who had not yet been exposed to the sight were overwhelmed by the vision of skeletons naked or in striped pyjamas. In Türckheim, on 26 April, Robert Hort found a cluster of camps with 15,000 Jews awaiting deportation to Dachau; in Ravensbrück two days earlier Albert de Cocatrix had found 10,000 women from ten different nationalities, and dozens of young children in hiding. It took two weeks to coax them out and convince them that they could play and talk without fear of being discovered by SS guards. When women from Ravensbrück arrived by truck in Switzerland, the mayor of the village on the border had all the village bells rung; several of the women crept out of the lorries and knelt on the ground.

On the roads, in the extreme chaos settling on liberated Europe, the delegates encountered German civilians fleeing the advancing Russians, pushing wheelbarrows and prams with their belongings, and confused Wehrmacht soldiers not sure where to go. Among them were columns of ragged, emaciated survivors of the camps, guarded by SS men ordered to move them on to other camps away from the front line. Many commandants had chosen to ignore the International Committee's request to keep the inmates where they were, to be treated and fed by the Allies as they arrived. A quarter of all the marchers who left the camps would die. Willy Pfister, who came across a column in an area not yet liberated, was reduced to driving alongside, feeding the starving men and women as they stumbled along, unable to do anything to help those who could not keep up and who were shot by the guards and left to die by the roadside. Once they realized that the men with the Red Cross armbands came from the International Committee, some of the marchers fell to their knees and begged them not to leave them to die. Pfister was talking to an SS guard when moans were heard from a man lying nearby who had been shot. The officer interrupted the conversation, strolled across, shot the man in the head, and wandered back to resume talking.

And now, at last, the mystery of Theresienstadt (Terezin) was solved. In June 1944, Dr Rossel, a delegate attached to the Berlin office, had been taken to see Theresienstadt, an eighteenth-century fortress town on the road from Prague to Dresden. With him went two members of the Danish Red Cross, searching for 400 Jews recently deported from Denmark, and several high-ranking German officers and members of the German Red Cross. They were taken all round the old fortress city with its deep moats, they talked to the Jewish council of elders who were said to be running it, and took some photographs. Afterwards they went to a dinner given by Reichsprotektor Karl Hermann Frank. Rossel had undertaken not to make public his impressions.

As it happened, they were good. His fifteen-page report to the International Committee in Geneva described a clean and cheerful place, in which the inhabitants looked well fed. 'In the ghetto it is even possible,' wrote Rossel, 'to get hold of things almost unfindable in Prague.' The surgery was well equipped, the library adequately stocked and there were several orchestras. The canteen was spacious, he added, with people served promptly as soon as they turned up for meals by a young girl in apron and cap, 'as in a restaurant'. The published report, with its passing reference to the possible 'Potemkin' nature of what had been seen, was so prudently and cautiously phrased that there had been an outcry of protest from Jewish organizations around the world. However, there the matter had rested. No other delegate had been able to visit Theresienstadt since.

On 6 April 1945, Dr Otto Lehner and a delegate called Paul Dunant were admitted into the ghetto. In keeping with Kaltenbrunner's instructions about 'voluntary hostages', Dunant had been named specific delegate to the camp. At first he, too, was astonished to find conditions so apparently good. German officers accompanying him explained that Himmler had wished to give the Jews the opportunity to organize their own communal life, with a view later to setting up a Jewish colony somewhere totally apart from the German population. While waiting permission to take up his appointment, Dunant observed the arrival of

open trucks from the east. Two thousand skeletal figures were found
to be in them; forty-seven were already dead. They had had nothing to
eat for twelve days, and brought terrible stories with them. Dunant was
able to prevent some of the more eminent hostages held in Theresienstadt from being taken off to Berlin for the Germans to use as hostages
to bargain with. When, on 2 May, he was finally allowed into the citadel,
he found 5,000 prisoners, most of them Czech Jews in terrible conditions.
'These poor people,' Hedwig Ems, a woman who survived Theresienstadt,
wrote later, describing the scene, 'were in a pitiful state, and Dunant
asked: "Are these people?"' Later, Dunant reappeared, having protested
vigorously to the German officers. He came, says Ems, 'as an Angel of
Salvation . . . Through his presence the last attack on us was prevented.'
Shortly before his arrival, plans had been made to dig an enormous pit,
larger than those at Buchenwald, where 10,000 Jews had been shot only
days before liberation by Patton's Third Army.

Nearby, Dunant found other apathetic and dying prisoners. On 5 May,
Theresienstadt was placed formally under the International Committee;
the SS flag was lowered, the Red Cross flag hoisted in its place above
the citadel. Dunant's task was almost overwhelming: nearly half the
13,000 people he found, once he had counted numbers throughout the
fortified village, were ill with typhus, or in quarantine. On 8 May, at
nine o'clock at night, the Russians arrived.

It was only on entering the citadel that Dunant discovered the extent
of the hoax perpetrated on the International Committee in the summer
of 1944. Survivors told him how, two months before the delegates' visit,
the names of streets inside Theresienstadt had been changed to make
them sound more picturesque; how halls had been emptied of bunks
and designated as elegant meeting rooms; how barbed wire fences had
been concealed, lawns laid out and flower beds planted; how model
schools had been opened; and how the SS had filmed it all, to use as
propaganda. In fact, as the International Committee had always suspected, Theresienstadt had been a transit camp where the young and
strong were selected for labour, and the rest sent on to the gas chambers.
Of the 140,000 people who had passed through Heydrich's 'paradise
ghetto', none is known to have survived.

*   *   *

Once the war had got under way, there had been a push in Germany to recruit new members for the German Red Cross. It was not long before over three-quarters of a million people, all with their Red Cross uniforms or Red Cross badges, were engaged in war work of one kind or another, taking part in military-style parades on Sundays. Something of the vigour and eagerness of the German society made its way into the pages of the International Committee's *Review*, which carried regular and appreciative reports of German nursing programmes and inventions, just as it carried everything else, without comment or analysis. One, early in the war, described a new order that had just gone out: anyone keeping horses, cows and over ten pigs was obliged to keep one Red Cross veterinary box; if more than twenty animals, this had to rise to two boxes. Discussing their dealings with the German Red Cross in the autumn of 1939, Chenevière observed that 'it is difficult to refuse the German Red Cross something at this moment because it is so much ahead of the other Red Cross societies when it comes to the organization of its services'.

Something of a bad smell must, however, have tainted the German Red-Cross from relatively early in the war. When, in 1940, the Duke of Saxe-Coburg, still nominally president, paid a visit to America, there was consternation in some of the larger chapters of the American society which he had planned to visit. In New York, Mrs Davison offered to hold a small private lunch for the duke, but her suggestion was turned down when no high-ranking male guests could be found to accept, and it was thought that the duke might be embarrassed 'to be entertained at a luncheon of seven ladies and no men'. When A. J. Berres, manager of the Detroit chapter, sent a photograph of himself and Saxe-Coburg for publication in the Red Cross magazine, its editor, H. C. Thompson, replied drily that 'at this juncture in world affairs, National headquarters does not seem to be very Duke-minded'.

The International Committee itself, however calm on the surface, was clearly becoming increasingly uneasy, and some of this unease came across when a letter arrived from an American lawyer on behalf of a client who wished to leave the German society some money in his will. Was there, asked the lawyer, any 'substantial difference between the charitable nature, aims and functions of the present German Red Cross society' and the American one? Jean Pictet's answer was a model of evasion. He devoted many paragraphs to the German society's excellent statutes; just three words 'in essence similar' in answer to the question about differences.

How much did Pictet really know? In 1936, at the same time as he was made acting head of the German Red Cross, Dr Ernst Grawitz, editor of a series of short books entitled *Eternal Doctors*, had been appointed head of the SS health services by Himmler. It was an important post, and he had many doctors and medical helpers under him. Grawitz was crucial in pushing through the Nazi medical ethos of *Gleichschaltung*, and doing away with 'exaggerated compassion' for the weak. He was known to support the view of doctors as 'protectors of life', which in his case meant euthanasia and racial breeding. In the summer of 1942, by which time he had been acting president of the German Red Cross for six years, Grawitz recommended to Himmler the use of gas chambers as the best way to go about mass killings. He regarded Zyklon-B — which was later to be transported around Germany in Red Cross vehicles — as a superb technological achievement because it allowed 'humane killing'. Humanity to him seems to have meant mass murder with technical efficiency. In Auschwitz, 'selections' were conducted by camp physicians, under the authority of the chief doctors of the camp, men appointed by Grawitz. It was on his orders that selections were carried out by doctors in the first place and that only exceptionally fit Jews were sent for labour. There was no point in sending the others, argued the Red Cross president, 'since they would in the end have to be killed'. At the Nuremberg doctors' trial, in the autumn of 1946, it would be said that Grawitz was an expert in developing 'medically the best methods for killing'.

One of the doctors under Grawitz — it would later be estimated that two hundred German doctors took an active part in what were described as medical war crimes — was a talented surgeon called Karl Gebhardt, a solidly built man with little round glasses and fair hair that rose in a thick bush about his head. Gebhardt was a childhood friend of Himmler's, his personal physician and his principal adviser in medical matters. He had also been the senior German doctor for the Olympics, and was given the highest SS rank of *Oberstgruppenführer*. When, in May 1942, Reinhard Heydrich was shot by Czech agents of SOE, Gebhardt was flown to the hospital in Prague where Czech surgeons were removing pieces of shrapnel from his body. Hitler's personal doctor, Theodor Morell, had proposed using sulphonamide preparations that he mixed and used himself, but Gebhardt took the decision not to call on Morell and to trust the expertise of the Czech surgeons. Within two weeks Heydrich was dead of gas gangrene, and Gebhardt was in disgrace.

One way to rehabilitation was clearly to test the efficacy of sulphonamides, and to prove that people still died of gas gangrene, whether or not they were treated with them. German soldiers at the front were dying in great numbers from gas gangrene and no cure had as yet been perfected. Gebhardt now declared that 'in principle, when the well-being of the nation is at stake, experiment on human beings is permissible', and that 'concentration camp prisoners could not be left undisturbed while soldiers were dying at the front and their wives and children suffered air attacks and bombardments'. Together with Grawitz, and under the authority of Himmler who, as head of the SS, was in a position to provide him with limitless numbers of subjects, Gebhardt set about his first medical experiments. Auschwitz, Buchenwald, Dachau, Neuengamme and Ravensbrück were chosen as the main camps for the medical work. The doctors who worked in them would be described during the Nuremberg trials as having committed 'murders, brutalities, cruelties, tortures and atrocities'.

Gebhardt's first concern was with sulphonamides, for which great claims were being made by the Allies. Testing started at Ravensbrück. A first group of thirty-six Polish women – nicknamed 'rabbits' – were opened up, the wounds infected with various bacteria and then filled with wood shavings and ground glass, and closed again. Then treatment began. Early in September, Grawitz visited Ravensbrück to be told that all the women, though sick and for the most part permanently crippled, were still alive.

Grawitz, who might well have found himself responsible for Gebhardt's failure, ordered that another twenty-four Polish women be brought to the infirmary. This time, to make the wound more severe and more like the kind of wound soldiers received in battle, he had the women shot in the legs and the circulation of the blood through the muscles interrupted by tying off the muscles at either end. All but three died. At Nuremberg, the survivors told of infections that would not heal, of excruciating pain, of permanent injuries, and the slow death from gangrene and haemorrhage of their companions.

While the sulphonamide experiments were being conducted at Ravensbrück, a new series was started on bone, muscle and nerve regeneration and on bone transplants, possibly the most barbaric of all the experiments. Once again, Gebhardt was in charge. Selected women had their bones broken. One sixteen-year-old girl called Barbara Pietczyk had her tibia removed, piece by piece. Another had the muscles from her legs torn out, again piece by piece. Whole limbs were removed, and shoulder blades, mostly from women who had already gone insane and who were then killed; these limbs were then taken to nearby SS hospitals to see if they could be grafted on to wounded German soldiers.

All through the war, while Grawitz was denying all knowledge of the concentration camps to Huber and the International Committee, he, Gebhardt and others were busy conducting these obscene experiments on their inmates. Men, women and children were infected with jaundice, spotted fever, malaria and tetanus; subjected to extremes of altitude and cold; had parts of their bodies amputated and infected. Searching for 'forty healthy test subjects', Grawitz and Gebhardt discussed racial differences and agreed that there was no point in using gypsies as anything but control subjects, since they would yield results scientifically inapplicable to real Germans.

In the spring of 1945, as the Russians approached Berlin, Grawitz committed suicide. His successor as head of the German Red Cross, appointed by Hitler, was Gebhardt. The new Red Cross president was one of seven medical men sentenced to death at the doctors' trial.

FIFTEEN

Piercing the Darkness

After the concentration camps of occupied Europe, the war in the Far East was the International Committee's greatest nightmare. As Louis Calame and Sidney Brown had noted during their travels in China and Japan in the 1930s, there was something very particular about the Japanese attitude towards humanitarian concerns. Though among the most ardent of Dunant's early followers, the Japanese did not view the Geneva Conventions in quite the same way as the Europeans, at least not after the early 1930s. Their intransigence and brutality in Manchuria and Nanking should perhaps have provided an early warning. As in Germany, when military leaders and the Kempetei, a Gestapo-like police force, gained control of the government, the Japanese Red Cross society had rapidly taken on a new guise, more interested in drilling soldiers and holding 'frugality campaigns' than in the impartial nurturing of wounded soldiers. Though a number of old-fashioned members remained, they were unable to do anything. What would be incomprehensible to Geneva was the speed and absoluteness with which former advocates of humanitarianism now abandoned their international commitments and turned obediently to military nationalism.

For the Japanese, a prisoner-of-war was an object of shame and the prisoner-of-war code an aberration. The disgrace of being taken prisoner was so great that you did not want to receive loving messages or packets from home; on the contrary, you wanted to lie about your name and make certain that no one ever heard that you had survived. This was as true in the 1940s as it had been in the middle of the nineteenth century, when prisoners were routinely executed. The Japanese minister for war, reflecting the intensely militaristic spirit of the times, observed that any soldier who failed to carry out the task assigned to him deserved to die. Leaving for their units before Pearl Harbor, the young Japanese soldiers had taken part in traditional funeral rites – entrusting a lock of hair and piece of fingernail to their relations – and were not expected home unless victorious. For the foreign soldiers and civilians who would fall in their thousands into Japanese hands, the Geneva Conventions would amount to virtually nothing.

In September 1941, 60,000 Japanese troops had disembarked in Indo-China. Three months later, they mounted simultaneous attacks on Pearl Harbor and Hong Kong. At the end of December, Hong Kong capitulated, rapidly followed by Sarawak, Borneo and then Singapore, where the GOC, Lieutenant General Arthur Percival signed an unconditional surrender and 70,000 men were taken prisoner. Five days later, the Japanese landed in Timor and began encircling the Dutch on their islands. Sumatra was taken by parachute troops. Java fell in March. On 6 May, the Philippine islands surrendered. By early summer, all fighting men and most foreign civilians had been marched away to captivity in camps that soon spread across an area considerably larger than Europe, while their captors were now in control of virtually the entire coastal area from Singapore to Vladivostok. Geographically, the men – and the interned women and children – were many thousands of miles from home; psychologically they were at sea, in the hands of people they had long despised, who spoke a different language and had a very different culture, their own having collapsed with humiliating speed before the Japanese invasion. All this would tell, mentally and physically, in the months and years to come.

The first news from the Far East, once the International Committee in Geneva had put out its customary offers and reminders, was almost reassuring. The Committee already had a base in Shanghai, from which it had organized relief for China. The prospect for shipping supplies looked good, with the idea of using Macao as a depot. Dr Fritz Paravicini, the long serving delegate in Tokyo and with a Japanese wife, though already in his late sixties, was accepted as accredited representative by the Japanese, among whom he had many friends and contacts. On 5 February 1942, came the reply to the Committee's letters. Even though Japan had only signed, and not ratified, the 1929 Prisoner-of-war Convention, it professed itself willing to apply it – '*mutatis mutandis*' other things being equal – to all prisoners, and it would extend the same privileges to internees. Furthermore, it undertook to respect the customs, food and dress of the people it took prisoner. Remembering the Russo-Japanese war of 1905 and the scrupulous behaviour of the Japanese towards their Russian captives, the British, Americans, Australians, Dutch and New Zealanders, all of whom had citizens now prisoner in Japanese hands, had reason to feel a little reassured.

But not for long. 'Mutatis mutandis' had a sinister ring to it. It meant that the Japanese could decide at will what to do and which articles of the Conventions, to respect, 'necessary changes having been made'. A few visits to camps in Japan by the known and trusted Dr Paravicini would be allowed, but none to those in occupied territories, which the Japanese, like the Germans, decided did not fall under the Geneva Conventions. As Dr Paravicini was soon observing with considerable despondency, the war in the Far East was a matter of life and death for the Japanese 'and anything that does not contribute to its progress is superfluous and must wait'.

Then, early in February, came the first alarming reports. A British official who had managed to escape from Hong Kong reported in a telegram to the Foreign Office in London, forwarded to the International Committee, that Europeans in the city were 'now nearly all interned with little rice and water only and occasional scraps of other food . . . British dying like flies'. The Swiss consul's attempt to get permission for a visit by an International Committee delegate resulted in total failure.

> No permission is granted yet to collect European dead; seventeen Royal Scots were found shot, their hands tied behind their backs . . . One entire Chinese district has been declared brothel regardless of classes of residents; many European women raped, some afterwards shot or bayoneted.

According to this British official, the Japanese had been heard to say that they intended to let all the Europeans die so that 'no one could tell the story'.

There was more to come. On 30 March, another report was forwarded by the British to Geneva: the food rations in the Stanley Prison in Hong Kong, where all the foreign civilians were being held, were 'inhuman'. Beri-beri, dysentery, cholera, typhoid and typhus were spreading. The Canadians were also hearing rumours. Their cable to Geneva reported prisoners-of-war 'held in Kowloon under atrocious conditions . . . it is stated that they are without adequate food and drinking water, that most unsatisfactory conditions prevail . . . Request International Red Cross Committee make every effort to secure independent report.' Fears now grew for all the other foreigners, civilians as well as soldiers, believed to number nearly 400,000, scattered in camps throughout the Far East.

The International Committee was already doing all it could. Though painfully overstretched in Europe, it was pressing the Japanese authorities hard. *Mutatis mutandis* had so far resulted in a complete lack of cooperation, prevarication over the appointment of delegates, silence over prisoners' correspondence, and a no to all camp visits and parcels. With virtually no Japanese prisoners in Allied hands — when a Japanese garrison at Atton, in the Aleutians, fell to the Americans, only twenty-eight out of the 2,600 soldiers were taken alive — the whole concept of 'reciprocity', so dear to Geneva, became meaningless.

In March came one concession, over and above the recognition of Paravicini in Tokyo. The International Committee was informed that it might appoint a man to Shanghai. Following their customary practice, they asked the local Swiss consul for the names of reliable Swiss citizens and settled on Edouard Egle, director of a firm of importers and engineers called Siber Hegner & Co. Ltd., who spoke excellent English, German and French. Meanwhile they put out feelers for a second delegate on Chinese territory, lighting on a man called Zindel in Hong Kong, after tracking down his uncle in a village in Switzerland. His nephew, the uncle told them, had been a diligent employee of Arnold Trading & Co. in China for the past twenty years, was competent, serious, hard-working and had an 'honest and open nature and healthy spirit'. Did he, asked Geneva, 'possess the necessary qualities for such a task?' Yes, replied his uncle, he did indeed.

The three men, Paravicini in Tokyo, Egle in Shanghai and at least in theory Zindel in Hong Kong — for the Japanese had yet to pronounce on his appointment — were now accredited delegates. The International Committee searched the Far East for other likely reliable Swiss citizens, settling on a Mr Surbek in Sumatra, a Mr Weidman in Batavia and Dr Matthaeus Vischer, a doctor and medical missionary, specialist in tropical medicine, in Borneo. Dr Vischer, who had arrived in Borneo in 1927 with his wife and a one-year-old daughter, was running a mission hospital. Trapped by the war in the Far East, he had already offered his services to the Committee. On 19 March, the Committee asked the Japanese Red Cross to watch over the 'well-being' of its delegates. The society repeated that only the delegates in Japan, Shanghai and Hong Kong would be recognized.

Shanghai in 1942 was an open city, with over four million Chinese and almost 100,000 foreigners – Russians, British, Germans, Austrians, Americans, French, Swiss, Scandinavians and Portuguese; their numbers had been recently swollen by the 18,000 Jews who had been able to escape from Nazi persecution in Europe and found refuge with the two small local Jewish communities, Sephardim who had come from Baghdad via India in the early nineteenth century and Ashkenazim from Russia. The city was crammed, unhealthy and short of food. The news that reached Geneva via Egle was not good. Though it would be some time before forcible internment, the Japanese had already made it plain that all enquiries about internees would have to go to the Japanese consul, all those about prisoners-of-war to a liaison officer of the Japanese army. There would be no question of any camp visits. Egle's mail was being censored. He had been forbidden to make any enquiries about those arrested by the Kempetei. No one would provide him with lists of the prisoners, and the Japanese wanted no relief or parcels from abroad. Shanghai, reported Egle, was full of desperate people, either frantic for news, or destitute, their regular sources of income cut off. Hoping that the Japanese would soon relent, Egle increased his staff, taking on two Swiss assistants, a Chinese accountant and typist, two messenger boys, two coolies and Miss Satoh, a twenty-seven-year-old Japanese woman, 'my star acquisition, a charming and most helpful personality'.

On 16 May, Egle sent the Committee a revealing letter. It was both prescient and depressing. He had been told that he might now plan a trip to Hong Kong, where the entire British community was said to have been interned, though there was no word from Zindel. This visit would, Egle suggested, set the tone for all future delegations to the Philippines and the Dutch East Indies. 'You may possibly blame Dr Paravicini and myself that we are not adhering to the modus operandi laid down by the ICRC,' he wrote, but this simply cannot be done. With the war, the Far East has undergone a change which never more will be reversed . . . and we have to adapt ourselves and make the best of it . . . The Japanese Empire has established itself as protector over all nations in the Far East . . . and will not stand any interference with their plans and ideas as to how things should be run . . . We have to realize that we are more or less the guests of the Japanese authorities, that we can lodge pleas for favours, but are not in a position to DEMAND anything . . .

Any wrong move, he warned, any delegate 'who would not know how to pay due respect to the feelings and aspirations of our Japanese friends', would have drastic repercussions.

And now matters appeared to grind to a halt. In a climate of intense mutual distrust, with rumours flying about, with hundreds of foreign residents resorting to every kind of tactic to get news abroad or aid in, the Japanese dug in their heels. Suspecting that Egle was simply protecting enemy interests, they began to doubt the neutrality of the International Committee itself. There would, for the time being, be no visits to Hong Kong, no inspection of camps, no lists of internees or prisoners, and no news of Surbek, Weidman or Vischer.

What was more, the Japanese Red Cross, once so vigorous in imitation of European humanitarian endeavours, now lost all separate identity, its nurses and doctors pressed into service for the army, the senior people with sympathy for Geneva silenced. Prince Tokugawa and Prince Shimadzu, who had sat through so many meetings and ceremonies with foreign Red Cross dignitaries, and who continued to feel themselves part of an international brotherhood, were reduced to discussing arrangements over transport. The foreign section, once the pride of the imperial court, was put into the hands of a director, a secretary and three volunteers, none of whom spoke anything but Japanese. The *Huryojohokyoku*, the official prisoner-of-war information office, was discouraged from pestering the authorities for lists of names 'which appear to have no vital connection with the prosecution of the war'. For all the renowned manners and courtesy of the Japanese, no effort was made to conceal their contempt for the International Committee or for its delegates: to every question came back approximately the same answer: 'the time has not yet come to contemplate the carrying out in practice of this scheme.'

Six months had passed since Pearl Harbor, and nothing of any importance had yet been achieved for the foreign captives by the International Committee. The American State Department, via the Swiss government and its minister in Tokyo, sent a stiff communiqué to the Japanese government about the continuing violations of the Geneva Conventions, with 'a most emphatic protest' at the 'inhumane and uncivilized treatment accorded American nationals'.

The names of less than five per cent of the estimated number of prisoners and internees had been transmitted to Geneva. Anxiety, frustration and their own pressures at home were causing both the British and the American Red Cross societies to become increasingly impatient with Geneva. In the corridors of the Red Cross society in London, as in the prisoner-of-war department of the Foreign Office, there was much talk of 'unreliability'. Miss Sidney Jeanetta Warner, in charge of prisoners at the British society, speculated that the time might have come to bypass the Committee altogether and try to pander to the Japanese Red Cross's 'amour propre' directly, by making it see how very strong it could, and should, be in these circumstances. But now came an incident guaranteed to provoke the sceptical allies still further.

Early in July 1942, Egle at last received permission from the Japanese High Command to visit Hong Kong. He was received 'affably' by a Mr T. Oba of the Foreign Affairs Bureau, 'one of the finest gentlemen I ever met in my life,' and, together with Zindel, taken to Stanley Camp and allowed to 'wander at will'. Nicknamed by the internees the 'bag', Stanley was where all interned civilians would spend the entire war, replicating life in the colony before the Japanese occupation, with the leading merchants and bankers in charge.

Egle and Zindel were, as they soon reported to Geneva, agreeably impressed. Things in the camp were not as they had feared. 'I found everybody so cheerful,' wrote Egle, 'as if they were spending a holiday in a summer camp. Most of the people were in bathing suits or shorts, sunbathing, reading, lawn-bowling etc. It is a pity that there is not more shade in the way of trees. For some obscure reason the British forgot to plant any.' Egle went on to praise the wonderful views over the sea, the opportunities for exercise, and the provision of delicacies no longer to be found in Shanghai. 'I believe that ninety-nine per cent of the inmates, once the time comes for their liberation, will leave the camp with a profound feeling of thankfulness and respect towards our Japanese friends . . . Stanley Camp could be taken as a model for any internment camp by any nation in the whole wide world.' Egle must have been a delight to his Japanese hosts. He was impressed wherever he went. In a second camp he remarked on a 'nice little cemetery', lots of books, fly-papers, and the fact that the hospital contained as many nurses as patients. During his rounds, he was interrupted by an internee trying to present him with a long typed list of complaints. 'I felt,' he observed to Geneva, 'that the way the matter was brought up was somewhat tactless and I considered that Colonel Tokunaga was perfectly right in requesting that such complaints should be submitted to him first . . .' In a further letter he mentioned that some of the inmates in Stanley looked much better now that they had lost weight, 'sun-bathing, tanning the skin, a bit of physical exercise'. As for Zindel, Egle was full of praise for his new colleague, saying that he had a 'sympathetic understanding of the new order in East Asia' and that he was singularly fortunate in having 'such extremely nice people as Colonel Tokunaga' to deal with.

It is not surprising, perhaps, that when Egle's report finally reached London at the end of August, it was greeted with irritation and disbelief. It was, remarked an official in the Foreign Office, 'surely too good to be true and seems to confirm our doubts about the reliability of Egle'. A note has been added, in another hand: 'Yes, we have to take Egle's reports with *pounds* of salt.' British fears that all was not well in Stanley were soon confirmed. A secret message, transmitted to London, dismissed the International Committee report as 'completely misleading'. Far from being the summer camp Egle had portrayed, Stanley was in a terrible way, with funds almost exhausted, reserves of clothes dwindling and food rations constantly cut.

Was Stanley another Theresienstadt, the delegates duped by clever propaganda? As with the Czechoslovakian camp, the full answer would have to wait until the end of the war.

Not everyone, however, took Egle's report at face value. In Geneva, the Far East section of the International Committee was headed by a man called Mouravieff, who had a Swiss father and an English mother, who spoke perfect English and knew the Far East well. With him was Marguerite Straehler, who spoke Japanese. Both suspected that Egle was labouring under terrible difficulties, and that his reports were being heavily censored, even if it was not until later that they learnt that the Japanese were doctoring them regularly to present a more glowing picture. Over the months to come, Mouravieff would become a keen student of the Far Eastern report, learning how to read between Egle's lines and what to deduce when questions he sent were studiously ignored. Knowing what risks the delegates were running and how easily they could be accused of spying, he took to sending his questions directly to the Japanese, rather than going through the delegates. Though Egle continued to have his critics, his reputation was somewhat restored when a message was delivered in person by the International Committee delegate in London to the War Office, explaining the immense delicacy of his position. 'The great value of having International Red Cross delegates on the spot,' R. E. A. Elwes in the War Office wrote to G. A. Wallinger in the prisoner-of-war department of the Foreign Office, 'is *not* that they should report to us but that they should organize supplies and welfare as far as the Japanese will permit'.

However, relief, as rapidly became clear, was no easier to arrange than letters or prison visits. The Japanese were not greatly concerned with keeping their prisoners fed or healthy. As rations were reduced, month by month, the Committee, badgered by the national Red Cross societies of countries with internees in Japanese hands, devoted hours to schemes that might prove acceptable to the Japanese. There was no real lack of supplies, the allied governments being willing and able to produce and pay for them, and no shortage of ships, but the Japanese were adamant that no neutral ship could enter their waters. A plan for a halfway depot somewhere in the Pacific from which the supplies could be taken on by Japanese ships worked briefly, as did the transporting of relief in ships used for the exchange of diplomats, but both foundered after one of the feeder ships, the *Awa Maru*, was torpedoed. Postal arrangements started badly and got worse; the very little that got through to the camps or out to the west took as much as a year, travelling via Lisbon, Geneva, Trieste, Istanbul, Moscow, across Siberia, Mukden, Korea and Tokyo. Parcels piled up undelivered and looted by guards. Once again, it would fall to individual delegates to test the obduracy of the camp commandants and to see just how far it would be possible to go.

At the end of March 1942, having machine-gunned close to 20,000 local Chinese or drowned them in junks sunk in the harbour, the Japanese rounded up 3,000 Europeans in Singapore and marched them off to Changi jail, a prison fortress seven miles to the east of the city. With the women and children the guards set a slow pace, having been told that European women were not accustomed to exerting themselves. At midday, there was a break for sardines and army biscuits. As they walked past the rubber estates, the women sang 'There'll always be an England'.

Changi was a large, modern, concrete building standing on the site of former British barracks and surrounded by double walls and barbed wire. By standing on a bench, it was just possible to see coconut palms, rubber trees and the sea. Erected for 600 prisoners, with cells eleven feet by seven, it soon contained over 4,000 internees, men, women and children accustomed to servants, an intense social life and great comfort. Many were without beds or mattresses; latrine buckets and garbage pails doubled as cooking pots. Women who failed to bow properly to their guards were slapped. Changi was noisy, filthy and in wet weather the rain blew in. The walls sweated. The internees kept boredom at bay with lectures, six-a-side soccer, choirs and glee singing, and by discussing Bertrand Russell's recently published *The Conquest of Happiness*. There was a flourishing amateur theatrical life. As the weeks passed, and medical supplies and vitamins ran out, the mood soured. When the internees were suddenly accused of running a spy ring, classes and lectures were banned and the purported spies taken away and tortured.

H. M. Schweizer was the managing director of two Swiss trading firms in Singapore, Diethelm & Co. Ltd., and Hooglandt & Co. Son of a post office worker in Zurich, he had started his career as an apprentice to a textile company. He was now forty-three, married, with no children. To judge from his long report, written only after the war, he was a brave, humorous and resourceful man.

Approached by the International Committee as a possible delegate to Singapore before the city fell to the Japanese, he had been neither formally appointed nor briefed as to his duties when Singapore was occupied. The Japanese refused to recognize him as an official delegate, and he was far from certain about his role, but borrowing a manual on the Geneva Conventions from the Australian Red Cross representative, Lt Col. Roberts, he learned its articles by heart and went off to visit the Japanese high command. There he demanded lists of internees, names of prisoners, the setting up of a family message service and some means for tracing missing people. The Japanese refused them all. So Schweizer set about improvising.

At first, helped by making contact with internees sent into Singapore from Changi to mend roads and keep the electricity supplies serviced, Schweizer was able to set up both an above board delivery of food and medical supplies to the camp and an underground network. He got hold of a two and a half ton lorry, had it painted blue with a red cross on it, and negotiated deliveries. The Japanese responded by ordering him to remove the red cross and forbidding him to use the title of delegate. He changed it to 'neutral agent on behalf of the Red Cross'. He recruited helpers among the Swiss residents and made certain that he was on good terms with the Japanese officer in charge of internees, a former diplomat to London called Asahi, who had written a book on economics. He also managed to win over to his side a Japanese sergeant major called Fujibayashi, a former teacher of English at a high school in Tokyo who wanted to learn German. Schweizer offered to give him lessons; the two men were soon playing chess regularly and discussing the Geneva Conventions. One of Fujibayashi's jobs was to translate into Japanese all outgoing messages and in this capacity he became extremely helpful to Schweizer. It was only after the war, when Fujibayashi was an Allied prisoner, that Schweizer learnt that he had been a member of the Kempetei, and had risked his own life to help the internees. Fujibayashi died in captivity, 'a fine Nipponzin with a broken heart'.

When funds from Geneva failed to arrive, Schweizer arranged for loans from Diethelm & Co. For eighteen months, he kept up his work, despite no contact with either Geneva or Paravicini in Tokyo. Prince Shimadzu, vice-president of the Japanese Red Cross, did come through Singapore on a visit of inspection, but during a private interview explained apologetically that there was nothing he could do beyond carry a letter out for the International Committee. In Geneva, Mouravieff was well aware of Schweizer's almost impossible position and at one point, when the Swiss businessman risked arrest and possible execution, circulated reports about his work on the committee's behalf, thereby shaming the Japanese into 'the necessity of a cautious attitude towards my person'. When a message got through to Geneva, saying only that Schweizer was using their funds 'judiciously', it was Mouravieff who recommended refraining 'from asking him more detailed questions', though the information that he managed to extract from Schweizer's careful words was not reassuring – malnutrition among detainees, cruel behaviour by camp guards, lack of vitamins leading to poor sight, skin diseases and general debility. And so Schweizer went on improvising. When Singapore ran out of imported foreign food, he bought peanuts, Indian meal, the occasional live pig, and talcum powder which the internees used in cooking; it had a sweetish and not disagreeable taste. The number of internees in Changi had now reached 5,000, as Jewish refugees and stateless people were brought in to join the Europeans. Every tin of condensed milk, every salted fish that went to the internees, he wrote later, was regarded by the Japanese as help to the enemy, and that in turn was considered treason. Though never physically tortured, he was regularly picked up and interrogated, verbally bullied and threatened sometimes for eight to ten hours at a time in dungeons under the Kempetei headquarters, 'with my head nearly bursting and every muscle hurting' from tension and terror. There were constant attempts to trap him. After Lt. Col. Roberts was arrested, accused of having 'acted against Japanese military orders' and vanished into 'torture chambers like those of the middle ages', he was approached by a 'pretty Eurasian woman' who told him that she had ways of contacting Roberts and had secret channels to the camps. She was insistent, returning to see him again and again, but Schweizer kept telling her that he could do nothing without permission from Geneva and the Japanese authorities. Later, he learnt that she had close connections with high-ranking Japanese officers.

On 10 October 1943, Japanese ships in Singapore harbour were torpedoed and sunk. The Kempetei decided that the internees were responsible for the submarine commando raid. Fifty-seven were taken away, questioned, and tortured. Twelve died, one having been beaten almost continuously for 144 hours. All the Japanese guards known to have shown lenience towards the civilians were replaced. Schweizer himself was arrested and questioned and for several weeks supplies to Changi were stopped. Hearing from a post office worker that there were rooms stuffed with undelivered Red Cross mail, he had a telegram from the International Committee blown up into a poster and prepared to distribute it around Changi. The Japanese forbade it. Then, at the end of 1944, news came of a large sum of money deposited in his account from Geneva. He was again arrested and discovered to his surprise that, given the compartmentalizing of Japanese affairs, no single office or department had a full picture of his relief work. But this time the Kempetei had had enough. All further supplies to Changi were cancelled. Schweizer had no choice but to obey, though he was able to arrange for some small items to make their way in via an Indian firm. 'I became,' he wrote later, 'almost desperate because of my helplessness.' He was lucky to be alive.

Schweizer was not the only unofficial delegate to risk his life for the internees. Werner Salzmann was another manager for Diethelm & Co. Ltd., working in Bangkok. Seventeen months after the Japanese occupation he was asked by the International Committee to take on the duties of unofficial delegate, all negotiations with the Japanese for an accredited representative having failed. Salzmann accepted and, like Schweizer, set about exploring the limits of his new job. He, too, soon realized the extreme precariousness of his position.

Prisoners-of-war in Siam were in a particularly appalling position. In 1942, the Japanese had decided to build a railway line to link Siam to Burma, joining two existing lines separated by several hundred miles, which would enable them to cross Burma and invade India. It was to start some seventy kilometres from Bangkok. Engineers had earlier estimated that the line would take five to six years to build. The Japanese decided to allow eighteen months, then reduced it to twelve when they found that they were running late. Sixty-one thousand allied prisoners-of-war, some sent from Singapore and the Dutch East Indies, were put to work together with 250,000 Burmese, Malays, Thais, Chinese, Tamils and Javanese.

The 'death line' along the River Kwai, as it was soon known, ran through dense virgin jungle, with trees up to fifty metres high. The climate was tropical and unhealthy. The monsoon brought ceaseless rain, mud and putrefying vegetation. Clothes and shoes rotted. Work lasted sixteen hours a day; the sick were carried to the site sitting or lying. For a while, the Japanese respected the prisoner-of-war code that prohibited officers from doing manual labour, but when progress seemed slow, officers who refused to work were threatened with execution. 'Death called to us from every direction,' wrote Ernest Gordon, who survived the railway to write his memoirs. 'It was in the air we breathed, the food we ate, the things we talked about . . . It was so easy to die.' The bodies of the men who did succumb were left by the tracks or put into barges to float down the river, 'starved, overworked, corrupted with disease – no more than skeletons covered in skin'. A Chinese pastor called Marcus Chang reported seeing half-naked prisoners of 'skin and bone, unshaven and with long matted hair'.

Bangkok was full of rumours about the 'death line'. Salzmann heard them from colleagues at work, friends at the sports club, the Chinese who ran canteens in the camps and from doctors who smuggled news out. During his own trips up country he had seen for himself distant emaciated figures labouring in the jungle. By the autumn of 1943 he was no longer in any doubt that prisoners were dying in their hundreds. Knowing that he was watched, and that if he was caught smuggling information out of the country he would certainly be arrested and tortured, he decided to put together just one report. In it, he described prisoners without shoes or trousers, working in the jungle in terrible conditions; he told how dysentery, beri-beri, diphtheria, cholera, typhoid, and tropical ulcers were rife; he reported rumours that three-quarters of the men were suffering from malaria and that the prisoners were now reduced to eating rice and a little salted fish. There was no meat, no vegetables and no eggs.

Using a secret courier, nicknamed 'dog lover', and a highly secret route – he refuses to this day to divulge any further details – Salzmann managed to get his report back to the International Committee in Geneva, who forwarded it to London. Coming on top of other reports, it confirmed what was already suspected. Anthony Eden made a statement in the House of Commons, based on what he referred to as 'reliable neutral sources'. Intense pressure was now put on the Japanese from all sides; it had little effect. To every request for information the same reply always came back: the prisoners-of-war were being treated fairly and the sick given good medical care. Salzmann, realizing that it was too dangerous to do more, returned to trying to get relief into the camps: a little food and a few drugs did get through to the prisoners. As with Schweizer, it was all a question of making deals with the Japanese, knowing whom to trust and whom to avoid, raising money in long-term loans, forging contacts with middlemen, relying on messages scribbled on strips of lavatory paper and riding around Bangkok on his bicycle, from warehouse to warehouse, in search of food. As in Singapore, his employers, Diethelm & Co., proved extremely helpful.

By the end of 1944, the Allies had received enough reports, both from the International Committee and from their own private sources, to realize how desperate matters had become. There was still virtually no mail, no lists of names, and very little relief to the camps. There was no official delegate in Singapore, Java, Sumatra, Borneo, Manila or Bangkok. Any mention to the Japanese of the Geneva Conventions produced anger. 'You ask too much,' a furious Japanese colonel told Schweizer. 'You must not be impertinent with Imperial Army.' The firebombing of Tokyo in March 1945, when sixteen square miles were destroyed by incendiary bombs, leaving 100,000 dead and over a million homeless – 'scorched and boiled and baked to death' as the man who masterminded the operation put it – only served to curtail the International Committee's activities still further.

In December 1944, Zindel in Hong Kong, visiting an officers' camp in Argyle Street, was slipped a message wedged into a sliver of bamboo. It contained details of the deterioration of conditions inside the camp. As he was finishing his rounds, a prisoner called Captain Barnett shouted out to him: '*Nous mourrons de faim.*' Challenged by the guard, he repeated it in English: 'We are dying of hunger.' The interpreter slapped him across the face. Judging that it would be best for Barnett if he said nothing, Zindel continued calmly on his rounds. As he left, he mentioned to the camp commandant that he was concerned about the food. The commandant lost his temper, shouted and warned that if any word of criticism got out, all supplies to the camp would be halted. Later, Zindel heard that Barnett had been badly beaten up. He managed to get this last bit of evidence of Japanese brutality out to Geneva. From all over the Far East, the reports were now all the same – reduced rations, cruel guards, whose slaps, blows, kicks and beatings the internees never learnt to anticipate – and rapidly spreading illness and disease, what an internee in Changi jail called H. F. MacKenzie would later describe as an 'atmosphere of dark terrorism'.

Throughout this time the national Red Cross societies of the countries whose citizens were internees remained sceptical about the International Committee's efficiency in the war in the Far East. Exquisitely courteous exchanges between Huber and the Japanese Foreign Office only served to deepen their mistrust. On 10 October 1944, for example, Huber expressed in a cable to General Maroru Shigemitsu his 'desire to render all possible assistance for the welfare of those prisoners-of-war detained by the Japanese'. The general replied that he had 'examined with careful consideration and deep sympathy humanitarian proposal which your committee made in traditional red cross spirit', adding that, 'this moment presents practical difficulties . . .' There was no further communication from Geneva. The American Red Cross in particular had never really accepted that the Swiss delegates were doing all that they could. Telegrams crossed the Atlantic with suggestions that the Committee be 'goaded' into doing more. These doubts and criticisms were silenced only after meetings with Huber and Burckhardt in Geneva, from which the Americans and British who attended them emerged agreeing that their 'slow and painful process of persistence' was all that could be attempted at present, given the prevailing 'militaristic, obstructionist Japanese policy'. 'It appears,' said one somewhat grudging note, 'that they have for a long time been trying to pierce the darkness . . . which envelops the Philippines, the Dutch East Indies and Malaya.' As one British Foreign Office memorandum now put it:

> The plain fact is that for the last ten years Japan has broken every treaty of importance – instruments of more importance than the Prisoner of War Convention. She has almost forgotten how to observe a treaty. How, then, will she ever be persuaded to observe a treaty now, except by one thing – fear of the consequences?

Just the same, the slight contempt felt by the Allies towards the International Committee never quite went away. It comes across in their reaction to the death of Dr Fritz Paravicini in the winter of 1943. A note that did the rounds of the Foreign Office in London observed that Paravicini was 'a large, soft, sensual, subtle looking fellow of, I think, Swiss-Jewish extraction', to which someone has added, in brackets, 'When I knew him he was thin and rather ascetic!' A new man, it was agreed, should be 'a) of the highest integrity, b) with a core of steel, c) subtle and sagacious'. Not long before, the Australian Red Cross had dismissed Paravicini as a 'nice old man . . . who lacks the energy and forcefulness necessary for this work'. The unfortunate doctor bore the brunt of much of the widespread dissatisfaction with the Committee's impotence: when the prisoners in Omori camp in Japan heard of his death, they are said to have cheered.

With the death of Dr Paravicini his assistant, Fritz Bilfinger, who had worked in Shanghai before the war for the Chinese Aluminium Rolling Mills Ltd, was made acting delegate to Tokyo. In September 1944 came the news that Dr Marcel Junod would be acceptable to the Japanese as Paravicini's formal replacement. After innumerable delays, caused by confusion over visas, Japanese obstructiveness and the sheer difficulties of travelling across the world in 1944, Junod and Marguerite Straehler who, speaking good Japanese, had been chosen to accompany him, reached Manchuria on 6 August 1945. They had been on the road for over two months, passing through China, Egypt, Persia and Moscow.

Their first visit was to Hoten Branch Camp, Seian, where the Japanese had put their highest-ranking foreign captives; among these were General Percival, GOC in Singapore, General Wainwright, American commander in the Philippines, and General Starkenborgh from the Dutch West Indies. The visitors were told that they would be allowed to speak to just one of the prisoners and then only ask him about his health, whether he had a particular request to make and a short message for his family at home. 'On your attitude today,' Junod was told, 'will depend the whole future of the International Red Cross delegation in Japan.' He and Mlle Straehler were taken to a room in which the fifteen most senior prisoners were standing motionless. The Japanese commandant rapped smartly on the floor with his sabre and the detainees, in total silence, bowed low. General Wainright had been elected spokesman. His answers, Junod noted later, were dignified, brief and bold. Mlle Straehler found the 'imposing of oriental customs on American and Allied officers . . . deplorable'. There was no further conversation and in any case Wainright was totally deaf to argument. But then General Percival insisted on being allowed to speak asserting that he, not Wainright, ranked highest. Reluctantly, the Japanese granted him a one-minute statement. Junod and Mlle Straehler left Seian depressed, with Percival's last words ringing in their ears: 'Promise me to come back. Promise me to come back.'

That same day, 6 August 1945, even as the delegates were getting a taste of what they feared awaited them in Japan, the Americans dropped the atom bomb on Hiroshima. No public announcement was made, and it was not until 9 August, the day the second bomb was dropped on Nagasaki, that Junod and Mlle Straehler reached Tokyo and heard from friends what had happened. There was talk of 100,000 dead, of bombs descending by parachute, of a typhoon of glare, heat and wind that left behind it a sea of fire.

On 15 August, for the first time in Japanese history, the emperor spoke on the radio: he told the Japanese people that he had agreed to an unconditional surrender. Junod, the most experienced of delegates, marshalled his small forces, got the Japanese to agree to the formal recognition of International Committee delegates throughout Indo-China, Siam, Singapore and the Dutch East Indies, approached the protecting powers, Sweden and Switzerland, for extra men, made up seven teams of three people each and went to call on the Department of Foreign Affairs and the War Ministry. From information painstakingly put together in Geneva over the last three years, he believed there to be forty-three prisoner-of-war camps in Japan, Formosa, Korea and Manchuria; he now learnt that there were in fact 103. He knew of 27,000 prisoners-of-war in Japan; he was told of 34,000. As for civilian internees, figures suggested as many as 200,000, from the very elderly to babies born in the camps.

On 27 August, Junod reported to General MacArthur that plans were in hand for the evacuation of prisoners and internees. That day, delegates left for the camps, achieving in just a few hours what their predecessors had not managed to achieve in over three years of war. 'The delegate,' Junod ordered his troops, 'shall manifest throughout his mission a spirit of objectivity, impartiality and conciliation . . .' One of Junod's fears, as he impressed on the men the need for speed, was that the Japanese guards and camp commandants, disobeying the emperor's orders, would massacre the prisoners before the arrival of the Allies. All over the Far East, the long-desired lists of names began to be assembled — lists of the prisoners-of-war, lists of internees, lists of the sick, lists of the dead. Once again, International Committee activity would range from dealing with huge problems – the evacuation of entire camps – to small details, the obtaining of a particular drug for an individual prisoner. As the survivors surfaced, there was a desperate need for news. The delegates began to send the first of many cables, reflecting something of the anguish in which the captives had lived: to a Fran Pastor Johannes in Westfalen from a Mrs K. Moller in Sumatra, 'Am alright how are my children?'; to a 'Family Ludwig' in Hessen-Nassau from a Marie Brastagi: 'Haensschen died otherwise everything alright please send news of yourself and Fritz.'

An extraordinary silence seemed to have settled over Hiroshima and Nagasaki. Two weeks had gone by since the bombs had been dropped and there was still no information on the numbers of dead or the condition of survivors. Junod, assessing in his mind what supplies and medicines might be needed, remembered a phrase that had stuck in his mind when reading a paper put out by the Americans describing their atom bomb: 'for seventy years at least the radio-activity of the earth around the scene of the explosion will prevent all forms of life from existing there'.

On 2 September, Bilfinger, who had been despatched by Junod to Hiroshima, sent a first cable to Tokyo. It was very bleak.

> Situation horrifying. 80% of town razed. All hospitals destroyed or severely damaged ... Many victims, apparently recovering, suddenly experience fatal relapse owing to degeneration of white corpuscles and other internal injuries. Deaths occurring now in great numbers. More than 100,000 injured still in provisional hospitals in neighbourhood ... Urgently need large supplies bandages, cotton wool, ointment for burns, sulphonamides, blood plasma and transfusion kits ...

Even to a world that had witnessed the destruction of Dresden and Coventry and the firebombing of Tokyo, the devastation at Hiroshima carried a peculiar revulsion.

Junod took the cable and a number of photographs of the scorched city to Supreme Command headquarters and asked, in the name of the International Committee of the Red Cross, for food and supplies for the victims. Five days later, on 7 September, Colonel Sams, the officer in charge of assistance to Japanese civilians, brought MacArthur's reply: the US army was not prepared to organize relief to the victims of Hiroshima and Nagasaki, but it would provide fifteen tons of medicines and food, and transport it on six army planes, with a commission of American experts and doctors. Junod was to accompany them, and take charge of deliveries.

Junod left several versions of his first reactions to Hiroshima, before he set to work. It was a memory to add to the many that had haunted him since his earliest days in Ethiopia, over ten years before. The most detailed was in a long article, found among his papers only after his death in 1961. We 'witnessed a sight unlike anything we had ever seen before. The centre of the city was a sort of white patch, flattened and smooth like the palm of a hand. Nothing remained . . .' He went on to describe the silence and desolation of the ruins, railings ripped from bridges, trees with charred and flayed trunks, a hospital set up in a half-demolished school where the 'injured often have uncovered wounds and thousands of flies settle on them and buzz around' and where there were patients 'suffering from the delayed effects of radioactivity with multiple haemorrhages' needing transfusions. 'But there are no donors, no doctors to determine the compatibility of the blood groups; consequently, there is no treatment.'

It was the camps, both prisoner-of-war and civilian, that most concerned the Allied command and the Red Cross teams that followed close behind the troops. Many of the first reports that now started to come out of the camps came from Junod's new delegates and from the men who had tried so hard, at such personal risk, to bring out news during the years of war. Working on their own or in pairs, they hastened from camp to camp, in a growing state of despair and urgency, realizing how little time was left to save men and women on the very edge of starvation.

Schweizer, finally confirmed as official delegate in Singapore, was now in a position to demand where he had previously been able only to beg. In one camp he discovered many thousands of British, Americans and Dutch, ill, hungry, frightened, depressed, their clothes in shreds and longing for news. They asked for newspapers, however old. Nearby, he found a camp with Indian prisoners; 1,700 of them were ill, 400 seriously, with beri-beri, tuberculosis and malaria. Everywhere, survivors were hungry. 'Suggest Singapore General Hospital be placed at their disposal as treatment and dispersal centre for sick and decrepit . . . inmates will require complete refitting specially suggested flannel trousers, sports coats, pullovers, woollen jumpers, pyjamas, towels . . .' While he waited for Allied supplies, Schweizer drew on a stockpile he discovered of unde-livered Red Cross parcels and roped in the entire staff of Diethelm & Co. Ltd, to help him collect sixty tons of relief. They distributed 16,000 loaves of bread, forty-nine live animals and ninety cases of medicines, the money to pay for them lent by his firm and by friends.

In Bangkok, Salzmann was at last discovering the full tragedy of the 'railroad of death' camps. The cables he sent divided the survivors into seriously ill, moderately ill and slightly ill; there were virtually no 'fit'. The reception he was getting, among inmates who had seen no European outsider in three and half years was, he reported, 'tumultuous'.

What most concerned him was the condition of the vast Asian labour force brought in to work on the railway and now dying in the jungle of starvation and lack of medical care. It would be said that over half of the Burmese, Tamils and Malays conscripted to work on the line died there. No one had known much about them; and no one, now, seemed to care. Even as the evacuations began, orders came from military High Command to pay little attention to them, as they were said to belong to the 'Asiatic sphere of co-prosperity', the economic union forced on the region by Japan in the 1930s. Together with the Siamese Red Cross, Salzmann appealed for supplies and took charge of getting help to the 16,000 people, many skeletal and barely alive, found on the tracks.

From an American Red Cross team, which went into a camp at Omori in Japan ahead of the allied forces, came a flatly written but vivid account of the prisoners.

> a lot of men standing on a dock, nude . . . The prisoners were hysterical . . . our men went on in and found a horrible situation – suffering and starvation, most of the men were nude, and a good many of them were sick in the dispensary . . . Admiral Boone stated that we have no piggery in the United States to compare with that place . . . The prisoners were emaciated, and the buildings were filthy and dirty – they had mud floors . . .

and cubicles . . . which were lined with very, very sick people lying on them. There was no matting, and they had no blankets . . .

Marie Adams, a field director for the American Red Cross, caught in the Philippines by the Japanese invasion, had spent the war in a camp for internees outside Manila. It was from her that now came details of what civilians had gone through as their rations were reduced, month by month.

> During the last month, we had no rice. Consequently, we served at noon a half cup of hot water in which had been boiled greens . . . or the heart of the banana stalks or carrot peelings left over from the previous night's supper . . . at night we would have four or five tablespoons of mush, either of corn or rice or soy beans . . . We had no sugar for six or eight months before the liberation, nor any fresh fruit . . . More and more internees were becoming acutely ill with beri-beri, pellagra and just plain starvation . . . Irritability is one of the first symptoms of starvation . . . we were all cross, irritable and edgy . . . I ached to the ends of my fingers and toes, with the most horrible ache that I have ever experienced . . . Many had horrible skin conditions. Tropical ulcers and boils were developing everywhere, and infections were on the increase . . . Sanitary conditions became indescribable because none but the most essential tasks could be done by the starving internees . . . 1,800 women stood in line for the bathroom . . . the situation aggravated by the fact that nearly everyone was suffering from dysentery or diarrhoea . . . Men, during the last week or two of the camp, were dying, either so completely emaciated or so bloated one could scarcely recognize them . . .
>
> If we had not been liberated when we were, I believe that the majority of the internees would have been dead within three or four weeks . . .

One of the last camps to be evacuated was Ofuna, in Japan, towards the end of September. Junod had heard of it almost by chance, in the Ministry of Foreign Affairs. When he got there he found 135 naval and airforce officers, sent there early in the war for questioning. Some had spent up to six months in solitary confinement; all had been repeatedly beaten with wooden clubs, leaving a number with unmended breaks and fractures. The prisoners had had no contact with the outside world since the spring of 1942.

Relief, flown in from all sides by the ton, now began to reach the camps, with parachute drops of milk, sugar, butter and chocolate. Junod, learning from his delegates how near the end many of the captives were, pressed the Americans to move faster. While the Japanese soldiers, renamed 'surrendered enemy personnel,' were marched away into captivity — though not as many as had been expected, retreats being marked by the sound of shots and explosions as they chose suicide over capture — evacuation of the survivors got under way. It was carried out at impressive speed, the soldiers and civilians alike rescued, treated, clothed and sent on their way within a few weeks of release.

Not many found the process easy. News from families, reaching them sometimes after three years of silence, was not always good. Some of the men, who had been tortured or left for weeks at a time in punishment blocks, emerged depressed, anxious and restless, driven by acute claustrophobia to spending most of their time outdoors. Dysentery, malaria, beri beri and tropical sores had left digestive problems, skin infections, bad sight. All had lost weight; some had shrunk into old age. Those who had been beaten had back injuries. Lady Mountbatten, who travelled around the Far East in October for the British Red Cross, of which she was superintendent-in-chief, wrote to a friend about the civilians who had already been elderly when interned by the Japanese early in 1942. 'One sees little future for them, either at home or overseas, and they will need a good deal of help and sympathy. Many of them are permanently broken in health and many homeless, and are really too old to start all over again.'

American Red Cross personnel now arrived from the United States to coax a new unmilitaristic Japanese Red Cross Society out of the ashes of the warrior-like wartime organization. They were confused to find Japanese prisoners-of-war more interested in remembering the five imperial doctrines — patriotism, etiquette, martial courage, truthfulness and austerity — than insisting on their right to certain comforts, and disturbed that the Japanese seemed to have no word for 'volunteer'.

Before long, the carefully named 'consultant on volunteers' had been rechristened by the Japanese as 'drafter of volunteers'.

Junod and Mlle Straehler, reminding everyone they met, victors and captives alike, of the articles of the Geneva Conventions, walked for miles around the ruined streets of Tokyo calling at offices and military departments until they were able to commandeer an old taxi that belched black fumes to drive them around. They were looked after by the former chef of the Imperial Hotel – he had made his name in Suvretta House in St Moritz – who now proved imaginative at procuring missing supplies. Junod noted that every Japanese he met seemed to have sunk into 'apathy, stupor and nonchalance' and that they seemed to prefer to camp in the ruins of their cities rather than make efforts to build new homes. He got on well with the Americans, though he complained that they had little time for 'pretty phrases'. When he asked Prince Shimadzu why he had never helped the delegates to get inside the camps, the prince replied that had he done so he would have been beheaded.

It was only in the autumn of 1945, when the camps were at last empty of allied captives, that the men who had acted as delegates for the International Committee in the Far East were at last able to explain their silence, their apparently approving reports and their seeming lack of co-operation. They had not, it turned out, been duped; there had not been another Theresienstadt.

On 2 October, Zindel wrote an eleven-page report from Hong Kong.

> I found the Japanese in general, and the Japanese military authorities in particular, extremely sensitive to anything implying criticism . . . I could study and admire at leisure every piece of poultry or cattle . . . but it required a special effort on my part to get close even to a comparatively small portion of the prisoners-of-war in the camps. If I continued my camp visits under such humiliating circumstances, it was because of the knowledge that, had I left the camp under protest, my future activities on behalf of the prisoners-of-war would have come to an abrupt end.

Zindel went on to explain how he had been kept under constant supervision, suspected of being a spy; how he had discovered that a dossier was being built up on him; how he was shadowed and his servants questioned. His response, he wrote, had been to adopt a particular

manner for dealing with the Japanese, one that was patient and circum-
spect but never servile or intimidated.

It must have been wonderful, after so long under a faint cloud of
disapproval, to receive a letter like the one Zindel was now sent by Kay
Neckerman, Danish consul to Hong Kong. 'Few people are able to realize
the difficulties you have been up against . . . to me it is absolutely clear
that you have achieved much more than anyone could expect . . . and
I do hope you will get the recognition you deserve.'

From Schweizer came a letter to Geneva, expressing profound relief
at being able at last to speak out after so many years of silence. He was
also able to reassure the Committee that he had kept a 'complete and
accurate account of all monetary transactions' as well as 'a book of notes
and references'.

One by one, the International Committee's men in the Far East, cut off
from their colleagues for over three years, officially as well as unofficially,
emerged. All of them, that is, except for Dr Matthaeus Vischer and his
wife Betsy, from whom nothing had been heard since the day the
Japanese occupied Dutch Borneo. Questioned by Junod as to their whereabouts, the Japanese were evasive. Finally, they admitted that the couple
were in fact dead, executed after having 'confessed to having taken part
in a great anti-Japanese plot'. When Junod was able to track down the
naval prosecutor who had conducted the 'investigations' at Bandjarmasin, he was told that Vischer had owned a revolver, that he had tried
to get in touch with the enemy by wireless in order to transmit secret
information about numbers of troops and vital buildings, that he had
set up a secret organization, planning to take over Burma, that he had
been sent money from abroad and made attempts to contact submarines.
When he heard that the Vischers had 'confessed', Betsy having agreed
that she had 'accompanied her husband in the conspiracy discussions',
Junod could only wonder at the torture they must have suffered first.

Later, he learned that the hearings had taken place in Japanese, that
there had been no interpreter and no defence lawyer, but that questions
'were put to him in a gentlemanly manner'. On 20 December 1943, Dr
Vischer and his wife, wearing clothes described as 'skimpy,' had been
beheaded with a sword.

When at last he managed to talk to other people who had been
interned in Bandjarmasin, Junod heard that the doctor had been a

conscientious and much loved man, that he had treated people in the camps both as a doctor and a dentist and that he was known to have been very strongly anti-Japanese. Vischer, it seemed, had been cautious; his wife had not. Betsy, the former internees told Junod, had gone to great lengths to get hold of food, tobacco and clothes for the internees, riding with them to the camp on her bicycle and tipping them out on to the ground, paying no attention to the guards. The doctor, one Dutch woman told him, had kept telling the internees to take care. 'Mrs Vischer took very little. She just went on throwing parcels to us over the wall.' Whether or not the Japanese had really believed that the Vischers were plotting, no one knows; but it is clear that they found Betsy's attitude disrespectful and were well aware of the antagonism the doctor felt towards them. The Vischers did not die alone: twenty-four other people were shot for their part in a 'plot' against Japan. It was, said Junod, 'the most serious and most tragic incident in our history'.

The other fourteen Swiss doctors, missionaries and businessmen, who had attended so zealously to International Committee affairs in the Far East and who, like the Vischers, had done their best to get hold of lists of detainees, take supplies into the camps, and keep in touch with Europe – as the Geneva Conventions specified – must have marvelled at their own survival.

The war was over. On 7 May, Admiral Dönitz had ordered the German forces to capitulate; on 14 August, the Emperor of Japan announced his country's surrender.

Between fifty and sixty million people were dead, twenty-five million of them in the Soviet Union alone – it would later be said that the figure was far higher – and three million of those were German prisoners-of-war, unprotected by the Geneva Conventions. The numbers soon lost their power to shock, though the figure of nearly six million Jews murdered by the Nazis, from sixteen countries, kept its resonance. There were just two survivors from Chelmo, one of the six extermination camps of the Third Reich. From the railway of death in Burma and Siam, 15,000 Allied prisoners of war, 'cooked and blinded' by heat and glare, as one survivor put it, never came home.

Even as the paper of Japanese surrender was being signed on board the USS *Missouri* in the Bay of Tokyo, fires burned brightly day and night as Japanese civil servants incinerated incriminating documents, papers relating to the atrocities in Nanking as well as to the torture of Allied prisoners-of-war. 'Personnel who mistreated prisoners-of-war and internees', said a secret cable that went out to Japanese field commanders, as the Americans were closing in, 'are permitted to take care of it by immediately transferring or by fleeing without a trace.' Just the same, 920 Japanese were sentenced to death for violating the Hague and Geneva Conventions in the Tokyo war trials between 1946 and 1948, where the principle laid down first in Nuremberg at the end of 1945 – that natural law, man's innate sense of right and wrong, has a legal place in human affairs – was upheld. At Nuremberg as in Tokyo, despite lawyers who wondered how far crimes against peace constituted true crimes under international law, aggressive war was accepted as the 'supreme international crime' as was the applicability of Article 26 of the Geneva Convention which laid responsibility for the treatment of prisoners-of-war at the door of the commanders-in-chief of belligerent armies. Though the Japanese committed their atrocities as part of their conduct of war – and not, as the Germans had, as steps towards a planned genocide – they came out of the war more hated, not least because the Allies went on distinguishing between 'good' Germans and the Nazis, and because the Japanese had shown such extreme brutality towards their allied prisoners; twenty-seven per cent of the prisoners in Japanese hands died. During the infamous Bataan death march in the Philippines in April–May 1942, 10,000 of the 76,000 American and Filipino soldiers who set out to cover 120 kilometres failed to survive. And there was anger, after the war, that so many Japanese had been allowed to commit suicide – more than 1,000 officers alone – before they could be brought to trial.

Ernst von Weizsäcker, secretary of state in the German Foreign Ministry and Burckhardt's boyhood friend, acquitted at Nuremberg on the charges of planning to wage aggressive war, was sentenced to seven years for his complicity in the deportation of Jews from occupied Europe. On appeal, his sentence was reduced to five years; Burckhardt gave evidence on his behalf. At Nuremberg, no attempt was made to investigate the German Red Cross.

*   *   *

The International Committee had gone into the war in 1939 with nineteen collaborators, working in cosy harmony in the Villa Moynier on the lake. In the spring of 1945 there were 3,650 of them, all Swiss, 2,000 of them unpaid volunteers, working in five separate buildings. Altogether, the International Committee had distributed and forwarded 470,000 tonnes of relief to prisoners-of-war and internees; delivered twenty-four million parcels; arranged for the exchange of 120 million Red Cross messages between prisoners and their families. By April 1945, nine million letters had passed through the agency. During the six years of war, some 150 delegates had carried out many thousands of visits to camps across all five continents.

In 1996, after the Office of Strategic Studies in the United States – the precursor to the CIA – opened files which had been classified for fifty years, charges were made of corruption and German infiltration of the organization. One delegate would be judged guilty of illicit dealings in funds probably looted from victims of Nazi persecution; another of gullibility and foolishness. Louis Haefliger in Germany was acknowledged to have been too vainglorious, and Paravicini in Tokyo; somewhat compliant and it had clearly been a mistake – though unwitting – to employ Dr Hans Meyer, who had been an assistant to Dr Gebhardt of the German Red Cross in 1943 and 1944. But delegates, for the most part unrecognized, unrewarded and unremembered, were the true heroes. When, in the late 1970s, the historian Joseph Lador-Lederer produced a critique of the International Committee, he concluded that the 'overall picture which thus emerges is one of timidity at the higher echelons and of great courage of the delegates in the field'. And not only that of recognized delegates: as Schweizer insisted in a long report written after the war, nothing would have been possible without the 'great, selfless, and courageous help' of his Swiss business colleagues. Far from Geneva, totally unprotected and at the mercy of sudden Japanese displeasure, these unnamed and long since forgotten men and women were extraordinarily brave.

There would be a reckoning, an examination of how the Geneva Conventions had stood up to a war that proved more murderous than any one of its participants had expected, and a detailed investigation of all the International Committee had been able to do and all that it had failed to do; but not yet.

As the fighting stopped, only Burckhardt thought to lay down a marker for the future. It had been the International Committee, he noted, that had been the 'first, the only institution which has been able, however late, to penetrate at last the concentration camps and ... save a large number of these unfortunate deportees and political prisoners, protected by no Convention' – perfectly true, but begging a hundred questions.

In October 1945, the International Committee was awarded its second Nobel Peace Prize. Not long before, Huber had sent out the organization's 370th circular, a document as morally weighty as any in its history. 'Total war,' he declared,

> has given rise to new techniques. Does this mean that we must admit that individuals can no longer be legally protected and will henceforth be considered merely as an element of a community at war? This would signify the collapse of the principles underlying international law ... If war denies value and dignity to the human person, it will move ineluctably towards total devastation, since the human mind, which exploits the forces of the universe, seems bent on inventing ways to speed the headlong rush to destruction ...

With the return of peace, he wrote, the moment had come to 'protest against this overthrow of human values and to turn the light of man's conscience, frail though it will be, to pierce the darkness'.

SIXTEEN

Surviving the Cold Winter

'Europe is on the move. The exiled peoples are going home. The roads are filled with men and women of a score of nations ... Frequently they pause and rest in the warm sun, for the end of the shooting finds Europe not only injured but very tired,' wrote a correspondent to *The Times* on 18 May 1945. For the delegates of the International Committee, the summer of surrender did not bring the end of their war, nor even a dropping off in their duties. On the contrary, they had never worked harder and the Geneva Conventions had never been more necessary. As the prisoner-of-war camps were emptied of allied soldiers and the internment and concentration camps cleared of Hitler's unwanted human beings, so they filled up with German and Axis soldiers, now prisoners in their turn; they too needed visiting and often protecting from their Allied guards with scores to settle.

And there were the refugees, the displaced people – the DPs as they were soon known – driven from their homes by the bombing, by the advancing Russians, evacuated from camps and desperate to get home, and the former prisoners-of-war, released at the rate of 22,000 a day in the British zone of northern Germany by the end of May. Sometimes the columns of people stretched 80 kilometres or more. Determined to get food and medical supplies into liberated Europe, the International Committee set up a transport network of trains, trucks, vans, anything that could still be made to move. A first convoy of railway wagons filled with supplies left Switzerland on 6 March. It took forty-three hours and ten minutes to cover 330 kilometres, and the engine had to be changed three times. The German railways were now run by women and foreigners: where there was no one in charge, the delegates learnt to run the trains themselves. The depots, into which the provisions were unloaded, were heavily guarded by former prisoners-of-war, for the most part officers and 'men of confidence'. It was not entirely clear to anyone at this stage how great a part the International Committee, the League of Red Cross Societies and the national Red Cross societies themselves, already jostling for power in the post-war world, would play, but they had been ready for many months. Now, with liberation, they were eager to act.

Everywhere the delegates and civilian relief workers of the national societies went, they encountered slow-moving seas of people, Slovenians, Slovaks and Romanians flowing down through Yugoslavia into Italy, Cossacks making their way along the Garl river towards Lienz, ethnic Germans expelled from central Europe after the Potsdam agreements, confused casualties of Europe's newly drawn boundaries, slave labourers brought to the Reich from Poland to build the Wehrmacht fortifications and now going home; and a few Jews, though there were not many left. Poland alone had lost 97.5 per cent of its pre-war Jewish population.

In this sea of people there were soldiers, old people, whole families, lost children in rags and no shoes, Communists, ex-stormtroopers, shell-shocked survivors, gangs of marauding youths. Some were ill, some had suitcases, some pushed wheelbarrows, some rode horses. One family crossed the Rhineland on a camel taken from a German zoo. By the early summer of 1945 there were said to be forty million people adrift and on the move across Europe; they needed food, clothes, shoes, medical care and somewhere to sleep. They were ill with typhus, scabies and TB. And they were, in great number, stateless, and did not know who they were. 'Citizenship,' wrote Hannah Arendt, 'is no longer regarded as something immutable, and nationality is no longer necessarily identified with state and territory.' Many did not want to go home, even had they known where it was and how to get there.

Europe itself was not in a position to care for all these people. War had eaten into world reserves of food, livestock had long since disappeared, agriculture was devastated and the protracted fighting and bombing of the last year, as well as Hitler's scorched-earth policy, had left the continent in ruins. From the Volga to the Atlantic, there was chaos, illness and hunger, especially in Germany, the Balkans and eastern Europe. In Würzburg only one in every five houses was still standing: in Warsaw not even one in ten. In the Polish province of Kielce, 146,000 people were living in hollows dug from the rubble that had once been their homes. Along a hundred miles of previously built-up Yugoslav highway, there was not a single building left. The smell of corpses wafted up from bombed basements, cellars and sewers in the devastated cities along the Rhine. Cologne's great cathedral, wrote a reporter for the *New York Times*, was like 'the sprawling skeleton of a giant animal'.

Plans for the relief of post-war Europe had been debated at length. It had always been accepted that it would start in the hands of the military, with the Red Cross and other charitable organizations on hand to help. As early as 1940, Churchill had set up a committee of surpluses, to accumulate provisions for eventual liberation; it became, in 1941, the Inter-Allied Committee on Post-war Requirements, based in London. Preparations had intensified at the time of Operation Overlord, the allied landings in France, and in June 1944, two days before D-Day, SHAEF (Supreme Headquarters, Allied Expeditionary Force), had issued its first instructions for dealing with refugees. Eventually, it was agreed, relief for displaced people would be handed over to the UN Relief and Rehabilitation Administration (UNRRA) founded by forty-four allied governments to help countries liberated from Axis occupation. The task was assumed to be far too large for any one organization – even the International Committee.

As it turned out, there were more refugees, in a worse state, than had ever been expected. In August 1945, 17,500 homeless people entered Berlin every day. From Bayreuth, the International Committee delegate, J. Pfeiffer, wrote to say that typhoid had broken out among the Poles, Lithuanians, Estonians, Ukrainians and Hungarians who filled the city, and that the death rate among children was rising sharply. 'There is a no-man's land between the American and Russian lines and it is filled with thousands of people from every nationality, in an advanced state of malnutrition . . . Most of them want to get away from the Russians, but the Americans don't want them.' From Baden-Baden, where the delegate, Denis Favre, had been sent, came a resumé of conditions in the DP camps he had visited. 'Treves-Faven, 4,545 people. Camp contains about 1,200 people too many. There is not enough milk for the children, women or the elderly . . . Infirmary filthy . . . Atmosphere terrible.'

With the prisoners-of-war, and those who had somewhere to go, the military acted with great speed, repatriating 80,000 people a day during the summer months of 1945, by truck, train and even barge. When

SHAEF wound up its operations in July, leaving western Germany and Austria under the military command of British, American and French zones, many millions of displaced people were already home. But they had been the easy ones, and those now left to UNRRA, to the military in the zones of occupation and to the vast assembly of willing organizations, of which the International Committee and the Red Cross societies were the leaders, would prove awkward, desperate and often intractable.

Among these were the children. A British Red Cross team, reaching Rotterdam with the Allied troops, came upon a small hospital. Among its 300 child patients were ninety babies, 'tiny, discoloured creatures with stick-like limbs, clawed hands and large heads'. The wards were almost totally silent, but if you listened hard you could just hear a persistent background sound of soft whimpering. The older children were found 'thoughtfully scratching one twig-like arm with the little purple claw of the other'.

Plans had long been under way for a rescue operation for Europe's children, whose suffering, a Save the Children Fund report suggested, 'has probably never been surpassed, and seldom paralleled on the long Via Dolorosa of the human race'. But no one had quite expected what now faced them. Every place freed by the Allies revealed abandoned, hungry, frightened and sick children, apathetically crouching in the ruins of buildings, starving to death in deserted schoolrooms or hospitals, or roaming the roads in search of something to eat. Reports were soon reaching the Red Cross societies of 700 orphans found in prisons in Lódź, in Poland, of 60,000 Dutch children with neither homes nor parents. From the Russian zone came news of 1.2 million refugee children, many of them sick or malnourished. The International Committee, quickly perceiving that this was an area in which the wide vision provided by their scattered delegates could prove helpful, started collecting statistics. They put out a statement saying that they estimated that thirteen million children in Europe had lost their natural protectors. Three million of these were in Poland. 'We cannot . . . in view of information which is continually brought to our attention,' the International Committee cabled the American Red Cross, 'remain indifferent to situation war victims especially children who are affected by this immeasurable distress.' The left-wing publisher Victor Gollancz, launching his Save Europe Now campaign, wrote: 'It is not in accordance with the traditions of this country to allow children – even the children of ex-enemies – to starve.'

Not all damage was, as the medical experts and psychologists pointed out, physical. Intensive feeding programmes could do much to keep at bay new cases of rickets, and children emerging wan and very frail, looking several years younger than their age, regained weight at a satisfying speed. But their mental health would prove slower to cure, particularly when they had spent the war years working as slave labour for the Nazis. It was clear to the International Committee, as they took stock of who the children were, that those of an age to work had been allowed to live, while those too young had been left to die. One relief worker described thirty Polish girls who had worked on farms in Germany: 'Most of them were in rags, all showed marked effects of malnutrition and mental anxiety. Their hair was a mat filled with lice. All had skin infections, two so seriously that they were unable to wear shoes . . . Some were so confused that they thought themselves German.' Another came across a fifteen-year-old Romanian boy whose parents and baby sister had died at Oranienburg, while he, two brothers and a sister were sent to Auschwitz. During a march to another camp, the two younger boys were kept back by guards; his last sight of them was 'huddled together on the roadside'. His remaining sister disappeared into Gleiwitz concentration camp. The boy himself was rescued by the Americans while on his way to Dachau. He was now completely alone.

Some of the children gathered in by the Red Cross and UNRRA were found to be mute; all were wary and suspicious of things the relief workers found hard to anticipate. They refused to eat ice cream, because it was cold and looked odd, they shrank from physical contact and they seemed indifferent to death. They appeared to expect nothing from adults. Children became the subject of one of the International Committee's first post-war appeals, after Huber convened a gathering of children's organizations in Geneva in the early autumn of 1945. It was addressed not only to governments and national Red Cross societies but to the whole world. 'Only an immediate and concerted effort can avoid an unprecedented catastrophe. The situation is so serious in many parts of Europe that we are obliged to issue this cry of alarm . . .' From all over the world, special funds, earmarked for the relief of children, started to arrive.

* * *

It was in the field of civilian relief that the International Committee and the Red Cross societies really came into their own. It was work they knew well and they had spent the years of peace preparing for it. From the moment the Allies landed in North Africa, both the American and the British Red Cross societies had sent teams close behind, first to act as hospital visitors and provide 'comforts', later to take relief to those devastated by the war. Remembering the epidemics and famine that had followed the First World War, they sent 'spearheads' in khaki dress with special berets and badges to follow behind the troops, like the early Red Cross commissioners of the Franco-Prussian war, to survey what would be needed and hand out instant emergency help. When the Allies reached the toe of Italy, the British Red Cross set up a depot in a Pirelli warehouse in Bari: when they reached Rome, the British took over Prince Boncompagni's Villa Aurora, while the American Red Cross occupied the Hotel Berberini.

In September 1943, the decision had been taken by the Allied military high command to put all civilian relief into the hands of the American Red Cross. There had followed a conciliatory letter to the British Red Cross from Norman Davis, president of the American society, saying how much he would value British partnership. The rivalry that inevitably followed, with the British complaining that they had been turned into poor relations, was not really dispelled until the closing months of the war. Mindful of North Africa, which the American Red Cross had in fact reached some weeks *before* the British society, a British Red Cross advance party landed on the French coast on 11 June, five days after D-Day, followed by the first welfare officer on 19 July. In their wake came a motor ambulance convoy, a mobile chiropody unit and supplies, the dominating feature of Red Cross life: in the two weeks after D-Day, five million cigarettes, 25,000 toothbrushes and 29,000 pairs of pyjamas were taken across the Channel and distributed to field hospitals. A Major Guise took over the Château de Cambrai, filled a nearby barn with his Red Cross stores and went to reconnoitre his surroundings.

The International Committee had agreed to set up delegations in each of the three German zones of occupation with a fourth in Berlin. Delegates were despatched from Geneva to run them. Vlotho, a sixteenth-century town of half-timbered houses near the British military headquarters at Bad Oeynhausen, not far from the Cologne—Berlin autobahn, was made the base for all relief work in the British zone, and it was here that twenty-three national Red Cross societies and many other voluntary organizations working with them gathered. From the International Committee in Geneva, after his stint in London, came Nicholas Burckhardt whose job was to oversee the trains bringing relief into Germany, making certain that each had a delegate on board to prevent looting and hijacking. (The wagons were labelled 'books'.) Burckhardt made friends among the railway staff, for they were often the only ones with working telephones. By the late summer of 1945, Vlotho had become a miniature Geneva. The end of the war had revealed a huge number of undelivered Red Cross parcels, and these were now handed out to civilians as relief, the American ones (liver paste, luncheon meat, tinned salmon and coffee concentrate) considerably more popular than the French (nougat, Maggi soup and dried vegetables) or the Italian (concentrated jam, potato powder, butter and vitamins).

Vlotho was chaotic, busy and good-humoured. Young men and women who had volunteered as drivers found themselves cooking, running de-lousing programmes and coaxing apathetic refugees back to life. A meeting of ten relief teams under the British Red Cross on 24 August 1945 conveys a picture of energy and competence; and just a little smugness. There was talk of the terrible slowness of the official channels, and of effective ways of scrounging. There was a comparison of the different nationalities of the refugees and agreement that, though in need of constant supervision, those from the Baltic states were the most cultured. There were shared complaints about the amount and variety of bedbugs, lice, fleas and assorted vermin. Where all were as one was on the hopelessness of UNRRA, soon, Burckhardt remembers, nicknamed You Never Really Relieved Anybody.

From the minutes of meetings of the British Red Cross, whose committees continued to be dominated by retired diplomats and soldiers, come across the clear, shrewd voices of competent women officers who travelled around Europe patrolling their beats with humour and determination. Even translated into the neutral language of the committee, they still breathe fire. Sidney Jeanetta Warner, director of the Foreign Relations Department, was one of them, a woman who looked formidable in her uniform and spectacles, but who gives the impression on paper of being shrewd and kindly. Soon after the surrender of Germany, Miss Warner set out for the Continent: she was appalled by the destruction of Hamburg, and watched chains of German civilians shifting rubble from what had been their homes, admired Belgian Red Cross resourcefulness and reported on the Swedish Red Cross handing out gruel and carrot soup to children. She reached Berlin through the debris of abandoned tanks and cars, and visited the ruins of the Chancellery, 'the pavement torn up and smashed, what furniture remains destroyed and ripped to pieces ... papers, books, desks and most nouveau-riche looking chandeliers made one feel that most evil and degraded human beings must have lived there ... Added to this, there is, of course, a pervading smell of rotting wood, if not rotting bodies.' Everyone was worried about the coming of winter. Ella Jorden, a medical missionary in China at the time of the Japanese invasion, and later interned by the Japanese in Shanghai, went off to work with German refugees from East Prussia, and found them living in bunkers, 'grey-skinned people, whose lives were spent sleeping and walking in labyrinths of air-raid shelters ... a sullen army of helpless humans, living in conditions which would be condemned by any livestock inspector.' Not all the victorious countries felt much sympathy with the idea of taking relief to Germans, Victor Gollancz remarking that the Germans were being starved 'not deliberately in the sense that we definitely want them to die, but wilfully in the sense that we prefer their death to our own inconvenience.'

By August, the British Red Cross had 900 people working in north-west Europe, doctors, drivers, mechanics, dietitians and shorthand typists, camping in the ruins of chateaux, in tents, in college halls and naval barracks, doing everything from serving tea to taking down letters. Wherever they went, they found child refugees covered in impetigo, eczema, boils, ulcers and burns. An air of urgency hung over everything they did, as the numbers of displaced people never seemed to go down, as supplies were used up and petrol ran low. Lists and instructions multiplied, as if forms and documents, properly filled in, could somehow be made to contain the chaos, though the methods adopted then are still considered the most efficient. 'Who has been displaced?' read one form. 'When? Where? Why? Who, while displaced, has died? ... married? or had a child born? Who, having been displaced, remains displaced? Where? Why?' It seemed, sometimes, to have an Alice in Wonderland quality to it. *Over to you*, a British Red Cross magazine that ran for just a few issues, remarked on how little joy there now seemed to be among the exiled who were going home.

Joan Couper, one of a British Red Cross team of ten women and seven men who had followed the British army during the Italian campaign, found herself in Piedmont when the war ended. The diary she kept is a mixture of ruefulness and exuberance: terrible roads, magnificent views. 'Foggia: visit remote villages: "Are you Christian?" Guard against grateful recipients . . . Typhus protection – 5 squirts. Florence: Rescue Berenson [The noted art critic, by then eighty, who had passed the war years in Italy] . . . Jewish children in convents . . . DP with hens, mud, chains. Bologna: shaven headed women . . . DPs walking home: food points.'

Most of her work took her to camps of civilians awaiting repatriation, but at one point she found herself visiting British and American residents who had sat out the war in Italy, in ever-growing penury, in Fiesole and San Domenico above Florence. Breaking them down into

1. elderly women, often retired governesses in need of help . . .
2. well to do foreigners, with houses and property, would manage if could be tided over with emergency rations . . .
3. a number of Marchesas and Principessas, British or American married to Italians, for whom 2. would apply, and
4. nuns, 2 convents for English speaking nuns, very willing to help.

Besides these, she noted that there was a 'rather nebulous mass of Italian-speaking persons who produce British passports . . . but make demands in a distinctly Italian manner . . . one has a grandmother dying from colitis who was in urgent need of 6 tins of corned beef . . .' By October, Joan Couper had unearthed '1,125 Allied Nationals' in the hills above Florence, set up a local committee to liaise with the British Red Cross, under a Mother Superior, the British chaplain and 'two or three people with a large acquaintance', organized for a 'family of 5 Cypriots [to be] removed from a fastness in the wild wet wood above Firenzuola', requisitioned an abandoned shop to act as centre for supplies, taken on a part-time cleaner and persuaded a local butcher to cut up meat into rations in return for some extra food. A Miss Turner, with a car, was put in charge of ferrying rations to 'invalid ladies, living some distance away'.

According to Miss Couper's timetable, Mondays were ration day for 37 Dutch, 12 Norwegians, 4 Danes, 57 Greeks, 13 Czechs, 27 South Americans; Tuesdays were the turn of Poles and Russians, while Wednesdays were devoted to 97 Yugoslavs, 18 Belgians, 7 Chinese and 27 'Other Nationalities'. It is impossible not to feel that she was enjoying herself. By November, rations were flowing so smoothly that she permitted herself a trip 'further afield' battling against formidable odds of 'mud, broken bridges, chains, white bullocks, really Kingly pot-holes' to ferret out more Allied nationals. Two young Poles were discovered in the care of some outlying nuns, and an elderly lady in a psychiatric hospital, 'Allied, but exact nationality a little obscure'. A Marchesa Bottini had been attached to her as interpreter, and the two ladies managed to see off a marauding rival field officer, who was thought to have designs on her patch. At times, Miss Couper would have passed as a character from the novels of E. M. Forster.

Mrs Thorold, of the British Red Cross, started her refugee work in Germany and in the early summer of 1945 was posted to Odessa. Having unnerved one officer – he expected 'something resembling a She-Bishop' – she turned out to be charming and highly efficient, quickly winning over even the normally suspicious Russians. For three months, with two other Red Cross ladies, Mrs Thorold distributed chocolate and cigarettes to former prisoners-of-war, paid daily visits to those in hospital, called on mothers and babies, and transported people around Odessa in her car, including 'one lunatic and one inebriated American'. In her report for the British society she praised her two companions, Mrs Veale and Miss Macrae, for their 'excellent work', but commented that they were not 'very suitably equipped for rough and sometimes dirty work' and expressed reluctance to 'spoil their good clothes'.

During the years of war, American Red Cross chapters across the United States had been knitting and sewing steadily. Thirty-four million garments had been turned out and sent to serving American soldiers and the needy civilians of Europe. Stocks were now running low, and the American Red Cross spent a million dollars on buying textiles, wool and cotton so that the knitters and sewers could keep on working. By the late summer of 1945, the American society had 2,200 people stationed in Europe, distributing relief and medical supplies, and working, according to their statutes, on behalf of American soldiers in the field, and not only as the British society was restricted to doing, with wounded prisoners-of-war. While none of their supplies could compare with the major relief programme run by UNRRA — despite the scepticism of the volunteers in Vlotho — it was now moving supplies to over twenty countries in three continents, with 15,000 professional staff and 35,000 local recruits — the American Red Cross had, like the other societies, carved out its own niche. If the British sometimes sound a little bossy, the American tone was upbeat and somewhat sanitized. The clubs started for the American soldiers in Britain had followed close behind the American troops when they crossed to Europe, and were now highly professional outfits, skilled at turning disused theatres and half-ruined inns into craft shops, libraries and bars, and importing ping-pong tables, pianos and Victrolas for 'impromptu stunt features'. As the fighting ceased, so the Clubmobiles and their doughnut girls were perceived as ever more important, to protect exhausted and 'let-down' soldiers 'against that terrible mental and physical strain', particularly in places where they were not allowed to fraternize with locals. In the memos that sped across the Atlantic, there was much talk, along with calls for spare felt for pool tables and juke box parts, of whether or not the time had come to 'screen *Fräulein* for our dances'. So far, wrote W. A. Stephens, commissioner in Germany, 'we have used only DPs or American girls, but the DP girls are often of less desirable calibre than the better class German fraulein would be'. When the American Red Cross announced that it would at last be getting out of doughnuts and food, there were squawks of protest that the 'two things that a man away from home in a foreign country has always looked for first in a Red Cross club is something to eat, and then an American woman with whom to talk.' (When prisoners-of-war and internees emerging from the camps were not all found to be in good enough shape to digest the ubiquitous doughnut, there were many consultations with dietitians, after which the Clubmobiles offered egg nogs, made with powdered milk and powdered egg, instead.)

The memoirs of Kitty Gillman of the British Red Cross, who sailed on board the *Gripsholm*, repatriating troops from Algiers to Britain, gives a flavour of the rivalry between the American and the British societies, and their very different styles. On board she found a Mrs Caffrey of the American Red Cross and soon established that she had 'no idea about dealing with large numbers of soldiers . . . Had I been on board sooner, everything would have been easier . . .' The supplies belonging to the British, American and Canadian societies got muddled up, Mrs Caffrey proved incompetent at dealing out 'comforts', the Canadians had the best chocolate but the Americans had slippers, while the American ladies envied the British their 'chic brown and white trouser suits'. The American soldiers, Kitty Gillman noted happily, did not much care for 'their civilians. So I mothered them in the best way I could.'

Most of the vast sums of money spent in liberated Europe by the various Red Cross societies came from donations. In Britain, £1m was raised every month well into the sixth year of the war. Small repeated appeals, like the 'penny-a-week', brought in £20m. Auctions were always good as fundraisers, though few, perhaps, were as imaginative as a sale held in Chile at Punta Arenas one Friday night by a women's committee. The report of the event spoke of 'ten sheep, a dozen sheep's tongues, kidneys and livers, twelve chickens, two ducks, five pork brawn, five sacks of cabbages, two sacks of turnips, potatoes, celery, parsley, five large fruit cakes, swiss rolls, buns, scones, tarts, pies, apples and home-made sweets'. To all Red Cross societies all over the world, destined for despatch to post-war Europe, came the most random and varied of gifts in kind, from Wellington boots to fishing rods, billiard tables to aspirins. In London, the British Red Cross opened a bonded store for tobacco, cigars, cigarettes and playing cards (then subject to duty). There was always a shortage of hot water bottles.

In 1939, the International Committee had employed just two people to deal with relief supplies; by the end of the war it was running the biggest single relief operation in the world after UNRRA. Though that role was quickly taken over by the major feeding programmes operated by the Allies, the International Committee, like the national societies, moved into areas either overlooked by everyone else or simply too unpopular for others to wish to take on. From early in the summer of 1945, it had a travel document service, providing rudimentary papers that enabled displaced people to move around. When it became clear that 14 million members of various racial minorities would be expelled from their countries of original domicile – like the Germans of Poland,

Czechoslovakia and Hungary — they launched a determined campaign to make certain that they received treatment as good as that handed out to civilian internees. As the winter of 1945 set in, the weather soon producing the harshest cold and rain for many years, the Committee again took on one of the roles it knew best, that of appealing to the world's conscience. As ever, the language it used was sonorous. There was, it said, a 'catastrophe menacing ... millions of people who are starving, without shelter, insufficiently clothed, ill-protected against epidemics, enfeebled by privations of every kind. These disinherited will be unable to survive the coming winter ...'

In 1948, UNRRA would be wound up, and the million or so refugees who had still not found homes, who could not be repatriated and to whom the West continued to feel some kind of obligation, were handed on to an International Refugee organization, set up for a five-year lifespan by the newly created United Nations. By the time their mandate was up, 177,000 'hard core' refugees remained in Austrian and German camps. They were, for the most part, ill, depressed, difficult; some disturbed, some politically suspect, some with TB or paralysed, destined to live out the remainder of their lives in camps. No one wanted them, not even the UN High Commissioner for Refugees, who inherited the task of caring for them. He, too, was supposed to have a limited mandate: long before it fell due, it was clear that these refugees, Huber's 'disinherited', were here to stay.

*   *   *

Sigrid Bork, born 1940. Brown-grey eyes; dark blond curly hair. Our daughter is extremely sensitive. She keeps her mouth open because she has trouble breathing through her nose ... The last time we saw her she was wearing a small black coat, red slippers, a blue cap, dark grey muff, red scarf, grey-brown gloves ... On 2 March 1945 we had to leave her in a hospital because of suspected diphtheria. From there she was taken away by nurses. These nurses might be able to tell us where she is, but we can't find their names ... Who can help us?

This cry, signed 'Getrud Bork. Mother', appeared on a poster in the early summer of 1945. Alongside it was a passport-sized photograph, showing a startled, round-eyed child, her mouth a little open.

Sigrid was just one of 298,000 children lost on German territory during the final months of the war and the summer of liberation. Thirty-three thousand of them were 'foundlings', children picked up by the roadside or lifted from the bodies of their dead parents to which they were clinging, so young or so confused that they could not remember or say their names. Posters, with rows of small faces and the anguished pleas from distraught parents were to be seen in 1945 in every post office, bus terminus and train station. Refugee centres were full of men and women holding snapshots, battered, faded little photographs, left over from family holidays or kindergarten gatherings, wandering round and round, asking all new arrivals whether they had ever seen their child.

There was Bruno Schwarz, who stares out anxious and waif-like from his photograph, his ears protruding from close-cropped hair. 'Born 4.3.42. Eyes blue, hair very fair. The child was wounded in Heiligenbeil, East Prussia, and taken to the district hospital.' There was Stella Falck, a 'quiet and calm' child with a particularly deep voice and a doll which had real fair hair, could say Mummy and Daddy, and to which she was very attached; Siegfried Rzegotta, a solid, plump baby, 'born 1.7.43., eyes pale blue, hair fair . . . last seen in February 1945 . . . wearing a dark blue romper suit with his full name printed on it'; and Norbert Wolf, a laughing fair child in a peter pan collar, 'born 8.6.42, eyes blue, hair blond. Went missing on 7 May 1945 on the Czech border.' The descriptions give little away: one can only guess at the anguish of their parents.

Then there were the missing adults, parents sought by 'foundlings' with numbers but no names, whose faces peer blankly from posters headed 'Who am I?' Number 337 looked Scandinavian, her straight blonde hair parted on one side and held back with a clip. 'Name: unknown. Born c. 1940. Eyes blue, hair fair. The child tells us that she is from the Schosberg area. Her mother was bleeding profusely in Kolberg. Nothing else is known.' Dark-haired Number 9, who thought her name was Marlis had been rescued by a sailor from the *Memel*, when the ship went down. Her mother and three brothers and sisters were believed to have been drowned. Some of the lost children at least knew their names, like Peter Podbielski, who wasn't sure of his age, but knew that he had siblings. 'The child says: "Mother went shopping and never came back".' With these lost children, a whole new tracing method was worked out, the smallest detail prised from make of clothes, habits, scars, birthmarks.

The lost were not of course all children. The war had parted wives from husbands, brothers from sisters, soldiers from civilians; in the sea of dispersed people they searched for each other like players in some ghastly game of blind man's buff, groping round Europe. Alongside the soldiers, whose faces, like those of the children, stared out of posters hung in all the places in which refugees might congregate, were descriptions of appearance and character. Wolfgang Mehlhose, a serious, square-faced young man in rimless spectacles, 'last heard of 3 March 1945 from a bridgehead on the river Oder. Said to have been taken prisoner at Alt-Tuchend.' Mehlhose was twenty-one. Near him on the same poster was thirty-eight-year-old Sergeant Josef Graf, studious in collar and tie, a porcelain painter 'seen in May 1945 in Auschwitz, most probably left there on 25th or 26th May 1945 for Siberia. Since then there has been no news.' From graves, from interviews with survivors, from military records and hospital registrars, a hunt for the dead, as for the living, began.

Few documents give a better idea of the dispersal of people by the Nazis and the difficulties that now faced the searchers, than the accounts of the liberation of the concentration camps. It was not just a question of age or nationality: there were a dozen different languages and dialects, any number of illnesses, both physical and mental.

Sandbostel lay between Hamburg and Bremen. As the Allies advanced across Europe and the Germans drove their political detainees by forced marches northwards, its camp became a receiving centre for thousands of sick, exhausted, dying people. The British reached Sandbostel on 29 April 1945. They had not been expected so soon.

The camp contained about 6,000 people. Typhoid had broken out, and as the detainees died their bodies had been piled into mass graves, without identification. Two weeks earlier, a transport full of prisoners from the camps had been refused admission; it was still there, near the gates, but very few of those inside the cattle trucks were still alive. In the camp office, three tonnes of unsorted papers were found, most of them admission cards. There was no death register.

Bit by bit, order of a kind was imposed on the living. The sick, who tended to wander at will, often naked, were given identity tags — yellow for typhoid, blue for TB, pink for everything else. The tracers now turned their minds to the dead, the thousands buried in unmarked pits, and the missing, those for whom admission cards had been found but for which there existed no word of whether they had died or been transferred. What had happened to Comdt. des Plas, of the French Resistance, arrested in July 1944, who had written to his wife shortly before the Allies arrived saying that he was in good spirits, expected to be liberated any day, but was 'physically low'? To Chaim Langleben from Wilno in Poland, of whom nothing was known except his age, fifteen? Or Louis Octave Daniel, born 1900 in St Brieuc, last seen alive a few days before the arrival of the British?

Not far away lay Neuengamme, a concentration camp built in 1940 by the Nazis for 2,000 inmates, and filled as the war went on with between 7,000 and 14,000 prisoners. When it was liberated by the Allies, in the spring of 1945, it was found to contain 38,000 men and 10,000 women, Russians, Poles, French, Germans, Dutch, Yugoslavs, Italians, Spaniards, Greeks, Hungarians, and 1,150 people of 'other nationalities'. Some had already been in the camp many months; others were being prepared for departure when the Allies surprised the German guards by their arrival; others again were parked in railway carriages nearby, await-ing further deportation. A few lay dead. The convoy of lorries about to take them to Belsen had been hit by bombs. There were packed goods wagons, ready to carry loot to nearby safety; in the camp itself, fires had been lit to burn incriminating documents which would have helped identify the dead, who now lay in shallow mass graves. Hundreds of prisoners had been drowned in the previous weeks, when the Germans tried to move them by barge to other camps.

Neuengamme had seen many executions; and it had been one of the camps used by Gebhardt and his colleagues for medical experiments – particularly tests on six-year-old children for tuberculosis.

The Allies arrived to find total confusion. One of their first concerns was to try to discover who was in the camp and the names of those who had died there. Dozens of relief workers set about the enormous task of taking down the details of the living, hampered by foreign names incorrectly spelt, false names given to spare families pain, either at the time of arrest or now because they did not want to be sent to what had been their homes, by the uncertainties of central Europeans, who no longer knew what new nation they belonged to, and by Jews, who said only that they were Jewish. When after many weeks a tally was at last made, the Allied searchers found themselves short of nearly half the names of those they believed to have been in Neuengamme. The difference of 36–37,000 'male subjects in the average age of 17 to 45,' says the report, 'are the dead of Neuengamme'. Finding out who precisely the dead were, and how and when they came to die, became one of the many tasks taken on by the Red Cross in the wake of the war.

By the summer of 1945, the International Committee had come a long way in the field of tracing. They knew how to unravel names, had learnt which letters were easily distorted and how sounds were transcribed in dozens of languages, were good at working out that a lost Italian whom the Germans called Dell Dea was much more likely, given writing styles and their own instinct for what belonged with what, to be Dell'Oca; they were experts at who to contact where, and who might help with their enquiries.

But this was a task of a different dimension. It involved not only the military, but civilians. One in every four Germans was said to have been lost, or to be seeking a lost relation. The International Committee was not so much unprepared as overwhelmed, for preparations had been going on both in Geneva and in various national Red Cross societies for many months. The story of the British Red Cross tracing programme, and its close work with Geneva, gives a picture of how close, in 1945, the Red Cross world had become.

In May 1940 there had been a Wounded, Missing and Relatives department in London. With the fall of France its work had grown at such a rate that it had taken on 470 searchers, recruited on the basis of their tenacity, tact and commonsense. Muriel Monkhouse, who died in 1997, in her late eighties, joined the foreign relations department in June 1940, when the first of what would become 30,000 French enquiries came in. The office then consisted of a few French speakers, and three professional typists. All were volunteers. Muriel Monkhouse was told: 'Stay three months and you will get a badge.' She stayed fifty years. Sydney Jeanetta Warner had been to Geneva, seen the tracing department and returned to instil not only the methods used by the Swiss, but their addiction to confidentiality. She was, says Muriel Monkhouse, a 'martinet, one of those people you instinctively knew when they were in the building. People who disagreed with her tended to disappear overnight.' When

Mlle Ferrière visited London, she came to see the British tracing service. Muriel Monkhouse can remember her saying: 'Never forget that you are privileged to do tracing.'

There had been a meeting in London early in 1943 between the army, some of the allied commands and the foreign relations department of the British Red Cross, with a view to anticipating problems of tracing that might arise once the Allies landed in Italy and began their march north. In close co-operation with Geneva, where Mlle Ferrière and Melchior Borsinger, the young diplomat who had joined the International Committee just before the war, watched over the tracing departments, bureaux staffed by specialist tracers had followed close behind the Allied forces as they made their way up Italy – and by the summer of 1945 in Italy alone, 106,220 dispersed people from seventy-two nationalities had been registered. Everywhere the army went, trained tracers went with them. SHAEF asked the British Red Cross to set up tracing bureaux in the British zone in Germany, while all over Europe other tracing offices, run by the churches, by voluntary societies, by charities, under the name of *Suchdienst* – tracing service – all in close touch with the International Committee, now opened. It was a formidable task, and addressing it proved to be one of the success stories of Red Cross co-operation.

No war had ever dispersed so many civilians. Many had left their homes without time to make plans or arrange for ways in which they could be contacted. Others had simply been arrested and disappeared. Early in the summer of 1943, the agency in Geneva had produced a standard card, similar to the one for prisoners-of-war, which people parted by the fighting could use to notify their whereabouts to a central register set up in Geneva. The scheme was publicized through the national Red Cross societies and, on their travels backwards and forwards across Europe, delegates had distributed cards widely. By 1944, completed cards were pouring into Geneva: the numbers increased rapidly when it was announced that the cards did not need stamps. With the end of the war, UNRRA had asked the International Committee to act as a central tracing bureau, into which all other tracing operations would feed. Geneva, it was thought, would become the immense central switchboard for the lost.

On paper the arrangement sounded excellent. But in 1945, matters did not proceed altogether smoothly. Though the International Committee went ahead and began to distribute their P10 027 cards in the dispersed persons camps, the Allies continued to delay formally appointing the Committee as lead organization, not least because agreement could never be reached as to the scope of the tracing. The Allies instinctively did not want to waste much time on their former enemies, while the International Committee protested that to restrict tracing to members of the allied nations was in breach of its mandate.

UNRRA now went ahead set up its own central tracing bureau at Höschst near Frankfurt and began to distribute its own cards throughout the three western occupied zones. Tracing systems proliferated and as the months passed, duplication and chaos grew. The two main tracing centres, Frankfurt and Geneva, each filled their own vast indexes, grappling as they had done during the war with names of soldiers, with 25,000 English 'Smiths' and 40,000 German 'Müllers'. Women were found to excel at tracing work, something in their doggedness responding to the meticulous and detailed nature of the job. But even they, for the most part, proved totally unsuccessful in penetrating the mystery surrounding the prisoners who had vanished into captivity in the Soviet Union and the Baltic states. In September 1945, a tracing bureau was theoretically opened in Moscow; enquiries flowed in; very little ever came out.

Tracers were now everywhere, sometimes pursuing their own leads, at others in contact with Geneva, Frankfurt, London, or anywhere else that might prove helpful. Though in the years that followed missing people in their thousands were traced, children recovered, extremely complicated cases solved by dint of laborious hard work carried out by Muriel Monkhouses all over Europe, it rapidly became clear that some kind of overall authority was needed.

Arolsen is a small town in the central German region of Hesse, once the seat of the princes of Walbeck. Their castle, a fine eighteenth-century building surrounded by forests, stands in a hollow, falling away towards a lake. The town is full of trees, wide avenues and small, detached houses; there is little traffic. It was here that, in 1946, UNRRA brought its records on missing and displaced people, here that the tracing bureau, transferred to the International Refugee Office, was rechristened the International Tracing Service, and here that, after the Allied High Commission for Germany was disbanded in 1955, it was given to the International Committee to run and keep safe in perpetuity. As it had long hoped, the Committee at last became the depository for the files on what have become over fourteen million people, victims of the Nazi extermination and concentration camps and of deportations to forced labour in the Reich, as well as displaced people who were in the camps after the war, or who emigrated with the help of the International Refugee Office. Arolsen is a monument not just to the immense Nazi machinery of repression, but to the German love of order and efficiency. When, towards the end of the war, paper ran out, camp records were kept on the back of cigarette packets. Together, these documents provide the details of how the camps were run, throwing light where the *Nacht und Nebel* decree once brought darkness. It is doubtful that any other nation would have left such a legacy.

The town was geographically perfectly placed. It had been loved by Goering for its accessibility and good train connections and now stood at the centre of the four Allied zones of occupation. Vast barracks, left over from its days as a garrison for the Wehrmacht, provided ideal space for the mountain of documents, shipped here first by UNRRA and later by the public prosecutors at Nuremberg, who were delighted to have a safe archive for the papers they had accumulated during the trials. Since that day documents have never stopped coming – from new trials, from archives unearthed in the East after the Berlin Wall came down, from papers found tucked away in basements in private collections over the years, from forays made by the searchers to other countries and other collections, and from constant consultation with the tracing departments of the national Red Cross societies. The International Tracing Service is the second largest employer in the area, after a local factory: fifty years after the end of the war, there are still nearly 400 people on its staff, paid for by Germany. The director of Arolsen is always an International Committee delegate, guarantor of neutrality.

Arolsen lends itself to statistics. It is hard to find other ways to convey its sad, odd tone, a mixture of sterility and overwhelming tragedy. The buildings, unremarkable long white houses, several storeys high, running down one side of a tree-lined avenue, are silent, clean, free of dust. The staff move around the long, straight rows of buff-coloured files and boxes quietly, to the faint hum of an air conditioner which keeps the temperature constant. The feeling is not of an archive but a laboratory. Over nineteen kilometres of boxes run through the buildings, holding some forty-five million separate pieces of paper. Most of the fourteen million people to whom they refer are of course dead, for what is kept here reflects both the numbers who died in the camps and those who survived and later sought confirmation for pensions or insurance, since time spent in the service of the Reich counts double in compensation terms. More haunting is the fact that the records of only two million of the fourteen million people whose wartime repression and anguish are so painstakingly preserved have ever been consulted. For the other twelve million, the knowledge is there but no one has ever asked for it.

Lately there has been an increase in enquiries – from eastern Europe after the fall of the Berlin Wall, and from people who were children in the camps or who did forced labour. Now, nearing retirement, they need proof that they were indeed, as they claim, victims of the Nazis. Others, nearing their own death, wish to receive confirmation of the deaths, in Nazi hands, of relations whose loss they have never faced up to. The hunger for records of all kinds, documents, birth certificates, photographs and wills, has long been recognized as important in the battle fought by refugees to come to terms with their past lives and rebuild new ones. Inundated by these enquiries, the ITS operates with a two-year backlog; priority is given to enquirers over the age of eighty. To every visitor statistics keep being offered: 3,000 documents are processed through the thirty-two separate departments on any one day, where they might be joined, as they were in the First World War, in 'concordance' – now known as a 'meeting'. In 1967, all names were reduced to a simplified form, half phonetic, half alphabetical, to bring some order to the 352 variations of the name John, or the 156 Schwartzes. Now, in the mid-1990s, nearly all letters come from survivors of forced labour, wanting to benefit from bilateral agreements signed by Germany after the war that they would compensate all those deported. The International Committee certificate is the only one accepted as proof of deportation. Since the early 1960s, Arolsen has also helped provide proof of injuries suffered by those on whom the Nazis conducted their medical experiments, a 'neutral commission' consisting of a German doctor, representatives from Poland and Hungary, and delegates from the International Committee acting as judges.

In all of Arolsen's silent buildings there are no rooms fuller of ghosts than the ones reserved for the concentration camps. On Himmler's orders, many records were destroyed as the guards pulled out and the Allies advanced, but not all commandants had time to carry out his instructions. There is almost nothing for the extermination camps of Belzec and Treblinka: even the Germans saw no point in registering those about to die. For Buchenwald and Dachau, the records are virtually complete: who went there, when, how and often why; what work they did and what money they had with them; who was ill, with what and for how long; who died, who was transported, who, on liberation, was still alive. There are death lists, transport lists, work lists; behind each, neatly recorded in ledgers, lies a story.

As the Allies closed in on Auschwitz, the survivors were packed on to a transport for Buchenwald, their names, ages and professions meticulously recorded. Their train left Auschwitz on 26 January 1945; all on board were men. Some were 'political', and among these were some Jews; some were French Jews, among them an electrician, a fitter, a tailor, a bootmaker, a clockmaker and a cook. There were seven Dutchmen – a radio technician, an electrician, a carpenter, an architect and three fitters; four were from Amsterdam. There was a twenty-three-year-old Spaniard and a thirty-three-year-old Romanian furrier. When the train reached Buchenwald, several were found to have died en route.

Buchenwald was surrounded by sub-camps. Every day, morning and evening, its inmates were counted. On the evening of 4 March 1945, there were 84,226 men; six days later, due to some departures and some deaths, the number had dropped to 80,900. Buchenwald was liberated on the 11th.

The Germans were particularly thorough when it came to trains carrying the deportees which, on Himmler's orders, had priority even during the frenzy of retreat. On 27 July 1942, according to yet another register, train number DA901 left Le Bourget-Drancy outside Paris at 8.55 a.m. Its destination was Auschwitz. There were 1,000 Jews on board, many already transferred from other camps. Rations of potatoes, bread and beans had been calculated for a fourteen-day journey. Pages of this ledger opened at random list number, nationality and occupation of those on board line by line. Many were elderly; there were several shoemakers and apprentice dressmakers. This ledger has, however, always baffled Arolsen searchers. Some names have faint pencil marks running through them and at the end there is a new list of names, apparently added later. Did those with pencil marks die on the way? or before? and were they replaced at the last minute? From that transport there were probably no survivors.

For Gross-Rosen, the camp in what was then Silesia, almost no document has ever been found. There is, however, a list on lice. Every few days, prisoners were checked for lice and the number found recorded on lice control cards, later copied into a register. In these faded pages, now flaking away from the ledger's spine and filed in boxes in a row on shelves in a quiet grey room, the scene comes alive, men and women standing in a line, their heads lowered for inspection. On 2 November 1944, number 30,705 had just one louse; number 70,730 had ten. The ledger is all there is to tell who was in Gross-Rosen that day.

Arolsen is not only about statistics; it is about lives, some still being lived. Not long ago, a woman wrote from France to ask for help in tracing her natural parents. She was the daughter of two foreign workers, of whom she knew only the names and the place where they had worked in 1945. She had no memory of them, having been adopted by a nurse in whose care her father had put her at birth. Consultation of the card index told searchers that the mother had been seventeen when she gave birth, that she was Greek and that she had not wanted to keep the baby. The father was Dutch. The tracers contacted the Greek Red Cross, who tracked down the mother, now married and with another child. Having always regretted her decision, she was delighted to be reunited with her daughter. The Dutch Red Cross discovered that the father was dead; but his widow was willing for his daughter to visit the grave.

Arolsen is a closed archive. One day, says the International Committee, it will be opened to historians. Until then it remains a place of record, the most complete written record of the Nazi deportations, to be consulted by the living, in search of the dead or of their own past.

No corner of the tracing work was more poignant than the search for stolen children, whether for the young boys taken from their schools or as they worked in the fields as slave labour, or those selected for the Germanization programme. As the fighting stopped, parents clamoured for their stolen children, many last seen three or even four years before. Not all, when found, would want to go home. German had become their first language and they had no memories of the frantic women who now appeared and claimed to be their mothers. Only slowly, bit by bit, did the Allies piece together the scale of the Nazi's racial ambitions. Documents captured in liberated towns first suggested that there might be as many as 50,000 stolen children, once Swedish, Czech, Norwegian, French, Dutch and above all Polish but now, in theory, German. By 1946, there were 200,000 enquiries from Poland alone.

In order to cope with the sheer number of stolen children special child-search teams were formed under an American woman called Eileen Blackie, who had been a friend of Eleanor Roosevelt; they worked closely with the International Committee and the Red Cross societies of the countries concerned. Bavaria, an area to which a number of the kidnapped children had been taken, became the centre for the first team of searchers. Within a few months of peace, nearly 1,000 of the kidnapped children had been found and returned to their families. More teams were now set up, with linguists in particular demand: by the time the search programme reached its peak, twenty-seven languages were being spoken. One of the hardest assignments, they soon found, was the search for babies born to women brought to the Reich for forced labour, who were taken from their mothers at birth for the *Lebensborn*, the fountain of life programme. These babies, as Roman Hrabar sees it, were 'kidnapped even before they were born'.

Dr Hrabar is a Polish lawyer, a distinguished-looking man in his late eighties who wears old-fashioned suits and has old world courtesy and manners. In 1945 he was working for the social welfare department of Katowice, an important crossroads for refugees moving east and west. Hrabar had been a member of the Polish Red Cross before the war and had been arrested by the Gestapo in Cracow but saved from the concentration camps by the arrival of the Russians. In 1945 he was in touch with dozens of Polish parents searching for their stolen children. When UNRRA approached him to join the child-search team in Heidelberg, he went willingly. Apart from Polish, he spoke English and Italian learnt from his mother, and German from his student days in Munich.

Heidelberg, and later Wiesbaden, became centres for the child-search teams. Like the original team of Nazi kidnappers, who had been experts in the subtle traits of racial value, these new post-war searchers became detectives, skilled at working from the smallest clues, trying to understand the thinking in the Nazi minds as they took the children. They were much helped by the German sense of order and the German love of records.

Military orders had been issued to give the searchers automatic right of entry into homes and schools. They had been told to interrogate whoever they wished. It was a slow, often frustrating process with sudden, overwhelming rewards. Though the German authorities had been ordered to give up all papers relating to the Germanization programme and to any births to foreigners that had taken place during the war years, many of the relevant papers had been lost in the bombing or destroyed by officers reluctant to see racially valuable children lost to the Reich. Figures were falsified and the painstaking process of identification was frequently thwarted by last-minute denials and disappearances. Hrabar kept travelling, knocking on doors, questioning, searching homes, checking, talking to witnesses, endlessly in contact with other searchers working from lists put together by the International Committee and UNRRA, from information provided by parents, grandparents, aunts, uncles. Sometimes he just stood in playgrounds watching children he suspected to have been kidnapped, listening for words in foreign languages that might give them away. There was an unhoped-for break in 1946 when missing documents turned up in the Ministry of the Interior in Warsaw, giving both the original names of a number of stolen children and their new German names and addresses.

It was from these papers that Hrabar was able to break one of the codes under which the kidnapped children had been processed: faithful to their sense of order, or perhaps simply lacking imagination, the Nazis had used the same first letters of both Christian and surnames, and sometimes even the second and third letters.

Hrabar remembers his successes with immense pleasure. One case he talks about with particular fondness. Two small sisters, Alodia and Daria, came from the Zamość area. Alodia was five and Daria four when their father, a doctor accused of trying to poison a local Gestapo garrison while working for the resistance, was arrested on 9 September 1943 and executed in the town square. Their mother was put on a train for Auschwitz. The two girls were taken by the Brown Sisters to Łódź concentration camp, where they were measured, inspected and decreed racially valuable. From Łódź, they were moved to a *Lebensborn* home in Poznań. Alodia, by now known as Alice, fell ill and was taken to a hospital in Kaliść just at the moment when the girls' uncle had picked up their trail and was close behind. He reached the hospital too late. Only days before Alice had recovered sufficiently to be handed over to a German foster mother, who had wanted to take Daria, now Doris, as well but had been told that it was against the *Lebensborn* policy to take two children from the same family. Alodia/Alice went to Mecklenberg in Germany, Daria/Doris to a town in Austria.

The papers dealing with the two sisters were among those found in Warsaw. Hrabar now had names to work with, though not addresses. Meanwhile the girls' mother, who had survived Auschwitz and Ravensbrück, had come home and was able to provide him with photographs and details of the girls' appearance. She too began to search for the children. Clue by clue, Hrabar traced them to their new homes. Both foster-mothers were sad, but made no fuss. On 6 November 1947, Alodia arrived home on a Polish Red Cross train, with a label tied round her neck. She was nine, and remembered nothing of her mother beyond blonde hair, which had since gone white. Daria arrived a week later. With considerable difficulty the three built a new life together.

There were, however, many thousands of unhappy families. Many of Hrabar's searches led him to the gates of concentration camps; 'T' for 'tot', dead, was stamped on the files. And even when traced not all the children would agree to come home, while those who were forced to do so were sometimes wretched. Among those forcibly repatriated were children who genuinely mourned kindly German women who had done all they could to love and care for their adopted children, who now refused to speak their mother tongue and bitterly resented the poverty of their post-war homes.

At Nuremberg, Dr Hrabar and other searchers provided evidence for the Germanization programme, taking four kidnapped children with them as witnesses. A number of German officers, found guilty of the theft of Polish children, received long prison sentences. Nevertheless, in 1948 the child-tracing operation was abruptly wound up, despite the protests of Mrs Blackie, Dr Hrabar himself and many of the other searchers. Of the 200,000 kidnapped Polish children, barely 30,000 had yet been traced. There were many clues waiting to be followed up. Later, Hrabar was shown a secret memorandum circulated among the senior officers of UNRRA. It said that it was no longer policy to add to the 'biological military strength of the enemy', a phrase that had uneasy overtones of the Nazi's racial designs; he took it to mean that Poland and the Soviet satellite countries, and not Germany, were the enemy now. Hrabar himself went on searching as and when he could, believing that to avoid future genocide, people must know and understand the past. How, he asks, could this have happened, in the centre of civilized Europe? Today, Hrabar believes himself to be the last historian of Poland's stolen children.

Among Hrabar's contacts were members of the German Red Cross, people Hartmann, who had taken on the title of 'acting president' after Gebhardt's arrest, called the 'old guard'. These men and women, Hartmann assured Huber in long and somewhat plaintive letters written in the summer of 1945 to Geneva, had done all they could to 'preserve the true spirit of the Red Cross' during the dark years of war. 'A great number of Germans of all ages,' he wrote on 18 June 1945, now needed to find 'some kind of forward-looking occupation, with a moral dimension . . . they wish, dare I say it, to restore their own sense of pride as human beings and harness it to active and practical humanitarian work – and where better than in the Red Cross?' Just the same, the German society was in trouble. Its coffers were empty and its vehicles had been commandeered by the Allies. Colonel Paul Draudt, who had done so much to broker an agreement between the League and the International Committee, had been killed in the bombing of Darmstadt in November 1944. The Duke of Saxe-Coburg, who, though weak, had proved a mild force for good, was going blind. Of the former presidents, Grawitz had committed suicide to avoid arrest and certain execution and Gebhardt was about to be indicted for crimes against humanity. And which of its five million members could be said not to have been tainted by the Nazis? More than that, as a long memorandum circulated around the International Committee in June 1945 put it, the society itself could not really be said to exist since the German state itself, no longer fulfilling the three criteria of statehood – a people, a recognized government, a territory – had legally disappeared; and no one, for the moment, quite knew what shape a new Germany might assume.

Unlike the Polish society, the German society had spawned no free Red Cross in exile, which would now have been in a position to return to liberated Germany and take office. There was at least one attempt at an internal coup, when Rudolph Nadolny, Germany's pre-war ambassador to the Soviet Union, pronounced himself to be the new president of the German Red Cross, but his claim was quickly silenced. Matters seemed to reach an unprecedented low when Hartmann was arrested by the Americans in the summer of 1945, together with the entire local Red Cross staff, on the grounds that he had done nothing to help the detainees in concentration camps. It took all Huber's powers of persuasion, as well as the testimony of several relief officers that Hartmann had been 'correct' in all his dealings, to get him released.

Though the International Committee was anxious to retain some control over the German society's fate, decisions about its future were taken, peremptorily and with embarrassingly little consultation, directly by the Allies, each zone adopting its own different policy. The British and the Americans, who both felt that the German Red Cross had been 'Nazified throughout the whole of its organization' and nowhere more so than in Berlin, started a thorough process of investigation, checking every member and expelling those they called 'undesirable elements'.

There had been friendly links, before the war, between the American, British and German societies and these now paid off as aristocratic families resumed contact and their members rekindled the old local branches, just as they had always done in the past. These local initiatives, the Allies agreed, should slowly be coaxed back into life. 'Purification,' Nicholas Burckhardt wrote to Geneva from Vlotho, 'needs to be done in a friendly manner and with a lot of tact.' Foreigners living in Germany were particularly prized, and Princess Marguerite, born English and married to Prince Ludwig of Hesse, increased the work she had long been doing for the society in her area and became its president. Anton Schöling, who was a young lawyer in 1945 and would become secretary-general of the German Red Cross between 1958 and 1976, persuaded the Americans to let him and a former local Red Cross branch look after 5,000 refugees taking over what had been the convention halls once used by the Nazis in Nuremberg.

The French, after a report that in their zone the German society had been a 'political organization working underground against the Nazis', were more forgiving, briefly dissolving the Red Cross branches but then allowing former members who had been screened and found clean to resume their work under a renamed organization. The Russians, after an initial period of apparent lenience, suddenly ordered all German organizations with the faintest taint of a Nazi past to be closed, and the German Red Cross with them. It was not until after the foundation of the German Federal Republic that a new national German Red Cross society was formally reborn, on 26 February 1951.

Both Hartmann and Schöling understood that the only real way to regain respectability was through work and to that end they committed themselves, aided by members known to have remained loyal, to tasks they knew they could do well. Tracing was one of them. Through their own files and offices they were able to put together the posters of the lost and dispersed people that now hung in every railway station. By 1948, with the help of Caritas and the Protestant churches, 230 books of the missing, with 900,000 names and photographs, had been published.

Slowly, and more slowly as the time went by, some of the missing were traced and came home, though nearly three million refugees of the forty million adrift in Europe in the closing months of the war died in the turmoil that followed it. Neither Wolfgang Mehlhose nor Josef Graf, the two young soldiers from the posters, was ever heard of again, though in time their families received a 'military expert opinion concerning their presumed fate', a euphemism for death. Some of the parents of lost children were more fortunate. Norbert Wolf, the little boy in the peter pan collar, was traced and reunited with his parents. Peter Podbielski was discovered in a children's home in Lübeck and returned to his father. Foundling No. 9, the dark-haired little girl who called herself Marlis and whose mother, brothers and sisters had gone down in the *Memel*, was recognized by her father from her poster. There was some doubt that she was the right child, for he remembered a girl with blue eyes and light blonde hair, but when he saw her, he knew at once that one of his children had survived.

Bruno Schwartz, the waif-like little boy with protruding ears who had been left in a doctor's care in the hospital in East Prussia while his mother Therese took his sisters to safety, died of his wounds. After the war, his mother waited for him in the West, begging the various tracing services to find him and endlessly trying to discover the names of nurses who had worked in East Prussia and might have come across him. Only in April 1958, when the boy would have been sixteen, did she learn the truth. The director of a cemetery in Celle wrote to say that they had found a grave with the name of Bruno Schwartz. Therese Schwartz, fleeing with her daughters from East Prussia, had lost another son, aged six, in the bombing. Her husband, missing in Romania, has never been found.

Siegfried Rzegotta, whose plump face stares so beseechingly from his poster photograph, last seen in his blue romper suit, never came home. In 1956, his mother Irmgard finally heard from a nurse called Christine Heuber, who had evacuated a group of children from a home late in June 1945 that Siegfried had been among them. Sometime in the frantic journey towards safety, the boy's heart had simply stopped beating.

No one ever came forward to claim foundling No. 337, the Scandinavian-looking little girl. In time, she was given a new name, Gertrude Voss, and a date of birth, 30 March 1940. All attempts to find her real identity failed. In 1976 she wrote to the German Red Cross to say that she was not interested in any further tracing.

SEVENTEEN

One Reference to God

On 8 June 1945, M. de Reynold, a delegate stationed in France, visited the camp of Montreuil-Bellay, where German prisoners-of-war and civilians arrested by the Allies after liberation were being held. He went home that night and wrote a long, confidential report for the International Committee. He had found, he said, dirt, shortage of food and such extreme hostility towards the inmates from their French guards that many were severely depressed. There were no washbasins and no furniture of any kind. Women and children were sleeping on the floor. There was no refectory: meals were taken standing. 'The internees have only the blankets they arrived with,' de Reynold wrote, 'and not always those, for many were stolen before they got here.'

The barracks in which the sick men were held – almost all the men were ill – were like a '*cour de miracles*', he went on, full of the disabled, the blind and the paraplegic. Many had ulcers, abscesses, dysentery and impetigo. Several were over eighty. 'I cannot understand,' said de Reynold, 'why so many elderly, ill, maimed, infirm and paralysed people, as well as young boys and girls and even children are interned under these conditions . . .'

Since the camp kept no list of the names of those it was holding, no one knew how many it contained. Among the women, de Reynold observed 'quite a large number of prostitutes who, physically and morally, have done much to poison the camp'. The guards were letting in men from outside, and the women were offering themselves in exchange for food. Venereal diseases, according to one doctor he had spoken to, were spreading. 'It is a heartbreaking and tragic experience,' de Reynold continued, 'to see on one side a number of women and even young girls relatively well fed, while on the other are those who have retained their dignity – the ugly, the old, the children and the men, who drag themselves painfully around the camp, lifeless and haggard, for these people are hungry and are slowly starving to death.' Even allowing for a certain Swiss prudishness, the picture he painted was shocking.

De Reynold's report, which reached Geneva a few days later, was not altogether unexpected. Nearly a million Germans had been taken prisoner in France in the closing months of the war; many of the men assigned to guard them had suffered from German brutality and now found it hard to resist getting even. Rumours had been reaching the International Committee for weeks about the harshness with which former members of the French resistance, some of them boys no older than sixteen, were treating Germans who fell into their hands. A note about a troop of German soldiers captured by the resistance, by a Herr Grueneisen of the German Red Cross, described the men in rags, their uniforms, shoes and warm clothes taken from them, their heads shaven, their hair pulled out, bullied, beaten, threatened and paraded before angry local people who spat on them. From a camp at St Louis, a German prisoner managed to get a letter out to a Pastor Leuschner in Basle about comrades who were dying: '. . . today's total is 68, about one per day . . .' The pastor's own report spoke of sick and wounded men, left idle for months, with no news of their homes or families, of amputees without proper medical care, and of constant hunger. He also described a wedding feast that had been arranged for a former German commandant of St Louis who had evidently made friends with the French and which took place the same day that six German prisoners, who had died of starvation, were buried. The black market, according to Leuschner, had yielded two sumptuous meals — hors d'oeuvres, consommé, fish, veal, cheese, cakes, ice cream, and several different wines and liqueurs.

From Périgueux came a letter describing the death of a fifteen-year-old German boy, exhausted by a fourteen-kilometre march, who had been battered by a guard and his body buried near a rubbish tip. 'I beg and supplicate you to intervene,' wrote a man called Auguste Gautier, who lived near a German prisoner-of-war camp near Châteauroux, 'as urgently as possible to bring an end to the cruelties inflicted on German prisoners, swindled, starved, without sanitation, without help, dying at the rate of four or five every day.'

By August, stories of brutality against the German captives were reaching Geneva by nearly every post. Jean Courvoisier is a tall, stooping man in his eighties, for whom the years spent in France immediately after the war were among the most unhappy and distressing of his life. In 1944, demobilized from the Swiss army for reasons of health, Courvoisier heard that the International Committee were looking for delegates to go as 'voluntary hostages' to the concentration camps just before they were liberated. He sent in his name. The Committee despatched him not to Germany but to Lyons where he set up an office and a storeroom in his hotel bedroom. His first task was to visit a hospital taken over to house captured Germans, many of them severely wounded. which so appalled him that he considered resigning. 'The French resistance were acting as guards. There were no medicines, and the German nurses were constantly raped. One doctor insisted that I attend an amputation to show what it was like when there were no anaesthetics. He used newspapers for bandages.' Even now, Courvoisier finds it hard to talk of those days.

> Lyons was tough. In the streets, Germans were holding out empty tins and begging for food. Collaborators, even the women, were being hanged and their bodies left in dustbins.
>
> One day I received a letter from a lawyer. He told me about a camp for German civilians, most of whom had fled from the Nazis in the 1930s. He said: 'Come and see for yourself. Appalling things are happening,' I went at once. I found a German woman giving birth on the floor. The 'man of confidence' appointed by the internees kept saying to me: 'Go to the basement, go to the basement.' I cannot tell you, even now, what I saw there.

Though it was by now ten at night, Courvoisier went to find the local mayor.

> It was freezing cold, and totally dark. I knocked on his door. When he saw who I was, he said: 'You have come to talk about the German prisoners.' He told me that his two sons had been shot by the Germans. Then he said: 'I'm French. This can't go on.' He called the local police, and I told them what I had seen. They agreed to take over the camp. I went back to Lyons and talked to the French Red Cross. I explained that even the children were dying. They told me to come back in an hour. When

I got back, they had filled a lorry with food, but they didn't want to be seen driving it. Everyone was terrified of being taken for a collaborator.

The International Committee had twelve delegates in France in 1945 with headquarters in Paris and offices in various cities run by single delegates, each with a car and a driver. Many were little older than students. During his first few months, Courvoisier visited 23,000 German prisoners and internees. Explaining apologetically to Geneva that he was doing his best to get the 1929 Convention applied but that the realities of war made his task more or less impossible, he told them a story. Not long before, four German prisoners-of-war, working on a dam near Lyons, had escaped. The French had seized another prisoner, taken him to the top of a rock eighty metres high, and thrown him off, as a warning to the others working below.

Courvoisier fell ill and went home to convalesce at Vevey. He took the opportunity to write down the issues that had been bothering him on his rounds: the fact that repatriation for the German prisoners never seemed to come any closer; that boys as young as twelve were doing forced labour; that priests and doctors, 'protected personnel' under the Conventions, were not being released to go home; and above all that the Germans, both civilian and military, were being held in impossibly harsh conditions – no news from home, no medicines, no parcels, no books, no religious services. Wherever the French resistance had been most active and the German army most punitive, the prisoners were faring the worst. Was this not in breach of the 1929 Prisoner-of-War Convention, according to which prisoners had to be repatriated at a reasonable speed, fed and sheltered at the same standard as troops and allowed to send and receive mail?

France itself, in 1945, was seriously short of food. The French were reluctant to see much of it go to the Germans. As rations to civilians dropped to as little as 1,200 calories a day, so those to prisoners dropped too. 'There are numerous despairing pleas from men who are all skin and bones and tortured by hunger,' wrote Courvoisier to Geneva. 'But they are all convinced that a visit by a delegate means that they will soon go home.'

In this the German prisoners were wrong. France had seen its economy ruined by five years of war, its agriculture reduced to chaos, its towns and villages razed. German manpower was going to put it right, whatever the articles of the Geneva Conventions. A working day for the Germans now put to work in fields and factories and to rebuild roads and railways often lasted sixteen hours. Everywhere Courvoisier went he was greeted with cries: 'We need blankets, uniforms, underclothes, shoes!' Above all, they needed food. As he travelled round his beat, Courvoisier noted signs of increasing malnutrition. Many of the deaths he described were due to starvation.

The conditions in which the Germans were held were not the only breach of the Geneva Conventions. By the end of the war, the soil of France had been planted with some thirteen million mines, laid in three sweeps across the country: the first in preparation for the Allied invasion, the second in the face of advancing troops, the third by the Allies themselves, to repel a German counter-attack. As French farmers returned to their fields, they were being maimed by unexploded and concealed mines. So the German prisoners were drafted in to march across the fields with steel probes, poking the soil. When they hit a mine, it exploded; when the fields appeared clear, the prisoners were sent back to plough the earth and detonate anything not detected earlier. Later, the French would admit to 2,500 German deaths caused by mines. Courvoisier, called again and again to intervene – there was no ambiguity in the wording of the 1929 article that forbade the use of prisoners-of-war for dangerous work – believes there were more like 20,000 deaths. Those who tried to escape were punished brutally. Another delegate, a man called E. Filliettaz, wrote that when caught, the Germans were beaten up, both by their guards and by the farmers, then fed only once every other day and their workload increased. One of Filliettaz's jobs one day was to locate the mass graves of German prisoners-of-war, shot in batches of forty in the Haute Savoie. 'Generally speaking,' he noted, 'their conditions have no resemblance to those laid down in the Geneva Conventions.'

A note of weary desperation and helplessness comes through these reports from France, a tone not found in many of the International Committee archives. Like Courvoisier, all the delegates were constantly confronted by the fact that there was absolutely nothing that they could do to force the French to stand by the Geneva Conventions. Not surprisingly, then, the German prisoners, who had started out so admiring of the International Committee, grew disillusioned with its powers when none of the things they asked for – letters, better food, protection – were forthcoming.

Some of this disillusionment was reflected in the delegates themselves. The war had gone on too long, with too many pressures. They were exhausted and their morale seems to have sunk to the point that delegations in liberated Europe, once renowned for their probity, now became slightly tarnished by rumours of petty pilfering. Visitors from Geneva returned to report stories that the office in Frankfurt was '*pas sérieux*,' that secretaries came and went as they pleased, that drivers took the cars for their own use. Mrs McCready, attached to allied headquarters and who had been partly responsible for the International Committee's headquarters in Frankfurt, wrote a sorrowful letter to Jean-Pierre Pradervand whom she had known during his earlier work as delegate in North Africa and Washington. She was leaving her job and she wanted to warn him before she left that there was a great deal of bad feeling in Frankfurt between the Americans and the International Committee delegates. None of the things promised under the Geneva Conventions were being done, though the blame for this lay principally with the Americans.

> As you will gather . . . something is wrong . . . A series of articles in the Army Press unfavourable to Switzerland . . . did nothing to help. I remarked a growing dislike of the Delegation and almost a contempt for the Committee, which was described as a 'racket' and a 'gravy train'. The removal of most of the Delegation personnel from Headquarters to live with a German family outside Frankfurt, while continuing to claim messing facilities, office space, furniture, typewriters etc, did not please the authorities . . . In five years working with neutrals . . . I have never experienced national awareness but have always felt everyone was trying to help those who suffered. In Frankfurt it was the opposite and of course, it became odious for everyone.

Then, in the summer of 1945, came a scandal of another dimension.

Technically, the Americans were responsible for the Germans they had captured. But since they did not want them and the French did, the decision was taken to transfer 400,000 prisoners to France to make up the million workers the French estimated they needed to put the country back on to its feet. Switzerland, which had been the protecting power for the Germans, had been informed by the Americans on VE-Day, when the German government was abolished, that they no longer held that role. One result had been that visits by International Committee delegates to American-run camps had been severely curtailed, though the Americans continued to reassure Geneva that they would treat the prisoners according to the 1929 code. The Germans who were now transferred to France from American-run camps at Chartres and along the Rhine arrived emaciated, barely able to walk, many seriously ill with malnutrition. They wore rags, their clothes and personal belongings having been taken away from them. Few weighed over 42 kilos. 'Anyone who isn't fit for work is dismissed out of hand, put into civilian dress (of a meagre kind), cast out into the street, without belongings, without papers,' de Reynold warned the International Committee from Baden Baden. 'These people are dying. The Americans send to the French all those in a bad state of health. What's more, they seize on anyone to make up the numbers, they shove even women and children in a uniform, saying that they had belonged to a Nazi organization.' Very few of the Germans were sufficiently healthy to do any work, those in mining detachments so feeble that they were a danger to themselves and all around them, and doctors began to say that a catastrophe was in the making. The Americans, trying to explain away the men's condition, said defensively that they had already been in French hands for some weeks during which time the supplies they had had with them had been looted. It was all a far cry from the doughnuts and the Clubmobiles.

As urgent reports flowed back from the delegates to Geneva, the International Committee took the almost unprecedented step of sending a cable to the State Department in Washington. It was clear and firm, with few of the usual conciliatory phrases. 'Alarming reports health thousands German prisoners transferred from American camps to French authorities . . . arrived French camps state extreme weakness resulting prolonged undernourishment . . . consequence is overpopulation of French camps by unfit for whom detaining authorities lack requisite means of building up their health.' What they proposed was that the United States should immediately send emergency relief and halt all transfers until the men's health was stabilized. The Americans were also advised to 'increase prisoners' rations in American camps Europe to obviate prolonged undernourishment and aggravation general health'.

Jean-Pierre Pradervand, chief delegate to France, judged the time had come to act. He returned to Geneva and, before a special meeting of the Committee convened on 21 September 1945, gave a summary of what he believed was going on. The minutes record him as saying:

> Of the 600,000 German prisoners-of-war in French hands, roughly 40,000 are not fit for work. The French government has agreed to repatriate these. Another 150,000 must be considered unfit due to malnutrition. The situation continues to get worse with the arrival of prisoners-of-war transferred from the Americans and who are turned over to the French for the most part in very bad shape.

Pradervand told the Committee that he had been approached by the French commandant of the camp at Thoré, where some of the former American-held prisoners were now based. 'Of the 20,000 prisoners in his care, 7,000 are in a seriously bad way.' Delegates despatched to Thoré had returned to report, Pradervand continued, that '2,000 prisoners are beyond help', even with intravenous injections of plasma; '2,000 others are in a very serious condition, but could be treated. 3,000 are severely malnourished, but could be fed by mouth.' What was happening at Thoré, he suggested, was probably happening in camps all over France and Germany.

Four days later, acting entirely on his own initiative, Pradervand took a further step. 'I summoned the delegates under me,' he explained, 'and told them that what I was going to do next might well result in all of us being expelled from France. I wrote personally to de Gaulle, describing exactly what I had seen at Thoré, warning him that many of the German prisoners were not likely to survive the winter.' On the day of his own visit, he told the general, there had been twenty deaths and no coffins in which to put the bodies. 'Together with my letter, I sent photographs, a list of the regulations to remind him of France's commitments under the Geneva Conventions, and some suggestions for immediate action.'

Next, Pradervand went to Frankfurt to talk to the Americans. Articles began to appear in the French newspapers, calling for an end to the 'politics of vengeance'. 'It is our duty,' wrote a correspondent of *Le Figaro* on 19 September, 'to judge the hideous crimes of the enemy and to take every measure we can to make certain that they will never again take another step in the direction of such crimes. But it is also our duty not to imitate him.' There was talk of Thoré being another Dachau. In 1995, Pradervand was in his eighties and had retired after a distinguished career in Swiss politics, almost blind but still full of fire. 'To be a good delegate,' he said, 'you had to be independent. I was a civil servant on holiday, lent to the International Committee by my canton and paid by them. At any moment I could simply have quit.' Like Born or Brown before him, Pradervand proved what single delegates, released from the constraints of Geneva, could do if they chose to.

At last something was done. General Buisson, head of the department dealing with Axis prisoners-of-war in the Ministry of War in Paris, added his voice to that of the International Committee. In America, Henry Dunning of the American Red Cross wrote that the 'situation of the German prisoners-of-war in France has become desperate and shortly will become an open scandal'. The American military now released more food – there were numerous prisoner-of-war parcels that had never been delivered, containing high-calorie provisions – and undertook to halt transfers. Between the 6th and 20th of October. 2,996 tons of provisions were sent in by lorry, together with warm clothes and medicines. The older prisoners-of-war, as well as the sick, were repatriated to Germany. Drugs came with Dr Calpini from the International Committee stores in Geneva, 510 tonnes of tuna arrived from Portugal. By November, the Red Cross delegates had been increased to twenty, with thirty-six assistants and drivers. By early December, 50,000 German prisoners-of-war were back under American supervision. Bit by bit, the great mass of German prisoners-of-war and civilians was sorted out, first into numbers and lists, then into groups – the aged, the infirm, those weighing less than 50 kilos – and finally into individuals. No one really knows how many Germans died as a result of American and French brutality. Reports suggest a minimum of 314,241, which was the number of the missing and not accounted for by the time all who wanted to go home were repatriated. Pradervand concedes it may have been 80,000.

Pradervand's own story is interesting. Sent to Algiers in 1943 by the

International Committee — which had four delegations and about a dozen delegates in North Africa — he was there at the same time as a man called Georges Graz, a mining geologist working in the Congo until taken on by the International Committee and sent to the Spanish Civil War. In April 1943 Graz had been appointed general overseer for the Committee in North Africa. On the night of 14 October he was arrested in his room at the Hotel Aletti. Graz had been, it transpired, an old school friend of a man called Jean-Roger Pagan, who had visited him from time to time at the Aletti, where Graz had spent five weeks ill in his room; Pagan had helped him type up a few Red Cross letters. Pagan had now been caught spying for the German secret services and had confessed to having been sent to Algiers to study American concerns and to identify important landing sites. During questioning, he had mentioned, among other Red Cross people, the name of Graz as an associate.

Graz spent four days in detention, accused of spying on the movements of French troops. He was interrogated in *conditions pénibles* until on 18 October, he was released, after the intervention of the Swiss consul, the Commission of Foreign Affairs and the International Committee. On the 20th, he was taken before Pagan, who repeated his accusations. Just the same, Pradervand managed, as he told me in 1995, to get Graz released and sent back to Geneva. In Graz's room had been found a long report written for Chenevière, largely about the political situation in North Africa. It included several damning remarks about the relations between the Americans and the French, a few critical observations about the French, and some digs about American behaviour in Tunis.

Pagan was executed on 2 December 1944. Before he died, he told a Swiss official who had been to visit him in prison that he regretted having named his old school friend Graz. There was, he said, no truth in his earlier accusations.

However, suspicions had been kindled about what the International Committee was up to in North Africa. The papers in the American secret service files, declassified in 1996, base much of their case against the Committee on Pagan, Graz and Pradervand, who was said to have lived at the Aletti (as did many of the foreigners who went to Algiers during the war) and to have been a member of its officers' mess. The tone of the OSS report is one of mistrust and distaste for the whole

International Committee. Writing about Pradervand, it says that 'he is in very close touch with those who are known to have German connections. Through these contacts, he cannot help but have accumulated valuable information which German IS agents will have no trouble extracting when he clears through them on his forthcoming return to Switzerland.'

The International Committee's verdict on Graz in 1996, after exhaustive enquiries, was that he had been 'imprudent'. There was never any question at all that Pradervand would have lent himself to any illicit activities or that he was a spy, a view borne out by thorough research. But it is possible to speculate that in 1945, when Pradervand orchestrated the campaign to improve conditions for German prisoners-of-war in American and French hands, he was regarded as an unpopular and suspicious figure by the Allied secret services.

Even after the appalling treatment of German detainees had been exposed, and new standards agreed and put in place, the French still found it hard to treat their captives with decency. They agreed to repatriate many but sent them home in sealed carriages without water or food. When the trains reached Tuttlingen where the men were to get off, the prisoners were simply pushed out on the ground, however 'ill or mad'. In December, a convoy arrived in Baden Baden bringing freed German prisoners from Rennes. The journey had taken four days and four nights and the prisoners spent them in locked cattle wagons without food. Four men died on the journey, eight more on arrival. All through the winter of 1945 delegates were forced to abandon their other work and rush to crises, cabling Geneva who, in turn, brought pressure to bear on the French government. Accompanying these prisoners were the 18,000 German civilians, at last repatriated if, for the most part, destitute. Many were German women, brought back with babies by French soldiers at the end of the war and then abandoned.

Not all the Germans, of course, were in a position to leave. When the Allies liberated France, they had arrested and put into separate prisons German soldiers they believed to be guilty of war crimes. Though they played no active role in the cases that were now brought before military tribunals, International Committee delegates were allowed to attend the trials as observers. (There was no International Committee presence at either Nuremberg or the Tokyo trials.) Courvoisier, in Lyon, an area remembered for its bitter war and equally bitter reprisals, was appalled to find the prosecutors demanding the death penalty for every charge. He recalls a young German lieutenant, brought before the tribunal for an act of reprisal, who kept repeating: *'Ich bin unschuldig'* – I am innocent. At 4 a.m. next day he was shot. A little later, the guilty man was found.

Two thousand two hundred Germans, Gestapo, SS and Wehrmacht, who had given orders to shoot partisans, were tried in France, where the Nuremberg rules were brought into play alongside French law. Arguments, between prosecutors and the defence, turned on whether the men in the dock had only obeyed orders or whether, knowing that they would be shot if they refused them, they had no choice but to obey. As time passed, the International Committee assembled a legal team and the trials, conducted earlier in a spirit of hatred and retribution, were made fairer.

Even then, there were many cases that seemed to fit nowhere in the normal process of justice. Madame P. A. van Laar, a Swiss citizen trapped in France by the war, had been refused work by the French Red Cross on the grounds that she was foreign and had finally kept her two daughters alive by working for the German Red Cross. On liberation, she was sentenced to two years in jail. The delegates could do nothing for her.

France was not the only country to hang on to its prisoners-of-war long after the fighting stopped. In Britain, as in Belgium, Germans were hard at work well into 1948. Not all, when the moment came, wanted to go home. The International Committee, mindful of the rules it had worked so hard to set up, continued to watch over them, from time to time issuing protests about men leading a 'miserable existence'. Two years after the end of the war, it claimed that the 'exercise of their civil rights is practically nullified; their home life has been destroyed ... in short, they are kept beyond the pale of human society.'

From September 1947, prisoners were offered labour contracts by France, Belgium, Luxemburg and Britain, where the government had argued, as the French had done, that since Germany had used slave labour so ruthlessly during the war, keeping them on was 'some form of compensation'. By 1950, eleven years after the outbreak of war, all those wanting to go home had left.

For the delegates of the International Committee in Europe, only then was their war finally over.

On Easter morning 1948, 120 members and employees of the International Committee, bringing with them friends and relations, made a pilgrimage to Solferino. In coaches hired for the occasion came people from the League, from various national Red Cross societies and a number of Italian dignitaries. Together they walked up the long alley, between the row of cypresses, towards the sanctuary where the bones of the soldiers who died in the fighting of 1859 had been collected and stacked, one on top of the other, held in place by wire mesh in piles that reached from floor to ceiling. It is a sombre and uneasy place, as it was intended to be: bones mixed with bones, *tutti fratelli* in death. As the Easter bells rang out the pilgrims gathered round to hear speeches in memory of the Red Cross founders and in celebration of the great humanitarian work that had been their legacy. The old ruined tower, over which the Italians and the French had fought so hard at such enormous cost, was, the visitors agreed, the true heart of the battle of Solferino. It was here that they decided to lay a marble plaque, to mark the spot of Dunant's inspiration.

Among the Committee members and the delegates, however, there must have been some who wondered a little ironically whether the prevailing tone of self-congratulation was altogether appropriate, whether the Red Cross movement, far from being a happy and united band, was not in fact about to splinter out of control. The years immediately following the Second World War should have been a time of satisfaction – was there not the Nobel Peace Prize to prove the value of their work? In fact those very years had been the International Committee's lowest hour: and in the spring of 1948 it was far from clear that it would survive.

Long before the fighting had stopped, the International Committee had begun to apologize. At issue here was the question of the concentration camps and whether the Committee had done all that it could to save the Jews in Nazi-occupied territory. Burckhardt, in an article published in the *Review* in May 1945, was one of the first to strike a note which fell somewhere between apology and defiance. In his wake came

Huber with Frédéric Siordet and Edouard Chapuisat, each adding a little to the debate but taking their cue from Burckhardt's tone. Siordet noted piously that the issue had been the 'most difficult problem encountered by the International Committee on the painful road that its activities call it to follow'. Chapuisat helpfully added that he had calculated that the Committee had given 32,361 hours of work to the concentration camps – the equivalent of fifteen years of someone's life. A tetchy note pointed out that it had been a mistake to assume that the Committee had any real power in wartime and that it would have been 'sadly sterile' to make too public a statement over the camps. 'No protests and no threats,' insisted the booklet on the concentration camps put out soon after the war, 'have ever changed methods of barbarism or lessened the destructive powers of modern weapons.' All that would have happened, had the Committee spoken out, was that 'the very people whom it wished to save' would have been abandoned to their fate. The message was strangely defeatist.

The impression this defensiveness gave, expressed even before any serious attacks were made on the Committee, was not helped by the fact that the organization itself was at a low ebb. The wartime strength of some 3,500 people had dropped away abruptly to under 400; donations were sharply reduced, though vast claims were still being made on the organization; and the Committee was trying to pull back from a deficit of over three million Swiss francs at the end of the war. It had not emerged very well from the post-war relief programme either, its claims to co-ordinate tracing usurped by UNRRA and its relief efforts dwarfed by those of the Allies. Burckhardt had left the Committee to take up his appointment as ambassador to France, de Gaulle having asked for him in person, saying that he wanted to have someone to discuss Richelieu with – Burckhardt's literary reputation in France was founded on his excellent biography of the French cardinal – and the Swiss were eager to send someone to mend bridges between the two countries.

In 1946, Huber was seventy-two and in poor health. The decision was made for him to turn the presidency over to two vice-presidents, a much liked but elderly and self-effacing doctor called Ernest Gloor, and Martin Bodmer, who had a passion for committees and who is remembered principally for a magnificent library he donated to the City of Geneva.

There had been other changes, of a profound nature, throughout the

Red Cross generally. Prince Charles of Sweden, president of the Swedish Red Cross since 1903, one of the early statesmen of the movement, had at last retired, at the age of eighty-two, after giving a last, eloquent speech. 'The only true path to peace . . . is the creation of a more perfect breed of men: less egotistical, reflective, wise and fully conscious of their responsibility for what happens on earth . . . We get, in the end, the world we deserve.' Pioneering figures, like the Americans Ernest Swift and Norman Davis or the German Colonel Draudt, were all dead and the war, which had left the protagonists exhausted and bereft of resources, had also sapped the world's charitable spirit. Of the seven and a half million people who had joined the American Red Cross during the war, six million had faded away. 'The spirit of the times,' Huber wrote in a despondent letter to Burckhardt, 'makes me feel helpless. Often I see everything in imminent decline. Law is trodden underfoot all over the world.'

As peace returned to Europe, however, the Red Cross societies, kept apart by six years of war, were anxious to meet, to discuss their experiences, and talk again about what path they should pursue in the post-war world. Not everything they said was friendly. In the corridors of the many gatherings that now took place, there were mutterings about the Committee's failure to help the Jews. Jean Pictet, today an upright, lean, active man in his early eighties, with straight white hair combed back, his manner at once direct and unexpectedly sentimental, was then just emerging as the philosopher of the organization. He remembers countless acrimonious debates and constantly being challenged by people whose tone was decidedly hostile. 'I travelled around, under real pressure, trying to describe what we had been able to do. I was bombarded by attacks.'

The gist of the hostility was perfectly straightforward. The International Committee was not the only humanitarian organization in the world, but under Huber it had gone out of its way to develop a strong moral voice. Why then had it failed to speak out over the concentration camps? True, the Allies and the Vatican had said and done very little; true, the International Committee, as Burckhardt had spelled out, had done more than most, its special service of relief to the concentration camps sending some 750,000 packets to their inmates. But why, given its role as guardian of the Geneva Conventions, had it done nothing when they were so comprehensively violated? At the meetings, there was talk of anti-Semitism, of pro-German sympathies – people remembered Burckhardt's time as high commissioner for Danzig and wondered whether he hadn't been a little too willing to act as intermediary for the Germans – and of far too close a tie with the Swiss government. 'When I said that the International Committee had remained absolutely independent of the Swiss government, everyone laughed,' Pictet remembers. In the late 1940s, the International Committee was widely perceived to be in Berne's pocket and when Berne was discredited so was the Committee. Philippe Etter's presence at the famous 1942 meeting was now agreed to have been a determining factor in the Committee's failure to act.

Faced with these mounting criticisms the Committee reacted, according to many people today, too hastily and too apologetically. 'I begged Huber not to go in for self-flagellation,' says Pictet. Members argued in such a way as to give a distinct feeling that they were protesting too hard; they also kept contradicting themselves. Arguments, speeches, self-justifications tumbled out, one after another. They had not, they insisted, ever known for certain what was happening in the camps, since the Nazis categorically denied them access; and a public statement might have jeopardized their entire work on behalf of prisoners of war – the only thing for which they had a mandate under international law. Those limits, they added, had been imposed on them by the very governments which now attacked them. What was more, they now pointed out, they had entered a twentieth-century war governed by principles drawn up in the nineteenth. The Committee owed its power to its credibility and its credibility was based only on its neutrality and discretion. It had spent the first forty years of the new century trying to adapt – to chemical warfare, to weapons of mass destruction and, more profoundly, to a changing philosophical and political view of the nation-state. Year by year, the Committee had fought and lost critical battles – against the Bolsheviks, against the Fascists, against the Nazis – while clinging on to a belief that it was more important to help prisoners-of-war than to criticize a regime. Their resources were few and they admitted that they had not perceived early enough the scale of the disaster.

Bit by bit, a campaign of vilification grew. The excellent work done for prisoners-of-war was forgotten, as was the fact that the Committee had not been alone in failing to understand and confront evils with which nothing in its experience had equipped it to deal. Critics asked why the Committee did not simply admit to having made a mistake, apologize and explain why. A bad mood seemed to settle over the entire Red Cross movement, fanned by memories of how little notice the International Committee had taken of the national societies, and there came a moment when Yugoslavia seemed to be suggesting that the Committee should face some kind of Nuremberg tribunal. Count Bernadotte, president of the Swedish Red Cross after Prince Charles stood down, voiced aloud what many were saying in private: that the International Committee had suffered from not being truly international, and that what was needed now were members from countries other than Switzerland who would of course resign if their own countries went to war, to ensure neutrality. This proposal was supported by the Russians, who were leading the attack from the East, blaming the Committee for its failure to help Russian prisoners-of-war and saying that they wanted to have nothing to do with such 'monarcho-fascists'. (As it happened, Bernadotte himself was not altogether trusted. Though his campaign to save a number of Jews early in 1945 had earned him gratitude, he was suspected of having personal ambitions to turn Sweden into a permanently neutral Switzerland of the north, with himself at the head of a Swedish Red Cross, which would rival Geneva in world influence, suspicions that only grew when he appeared at a meeting wearing a military greatcoat and cap festooned with red crosses.)

The League, eclipsed during the war years and now anxious to make its mark, was not altogether sad to see the Committee under assault. But it, too, was in some disarray despite having not only contributed to the relief of civilians with the Commision Mixte but having responded generously to calls for help in famines like the one that took a million and a half lives in Bengal and South India between 1943 and 1945. There was no avoiding, now that the war was over, the question of the erring national societies, suborned by totalitarian regimes. Representatives of the German and Japanese societies were noticeably absent from these post-war gatherings.

Something of the movement's fears of disintegration had already been expressed at one of the earliest post-war meetings held in October 1945 and attended by fifty-three national societies. The occasion had been a fascinating mixture of self-deception and honesty. The conference president, a Dr de Muralt, had opened the proceedings with a declaration that during the 'violent whirlwind of passions, when the hatred of the peoples had reached its paroxysm . . . there was not a single dissident society.' All might, perhaps, have been kept tightly within the realm of make-believe, had not de Rougé, still secretary-general of the League, unwisely risen to say that, as he saw it, this was a parliament in which all views should be expressed and all delegates 'explain their ideas in all freedom and without reticence'. Some were only too happy to do so.

It was Vittorio Minnucci of the Italian Red Cross who put the problem most plainly. The Italian society, he said, had during the war been the victim first of collective policy, then of an occupying power, and finally suffered 'from a terrible political and military servitude'. Its 'lamentable experiences' at the hands of the Fascists should, he said, serve as a warning to others. The only way to prevent this happening in the future, he continued, was for the International Committee not just to threaten expulsion from the movement but have the power to carry out the threat. Tough speeches followed, reminders that the constitution precisely allowed for expulsion in case of 'political or sectarian activity', which were fielded and dodged by both the League and the International Committee who were now united in their desire to keep away from politics. But it was repeatedly taken up by delegates who insisted that the Germans would have modified their behaviour had the Red Cross taken a tougher line.

In later years this first meeting would be remembered as prescient. Though no conclusion was reached about errant societies, enough of a marker had been put down to keep the debate fresh and constantly re-examined at future conferences. Other points of lasting relevance were a warning that the Red Cross was likely to 'suffer for some time yet' from competition from the many new oganizations that had sprung up during the war, and also that refugees were now a world phenomenon and very unlikely to disappear. Huge questions were at issue here, more readily raised than answered at a moment when tempers seemed so frayed. The post-war meetings were mirrors to the disunity of the movement.

In July 1946, the League met in Oxford. The American Red Cross had a new chairman, Basil O'Connor, appointed after Davis's death in 1944, a resolute and clear-sighted man. For twelve days delegates talked all day and much of the night about principles and the need to have some mechanism by which errant societies might be expelled; about the League's relationship with the new United Nations; about whether to return to Paris or stay in Geneva: and about the over-riding importance of drafting a fourth Geneva Convention for civilians. Somewhat to the dismay of some of the League's more haphazard workers, 'organization and method' specialists were appointed to introduce American business practices into the movement. The Oxford gathering was crucial and long remembered, less for any specific resolution than for its spirit: a determination to use the experience of the war which had just ended to build a stronger, more united Red Cross.

There was another meeting, which Riegner remembers well.

In 1946, I was invited by the International Committee to come to a meeting to discuss a possible revision of the Geneva Conventions. I went, and found fifty representatives from all the non-governmental organizations who had been involved with the International Committee during the war. Ostensibly, we were there to talk about the future. I was the only Jew. I saw the agenda and noticed that every item concerned voluntary organizations. So I put my hand up and said that there were other matters that I would like to raise in any discussion about another Convention — and particularly the fate of civilians in occupied territory. I was told that I could have my say later in the day.

The day passed. As the meeting ended, a vote of thanks to the International Committee was proposed, for everything that it had done during the war for 'prisoners-of-war and civilian internees'. All the International Committee grandees were there. I suddenly realized that this vote of thanks was the real purpose of the meeting, and that the Committee had drafted it itself.

I asked to speak. I said that I fully agreed with a vote of thanks for the work done for prisoners-of-war — but that the words 'civilian internees' should be omitted. There was total silence. No one supported me. Not the World Council of Churches, not the Catholic organizations, no one. Then the grandees began to argue with me. I stood my ground. I just kept saying that they couldn't expect me to thank them for protecting people they had failed to protect. The argument went on and on. At last, someone came up with an idiotic proposal: why not exchange the words 'civilian internees' for 'assimilated people'? I laughed. The words didn't make any sense. Then I said, 'Well, if that makes you happy . . .' and 'assimilated people' went in.

Matters reached some sort of crisis at the seventeenth international Red Cross conference, held in Stockholm in August 1948. It was almost exactly ten years since the movement had met in London for its painful last pre-war gathering. Time was taken to mourn the dead and to make a tally of the successes. The International Committee had much to be proud of and it took pains to put its record across. Frédéric Siordet had been asked to prepare a 'short account' of the Committee's wartime work. It has Burckhardt's defensive tone, but also a certain defiance. A number of passages are particularly revealing. Returning yet again to the concentration camp theme, Siordet wrote: 'Tell the world? By what means? . . . Geneva knew neither more nor less than anyone else: rumours, stories, conjectures based on tales told by the few victims who escaped from these hells on earth, in so far as the lips of the survivors were not sealed in terror.' He went on: 'The prisoners of the East European theatre, the concentration camps and the Far East: did the Red Cross fail in regard to all these? It was far more, and much worse than that. The civilized world itself had failed.'

Count Bernadotte was the president of the conference, and he made generous references to the International Committee, while being wooed in the corridors to abandon his plans for a more representative body with members drawn from other nations. In fact he had already had a change of heart. His earlier enthusiasm for the Soviets had given way to mistrust as they continued to attack the Committee for failing to help Russian prisoners-of-war, conveniently forgetting their own failure to ratify the Geneva Convention, which had made it impossible for the Committee to act, and as they turned on the Swedes for selling arms to the Germans and for the award of the Nobel Peace Prize to the Committee (even though the Swedish Red Cross had not been involved in the award). The Russians were again in belligerent form, deftly playing the League off against the International Committee. Bernadotte abandoned his idea for a reformed Committee and suggested instead that there should be some kind of co-ordinating body to make it more effective. For Bernadotte, the most important job for the Red Cross now seemed to be that of campaigning for peace and making itself known throughout the world. He was not alone in sensing that one of the major wartime problems had been that so few people had heard of the International Committee.

Once again, the good humour with which the conference opened soon soured. Bernadotte's pleas for 'friendship and comradeship ... both inside and outside the conference rooms' which always 'unite the members of a good and happy family' were quickly ignored as a message was read out from the Soviets – who, together with the Bulgarians, Poles, Romanians, Czechs and Yugoslavs had turned down the invitation to attend – accusing the International Committee of failure to protest against Nazi crimes and of an 'unfriendly attitude towards the Soviet Union'. This was no happy family. Even loud calls for the meeting to stick to the agenda, a fulsome speech of thanks by the Greeks to the Swedish Red Cross for its relief to famine areas in 1942, and the presentation of a bust of Athena Hygeia, Minerva, Goddess of Health, could do nothing to dissuade the Lebanese and the Israelis from clashing bitterly over Palestinian refugees.

It was left to Paul Ruegger, the International Committee's newly appointed sixth president, a thin-lipped, slightly precious figure, but formidably intelligent – he was said to dictate letters to three secretaries simultaneously, in three different languages – to deliver a skilful plea for unity and for members to stop looking at the past and prepare instead for the future. Ruegger had been Switzerland's youngest ambassador before the war, the International Committee's first Catholic and a pupil of Huber's; he had been declared *persona non grata* by Mussolini, who rightly suspected him of strong anti-Fascist feelings. All his talents were now needed. Helped by Bernadotte's decision to back the Committee, he managed to swing the vacillating conference behind a decision to leave the International Committee's role essentially untouched. Even if, at the next great international gathering in Toronto, in 1952, there would be fresh attacks on what the Soviets chose to call the *soi-disant* International Committee, the organization had survived. It would stay in Geneva and in Swiss hands.

Would it have made any difference to events in the Nazi-occupied territories if the International Committee had spoken out? Most commentators argue that it would, that Huber's prestige and integrity had lent the Committee enormous moral weight, and that speaking out was the Committee's last and most effective weapon. Even a half-way measure – a diplomatic intervention, a visit by Huber and Burckhardt to Berlin, a personal letter to Hitler – might have achieved something. They are to be reproached, Riegner believes, for never really exploring ways to intervene, nor trying to exercise the 'right of initiative' invested in the Committee by its statutes, and because they were not bold enough to risk offending the Germans. The fear of German invasion, though doubtless real at the time, looks foolish now. By evading the appeal, by failing to adjust to circumstances beyond its control, by not having the courage to risk its own future in providing this 'minimum of humanity', the Committee could not but call into question the reason for its own existence.

The decision taken by the Committee, on 14 October 1942, which set the tone for all that followed, was not unexpected – the policy of caution and non-confrontation had been fashioned long before in dealings with Mussolini over Ethiopia and Hitler over the concentration camps of the 1930s – but it did weaken the organization. Huber's sleepless nights of anguish were irrelevant. When called on, the Committee had neither risen to the occasion nor been great enough to recognize and confront new challenges. It was this – the fact that it decided not to try – and not its failure, that would leave its mark long after the world had forgotten all the remarkable work it carried out during the five years of war.

The passions that went into the concentration camp debates may have been at least in part responsible for the sense of urgency which now went into the revision of the Geneva Conventions and particularly to the translation of the weak Tokyo draft of 1934 into a tough and binding agreement on protection for civilians. The war had seen civilians arrested, interned, deported, tortured, starved, bombed and murdered. Quite apart from all the men, women and children massacred by the Nazis, 67,000 British citizens had been killed in air raids, 18,586 of them in Coventry, a quarter of a million German civilians had died during the allied bombing raids over Germany between 1943 and 1945, and at least 340,000 Japanese civilians were dead. Stuttgart had been bombed fifty-three times – sixteen victims for every hundred tonnes of bomb. It was no longer possible to stall, to hark back to Moynier's day when it was still reasonable to argue that the Convention was an instrument best left alone and that any tampering could only lead to a weakening rather than a strengthening of its powers. There was no talk, interestingly, about the futility of the Geneva Conventions and whether they should be abandoned: on the contrary, there seemed to be an extraordinarily united belief that the Conventions could be made to work, providing they were correctly worded. In any case, the laws of war and Dunant's humanitarian legacy were all that stood between man and the increasing barbarity of war.

On 15 February 1945 Huber had announced that he was starting talks aimed at adding to the Conventions, and that he had identified three priorities: the protection of civilians, the protection of the victims of civil wars, and the addition of some kind of monitoring mechanism – harking back to Moynier's tribunal – in which the International Committee would have a role to play. It was imperative to act quickly, Huber insisted, before the expertise developed during the war years evaporated and the specialists in military and international law returned to their civilian lives. In September he wrote to the US State Department and to the foreign offices of Britain, the USSR, China and France, asking them to send representatives for initial discussions in Geneva. In a circular put out on 5 September, Huber was at his most eloquent:

> Totalitarian war has bred new techniques. Has it therefore to be admitted that the individual must cease to be legally protected and must be considered as simply an element of warring collectives? . . . If war denies [man's] worth and dignity, it will proceed to unlimited destruction, because the intelligence of man, as it progressively seizes the forces of the universe to make use of them, seems only to accelerate along this fatal road . . . But the Red Cross ideal remains an incarnation of the ideas of the intrinsic worth and dignity of people.

Meetings to discuss the Conventions now began in earnest. The problems they faced were enormous: no modern war had ever been as long, as intense, as murderous or as widespread; never had the Red Cross emblem been so profoundly violated: and never had prisoners-of-war or civilians been so barbarically treated. The International Committee itself, on the basis of these talks, prepared four draft Conventions, which were duly approved at Stockholm in the summer of 1948. A diplomatic conference called by the Swiss confederation – the accepted method for convening these gatherings – was set for the late spring and summer of 1949. Like all such events, it provided a theatre of political intrigue, fine speeches, horse-trading and a constant clash between humanitarian ideals and military realism. The International Committee, present only as observer, nevertheless exercised considerable background influence, not least because this ostensibly most apolitical of institutions was more politically astute than many of the numerous delegates who converged on Geneva.

A good deal of national mental baggage arrived with the delegations, which varied enormously in size, experience and the amount of power and responsibility conferred on them by their governments. All agreed that some humane limitations on the conduct of war were crucial; but the question was how much was not only desirable but also achievable.

A vast number of separate issues were under debate. There was the question of prisoners-of-war and the drafting of a revised 1929 code to take in the very different treatment of prisoners seen in the war throughout Europe, North America and the Far East. There was the relatively uncontentious examination of the treatment of sick and wounded prisoners which also led to a revising of an earlier Convention. Then there was the highly political and controversial subject of civilians in war, given not simply aerial bombing of cities and the atrocities committed but also the development of weapons of mass destruction, the invention of atomic warfare and the daily violations of the red cross emblem. And there was the topic of civil and internal wars, much talked about, never properly addressed.

From Britain came delegates grateful to the International Committee for their assistance to British prisoners-of-war but reluctant to extend the Conventions too far to cover civil wars, and sensitive on the subject of economic blockades. They soon won a reputation for high-handedness. From the United States came military men, wary of too many blanket concessions to civilians, and defensive in discussions of indiscriminate bombing. From Australia came the tough and adroit Colonel W. R. Hodgson, very experienced at handling Soviet diplomatic manoeuvring. From Poland came a delegation that seemed to early observers to be a stalking horse for the Soviet bloc, and which appeared willing only to discuss peace. The Soviets had never replied to the Swiss invitation and there was considerable surprise when, on the opening day, a strong Soviet team appeared, bringing with them delegates from seven satellite countries. All proved quick to make disparaging references to the '*soi-disant*' International Committee. In the corridors, the League intrigued, scrabbled for a footing, and made common cause with the Americans, still seeking to find ways of diminishing International Committee power; while Mgr Bernardini, papal nuncio to Switzerland and head of the Holy See delegation, kept pointing out that 'in a humanitarian convention there should be at least one reference to God', even if it annoyed the Russians. Like horses lined up before a race, the players jockeyed for position, lobbied, nobbled and bartered.

Given the range of subjects to be covered and the acute differences of opinion and desires, a remarkable amount was achieved in the fourteen weeks. A new Convention of 143 articles and five annexes, strengthened the law on the treatment of prisoners-of-war and covered every moment from capture to release or death; though there were acrimonious disagreements about who exactly counted as a prisoner-of-war and whether or not those indicted for war crimes should benefit from the Convention. With the shadow of the deaths, at German hands, of thousands of Italians who had joined the Allies in 1943, it was agreed to extend the definition of 'prisoner-of-war' to cover 'organized resistance movements' in occupied territories. Even so, the new Convention contained what would be regarded as only a weak reference to fighters in civil wars: the only relevant passage was Article 3 which guaranteed rights to anyone rendered *hors de combat* in a civil conflict. The sick and wounded also saw their protection re-examined, slightly strengthened and endorsed.

But it was the new Convention on civilians that really focused the delegates' minds.

At the heart of the just war tradition, as well as the modern laws of war, lay the question of non-combatant immunity. Long before the Second World War, it had been accepted that any injury to civilians was justifiable only if indirect and unintentional. The difficulty came in identifying the moment when military action ceased to be justifiable and became indiscriminate; and the Second World War had been fought under rules singularly inappropriate to high altitude bombardments and weapons of mass destruction. A combination of what was now known as total war and an absence of clear, legal definitions and standards, had effectively rendered civilians appallingly vulnerable. For the International Committee, indiscriminate bombing was absolutely illegal in that it contravened the most basic tenets of international humanitarian law. Its other major concern, as reflected in the drafts it had prepared for the conference, was of course the fate of civilians in enemy hands.

In 1949 it was still just possible to dream. Through the debates on economic blockades and on banning nuclear weapons, a number of articles emerged, agreed on one by one. Though often watered down, these new articles did provide a new standard in humanitarian law. As many present had anticipated, it was the subject of internal wars that proved the most contentious. The desire to protect the victims of civil wars dated from the Washington conference of 1912, when it was loudly condemned by the Russians. Where they once again clashed with the West in 1949 was over the suggestion that each Convention be equally applicable to national as well as international wars. Debates on this topic were made all the trickier by the fact that, even as the delegations were meeting in Geneva, Britain was in a state of civil conflict in Malaya, the Netherlands were on the verge of losing Indonesia, the French were fighting the Viet-Minh in Indo-China and the Greeks were in the middle of a fully fledged civil war, government forces and communist guerrillas alike behaving barbarically towards their prisoners.

On 12 August 1949, the new Conventions were ready for signature and ratification. Under them came new goals, new propositions, new rules and new definitions – 'grave breaches' common to all four Conventions, included 'wilful killing, torture or inhuman treatment, including biological experiments [and] wilfully causing great suffering or serious injury to body or health', though the question of just how to humanize wars that had become totally destructive was a philosophical debate that was never really addressed. A hint of human rights had made its way into Article 3, with a statement about minimum humanitarian rules in internal conflicts, and the proceedings adjourned with an increased recognition that states were henceforth not to feel quite so free to treat their own citizens with such little regard for their rights. The long-held principle of 'reciprocity' had been killed off – it had proved singularly ineffective in the war – and in its place, common to all four Conventions, had come an undertaking to 'respect and to ensure respect for the present Conventions in all circumstances'. Earlier rules of war had been vague on enforcement. States themselves, it had been understood, would be their own policemen. By 1945, it had become clear to everyone that some mechanism to ensure compliance was essential – and this conviction did translate itself into a range of new undertakings about education for the armed forces on the rules of war and about dissemination generally. More than that Article 1, common to all four Conventions, made it a duty for states to ensure the rules were implemented not only in their own territories, but everywhere, whether they were involved or not.

Atomic weapons and non-directed missiles, the diplomatic conference decided, were simply beyond their competence and belonged more properly with The Hague, though many delegates expressed their grave anxieties about the threat posed to civilians now and in the future by discoveries in the field of atomic energy.

Article 3, common to all four Conventions, was widely regarded as a genuinely revolutionary legal move. States signatory to the Conventions would in effect agree, in circumstances in which their authority was flouted, that their behaviour towards any rebellious sector of their population would be governed by international humanitarian law. Contracting parties would bind themselves to treat humanely 'without prejudice or distinction as to race, colour, religion or belief, gender, birth or fortune, or any similar criterion' all individuals 'not taking direct part in hostilities, including members of the armed forces who have laid down their arms and those persons who have been rendered *hors de combat* by nature of illness, wounds, capture or for any other reason whatsoever'. At all times and in all places, Article 3 continued, were prohibited:

a. attacks on life or body, especially murder in all its forms, mutilation, cruel treatment, torture and torment;
b. the taking of hostages;
c. attacks on personal dignity, especially humiliating or degrading treatment;
d. condemnations made and executions carried out, in the

absence of prior judgement by a properly constituted court supported by judicial provisions recognized as indispensable by all civilized peoples.

In the years to come, Article 3 would often be quoted, though not always to much end, for the diplomatic conference did not choose to include a precise definition of where it would or would not apply, and states would interpret its applicability fairly randomly. For the International Committee, what would now be known as its 'right of initiative' was spelt out, having for so long simply been one of its informal ways of operating – the 'right' to offer its services, wherever and in whatever circumstances it felt it could be helpful, with the tacit understanding that states would not take offence. Nothing, however, was said about enforcement, and though the International Committee had the 'right' to be there, there was nothing it could do to oblige anyone to listen to what it said. The Geneva Conventions of 1949 remained in essence what the earlier ones had always been: a set of rules, against which could be made appeals for decent treatment during armed conflict. And that in itself was something. As Telford Taylor, a counsel for the prosecution at Nuremberg, put it: 'If it were not regarded as wrong to bomb military hospitals, they would be bombed all the time, instead of only some of the time.'

Something of the world's disgust at the violence and cruelty of the war that had just ended was reflected in the fact that by 31 December 1949, fifty-five states had signed the four new Geneva Conventions. Frédéric Siordet called them a 'monument to humanity', but warned that they should not be allowed to crumble into a 'useless, melancholic' ruin 'evocative of good times past'.

EIGHTEEN

Affairs of the Heart

The men and women gathered in Geneva in the summer of 1949 could not have foreseen the complexities and varieties of the armed struggles about to break over them. The wars they dreaded and had now legislated for — major wars between major powers, classical 'international armed conflict' — were in fact already over: the last old-fashioned declaration of war was that of the Soviet Union against the Japanese on 8 August 1945. Instead, there would be wars of decolonization, revolutions, nationalist and ethnic struggles, terrorist attacks and further genocides, involving ever more sophisticated and ever more available weapons, which would end, not in peace, but in fragile and temporary ceasefires. And these civil wars would be notoriously savage, each side denying the legitimacy of the other, with very little concern anywhere for the laws of war.

In some ways, the 1949 Geneva Conventions would turn out to be more a commentary on the old world and the old ways of waging war, an expression of the laws humanitarians would have liked to have seen in the past, than relevant to the world that now faced them. Dunant would, just, have felt at home; but probably never again. There would be no more of his kind of war, with a beginning and an end, readily identified enemies and recognizable weapons.

The end of the 1940s was a time of reckoning for organizations like the Red Cross. A new order, based on international co-operation, was in the air. The war crimes tribunals in Nuremberg and Tokyo had at least made the point that the laws of war were applicable not only to states but to individuals who carried out their orders, and if there were some who dismissed the verdicts as 'victor's justice', the principle of personal accountability had been laid down. The birth of the United Nations and other inter-governmental bodies promised a world, as Geoffrey Best puts it in *War and Law since 1945*, 'more generous, more just and above all more peaceful', and even if that soon proved illusory it seemed for the moment possible.

The International Committee itself had reason to feel satisfied. Having wisely waited to undertake a full revision of its own structure until the diplomatic conference of 1949 had made such a revision impractical, it had emerged intact, confirmed as the major organization dealing with protection, its 'right of initiative' upheld and with a further brief to develop new laws for protection together with the UN and the League, as well as to help apply the laws through its reports and visits to places of detention. As before, it remained the custodian of the Geneva Conventions, responsible for the victims of war and the co-ordinating organization in wartime; it had also been given a more prominent role in the distribution of relief. The League, which since the important Oxford meeting in 1946 had adapted a more assertive stance, remained the leading agency in peacetime – a distinction doomed to disaster in an age of continuous, ill-defined warfare. And the 1949 Conventions had given the Committee a new, stronger set of rules with which to challenge governments and pose awkward questions, though the skills, courage and imagination of its delegates would remain as important as they had ever been. All this was a just reward for its six years of work with prisoners-of-war, its immense and imaginative relief programme and a tribute to the effort and legal skills it had put into the long months of preparatory sessions for the revised Conventions. It was both a decided victory over its critics, and something of a surprise, given the Committee's impossible and unhappy position after attacks made on its inaction with regard to the concentration camps.

With the end of the war, and in recognition of the immense tasks that faced the organization in the post-war years, came a formal shift of power within the International Committee itself, away from the co-opted and predominantly elderly members who once again met only every three or four weeks at best and into the hands of a full-time, properly paid general secretariat. Both Huber, before his retirement in 1947 and Burckhardt before he decided to stay on in Paris as Swiss minister, had worked on the International Committee's new structure. Huber told a meeting of the Committee, on 3 January 1946, that he felt that it had become essential to distinguish clearly between the Committee members, who would 'control and decide the main courses of action', and a 'managing body', which would 'perform the executive functions and administration of the day-to-day work'. As President, Paul Ruegger, devout, close to Vatican circles, superstitious by nature and somewhat vain, given to self-aggrandizing gestures, was not liked by everyone; there were rumours, never substantiated, that he had had a hand in the Swiss government's decision to stamp the letter 'J' into the passports of German Jews who wished to travel to Switzerland before the war. Just the same, everyone recognized his skills as a diplomat and believed they could only be useful in the uncertain months to come.

Several distinguished members had died during the war – Guillaume Fevre and Giuseppe Motta among them – and others were now brought in to take their places. An international lawyer, Professor Dietrich Schindler, was invited to join the Committee, with an eye to the necessity for good international legal brains; René von Berchem, grandson of the former acting president Edouard Naville, agreed to serve, as did Léopold Boissier, secretary-general of the Interparliamentary Union and son of Colonel Edmond Boissier, former vice-president. Family connections had lost little of their usefulness, and nor had social standing, most candidates belonging to Geneva's traditional and exclusive clubs like Le Cercle de la Terrasse. Of the twenty members who now made up the Committee, only nine had been in office before the war. Another newcomer was Jean Pictet, rewarded for his wartime work, a rare promotion from staff to board. Despite Ruegger's willingness to consider the question, the Committee fought off attempts to open its doors to foreigners.

The organization, having shed its many wartime volunteers, had also lost some of its best delegates, men like Maître Lalive of the Commission Mixte, who decided to return to his legal career, and Marcel Junod who went back to his hospital work. It was clear to those who remained that the Red Cross would now once again be polarized, as it had been in the days of Dunant and Moynier, between those who favoured what Pictet calls '*la diplomatie raisonnée*' and those who continued to insist that there should be no restrictions on International Committee work and that its motto should be '*le coeur qui ne se limite pas*' – an issue soon to challenge the organization's resources. In 1949 it was still possible to view humanitarian concerns and human rights and the laws of war as facets of the same principle and for one organization – the Red Cross – to preside over them both. New non-governmental bodies like Oxfam had been born and would soon assume some of the same responsibilities. Others, like Amnesty International, were not far in the future. But the days when the supremacy of the international Committee would be challenged still lay far ahead.

As for the role of the Committee as the moral voice on humanitarian matters, it was now once again redefined in a long article by Huber, written for the *Review* in January 1947. Should the International Committee respond by public protest, he asked, when confronted by grave violations of the Geneva Conventions? No, he went on, because 'all protests are equal to judgements and impartial judgements cannot be reached in wartime . . . because they are open to misuse and propaganda . . . and because they are ultimately futile'. Was it therefore better to indulge in futile public protests than to take relief wherever it could be taken? The International Committee was a relief organization 'committed to its original principles of universality and neutrality' and nothing that had happened in the Second World War, insisted Huber, made him question that commitment.

As if to reinforce his words, to make the Committee's position for ever clear, Pictet was now asked to draw up what became known as the seven 'fundamental principles'. Dunant and Moynier had never really seen the need to spell out their beliefs: they knew each other well and understood instinctively what led them to say the things they did, and very little had ever been laid down until fifty years after the birth of the movement; even then only four essentials – charity, universality, independence and impartiality – were mentioned. Pictet now added humanity, neutrality, voluntary status and unity, and dropped charity, at least as a word, for the charitable impulse behind the Red Cross work was not in question. He took care to insist on their firmly unsectarian character, saying that they were 'acceptable to all men, whatever their outlook on life'. Of his seven principles, much debated and finally accepted by the entire movement in 1965, only neutrality has caused lasting difficulties, though unity, in this most disunited of all organizations, remains one of Dunant's least successful dreams. Pictet defined neutrality in simple terms: the Red Cross, he said, should 'never take sides in hostilities or engage at any time in controversies of a political, racial, religious or doctrinal nature'. In return for being allowed access to detainees in all places and in private, and permission to carry out its usual work of assistance and protection, it would undertake not to pronounce on the violations it witnessed. 'Discreet persistence' and not outspoken condemnation, 'ad hoc diplomacy', delegates acting as they saw best and seeking justification later, would remain the key to International Committee work.

What the Committee needed now was a new cause. They soon found one in the atomic bomb and they would return to it again and again in the years to come. As with poison gas in 1918, the atom bomb was a weapon that could be criticized without having to single out any one country for attack. At successive Red Cross gatherings, resolutions were carried prohibiting these new 'non-directed' weapons 'which imperilled the very future of civilization'.

It was a more professional, more internationally-minded body, with a clearer division of jobs and responsibilities, that now set about identifying its post-war priorities. And it was not only the structure that was different: the organization had acquired a new style. It may have been at least in part the hostility expressed towards the International Committee at the end of the war that made it now, like a sea anenome, shrink back from exposure. Certainly, no report written after 1945 was ever again so open or so full of opinions, nor any delegate so candid. The Kafkaesque word 'nettoyage,' cleansing, was coined to describe what happened to the reports that arrived from the field before they were published in the Review, effectively turning what had often been passionate, discursive, sentimental and even funny documents into tight, neat statements. From the very earliest days, when Appia and van de Velde sent back their colourful war reports from Holstein and Schleswig, to the end of the Second World War, the history not just of the Red Cross movement but of the growth of the humanitarian spirit generally, could be read in the Review, month after month as it unfolded, sometimes with a candour surprising in an organization as wedded to discretion as the Committee. Louis Calame, Sidney Brown and Marcel Junod had all made their views felt.

After 1945, individual voices disappear; the house style becomes neutral and bland. Reports, once fun to read, turn into chores. The International Committee itself, as Geneva became the world capital for humanitarian concerns, appeared to turn inwards towards bureaucracy and hierarchy, to become a more restrained place, so fearful of exposure and criticism that its very name became a byword for secrecy, though the delegates whom it continued to recruit seemed to lose none of their gung-ho charm and sense of adventure. There would be no more of the light-hearted gatherings described by Pictet in the late 1930s, at which people played games and made up rhymes about those in the field.

In September 1948, soon after the Stockholm conference, Count Berna-dotte returned to Palestine where he had taken on the job of mediator between Arabs and Jews for the United Nations, to initiate a vast relief plan for the ever growing number of refugees in the area. (In some quarters, Bernadotte's appointment was seen as another step towards his goal of taking over the presidency of the International Committee.) On the 17th, he went to Jerusalem to see Jacques de Reynier, appointed to Palestine after working with the German prisoners-of-war in France, and to meet a number of Arab leaders. The party set off back at about five in the afternoon in three cars, two bearing the UN flag, the third that of the Red Cross. Count Bernadotte was travelling with his three assis-tants in a UN car. At the first gate entering the Israeli section, shots were heard. Bernadotte died in hospital that night. Pierre Gaillard, another delegate to Palestine, arranged to transport the body to Haifa, where a plane was waiting. Fearing trouble if it travelled in an Israeli ambulance, he got hold of an old British Red Cross vehicle and drove it himself through the Arab lines.

For the Red Cross movement, as for Sweden, Bernadotte's death was devastating. In Israel, there was a sense of catastrophe; never had the UN presence felt so frail. The plane paused briefly in Geneva, where his coffin was placed on a bier on the runway, and friends and colleagues from the International Committee and the League came out from the city to pay their respects. The funeral was held in Stockholm's Gustav Vasa Cathedral, attended by royalty and the representatives of dozens of national Red Cross societies. After a funeral march to the drums of Bernadotte's former regiment, the crematorium doors opened and trumpets sounded. Later, the ashes were carried to a wooded cemetery by the light of flares. For many of those present, Bernadotte had been a figure of firmness of purpose in a movement still very much at sea.

Palestine was to be the International Committee's return to grace. Events there would give it the chance not only to restore its credibility and dispel any lingering taint of anti-Semitism, but to press ahead with duties strengthened by the Geneva Conventions. The British, as they pulled out, asked the Committee to provide a medical programme. Palestine was also to be the place where the International Committee and the League would demonstrate that relations between them could, despite mutual wariness, be harmonious. Given the intense bitterness and violence of the Palestinian conflict, the fact that it involved people highly critical of the Committee's wartime achievements – the Jews – and that the needs of those being made destitute would become limitless, the Committee emerged surprisingly unscathed, if a little bruised. There was no national Red Cross society in Palestine to help – or indeed hinder – its work, plans to start one having foundered both on the apparently insurmountable problem of getting Jews and Arabs to collaborate and because the Jews wished to call their society the Magen David Adom, the Red Shield of David, a name the Committee was not prepared to recognize. Exchanges on the subject, between British officials and various Red Cross societies before the war had been adamant: as G. W. Heron, director of the medical services in Jerusalem had put it, a 'Red Cross organization in Palestine' was neither 'necessary nor desirable'.

The years of the British mandate had been marked by repeated acts of terrorism by illegal armed Jewish groups, extremists who had no wish to see Jerusalem turned into an international city. The Stern Gang (Lehi), co-founded by the future prime minister, Yitzhak Shamir, were soon identified as Bernadotte's killers. By 1947, Britain had decided to end its mandate, announcing that it would withdraw its troops on 14 May 1948. The United Nations had voted for partition, favoured by the Zionists, opposed by the Arabs. It was plain to everyone that conflict between Jews and Arabs was unavoidable.

The International Committee had been keeping watch on the region for some time when, early in 1948, it received a request from the high commissioner for Palestine to send doctors and nurses to take over the hospitals when the British left. This was a role it knew it performed well, and Dr Roland Marti, veteran of the Spanish civil war and the German camps and now head of the medical division, left for Cairo to talk to members of the Arab League and senior figures in the Egyptian government before travelling on to Palestine.

On 12 March, anticipating violence during the withdrawal of the British soldiers, the International Committee sent out its customary appeal to both sides to respect the Geneva Conventions and received reassuring replies from both Arabs and Jews. Tensions were, however, already high, and rising all the time. On 9 April, the Stern and Irgun gangs attacked an Arab village west of Jerusalem called Deir Yassin. De Reynier described in a report how 254 men, women and children had been massacred and their bodies stuffed down a well. Arabs, he wrote to Geneva, were fleeing their homes, driven by stories of atrocities reported in the Arab press and by the savagery of the Zionist gangs bent on reducing Arab numbers while there was still a chance. By the time Bernadotte died, many thousands of Arab families had lost their homes, their possessions and their means of livelihood. The day before his death, Bernadotte had issued a statement: 'The right of innocent people,' he had declared, 'uprooted from their homes by the present terror and ravages of war, to return to their homes should be affirmed and made effective,' words unlikely to make him popular with the Zionists.

With the departure of the British, Jerusalem became a battleground. For the International Committee the city presented a chance to test yet again their idea about safety zones, places of absolute neutrality over which the Red Cross flag would fly and where non-combatants could gather to escape danger. Three different sections of Jerusalem were declared security areas – the King David Hotel, the YMCA hostel and former Terra Santa hospice as the first zone; Government House, the Arab College, the Jewish Agricultural School and part of Allenby barracks as the second; and the Italian School and Hospital as the third. Civilians flocked in search of safety and the Committee embarked on negotiations to have the entire city declared a safety zone.

But the hope was illusory. The zones proved no more effective than they had anywhere in the Second World War. A nurse, a member of an International Committee medical team, was wounded, as was Pierre Gaillard, knocked out when a bullet ricocheted off his windscreen and hit him as he was leaving the Arab quarter; another delegate was assaulted. The Committee issued an appeal. Fifteen days after assuming the presidency, Paul Ruegger came from Geneva in Jerusalem and scored a few small successes with evacuations and releases of a number of both Arab and Jewish women and children; he returned to Switzerland convinced, like Gaillard, that political detainees would become one of the International Committee's major future concerns. A truce which had been negotiated by Bernadotte held briefly. But then the King David Hotel, occupied then vacated by the UN, was taken over by Jewish forces and attacked by the Arabs; building by building, the first safety zone was overwhelmed by armed conflict. The Committee lowered its flag and pulled out. In July, the Italian Hospital and School had to be abandoned. Safety Zone 2 held for longer but was then cut off by the crossfire between the Jewish and Arab forces, and abandoned. Delegates returned to concentrating on repatriating the sick and wounded, visiting prison camps, tracing missing civilians and trying to set up a communications network for captives and their families. These were dangerous times and Jean Courvoisier, who had also been posted to Palestine, often found himself crawling across no man's land trying to rescue civilians stranded by heavy crossfire, with nothing but a red cross armband and a small flag for protection. Stories of the courage of the delegates began to reach Geneva. After a night of heavy fighting in Jerusalem the UN had brokered a cease-fire, but no one dared collect a number of wounded men who lay between Jewish and Arab lines because they had fallen in a minefield. A Red Cross delegate, André Durant, alone and in total silence, set out to collect them. There were shots, then an explosion. Durant lay for an hour, having lost his right arm, before being rescued by Israeli soldiers.

During the late 1940s, the International Committee delegates, as they went on their various visits around the world, kept warning that numbers of refugees were growing and that this was not a passing problem. Conflicts breaking out in Burma, Indonesia, Greece and Indo-China were all causing vast displacements of people; and in Palestine the delegates' fears were soon confirmed. Most Arabs had taken refuge over the borders in the Arab territories, where many of the towns and villages had seen their populations double in a few weeks. By the late summer of 1948 they were thought to contain some 400,000 homeless and increasingly destitute people. Another appeal, this time for relief, went out from Geneva. It brought in generous donations of money, food and medicines. But it was never enough. The refugees, whose numbers were consistently underestimated, and whose rations had been settled at somewhere scarcely above malnutrition, were always hungry and always prey to disease.

Ella Jorden, the intrepid medical missionary interned by the Japanese who had worked for the British Red Cross repatriating slave workers to the European countries from which they had been taken by the Germans, arrived in Jordan where the small Jordanian society had been overwhelmed by refugees crossing the border from Palestine. In a valley in the desert she found a camp with 17,000 people crammed into 1,400 tents, and a small team of British Red Cross doctors to care for them. Smallpox had broken out and there were dozens of cases of pneumonia and malaria, despite an intensive programme of spraying with DDT. Many of the children had conjunctivitis. The valley was full of snakes and large spiders. Rations were minimal. Ella Jorden was soon reporting that the refugees were too 'inert and homesick' to make any efforts to improve their surroundings, preferring to wear the clothes they had arrived in until they fell apart and absolutely refusing to try out new food. A Swiss gift of several tonnes of Gruyère cheese was left untouched, the refugees insisting that they could not eat anything full of holes. Unwanted girl babies, Ella Jorden noted, were left to starve to death. From other camps, run by other Red Cross societies, reports were the same: hunger, disease, apathy.

All through 1948 the refugee numbers kept growing, increased by the poor, those who had lost not their homes but their livelihoods, but who were excluded from the relief programmes by the accepted definition of a refugee – someone who had fled his home on account of war or troubles. In the autumn, the UN at last voted a relief package worth $30 million. Sir Ralph Cilento, in charge of UN relief, announced that he believed that the number of refugees now stood at over three-quarters of a million. Trygve Lie, secretary-general of the United Nations, approached the International Committee, the League and the American Quakers, asking each to take an area in which to distribute relief. The International Committee was given the regions under the command of the Jewish forces, and central Palestine, from Jenin to Hebron, an area with some 300,000 refugees. Ninety-two Swiss delegates, doctors and nurses were sent out with blankets and medicines. They recruited local people to help them. The League was soon housing, feeding and caring for people dispersed over some hundred thousand square miles of desert, having called on the resources of twenty of its member societies and recruited nearly 1,000 staff, many of whom were experienced in refugee work from Europe in 1945. An International Committee nurse, arriving in Gaza, sent a description to the *Review* of her first sight of the camps. 'I had thought,' she wrote, 'I would have found misery, but of a limited kind. Alas, the misery is without limits and my impression is that our relief is nothing but a drop of water in an ocean.' There were, she noted, no new clothes, no shoes, no vegetables and no fresh fruit. 'Only one thing is expanding: the cemetery. Every morning new palm fronds shelter new graves.' Early on, the UN Relief to Palestinian Refugees (UNRPR), had warned against giving food to people who were not bona fide refugees, like nomads or villagers. A report, lamenting the lack of a proper census, noted: 'Self-interest and greed followed the appearance of foreign relief . . . the numbers of refugees increased as if by magic . . . Weeding out meets with stubborn resistance, both passive and active: lies, cheating, personal attack.' For the International Committee delegates, battling to make inadequate supplies go round hungry children and adults reduced to the verge of destitution, the distinction between real and false refugee tended to lose its meaning.

From the very beginning, Palestine had been a dirty war. For all their earlier promises, neither Jews nor Arabs had paid much attention to the Geneva Conventions. The emblem had been ignored, hostages taken and murdered, atrocities committed daily. As Gaillard was soon remarking, it was not so much a question of having enough doctors, but of preventing ever growing numbers of 'disappearances'. Looking back on those days now, he believes them to be the first example of 'ethnic cleansing'. When in the spring of 1949 an armistice was declared, the International Committee, whose duties officially ended with the ceasefire, pulled out handing over its work to the new UN organization for refugees in the Middle East. Its experience in Palestine had not altogether improved its image, and it would be accused later of having failed to understand the 'cultural and religious context'. In a critical survey of the International Committee in Palestine, published in 1996, Dominique Junod, Marcel Junod's niece, would write that de Reynier in particular was conditioned 'by his taste for strategy and prestige, and perhaps also by his anti-Jewish prejudices'. Both the diplomatic conference leading to the new Geneva

Conventions and the UN had ducked the question of ultimate responsibility. Palestine, the Committee now warned, spurred on by the delegates returning from the field, should act as a reminder that responsibility for refugees fell to all nations and that it was not going to be enough simply to act in the 'spirit of the Conventions'. With a touch of smugness, they now identified themselves as men 'imbued with the humanitarian spirit ... who, remembering that they are first human beings dealing with other human beings', were well placed to 'attenuate the hardships'.

If this was a dry run for things to come, however, it did not augur well. A troubled peace was turning out to be as dangerous, costly and painful as official war.

The neutral, apolitical nature of the International Committee is a refrain sung continuously since the day that Dunant wandered among the wounded Austrians and French on the battlefield of Solferino, taking no account of their nationality. Yet humanitarian work cannot avoid a political dimension and the threads of political intrigue that run through it seldom fail to leave their mark. In 1950 a war broke out that was not only to challenge the 1949 Geneva Conventions – it would be the first test of Article 3, the extension of protection to victims of civil wars – but would plunge the International Committee into a bitter ideological conflict in which both sides saw themselves as representing the force for good, while the Committee itself was branded as politically partisan.

On 25 June 1950, North Korean forces crossed the 38th parallel and the war in Korea began. The UN Security Council declared North Korea to be the aggressor and called on member states to help the South. When UN troops reached the Chinese border, China counter-attacked. President Ruegger sent off his cables to the governments of both North and South, reminding them of the existence of the Geneva Conventions. Syngman Rhee, president of the Republic of South Korea, replied that the South was 'proud to be a signatory' and would live up to their standards: the North, which was not one of the sixty-one countries which had signed the 1949 Conventions, remained silent. More cables went off; the silence continued. A Korean speaker was found in Geneva and a brochure on 'advice to nurses' was translated from French and sent off to Korea: it would, the Committee suggested, 'surely be of intèrest to you and useful for your society'. There was no reply. The UN forces agreed to be bound by the Conventions. China announced that the International Committee was nothing but a 'capitalist spy organization' trying to use its special privileges to obtain 'strategic intelligence' – much the same argument and language China was to adopt at the international Red Cross conference in Toronto in 1952.

Soon some 170,000 North Korean soldiers had been taken prisoner. A delegate called Frédéric Bieri was despatched to South Korea to begin prison camp visits and to embark on a routine of checking conditions and reporting needs perfected by many delegates before him. Before long he was advising Geneva that he was busy negotiating for dried octopus to be added to the prisoners' diets and that he had provided a number of volley-balls to the camps. Jacques de Reynier and Jean Courvoisier had now been appointed delegates to the North and prepared to leave for Korea.

The persistence with which the International Committee continued to woo the North was impressive. More cables were sent, respectful but insistent. In January 1951, by which time there had still been no reply, President Ruegger suggested visiting the North in person. Overtures to China, where he proposed to touch down on his way, were instantly rejected by Zhou Enlai, the premier and foreign minister of China, who said that there would be no stopping in China until North Korea had given the go-ahead to an official mission. Messages for the North concerning Ruegger's trip were transmitted over short-wave radio on 9th and 10th January in English twelve times, six times in French and ten times in Korean. The silence was still not broken. A visit to China was at last brokered, but when the International Committee announced that the Chinese had agreed to forward to the North Korean camps the medical supplies that the Committee had gathered, the Chinese retorted that it was all a mistake and that they had no intention of doing anything without North Korean permission. A trip to Moscow to see the North Korean ambassador, led by Ruegger, ended in humiliation when the ambassador refused to see him.

After months of delays, Jean Courvoisier was suddenly given a visa for China and permitted to proceed as far as Tiantsin; but there he stayed. De Reynier had still not left Geneva. The Committee, having discovered an expert in Korean calligraphy, asked him to prepare a courteous greeting for the elusive Korean ambassador to Moscow: 'O Excellency! We wish you good health in this beautiful season of sprouting cereals!' There was no reply. Perhaps, inquired the Committee next, the North might be willing to accept a 'different way' of doing things? The silence remained total. Ninety-one thousand names of prisoners-of-war held in the South had been given by the UN forces to Geneva; the North admitted to holding 110.

Bieri, who was soon joined by de Reynier, was hard at work in the South. The early reports on conditions in the camps were good. But as the months passed, overcrowding grew more acute and the Koreans guarding the prisoners remained hostile towards them. De Reynier returned from visits to two prisons in Seoul in which civilian internees had been placed, reporting that he had seen 9,200 captives 'in a state of semi-starvation'. He had also come across fifty dead bodies. Water was rationed and many of the prisoners seemed ill; some bore evidence of having been beaten. He had also seen women with babies strapped to their backs being marched off to interrogation. When taxed with these incidents, the South Korean authorities insisted that only 'criminals, suspects, traitors and collaborators' were arrested, though the minister for justice admitted that as 'communists think only of killing' you had to 'kill them first, before they had an opportunity to kill others.' Harsh treatment of civilians, particularly women and small children, was in clear breach of the Geneva Conventions, warned the Swiss delegates. Before long, an apologetic note was delivered from the foreign ministry: 'We are engaged in a life and death struggle and we are sorry to say that the conditions everywhere are not what they were before the war'. Together with their reports, the delegates sent photographs back to Switzerland. On the Committee's recommendations, special camps were set up for civilian internees.

Because there were so few delegates, it was some time before it became clear that a deep and bitter ideological division between the men in the camps was beginning to cause problems. Most of the guards were Korean, not UN, troops and in any case the foreign soldiers spoke no Korean and were not greatly concerned to understand their prisoners' culture or history. The speed with which the men had been captured had not allowed for a very precise registration process. As feuds between communists and non-communists simmered, the authorities realized that some 21,000 of the men being held were Chinese and that, along with the North Korean prisoners, there were also some 49,000 South Koreans captured during the fighting or rounded up later on suspicion of being Northern soldiers in disguise. These men naturally viewed communism and their futures very differently. The increasingly volatile mood of the camps was not improved when every prisoner was issued with a sports shirt and Bermuda shorts, dyed a nice red colour: no one had thought to consult the Koreans or they would have discovered that the red chosen was the very one used by the Japanese as prison dress for criminals during their occupation of Korea after 1910. The prisoners-of-war threw the shorts at the guards, first wrapping rocks up inside them. One injured a South Korean guard, and his colleagues opened fire, killing three prisoners.

Pusan Camp No. 1, where 135,000 Korean prisoners lived through the first winter and spring of captivity, was broken down into enclosures, surrounded by barbed wire fences. Many of the men had been malnourished at the time of capture and many had dysentery. The food they were given, though for the most part of sufficient quantity, was very bland for Korean taste and made the dysentery worse. Cases of malnutrition increased. The compounds were filthy and the louse population grew, the Americans complaining that Korean lice defied the strongest DDT. Quasi-official police forces began to emerge within the camps from among the stronger prisoners, tolerated though not sanctioned by the UN command.

The UN authorities were aware that the conditions in the camps were in breach of the Geneva code and efforts were made to improve both buildings and sanitation. Just the same, released prisoners described overcrowding, constant hunger, lawlessness and brutality that verged on sadism. As communists and non-communists struggled for control of the compounds, so the self-elected camp police resorted to ever greater violence, roaming the camps under cover of darkness, beating up and sometimes killing their ideological enemies. 'Under the present circumstances,' a delegate reported to Geneva, 'the prisoners are excitable, unstable and restless.' Riots broke out, which turned the compounds into battlefields. UN guards and camp commandants, though for the most part intent on following the Geneva Conventions, could not but help finding the articles somewhat inappropriate when dealing with a prisoner-of-war population divided along ideological lines and bent on destroying the other side. The decision taken not to intervene only led to more brutality. One of the UN's few genuine attempts at interference, an educational plan called Civil Information and Education, an unashamed paean of praise for the charms of capitalism – 'an ideological orientation towards an orderly, responsible, progressive, peace-loving and democratic society' – only served to promote the anti-communist factions, which in turn led to reprisals from the communists. Sears Roebuck catalogues were handed out to show the desirability of all things western.

Bieri and de Reynier were doing their best to follow the ebb and flow of ideology within the camps, and to intervene when brutality seemed to be getting out of control, but there was not a great deal they could do. When a riot broke out in Koje camp early in 1952, troops went in and restored order with what was later admitted to be undue violence. Sixty-nine prisoners died; 142 were wounded. The UN now announced that the delegates would be barred from certain camps until their safety could again be ensured, which led to a direct confrontation between the International Committee and the UN. A visit by Dr Otto Lehner, the delegate to Berlin kidnapped by the Soviets in 1945 and now chief delegate for the Far East, was somewhat marred by a long article that appeared in a Hong Kong paper, saying that Lehner had been personally responsible for a 'scandalous report describing the pleasures and benefits of life in Hitler's concentration camps'.

By the summer of 1952, life in the camps had become almost intolerable. Ideological groups had taken over a number of Pusan's compounds and were imposing rule by terror. American guards intervened by cutting off all supplies while opening a new compound with food and water nearby to which the rebels were invited to move, having been sorted and screened. Eventually troops were sent in, with tear gas and stun grenades.

The Chinese Red Cross suddenly decided to open its own verbal assault on the UN forces. While accusing the Americans of mistreating prisoners, using poison gas and bombing well-marked Red Cross hospitals in the North, they issued reports and pictures showing how excellently the North Koreans were treating their own captives. A letter sent to President Ruegger included a long message signed by 1,362 British and American prisoners. 'All of us are safe and sound and looking forward to the day when we can return to our homes and our loved ones,' it said. 'Indeed, our only danger is that we may be bombed again by American aircraft . . . Our fear is not that we will suffer as prisoners-of-war but that we may be blotted out by the same group of selfish warmongers who sent us out here in the first place.'

What the International Committee delegates rightly suspected but had no way of proving, was that the prisoners being held in the North were in fact in a very bad way, particularly some of the young UN soldiers, who had been utterly unprepared for hardship and were now frightened, hungry and succumbing to pneumonia and dysentery. Under what the Chinese called the 'lenient policy', soldiers who they claimed should have been executed as war criminals – for was this not an 'unjust' war? – were in fact being given the chance to repent their crimes. A 're-education' campaign was in full swing, and it involved physical violence, solitary confinement, starvation as well as 'incentives'. As one later much-quoted Chinese officer put it: 'We will keep you here 10, 20, 30 or even 40 years if necessary, until you learn the truth, and if you still don't learn it, we will bury you so deep that you won't even stink.' The 'progressive' prisoners, the ones who accepted the wisdom of Marx, Engels, Lenin and Stalin, were treated better than the 'reactionary' ones, who were told that they would no longer be able to benefit from the 'lenient' policy. Not surprising, then, that many opted for the 'correct' answers in the questionnaires they were given to fill in. To help fix their minds, personal indoctrination sessions and compulsory singing of communist slogans were introduced as well as visitors, books, newspapers and films with a pro-communist slant. A number of western journalists known for their sympathy towards communism were invited to inspect the camps, and most returned home afterwards with praise for their conditions. 'Prisoners get more meat, more fat and more sugar,' wrote Jack Gasser, a member of the British Communist Party, in the *Daily Worker* in March 1952, 'than anyone in Britain receives from a ration book'. Both Mrs Monica Felton, Chairman of the British Assembly of Women, and Alan Winnington, also of the *Daily Worker*, returned to London to describe massacres, torture, brutality and rape suffered not in the North but by prisoners held by the United Nations. (In 1952 Mrs Felton received a Stalin Peace Prize in Moscow.) Meanwhile the North, continued to refuse the International Committee permission to visit their camps, pointing out that conditions were so good that there was no need for inspection.

The first mention of bacteriological warfare came in late 1951. Typhus was reported in the North, probably brought by the Chinese volunteers, but quickly attributed to American dirty tricks. On 27 February 1952 the Hungarian Red Cross sounded the attack in a strongly worded cable to Geneva, declaring that the Americans were 'throwing from their planes infected insects' and causing 'massive deaths' with bacteria. Further cables from Poland, Bulgaria and Romania spoke of a 'war of bacteriological extermination'. The International Committee passed the cables on to the American Red Cross.

The story of the American troops dropping infected bugs has never been totally cleared up; but while it lasted it provided the North with a wonderful opportunity to spread confusion. Later, in a long document published in Peking in 1953, written by the Chinese Red Cross and titled 'Concerning bacteriological warfare in Korea and China', the charges were spelt out. Seven hundred and seventeen rat-like animals were said to have been spotted in places where they had never been seen before at that time of year immediately after a low-flying American plane had been heard. 'In the morning,' so the report said, 'the villagers found many of the voles dying or dead in their houses and courtyards, on their roofs, and even on their beds.' Anthrax, continued the report, had been dropped using insects, spiders and the feathers from chickens as carriers. Cholera had been spread by marine molluscs which suddenly appeared in the middle of the countryside. There were photographs of women wielding chopsticks and crouching on the ground 'insect catching . . . to exterminate the insects dropped on the snowy ground', as well as descriptions of odd-looking 'wolf-spiders' which, when ground up and injected, caused instant death to a white mouse, a duck, a chicken, a pigeon, a guinea pig and a rabbit. Photographs showed guinea pigs with enlarged spleens.

The Americans reacted furiously to the charge. A communiqué from the State Department reached Geneva on 11 March, denying the story and asking the International Committee to carry out an investigation. The Committee asked North Korea for permission to send a commission of 'morally and scientifically' independent people and began to search for respected epidemiologists and entomologists. The Committee now also issued one of its rare statements to the press, on 31 March 1952, setting down the true order of events, accusing Radio Peking of broadcasting 'a tendentious and damaging report' and saying that China's accusations 'were clearly contradicted by the facts and that the ICRC categorically denies them'. The weeks passed, but nothing was heard from the North. Fifteen of the states supplying forces to the UN Command were parties to the Geneva protocol of 1925 banning poisons and germs in war; South Korea, North Korea and China were not.

The North Koreans were not being idle. Deciding that the International Committee was 'not sufficiently free from political influence' to be capable of producing an 'unbalanced inquiry', they decided to set up a scientific commission of their own. A number of experts from Sweden, Italy, Brazil and the USSR, including Joseph Needham, the historian of Chinese science, from Britain, agreed to travel to Korea, take statements from captured American airmen and examine the voles and chicken feathers. They returned to produce a 700-page report, complete with laboratory tests, autopsy findings, maps and photographs. It is an odd, but thorough, document. Their conclusion was that bacteriological weapons *had* been 'employed by units of the USA armed forces, using a great variety of different methods for the purpose, some of which seem to be developments of those applied by the Japanese army during the Second World War'.

Few experts today are willing to go quite so far, though most concede that the reports from North Korea unquestionably contained a number of facts and findings that have never been explained. In the late 1930s, a Japanese army surgeon called Ishii Shiro was known to have set up Unit 731, described as a 'water purification plant'; it had insect breeding facilities, a prison, an airfield and a number of specially designed aircraft. Rumours circulated that Shiro's results were so impressive because he was able to experiment on human beings as well as laboratory animals, using Chinese prisoners, some Russians and a few 'half-breeds', and that he had perfected a way of spreading the plague by dropping rats and voles from low-flying aircraft. Infecting feathers with spore diseases, was, so it was said, Shiro's idea. By 1945, Japan was believed to have a huge stockpile of germs, vectors and delivery equipment.

At the Tokyo war crimes trial, not a great deal was said about Ishii Shiro, bacteriological diseases or Unit 731. But to this day journalists and scientists continue to turn up clues about the unit and its experiments, and to point to odd similarities between the Japanese programme and bacteriological experiments known to have been carried out in the United States. Korea, they say, may have provided an excellent dry run.

By the time the international furore over the voles and the germs had died down, the UN had other things on its mind. As negotiations for an armistice at last got under way, the communists suddenly appeared to take an interest in the prisoner-of-war Convention. In July 1953, Zhou Enlai announced that though the code contained a number of articles he disagreed with – all foreign soldiers were, in Chinese eyes, war criminals to whom the Conventions did not apply – he was willing to embrace the others, and particularly General Article 118: 'Prisoners-of-war shall be released and repatriated without delay.' Once they had thought through the extent to which the word 'repatriate' can be ambiguous, the UN and the delegates saw all too clearly the trap that was being set for them. While the West argued that Article 118 was designed to protect prisoners, in that once released the prisoners were to be set free, the communists argued that what repatriate really meant was that *all* prisoners should be returned to the country for which they were fighting without delay. Many of those held in the South had no intention of going back to North Korea.

It took many months, considerable bitterness and the skills of all parties combined, International Committee delegates included, to find and put through an acceptable compromise. Once the armistice talks were agreed delegates were at last allowed to visit camps in North Korea, but the visit proved as farcical in its own way as that paid to Theresienstadt in 1944. Screening the 170,000 men in UN and South Korean custody turned into a succession of misunderstandings and recriminations. Sessions to discuss procedures were interminable and ill-tempered and the stalemate only aggravated the country's economic decline and food shortages. It was not until August 1953 that some 76,000 North Koreans who stated that they wished to go back to the North were sent home, leaving almost 23,000 non-communists who refused to go with them and were put into the custody of an agreed Neutral Nation Repatriation Committee, under the Indians. Various face-saving formulae to account for the reluctance of so many to return to communist rule were somehow found.

Reports were now published by the Chinese Red Cross about the terrible conditions of their returned prisoners – men incapacitated and crippled by 'wrong amputations by the US medical personnel', stories of beatings, stabbings, starvation rations, carried out by the UN and South Korean forces alike. Two thousand six hundred captured Chinese volunteers were said to have been murdered, after being used as live targets or having their hearts cut out. Survivors reported 'four or five ounce dumplings made of mouldy barley, not much larger than an egg', maggoty vegetables, and having their 'limbs crushed with wooden bars'. One volunteer said that he had seen 'with my own eyes a man thrown off a lorry' and how the other lorries then drove over his body, one after the other. 'Tears of fury and sorrow,' he declared, 'fell from our eyes.' There were descriptions of massacres, of 'pools of blood', of being tattooed with 'reactionary slogans' and of those who refused being told: 'You will leave a piece of your flesh behind.'

Wisely, the International Committee said little, beyond taking the unusual step of publishing two sober, comprehensive and very long volumes detailing every phase in this confused war, including letters and telegrams sent and received. For the Red Cross movement as a whole, the Chinese Red Cross's unquestioning acceptance of its government's ideological position after the communists took power provided unwelcome proof that the much criticized and total subordination of the German, Japanese and Italian Red Cross societies to their totalitarian governments before and during the Second World War had not succeeded in preventing others from doing the same.

From the North now came nearly 13,000 prisoners, of which 3,500 were American and 1,312 from other UN member states, many dazed by the 're-education' programmes and some far from clear as to where their loyalties now lay. Some 16,000 prisoners were said to have died while in captivity in the North.

When the screening was over and the last of the prisoners had gone home – the eighty-eight men for whom no home was found were finally taken back to India by the Indian Red Cross – delegates returned to Geneva to take stock of what they had been through. The International Committee's verdict, drawn up for the benefit of outsiders, was not as bleak as that painted by others. After all, one side at least, the UN forces, had done much to adhere to the Conventions, and Article 3 had been tested and found workable. Yet the Korean war had proved all too convincingly the powerlessness of the International Committee and the Geneva Conventions in the face of a flat refusal by a government to co-operate; even those theoretically accepting the prisoner-of-war code had condoned, not just poor conditions, but brutality. But the delegates had again shown the value of persistent, scrupulous reporting, even if several returned to Geneva to observe that the International Committee's role in the repatriations had been 'far from glorious', in that it had been forced to condone practices no one could regard as fair.

Just why such a war had broken out in the first place, and how such wars could be prevented, was not, however, their business. On these matters the Committee remained silent, again demonstrating that its interest in war lay in its conduct, as Dunant had made plain, and not in war itself.

If Korea had shown a Red Cross world at war with itself, its national societies torn along ideological lines, the eastern bloc members supporting the Chinese and eager to parrot the politics of their governments and to condemn the International Committee itself for being partisan, the revolution in Hungary was to prove what harmony could achieve. It was not only the largest relief operation of its kind yet mounted by the Red Cross, working closely with the UN high commissioner for refugees and the various relief organizations, but it was also carried out faster and more efficiently than anything that had gone before. Old animosities were forgotten in the scramble not only to save lives but to make them bearable.

On 21 October 1956, Władysław Gomulka, communist party first secretary in Poland, dissolved the security police and collective farms, set up workers' soviets and proclaimed a socialist state free from Kremlin rule. There was no Soviet military attack. In Hungary, a country with a real tradition of human rights dating back to the Middle Ages, the liberals who had managed to survive ten years of oppression under a puppet government run by Moscow and the terror tactics of the AVO secret police, watched developments in Poland and wondered. Over the next few days a revolution was born, sparked off by an anti-communist and anti-Russian demonstration by university students and writers, and very quickly taken up by most of the rest of the Hungarian population including large sections of the ordinary police and the army. By the evening of 23 October, over 300,000 people, many of them in lines of six abreast, were marching through Budapest. The AVO security men opened fire but the reformers pressed on, attacking all AVO men they found. Calls for Hungarian troops to restore order ended as many of the soldiers joined the demonstrators. This time the Russians did react and sent in their own soldiers; unarmed Hungarian civilians, some no more than children, clashed with Russian troops.

The fighting lasted for several days. On 30 October, Moscow Radio broadcast a Soviet declaration that their commander-in-chief in Hungary had been ordered to withdraw and that they were prepared to discuss the evacuation of all Soviet troops with Colonel Maleter, one of the heroes of the revolution. Among the Hungarians there was heady and disbelieving talk of independence, neutrality, democracy and even getting out of the Warsaw Pact.

The spirits of the revolutionaries were high, but there had been many casualties and supplies of food and medicine were running low. A telegram arrived in Geneva from the Hungarian Red Cross, the national society that had led the attack on the International Committee in Korea only four years before. 'Have lost all vehicles, need as far as possible ambulances, lorries, surgical instruments, X-ray equipment . . . baby foods, condensed milk, fats, building materials, timber, cement and glass.'

The world had been following the fighting in Hungary with horror and sympathy. Offers of help from national Red Cross societies were already pouring into the Committee, which now reacted with speed. Hungary was surrounded on three sides by communist countries – Czechoslovakia to the north, Russia and Romania to the east, and Yugoslavia to the south. To the west lay Austria, which now became the willing and generous gateway for an immense relief operation. An immediate airlift was arranged by the International Committee to take emergency supplies, including blood plasma and concentrated food, from Vienna to Budapest. The Committee announced that it was receiving new offers of help every hour.

On 1 November the Hungarians still believed that they had won. Next morning Budapest awoke to the sound of jet bombers, mortars and tanks, apparently impervious to the barricades of cobblestones and the soap smeared on the streets to deter them. Imre Nagy, who had been made chairman of the Hungarian People's Republic, broadcast over the radio that the Soviet army was attacking. After a final playing of the national anthem and an appeal by the Writers' Association – 'Help Hungary! Help the Hungarian writers, scientists, workers, peasants and intelligentsia. Help! Help! Help!' – the free radio of Budapest went dead. In one of the last telephone conversations with the outside world, the Hungarian Red Cross asked the International Committee to secure respect for the fourth Geneva Convention for the civilians trapped in the capital. The Committee put out an appeal over the radio for the wounded to be collected and taken to safety. Just the same, thousands of civilians died.

With Budapest airport closed, the International Committee grounded its plane in Vienna, halted the flow of supplies and asked the national societies to stand by. Even so, forty of them, from countries as far apart as Argentina and Pakistan, already had supplies in transit and soon Red Cross staff in Vienna were disappearing under a mountain of goods, all of which needed unloading, checking and repacking. The focus of their work now moved to the border between Austria and Hungary, across which, from the evening of 4 November, refugees flowed: men, women and children, frightened and desperate, dragging behind them suitcases and wheelbarrows, much like the Jews who had marched to Hegyeshalom in the closing months of the Second World War. The village of Andau, near the border, saw 55,000 people pass in the next few weeks. It was, so people said, the largest flight of civilians in Europe since the Spanish civil war. In the *Review*, the International Committee referred to itself as the 'footbridge which continues to exist when other bridges have fallen'.

Herbert Beckh was one of two International Committee delegates who had managed to reach Budapest before the Soviets invaded. He was a stout, balding man with glasses and a double chin; he was also dignified, unflappable and industrious. With the remarkable reserves of energy that these Swiss businessmen-turned-delegates seemed to possess, he now embarked on an almost frenzied mission to help refugees escape Soviet reprisals, to organize the flow of relief to the capital, to set up an information bureau and a tracing office, as well as exerting continuous pressure on the authorities to allow him to visit people taken prisoner.

It was dangerous, uncertain work and there was something of Born in Beckh's doggedness. No one was sure who was in charge or where sympathies lay. All Geneva could do was remind both Hungarians and Soviets about the neutrality and immunity of Red Cross personnel.

In Budapest there was no coal and no milk. With supplies of food and medicines dwindling rapidly, with winter setting in and many buildings destroyed in the fighting, the Committee now concentrated on getting convoys of relief through. The first, accompanied by an Italian and a Danish unit, consisting of some 166 doctors, interpreters, delegates and drivers, was ready to set out from Vienna on 8 November, all sixty-five vehicles painted white with red crosses. The plan was to drive to Budapest and hand over supplies, if possible directly to Beckh and his colleague, and if not to what remained of the Hungarian Red Cross. Instructions went out to give nothing to 'non-qualified persons'. After various delays the convoy reached Budapest, unloaded, and set off back to reload and make the same journey again. Feeding programmes were started, for babies and small children, and sheets of glass arrived for the thousands of shattered windows through which the snow was now falling. In February, the International Committee announced that it had just despatched its fiftieth convoy. There was no shortage of supplies. Hungary's revolution, with its pinched refugees and daring students seemed to strike a particular chord in western minds, their losses captured in the many pictures of families trudging through the sleet and made more poignant by the overtones of the Cold War.

The revolution in Hungary also marked an excellent moment in the Committee's traditionally uneasy relationship with the League. Relief was now split into two, the Committee concentrating on Hungary itself – the war zone – while the League looked to the refugees increasing every hour in Austria itself. The League rapidly recruited 650 volunteers to run reception centres and appointed a new 'delegate-co-ordinator'; the International Committee took on 151 people. Vienna became a vast encampment of refugees, international organizations, UNHCR officials and supplies. The 1000th truckload of relief to reach the city brought goods from Germany, Italy and Britain; that same day, twelve aeroplanes landed with a million kilograms of rice from Spain. America sent cheese and blankets and many of the relief parcels whose contents had been so carefully worked out during the war; the British supplied condensed milk. Seed potatoes, barley and oats came from the Food and Agriculture Organization in Rome. Over a thousand tonnes of flour travelled by river. Austria was accustomed to refugees, and particularly Hungarian refugees, but this was the second time in a little over eleven years that overwhelming numbers had crossed their border in search of asylum. On a single day, in the autumn of 1956, 8,000 refugees came across, some of them soaked and frozen, having waded through icy marshland. Before many weeks had passed, there were some 169,000 people living in camps, in shacks, barracks, hospitals and castles, fed by more than thirty national Red Cross societies from all five continents, and by the UNHCR. The Austrian Red Cross imaginatively arranged for the Hungarian children to have vouchers with which to choose their own clothes, instead of just giving them handouts. In the camps, Red Cross staff arranged sports, orchestras, film clubs. 'Idleness,' noted the *Review*, 'is the worst enemy of the refugee.'

So obviously efficient was the entire operation, the only one east of the Iron Curtain between the end of the Second World War and 1981, that for once neither League nor International Committee had any difficulty in repelling the usual attacks. A false rumour was put out by an American newspaper that the Soviets were looting the relief. Based on a letter sent by a priest in Hungary to a colleague in St Louis, it was soon proved inaccurate. But they could do nothing to prevent the new Soviet-backed Hungarian authorities from imposing heavy customs duty on the supplies going in, which reached seventy per cent in the case of tea and coffee. Donors were advised to switch to gifts on which there was no duty – a strange collection of things that included pork, aprons, children's shoes and soap.

The closing day for relief action was set for 30 June 1957, though the tracing of the missing would go on for many years. A new operation, the resettling of Hungarians unable to return home for political reasons in countries throughout Europe and North America was under way, masterminded by UNHCR, which succeeded in placing refugees in thirty-five countries. Britain took 12,000 and some of these were flown in by the British Red Cross in an operation which was in its own way another model of co-operation; independent charter companies, who seconded pilots and planes to bring the refugees in, were noted and Red Cross volunteers were on hand to meet and look after them. 'Even Geneva,' commented W. E. Casley of the Aeronautical Information Service a little tartly, 'has been forced to admit a certain reluctant admiration for this country.' Asylum, commented the Austrian minister of the interior, Oscar Helmer, 'is an affair of the heart'.

The Hungarians did not die of hunger, nor of avoidable diseases. But their moment of freedom was short. This time there was no Soviet pulling back. Imre Nagy was arrested, convicted as a traitor and executed. Hungary returned into Soviet hands, with a new 'revolutionary peasant-worker' government and a puppet premier, János Kádár. Arrests, deportations to the Soviet Union and executions began once again. Those who had managed to reach safety abroad and find homes were fortunate. With the numbers of refugees now swelling all the time throughout the world, others would soon not be as lucky.

Herbert Beckh had tried very hard to visit prisons. The new Hungarian regime refused to let him in. From time to time, as the days passed, he was able to intervene when he witnessed arbitrary arrests, sometimes saving men and women from immediate execution by being firm and calm and quoting the Geneva Conventions. It was another case of the impotence of the accord when it came to government obduracy, and the power of individual delegates.

But this was really the Committee's only failure. Geneva had every reason to feel content with the relief operation. The Hungarian revolution had provided it with the chance that it had hoped for in Palestine to prove not only its unique neutrality but its efficiency. Thirty-six national societies and eleven governments had listened to its appeal, sending over fifty thousand tonnes of relief, and useful lessons had been learned about the need to standardize medical supplies so that doctors in less developed countries were not baffled by new drugs. As a display of co-operation, it was judged to have been a model for what could be achieved if the world was prepared to act in harmony, much as Born, Lutz and Wallenberg had shown what might have been accomplished for the Jews throughout occupied Europe if the Allies, the Vatican and the International Committee had chosen to act together.

Yet, looked at with hindsight today, when international politics and public relations have come to devour most emergencies, when refugees and asylum are to do with politics and are no longer affairs of the heart, the Hungarian episode has an air of innocence.

*   *   *

France's record with its prisoners-of-war had not been good in the post-war years, tarnished as it was by the stories of brutality towards the conquered Germans kept captive on French soil. In 1954, barely seven years after public indignation and the International Committee's intervention put an end to the slow starvation of German soldiers and internees, France became involved in another conflict, soon renowned for its brutality. The eight-year war in Algeria would not only provide a crucial test for Article 3 of the Geneva Conventions and herald a decade of wars of national liberation, but would bring to the fore what has become in recent years one of the most disturbing issues in human rights and humanitarian law: torture. For many of the French, who remembered all too well the concentration camps and the years of Nazi occupation, the war in Algeria would spell a particular kind of shame.

On All Saints Day, 1 November 1954, Algerian nationalists, despairing that the end of the Second World War had brought not liberalization and equality but an implacable return to French nationalist *pied noir* rule backed by strong French military forces, launched a revolt. The 'night of the long knives', as it was soon called, failed to lead to the popular uprising they had hoped for but as French reprisals triggered increased Arab attacks, so the two sides hardened. The first Algerian nationalist targets were French police stations and military barracks; after that, they turned to civilians and Muslims sympathetic to French rule. In January 1955, judging that the numbers of Arab detainees in French hands was reaching a disquieting level, the International Committee offered its services to both sides, quoting Common Article 3.

The French prevaricated at first. Algeria, they said, was a part of France and its internal conflicts a matter for the French alone; the troublesome Arabs they were detaining in special camps set up on General Salan's orders were only 'rebels'. Then, almost unexpectedly, they sent word that they were prepared to abide by Article 3. This concession was crucial, because it marked a tacit recognition that men and women they called terrorists had none the less found a place under international law as being identifiable people 'in the hands of a power that regards them as an enemy'. France now agreed to allow the Committee to send a delegation to Algeria and to visit detainees without witnesses as long as it was accepted that they would confine their questions to the conditions under which the prisoners were held — and refrain from questioning anyone about the reasons for their arrest — and that their reports would remain confidential, for the eyes of Geneva and the French government alone. The detainees, France insisted, were not prisoners-of-war and would not be called such; but for the duration of this war they would be treated as if they were. For several weeks, from the end of February to mid-April 1955, delegates visited forty-three places of detention in Algeria — of which there were now hundreds, ranging from interrogation centres to vast camps.

One of the delegates sent to Algeria was Pierre Gaillard, the mountaineer, now head of the Middle East section at the International Committee in Geneva. Like President Ruegger, he had long been warning the Committee that political detainees were a subject about to pose terrible problems, and he saw in the Algerian conflict the perfect opportunity to test the limits of Red Cross power using the 1949 Conventions. If the Committee seemed to have been dragging its heels — its power as the decision-making body remained strong, if not absolute — it has to be remembered that these were the years of the Hungarian uprising, Castro's landing in Cuba and the Suez crisis, all events in which the Committee was to some extent involved. 'It was extremely hard,' says Gaillard today. 'There was considerable resistance to our visits, particularly to prisoners held in pre-detention, and it was only through conversations with prisoners that we were able to start putting together a list of places where people were being held and assess how they were being treated.' The conditions of civilians rounded up in immense 'resettlement' camps — there was talk of over a million, held behind barbed wire, in camps very like the German concentration camps of the 1930s — were also disturbing, as were those of the refugees who had fled the fighting to find extreme poverty along the borders with Morocco and Tunisia.

The war in Algeria became exceptionally brutal very quickly. Even though the French government had publicly announced that interrogations were to be conducted without physical violence and that 'every offence against human dignity' was 'vigorously forbidden', more and more mutilated bodies of Algerian Muslims began to turn up in ditches and along the roadsides. As nationalist attacks increased, so the French came to regard every Arab, even boys and old women, as potential killers and to act accordingly.

In the summer of 1955, the Algerian nationalist army, the FLN, declared war on French civilians. On 15 August, in the great heat of a north African summer day when French families were on holiday by the sea, they threw grenades into a café in Philippeville, a coastal city with many thousands of French inhabitants, and dragged motorists from their cars to cut their throats. At Aïn-Abid, not far away, thirty-seven French civilians were slaughtered with sickening brutality, disembowelled or cut up into pieces. French retaliation was immediate, just as sickening and on a far greater scale. Men, women and children were murdered and mutilated. Soon, bulldozers were needed to scoop up the bodies of the dead for burial. Ain-Abid, with its evidence of careful FLN planning, was a turning-point for the French military. After this, determination to crush the rebellion pushed aside what few liberal constraints remained.

Torture was a subject of great relevance to the International Committee. Both the Stockholm conference and the 1949 Geneva Conventions, as well as the Universal Declaration of Human Rights, had come out in clear condemnation of torture, declaring freedom from such violence to be one of man's fundamental and inalienable rights. As a Russian delegate to Stockholm had put it, to unanimous approval, torture was one of the 'darkest stains in the history of mankind', a sentiment readily endorsed by the French, who had proscribed it at the time of the French Revolution and added an article to its own penal code prohibiting it on the pain of death. Torture, as the International Committee delegates had long since recognized, thrived where prisoners were held in secret, and particularly during the first days of detention and interrogation. Prison visits were one of the only weapons against it. Gaillard had quickly perceived how the torture of detainees in Algeria by French paratroopers was taking hold. 'We knew what was happening. We knew that the French were torturing people to get information. We took doctors with us. But it was very hard: often those who had been seriously tortured were simply killed so as to leave no trace.'

At the height of the battle for Algiers, in the early months of 1957, torture was put into the hands of 'experts' among General Massu's paratroops, men who perfected the use of the *gégène*, an army signals magneto with electrodes that could be attached to the genitalia. The experts seemed to need very little rest, either night or day. The *gégène* was the ideal torture weapon, leaving no marks except in cases of exceptional savagery. In France, the stories of torture that surfaced occasionally in the papers were vehemently denied by the government. 'There have without doubt been a very few acts of violence, and they are to be deplored,' Guy Mollet, the prime minister, told a meeting of socialists in La Marne on 14 April 1957. 'But they came, I can assure you, only after attacks and atrocities carried out by the terrorists . . . And these, I repeat, could almost be counted on the fingers of one hand.' As for comparisons between the French army and the Gestapo, made by outspoken liberal lawyers and journalists, these were 'scandalous'.

In 1957, a young Swiss called Laurent Vust, who had grown up in Algeria and whose father, the local representative for Nestlé, had been made an International Committee delegate with Gaillard, was asked whether he would be willing to join the missions of inspection. Vust was training to be a lawyer.

> They were on the seventh mission when I joined them. One of the first prisoners I saw was a young man in an interrogation centre. He was crying. He had just been tortured with the *gégène*. It was also on the first day that I saw my first corpse in a prison. One of the prisoners came up to me and pointed to a group of men. Look, he said, those men have been tortured. Can't you do something? Aren't you from the Red Cross?

There was in fact very little that Vust and his companions could do. Beyond complaining to the French officers – at which Gaillard was said by Vust to be excellent, combining utter firmness with an agreeable manner – the delegates were bound by their mandate, which allowed them only to insist on private talks with the detainees. However, they used these talks to discover other holding centres around Algiers, which they would then try to visit without prior announcement. 'There were enormous numbers of these places,' Vust remembers,

> at which terrible things were happening. It was a sad and painful process. In one prison, because I knew a bit of Arabic, I asked a whole group of prisoners standing together: 'Who here has been given electric shocks or water torture?' Every man in the room put his hand up. And when we were allowed private talks, we often thought the rooms were bugged and that the men we were talking to would be punished after we left. The French

Algerians who knew what we were doing hated us. We couldn't use red cross markings on our cars – it would have been too dangerous.

After every mission the delegates wrote their prison reports – which had changed remarkably little since the First World War – and sent them to Geneva. From there they went to the French government in Paris, after which no more was heard. It was, as Léopold Boissier at the International Committee in Geneva told a press conference, a highly delicate matter, working in situations 'so little defined by law'.

And there matters might have remained; torture known beyond all doubt to Swiss delegates powerless to intervene. One can only guess at Gaillard's anguish and sense of frustration. But then, in 1960, came a leak. To this day no one knows for certain – or is prepared to say – where it came from, but on 5 January *Le Monde* published a long article on the war in Algeria, lifted from the most recent 270-page International Committee report and quoting it more or less verbatim.

> . . . '10 prisoners speaking French chosen at random' reported a delegate who had been to see a camp in the Kabylie 'are absolutely terrified. They begged us not to disclose what they had told us, for fear of being beaten, or even killed, in reprisal.' The delegate to the transit centre of Bou Gobrine described how 'several prisoners complained that they had been tortured during interrogations after capture (water, electricity).' From the transit camp of Bouzareh, in Algiers, the delegate wrote 'We can confirm that torture appears to have been carried out on the prisoners, more or less systematically, from the time of their first interrogations.' In the military camp 'des Chênes' the delegate saw '3 prisoners with signs of recent contusions (severe bruising of the face and around the eyes)'.

The story was picked up by other newspapers. Jean-Paul Sartre called the torture in Algeria 'a plague infecting our whole era'. Laurent Vust remembers *Le Monde*'s synthesis as 'very good and not at all exaggerated'.

The cautious, sober tone, the unsensational litany of cruelty, hardship and above all torture, was confirmed in page after page of careful description: the French paratroopers in Algeria had, in their war against the

Arabs, resorted to systematic physical brutality. The information was neither new or unknown – brave reporters and lawyers had been saying as much for many months. But there was something in this cool Swiss analysis, set out pedantically and almost monotonously without adjective or judgement, that made it not only believable but repulsive. Later, the French public would hear all too many details of young French soldiers turned torturers by their sergeant majors – men referred to as '*gros durs*' who were '*sympathique et chic*' to their own troops – who had taught them how to slit men's throats and throw recalcitrant captives alive from helicopters into the sea, just as they would read all too many descriptions of paratroopers drinking champagne from the skulls of their victims or cutting off their ears to wear as trophies. These images were sickening, too; but the voice of the Swiss delegates was different. What was more, it came at the right moment, when the mounting rumours of torture needed authoritative corroboration. How important was it that it came from the International Committee? 'They were a help, but not crucial,' is all that Dr Moussaoria, one of the leading figures among the Algerian nationalists, is now prepared to say. 'On their own, the International Committee were simply not powerful enough to dare to take the French government on.' Others believe the Committee's leaked voice to have been decisive. Jacques Moreillon, author of an excellent work on political detainees and a senior member of the Committee during the 1970s and 1980s, rising to be secretary-general, says that the Committee's report was crucial.

> Had the French paid any attention to the reports before *Le Monde* published their article? Who knows? It probably depended on who read them. But when *Le Monde* got hold of our report – perhaps from a civil servant in the Quai d'Orsay who found what was happening in Algeria unacceptable – and all the world was able to read about the things the Red Cross had witnessed, then the French government had to do something about it. Quite apart from anything else, it was impossible for them to deny it.

From the spring of 1960, torture in Algeria did decrease. After the publication of the International Committee report, a number of French officials were forced to resign. Public opinion, outraged by the mounting evidence of atrocities which now bombarded the newspapers from all sides, was such that some action had to be taken, even if General Massu insisted that, given what was happening in Algeria, he had no alternative but to use all methods he had available. (Much later, when questioned about Algeria, Massu gave his famous reply: 'In answer to the question: "Was there really torture?" I can only reply in the affirmative, although it was never either institutionalized or codified . . . I am not frightened of the word.')

The Vusts, suspected of their part in the report, were in some danger and, Laurent Vust believes, were saved only from *pied-noir* retaliation by a mechanic friend of his father's, himself a member of the French armed resistance, who vouched for his loyalty. The International Committee itself was forbidden to return to Algeria for a year, but when they were allowed back in delegates found that many of the officers they met were far more helpful, themselves revolted by some of the facts that had been made known. Accounts of torture, in the early 1960s, still had the power to shock. The International Committee delegates were now given a general as escort, rather than the lieutenant of their earlier visits, and lent a helicopter in which to travel around. In any case, the war was slowly drawing to an end.

The leak in *Le Monde* had done more than play its part in revealing the use of torture by French soldiers. It had demonstrated one of the fundamental contradictions in International Committee work: that the price paid for being allowed to be a witness is to remain silent about what is seen, hoping to effect change through moral pressure. If that fails, only exposure is left and exposure, used only extremely rarely by the Committee and as a very last resort, is an unreliable weapon leading both to public fatigue and to the banning of International Committee missions, which can leave victims even more vulnerable than they were before. This delicate instrument, like the right of initiative, is a question often best left undefined. In Algeria, the matter was taken out of their hands — and became all the more powerful for that.

Ben Bella and a number of other Algerian leaders, men like Mohammed Khider and Hocine Ait Ahmed, had been taken by the French and locked up in the Château de Turquant in mainland France. There they were allowed to move around more or less as they wanted, and their doors left unlocked, until a decision was suddenly taken to confine them to their rooms. In protest, and to improve prison conditions of all Algerian detainees, they went on hunger strike. So too did 5,000 other Algerians in French hands. The government responded by sending in doctors. The hunger strikers refused to see them. Then came Mme Laporte of the French Red Cross. They refused to see her too. Pierre Boissier, a senior International Committee delegate, arrived to see Ben Bella. After talks, he set off to visit other Algerian detainees in other prisons. He returned to report their conditions satisfactory. It says something about the credibility of the International Committee that Ben Bella now called off the hunger strike, ordering the other Algerian detainees to do the same.

This was in late November 1961, and the war was very nearly at an end. On 18 March 1962, a cease fire was finally agreed. For a while, the fighting in Algeria went on, as embittered French *pieds noirs* made last frantic efforts to jeopardize the settlement. And then it was all over. A million Algerian Muslims were said to have died in the seven-and-a-half years of the war. Well over a million French Algerians opted for new lives in France and for a while the French Red Cross ran twenty-four-hour reception centres in Marseilles, Toulouse, Lyons and Bordeaux.

For the Red Cross movement, Algeria had been not just a first-hand experience of torture and of a war of independence — and as such a dry run for those soon to be waged in Angola, British Bechuanaland, the Cameroons, British Somaliland and the Belgian Congo — but another chapter in their growing involvement with refugees. As in Hungary, the war had given them another opportunity to prove how efficiently the International Committee, the League and the national societies could work together when faced with waves of people on the move. With the independence of Morocco and Tunisia in 1956, refugees from the war in Algeria had begun to swarm across their borders. Most had been women, small children and the very old. They had arrived exhausted, frightened, ill and very hungry, having kept themselves alive by eating grass and the prickly pears they found growing in the oases in the desert. Visitors to the scattered refugee encampments remembered the starving child survivors of the German camps, their bellies distended and their arms reduced to sticks; the first of the images of modern famine which would later become all too familiar filled the western newspapers. The Moroccan Red Crescent was hastily incorporated into the League's fold, and national societies began to pour aid into the area. Compassion fatigue had not yet settled on the West. Tent cities rose among the dunes and were soon home to more than a quarter of a million refugees – over half of them children under fourteen – supported by forty-two national Red Cross societies. Children all over the world raised money to contribute to the Junior Red Cross's gift of 160,000 tins of condensed milk every month.

With the ceasefire came the complicated task of repatriating refugees to a country in which much of the population had been reduced to the edge of destitution by the long war. Four million of Algeria's nine million citizens were reported to need help. Two-thirds of its doctors had fled the country or been killed. Few of the normal services were working. The returning refugees found their villages and houses ruined, their flocks long since slaughtered and eaten and their fields filled with unexploded mines. The League, the Quakers, the churches and aid organizations everywhere joined forces to send in food, open milk stations and distribute seed to farmers. The Algerians did survive; but only just.

Not all Algerians who had survived the war survived the peace. General de Gaulle had never been greatly interested in the fate of the Harkis, the 180,000 Muslims, *anciens combattants*, defectors from the FLN or men simply sympathetic to the French cause, who had chosen to take up the offers of good pay and fight with them against their fellow Algerian Muslims. The French called these men loyal; the FLN regarded them as traitors. Very few of the Harkis, who had been warmly and repeatedly promised new homes and new lives in France in the event of the war going against the French, were actually granted them; and in any case many were seduced to stay in Algeria by assurances that the past would quickly be forgotten in the new Algerian state. Disarmed and abandoned by the French, the Harkis were put to work clearing the mines that had been laid along the border with Morocco. Many died there.

Stories were soon heard of whole Harki families dragged from their homes and put to death, of men castrated, buried alive or dragged by ropes along the streets from the backs of lorries. Laurent Vust, who had by now left Algiers for Geneva, remembers being told of a Harki slowly boiled alive in a cauldron. For Pierre Gaillard, one of twenty International Committee delegates who had been asked back by both the Algerians and the French to search for the 'disappeared', many abducted after the war had officially ended, these stories were acutely painful. As with the atrocities perpetrated by the French paratroopers on their Algerian captives, he was appalled by what the Algerians were now choosing to do to their own countrymen.

But this time there was absolutely nothing he could either say or do. The Harkis did not fall under the Red Cross mandate and their fate is only briefly touched on in the monthly *Review*, though the International Committee did put out a radio appeal in the summer of 1962 saying that it was 'profoundly moved by the distressing acts of cruelty'. It is estimated that more than a hundred thousand Harkis were murdered.

On 1 January 1960, Max Huber died. He was eighty-five and had been ill for many years. The eulogies delivered at his immense public funeral reflected the place this modest and tormented man had come to occupy in the minds of the Red Cross and the Swiss alike. For the Swiss Huber had been an exceptional international jurist and scholar, the man who had helped reconcile national neutrality with membership of the League of Nations, a figure of world stature in a country, as one cool observer noted, in which there were not many such people around. Huber had also been, as his long-time admirer and friend Jean Pictet put it, 'the moral and legal conscience of the Red Cross . . . during a quarter of a century'.

Huber, all agreed, had been a good man who was convinced of the goodness of others. Less puritanical than Moynier and far less self-righteous, but also capable of great practicality, he left a legacy of belief in the dignity and liberty of man. And Huber was not, friends were quick to remark, without humour. Though he had been known to sit through dinner parties without uttering a single word, Jean Pictet recalls great belly-laughs in private in his office and the pleasure he took in describing the Red Cross president's position at meetings as a 'bag of fleas'. Huber saw his job, he once confided to Pictet, as that of the 'drains of the organization, without which the kitchens would soon flood'. Outside the theological world, few men have written more revealingly and with more anguish about their own doubts. 'Was I made for action?' Huber had speculated in 1946, in the wake of the criticisms of the

Committee's wartime performance. 'I feel myself to be, in many ways, related to Erasmus. Like him, I always see the bright and the dark side of things. Yes, I am inclined to fear the action that cuts through things: bottomless neutrality, which poses so many problems, governs my reactions.' Huber, moderate in all things, weighed down by an oppressive burden of personal guilt and responsibility, may simply have been too anguished to lead the International Committee decisively through its darkest wartime hours.

Huber had given twenty-four years of his life to the International Committee and been its president for nineteen of them. He did not live to see the end of the war in Algeria, but he did survive long enough to see sixty countries ratify the 1949 Geneva Conventions, to witness the mounting refugee problem taken seriously enough for the UN to declare 1959 World Refugee Year, and for the Food and Agriculture Organization to announce a freedom from hunger campaign. And he did observe the growing number of new international humanitarian organizations which would often, in the years to come, turn to the International Committee as their model. The world he left behind was a very different place from the days when he had first taken notes at Gustave Ador's elbow soon after the First World War. The 1950s had shown that the long years of war would not be followed by any kind of peace. If this posed challenges the Red Cross would find hard to meet, Article 3, the important addition to the 1949 Geneva Conventions on 'armed conflicts not of an international character', had already proved its worth in a string of internal conflicts.

For the Red Cross movement generally, the years between the end of the Second World War and Huber's death had been quarrelsome ones. Bitterness and rivalry had marked both major international conferences of the 1950s and politics invariably now invaded every gathering. In 1952 in Toronto, the International Committee had been accused by the Czechoslovak delegation of being nothing but a 'blind for the crimes of the aggressors' — a barely disguised reference to the wartime charges of partiality. In Delhi in 1957, with the Cold War at its height, Taiwanese and mainland Chinese delegates had sniped at each other over territorial claims dressed up as seating arrangements and there were heated exchanges over weapons of mass destruction; western delegates argued that these were topics best left to the political arena of the United

Nations while others claimed that the destruction of humanity was a moral issue the Red Cross could not afford to ignore.

Yet 1960, the year of Huber's death, found both League and International Committee as robust separate organizations. The League, which had given itself a new structure and a new executive committee of governors, had moved into larger premises in Geneva, having abandoned all thoughts of returning to its pre-war quarters in Paris now that Switzerland had effectively become the home of world humanitarian affairs. Winds, floods, broken dykes, hurricanes and earthquakes which had struck parts of the world particularly hard in the 1950s had brought in generous new funds and the budget had doubled in a little over ten years. A Canadian barrister from Winnipeg, John MacAulay, had recently taken over from the long-serving Bonabes de Rougé as chairman and a forty-three-year-old Swede, Henrik Beer, once assistant to Count Bernadotte, was embarking on what would be a popular twenty-year reign as secretary general. It was Beer who would later compare the League to an 'international fire brigade' and its delegates to latter-day Henri Dunants.

The International Committee, now no more than a quarter of a mile away across Geneva under its new president Léopold Boissier, was widely regarded as a place of some international importance, in which diplomacy was practised with ever greater finesse. When delegates travelled, they were treated with courtesy and respect.

On 8 May 1963, the Red Cross turned 100. A centenary symbol was dreamt up, a red cross or crescent beside an oil lamp suggesting, with the true Red Cross blend of fervour and sentimentality, mercy and the flame of life. Stamps were published all over the world with this motif and a number of Air France planes added it to their livery. Red Cross birthdays were always taken seriously, but as the 100th approached fourteen new societies rushed for and were granted membership while existing societies all over the world embarked on a frenetic race for a truly memorable celebration. (The most imaginative was perhaps the Thai Red Cross which sent 500 of its most poisonous kraits, king cobras and vipers to Geneva to be milked for their venom in front of admiring visitors to a Red Cross exhibition.)

Swiss soldiers, in the uniforms worn at Solferino, paraded through the city. That autumn, the League and the International Committee were jointly awarded the Red Cross's third Nobel Peace Prize, while plans were made to erect a monument to Dunant in Geneva, an angel with widespread wings, giving the impression of 'movement, of flight towards places where the wounded of conflicts . . . are to be found'. There would be no shortage of wounded in the years to come.

NINETEEN

Men of the Red Cross

The civil war in Yemen was to provide the International Committee, and particularly some of its more romantic and independent-minded delegates, with one last, old-fashioned, war. There would of course be others, in the years to follow, in which identifiable enemies would line up neatly, one force against another, using weapons acceptable under the Geneva Conventions, and where the Committee would be seen to exercise all its traditional skills. But never again would delegates seem so isolated or so free. For Laurent Vust, veteran of Algeria and sent to Yemen not long after the war began, it was 'virgin territory for adventurers'.

Yemen is one of the hottest places in the world. There are times when temperatures rise to over 50°C in the shade and when the blackened rocks seem to tremble in the intense heat. It was here, in the autumn of 1962, after the death of Imam Ahmed and the overthrow of his successor, Imam El Badr, that war broke out between the royalist forces camped out in the mountainous north and the republicans under President Abdallah Sallal, supported by the Egyptians and with their headquarters in Sana'a. The Yemenis knew nothing of the Geneva Conventions. By December, a first International Committee mission had been able to visit both sides and reach basic agreements over the treatment of prisoners-of-war, traditionally despatched speedily as cowards. They were also able to promote the setting up of Red Crescent societies in the area in time for the 100th anniversary of the Red Cross movement, a fitting moment to bring the hitherto unpenetrated Arabian peninsula into the fold. In the wake of the delegates from the Red Cross came the doctors who found a country untouched by modern life. Very few Yemenis had ever seen a doctor or heard of medical treatment. As the doctors and nurses travelled around, exchanging their lorries for mules as they neared the mountains, they realized that much of their work was likely to be not with the wounded but with ordinary Yemenis, infected with the kinds of diseases long since eradicated or controlled in the West. With the war becoming fiercer and crops and fruit trees destroyed, illnesses were spreading rapidly, as civilians abandoned their homes and with them what little hygiene they had practised before. Gangrene, malaria, tuberculosis and typhus spread.

The Yemenis were delighted with their Swiss visitors, particularly when they wore their crisp white clothes. Once the Arab men had made it clear that any examination of a woman would have to be carried out when she was fully dressed and injections given through clothes, they were eager to line up for pills and poultices and even operations, since the greater the treatment, the more it seemed that they were being singled out for special attention. A pill was good and an injection better; but an operation was agreed to be best of all.

When it became obvious that a field hospital would be needed, close to the fighting, delegates set out to survey no man's land, currently supervised by the United Nations, and found a spot on a small plateau surrounded by the spurs of a volcanic range, conveniently separating the Yemen from Saudi Arabia. Here, at a place called Uqhd, about fifty miles south of the Najran oasis, a hospital was created. It consisted of a new invention called a Clinobox, a prefabricated surgical unit with an operating theatre, which had been flown in on an American cargo plane and then hauled the last 660 miles by truck. With it came seven doctors, four male and five female nurses, two pharmacists, a radiologist, two telegraphists, several technicians, a quartermaster and his assistant, and a cook who produced a great deal of spaghetti.

Soon a neat compound was in place, white tents surrounding the Clinobox, everything covered in the distinctive Red Cross emblem. Wounded as well as the sick began to appear, carried in by comrades who had marched for days to sample this exotic experience from the West. Casualties from the war included many with acute nervous shock from the bombing. Staff had to struggle to make the soldiers put down their weapons, as the Geneva Conventions insisted on hospitals being free of arms. Away from the safety of Uqhd, roving medical teams, crossing hundreds of miles of desert on the backs of donkeys, found themselves stopping to operate on wounded Bedouin, having to give

priority to those who pressed their claims with guns. By night, the
doctors slept in caves in the mountains, trying to keep themselves and
their equipment away from the sand that blew up regularly into sudden,
ferocious storms. The 'virgin territory' for adventurers proved virgin for
antibiotics as well and recovery was sometimes startlingly rapid. 'It is
doubtful,' noted the annual review of the International Committee for
1963, 'whether Europeans had ever set foot there before.'

André Rochat is one of the strangest delegates ever recruited by the
International Committee, a man who seemed to combine an almost
fanatical worship of Red Cross principles with as strongly held a personal
vision of how they should be applied. Rochat was thirty-eight when he
first went to Yemen in 1963. Earlier in his life he was said to have served
as a captain in the Swiss army and to have been a maître d'hôtel for
the Monaco royal family. He was recruited in Geneva through good
Swiss connections, hastily briefed on his duties and informed that if he
failed in them he would be disowned, and given a diplomatic passport.
As he left Geneva, Pierre Boissier said to him: 'We will do all we can to
help you carry out a difficult task. You will need courage and irreproachable behaviour. And never forget what you represent.' Rochat was tall,
thin and elegant, with dark, straight hair combed back, and somewhat
haughty in manner. In appearance, he reminded people of Marcel Junod.
More than any delegate since Dunant himself perhaps, he felt that he
had received a call. The Red Cross was his mission.

Agreements over the treatment of prisoners-of-war had been drawn
up with the Yemen Arab Republic and the Egyptians, and with the main
royalists, but some of the tribes in the north were still largely unknown.
It was said that they were holding Egyptian captives in atrocious conditions so, taking with him an assistant – he would later say that he
never travelled without an assistant, to act both as witness and pupil –
Rochat set out across the desert to the northern mountains, accompanied by donkeys laden with a tonne of food. After some days, he reached
the Imam's headquarters and was directed towards the Imam's cave. The
story of their meeting has entered Red Cross lore. Calling for water,
and a cave of his own, Rochat announced through an interpreter that
he would have to prepare himself for the royal interview and that he
needed to dress for the occasion. From his luggage, he took a white
linen suit, a white shirt and a tie. He washed, changed, combed his hair.

'Only then,' Rochat says, 'was I in the right condition to carry out my mission — as a formally accredited diplomat, calling on a head of state. We met, exchanged courtesies and reached an agreement. That was how things were done.' Though respect for prisoners on either side in this war would never be great and most continued to be manacled and their wounds left untreated unless a delegate was actually in the vicinity, Rochat was able to secure some improvements in food and surroundings for the Egyptians he found squatting in terror on the floor, and was later able to arrange for the exchange of a number of men from both sides.

Not everyone liked Rochat, who was to spend much of the next five years under white flags with red crosses roaming Yemen on camels, crossing vast stretches of desert at the head of convoys of prisoners on their way to be exchanged, learning Arabic from the Bedouin, and conducting medical teams from Europe and North America in and out of the areas where they came to work. Stories reached Geneva about young delegates made to kneel at Rochat's feet before being accepted as fellow officers, about packs of recalcitrant donkeys dragooned into straight lines as if they were army horses, about imperious behaviour and theatrical and extravagant ways. Rochat himself says: 'I never made friends among my delegates. We never said "tu" to each other. They feared me, but they admired me. It's very tough, the silence of the Red Cross.'

Rochat is now in his early seventies, an upright, military looking man. He lives in an imposing villa above Vence on the Riviera, with formal gardens overlooking the sea and views across to the mountains. He has eight Burmese cats and his rooms are full of jewellery, cups, coverings, and carvings brought back from Yemen. On the walls of his study hang framed photographs of himself during the war, riding camels or surrounded by Bedouin. In the photographs he is never smiling. 'When I arrived in Yemen,' he says,

> it was still a white spot on the atlas. It was unknown. I quickly saw that unless I understood the minds of the people who lived there I would never be able to do anything. Emirs, kings, ministers, tribal people, revolutionaries, Egyptians trained by Nasser — imagine all this, it was an enormous task. I had to become a

man of the people. I had to be seen to know, to understand and to respect the people – but not to be too modest. What an honour! What a challenge! Everything had to be created. I had left Geneva proud and confident. Now I discovered that I was naked. What a magnificent destiny to be a man of the Red Cross!

During the five years of their presence in Yemen, the International Committee sent 500 people into the field, each medical team taking leave after a two-and-a-half-month stint, which was as long as a European was thought to be able to stand the heat. In the pages of the *Review*, work there was regularly described as 'hazardous'. Apart from Vust, who was badly burned in a plane crash, one delegate was wounded when his medical team was ambushed and others grazed when attacked from the air. A few fell off their mules and fractured bones. For a while most of the work was carried out at night, under cover of darkness.

A cease-fire of sorts was signed at Jeddah in October 1965 by King Faisal of Saudi Arabia for the royalists, and President Nasser for the republicans. It was repeatedly broken and though the hospital at Uqhd was dismantled after a few years, roving medical teams continued to take their infirmaries to distant outposts where epidemics were thought to be breaking out. Rochat now set about negotiating the release of forty-four royal women and children, held under house arrest in Sana'a since the beginning of the war.

Then came rumours of an air attack on civilians, carried out by republican troops and Egyptians. Rochat thrived in these situations. The role of the delegate, he would tell the young men sent out from Geneva to join him, is to be a 'noble adventurer, a doctor and a priest all at the same time'. He set off on his camel to find out what had happened, and was soon able to confirm not simply that civilians had been bombed, but that they had been attacked with gas – the first case of poison gas since the Italians used it on the Ethiopians in the 1930s. 'The four survivors who were in the contaminated area are all in pain from their eyes and are almost blind,' he reported to Geneva. 'All have pains in their chests and none shows any sign of a wound. The doctors . . . stress that all the evidence leads to the conclusion that oedema was caused by the breathing of poison gas.' Rochat's report was sent, as was customary, to Geneva and to the parties at war. Somewhere along the way, as with the Algerian report on torture, it found its way into the hands of the press, this time the *New York Times*. The International Committee, possibly remembering its lack of intervention in Ethiopia, reacted with a public protest, saying that they were 'extremely disturbed and concerned'. In best Committee style, they also refrained from actually naming those using the gas. There was a great deal of publicity; the International Committee was nowhere criticized for its outspokenness; and there were no more reports of gas.

In the years since then, cease fires have been signed and broken in Yemen and in 1994 the International Committee again sent delegates to the area; again they found untreated wounds and sick civilians. But Rochat is not the only man who remembers the first years of the war in Yemen as a time of excitement and bravura. Pierre Gaillard, another veteran from the war in Algeria, recalls trying to make an agreement with the Imam that his prisoners would be spared. 'Without really understanding why it was necessary,' Gaillard says today, 'he accepted, and said that the only way he could be sure that prisoners would not be killed would be if he offered a gold piece for every prisoner delivered to him alive by his men.'

Gaillard, like Rochat but also like many of the earlier delegates, has no doubts that it was far better to be a delegate in the 1960s than it has since become. 'We were sent off and we were free. We made the decisions. True, Yemen was the first war in which regular radio communication was established with Geneva. Just the same, we got away, we did things on our own.' Rochat is more forthright. 'The headquarters in Geneva are the enemy,' he says, putting into concrete terms the hostility often felt by delegates in the field towards the decision-makers in Geneva. In Red Cross terms Yemen was a delegates' war, as Ethiopia and the Spanish civil war had been, perhaps the last true delegates' war. Even the more bureaucratic members of the organization, who watched the war in the Yemen from their desks in Geneva, praised the delegates for their courage and the work they carried out for its inventiveness.

For Rochat, Yemen was not the start of a glorious career with the International Committee, though by the time his part in the war was over and he was sent to other conflicts, something of the life of the roving delegate had settled into his imagination. He was never to lose it. But, like Sidney Brown in the 1930s, Rochat did not quite fit in with the orderliness, obedience and sense of hierarchy that rules the Committee. He was not sufficiently self-effacing and far too prone to take control where the Committee would have preferred to see restraint.

'They wanted to get rid of me at once,' he says now, 'but they didn't quite dare. They offered me jobs in Geneva – I was a field man. But a free man is dangerous, and far from Geneva a free man is a man to fear. And then they dismissed me. At first I thought I would die. It was terrible to have risen to the top, and then to have it all taken away. A terrible experience.' When he left, Rochat cut himself off altogether: he never spoke to former colleagues again and never returned to the former Carlton Hotel, the great white building overlooking the original United Nations headquarters that had become the International Committee's headquarters. Twenty-six years later, he still finds the exile almost unbearable.

The 1960s were bringing a marked change to both the style and the tempo of the Red Cross movement. The framework of humanitarian law was now more or less in place, even if it was widely recognized that the right of initiative remained one of the International Committee's most delicate and important weapons. As with case law, action and exploration moved ahead of codes and rules and was then used to set precedents; and the delegates now joining the Committee quickly understood that, in a world in which intervention was no longer regarded as interference, it would be up to them to push into uncharted areas, establish ways of working that could lay the trail for those who came behind. There was much new ground to chart. The very nature of war itself had changed, and was changing all the time – hijackings which became a popular terrorist weapon in the 1970s, the taking of hostages, bewilderingly murderous new weapons, enemies whose identities remained shadowy. In Geneva, the Committee was constantly reaffirming its old principles, discussing them at the international meetings, drafting new rules in the light of new world events.

Increasingly there were doubts, not about the worth of the Geneva Conventions, but about how widely they were actually known. The old arrogance, the cosy certainty that because they had been drawn up and ratified by kings and rulers their articles would be obeyed, had long since vanished. Was it possible that no one really understood what the Convention was all about? And if that was so, how was the world to be educated in its responsibilities? As the savagery of the conflict in Algeria had shown, Dunant's plea about 'humanizing' war was becoming ever more necessary.

In April 1959, the need for teaching the rules and laws of war to the military had been debated at length by delegates to an international congress on the neutrality of medicine in times of war, who had spoken regretfully of the 'moral barbarism' of the 'blood-stained' times in which they were living. The International Committee was putting considerable efforts into finding ways of getting information into military academies and nursing schools, and there was much talk in the corridors of the old Carlton Hotel of capturing the 'minds and hearts' of all involved. Jean Pictet, Huber's heir as moral tutor to the organization, took charge of running courses in humanitarian law at the University of Geneva. When, in October 1965, 580 representatives of ninety-two national societies and eighty-four governments met at the Hofburg Palace in Vienna for the twentieth international conference, bickerings over world peace were settled at remarkable speed and delegates turned obediently to long discussions on the nature and content of humanitarian law and how to teach it. Dissemination, as it would come to be known, was to be an ever more central concern in the years to come.

In 1967, a terrible year for the International Committee, there were wars across Africa, Asia and the Middle East and few of those watching from Geneva believed that peace was likely to return soon. Delegates were being stretched ever thinner and the same men would now hasten from place to place with very few pauses, in the hopes of doing something to mitigate the cruelties of victors and losers alike.

Pushed by Gaillard and President Ruegger, the International Committee had long been concerned about political prisoners and carried out missions to visit those detained for their opposition to the governments of their countries. This role had repeatedly been endorsed at various meetings of the movement in the 1950s. Its right to ask states for access to prisoners had been explicitly approved by Common Article 3 of the 1949 Conventions with regard to 'non international armed conflicts'. But not until the 1960s, when spreading political instability throughout much of the world appeared to be leading to the detention of ever larger numbers of people, did delegates routinely add the victims of 'internal tensions' to their regular visits. Where the legitimacy of governments is frail, they found, there you find large numbers of detainees, often in conditions of extreme wretchedness. They moved into this field, as they did all things, gradually, helped by international interest in the outspoken reports published by Amnesty International, since its founding in 1961, and gradually began to perceive how helpful it could be to act in concert with other non-governmental organizations whose mandates were very different from their own. Though there was still great reluctance to agree on the precise nature of a political prisoner – terrorist, criminal and bandit to some, freedom fighter and hero of the resistance to others – the term was now generally accepted as covering someone who had committed a crime against 'national security' or who was being per-secuted for political reasons. The International Committee, acting on its customary basis of ad hoc diplomacy, announced that what mattered to them was that the person was actually in detention – not why he was there. They modelled their visits to political detainees on their established pattern of visits to prisoners-of-war, and constantly sought better prison conditions. Internal conflicts in Israel and South Africa would later teach them a great deal about political detention, but it was in Greece, in the late 1960s, that the immense complexities and subtleties of their role as prison visitors became clear, and it was there, in the barracks and fortresses of Athens and the outlying islands, that a code of practice was evolved. What was seen and learnt then has been passed down over the years from delegate to delegate. The pattern has remained largely the same: visits to all places of detention; discussion with com-mandant; talks alone with prisoners; return for a second discussion with commandant; report to Geneva and government in question; a second visit when requested. In return for all this, the International Committee undertakes to say nothing in public about what it has learned, unless the circumstances do not improve. Then, but only then, a public protest *may* follow.

On 21 April 1967, twenty military officers in Greece, backed up by 150 tanks and 3,000 soldiers, staged a coup. It took them little over two-and-a-half hours. They called their military takeover 'Prometheus', after the name given to Nato plans drawn up earlier as a contingency against the possibility of a communist take-over. Warning of an imminent threat to national security from the communists, the colonels proclaimed martial law, suspended civil liberties and set about tracking down and arresting some 6,500 'unreliable anti-Greek elements' before sending them off to places of detention memorable from the days of the recent civil war. The king swore in a new government of the colonels, who undertook to protect 'Christian, western democratic' values. Repression spread. Greece turned into a garrison state. On 3 May, the new Greek government informed the Council of Europe that it had no alternative but to suspend all fundamental rights during a state of emergency.

The military coup in Greece was the first witnessed in Europe since the end of the Second World War. European political leaders were far from comfortable with what was happening, particularly as stories of torture began to leak out of the barracks and detention cells in which the 'unreliable elements' were being held. As a member of the Council of Europe, Greece was party to the European Convention on Human Rights and tales of torture and the suspension of civil liberties did not sit easily with claims of being a constitutional democracy. Some of the Scandinavian governments were soon declaring that they could see no evidence of any threat to Greece's security from the communists or anyone else. When Amnesty International returned from a mission to Greece with alarming first-hand reports of ill-treatment of detainees, unease grew.

The International Committee had not wasted time. Seven days after the colonels' take-over a first delegate, a man called Germain Colladon, distant relative of the Dunant family, arrived in Athens. He was well received. The Committee's standing among the Greeks was high, from the generosity of their wartime deliveries of food to the starving islands. Colladon visited Yioúra where several thousand people were being held, among them one child. He came home with accounts of poor conditions and received assurances from the colonels that these would be improved. Though in his private reports to Geneva he added that he was afraid that delegates would encounter great difficulties in trying to locate all prisoners, and though he was clearly wary of Greek duplicity, Colladon himself was not popular among the families of the arrested men. He was elderly and gave little sign of energy or determination. 'A wrinkled old man with a whispery voice was ushered into the living room,' commented one wife dismissively, 'physically in danger of being blown out of the window by a dog's loud bark, and my heart sank when I saw whom I would be dealing with.' When a smug report appeared in the Greek papers stating that the International Committee was satisfied with prison conditions, there were outraged protests, not least from Geneva. The Committee hastened to remind the colonels that one of the quid pro quos of its own discretion about what was seen was that any report that it sent to the Greek government had to be published in full or not at all. Extracting the reassuring passages for publication was not acceptable.

Missions continued, delegates doing what they could to track down missing detainees and trying to improve food and medical conditions on the two island camps at Yioúra and Leros, but criticisms both of Greece and of the performance of the International Committee itself began to mount. The Swiss paper *Die Tat* referred to Colladon as a 'fool who lets the Greek government pull the wool over his eyes'. Meanwhile Amnesty International, whose mandate did not commit it to secrecy, continued, until banned from the country, to produce further evidence of torture inside Greek police stations. This paradox – knowing precisely what was happening but being forbidden to use that knowledge publicly – had haunted delegates before and would haunt them again. Something of the dilemma the International Committee had to live with came to light when the Council of Europe, pressed by member states, approached the Committee for reliable information as to what was going on inside Greek jails. The Committee refused to co-operate, just as it had refused to help the League of Nations over Italy's use of poison gas in Ethiopia in the 1930s. A plenary session took place in Geneva on 5 October 1967 among members of the Committee who were again split, as they had been on that October day twenty-five years before when they were asked to vote on the question of whether or not to make public what they knew about the concentration camps. Some argued for speaking out, not least in order to defend their own reputation from attacks of inefficiency and complicity; others held that secrecy must prevail. Prevail it did. In the Greek newspapers, the colonels continued to hint that the International Committee was far from dissatisfied with prison conditions.

In January 1968, Laurent Marti was named head of the delegation to Greece. Marti was an interesting figure, a former journalist for Swiss radio and the *Journal de Genève*, who had been much taken with the life

3505 **Rzegotta** Siegfried, geb 1. 7. 1943; Augen hellblau, Haare blond. H. Anschrift: Breslau, Sternstr. 51. Er befand sich Februar 1945 in Janowitz, Kr. Hirschberg, Riesengebirge, NSV-Garten, Sanatorium, und trug eine dunkelblaue Küblerhose mit vollständigem Namen. Mitteilungen erbeten unt. EK 30161 an die DSZ.

3530 **Schwede** Karin, geb. 22. 8. 41; Augen blau, Haare blond. Nach dem Tode der Mutter wurde das Kind von einer Fischersfrau Engelke aus Tawe/Ostpr. mitgenommen. Mitteilungen erbeten unt. EK 30171 an die DSZ

3531 **Wolf** Norbert, geb. 8. 6. 42; Augen blau, Haare blond. Das Kind ging am 7. 5. 45 an der tschechischen Grenze bei Reichenberg-Gablonz verloren. Mitteilungen erbeten unt. EK 301/2 an die DSZ.

3532 **Schwarz** Bruno, geb. 4. 3. 42; Augen blau, Haare hellblond. Das Kind wurde am 25. 2. 45 in Heiligenbeil/Ostpr. verwundet und dem Kreis-Krankenhaus über geben. Mitteilungen erbeten unt. EK 3173 an die DSZ

3737 **Schröder** Jürg-Detlef, geb. 17. 4. 42; Augen blaugrau, Haare mittelblond. Das Kind wurde einer NSV-Schwester auf dem Bahnhof in Stargrad/Pom. übergeben. Mitteilungen erbeten unt. EK 30177 an die DSZ

337 Name: **unbekannt**, geb.ca. 1940. Augen blau, Haare blond. Das Kind gibt an, aus dem Kreise Schloßberg zu sein. Die Mutter habe in Kolberg stark geblutet. Alles weitere ist unbekannt

371 Name: **Kwielitz** Traute, geb. ca. März 1941. Augen blau, Haare blond. Das Kind kommt anscheinend aus länd- lichen Verhältnissen. Mutter angeblich tot. Ein älterer Bruder Ernst von den Russen verschleppt

380 Name: **Kuhn** Hildegard, geb. 8. 11. 38. Augen braun, Haare dunkelblond. Kommt aus Birkenwalde, Kr. Samland, Mutter angeblich tot. Vater Max Kuhn zuletzt beim Volkssturm

381 Name: **Podbielski** Peter, geb. 16. 4. 43. Augen blau, Haare blond. Stammt aus Johannisberg. Geschwister: Edith und Günther. Die Kinder sagen: 'Mutter ist einkaufen gegangen und nicht wiedergekommen'

495 Name: **Sarnowski** Hartmut, geb. 24. 5. 43. Hartmut hat noch einen Zwillingsbruder

500 Name: **unbekannt** Klaus, geb. ca. 1942. Augen hellblau, Haare hellblond. Ueber die Herkunft des Kindes ist nichts bekannt

One of the posters of the lost and missing children put up in post offices, bus terminals and stations in 1945. Some 298,000 children were lost on German territory during the final months of the war

Friedrich Born, the exceptional
delegate to Hungary, 1944-45

Both the League and the International Committee sent convoys
carrying relief donated by more than thirty societies during the
Hungarian revolution

Hungarian refugees in a camp at Tratzkirchen in Austria. The Hungarian revolution was said
to have caused the greatest flight of civilians in Europe since the Second World War

Jacques Moreillon, the lawyer who
rose to be the first director-general of
the International Committee in the
mid-1980s

Jean-Paul Hocké was recruited as a delegate in the
Biafran war. He later became director of operations
during the Cambodian relief programme

Jean Pictet joined the International
Committee during the Spanish Civil War
and went on to draft its statutes

Melchior Borsinger, one of the International
Committee's longest-serving and most-loved
delegates

A Red Cross observer monitors an exchange of wounded prisoners between North and South Korea towards the end of the war in April 1953

A rare photograph of American prisoners-of-war in North Korea taken in September 1950. For many months the North denied taking any prisoners at all

Left Frédéric Bieri distributing cigarettes to prisoners from North Korea in Pusan camp in July 1950. Pusan was later the scene of violent confrontation between prisoners and guards

Women in Sana'a in the Yemen examining International Committee relief in 1964. Before the arrival of the Red Cross very few Yemenis had ever seen a doctor or heard of modern medical treatment

Transporting relief into the Yemen in 1965: an International Committee lorry carrying four tonnes of clothes donated by the Swedish Red Cross

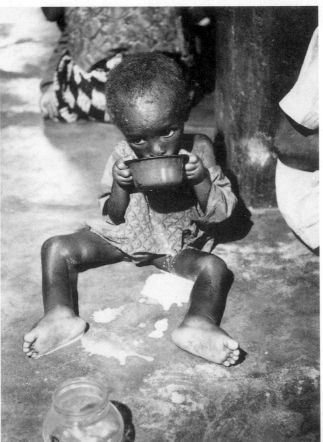

The Swedish Red Cross
distribute food at Udo, a
camp in Biafra

Biafra where starvation
prompted talk of
genocide, 1967-70

Over Cambodia's border with Thailand thousands of Cambodian refugees were looked after by thirty-seven relief organizations. This photograph shows the camp of Khao I Dang, 1979

Below Despite the rain, there was a desperate shortage of water for the camps. In one week alone in 1979, four million litres of water were delivered by aid agencies

Above Tracing the missing has been one of the International Committee's most important activities. Khmer refugees searching for their families at a missing persons centre in the camp of Nang Samet, 1980. By the end of February 1981 the International Committee had handled 45,000 enquiries

Left An International Committee nurse-delegate monitoring the growth of children in Ethiopia in 1988

Below Families searching for disappeared relatives in Cyprus in 1974.

The old Carlton Hotel in Geneva, today the headquarters of the International Committee

of the Red Cross delegates he met on his many trips abroad. He was cynical, well-dressed — all early stories of his exploits contain references to well-cut suits and watches with crocodile straps — and had all the gung-ho charm of the adventurer school of delegates. Like Rochat, he was also a little arrogant.

By the end of February, Marti had taken a flat with a view over the Acropolis and paid forty-three visits to twelve detention centres. He was able to describe, in detail, conditions at Leros, Lakki, Patheni and Yioúra. As his determination to help the prisoners become known, so the families of the arrested men began to contact him to make certain that he knew all the names to ask for and all the places to visit. And though the Greek government continued to hint that he was satisfied with all he saw, Marti himself paid little attention and continued to push hard for overcrowding in the prisons to be reduced and to be permitted to distribute relief to the more destitute families. When offered prison visits only in the presence of guards, he refused them. His only real card, and one that he was temperamentally suited to play with great gusto, was his threat that he would pull his delegation out of Greece very publicly unless his demands were met. The colonels, anxious about their standing in the Council of Europe, made some gestures to oblige him, agreeing to close a particularly appalling prison camp at Yaros and to release 400 sick and elderly detainees. If the International Committee had taken a while to enter the field, it was by now an energetic player in the game.

It was Marti who first came across a twist in prison visiting that was to present the International Committee with a new dilemma. Not all the political detainees, he discovered, welcomed a visit from a Red Cross delegate. Neither did they want the appalling conditions in which they were being held to be improved. 'Many of the detainees were clever, highly educated people,' Marti recalls. 'They pointed out to me that they were waging a war against the colonels and that if I forced them to improve prison conditions then that would lead to an improvement in their image — thereby helping them to remain in power.' As he travelled around the camps, Marti was repeatedly told to go away. 'We want to be martyrs, we even accept torture,' Marti remembers several men saying to him. It came as a surprise; he retired to think. Later he went to find the men who had refused to talk to him. He reminded them of two things. The first was that if he did nothing, they might well find themselves in the same cells in ten years' time, without blankets, medicines, books or visits from their families. He also pointed out that it was all very well for them to take this rigid position but what of the other men who wanted their conditions improved? He gave them fifteen days to reconsider. When he went back, they agreed to co-operate.

The stories of torture did not go away. Even after it was banned from Greece in the spring of 1968, Amnesty International campaigned hard from London to bring pressure on the colonels to put an end to the ill-treatment of their detainees. As was now widely known among those who had studied torture, the dangerous moment for prisoners was the first few days after arrest, when they were held incommunicado in police stations and military barracks. It was then that interrogation was carried out and then that coercion was used. Marti pressed the colonels hard to be allowed to visit the police stations; the colonels prevaricated. Marti's position was made trickier when Anthony Marreco from Amnesty International reported highly critically on a visit to the notorious Bouboulinas Street police station, during which he had taken down clear statements about torture. Marti had visited the same police station some six days earlier and, though he too reported allegations of torture, his report was used by the Greeks to imply that he had not altogether believed what he had been told. In newspapers across Europe, journalists turned their disbelief and outrage against the International Committee. When, in May 1969, *Look* magazine published a long article under the title 'Government by torture', Red Cross credibility reached a low point.

The acting president of the Committee, in the summer of 1968, was Jacques Freymont, the writer and academic, head of the Institut Universitaire des Hautes Etudes Internationales. Freymont believed that delegates should receive an almost military kind of training. He and Marti went to see Colonel Papadopoulos, new head of the Greek government, and asked him for a written agreement under which Red Cross delegates would be permitted to make unannounced visits everywhere they chose to go, and would also be allowed to distribute relief to the families of detainees. The colonels, at this stage, still needed the Red Cross, particularly as they were under investigation by the European Commission on Human Rights, which was monitoring Greece's violations for the Council of Europe. Even though the monitoring process and the International Committee were entirely separate and independent, the Red Cross verdict mattered. On 4 November, Greece signed an 'administrative agreement under public law', the first document of its kind ever drawn up between the Committee and a sovereign state, accepting its right to act on behalf of political detainees. Under it, Marti's delegation to Greece was made permanent with an office of nine people and delegates were given permission to visit places of detention as and when they wished to and to talk to detainees in private. The agreement was to last a year. In return, the International Committee undertook to remain silent and not pass judgement.

Marti's deputy was a young lawyer called Philippe Grand d'Hauteville. Jacques Moreillon would later say that d'Hauteville was probably too honest to work with modern governments in that he had trouble in believing in the moral bankruptcy of those he had to deal with. D'Hauteville had been on the earlier mission to Greece with Colladon and later played a part in the interminable wranglings over the written agreement. 'Marti began to open doors,' he says now.

> We split up into two teams, each with one delegate and one doctor, and we began to push hard to visit the places we had long known about but never got into.
>
> In one former hotel we found a number of high-ranking military officers, heroes of the civil war, kept in the most atrocious conditions. The shutters on to the street were kept permanently closed. These men hadn't seen daylight for almost six months. They had been kept on their own, and forbidden to speak to anyone. Several looked to me as if they had lost their wits. Others seemed to have turned green in the dark. One admiral told me that he had had terrible toothache for months and that finally the pain had been such that he had levered out the rotten tooth with a fork.

Marti and d'Hauteville went to call on Papadopoulos. 'I don't know how much he really knew about what was going on. He listened to us in silence. Then he said: "As a Greek and a Christian I will order this to stop." A few days later, when I drove past the hotel with my children, I saw that the shutters had been raised.'

Some of the camps, says Marti, were extremely difficult to visit, particularly in winter when the cold was intense and the sea very rough.

Leros, where detainees were held in an old barracks, involved an eighteen-hour journey from Athens, and when Marti arrived for his third visit he found the prisoners so angry about the little that he had been able to achieve for them that their shouts of fury drowned his conversation. D'Hauteville, who was with him, wondered whether they would get away from the island alive.

Marti's interventions were not all failures. When he went to visit Yioúra and found the prisoners in extreme misery, on a barren rock, many of them ill and cut off for weeks at a time, he made such a fuss that the camp was closed. However, he could not help wondering whether deals of this kind did not in some way play into the colonels' hands, and allow them to make too much in public of how humane they were.

Marti's complaints about conditions on Leros irked the colonels. They announced that his manner had become too vehement. To avoid being declared persona non grata, he left Greece, to be replaced by Max Stadler, another delegate in the Colladon style, with little of Marti's sense of purpose and energy. D'Hauteville, who had admired his former boss's firm manner with the Greeks, feared a slackening off in pressure, but before long, as rumours reached Geneva that the colonels were delighted with the new replacement, Stadler was recalled and d'Hauteville named senior delegate in his place. Like Marti, he pressed hard to visit prisons and camps where he sensed ill-treatment was continuing. 'Everyone came to see us. We became a sort of information centre and I learned a great deal. If I was forbidden to reveal what I heard or saw in the prisons and police stations, I could at least say publicly what I was doing.'

On 3 November 1970, the agreement with the Greek government came to an abrupt end. To its surprise and dismay, the International Committee was informed that it would not be renewed. The colonels no longer needed the imprimatur of the Committee's presence: they had withdrawn from the Council of Europe without waiting to be expelled and with it from their obligations under the European Convention on Human Rights. In any case the Americans, early critics of the colonels' harsh measures, had now chosen to forget them and had resumed normal relations with the junta with full military assistance. Within the Greek government itself, opposition to the agreement had been growing stronger, with more and more members arguing that it was intolerable to allow any foreign organization, even the Red Cross, to enjoy unrestricted access to Greek prisons. As an article in the Athenian newspaper *Kyzix Patson* put it, 'We would be only too happy if no one would interfere in our country's internal affairs.'

With Greece's withdrawal from the Council of Europe, journalists lost interest in the country's prisons. In any case, the numbers of political detainees had fallen and those who remained were gradually released. But for the International Committee, Greece marked the moment when political detainees became the subject of worldwide interest and when torture and abuses of human rights really entered the language of humanitarian law. Today, when torture has become endemic in over half of the world's countries, the issue has lost much of its power to shock; in 1968, it was still possible to believe that sufficient international outrage might put a stop to it.

But the Greek experience left an uneasy and contradictory message: that the Committee and its delegates had been tolerated only when perceived as potentially useful to the Greek colonels, and that once that usefulness had disappeared there was no mileage left in agreeing to their visits. On the other hand, the delegates had done much to curb torture and improve conditions for many of the 6,000 or so detainees and their families. And they now knew, with considerable clarity, that prison visits, like visits to prisoners-of-war, are best conducted according to a very precise and fixed code, laying down exactly what would be monitored and how, and the expected behaviour of both visited and visitors. The delegates had also learnt a lot about torture and what it did to people, though it would be some time before they would receive any formal training to help them understand fully its physical and psychological effects.

In January 1978, the historian Roland Siegrist visited Greece to assess how well the International Committee had performed after the colonels' coup. Not everyone he approached felt that they could speak openly. A few voiced fears that the presence of the Committee's delegates had in fact improved the image of the colonels in the eyes of the world and others said that they still failed to see the point of discretion and secrecy. Among former detainees and their families, however, the response was one of overwhelming gratitude.

It was left to the political historian and economist David Forsythe to point out that by the late 1960s, the international political dimensions of humanitarian work were beginning to take on immense importance. In a book published in 1977 he wrote: 'With the benefit of hindsight, it is possible to suggest – but not prove – that had the US been more concerned with civil liberties in Greece, the position of the ICRC might have been truly revolutionary instead of only provocative.'

Ask anyone in the humanitarian world to name the recent conflict which did most to shape the International Committee of the Red Cross to cope with the modern era and the answer is always the same: Biafra. The war between the educated, entrepreneurial Ibos of eastern Nigeria and the dominant Hausa of the northern provinces not only brought new players into the field of relief and aid but changed for ever the way that the Committee thought about itself and how it operated. After the civil war in Biafra, Dunant would have had trouble recognizing the movement he created.

The war in Biafra was the place and the time when politics were finally recognized to be fundamental to humanitarian work, where 'revolutionary humanitarianism' first emerged as a concept, though who coined the term no one is sure, and where the media played its first decisive role. In the 1990s, when the public has become inured to images of massacres and atrocities, starving children no longer shock. In 1967, the world had seldom seen pictures of children with distended bellies and stick-like arms and certainly not in any number. The first response was to remember Belsen.

The International Committee had never been greatly involved in Africa. Though the fighting in the Congo had drawn a number of delegates, few went willingly to a continent that seemed as yet remote from traditional Red Cross concerns. And in the summer of 1967, when George Hoffmann, senior delegate in Nigeria, warned Geneva that a 'holocaust is taking place, there are victims and care must be given to those who are not dead', the Committee was already deeply embroiled in Vietnam and the Middle East and was about to go into Greece. It took a while for them to understand the implications of Hoffmann's cable.

Nigeria is immense, about the size of Holland, Belgium, France and

Italy together. Declared independent of Britain in 1960, it had seemed to promise a future of stability and prosperity; for the West, it was the African country most likely to provide a model of democracy for others to copy. Britain thought of Nigeria as one of its most successful colonies and certainly not a place where a civil war would break out, despite signs of rising ethnic tensions as the Ibos felt themselves to be increasingly under threat. But in 1966 one coup was followed by another, and after a false radio report that some northerners had been killed in the east, northern troops went on the rampage, killing thousands of Ibo civilians and soldiers, hacking many of them to death. The Ibos who survived fled east, followed by an exodus of Ibos from other parts of Nigeria. The east had oil. A decision was taken to break away and set up an independent state of Biafra. Early assumptions that the easterners were so poorly equipped and trained that the war would be over in a few weeks disappeared as it became clear that the Biafrans fought well and that Lt Col. Odumegwu Ojukwu, who led them, commanded the support of over ninety per cent of the east. The Nigerian army, though many times the size, was poorly organized and General Yakubu Gowon, who now proclaimed a war of 'national unity', was not an effective leader.

The war was not, as expected, over in days. It became confused, with no battlefield and no defined front. Villages were destroyed and set on fire. Women and children, in ever growing numbers, were to be seen wandering around in search of food.

And then the famine began. Eastern Nigeria had always been self-sufficient in fruit and carbohydrates, importing meat from the northern provinces, salt from Niger and the dried cod that made up the bulk of its protein from Scandinavia. Nigeria now declared an embargo on the supplies of meat and salt, and imposed a blockade by land, sea and air on the import of fish. Biafra tried to increase its production of chickens and eggs, but as refugees from other parts of Nigeria flooded in and food stocks dwindled, so hunger grew. By the end of 1967, when Dr Edwin Spirgi, head of the medical Red Cross team at a hospital in Biafra, returned to Geneva to warn of imminent catastrophe, pictures had begun to reach the West of the victims of marasmus – in which people waste away into skeletons – and of the more deadly kwashiorkor, where lack of protein reduces small children to obscene contrasts of fleshless skulls and ribs rising above swollen bellies and legs, from which the flesh begins to peel away. Dr Bernard Kouchner, a young French doctor working for the International Committee in Biafra who would later play a crucial role in the development of humanitarian assistance, wrote an article published in the *Review* estimated the numbers of children with kwashiorkor to be at least 300,000. As missionaries and the churches appealed for help, so governments throughout the world hardened their positions on the conflict: Britain, the USSR and the Arab countries supported the federal government, the French, Israelis, Portuguese, South Africans, Rhodesians and Chinese the Biafran secessionists. The French supplied the Ibos with weapons, but also obliged the federal forces with the occasional planeload of guns.

The first to pay real attention to the fast developing disaster had been the Christian missionaries stationed in the east. As the war had grown harsher, they had carried food to distant villages and brought the worst affected back to feeding stations. The Catholic crusade grew rapidly to immense proportions. Most Ibos were Catholics – the northerners tended to be Muslims – and there was soon talk of a 'holy war' between Islam and Christianity.

By the summer of 1968, the West was growing used to pictures of starvation. The Nigerian Red Cross happened one day on a clearing in which they found over a hundred small children dying. A combination of the vast numbers of refugees adrift throughout Nigeria and the federal blockade on food was driving more than 2,500 people into hospital every week. On 22 June the *Sketch* published an article by Brian Dixon warning that three million children were near death. 'They sit,' he wrote, 'like decrepit old men.' 'If I had been a Jew in Nazi Germany,' declared President Nyerere of Tanzania, 'I'd feel the same as an Ibo in Nigeria.'

There had been talk of public relations and civil war before but no one was quite prepared for what was now to come. In late 1967, Biafra had turned for help to a public relations firm based in Switzerland called Markpress, best known for holding the Chrysler account. Markpress was an unexpected choice but, as it turned out, an inspired one: its owner and director was a Californian called William Bernhardt who had a small military moustache, a soft voice and a taste for well-cut English tweeds.

Bernhardt knew nothing about politics and still less about Nigeria, telling a friend later that when he received a call from the Biafran mission in Paris he thought that Biafra was the name of a brand of toothpaste. But he was hardworking, efficient and had a keen ear for the resonance of famine. Before long there were very few places in the world where the daily fate of the Biafrans was not known and discussed. By the time the war was over, Markpress would have put out more than 700 press releases and, at the height of the fighting Bernhardt was in daily contact with the House of Commons, the US Congress and – during the run up to the American elections – both presidential candidates. A world able to stay calm in the face of stories of torture in Algeria grew passionate with outrage. It was not long before there was talk of genocide. 'The agony of Biafra,' wrote the correspondent for the *Sunday Telegraph*, 'is an affront to the conscience of the civilized world.'

The International Committee had not been idle even if other, smaller non-governmental organizations had blazed the trail by simply hiring planes and flying into the area. Medical teams and delegates had been hard at work on both the federal and Biafran sides and all through the winter of 1967 and the spring of 1968 they had kept reporting to Geneva that prisoners taken by both sides were being massacred and that medical supplies as well as food stocks were running low. From Geneva, the Committee appealed to Gowon and Ojukwu to respect Article 3 of the Geneva Conventions relating to non-international armed conflict and were relieved when both not only agreed but declared that they would go further and apply all four Geneva Conventions – Nigeria was a signatory, but Biafra obviously not.

The fighting went on; hunger spread. In May, the Committee begged all concerned to respect 'urgent humanitarian measures' and to 're-establish peace in men's minds and hearts'. After Port Harcourt fell to the Nigerian forces in May 1968, which meant that the principal route for any imported food was now closed, delegates contacted Geneva to say that thousands of women, children and old people were fleeing the fighting, refusing to go home to their villages and suffering from acute exhaustion and hunger. Without at least 200 tons of food a day, they warned, the numbers of dead would rise dramatically. It was now that the full humanitarian implications of the war – and their political dimensions – became clear.

There was a great deal involved here and none of it was simple. It was not so much that the International Committee could not find enough food or medical assistance – by May 1968, nineteen national societies were pouring in supplies and dozens of other organizations offering help – as the fact that they were finding it increasingly impossible to get them into the country. The Biafrans and Nigerians alike had one main object in mind: to win the war. For Biafra this meant sovereignty over a seceded state; for Nigeria the prevention of such sovereignty. The high cost in lives, both implied, was unfortunate but probably inevitable. And while Nigeria was anxious to keep the world out, the Biafrans had quickly perceived that the surest road to victory was to draw in international support, and that pictures of starving children could help them do so. Whether the federal forces were really bent on genocide and were deliberately starving the Ibos to death was not at this stage obvious – but there was no doubt that people were dying. It was on this confusing and contradictory axis that the war turned and the relief agencies, long schooled in the Geneva Conventions' emphatic rejection of starvation as a weapon of war, were now buffeted by the ghastly prospect of raising and spending money in order to save lives, even if this meant prolonging the war.

The logistics of supplying relief on such a scale were themselves daunting. From the start, the churches had chartered planes to send in food, sometimes permitting weapons to travel alongside. The International Committee, on the other hand, was tied to its mandate: under the Geneva Conventions it had to seek permission from the government in Lagos for its deliveries to Biafra – Article 23 of the 1949 Conventions spelt out clearly that all delivery of aid in this kind of situation was to be subordinate to the agreement of the contracting power, who had to be convinced that the relief would go only to the civilians to whom it was destined and that enemy troops would derive no gain or advantage from it. The Committee was now constantly frustrated by the intransigence of the federal government, which at first insisted that relief flights could only land at Uli, an airstrip used by the Biafrans for military purposes. The Biafrans refused to neutralize it, as that would have prevented their military supplies from coming in. After further negotiations, the federal government agreed that the Red Cross planes could fly into Biafra 'at their own risk', which meant by night, and which was acceptable to the Biafrans as the relief planes acted as shields for the weapons being flown in by mercenaries; the federal forces proved reluctant to use their anti-aircraft guns on planes carrying relief. Gun-runners and food-providers now jostled for space above the darkened Biafran airstrips. A whole series of early flights made it into Biafra. Then a neutralized airstrip, clearly painted with immense Red Cross markings, was bombed by federal forces, leaving a number of workers injured and the runway destroyed. Just the same, negotiations and flights went on, with growing unease and bitterness.

The determination to beat the blockade took considerable courage. On 30 September 1968 two International Committee delegates, one a Yugoslav doctor the other a Swedish relief worker, as well as two missionaries from the World Council of Churches who had stayed on at a hospital during an attack by Nigerian forces, were shot dead as they lay on the ground. They had been lured into the open by a Nigerian officer who shouted out to them: 'Come out all members of the International Red Cross.' The two delegates were both thirty-two and married; their bodies were flown back to Geneva and buried in Red Cross flags.

The International Committee had handled the first year of the war well, remaining small and largely in the background. Hoffmann was a diplomat and good at brokering agreements. He was liked by both Biafrans and Nigerians. But as time went by and numbers of employees grew – 240 people in federal territory alone by the late autumn of 1968 – there was talk of the International Committee in Lagos being nothing other than another white European embassy. A rumour circulated about a consignment of relief consisting of twenty tonnes of cocktail sausages and biscuits. Some of the troubles of the Committee in the Biafran conflict would now stem from panic and over-reaction. More would come from their decision to go outside the regular staff and appoint as senior delegate to the war – they called him the ICRC High Commissioner for Nigeria – a former journalist, pioneer in international refugee work and Switzerland's former ambassador to both Washington and Moscow.

August Lindt was an interesting and highly able figure. Adventurous and energetic, descended from the wealthy chocolate family, Lindt was released from the Swiss foreign service for this high profile and delicate task. There was no doubting his abilities, but he was curiously unsuited to recognize or deal with the complicated and sensitive politics of the situation. He was also too impatient. It was his energy that finally forced through the 'at your own risk' concession for Red Cross planes to fly into Biafra, and his skills as a journalist that provided the media with memorable sound-bites, but it was also his arrogance that made the Nigerians deeply suspicious. For while Lindt maddened colleagues by never telling them where he was going, and he alienated everyone by conveying the impression that he alone would bring about a peaceful conclusion to a war in which everyone else was floundering. 'If he spoke to the Americans and Russians as he does to us,' a Nigerian diplomat complained to John St Jorre, who later wrote a book about the war, 'it's a wonder that Switzerland is still around.'

After Lindt decided to take a flight from Lagos without bothering to secure permission from airport control, he was abruptly expelled by the federal government to squawks of protest from Geneva. His unpopularity was not entirely his own fault. Despite the lesson that the Committee had learnt during the Spanish civil war that a single delegate for both sides invariably leads to suspicion and confusion, they had once again appointed one man to co-ordinate all operations. In his letter of resignation to the Committee, Lindt observed that his objectivity had not always been 'appreciated in this conflict where propaganda and psychological warfare play an important part'. In their reply, the International Committee spoke of Lindt's 'shining contribution to the history of human solidarity'.

And so the war went on, with relief operations constantly halted by sudden attacks on hospitals, by the weather, by the twists and turns of the war front and by the conflicting sweeps of political deliberations. In the West passions mounted about what was now widely being described as genocide, and the International Committee fretted about how little money remained in its rapidly depleting coffers. In *The Times*, a correspondent accused Britain with its sales of arms to Lagos of being at least partly responsible for the worst tragedy in the history of famine, and there was talk in the British papers of indifference, criminal apathy, callousness and an intent to further white supremacy. In November 1968 appeals for funds from Geneva had produced ten million Swiss francs. The Committee announced that it needed twenty-two million more, and nine of those urgently. In January 1969, a hospital run by the Red Cross at Wawo-Omama in Biafra was bombed by federal aircraft. The Committee protested. By April, greatly helped by supplies and medical teams from UNICEF and the World Council of Churches, the Committee was running the biggest relief operation they had ever mounted, employing many hundreds of foreigners, Swiss delegates, doctors seconded from the national societies and expatriates, as well as 2,000 Nigerians. They had 400 vehicles and various ships and aircraft, delivering over three million meals a week in Biafra, and they were carrying out an extensive vaccination programme. The dangers of famine in territory under federal control were at last receding, though in Biafra itself there were still areas where people were not being reached. At the end of May 1969, Jacques Freymont issued an appeal against a 'new and redoubtable danger: the weariness of public opinion'.

What Freymont did not know was that the International Committee's days in Biafra were numbered. At much the same time as he was speaking, Count von Rosen, who had flown into Ethiopia with Junod in the 1930s and was now a grandfather, was putting together a small freelance operation of his own to come to the aid of the Biafrans. Calling his mission Operation Biafran Baby, von Rosen flew a number of raids with light aircraft armed with rockets, wearing a golden baseball cap back to front to protect his neck from the sun. Von Rosen was a Swede. On the evening of 5 June, a Swedish Red Cross DC-7B, on its way to Uli in Biafra, was shot down by a federal plane. It had been carrying eleven tonnes of rice and the International Committee had been privately informed that its planes would not be attacked. On board were an American pilot, a Norwegian and two Swedes. Only two bodies were ever found.

The next day, flights into Biafra were suspended. The International Committee protested, blamed Count von Rosen for jeopardizing the entire relief programme with his freelance operation and pointed out that it had saved, up to that day, over two and a half million 'innocent victims of the war'. On 30 June, the Nigerian government announced that it had decided to bring to an end the Committee's mandate to co-ordinate the relief operation and that it would now be placed in the hands of a Nigerian rehabilitation commission instead.

In a long, stern statement, issued simultaneously in Lagos and London, the federal government strongly attacked those who had sought to 'use the humanitarian cover to sustain the rebellion' in Biafra and accused donors of causing more lives to be lost by indirectly prolonging the war. So-called 'mercy-flights', the statement continued, would no longer be used to carry messages between the secessionist regime and the outside world. The statement ended with a clear warning. There would be no further relief allowed into the country at all if the relief agencies failed to 'control their functionaries who engage in pro-rebel publicity stunts'. After a hasty visit to Lagos by Naville, the banker who had taken over from Freymont as the Committee's tenth president, and permission to make five last flights with medical supplies, the Committee turned over its activities to work 'in co-operation with the Nigerian Red Cross', though all through that autumn they continued to warn that 'the very existence of a generation is . . . in peril'. It was not only the ban that brought an end to the flights: the International Committee, re-evaluating what it had been doing, was forced to accept that Nigeria, the established government in a civil war, did have the legal right to set the terms of inspection for relief flights under the Fourth Geneva Convention. There was really no choice but to reject what had come to be called 'revolutionary humanitarianism', the taking in of aid without reference to those in power.

In any case, the war was fast coming to an end. In January 1970 fighting in Biafra ceased. Biafran resistance had simply collapsed under the combined weight of the famine, exhaustion and the supremacy of federal military power. On 6 February, the relief operations stopped and stocks were wound up. The International Committee and other relief agencies were now forbidden to take further supplies into Biafra, though several delegates were allowed in to inspect conditions.

The Nigerian civil war lasted almost exactly a thousand days. It had started in the summer of 1967 as 'history's least-reported war'. By the time the fighting was over, early in 1970, it had become the largest, most savage, best provisioned and most publicized conflict in the history of the African continent. Millions of words had been written about it, but it was radio and above all television cameras that had kept the spectacle of dying children before the world for almost its entire span. To this day the name Biafra conjures up images of hunger. It was the first television famine disaster of modern times. Some 600,000 people died, but never before had so much foreign aid gone into keeping the survivors alive.

For the International Committee, Biafra brought changes of a drastic and enduring kind. Never had the organization raised or spent so much money nor been confronted by so many difficulties. It had gone into the war controlled and run by a group of conscientious but hardly radical middle-aged men in Geneva, committed principally to assisting prisoners-of-war and political detainees, to tracing the missing and putting them in touch with their families and to monitoring the Geneva Conventions. It came out of it a leading relief agency, a role hitherto left largely in the hands of the League for peacetime natural disasters, its policies shaped by a new generation of energetic and ambitious men. Over the next twelve years, Jean-Paul Hocké, who was working for a car firm in Nigeria when he was recruited as a delegate early in the war, would become one of the driving forces in the organization, rising to the post of director of operations. Hocké had no doubts about the importance of relief in wars. Even if the final verdict on the International Committee's performance in Biafra was not altogether good – hindsight has judged it to have been unprepared and uninformed in the summer of 1968 when starvation reached its peak, and at times both expensive and inefficient (though this is possibly true of most relief operations in emergencies) – it had proved capable of conducting a relief operation of a totally unexpected size and complexity. The logistics of large-scale wartime disasters, particularly during civil conflicts, and a recognition that relief and assistance to prisoners-of-war must go hand in hand, that relief to civilians is a crucial component of modern wars – something never contemplated by Dunant – would now become central to International Committee thinking.

More than the logistics of relief, however, Biafra had brought changes in the way the world thought about the role of humanitarian agencies generally. The International Committee, accustomed to being the major and often the only player in the field, would not find all of them easy to accept. There was the uncomfortable debate as to whether the immense international concern for and generosity towards Biafra's starving children had not in fact prolonged the war, thereby increasing the suffering, and with it a realization that until the principles behind the delivery of aid were resolved, an operation of this kind would be doomed to confusion. In a war in which those who took in food by breaking the blockade were accused of supporting the resistance and those who respected Nigeria's sovereignty were judged to have helped the federal forces to commit genocide by starvation, there would be no winners and no easy answers. Other agencies, who had no binding mandate, at least enjoyed the freedom to chose where they would go. The International Committee, buffeted by visions of acute need on one side and its responsibilities under the Geneva Conventions on the other, spent much of the war uncertain as to its duties, only at the very end reaffirming its clear commitments under Article 23. It had gone on increasing its efforts to get relief into Biafra, even after Lagos withdrew its original permission over flights. Once the Nigerians challenged its stand by shooting down its plane, it had been faced with a choice: to remain aggressive and defy Nigerian policy, or suspend flights and seek to negotiate a new agreement, one that would preserve its traditional role of acting only with the consent of both parties. After painful soul-searching, it had opted for the second. As Jacques Freymont spelt out in an article written for the *Review* in February 1970, soon after the end of the war, 'that tenacity and that intransigence which we consider necessary must be contained by certain rules . . . The ICRC . . . cannot ignore that body of rules which itself helped to establish and for which it demands respect from states.'

No one could accuse the Committee of a lack of tenacity. But they could and did accuse it of political innocence, of a failure to see through Biafra's adroit propaganda, and of allowing itself to be manipulated by the political currents of outside governments, though it were not the only agency to be duped. 'A humanitarian motivation,' David Forsythe observed drily, 'is no substitute for political sophistication.' Humanitarian aid, it would soon be said, is really a modern extension of diplomacy. The International Committee, perceiving just how vulnerable it had become in this new world of humanitarian politics and how essential it was to define and redefine its goals in every new conflict in the light of prevailing political currents, would never be as guileless again. How far it would adapt, how fundamentally those in charge would prove able to mould Dunant's dream to cope with political constraints that no nineteenth-century philanthropist could ever have imagined, would determine to some extent the Committee's onward journey.

One of the doctors flown in early to Biafra by the International Committee as part of the contribution of the French Red Cross to the war had been Bernard Kouchner. Like many of those whose first experience of relief work was the starving children in Biafra's camps, Kouchner was devastated by what he saw, and soon frustrated by the ban on speaking out imposed by the Committee. Watching children die, he concluded, as did others, that what he was witnessing was nothing other than genocide by starvation. Kouchner had lost members of his family in the Nazi death camps and would later say that he was not prepared to condone a second complicity of silence. Returning on leave to Paris, he called on Jean-Paul Sartre and Simone de Beauvoir, and wrote, together with a fellow Biafra delegate, an article for Le Monde entitled 'Two French doctors returning from Biafra bear witness', and founded a Committee against Genocide in Biafra. Late into the night, he talked to friends about his idea for setting up a sort of 'anti-Red Cross', somewhere where the 'new humanitarians' could meet.

The International Committee was remarkably tolerant about Kouchner's outburst and he returned briefly to the field on its behalf. But out of Nigeria's blockade, paralysing the humanitarian efforts, was born the idea of 'sans-frontièrisme' and médécins d'urgence, the need to combine medical assistance with the duty of bearing witness and the feeling that the public must be kept informed of what is going on in the world in order that pressure is put on those responsible for atrocities. Others before Kouchner had found the International Committee's pledge to secrecy hard to bear, but it was Kouchner and his friends who finally defied the edict publicly. In December 1971 Médécins Sans Frontières was set up in Paris, a fusion of Kouchner's doctors and another group who had worked with the victims of Bangladeshi floods. While their drive was at first welcome to the International Committee, who drew on this pool of young doctors for their relief operations, their outspokenness and independence soon became irritating to Geneva, just as MSF quickly became dismissive of the Committee's caution and reluctance to give power to the men it sent to the field. 'This forced mutism,' wrote one MSF doctor, 'turns delegates into perpetual grizzlers.' 'There was arrogance on both sides,' remembers Romy Brauman, founder with Kouchner of MSF. 'We were young, ambitious, keen to carve out our own territory. The International Committee agreed with our insistence on speed and professionalism when it came to medical matters, but they found it impossible to accept that they were no longer alone in the field.'

MSF was not the only organization to grow and develop in the course of the Biafran war and in time the network would grow immense with separate organizations in many countries. UNICEF had played a large part in providing relief, adding their experience in servicing operations on the ground to the International Committee's skills at transport and delivery. 'We suddenly found that the world was full of competitive non-governmental organizations,' says Charles Egger, then UNICEF's deputy executive director for programmes. 'We realized that we had no choice but to pull up our socks, become accountable, co-operate. From Biafra date our meetings to explain to our committees what we had done and why we had done it. It was as much a period of learning for the Red Cross as it was for us.' After the war in Biafra, the International Committee would never be alone in the field and never free of the competition that has come to mark modern humanitarian work.

The International Committee would never feel entirely safe again, in the sense of guaranteeing the safety of its delegates. Men had lost their lives for the Red Cross in countless earlier conflicts, but Biafra was the first war in which Red Cross members were made targets for attack. Fourteen delegates, workers and pilots had been killed. Writing in the *Journal de Genève*, on 12 October 1968, Jean Pictet described the deliberate shooting of the two delegates outside the Okigwi hospital as a 'tragedy which must lead to the most serious thinking . . . Our times are marked by a hardening of hearts and declining of international morality . . . If one day the protective value of the Red Cross emblem should be doubted . . . the world would have regressed a hundred years.'

One aspect of the war that all sides remarked on was the enormous role played by the media, not all of it, or even much of it, good. The BBC was so profoundly hated by the end of the war in parts of Nigeria that if you wanted to call a man a liar, you referred to him as 'a BBC'. Markpress had invented a public relations exercise that would seldom be improved on, eventually forcing the federal government to employ media consultants of their own. How the International Committee would deal with what it traditionally regarded as the enemy – exposure – and the realization that it was ultimately unable to control what was said and reported, would also prove one of the most lasting and interesting debates to come. The press unleashed on such a scale was seen to be a dangerous and capricious animal: but could sufficient money any longer be raised without it?

As for the genocide, had it in fact taken place? After returning from a visit to Biafra in September 1967, the Irish writer and diplomat Conor Cruise O'Brien had warned that 'mass murder on a scale unprecedented as yet in Africa' was imminent. His conclusion, soon shared by others, was that after the 1966 killings the federal government had decided to eliminate the Ibos and it was at that moment that the word 'genocide', that most potent linguistic legacy of the Second World War, entered the vocabulary of the Biafran war. That people died of hunger in their thousands was beyond dispute, but in the end both sides were forced to take part of the blame for the starvation; that there were terrible mass-acres and air raids was also beyond question, but then massacres and air raids have marked all modern wars, and this had been a very dirty war. But when it was all over, and it became apparent that there had seldom been a more bloodless end to any war, it was recognized that the killings had in fact shown no genocidal pattern.

In 1971 the president of the International Committee was a successful banker called Marcel Naville, a popular and good-looking former member of the Swiss foreign office and grandson of Edouard Naville, head of the prisoner-of-war agency during the First World War. Family ties, in the 1970s, were still useful. Naville's New Year message was bleak: he spoke of 'civilian populations reduced to famine, women and children buried beneath the ruins of their bombed homes, burnt-out ambulances . . . statesmen and diplomats kidnapped or hijacked . . . escalation of hate and suffering'.

The International Committee had never worked harder, moving into new countries and new fields. An expedition to Brazil, led by a delegate called Serge Nessi and accompanied by three doctors, covered 12,000 miles in search of the Amazonian Indians and returned with careful medical notes and a warning that the West would cause immense harm if it imported hitherto unknown diseases into the area. A month taken at random – May 1973 – gives some idea of the range and imaginative capacity of the Committee as it now anxiously sought some coherent path between its historical commitments and the need to address Naville's world of disorder and violence.

That May, delegates visited military and civilian prisoners-of-war in Pakistan, India and Bangladesh, where they were also keeping an eye on non-Bengali minorities, increasingly discriminated against over jobs and housing. In India, a delegate oversaw the repatriation of a Pakistani prisoner-of-war across the border at a place called Wagah. One hundred and fifty delegates were regular visitors to the Indian sub-continent.

In the Philippines, the regional delegate for Asia, A. Tschiffli, inspected two camps holding 575 prisoners. In Sri Lanka, five 'rehabilitation camps', scattered at opposite ends of the island, were visited.

Israel was currently holding 108 Arab prisoners of war, Egypt ten Israeli prisoners and Syria three: a delegate saw them all and supervised the repatriation of a number of sick Egyptian captives across the Suez Canal at El Qantara, while at the same time conducting 125 people across the canal east to west, and seventy west to east in a family reunification agreement. In Yemen, a doctor and a delegate visited 450 detainees, taking with them medicines, soap and washing powder.

That month, Serge Nessi was off again, this time on a five-week mission to Barbados, Trinidad and Tobago, Colombia, Ecuador, Peru and Brazil, meeting representatives from government and local Red Cross societies, and inspecting prison conditions for political detainees. In Rwanda, the regional delegate visited eleven places of detention in a little less than three weeks. In Sudan, a relief service set up a programme to distribute 2,635 tons of flour. In Gambia, the delegate for West Africa embarked on a two-week mission to see 260 detainees, then crossed the border into Sierra Leone, and from there on into Liberia.

In Geneva, delegates were at last at work overseeing compensation for former Allied prisoners of the Second World War in Japan, where the government had finally agreed to a sum of £4.5 million to go to the families of dead prisoners and to survivors whom the Committee considered had shown signs of having suffered 'undue hardship'.

Records of the time show that by the spring of 1973 the International Committee had become a major distributor of relief in over fifty countries. Naville's warnings about the escalation 'of hate and suffering' were proving horribly accurate.

The International Committee itself, however, was embattled. Until the early 1970s it had been dominated by its traditional collegiate body of up to twenty-five co-opted Swiss citizens, all but a very few of them men from the middle or upper classes. Of the ninety-eight who served on the Committee between 1863 and 1970, thirty-seven had been lawyers, nineteen doctors, and six bankers. Their average age was sixty; their average length of stay 17.6 years. But Biafra had made it plain that modern wars, in becoming more anarchical and complex, had somehow left the Committee behind. Faced with astute professional soldiers and manoeuvring politicians and diplomats, the ageing Swiss co-optees sometimes appeared a little naive, cautious and decidedly ignorant of world political nuances. They were, as Oran Young in a study of humanitarian intervention noted drily, 'a group of very Conservative businessmen . . . more strongly anti-communist than most Americans'. As was suddenly painfully obvious, the challenges of the new world order were too great for part-time humanitarians, many of whom had seldom left Switzerland. There was talk of stodginess, of an overly deferential manner towards governments, of a lack of sympathy for the emerging human rights movement.

What was more, a certain randomness reigned over the workings of the organization. The legal experts in 'la maison' went their own way, developing law and doctrine which the delegates, making decisions in the field that seemed most appropriate to them at the time, seldom consulted or even knew about. The organization's archive, one of the most remarkable of all historical records which traces the very nature of war for over a century, was unsorted, secret and closed to the public; to some extent this reflected the deeply paradoxical attitude of the Committee itself towards the past, one of both ignorance and dependency.

In the summer of 1973 two joint presidents, a much-liked Geneva-born doctor called Eric Martin and Roger Gallopin, whom some found overbearing and a little too fond of luxury, took over from Naville, the search for a single figure with sufficient vision and toughness to hold the movement together having failed. Jean Pictet and Frédéric Siordet had both been approached and declined. The currents sparked off by Biafra, and by the questioning and sceptical mood of the 1960s, were making people in the humanitarian world uneasy. Biafra had demonstrated that civil war and natural disasters were often inextricably entwined: did it make sense any longer for the International Committee to stick to wartime relief and the League to concentrate solely on peace? Realizing their interdependence in the field, yet determined to remain distinct, the two organizations had signed an agreement to adopt a 'common attitude and to co-ordinate their activities' in April 1969, on the eve of the League's fiftieth birthday. As yet, the emollient words had produced little visible sign of mellowing. 'They steal our victims,' Laurent Marti would later say of the League, 'if near, they creep into our wars. Why? Because war has charm. They want to say: "It's *our* victim." '

Were the febrile new political winds stirring the humanitarian world about to compromise the neutrality of the movement? Within the Red Cross, more and more people were beginning to look at Oxfam, Amnesty International and Médécins Sans Frontières, wondering how right it was for the Committee to focus on war, when others were trying to address the basic inequalities in society. From Finland and Belgium came noises about too paternalistic an attitude, about values now outdated and inappropriate, while the president of the Norwegian Red Cross, a fiery military man called Major General Torstein Dale, went further, bluntly asking whether the world still needed the Red Cross at all. Huge shifts of power within the League, away from the traditional western societies, were now beginning to mirror changes in global politics with superpower competition switching away from Europe and towards the Third World, where many newly formed states were becoming quarrelsome and vocal players.

It was out of these cross-currents that now came two major developments. One was a call from the League for the Red Cross movement to pause and take stock, to ask where it was going and reflect the interests and concerns of its new members, to 'slough off a colonial mantle,' which had been one of the legacies of its founders. The other, which came from lawyers and military legal experts and reflected a growing feeling that international humanitarian law as it stood was too muddled, too little understood and too steeped in the past to make sense of the anarchy and complexity of modern war, was for a revision of the Geneva Conventions particularly with regard to civilians, who seemed to be faring worse than ever in these new wars.

What the League was proposing was indeed new and radical: a thorough, detailed analysis of the entire Red Cross to be carried out by an independent outsider. Nothing like it had ever happened before. The International Committee was far from keen, though in time it would prove a willing if sceptical collaborator.

The man chosen to carry out this delicate task was Donald Tansley, the ex-vice-president of the Canadian International Development Agency and a respected figure known to be impartial. In his brief, Tansley was asked to examine the 'image, status, tasks and co-operation' of all Red Cross and Red Crescent societies, as well as the League and the International Committee, and to make recommendations about the future. With funds from the Ford and Volkswagen Foundations and the Leverhulme Trust, a small staff and the help of twenty external consultants, Tansley set to work. In the autumn of 1975, having investigated twenty-three national societies in depth, visited forty-five countries and canvassed every government signatory to the Geneva Conventions for its views, he was ready to report. Appropriately enough, it was dubbed the 'Big Study'.

It is hard now, at a distance of over twenty years, to know exactly what people expected. Some clearly anticipated praise; others suspected there would be suggestions for a little tinkering with rules and performance. What no one really considered was the possibility that Tansley would be critical. What he had to say was far from pleasant. Dr Martin, after a first glance at the report, called the evaluation a 'pitiless inquisition'.

No one, it appeared, emerged from the inspection well. It was not so much that the world now presented the Red Cross with insuperable problems as the fact that the Red Cross was failing to deal with them. In a time of rising inflation, dwindling food stocks, population growth and resource scarcities, with signs of armed violence, terrorism and civil disobedience all on the increase, announced Tansley, the Red Cross movement was complacent, isolated and lacking in planning and professionalism.

The national societies were found to be patchy, inward-looking, dominated by their governments, with health programmes run by elites 'living in cloud cuckoo land'. Some were judged very weak indeed: yet no monitoring system had ever been set up to oversee them.

The League emerged as vacillating, without clear principles, ruled over by a 'cumbersome and costly' government structure, and too much in awe of the International Committee, its relations with which were described as bedevilled by mutual suspicion.

But it was for the International Committee itself that Tansley seemed to reserve his harshest remarks. The Committee, he said, spent far too little time on analysis, evaluation and proper planning; it was too self-satisfied, too rivalrous, too secretive and it was led by conservatives and traditionalists who remained bound to the 'monarchy, aristocracy and upper classes'. What was worse, it had retained from a bygone age an unnecessary and unpleasant taint of charity, which he compared to the handing out of old clothes in a world in which social security was recognized as more dignified and more helpful.

As for the Red Cross movement as a whole, Tansley concluded that it was uneven, unable any longer to speak with a single voice, and that its future lay in a return to its successful past as a provider of emergency relief in times of both war and natural disasters, at which it was capable of performing supremely well. By the same token, he said, it would do well to pare away at all the hundreds of different activities and functions that it had acquired over the years, many of which were redundant and confused. And, as a further sting in the tail, he mentioned that the League and the International Committee would do well to merge, at least to the extent of issuing joint appeals and sharing a number of common services.

The first reaction to Tansley's report was silence. Then, bit by bit, people began to sift through the conclusions and recommendations, mainly it seemed in order to pull out bits they liked or found acceptable. Many hundreds of thousands of words were written, commentaries were drafted, discussed, redrafted and debated. Two questionnaires and a series of follow-up letters went out to the national societies – only thirty-nine of which ever bothered to reply. The *Review* was filled, month after month, by long, weighty comments. In August 1977 a document prepared by the secretariat and entitled *The ICRC, the League and the Tansley Report* was circulated to the twenty-third international conference in Bucharest. And there, in a morass of differing opinions, prickly feelings and vested interests, Tansley's report sank.

It did not, however, vanish entirely without note, though it took many months and in some cases years for some of Tansley's remarks to boil to the top. The national societies did at least reconsider their position within the League and in time the need for 'integrity', for certain agreed standards, did enter Red Cross language, though how effective such a pious wish would have proved against, for example, the Nazis, is not clear. To this day, whatever the provocation and blatant disregard for

Red Cross principles, no society has ever been 'de-recognized'. Many of the national societies had felt themselves belittled by the report and some expressed considerable annoyance. Asked many years later whether, with hindsight, he would have gone about his report differently, Tansley is said to have admitted that he had not taken sufficiently seriously their power and importance.

The League made a conscious decision that it did not want to become the lead agency in disaster relief, as Tansley suggested, but preferred to maintain its scattered, laissez-faire attitude towards its members. It did, on the other hand, make some efforts to devise nutrition programmes for famine relief, and did take seriously the need to strengthen some of the national societies. It added Arabic to its official languages and a new general assembly of national societies, meeting every two years, was set up to replace the old board of governors. Tansley had offered the League a chance to slim down. It felt happier as a sum of unwieldy parts. In 1980 it launched the new decade with a slogan that could be read as a deliberate snub to Tansley. 'Everywhere,' it declared, 'for everyone.'

The International Committee, still smarting from being told that it was an exclusive Swiss club obsessed with needless secrecy, did take Tansley's words seriously at least in the sense that it launched an internal investigation. As for a merger with the League, no one, in the late 1970s, had any more appetite for closeness than at any other point in their long and rancorous history, though both sides recognized that co-operation during disasters was an efficient way of proceeding. It was a somewhat chastened but defiant Red Cross movement, blaming Tansley for the poor presentation of his document and the lack of a proper blueprint for the future, muttering that it was too busy coping with crises to find time to sit back and appraise its own performance, which now embarked on a revision of humanitarian law. To many, it seemed that Tansley might just as well never have happened.

Nor was everyone inside the International Committee keen on this revision of the laws. Some expressed fears, as Moynier had once done, that any fiddling would only make them weaker. At meetings and discussions there was much talk of an inevitable tussle between old colonial powers who refused to accept that imperial possession had been wrong, and the newly liberated states, who argued that their fight for liberation was a 'just war', and should be fought by the same rules as international wars, with the same status for freedom fighters as for soldiers. 'Armed conflict not of an international character' had found its way into Article 3 in 1949, but as the 1960s and 1970s progressed from one internal conflict to the next, so the calls grew to replace or supplement it with something considerably more forceful.

There was mention at first of passing the job of preparing this review of the laws of war to the UN; after some jostling it went to the International Committee in which many western nations had more confidence. Fearing that ninety years' of their work might easily be jeopardized by states deciding to renege on earlier commitments, the Committee quickly scotched a proposal simply to revise the Geneva Conventions and a decision was taken to draft two protocols, the first on international wars and the second on internal conflicts; and all involved made a resolution not to be too ambitious and thus end by sinking slowly beneath the weight of inevitable controversy.

Conference by conference, meeting by meeting, the International Committee coaxed the process forward. They drafted and redrafted proposals; they prepared reports; and they slipped in the word 'humanitarian' whenever possible, leaving an implicit assumption that anyone opposing it would be 'anti-humanitarian'.

In 1974, representatives of 121 nations and eleven national liberation movements gathered in Geneva for the first of four sessions. This conference would be unlike any that had ever preceded it for its length — four years — for the number of delegates of extreme cultural and national differences, and for the fundamental divisions between east and west. Two-thirds of the delegates came from Third World countries and, less concerned than the westerners about being labelled 'anti-humanitarian', they were swift to use the threat of walking out as a weapon with which to bargain.

Among those who came to Geneva were idealists who wanted to see so many legal restrictions that the military would never again be able to wage war, and pragmatists who wanted to keep it all very simple. There were soldiers, diplomats, politicians and lawyers, very few of whom knew anything about the huge new advances in military technology but who cared passionately about the law as it related to their own countries. For month after month, the experts hammered out questions of reprisals and nuclear weapons; they wrangled over 'proportionality' and how many casualties were acceptable; they debated the protection of cultural objects and places of worship; they discussed dams, dykes and nuclear power stations; they quarrelled over hunger as a weapon of war, and over damage to the natural environment; they complained that, despite all the talk in 1949 about the need to educate the military in the laws of war, very little had actually been done; and they agreed that the language of the new protocols should not sound like something out of the Middle Ages.

There were days when the conference became a struggle between north and south, others when Arabs and Israelis fought for supremacy, others again when the Soviet influence weighed heavy, many of the Third World delegates being Soviet trained. George H. Aldrich, the ambassador who headed the US delegation, loved negotiation and argument. Many of the developing countries, he observed gloomily, were being 'led by radical states bearing grudges against the wealthy countries and against the US in particular'. Personally, he observed, he saw the conference more as a 'hazard than an opportunity'.

What the experts came up with, after many thousands of hours of debate, did increase protection for civilians and did give 'a more universal dimension to international humanitarian law'. There was to be a ban on attacks on all non-military objectives and on the deportation of civilians from one country to another, and a renewed prohibition on weapons that caused unnecessary suffering. And among the dozens of other new rules, both major and minor, was an agreement that wars of liberation were to fall within the category of international armed conflict.

And when, on 8 June 1977, the two new protocols were adopted, with 102 articles in Protocol I relating to victims of international wars, and twenty-eight articles in Protocol II relating to those of 'non-international' ones, a sense of relief washed through the weary debaters. True, the protocols were not going to solve all problems – terrorism and nuclear weapons, for instance, were barely touched on – but it was agreed to be little short of miraculous that anything had been signed at all, given the presence of so many people of such passion and such ideological differences. 'International humanitarian law,' observed Hans-Peter Gasser, a senior International Committee lawyer, 'is neither *jus ad bello*, nor a set of rules for arms control, nor a blueprint for peace: it is *jus in bello*, intended to answer humanitarian needs caused by armed conflict.' The main achievement of the protocols, all agreed, was that at last there were more rules to protect civilians. The gap left by the 1949 Conventions was believed to be plugged.

Not everyone liked what had been accomplished. The Americans, who signed among the first but did not ratify, called the protocols a 'terrorists' charter'. W. Hays Park, the American international lawyer, was extremely critical, concluding that they contributed no advance in the law of war but rather a step backwards in the protection of war victims since the strengthening and clarifying of some issues had effectively weakened their position. The protocols reflected, he believed, the time at which they were negotiated, which was one of 'the tyranny of the majority' of Third World delegates. The military complained that, translated into six languages, with potential discrepancies between the different texts, there were 'myriad major ambiguities'. Some states argued that the protocols were fatally flawed since they had no proper instruments concerning weapons, while others kept repeating that all the International Committee had achieved was to politicize the laws. The western countries protested that the Third World nations had in the end decided to place security interests above humanitarian concerns.

As for the International Committee, there was a feeling that in 1949 and now again in 1977 it had been both loser and benefactor in its association with the law of armed conflict. States retained the last say on almost everything and the International Committee was accused of having sought what was most acceptable to states rather than challenging domestic priorities and national sovereignity.

In 1977, articles appeared in newspapers accusing Israel of torturing its Palestinian detainees. The finger of guilt was immediately pointed at the International Committee, as it had been in Algeria when *Le Monde* published the Red Cross report on French army brutality. The story of Israel and the International Committee is revealing of Geneva's methods and the terrible difficulties it faces, and a comment on the way the new protocols did very little to alter its day-to-day work. The Committee entered Israel ten days before the outbreak of the Six Day War in 1967, anticipating troubles from the rising tensions between the Israelis and their Arab neighbours; and it has never left. For thirty years the size of the delegation has fluctuated, month by month, up to a high of forty and down to ten, according to political and military developments. But it is the only country which the Committee has never judged sufficiently peaceable to enable it to withdraw all its delegates.

The story of the delegates' presence is not all about torture, though Israel is the country where the Committee fought hardest to get their delegates to see detainees as soon as possible after arrest. After intense lobbying, a period of 'within ten days' was finally agreed on in 1979; not entirely satisfactory, but considerably better than the thirty days it had been until then. That agreement has for the most part held.

Israel's relations with Geneva are about the art of the possible in the humanitarian world, about steady pushing until deals acceptable to both sides are forged, about determined lobbying for better conditions for the many Palestinians taken into custody year after year, about regular battles to prevent the demolition of Palestinian homes, about the delicate business of playing at what is now called a 'hierarchy of credibility', about acting as observer of what goes on, never open informer but always final moral witness.

'Israel is very special,' says one delegate who spent many of his years with the International Committee in the Middle East.

> It just isn't like, say, the Balkans. There isn't the same degree of brutality — that is physical brutality, though I'm not sure how you judge suffering — by millilitres of blood? It's very subtle in Israel, all to do with psychology, the constant need to forge the right relation with the Israelis, one of mutual trust, and not allow oneself to be manipulated. You have to understand words behind words, what is *really* being said, then decide how far to push, how soon to stop.

After a series of incidents concerning torture when the Israelis did nothing to curb the methods of their interrogators, the International Committee issued one of its rare public protests. Though it provoked almost no interest outside the Middle East, it did, for many months, alter the infinitely subtle relationship between delegates and the Israeli authorities. 'It was like a marriage,' says a long-term delegate. 'Everyone knew that a crisis was possible, but no one quite believed in it until it happened.

For a while, we returned to icy formality, and a very literal interpretation of our mandate.'

There are very few senior delegates working for the International Committee today who have not served at least once in Tel Aviv or Jerusalem, who have not driven down the backstreets of the occupied cities to take medicine and food to the families of the imprisoned or carried children injured in street fighting to hospital, who have not spent hours repatriating prisoners-of-war, backwards and forwards across the borders with Israel's Arab neighbours, sweltering in the heat of the desert while dreaming of Switzerland's cool green mountains, who have not spent hours badgering their way past hostile camp commandants to talk to apathetic or vengeful detainees, trying to determine who has been beaten up, who intimidated by threats of reprisals against families, who manipulated by well-placed Israeli spies. The years in Israel have been important in shaping delegates, in turning them into diplomats and negotiators, social workers and therapists, experts in logistics, fine linguists and practised nutritionists. Israel is the only country whose national society, the Magen David Adom, is not recognized, for all its efficiency and size; the simple reason for this is that it insists on its own emblem, the Star (literally 'shield') of David, and the International Committee has always cited confusion and divisiveness as its objections, so fuelling complaints of continuing anti-Semitism among those who still believe the Committee's concentration camp policy was dictated by an innate dislike of the Jews. In no other country does the Committee's wartime past surface so relentlessly.

Israel is also the place where women delegates first really showed how effective they could be among people with no tradition of female emancipation, and where they demonstrated that women often make better and more acceptable listeners to the accounts of men who have been physically tortured. The International Committee's record in Israel is really one of patience and the rewards that it can bring. Their standing with the Israelis has been high and there came a time when they were so much part of the landscape that they acted as a point of reference even for the Israeli military.

Have they prevented torture? Not exactly, people say, but they have prevented it from getting out of hand, they have improved conditions for innumerable prisoners and their families, and they have acted as a crucial voice for international standards and a warning that to neglect them can be foolish. This, at least, is what their admirers say. Their critics are more wary. They see Israel as a permanent reminder that confidentiality, seeing all, year after year, and saying nothing, can very easily become complicity.

TWENTY

La Maison

On 17 July 1979, François Bugnion from the International Committee and Jacques Beaumont from UNICEF arrived in Phnom Penh. They were the first two representatives from the western humanitarian world to visit Cambodia since the Khmer Rouge had closed the country to foreigners in 1975; and their journey was kept secret from the press, not least because the United Nations still insisted on regarding the Khmer Rouge as the legal government of Cambodia, despite a new, Vietnamese-backed government installed in the capital. Bugnion was a lawyer by training, a veteran of the Committee's work in China and Vietnam, a traditionalist and a puritan in the reserved and gentlemanly style of an earlier generation of Swiss delegates. Beaumont, who had served with the partisans in France, was persistent, energetic, keen to perform well and widely regarded as very skilled at delicate negotiations. Colleagues today remember that he had a real feeling for underdogs and a flair for sorting out messy situations. The two men, one cautious and somewhat anxious, the other eager and assertive, could not have been more different: they were to make an impressive pair.

From the window of their plane as it landed in Phnom Penh, they looked out at a scene of desolation: villages empty of all people and animals, roads pitted and rutted, fields left uncultivated. The airport was deserted. The streets, as they drove into the city, were full of rubbish and overgrown with thick, tropical vegetation. On the outskirts, casually pushed against or on top of one another, were rusting cars. It might have been the aftermath, many years later, of a nuclear explosion.

During the forty-eight hours the two men were permitted to stay by the new government of Heng Samrin, a former defector from the Khmer Rouge, they visited an orphanage without food or drugs and a hospital with 800 patients and three doctors. There was no soap, no sheets, no sterilizers; meals consisted of thin rice soup. The amount of drugs left in the hospital would, Bugnion reported, have fitted on to one small tray. Their interpreter was so weak with hunger that he fainted.

The degree of misery and starvation was shocking and far beyond anything Bugnion and Beaumont had been prepared for, but it did not come as a complete surprise. Ever since the Khmer Rouge had taken power in 1975, throwing the International Committee and UNICEF delegates to Cambodia out of the country along with all other foreigners, stories of cities emptied of people, of forced labour, of the steady purge of the professional and educated classes, of the execution of doctors and the destruction of medical equipment, of brutality and murder and starvation, had been brought over the border into neighbouring Thailand by refugees. Occasional articles appearing in western papers had warned of impending catastrophe – Nayan Chanda had written in the *Far Eastern Economic Review* about 'abandoned towns . . . littered with skeletons and the debris of war' while 'hundreds of thousands of tired and dazed people criss-cross the country seeking missing relatives'. But no one in the West was greatly interested, even after a French priest, François Ponchard, who had spent many years in Cambodia, produced *Cambodge: Année Zéro* where he described in detail what had happened to a country destroyed by nine years of war, revolution and Pol Pot. The International Committee, alerted by the anxieties of delegates in neighbouring countries, had on several occasions made offers of help both before and after the Vietnamese invasion of 1979, but had always been met by silence. What had brought Bugnion and Beaumont to Phnom Penh now, on their brief and secret visit, was a sudden plea from the new government and its foreign minister, Hun Sen. Three million of Cambodia's former population of a little over seven million were dead, Hun Sen reported, from torture, execution and starvation. The survivors were for the most part so weak that few would live without western help. In Geneva, the International Committee and UNICEF had agreed on this first joint exploratory visit.

After the forty-eight hours had elapsed, the two westerners were urged by their Cambodian hosts to hurry straight back to Geneva to report what they had seen. They were to tell the West that Cambodia needed food, medicines and money but not people: they would reconstruct their country themselves. Bugnion and Beaumont decided to retire no further than Ho Chi Minh City (the former Saigon), wishing to remain close at hand in order to press hard for a further permit to enter the country; they argued that forty-eight hours had not given them nearly enough time to assess what needed to be done. On 9 August, after frustrating delays and prevarications, they were allowed to fly back to Phnom Penh taking with them four tonnes of drugs and medical equipment hastily provided by Geneva – the first to reach Cambodia in over four years. They also took with them a proposal for a co-ordinated assistance programme, and representatives of the Food and Agriculture Organization and the World Food Programme. In time, though not before many miserable months of negotiations, this would turn into the largest relief operation the International Committee had ever mounted, far exceeding even Biafra. Cambodia was the manifestation of Naville's worst prediction for the future of the world – starvation, civil war, civilian casualties, superpower politics, nationalism – all rolled into one.

Biafra had opened the Red Cross to the new currents of competition, relief, politics and the media. In Cambodia, the organization would be transformed over eighteen months and become able to deal with them all. In the summer of 1979 the International Committee was still relatively small; by the time it pulled out of Cambodia, it had become an immense enterprise – at one point it had more than 800 people in the field – with teams of experts in transport, logistics, development and nutrition, many learning these new skills as they went along, obliged to act in close co-operation with a vast and multiplying new world of humanitarian and human rights organizations. The conflict in Cambodia would present the Red Cross with yet more confusion and dangerous political constraints, many of them shaped by America's earlier bombing of the country and by the century's shifting position as a pawn in Cold War diplomacy; no one any longer doubted that Dunant's dream was a highly political game and that sophistication was one of the more powerful weapons required. Cambodia would also give the International Committee the chance to restore its image of impartiality within the communist world; its help and authority had been systematically rejected in Korea and Vietnam, and its delegates continued to be seen as part of the bourgeois and capitalist bloc.

Political complications and the kind of media attention most hated by the Committee were not slow in coming. After a visit to Cambodia later in August by Jim Howard, Oxfam's bluff and genial representative, stories began appearing in American and British newspapers carrying details of Khmer Rouge atrocities and the impending starvation of those who had survived. Howard described children with 'eyes full of pus', fearful, bald, starving and too weak to stand. The *New York Times* carried a story by Seymour Hersh saying that in his long career as a journalist he had visited many ravaged countries, but never seen misery on such a scale. Accompanying his article was a photograph of two children crouching grimly together: the baby had the vastly swollen head and sparse hair of the mirasmus victim, familiar to readers from the days of Biafra.

The correspondent for the British *Daily Mirror* in Indo-China was John Pilger, who now visited Phnom Penh under the auspices of Vietnamese television and came back comparing Pol Pot to Hitler. He had been to Tuŏl Sleng, where the Khmer Rouge had photographed their victims before and after killing them; he called the torturers 'Gestapo' and the torture centre 'Auschwitz'. Though what Pilger described in a television programme that went out in the UK in October was not in essence so very different from the reports of other journalists, the stories of torture and massacre he told struck a particular chord in the West. Protests from the public grew louder, and with them criticisms of UNICEF and the International Committee, who were accused of having sat by and done nothing; secrecy was once again taken for inaction. To those in Geneva, it produced painful memories of the attacks that followed their silence over the Jews. One of Pilger's more accusatory — and unjust — statements had been that the International Committee was doing 'virtually nothing'.

In fact, UNICEF and the International Committee had not been idle. Bugnion and Beaumont had kept up incessant pressure on the new government to relax their hostility towards the outside world and to reach agreement on a programme of aid. The discussions were eased by Beaumont's skills as a negotiator, but endlessly blocked on the question of who exactly was to be fed western food. The new Kampuchean government wanted assurances that none would go to former members of the Khmer Rouge. Bugnion continued to repeat that under the International Committee's mandate all victims had to be helped without discrimination. And there, for the moment, the matter rested, the sense of crisis heightened by reports issued by Oxfam that Cambodia was full of 'emaciated Belsen-type walking skeletons' and that there would be over two million more dead by Christmas unless something drastic was done. Breaking ranks from colleagues fettered by their mandates, Oxfam now agreed to Phnom Penh's terms and gave assurances that no food would go to the Khmer Rouge, whether they were starving or not. There was nothing that Bugnion and Beaumont could do but watch, smarting under Pilger's attacks which they could not refute. Even a public appeal to the Heng Samrin regime and Vietnam, one of the new International Committee's president, Alexander Hay's rare utterances, did nothing to change the Kampuchean government's mind.

Not far away from Phnom Penh, on Cambodia's border with Thailand, another drama was being played out. This, too, was highly political and here it involved refugees.

The Thais were used to refugees. They had arrived from China after the outbreak of civil war there in 1946, and all through the Khmer Rouge days hungry, frightened and miserable Cambodians had been trickling across their borders. It was they who had brought the first stories of Khmer Rouge brutalities, stories which the Thais, who supported the Khmer Rouge as their bulwark against a possible Vietnamese invasion, were loth to hear. Just the same, camps had reluctantly been opened along the border, into which the International Committee and other humanitarian organizations had been taking aid. In the spring of 1979, however, the exodus increased. Some 200,000 people struggled over the mountains and out of the forests, escaping the fighting between Vietnamese and Khmer Rouge, overwhelming the Thais and placing immense demands on the resources of western donors. Of the 200,000, about 80,000 were given permission, of a temporary nature, to stay.

But their arrival coincided with the waves of Vietnamese fleeing by sea — the so-called 'boat people' — from their own increasingly repressive regime at home, and south-east Asia was now awash with homeless and destitute people whom no one seemed to want. When western governments criticized them for their inhospitality towards the refugees, the Thais were quick to point out that no one else seemed very interested in them either. No further refugees from either Cambodia or Vietnam, announced the Thai prime minister, General Kriangsak Chamanand, would be allowed to enter Thailand, as 'we have too many already'. At this point, there were 350,000 Vietnamese boat people in camps in the Philippines, Malaysia, Singapore, Indonesia and Hong Kong as well as in Thailand itself. As a number of south-east Asian countries began to tow the boat people back out to sea, there was talk of another Evian Conference betrayal, when western countries, in July 1938, refused to offer homes to the German Jews.

Francis Amar is a neat, quiet man. In 1977 he had been sent as chief delegate to Thailand by the International Committee, where he had devoted his time to relief work with UNICEF and the tracing of people missing in the long struggles consuming the region. Like the other westerners who listened to the refugees' stories of Khmer Rouge brutality, Amar had trouble believing all he heard. Never, in all his years in the Red Cross, had he heard of such cruelty. Because Cambodia was so effectively sealed off from the rest of the world, there was no way of checking on the stories.

One morning, as Amar was sitting in his office in Bangkok, one of his local delegates on the Cambodia–Thailand border rang to tell him that he had heard that Thai soldiers were rounding up the refugees and putting them on to buses. What should he do? 'Follow them,' Amar told him. 'See where they are going.'

The countryside that surrounds these camps is flat. But not far away at Preah Vinear is a cliff marking the border between the two countries down which twists a steep and narrow path. At the bottom, in 1979, lay a minefield. The Thais, who had decided that they were no longer prepared to be overwhelmed by the growing numbers of arrivals, were taking some 40,000 of the refugees with the idea of pushing them down the steep path and back into Cambodia. The International Committee delegate, stopped by Thai soldiers five miles away, did not actually witness these events, but before long he heard descriptions of desperate people clambering and slipping down the path and into the minefield where children and women were being killed and maimed. Amar, following the events from Bangkok, issued a strong protest to the Thai government. The Thai prime minister responded as strongly, vigorously protesting against unwarranted foreign intrusion in domestic affairs. The International Committee, which had played this game before, announced that they would be pulling Amar out of Thailand and, in a mood of high public resentment and bitterness, flew him back to Geneva. Nothing happened. Political negotiations between the UN, western governments and aid agencies and Thailand multiplied. In no man's land, sandwiched between the cliff above, ringed by Thai guards, and the minefield ahead, the surviving refugees clustered, with little food or water.

Though the immediate crisis was overcome and arrangements made for this unhappy group, the exodus of refugees from Cambodia into Thailand continued. Some were so weak that they died on the border itself, or arrived so ill that there was nothing that anyone could do for them. On 17 September, delegates from the International Committee and UNICEF were allowed to make, once again in secret, a first journey to Khmer Rouge areas along the border. They returned horrified, reporting seeing hundreds of people suffering from cerebral malaria reduced to eating bark and bamboo shoots. By now journalists were filing stories on what was happening and on the apparent unwillingness of the International Committee or of UNICEF to commit proper funds and people to the emergency. The articles began to fill western papers, particularly as within Cambodia itself the relief programme still remained blocked. The visit to the dying Khmer Rouge, despite efforts to keep it secret, had been picked up and broadcast by the BBC, leading to fresh and angry complaints in Phnom Penh that the International Committee and UNICEF were now violating the sovereignty of the Cambodian government. While their stock sank, Oxfam's rose, as it continued to distribute relief on the Cambodian government's terms. Political pressures continued to dictate every move, as the UN insisted on upholding the Khmer Rouge as the legitimate government of Cambodia, against increasingly bitter challenges by the Soviet bloc and the Vietnamese.

None of this was the International Committee's fault. The political situation was at a stalemate. In Phnom Penh, the new government continued to insist that no aid should go to the Khmer Rouge and was bent on obstructing all deliveries of relief to its own citizens until these terms were met; while at the same time making public pronouncements about the generosity of non-governmental donors and gifts of aid from the eastern European bloc. In Bangkok, the Thais were appealing, with growing urgency, for a major rescue operation for the refugees on their borders, some of whom were known to be Khmer Rouge though most were innocent civilians caught in the civil war. Without proper help for all refugees, said the Thais, they would have no choice but to keep the border closed, condemning the starving refugees still struggling towards it to death. Negotiations had entered a seemingly intractable stage.

It was now that new players entered the game. Bugnion and Beaumont had proved tenacious negotiators, but the International Committee had other cards to play. By the autumn of 1979 Jean-Paul Hocké, the former car salesman recruited to help in the Biafran conflict, was director of operations for the International Committee. What Hocké, an able and ambitious man, had perceived in Biafra was that not everything was yet fixed in the modern humanitarian world and that there was still room for new ideas and new ways of doing things, even in an organization as apparently staid and rooted in tradition as the International Committee. Hocké was a realist. He knew instinctively that to be successful and to attract donors there was no choice but to court the media and think in global terms. While Bugnion and Beaumont kept up their pressure in Phnom Penh. Hocké set off on a series of lightning visits to the area, to Washington and to the UN in New York, where the secretary general, Kurt Waldheim, was busy trying to broker agreements with all sides. Hocké was good with the Americans. A tall, somewhat gangling figure with the round face of a pug dog and an easy, casual manner, he came across as powerful and effective. His English was good. His descriptions of starvation were terrifying. While in New York the newspapers continued to talk about genocide – Pilger's cry had been taken up, not only by Anthony Lewis, who wrote in the *New York Times* of another 'holocaust', but by Bugnion himself, who returned to Geneva comparing Cambodia to Buchenwald. The talking continued, repeatedly coming adrift under conflicting rumours, prematurely publicized deals and accusations that the international organizations were using humanitarian relief as a way of interfering in Cambodia's internal affairs. During repeated and anguished meetings, International Committee and UNICEF delegates kept on reminding listeners that their fundamental principles committed them to neutrality and that to agree not to feed one section of the victims could only create a dangerous precedent. Hocké is remembered by people who attended meetings with him at the time as a forceful and sometimes harsh negotiator, causing some to worry that he might go too far and alienate useful collaborators. When the rift with Oxfam was at its height, Hocké had no hesitation in describing the deal it had made with Heng Samrin as 'a catastrophic breach of a vital principle'.

In the end agreement was reached, whether because of Bugnion's transparent integrity, Beaumont's energy, Hocké's anger and drive or simply because deaths from starvation were believed to be growing all the time. On all sides, concessions were made. In Thailand, General Kriangsak Chamanand announced that he would relax his strict border policy and accept the proposed refugee programme, including the building of holding centres for what they insisted on calling 'illegal immigrants'. In Phnom Penh, on 14 October, Bugnion took part in a crucial four-hour meeting. Though it was almost brought to a disastrous close when the Cambodians referred to the package he was proposing as '*aide empoisonée,*' they agreed to the immediate start of an aid programme, as long as the question of feeding the Khmer Rouge would continue to be debated in future meetings.

The international humanitarian world now plunged into action. UNICEF had been declared lead agency in the UN relief programme by Waldheim – by the late 1970s relief had become a question of careful worldwide planning – and FAO and the World Food Programme agreed to find food and ship it to the area, calculated on the basis of '2,250,000 persons in danger of starvation'. With it were to go sixty doctors, 200 nurses, 200 midwives for thirty-five hospitals and 2,000 village clinics, specialized equipment for surgery and supplies for orphanages. Daily airlifts were begun from Bangkok. A country was going to be rebuilt, virtually from nothing. A 'land bridge' would be opened at two points on the border with Thailand, to deliver rice to thousands of Cambodians who would come from inside the country to collect it. As for the International Committee, it now became the organization formally responsible for medical assistance. On the border, UNICEF and the International Committee would organize a food and medical programme. On 5 November, Waldheim called a pledging conference in New York at which governments undertook to provide US$210 million in cash and kind. It was an emotional occasion. Jean-François Poncet, the French foreign minister, spoke of children 'who have only known a life of suffering'. Andrew Peacock, the Australian foreign minister, called Cambodia a disaster 'possibly without parallel in modern times'. No one was tactless enough to mention the cliffs of Preah Vinear.

The aid people and the doctors, finally allowed to move out into the Cambodian countryside, reported misery on a scale not seen since the end of the Second World War: no roads, no transport, no services, no trade; but, interestingly, no actual famine. Of Cambodia's 500 trained pre-war doctors, only fifty-five had survived. The rest had been slaughtered, together with most of Cambodia's professional and educated classes, the main target of Khmer Rouge genocidal policies. Apart from tuberculosis, dysentery and malnutrition, there were many people with acute eye problems: in order to avoid being branded as intellectuals and executed, those wearing glasses had thrown them away. In what seemed a remarkably brief period of time, trucks, medicines, pens and paper, blankets, toothbrushes, toys, blackboards, sewing machines, cloth and cotton thread, fork-lift trucks, road builders and mosquito nets were pouring into Cambodia. Guy Stringer of Oxfam, somewhat embarrassed by his organization's earlier stand with its assumption that UNICEF and the International Committee would be obliged to pull out altogether, leaving them as main co-ordinating agency of the non-governmental consortium, apologized to Bugnion and turned his attention to exploring the possibilities of Oxfam's traditional work in development, now that others would be coping with the emergency. As a token of apology, Oxfam gave the joint mission a Landrover.

Nothing was ever said in a formal way about feeding the Khmer Rouge and it was tacitly understood that relief would go to all victims of the conflict without discrimination. The deal had proved as tough to conclude as any in the International Committee's recent history.

On the border, the refugees were sinking ever deeper into mud and misery. Those who continued to stagger and stumble over the border were sick, frightened and near death. With agreement over a co-ordinated relief programme at last reached, the international agencies, helped by a vast number of other non-governmental organizations, began trying to make their lives bearable. It was to be a muddled, costly and bitter process.

The border was now open and Thailand declared that it was willing to accept more refugees in two categories. There would be the 'illegal immigrants', to be placed in 'holding centres' under UNHCR supervision, and there would be the rest, in sprawling, ungovernable camps under the direct control of the various Kampuchean factions. These refugees were given no particular name.

UNHCR officials found themselves faced by the almost unbelievable task of creating camps for vast numbers of destitute people at great speed out of fields and bogs. There were very few roads or tracks and, though it continued to rain hard through October, no water. The aid agencies joined forces to buy water tanks, set up purifying systems, order bamboo and thatch, rope, mats, baby bottles. Few of the young men drafted in had any experience of building. From Bangkok foreigners came to volunteer their services. In one week alone, over 4 million litres of water were delivered to the area.

The Thais had asked the International Committee to co-ordinate medical relief. Like every other organization in this politically charged and chaotic conflict, they were ill-prepared. The condition of the new refugees crawling over the border was pitiful and some had to be abandoned to die there. A tent serving as a clinic in one camp collapsed in the monsoon rains and patients lying on straw mats in the mud were drowned. Once again the stories reaching the West were highly critical of the International Committee's performance: the Swiss were accused of turning away offers of doctors and nurses at the very moment when desperate refugees were clamouring for more medical assistance, and of refusing to accept outside estimates of the numbers of people requiring aid. After the International Committee spurned the offers of several planeloads of doctors landing in Bangkok, on the grounds that they had enough of their own, Médécins Sans Frontières spoke openly of 'imperialist behaviour' and 'humanitarian protectionism'. The Committee was furious and hit back.

Sa Kaeo, a camp forty miles from the border, became a byword for inefficiency. American experts advised the International Committee to build a hospital with 2,000 beds: the Committee put up one with 500; 3,000 were eventually needed. Drains and latrines became swamps in the torrential rain and under the ever-growing numbers of sick people. 'I have not seen a situation as humanly degrading as exists in Sa Kaeo,' wrote one relief officer. 'There isn't the remotest vestige of privacy as men, women and children defecate in full view of and within feet of the camp areas . . .' All through October, thirty people were said to be dying every day in the camp. Loud protests were heard again. Morton Abramowitz, America's ambassador to Bangkok, became a vociferous critic of the relief work, bombarding Geneva and Washington with telegrams about the inefficiency of both the International Committee and UNICEF. The Committee, he stated in one cable, was 'clearly remiss in anticipating needs', while UNICEF had 'played its usual belated-catch-up role'. The word genocide continued to make headlines and US President Jimmy Carter, despatching his wife Rosalyn to the border where she was photographed among dying refugees, called the Khmer Rouge the 'world's worst violators of human rights'.

Food, produced and delivered by the relief organizations, had rapidly become power in the hands of the different Khmer groups, some of whom were now running the camps under their own warlords with a grip of iron. No one was able to calculate precisely how many people were actually in the border area − some estimates put it at between 600,000 and 700,000. There were rumours that the food was being sold to Thai entrepreneurs, who sold it back to the World Food Programme. In a camp at Mak Monn, a man working for UNICEF worked out that eighty-four per cent of the food being delivered never reached the hungry people.

At the end of 1979, there were thirty-seven foreign agencies working along the border. By now the International Committee had issued an appeal for help and hundreds of foreign doctors and medical people arrived in Thailand, bringing with them every conceivable kind of drug and surgical technique. Many knew a great deal about medicine but nothing at all about refugees. While the American doctors pushed sophisticated and highly elaborate surgery and the missionary doctors invoked the help of God, the International Committee medical teams, desperately trying to maintain some kind of uniformity of service, urged more public health programmes and more reliance on traditional local remedies, mindful that soon the western doctors would be gone and that the local Thais could not but resent the preferential treatment going to the refugees. They were right: there were angry articles in Thai papers. Time was spent quietening the sometimes bossy Americans and repelling the help of organizations like the La Lèche League, who wanted to send lactating mothers to suckle the orphaned Cambodian babies. Once the worst effects of hunger and disease had been controlled, many of the refugees were found to be suffering from mental disorders, which they ascribed to forms of possession. Dr J. P. Hiegel, one of the International Committee's delegates, had studied psychiatry, and tried to set up medical programmes which combined western remedies with the services of traditional healers.

Within Cambodia itself, the relief organizations were fighting the same sort of confusion and apathy, attempting to impose some kind of order and structure in a country without electricity, telephones, roads or clean water, and where the educated classes were mostly dead, against a backdrop of increasing numbers of foreign visitors, come to report, advise, assist or simply look. Political rivalries between Cambodian ministries had to be understood and pandered to, and patience kept when they continually changed their minds. The many small organizations differed enormously in their methods and approaches, sometimes saying one thing while doing another. Cracks now appeared in the relationship between the International Committee and UNICEF, with the Committee accusing UNICEF of being too weak, and UNICEF claiming that the Committee was too confrontational. And though the deal with the Cambodians had apparently been accepted, it was not until 17 November, four months and many deaths after the day in July when Bugnion and Beaumont looked out of the window of their aeroplane at the deserted landscape below, that the Cambodian Foreign Ministry finally approved the aid package. Even then, Phnom Penh remained a city beset by rumours of impending famine and of supplies looted by the Vietnamese. While politicians discussed the implications of leaving nearly a quarter of a million refugees on the border as potential recruits for the hastily rearming Khmer Rouge, newspaper reporters continued to write about hunger. Oxfam's poster from Cambodia linked it to the Nazi death camps.

The massive relief operation creaked on. In Phnom Penh itself the aid workers continued to be kept away from ordinary Cambodians, segregated in a special hotel, while the Vietnamese seemed to be tightening their control on the country, complaining bitterly at the way that the UN continued to refuse to recognize the new government as the legitimate rulers of the country. With definite news of progress hard to come by and rumours that the food intended for starving villagers was making its way into the stomachs of city civil servants, came more protests from foreign donors about waste and incompetence.

In April 1980, the agencies announced that the present system of food delivery was 'catastrophic'. All the vast shipments of food were doing was keeping people barely alive, while a drought had hit local rice production and local stocks had almost totally disappeared. What was needed now, in order to keep people from leaving their villages, was to rebuild and extend agricultural production, a vast and ambitious proposal in a country in which the draught animals were all dead, the tractors, ploughs and tools gone, the irrigation dykes and canals collapsed, and where all but five agricultural technicians had been killed. Hocké and Jim Grant of UNICEF flew to Phnom Penh for more discussions, hoping to persuade the Cambodians to make helpful arrangements; they had little success.

None of the decisions made in this long and miserable saga was without difficulties, but the resowing of Cambodia brought friction to almost the entire range of actors involved. Just the same, experts did arrive to draw up plans for the delivery of rice seed and fertilizer, and for the repairing of the irrigation system. Fund raising efforts redoubled. After the jetty at Phnom Penh collapsed, causing a severe blockage in deliveries, an airlift was arranged and on 4 April the first flight of 3,000 tonnes of rice seed reached the country. Even the unco-operative authorities in Phnom Penh rose to the urgency of the situation, and a steady stream of ox carts taking seed from vessels and planes to outlying villages could be seen plodding along every road.

Distribution was further speeded up by the arrival of 1,000 trucks under the Joint Mission and more from the Oxfam consortium. Tug boats and barges arrived: then ferry boats. Roads were mended. By September 1980, just a year after the start of the emergency, prospects for the future of Cambodia looked reasonable. Those who had grimly predicted two-and-a-quarter million dead of starvation were now forced to admit that the famine, as in Biafra not so long before, had not been nearly as dire as predicted. Food had been distributed in vast quantities, but certainly not enough to have saved all from starvation, a fact which reinforced the feeling that the early visitors had been too easily led astray by their emotions and too ignorant about Cambodia's fertile land.

* * *

On the border, too, there had been progress. In the camps that now resembled precarious small towns — there were 125,000 refugees in the holding centre of Khao I Dang alone — people were at last no longer dying. They were, on the other hand, fighting. Food had become an important form of currency, with different Khmer factions looting supplies to sell on the black market or back across the border into Cambodia. Smuggling had become a way of life and there were stretches of the border where foreigners never ventured, and from where came stories of secret police terror tactics, or forced night repatriations, of Khmer Rouge warlords continuing to carry out 'crimes against humanity'. With the Khmer Rouge still recognized by the UN as the legitimate government of Cambodia, there was very little that UNHCR could do. Scores were settled with guns and hand grenades and the Thai guards, summoned by the relief organizations to help, proved unable or unwilling to improve security along the border. There had been talk for some time now in UNHCR circles of 'voluntary repatriations', but it was generally in private and not many of the refugees were believed to be willing to contemplate going home. The International Committee delegates, getting wind of what was being proposed, reacted fiercely: remembering the horrors of the cliff at Preah Vinear they announced that they would have nothing to do with any such plans and that they were far from sure that the conditions in Cambodia were such as to 'guarantee the safety and physical integrity' of anyone sent home — a stipulation under the Convention for refugees. As it turned out, very few refugees could be persuaded to go.

Then, on the night of 22 June, came an incident that triggered the end of the International Committee's central role in the area. Vietnamese forces, apparently in retaliation for the repatriations, attacked the camps and shelled a Red Cross hospital. The Thais and the Khmer Rouge fired back. In the crossfire, 400 refugees, scrambling for safety, were killed.

It was everything that the delegates had most feared. Regular distribution of food was now halted, while new criteria for the safety of civilians and relief workers were drawn up. It was agreed that the camps found to be entirely controlled by Khmer Rouge military cadres would no longer be provided with supplies, not least because they infringed the fundamental rules for humanitarian operations. UNICEF decided that it would henceforth distribute food only to children under sixteen and to women. The International Committee, while retaining its medical commitments, announced that it would be pulling out of food distribution altogether. Hocké had long been mistrustful of all association with the Khmer Rouge. And there were fears within the International Committee that the partnership with UNICEF was outliving its usefulness, the Committee feeling itself to be moving too far in the direction of development, UNICEF too much into crises. In any case, Kampuchea was shakily getting back on its feet and at least some of the refugees had gone home. The emergency, under the International Committee's mandate, was over even if not for the 160,000 or so remaining refugees, precariously clinging on in the ramshackle border camps, caught between opposing political forces. Though their official role as partner in the Joint Mission had formally ended, delegates from the Committee would not actually leave the area for many years, returning again and again as fighting broke out in the camps.

At the end of 1981, when the Cambodian operation was largely over, people settled down to look at figures. Over $600 million had been spent on relief, most of it donated by governments. The voluntary agencies had given another $100 million. In terms of money spent per head, it had been the largest relief operation the world had ever seen.

Humanitarian aid programmes are notoriously difficult to evaluate. Even Oxfam, which is scrupulous about evaluation, had great difficulty analysing precisely where the money had gone and how well and efficiently it had been spent. Oxfam emerged uneasy from Cambodia: there were those who said that it had acted precipitately and naively, and made too many predictions and too many concessions too quickly. An internal UNICEF investigation turned out to be so critical of the organization's performance that it was rapidly shelved. Among donors and public alike there were laments that there had not been better and more harmonious co-operation between the many who came to help, advise, feed and rebuild Cambodia. Not one of the organizations, in a conflict more politically tricky and more destructive even than Biafra, came out of the Cambodian operation unmarked. The delivery of relief had been for the most part chaotic, ill-organized and unco-ordinated, with the numbers of victims sometimes under- and sometimes overestimated, depending on who was counting and where. Politics had intruded at every turn.

The International Committee and UNICEF between them had spent just over $13m on health inside Cambodia during the months of their Joint Mission. When experts from FAO visited the country in 1983, they were not impressed. The health system, they reported, was 'disastrous'. In Phnom Penh there were water shortages, supplies of drugs were running low and there were not enough doctors. William Shawcross, in *The Quality of Mercy*, his fine book about the Cambodian conflict, reserves some of his more pessimistic remarks for the work of the International Committee. Inside Cambodia, he writes, the Committee was not only prevented from providing decent medical care but thwarted at every turn in their efforts to visit prisoners-of-war or political detainees, both by the Vietnamese when they invaded Cambodia in 1978 and by Heng Samrin. On the border they had fared little better, ultimately proving incapable of protecting the civilians who remained in no-man's land surrounded by minefields and at the mercy of the armed factions who ran the camps.

The International Committee does not view its own record so bleakly. Despite formidable odds, it had managed to put together and run a relief operation of unprecedented size. There was no question in anyone's mind that they had saved many thousands of lives, even if Hocké came to believe that the presence of so many humanitarian organizations in Cambodia may have achieved most by simply being symbolic of international concern. In the process the International Committee had turned into a new animal, the outline of which had been drawn in Biafra. It now had delegates who knew a very great deal about how to deliver relief in contradictory, emotionally charged circumstances where even the most primitive forms of transport are missing and no one agrees on who is entitled to food. From now on there would be few who did not accept that it had become, in fact as in law, a quasi-public authority.

Between 1979 and 1982, four million people and forty-five countries engaged in conflict. In 1978, the International Committee had eighteen delegations, scattered in various parts of the world. In 1983, it had thirty-six, a reflection not only of its commitments in south-east Asia, but of the growing demand for humanitarian intervention in a world constantly at war. What was more, it had been through a painful lesson on the difficulties of maintaining an impartial stand and on the pitfalls that lie along all roads in which political objectives and humanitarian actions are inextricably entwined. It had tested the uncertain waters of collaboration and found that these were not as unpleasant as they feared; it had also learnt about the need for accountability to donors, now that competition for money had come to dominate the relief world, and the importance of diplomacy and tact. 'We all learned this,' says Charles Egger, deputy director of the UNICEF programme during the Cambodian conflict. 'That how you negotiate is crucial, and that finesse, attention to form, and not bullying, tend to yield the best dividends.' It was during the long dinners that followed the negotiations with the Cambodian ministers that Egger understood the role played by manners and subtlety in humanitarian matters. 'In all our operational history,' said one high-ranking International Committee delegate in 1992, 'no other event has been as important. It was our turning point, and we are still living it today.'

In Geneva Jean-Paul Hocké — regarded by many as the architect of this new International Committee — was by now firmly in charge of operations, and operations for Hocké were essentially a mixture of protection and assistance, the assistance being the often necessary link into protection. To come to the help of people, you had to feed them first. Not everyone admired or liked the more professional, more glossy, more media conscious, more internationally-minded Red Cross, and a number of older delegates, who preferred the quieter ways of the old organization, slipped away. There were plenty of candidates to take their place. For them, Hocké was a hero. He had, believes Shawcross, been 'one of the most effective of all the aid officials who came to deal with Cambodia'.

And Cambodia had done something else. The horrors of Biafra could, just, be passed off as a unique and ghastly event. After Cambodia, it was clear to everyone that this kind of conflict — messy, bloody, political, with no clear frontiers and no easily identifiable enemies, in which civilians were slaughtered almost casually — would be the shape of things to come. Cambodia had also again brought to light, as the civil war in Nigeria had done, one of the most fundamental problems facing the International Committee: that of reconciling its duty to help all victims of war with obeying its mandate to respect sovereignty, of identifying a comprehensible and positive role for itself that was both faithful to its origins and yet able to cope with the grim demands of modern war.

When President Hay reviewed the activities of the International

Committee early in 1982, he spoke not of achievements but of failures
— the failure to visit and protect the victims of war in Afghanistan, to
monitor and assist during the fighting in the Western Sahara, to trace
people missing in Somalia and in the Ogaden, and to visit prisoners-of-
war in Eritrea. Preoccupation with failure, the need to evaluate constantly
and to anticipate the form and needs of future emergencies had become
part of the International Committee's daily life.

Among the Khmer straggling over the border into Thailand, day after
day, were thousands who had been separated from their families. Many
of these were children. Remembering 1945, when photographs of lost
children appeared on hoardings across liberated Europe, the International
Committee delegates interviewed and took pictures of those they termed
'unaccompanied minors'. Soon, all along the border, could be seen
posters covered in photographs; crowded in front of them were parents,
who came across from Cambodia to search for their lost children. Tracing
had long been one of the International Committee's most successful
activities; within months, almost half the children had found relations.
By the end of February 1981, the Tracing Agency in Bangkok had handled
45,000 enquiries. Delegates went on interviewing, visiting orphanages,
advertising.

In Cambodia itself, however, they made almost no progress. The new
Cambodian authorities did not want delegates roaming the countryside
asking questions. Since files and documents had disappeared under
Khmer rule, gone in the general destruction of the country's past, there
was very little that could be done to trace either the missing or the
dead, vanished during the years of Cambodia's isolation. Xuan was a
Cambodian woman whom the delegates tried very hard to help. Her
story says much about the enormous difficulties the International Committee now faced.

Xuan is Vietnamese, but she was born in Cambodia. She studied in
France, married a Frenchman and had two daughters. In 1957 she went
back to settle in Phnom Penh where, with her excellent French, she had
no trouble finding a job with the local International Committee delegation. Xuan's parents ran a restaurant and rickshaw business and
the family prospered. When her French husband died, Xuan married a

Cambodian and had four sons. Because she was a French national, the children took French nationality.

At six o'clock on the morning of 17 April 1974, Xuan woke to the sound of rockets: the Khmer Rouge were closing in on the city. She took her five children — her eldest daughter was studying in France — and with her husband sought refuge in the French embassy, together with hundreds of other frantic diplomats and Cambodians with foreign papers. On 20 April, the Khmer Rouge ordered all Cambodians to leave the embassy. Xuan had good friends in the foreign community and among the French but no one could be persuaded to issue her husband with the necessary papers. Once the boys announced that they wanted to stay with their father. Xuan had no choice but to stay as well. 'We left the embassy in tears,' she remembers.

Xuan's daughter was seventeen. It was decided that, with a French father, she would be safer with the French. What her mother was not to know was that when the French pulled out soon afterwards, they would leave her behind, and that the Khmer Rouge would quickly dismiss her as 'déracinée', rootless.

Xuan, her husband and the four boys joined the exodus from Phnom Penh, hounded by Khmer soldiers. They were almost the last to leave. The streets, she says, were already deserted and silent. They took the river road. They had been told where to go and for the next month they kept walking, driven by soldiers and sleeping under trees. The rice they had taken with them was soon finished. The boys, aged eight, nine, twelve and fourteen, were always hungry. One day they met a peasant who had just killed his last cow. He offered them a meal that cost as much as a government minister's salary for an entire year.

The Khmer gave them a small plot of land, on which Xuan's husband put up a shack. Xuan wove a roof out of bamboo. The boys went to work in the fields. That year the rice harvest was excellent, but just before it was due to be gathered, the family was ordered to move on again, to a more barren spot. This time the roads they walked along were covered with dead bodies. From time to time, they came across people they had known in Phnom Penh. By now a dog, large enough to feed a family for several days, cost an ounce of gold. The weeds from the river, their main source of food, gave the boys colic.

From this moment on, Xuan's life descended into a nightmare of endurance. The second boy sickened and eventually died. She was herself constantly ill. When Khmer Rouge soldiers arrived to ask why she was not working, they tried to trick her into admitting that she had been among the educated classes, by asking her questions in foreign languages. She told them she had sold bananas in Phnom Penh's market.

The youngest boy fell ill. She was in hospital with him when news came that her husband was dying. She arrived to find him unconscious, a small wound on his foot having gone septic. He died, she says, of starvation and despair. Her remaining middle son now caught beri-beri; the eldest went off to look for work and food further afield. One night, the eight-year-old, desperate with hunger, crept away to see what he could find. The soldiers brought him back unrecognizable, his back scraped raw by lashes. He lived, but four days before the Vietnamese soldiers arrived and rescued them, the boy with beri-beri died.

Xuan survived. She returned to Phnom Penh by lorry with one son and began to search for her eldest boy and for the daughter who had stayed with the French. She had friends among the new International Committee delegates did all they could to help her trace her missing children. Xuan herself searched, asked friends who had survived, checked lists. Her daughter was found; the girl's hair had gone totally white. She never heard of her eldest son again.

In 1979, Xuan and her two surviving children left Cambodia for Switzerland, where they settled and she joined the Central Tracing Agency in Geneva to work on Cambodian cases. Thirty people, right through the early 1980s, were kept employed full time, just on Cambodia, and Xuan stayed on. Three and a half million Cambodians had died in the fighting, famine and killings; ten years later, there were people still searching for those they had lost.

When Muriel Monkhouse, the British Red Cross volunteer, joined the foreign relations department in June 1940, soon after the fall of France, the idea that tracing might become a major activity for the national societies was entirely new. In Geneva, the painstaking sifting of spellings and records was nearly as old as the International Committee itself, born with Dunant on the battlefield of Solferino when he realized that the psychological anguish of not knowing what had happened to a relation could be more painful than any physical wound. As everyone in the Red Cross had long said, and repeated at international gatherings, the unity of the family was one of the 'loftiest and most generally accepted of mankind's fundamental rights', and tracing was a natural part of all Red Cross work, whether in peace or war. All this, Muriel Monkhouse knew and appreciated. What neither she nor anyone else could have known was that the nature of modern conflict would make tracing one of the Red Cross's most time-consuming and most important activities.

As the waves of lost people caused by the Second World War began to settle towards the end of the 1940s, the tracers wondered how long they would still be needed. The answer, as it turned out, was for ever and in ever greater numbers. Every war, every conflict, every major disaster, has parted people from their families, to add to those already missing from earlier disasters whose relations refuse to give up hope that they may still be alive. As the number of the missing kept rising, so the central agency urged national societies throughout the world to set up their own tracing services, co-ordinating them with Geneva. For some, like the German Red Cross, tracing proved a satisfying way of winning back respectability. Many people wait until near death to start searching for family members they have not thought about for years, by which time most traces have long since grown cold. Whenever there is an anniversary, a commemoration of a military victory, people still write asking for help in contacting relations they have neither seen nor heard of since 1939, not knowing having finally become more painful than certainty of death.

In 1956, a Hungarian refugee from Budapest called Nicholas Vecsey arrived in Geneva. Within a week he found a job with the International Committee trying to make sense of the 200,000 Hungarian enquiries about people lost in the revolution. He stayed thirty-five years, retiring not long ago to a house by the lake where he continues to act for the Hungarian Red Cross. In 1944 his sister worked for Friedrich Born, the delegate who tried so hard to save Hungary's Jews.

Vecsey turned out to be a gifted tracer, scrupulous, patient and dogged. It was he who first realized that centralized tracing from Geneva is all very well but that you need people working in the field during conflicts, collecting information on the spot, and he who began training specialized tracers who now make up an important element in many foreign missions. Over a period of ten years, he helped national societies set up their own tracing services, taught them how to co-ordinate with other services, produced a manual which became the Bible of the tracing world and made good links with UNHCR and other agencies. Vecsey worked in Biafra, where he travelled in planes delivering dried fish; in Jordan, where he was helped by twelve French-speaking nuns; in East Pakistan, Malaysia and with the Vietnamese boat people. Everywhere he went he realized how it helped to have been a refugee himself. 'One of the most passionate and important parts of my life,' he says,

> was talking to these people, hearing their stories. Only I, as a refugee, could understand that part of the condition of being a refugee was to look forward, to be positive, and that looking for people they had lost and had to believe would be found was part of that process.

It was after the exodus of the Vietnamese boat people, with hundreds of thousands of refugees scattered across a dozen countries and searching for someone they had lost, that he persuaded the International Committee to invest in a computer. Today, all missing people are recorded on this computer, which sifts through all possible spellings at a speed not dreamed of by the ladies in their neat hats who once sat at trestle tables in wartime Geneva. Yet Vecsey can't help wondering sometimes whether something hasn't been lost, whether the tidy and painstaking ladies mightn't have gone just that little bit further, given just that final check, that last attempt to replace a z with an s, or pondered whether an e might not be more likely than the a.

In the 1970s a new twist was added to the search for the missing, connected with a tactic that was fast becoming fashionable among the military dictators of Latin America: the 'disappearing' of unwanted people. Like the Nazis with their *Nacht und Nebel* decree, the Latin American soldiers had perceived that great power lay in making people 'disappear' and that families and entire communities could thereby be reduced to a paralysis of fear and obedience. The *desparacidos* of Uruguay and Argentina. Colombia and Brazil, have come to haunt modern times, as have the photographs of the mothers and grandmothers of the disappeared, whose mournful ritual of witness on Saturday mornings in Buenos Aires, at the Plaza de Mayo, has been copied by the families of those disappeared in Turkey's dirty war against the Kurds. 'Disappearing' people presented the International Committee with a new challenge, and it was among its delegates that the tracing of the lost began.

On 11 September 1973, General Augusto Pinochet led the Chilean armed forces in an attack against the presidential palace in Santiago and set up a military junta. Salvador Allende, the first democratically elected Marxist head of state, was killed. The first International Committee men on the scene were a doctor and a general delegate: they arrived to find 5,000 people locked up in Santiago's stadium and a growing list of people no one could find.

For a few days, everything seemed possible. Pinochet had taken power loudly reaffirming Chile's commitments under the Geneva Conventions, and there was no reason to fear complications.

Massimo Cataldi had joined the International Committee in the mid 1960s. He comes from the Italian part of Switzerland, a short, stocky, good-humoured man whose first language remains Italian, but his ease with languages, like that of all good delegates, is enviable. By December 1973, he was in Santiago, where his fluent Spanish made his job of drawing up lists of prisoners and searching the country for those who had so mysteriously vanished somewhat easier. It took him a few days to understand that something peculiar was going on.

> Why did Pinochet let us in? It was a mistake. He had decided to call Allende's supporters 'prisoners-of-war' − and under the Geneva Conventions we therefore had a right to be there. Then he discovered that had he called them 'political detainees' he could in theory have kept us out − but he needed to look good in the eyes of the world, and in any case, by then we were already there.
>
> We were amateurs then. We didn't know about 'disappearing' people, but we quickly learnt. We started drawing up names of missing people: families queued round and round our office building, day after day. There were soon so many that I could only see them in groups of 20. They filled in forms. Bit by bit, we had a list. Delegates travelled up and down the country. The

lists grew longer. For three months I worked all day, every day, until night fell and the curfew started. There was no time even to eat. There were always people waiting to see me.

Little by little, we got into most prisons. Some they told us about. Some we found for ourselves. They moved the prisoners all the time, to confuse us: we followed closely behind, making new lists, drawing up new cards. Sometimes prison directors denied that they were holding anyone. We insisted on seeing the cells and when we got there we never found anyone there, but we would see cigarette butts still burning on the floor. When we asked our drivers if they had seen anything, they would say that a refrigerator truck had just driven off at great speed. We protested to the authorities, again and again.

Once we knew who we were looking for, and whom to ask for, then at last 'disappearances' started to go down. They still used tricks against us, getting people to pretend to be those who were meant to be missing, but we learnt those too. We realized the importance of speed, the fact that once someone had been located then it is far harder for the military to 'disappear' them. The trick is to find them very quickly indeed after they have been taken.

The 'disappeared' were not Cataldi's only responsibility. Allende had given a home in Chile to some 12,000 people he called *amigos personales*, refugees from other parts of Latin America. Pinochet announced that they were no longer welcome. Thousands took refuge in the embassies, where the International Committee tried to sort out papers for them.

But the 'disappeared' were the cases that tormented him. After many months he had a list of over a thousand names, but knew that there were probably many others not accounted for, whose families were too frightened to come forward. On a return visit to Santiago, he set about checking. Some of the addresses he visited had been taken over by military families. At others he found people terrified to see him who begged him to go away. And in the end, once the sums had been done again and again, there were 650 names left on his list, those of people who had never turned up. Pinochet's new men stopped making excuses. They no longer denied the existence of such people. 'They said: it's normal. It happens everywhere.' Later, mass graves were found, in ditches, in ponds; later, too, 'disappearances' spread to Argentina, where the military rulers found the tactic useful in curbing resisters and where the numbers of those never found far exceeded the lost in Chile. 'But Chile,' says Massimo Cataldi, 'is the place where we learnt our trade.'

The last episode in the modern history of the International Committee and its tracing activity involves the longest of all modern wars, and one in which the Geneva Conventions were ruthlessly and systematically flouted. That the Committee and its delegates worked so hard is a tribute to their energy and determination. But for those who believed in the power of humanitarian laws, this conflict was both singularly depressing and something of a warning of things to come.

The International Committee already had a presence in Iran when, in September 1980, Saddam Hussein ripped up an agreement signed with the Shah over the Shatt al-Arab waterway at the head of the Gulf, declared it an Iraqi national river, and invaded Iranian territory. The Committee's delegates had been visiting the Shah's prisons and protesting at the violence used by the secret police, Savak, to extract information and false confessions. With the overthrow of the Shah in January 1979, all this now faded into the background as Ayatollah Khomeini's radical theocracy, based on Islamic Shi'ite fundamentalism, went to war against Saddam Hussein's nationalist Ba'ath government. Enmity between the countries went back to ancient rivalries and boundary disputes between the Ottoman Empire and Persia. The war between Iraq and Iran would be long, costly and murderous. At the height of the fighting, Iran would lose men at the same rate as the French and British losses in the First World War.

For a while at least, International Committee delegates were able to convince themselves that they would be allowed to practise their traditional wartime duties. There was something reassuringly open and above-board about the structure of this classic and conventional war, something few delegates had experienced in recent years. Though the various rules for preventing the outbreak of war or bringing it to a speedy end failed, there was nothing as yet in the air to suggest that the Red Cross role of 'neutral intermediary between the belligerents for all humanitarian questions' would not be honoured. Indeed, by mid-October, delegates were hard at work registering names of prisoners-of-war on both sides, undertaking searches, writing up reports and organizing family reunions and even the repatriation of the severely wounded. From the first, the numbers involved were vast; 45,000 Iraqis alone had been taken prisoner by the end of the second year of the war.

Any feeling of complacency soon vanished. True, both sides had signed the Geneva Conventions. But, as now became horribly clear, neither had the slightest intention of adhering to them. Before the war was a year old, both Iran and Iraq were concealing large numbers of prisoners, refusing access to camps, failing either to register all prisoners or to allow delegates to do so, executing captive soldiers, leaving enemy wounded on the battlefield and bombing towns and villages full of civilians. The Iraqis were said to be intimidating, torturing and then murdering their prisoners; the Iranians to be brainwashing theirs, coercing them into religious conversion in keeping with the promises made by Ayatollah Khomeini that he would carry the Shi'ite revolution throughout the Arab world. During this long war, the Committee would utter three of its rare public protests, taking a higher profile than it had done in many recent conflicts and condemning both sides for grave and unceasing violations. None touched a chord with the belligerents. From now until the end of the fighting, it would be a war of sudden attacks and stalemates, of concessions made only to be withdrawn, of tolerable relations rapidly replaced by vitriolic accusations.

In the years leading up to the war, Iraq had spent many millions of dollars on chemical production equipment. Its chemical plant at Samarra, north of Baghdad, had been busy turning out products for industry — but also thiodiglycol for mustard gas and phosphorus trichloride for nerve agents. In November 1983, Iran reported to the UN Security Council that its troops were returning from the front with wounds of a clearly chemical nature. By March 1984, casualties of this kind were growing rapidly. Iran sent human waves to the front: Iraqi forces were built only for mobile desert warfare. Chemicals were seen by the Iraqis as an antidote to these massed men, a way to redress the uneven balance, particularly as the Iranians were slow to issue protective clothing and, when it arrived, it proved ill-fitting due to the beards worn by their soldiers. When a medical mission arrived in Iran from the International Committee that spring, it reported seeing 500 soldiers with unmistakable chemical wounds.

Both Iraq and Iran had ratified the 1925 Geneva protocol on chemical weapons, but there was very little that anyone could do, beyond protest – which was what President Alexander Hay repeatedly did. It had little or no effect. The war was turning out to be more than ordinarily ugly. By now the International Committee had sixteen delegates in Iraq and fifteen in Iran. Reviewing his eleven years in office in 1987, Hay would describe a world in which there was an ever-growing gap between intentions expressed by states and their actual behaviour.

There was another group of missing people for whom the accumulated powers of the entire Tracing Service would prove powerless. To understand its complexity, one has to go back a little in time.

In March 1980, six months before the outbreak of the war, Saddam Hussein had sent out invitations to 1,400 leading Iraqi citizens, asking them to attend a discussion on the country's economic future. There was to be a reception afterwards in honour of a Ba'ath party anniversary and the guests were invited to dress formally. Eight hundred and fifty of those invited turned up. When the meeting was over, they were put on to buses which took them, not to a party, but to the Iraqi secret service headquarters. Here they were questioned about their families, friends and contacts, before being put back on to the buses and driven to the frontier with Iran, where they were deported. Their homes, possessions, valuables and documents were confiscated. The 550 people who had failed to attend the meeting were rounded up next day. For Saddam Hussein, this was another step in the on-going expulsion of all those with some distant Iranian religious or family affiliation, people from Iraq's many varied backgrounds whom he wished to be rid of in the months leading up to a war he had long been planning. To make quite certain there would be no fuss, he took the precaution of detaining at least one member of every deported family, to hold as hostage.

Most of these hostages were young men; none was under sixteen or over forty. A few were released within a few weeks and then deported; others, once the war broke out, were sent to the front and never heard of again. But one group, made up of doctors, lawyers, university lecturers and teachers, were labelled 'Iranian dissidents', and for these men, Saddam Hussein had other plans.

Kamal Ketuly is a research chemist, who came to Glasgow from Baghdad in the late 1970s. He was one of nine children, and his father was one of Saddam Hussein's deportees. In October 1980, not long after the beginning of the war, Ketuly received a telephone call telling him his parents had been granted asylum in Sweden. The family was now scattered: Ketuly in Scotland, part of the family in Sweden, a few members in Iran and the rest leading precarious lives in Iraq.

Not long after the family had been deported from Baghdad, Ketuly's younger brother Jamal came home on leave from military service to find the house boarded up. He heard what had happened from an aunt. While he was still trying to work out what he should do, he was arrested by the security services. They took him to Abu Ghraib, a prison infamous for its barbaric conditions. From time to time, news of him was smuggled out to the West. Then, one day in 1984, it stopped.

In Sweden, Ketuly's mother found the silence unbearable. She became deeply depressed and then developed leukaemia which killed her in April 1984. One of Ketuly's younger sisters, who had gone with her parents to Sweden, took her mother's death very hard. Three weeks after the funeral she killed herself, leaving a note: 'Every year,' she wrote, 'we say that next year will be better, and that we can all go home as a family, and that our brother will be released. This can no longer happen.' She was twenty years old. Not long after Ketuly's grandmother, worn down by worry and misery, had a heart attack and died, and his father contracted diabetes and had both his legs amputated.

The deportations and the taking of hostages did not stop with the outbreak of the war. They went on until 1987, in ones and twos, plunging more families into anguish and uncertainty. In Glasgow, Ketuly set up a centre for the missing people of Iraq, an office from where he lobbies members of parliament, the United Nations and the International Committee. Other exiled Iraqis have come to settle in Scotland, where they keep up a lonely vigil for the missing. There is a couple in their late fifties, the man a lawyer, the wife a former headmistress, who have seen eight of their relations taken as hostages. Three of them are her sister's sons, taken to Abu Ghraib on 21 March 1981. For the first few years, relations were allowed to take food and medicines to the prison once a month, queuing from long before dawn at the gates. In the spring of 1985, the brothers were moved to a camp in the desert. Here, conditions were better. A photograph taken of them during their stay shows three light-skinned pleasant young men, one with fair hair and green eyes, staring out with cheerful expressions.

In April 1986 an unexpected phone call from one of the young men told them that the brothers had been split up, that he himself had been moved to a training camp and would be given leave to visit them before very long. After that, he disappeared. Nothing has ever been heard of him again; nor of his brothers.

By then, the boys' parents were in Iran. Because their mother was so tormented by not knowing what had happened to them, the family felt that it was wiser to say nothing. That telephone call was the last sign that they were alive. They have decided to go on pretending that they still get news of the boys, that they are well, and that the day will come when they will be released. When the headmistress phones her sister in Iran, she gives her good news.

Then there is Hassam, a tall, earnest young man who was just thirteen, the seventh in a family of ten children living in some comfort in Baghdad, when the entire family, who had long been suspected of holding anti-government views, was arrested. They were given time only to pack suitcases. The war was four months old. After interrogation and six dirty, frightening and disagreeable months in prison, the family was sent on the long march across the border into Iran. Two brothers, aged twenty-six and twenty-four, were kept behind. They were seen once in Abu Ghraib. They, too, have disappeared.

The International Committee gives the same answer to all these people, and to the families of the 850 missing hostages Ketuly believes are somewhere in Iraq's jails: they do not know where they are and they have no way of finding out. Are they in fact dead? Ketuly does not think so. He feels that most are alive somewhere in Saddam Hussein's hidden dungeons and that with enough international pressure, and some luck, they will one day emerge. From time to time, he hears rumours, learns of drivers who were involved in the transfer of the hostages between the thirty or so prisons and camps where they are said to be held, and who can remember a name or two. Very occasionally, a mysterious little parcel arrives, with a tiny bag made of beads, in which the name of a hostage's mother has been delicately picked out. If they are ever found, will they still be recognizable? Some have been gone sixteen years.

The missing of the Iran–Iraq war are not confined to the hostages. When at last, through UN mediation, a ceasefire was agreed on 20 August 1988 and the International Committee embarked on the long, endlessly-postponed process of repatriation, the prisoners' 'right to be released' was again and again ignored. Neither side proved willing to repatriate 'without delay' the men they held. Not until he invaded Kuwait in 1990 did Saddam Hussein, needing Iran's support in the Gulf War, suddenly declare that the process would receive priority. By 1997 the men were still not home and month after month the International Committee continues to labour for their release. Promises are made and quickly broken. The politics of the situation, a complicated calculation involving the date on which the war is considered to have started and the numbers either side will admit to having killed, has meant that thousands of men remain unaccounted for. Some are known to have decided to stay in Iran; others are believed to be held under labels other than that of prisoner-of-war and do not therefore fall so neatly under the Geneva Conventions.

The Iraq–Iran war lasted nearly as long as both world wars together. It was a total war marked by some of the most vicious exchanges of modern times, including attacks on cities, use of child soldiers and the deployment of chemical weapons. A million people, soldiers as well as civilians, are said to have died in a conflict that ended with no victory for either side, except for Saddam Hussein personally who emerged in an even stronger position. A hundred and fifty thousand men were taken prisoner. The Security Council proved unable to identify the aggressor, shorten the war, impose a ceasefire or achieve any respect for international humanitarian laws. In terms of material destruction, the cost of the war is said to have far exceeded the entire combined national debt of all Third World countries. In terms of law and justice, and respect for the rules of war, the conduct of both governments as well as their leaders and soldiers, it raised many questions about morality and responsibility. It was a war in which the existing laws did not work. The International Committee fought its own long and hard battle. As the months of captivity extended into years, one of the delegates' main jobs was to try to alleviate the crippling boredom of the prisoners by providing looms, carpentry tools and sports equipment, much as they had in the Second World War. During the ninety-eight months of fighting, the Committee handled 13 million family messages, an extraordinary feat of efficiency and possibly the most important of all its activities. As Massimo Cataldi puts it: 'There is no family in Iraq or Iran who does not know of us.'

But for the missing hostages, the young men gathered up by the Iraqi security services so long ago − neither criminals, nor prisoners-of-war, nor internees but innocent bystanders, plucked almost at random from their families − they have been able to do nothing.

Jean-Paul Hocké ran operations for the International Committee for twelve years. He became its dominant figure and, say former colleagues, under his 'enlightened dictatorship' the logistics of handling major programmes of relief and protection were vastly improved; the International Committee to this day is superb at reaching the scene of a conflict at impressive speed even if Red Cross operations are neither the cheapest nor always the most cost-effective. Under him the medical programme became considerably more important, though not always in a harmonious way, the doctors refusing to regard medicine as politics and Hocké sometimes seeming to regard it as a sweetener, a way of getting a toe-hold in countries with obstructive leaders. He was no intellectual, so his colleagues say, preferring to act rather than analyse the implications of different courses of action; and he was extraordinarily dedicated, with a direct style.

Under Hocké, the Committee itself lost some of its authority. He never made much effort to conceal a certain contempt for the co-opted great and good among Switzerland's oldest families whom he accused of lacking vision, of being unable to stand back, work out where the world was going and act as true leaders. In 1985, Hocké left to become UN High Commissioner for Refugees where he soon made enemies among those more accustomed to the prevaricating and conciliatory UN ways. 'I was one of many who was orphaned when he left,' said one of those who admired him and felt his departure to be a blow to the Committee's future. He would have stayed at the Red Cross, but Hay decided to stand for a third term as president; it is no secret that Hocké had long had his eye on the presidency, even though the only precedent for such a move from management to the president's chair was that of Léopold Boissier, a far-sighted man many regard as among the finest of the International Committee's post-war leaders.

Not all the success of those years, which saw the International Committee evolve from an enclosed, somewhat solitary organization – a law unto itself – into an internationally-minded, competitive and media-conscious body, and its staff triple in less than a decade, was due to Hocké alone. It owed much to Hay himself, a highly cultivated man, whose apparently easy-going manner acted as an effective counter-foil to the more powerful personalities within the higher ranks and who came to be regarded as a father figure, good at listening but firm, and capable of rising to heights of anger and moral indignation at the villainy of man. Jacques Moreillon, the clever and scholarly lawyer who made the history, doctrine and internal management of the Committee his responsibility, was also central to the change. Moreillon and Hocké were distantly related and shared a student past: they were known as the two 'consuls', not always affectionately. After Hocké left for the UN, Moreillon took up the new post of director-general, immediately below the president, but he soon left to run the World Scout Federation; he too, it is said, would have liked the job of president. There were those inside the organization who found him a little dictatorial, though the delegates liked the way that he seemed instinctively to know how to bring out the best in them. (There was a third influential man in the 1980s, Alain Modoux, who handled press and information, leading to the inevitable joke that the Red Cross was run by a Trinity, under God the Father.)

During the Hay, Hocké, Moreillon years, relations with the League continued as fragile and uneasy as they had always been, with considerably better co-operation in the field than in the political minefields of Geneva, not least because the inherent contradiction of having two such close and rivalrous organizations had grown more absurd as the distinctions between peacetime and wartime blurred. As the League had always known and Laurent Marti crudely spelled out, war is a more sensational event than any peacetime disaster, and its victims will always attract more money and more attention. With every one of the League's many operations along the margins of a conflict, there were members of the International Committee who muttered about encroachment and complained about the way the League no longer did what it was supposed to do — co-ordinate the national societies — but had turned itself into another voluntary organization. For their part, those who worked for the League found, and still find, the members of the International Committee arrogant. The rivalry still obsesses both sides, much as it did in the fractious days of the 1920s.

In the national societies, the long-simmering unease about independence and autonomy, the fuse of which had first been lit in the days of Nazi hegemony over the German Red Cross, finally boiled over at the twenty-fifth international conference held in Geneva in October 1986. International gatherings had notoriously been settings for acrimonious bickerings — the question of the two Chinas and the recognition of Taiwan had rent the movement for decades — but this was different. It was, all agreed afterwards, horribly political, led to a great deal of breast-beating and caused Hay to put on record that this ill-tempered quarrelling should not act as a precedent for the future.

A number of societies had long been restive about South Africa's apartheid policies. Only the most artful and tenacious political manœuvrings by resolute conference chairmen, and promises of investigations into discrimination within the South African Red Cross itself, had managed to keep South Africa from being expelled before. These investigations had been discussed for years, against a background of rumbling dissatisfaction, though nothing had actually been done. The societies were no longer in a mood to prevaricate. Before the conference was more than a few hours old, government delegations led by some of the African democracies pushed through a resolution to expel the South African government delegates despite all Hay's pleas that the principle of universality was sacrosanct. Apartheid, declared forty delegations, was such a fundamental violation of the very essence of human dignity that the representatives of African states could not be expected to sit in the same room as people holding such racist views. The South Africans were to go, 'in the name of dignity'; otherwise they would leave themselves.

The response by Pretoria was to order the International Committee delegates out of South Africa, where they had been working among political detainees and in the black townships. In fact the fracas turned out to be less serious than Hay had feared, for the South African Red Cross was cleared of charges of racial discrimination and not expelled from the comity of national societies. And after the International Committee reminded Pretoria that its members had not voted for expulsion but abstained, the South African government changed its mind and allowed the delegates to stay. However, an important marker had been laid down: the days when western developed countries could impose their will on the Red Cross movement, and dictate which issues mattered and which were to be regarded as insignificant, were over.

Within the International Committee, the delegates had always been regarded as the organization's most valuable asset. As Jacques Moreillon put it in 1983, they were the Red Cross's trump card and the 'preservation and management of this capital is one of its most important and most difficult tasks'. It was in the delegates' skills as negotiators, their persuasiveness and authority with governments and rebel forces, that the success of the International Committee as the world's foremost humanitarian actor really lay. Though there was less talk in the 1980s of them as *combattants* or warriors, the men, and increasingly women, who joined the organization were no less adventurous and romantic, the mild manners and neat clothes of the best of them concealing a strange mixture of genuine compassion, vanity and steeliness, even if some still mourned the days when they were really free, before radio links forged an umbilical cord with Geneva.

Until long after the end of the Second World War the delegates had felt themselves to be safe. Often alone or in twos for weeks on end, in the thick of conflicts and at the mercy of sudden attacks, they had been able to take comfort in the knowledge that the red cross armbands they wore would be universally respected. For the most part they had been right. There were remarkably few casualties. The death of Georges Olivet, killed in the Congo in 1961 with two members of the Katanga Red Cross, had provoked concern and outrage but soon faded from memory. But in 1978 a consciousness of danger entered the Red Cross world. It has never gone away.

André Tieche, Alain Bieri and Charles Chabra, two delegates and a local employee working in Rhodesia, set out one day in a white car clearly marked with large red crosses to visit a clinic on the Mozambique border. Next day, their bodies were found in a desolate spot: they had been murdered. Enquiries were immediately launched. It emerged that Tieche, the head of the mission, had on this occasion been uncharacteristically foolhardy in that he had failed to go through the usual procedure of establishing that both sides in the conflict understood the nature and workings of the International Committee and its delegates. Though the identity of the killers was never finally established, the Rhodesian tragedy left a profound mark on the organization. It emerged very powerfully from the investigation that in the new kinds of conflict spreading around the world, the red cross emblem itself was losing its resonance. It was not only that many people had no idea what it meant: there was an uneasy suspicion that, far from being a shield, the Red Cross might be in the process of becoming a target.

The Rhodesian deaths would be followed by others and in the 1980s a number of Red Cross workers would be kidnapped in conflicts around the world, for the most part returned unharmed. But, added to a growing feeling that the complexities of the modern world were bringing challenges unheard of in the days when wars were wars and belligerents readily identified by their uniforms and guns, the awareness of danger served to make the International Committee more aware also of how new delegates should be recruited and trained.

Training had always been a somewhat casual affair, more a question of a few rules and principles and the suggestion that the skills needed by the delegate were best learned in the field and from colleagues. When Philippe Grand d'Hauteville was taken on in the late 1960s, he was interviewed by a 'nice old lady on a sofa with her cocker spaniel. She asked me if I spoke English and had a driving licence.'

With the late 1970s came more thoughtful recruitment policies, with two-week training courses where newcomers were screened and taught basic international law as well as a clearer appraisal of the risks involved in the work and how to handle the tensions of living constantly in danger. Recruits today are still picked for their idealism and desire to do good, and their obvious empathy with those they set out to help, even though it is accepted that this empathy will make them more vulnerable. But with these noble feelings must now go a balanced personality, the ability to work in a team, an absence of family problems, and steady nerves. Delegates are required to be interested, to want to learn more about themselves in order to understand others better, but not to be merely curious. They have to be able to sleep well so as to be alert by day to what they see and hear. They have to deal with the peculiar and ghastly smell of prisons, and live with the knowledge that however hard they try they will never be able to see everything. People suspected of humanitarian 'tourism' are firmly turned away.

Today, delegates come from all over Switzerland and a very few from abroad, the taboo on foreigners having at last been broken in the early 1990s, but only up to the middle ranks. The old preference given to Geneva's best families, particularly with those with names like Favre, Naville and Boissier, is reported to have disappeared, but many of the old names are still to be seen on the register and high-flyers in the business, medical, banking and academic world are as sought after as they ever were. Delegates have to be old enough to be 'mature' – at least twenty-six – but not so old as to have lost the capacity to adapt and learn (no older than thirty-five). They have to be efficient organizers, and at ease with themselves. Excellent French and English, a clean driver's licence and a university degree are no longer enough. Dr Barthold Bierens de Haan, a psychiatrist appointed by the International Committee goes to great lengths in his briefings to delegates to prepare them to cope with pressures and sights few can have dreamt of before. The fact that it took so long to make his presence possible is due to a lingering feeling among delegates that any trauma they suffer is as nothing compared to that suffered by the people they are trying to help, as well as to a certain instinctive hostility towards the need for any kind of psychiatric help. Certain rules – regular breaks, a minimum degree of comfort – now govern the day-to-day lives of delegates in missions that grow larger and more complicated all the time. 'Stress', both sudden and cumulative, and 'debriefing' are words that have entered the vocabulary of the organization. 'We prepare them for what could happen to them,' de Haan explains,

> so that they will not be surprised if they find that they suddenly cannot sleep or only want to be alone. We need people today who can express their emotions – and I sometimes think that

the Americans and the British are better at that than we are. Team life is crucial. We feel that the best way to support delegates is to have team leaders who are prepared and who can support their teams in the field.

Along with de Haan has come the appointment of an adviser on security.

It takes more courage to be a delegate today, particularly as night falls over some isolated, ill-protected encampment, surrounded by ethnic violence, hatred and contempt for the Red Cross and all it stands for. And it takes resourcefulness: the good delegate of the 1990s is not only fit, stable, discreet, adventurous and quick-witted, but versed in international humanitarian law and strong enough to withstand the envy and dismissiveness of rivalrous organizations, no longer so much an ambassador as a bringer of first aid to a dirty war. Dunant would like most of these warriors, particularly the *troisième combattants* in the Marcel Junod mould, for there are still a few who talk of it all not as a job but as a 'splendid adventure', though he would have doubts about the few who regard themselves as stars, running their own one-man shows, and he would be saddened to see that many do not share the fury of their predecessors at the injustices they see around them, nor their conviction that it lies in their power to put them right. Modern delegates are neither so angry nor so driven. Detachment is prized.

The number of delegates has doubled and tripled in recent years, bringing the figure to around eight hundred, with perhaps 100 new recruits every year. There are delegates general, created in 1970 to take charge of regions, and under them a hierarchy of other delegates, many now specialists in different aspects of the Committee's work – like tracing or relief. Applications remain high, with two out of every three delegates taken on under two- or three-year contracts that last two to three years but which can be extended. The quality of those who apply is not as high as it once was, according to the personnel department, when a stint with the International Commission was a passport to a good job in banking or the foreign service. 'Nowadays, during a recession,' said one long-time staff member, 'a background in the Red Cross is no longer perceived as so desirable by many Swiss companies. We are marked by a very strong aura, a feeling that we have developed a taste for adventure and power. We have become used to extraordinary things.' *La maison* is not held in quite the same awe as it once was, nor is the divide between headquarters and the field quite what it was when André Rochat roamed the Yemen on his camel and felt that Geneva was the enemy.

In 1986 a group of delegates staged a putsch, which is still barely known about outside the organization. By the standard of many coups it was a mild, good-mannered affair. But in an organization wedded to hierarchy and the notion of obedience and loyalty, the mutiny took on overtones of treason. It was a little as if some middle-ranking members of the Vatican decided to question the supreme authority of the pontiff.

This act of *lèse-majesté* had its roots in the Hocké and Moreillon days, though it did not burst through the civilized consciousness of *la maison* before Hay had been succeeded by Cornelio Sommaruga, an outspoken and somewhat contentious figure from the Tessin, with excellent contacts in the Anglo-American world, and a former, widely respected member of Switzerland's foreign service. Hay had brought with him to the presidency a wide understanding of banking; Sommaruga brought diplomacy.

The putsch was mainly about responsibility. The men and women who lived so dangerously in the field, often spending weeks on end taking decisions that affected the lives and security of thousands of people, were increasingly irked to find their views ignored when they returned to Geneva. Though they were greeted respectfully as heroes freshly home from battle, no one was much interested in what they thought about how the organization should be run. They now began to ask why, given that they shaped so much of the work of the International Committee when in the field, did they have no say in the day-to-day life of headquarters? But it also expressed a genuine feeling among delegates that, in his concentration on major relief programmes and the need to attract ever more money, Hocké had somehow betrayed the origins of the Red Cross, forgotten that the protection of all victims of conflict and the visiting of detainees lay at the heart of the Committee's role, and it was this, and not relief, that made the organization unique. 'At that moment,' says Carlos Bauverd, one of the rebels, 'a sickness entered the soul of the International Committee.' In the mid-1980s, Bauverd was not long back from medical work on the Cambodia—

Thailand border; his uncle was Jean Courvoisier, the delegate who had done so much for the German prisoners-of-war in post-war France, and Bauverd had grown up steeped in Red Cross lore.

All through the 1980s, as he and other delegates of his generation took part in the vast relief operations that kept the Red Cross at the forefront of humanitarian affairs, they went on wondering whether the path now being pursued by the Committee was the true one and whether the moment might not have come to pause and reflect on the nature of the organization itself. During the immense Cambodian operation discord had broken out between Hocké and Moreillon, Hocké inching ever more in the direction of development, Moreillon worrying that the organization was in the process of losing its way. When Hocké departed for UNHCR, his job as head of operations went not to Moreillon – who might have seen it as a base from which to consolidate power – but to André Pasquier, a high-ranking delegate in the Hocké mould but regarded as rather inflexible. Many of the younger delegates would have preferred Jean Hoefliger, the popular delegate general from the Middle East, but his independence of spirit was known to threaten some of the members of the Committee.

Halfway into his third term, Alexander Hay decided to retire. Pasquier had worked hard but he had been given little chance to redress an imbalance between relief and protection work that more and more delegates questioned. By now humanitarian relief work was big business, with many vested interests, and some felt sadly that the success of the modern International Committee was increasingly being seen in terms not of victims helped, but of kilos of food delivered.

What happened next is still cloudy. On Hay's departure, the Swiss government appears to have pushed for the appointment of Sommaruga, lending weight to all those who argue that the links between the government of Switzerland and its most important humanitarian body are far closer than has ever been acknowledged. Sommaruga has many admirers who praise his articulacy and achievements, and say that he is an excellent listener and a quick learner; he also has critics who call him a 'Catholic Cicero', with an ego the size of *la maison* itself, the drive of a military task-master and a habit of speaking out – at great length – without consulting anyone first. But even his critics say that Sommaruga has succeeded in doing things where a more emollient and humble man would certainly have failed. His job is not an enviable one.

The years 1987 and 1988 are remembered as deeply unhappy years for the organization when, overstretched in major operations in Angola and Mozambique and grappling with the unending conflict in the Middle East, it was also at war within itself; Pasquier and Moreillon were locked in administrative battle while outside, throughout the Red Cross movement generally, some of the stronger western societies tried to impose their own political concerns. From within, Sommaruga was busy imposing a style of his own, a way of doing things that reminded people uncomfortably of the Berne civil service and which clashed sharply with the individualism of many of the younger delegates. A number, sensing no future for themselves, left the organization. 'It was a haemorrhage,' Bauverd recalls. 'The best men were leaving and they were taking the history of the organization with them. That isn't something that can be taught, only learnt by imitation and familiarity.'

Among the unhappy delegates were men who had known each other for many years in the small and closed Swiss world which has in many ways remained the Committee's most fertile recruiting ground. In the evenings they met and lamented what they saw happening to the Red Cross. Before long the disaffected grew to well over 100 people, for the most part men in their late thirties and early forties, with some ten to fifteen years' experience behind them. Why not, they argued, write a letter to the Committee, setting out what they saw to be the problem, and urge a proper re-evaluation of the Committee's work and future? A letter was written. It was signed by twenty people, the feeling being that it was better for the more junior staff not to invite trouble. It called for a return to the International Committee's original mandate, closer links to the Red Cross movement generally, a more open and approachable attitude towards the public and an end to such expensive sidelines as the computerization of the entire organization. Marvelling at their own boldness, they delivered the letter to Sommaruga.

For a while, it looked as if consultations would take place. A working group was set up; talks were held. But as the weeks turned into months and nothing seemed to be happening, so attitudes hardened. A second, tougher letter was drafted and delivered. This time, events moved quickly. There were meetings, suggestions, offers. Rumours began to circulate that Pasquier would be removed from operations, that the structure of the International Committee would be examined and changed, even that Sommaruga himself might go. For a few heady hours, the Committee seemed to take the mutineers seriously. Then, as Bauverd puts it, the Bolsheviks were routed.

Within days, Sommaruga and Pasquier saw their positions strengthened. The ringleaders, bit by bit, were shifted to the sidelines; a few were removed altogether. Those who defy the International Committee are not readily forgiven. The mutiny was soon over. There would be no rethinking of the mandate, no return to an earlier framework, no winding-down of relief operations. It was in the hands of a more sober organization, among a generation of younger delegates who, some say, are less interested in history and conscience, less indignant about the world's injustices, less inclined to stir things up, that the International Committee now turned to face the future.

And that future was indeed daunting: the coming down of the Berlin Wall, the end of the Cold War, a sharp rise in ethnic and national violence, a proliferation of light weapons in the hands of terrorist groups the world over and the erosion of the nation-state.

———————————⌒———————————

TWENTY-ONE

The Landscape of War

On the day of my first visit to the International Committee in Geneva in May 1992, they were mourning the death of a delegate called Frédéric Maurice, whose car, clearly marked with a red cross, had been attacked in Sarajevo, and who had died soon after of his wounds. Maurice was thirty-nine, married, with two young children.

The day of my last visit, shortly before Christmas 1996, they were mourning six colleagues killed at point-blank range in their beds in the hospital compound of Novye Atagi in Chechnya just before dawn by masked men in military uniforms using guns with silencers. The dead, it turned out, had not thought to lock their doors, believing that a two-metre-high perimeter wall and armed guards posted around the hospital made them safe. They belonged to the new breed of delegate, five of them women nurses seconded to the International Committee by their national societies, the sixth a Dutch construction worker.

Both times, the Red Cross flag above the Hôtel Carlton in Geneva was lowered to half-mast. After the death of the delegates in Chechnya, a long line of humanitarian workers, on one frosty afternoon, marched in silence from the Place des Nations up the wide Avenue de la Paix towards the International Committee headquarters, carrying flowers. They came from church bodies and human rights groups, from vast international agencies and small non-governmental organizations, as if to say that Geneva, despite covetous eyes cast by Strasbourg, Bonn and New York, was still the world capital of the humanitarian world and that attacks on the Red Cross were attacks on them too. And in their respect for the dead there was also an expression of anger.

Nor were these the only losses. Despite close attention to new security procedures, three other delegates had been murdered in Burundi not many months before, their cars attacked as they returned from a journey to restore water to a refugee camp of 60,000 hungry and thirsty people.

In December 1996, in the Saint Pierre Cathedral in Geneva, President Sommaruga's message was the same as when he stood on the tarmac to receive the coffins on their return from Chechnya: the dead were brave people, fulfilling the original mission of the Red Cross, that of caring for the casualties of war; but this barbarity and contempt for the Red Cross and its flag was something that had to be stopped.

The sense of shock that had overwhelmed the International Committee in 1992 at the death of Frédéric Maurice in Sarajevo — part a horrified realization that delegates had somewhere lost their immunity in modern wars and part a very real affection for Maurice himself — had by the end of 1996 turned into a sober acceptance of danger and a feeling of being under siege. The 1990s have not been good years for the International Committee, despite budgets that grow ever larger and a staff that multiplies year by year. Many believe they are not likely to get better.

The end of the Cold War was widely heralded as the dawn of a more lasting world peace with greater respect for international law. In 1989 there was considerable rejoicing and a sense that the Geneva Conventions and all the agreements on torture, civilians and children, so long and so tenaciously fought for, were at last about to make their contribution to what many saw as a new world order. But there was not much time to rejoice. Of the many conflicts that have involved the International Committee since then, three — Somalia, Bosnia and Rwanda — have come to epitomize what the Red Cross faces today.

In October 1990, four members of the Red Cross were ambushed by armed men as they were driving away from delivering emergency assistance to refugees in the north-west of Somalia. One was seriously wounded and died; the other three were held by rebel soldiers before being released unharmed. The International Committee was by then the only humanitarian organization with a regular presence in the north-west, the others having pulled out one by one as the war between government forces and the Somali National Movement spread, intensified by ethnic tensions, different tribes aligning themselves with different sides and growing numbers of refugees crossing the border from Ethiopia. The war continued to escalate. In January 1991 a French rescue mission was sent in to take nine delegates and twelve Somali Red Crescent workers on board the warship *Jules Verne*, after the International Committee was forced to abandon its operations in Mogadishu because 'marauding fighters' were systematically robbing their vehicles at gunpoint, as well as looting relief and the personal property of the mission and its delegates. This was a new kind of anarchy.

Food shortages in Somalia rapidly became so acute that only one in every ten children was getting enough to eat. Faced with this desperate situation, the International Committee, with eighty delegates and 1,500 Somali Red Crescent helpers, began to reflect on the nature of famine and its manipulation during conflict, and to analyse the dynamics of access to food. Somalia was the conflict in which Mohamed Ali Barre of the Somali Red Crescent saved the life of a delegate called Wim van Boxelaere, who had been wounded by gunmen, and died himself of his wounds, as did several others during robberies, abductions or from land-mines; in which armed gangs pillaged warehouses and ships were unable to dock with desperately needed supplies of food; in which some 30,000 civilians were killed or wounded in the spring of 1992 in Mogadishu alone, due to the 'indiscipline of combatants and the total lack of respect for the most elementary rules of combat', as an International Committee report put it. The country slid further and further into chaos and famine. Drought made the famine worse, and war took the lives of over a quarter of the children under the age of five, while 800,000 Somalis fled into Ethiopia, Kenya and the Yemen. Disease spread as more and more people drank muddy water and ate grass, leaves and roots, and died as they queued for food at the 900 communal kitchens supplied by barges and helicopters feeding a million people a day. Roving medical teams flew to different parts of the country to take medicines and help to the ninety per cent of the population who had been dispersed by the fighting; the International Committee transmitted over a quarter of a million family messages in 1993 alone, and carried out a successful vaccination programme for nomadic herds. It was also the war in which armed humanitarian assistance – UN peacekeeping forces drafted into Somalia to 'establish a safe environment for humanitarian relief operations', by quelling the bandits and keeping the warlords from annihilating the civilian population – acquired a bad name after their actions led to fighting, reprisals, embarrassing political deals and a controversial and vacillating stand by the UN.

This was the first case of a forced armed intervention authorized by the UN Security Council; and it provided an urgent warning against using international humanitarian law as a basis for military intervention without thinking through what was to be achieved and how.

Somalia was also where 700 journalists arrived and television crews were seen stepping over dead bodies to get better shots. Somalia was the place where International Committee dissemination teams fanned out across the country, plugging the Geneva Conventions by every means they could devise, including the transmitting of a radio play called *Akara* with fifteen episodes showing how civil war can be avoided if the rules of war are respected; and where the International Committee, for the first time in its history, employed 2,600 gunmen to protect its delegates, convoys and warehouses. They called them a 'kind of police force', gave them 'food and work', and were troubled when people asked about the guns.

The first big year of Somalia, 1991, was also the year of the Gulf War, of a peace agreement in Angola after sixteen years of civil war, of deadlock in Mozambique, of work among civilian casualties of the Sendero Luminoso terrorists in Peru, of never-ending war in Afghanistan, of a bloodless coup in Thailand. On 8 May, Red Cross and Red Crescent Day, a 'chain of light' linked the Red Cross movement around the world. By the end of the year, just three years after the ending of the Cold War and its promise of so much peace, thirty conflicts had broken out. Deaths from wars were the highest in seventeen years.

Until Somalia, there was a feeling that wherever fighting was going on there was a case for sending in the military. Now it became clear that traditional armies cannot deal with anarchy and that it is very dangerous to confuse a humanitarian mission with a political and military one. A combination of new-found international co-operation, and the growth of violent factionalism by nationalist, religious or separatist movements, suggested the need to re-evaluate humanitarian assistance.

In Somalia, so it was said, 'Virtually no one with a weapon had heard of the Geneva Conventions . . .'

* * *

'Never before,' wrote President Sommaruga in the preface to the International Committee's annual review of 1992, 'had our activities in certain conflicts seemed so fundamentally questioned, nor had the rights of victims been so tragically flouted ... it is no longer simply war we are confronted with, but the very denial of humanity. We have reached the very depths of barbarity.'

In 1992, the International Committee, fully stretched in Somalia, was also at work in the former Yugoslavia where waves of refugees were fleeing from the fighting that had broken out in Croatia and Slovenia the previous summer. By early 1992, there were sixty delegates in many of the same places in which the first Red Cross envoys had served over a hundred years before. The same Balkan names would now be seen again in the pages of the *Review*.

By that summer, Bosnian Serbs, Bosnian Croats and the government forces of Bosnia Herzogovina were in a state of total war, made worse by complete contempt for the Red Cross emblem and the repeated targeting of civilians. Somalia had given the International Committee warlords, bandits and hunger. In Bosnia, delegates battled with rape, summary executions, deportations, hostage-taking, civilians caught in the crossfire as the front line constantly shifted around them, and the brutal treatment of detainees. It was to be a war of atrocities, of prisoners 'disappeared' into camps to which the International Committee was refused access, of sieges, of towns and villages bombed and blasted into rubble, of the total collapse of basic medical and social services, of the shelling of schools, hospitals and churches, of civilians made pawns in larger political strategies, of blockades and ultimatums. 'We kept thinking things could not get worse,' says one former delegate. 'Then they did.'

The war in Bosnia was where the term 'ethnic cleansing' entered the vocabulary. It was where the spectacle of destitute and terrified people, driven from their homes in midwinter, struggling through rain and snow with wheelbarrows and rucksacks, brought home to the West the fact that violations of the basic rights of human beings are not something that happen to other people, a long way away in some far-off continent, but can happen at any time, apparently out of nowhere, very close by. And it was where delegates saw and heard acts of barbarity none had imagined they would ever witness and later could not forget; where President Sommaruga appealed again and again for tolerance, compassion and respect for the Red Cross flag and the Conventions it stood for. Never, in its 130-year history, had the International Committee been as active diplomatically as in Bosnia and never had a president spoken out so often and so loudly. In Bosnia water became a weapon in the control and persecution of enemy communities. Queues for water made good targets for snipers. At the peak of the war the International Committee had 160 expatriates – the 1990s less formal and official-sounding word sometimes used for delegates, most of them, but no longer all, Swiss – and 800 local staff in the field, distributing relief, handling messages (150,000 a week, at one point), running medical programmes, restoring water supplies, doing what they could to curb forced expulsions, monitoring violations and, when the seemingly unstoppable violence led to deaths, protesting. If the war in Bosnia marked a peak of horror, it also saw remarkable co-operation among humanitarian organizations and within the Red Cross movement of an immense and generous kind. There were 102 national societies helping with the tracing programme alone.

When the Croatian armed forces launched their offensive in the north and south in early August 1995, the Krajina Serb population gathered up their possessions and took to the roads in the biggest single exodus since the start of the hostilities. One hundred and fifty thousand people were reported to be on the move. Some seven thousand others – the sick, the elderly, the resigned, for the most part women, old, bedraggled and distraught at being separated from their families – stayed behind. Delegates travelled from apparently deserted village to village, looking for signs of life, a thread of smoke from a chimney perhaps, a faint noise among the ruins, trying to coax terrorized people into the open.

In the war in former Yugoslavia, international humanitarian law was violated continually, systematically and without apology. The most solemn promises appeared to have lost all meaning. The siege of Sarajevo was the longest since that of Leningrad. The delegates who witnessed the fall of Vukovar and Srebrenica thought they had seen the depths of horror. All President Sommaruga's fears came to pass: a rising spiral of atrocities, and delegates in ever greater danger as roads were cut off and convoys shelled. It was horrifying, but not surprising, when Frédéric Maurice died.

The Dayton agreement, signed on 21 November 1995, followed by the

Paris peace agreement a few weeks later, ultimately succeeded in stopping the shelling and siege of cities and the slaughter of civilians. It gave the International Committee the job of visiting prisoners, protecting people from further expulsion and harassment and overseeing the release and repatriation of prisoners-of-war. It also put into their hands one of the saddest tasks in this long war: the tracing of the missing, and in particular the search for the 5,000 men who had fled the Muslim enclave of Srebrenica before the Bosnian Serb advance, and the 3,000 others said to have been arrested by their troops. By the end of 1996, the International Committee had collected 16,000 files on the missing. A year later they had been able to close only a thousand.

The International Committee already had twenty-six delegates in Rwanda when, on 6 April 1994, President Habyarimana died in an air crash and his country sank rapidly into Hutu-led massacres of Tutsis and their moderate Hutu supporters. Still heavily committed in Somalia and Bosnia, the International Committee set up emergency medical programmes while the Belgian UN force, which had lost ten men in the initial fighting, pulled out soon followed by all but 270 of the 2,500-man peacekeeping UNAMIR force. It did not seem to strike anyone as paradoxical that the modern obsession with memory, the enthusiastic commemoration of past struggles against tyranny, is not matched by determination to prevent it all happening again. By the end of April, the largest wave of refugees ever recorded by UNHCR – 250,000 people – had taken to the roads. Soon, the Committee's operation in Rwanda would overshadow all its other commitments for 1994.

A first medical team with 18 tonnes of supplies for Kigali was quickly followed by delegates, doctors, water experts, and relief. News bulletins from the front carried a litany of bloodshed: more dead, more wounded, more Red Cross workers killed or hurt, more orphans. In Kigali, the medical teams cleared bodies to keep epidemics at bay.

Events in Rwanda moved fast. In Bosnia, delegates had seen unwanted people driven at gunpoint from their homes. In Rwanda, they saw children hacked to pieces by machetes, pregnant women disembowelled, heads, arms, legs torn off and scattered as Hutu killers went on a rampage of carnage and destruction. Children died because they represented the future. Delegates schooled in the principles of silence and neutrality found themselves the sole witnesses of atrocities. Just sometimes they were able to act as a brake to further killings. Issuing a stream of reminders about the Geneva Conventions, they did what they could to intervene, negotiate, take Tutsis under their protection and make brave sorties to the churches, football stadiums and hospitals in which the terrified people were seeking refuge from the bloodshed. They were not always able to do much. Eight days into the massacres, armed militants halted a Red Cross ambulance on its way to a hospital and murdered the patients inside; later, orphans in Red Cross care were butchered. By the end of 1994 up to a million people were dead and two million more had fled over the borders into Tanzania, Burundi and Zaire. While the Rwandan Patriotic Front began to steer the country away from anarchy, delegates ran hospitals, provided relief, seeds and tools, installed safe water supplies, visited the first 16,000 suspected Hutu killers — the number would rise to over 65,000 — in jails in which conditions were deteriorating rapidly into a catastrophe of disease and deprivation. They were also wearily at work on dissemination programmes, noting bitterly that their carefully constructed educational programme of 1993, laid on for the Rwandan army, had achieved nothing at all beyond providing the world with another depressing lesson on collective indifference and ignorance when it comes to upholding the laws of war. The UN Security Council had failed to get states to take action to stop the killings but it did set up an international war crimes tribunal, as it had after Bosnia, to try those accused of genocide. The survivors of Rwanda's genocide feared that, having done nothing to halt the killings, the international community was not likely to be effective now. So far, they have been proved right.

On 14 December 1994, the International Committee issued one of its rare public appeals. Humanitarian pronouncements, like those made in the name of human rights, frequently reach sonorous heights. This one was no exception. It was also prescient. The appeal took the form of a warning. Without a proper international position on the genocide, and a co-ordinated, clear economic, military and legal response, the International Committee announced, the whole region of Africa's Great Lakes was likely to slide inexorably towards chaos. With the collapse of much of Rwanda's prison system, judiciary, police force, medical infrastructure and education, the country was in a fragile and desperate state, while over the border in Zaire and Burundi the Hutu killers were busy rearming. Those countries, overwhelmed by the waves of refugees, were themselves liable to explode unless some effective international solution were found. 'Hatred and bitterness,' declared the International Committee, 'must be put to one side before the desperate need for these people to live in peace and for their children to inherit a society from which will have been banished the intolerable alternative of being either victim or executioner.'

A third vision of modern conflict was now added to the warlordism and famine of Somalia and the ethnic cleansing and 'disappearances' of Bosnia: the separating of children from their parents. During the massacres of the early days, in the random chaos of the vast camps and in the bustle and confusion of the frenzied flight from the killers, many small Rwandan children had lost their families. By the end of 1994, the International Committee, working closely with the Save the Children Fund and other agencies, had registered 37,000 'unaccompanied' children. Most were between two, the age at which a Rwandan child could no longer be expected to be carried by his mother, and eight, still young enough to be easily lost in a crush. By the spring of 1996, the figure had risen to 67,000; six months later, it stood at 90,000. Since many of the children were too young and too traumatized by what they had seen and survived to provide any clues to their own identity, photographs were put up throughout the refugee camps, like those of the lost children of Europe in 1945 and 1946. In time, 22,500 children were reunited with their families. The search goes on. Modern technology came to play an ever-larger part in International Committee operations in Rwanda, a database being set up in Nairobi, keeping closely in touch with searchers throughout the region, transmitting over two million messages in what became known as the Great Lakes tracing programme.

In an independent evaluation of the international humanitarian response to the crisis in Rwanda, under the auspices of the Danish government and published in 1996, the International Committee was praised for the part that it had played in protecting Tutsis from the genocide, though there were stories about one International Committee worker persecuting those he was there to protect. The evaluation as a whole was not complimentary. Neither the United Nations, nor the various agencies, nor the non-governmental organizations had made any real effort, on any level, the report concluded, to produce a co-ordinated approach to the disaster, or one that was not short-sighted or egotistical.

These were not the International Committee's only wars, just as their delegates were not the only players in them. The years since the pulling down of the Berlin Wall have seen fighting in Afghanistan, Liberia, Uganda, Benin, Togo, Burundi, Sri Lanka, Colombia, Ethiopia, Angola, Mozambique, Peru, Sudan, Azerbaijan, Georgia and Armenia, and this list is far from complete. In 1994, Africa was so torn apart by violence that the International Committee reported that, for the first time in its history, it seemed to have come 'face to face with a number of violations that defied humanitarian reasoning'. Speaking before the UN General Assembly that November, President Sommaruga spelt them out: 1994, he said, would be remembered as a year of 'unspeakable suffering: entire populations threatened, starved, terrorized, massacred, turned senselessly into refugees'.

True, there had been the Gulf War, in 1991, in which the International Committee performed with distinction, having spent months coaching the Allied forces in their responsibilities and then despatching 600 staff to the war within a few days of its outbreak. But that is remembered in Geneva with a kind of nostalgia as a war in which clearly defined and recognizable enemies, wearing identifiable uniforms and badges of rank, faced each other across a known battlefield with conventional weapons. True, Margaret Thatcher complained that too little was done for the allied pilots taken prisoner by the Iraqis and paraded triumphantly on Iraqi television. But if not all the laws of war were scrupulously observed, at least they were seen to be relevant, suggesting that the problem lay not with the laws themselves, but in the need for them to be known, understood, learnt and respected. Those who relished the simplicity of that war and believed its advanced technology would make it a model of things to come, do not expect to see its like often again.

For the most part, the wars of the 1990s are marked by chaos and savagery. They have no beginning and no end. States have collapsed, leaving no clear line of authority, no identifiable leaders or soldiers with whom the International Committee can reliably reach agreements.

Respect for the Red Cross and its emblem, as for the humanitarian laws so painstakingly elaborated over the last century, has become negligible; indeed, as the deaths of the Red Cross people in Chechnya showed, the Red Cross has itself become a target for attack in countries in which it was for so long a symbol of repression and authority.

Water is a terrifying new weapon of war; the International Committee believes that contaminated water, or the lack of clean water, today causes as many deaths as do weapons. The 'disappearing' of people, once a tactic used by dictators at home to silence their opponents and dissidents, was carried into the field in Bosnia, where it was shown to be as effective and terrifying as during Hitler's *Nacht und Nebel* days. Civilians, who in the First World War made up just ten per cent of casualties, make up ninety per cent in today's wars, and most of these are women, small children and the elderly. The breakdown of states and the failure of the international community to control weapons has resulted in the spread of Kalashnikovs throughout Africa, south-east Asia and the former Soviet Union, with the result that rival factions can conduct their feuds with lethal firepower. Children as young as seven are now being recruited as soldiers in ever greater numbers: they are reported by Rädda Barnen to have fought in thirty-two conflicts in 1996. That same year the UN estimated that over a hundred million unexploded land-mines lay scattered throughout the world, most of them so small as to be invisible in grass. Once again, their victims are mostly women and children, gathering firewood or tending flocks.

The world that the International Committee faces today is an extremely uncertain one, perhaps more uncertain than at any other time in its history. The desperation of the world is putting huge burdens on resources: between 1985 and 1995, its spending on relief quadrupled to US$350m. Never have the services of its delegates and the monitoring powers of its mandate been more necessary, yet never have the delegates themselves been in such danger nor the Geneva Conventions more cynically flouted. 'We have become,' says one delegate, 'part of the landscape of war.'

One of the most obvious aspects of the new humanitarian world is that the Red Cross is no longer alone in the field. When Dunant wandered among the bodies after the battle of Solferino, he had virtually no rivals. The last ten years have seen an unprecedented explosion of human rights and humanitarian organizations. Styling themselves 'without borders', they are taking over where governments can no longer cope, doing jobs that used to be done by the UN agencies like planning new sites for refugee camps, bringing in their wake not simply more money, more concern and more relief for what appear to be ever-rising numbers of victims of wars and natural disasters, but also a new style, aggressive, vocal and highly competitive. At no other time in history have so many people apparently wanted to do good: at the height of the Rwandan crisis, 160 organizations descended on Kigali. Most of their workers were young, idealistic and impatient; they were also rivalrous and competitive for funds.

Not all of this new burst of humanitarian conscience fits agreeably or harmoniously with the International Committee, which has seen its supremacy questioned, competition for its funds and its moral authority challenged. Humanitarian aid, as Hocké rightly perceived in Biafra in 1969, is big business. In the bustle of this new order, the Committee and its delegates have been accused, with some justification, of arrogance, excessive secrecy and a refusal to collaborate. In 1993 the International Committee decided that it needed to improve its definition of its own corporate identity in order to design what it called an 'effective communications strategy', and commissioned an outside organization, Media Natura, to carry out a detailed study into the way it was perceived both throughout the Red Cross movement itself and in the wider humanitarian world. Many of the findings, like those recorded by Donald Tansley in 1973, were harsh.

Though most of the organizations interviewed expressed considerable admiration for the International Committee's speed and professionalism, there were complaints about smugness and aloofness; some said that they found the organization dull, cold, preachy and very Swiss. The non-governmental organizations in particular said that they were never quite sure whether the Swiss delegates were really 'one of them' or not. The very word 'delegate' was found irritating, people observing that it was nothing but a pompous way of saying 'field worker' – in itself revealing of the dwindling status of people who until recently viewed themselves as very like ambassadors.

Some of the donors to International Committee funds expressed ambivalence, praising the Committee's performance but adding that they were sometimes annoyed by the excessive legalism and apparent imperviousness to the outside world, and that they felt that they were entitled to more in return for their contributions. The International Committee, they said, preformed excellently against two of the most important criteria for investment support: it had an impressive track record and its clear mandate was attractive. But when it came to a third requirement, co-operation, the Committee fell down badly, though many who had worked with the delegates in the field admitted to a grudging admiration for their skill in letting others test the political waters first and make mistakes, then benefiting from their observations.

More interesting perhaps is the vision of the broader humanitarian world that emerges from the Media Natura study. It is one of mutual suspicion between the Red Cross movement, the UN agencies and the non-governmental organizations which at times borders on paranoia and rivalry; of anxiety that the high moral ground is being usurped by younger and more dynamic bodies; of wide acceptance that humanitarian action has become an instrument of foreign policy; of fear that the media are making war seem banal, violence normal and breaches of international humanitarian law trivial.

In 1973, Donald Tansley devoted a great deal of space to relations between the various components of the Red Cross movement; for the most part he found them troubled and rivalrous. Little seems to have changed in the last quarter century. The conference in Geneva in 1986 will always be remembered for its sourness and for the expulsion of the South Africans on grounds of apartheid. The twenty-sixth, due to take place in Budapest in 1991 – after Bogotá, the chosen capital, had to be abandoned because of civil war – was postponed at the very last moment when it became clear that a similar fracas was brewing over the presence of the Palestinians. Much anxious preparation, high-level diplomacy and horse-trading went into drawing up the agenda for the next, and many people turned up for its opening in Geneva in December 1995 fearful of further explosions and not at all certain if the Red Cross movement would actually be capable of weathering them.

In the event harmony was restored, no one tactlessly mentioned the PLO, the potential hazards over the naming of the various former Yugo-slav delegations were delicately negotiated and important resolutions were meekly slipped through on matters affecting civilians in war by a handsome turnout of 143 states. The fact that the conference took place at all was greeted with overwhelming relief, though serious, long, and in the words of one delegate 'almost unbearably tedious' speeches had to be sat through – inevitable, perhaps, in an organization of this size. In 1991, the League was rechristened the Federation, after remarks that the word 'league' reminded people of sporting clubs and crime syndicates.

Just the same, as Media Natura discovered, the currents of feeling between the International Committee and the Federation continue to run deep and bitter even though, in October 1989, a new accord had been drawn up between the two, specifying yet again and in precise detail the nature of each other's responsibilities. The Federation still accuses the International Committee of highhandedness and reproaches it for failing to recognize that there have been real improvements within the Federation in recent years when it comes to professionalism and performance; and that the dark years of the late 1970s and 1980s, when it expanded too quickly, without proper guidance, are long past. It is the Federation which has drawn up a ten-point code of conduct for disaster relief which includes not giving aid to further political aims and not acting as instruments of government policy.

In the International Committee, many high-ranking staff members still continue to dismiss the Federation as incompetent and too politically buffeted to be reliable, only as strong as its weakest national society and at the mercy of all their enthusiasms, however absurd and impractical. They repeat to each other Chenevière's old joke, *'La Ligue a tort'*, and wonder whether, as one man put it, the Federation is not still, as it has always been, 'the International Committee's greatest mistake'. There are some who say that the International Committee should long ago have absorbed the Federation, to become a single, powerful organization, though even they agree that it is now far too late. As one man put it: 'We have to fight for our own survival in the humanitarian world – let alone take on the rest of the Red Cross.' This seventy-five-year-old rivalry, rooted in very real fears and antagonisms, made more bitter by dwindling resources and the blurring of boundaries between war and peace, is increasingly seen as unseemly and undignified at a time when both organizations are struggling. 'The question is: can we be smart enough,' asks one senior member of the Federation, 'to become really successful partners?'

The irony in 1997 is that the number of current crises and disasters is down. Just as the International Committee remembers the Gulf War, so the Federation looks back on 1988 almost with nostalgia: fifty-one emergency appeals in a single year: floods in Bangladesh, hurricanes and typhoons in Central America and the Philippines, earthquakes in Nepal and Armenia, droughts in Chad, Mali, Mauritania and Niger, a plague of locusts in Algeria. Fund raising needs emergencies.

Some of the national societies, who have always felt themselves overlooked and despised by the International Committee, are indeed regarded as suspect by Geneva, where people cannot help remembering the total subjugation of the Japanese, Italian, German, eastern European and Chinese societies to their totalitarian governments, though real attempts are now being made to harness their strengths at times of major crises. The falling of the Berlin Wall has opened a whole new Red Cross world, one of great energy and great enthusiasm, but also archaic structures and more political turmoil. When members of the German Red Cross, one of the biggest and most active of modern societies, were at last able to cross the border and link up with its sister society in the former GDR, they found terrible conditions among the elderly and handicapped, many huddled together in unheated and dirty rooms. Vast sums of money have been spent, through the Red Cross, in improving these conditions. Throughout the former Eastern European bloc, there has been a clearing out of staff too closely steeped in the rigid communist ways in favour of younger people who have brought with them a freshness, a determination to implement the Red Cross message with a vigour lost in some of the older societies who find it increasingly difficult to recruit volunteers with the same sense of urgency. It is in eastern Europe, in the late 1990s, that Dunant would recognize the excitement of his early days.

The opening of the former Soviet bloc has also provided answers to the long unknown whereabouts of the missing German prisoners and civilians in the Second World War. Though a first agreement made with Moscow in 1957 revealed some information, it was slow and unsatisfactory work, many of the names having been wrongly transcribed. In 1991, the tracing services of the East and West German Red Cross societies joined forces, and began to work on a Russian card index of prisoners. An archive of files on eleven camps run by the Russian secret service in the

Soviet-occupied zone between 1945 and 1950 was found in Moscow with information on 123,000 political detainees, some of them boys as young as sixteen and seventeen accused of building up guerrilla groups. Bit by bit, the Red Cross in Munich started putting together a sad picture, following these boys from the camps of Buchenwald and Sachsenhausen, where they were taken after they had been emptied of their Nazi prisoners, tracing them as they were deported to Russia, then transferred to camps in Siberia.

Then, in 1992, arrived a first disc with data on German prisoners-of-war who had died in the camps; the Soviets, like the Germans, were found to have kept careful records. Since then a steady flow of microfilms of names has emerged, including a number of civilians, making it possible at last for what is known as an 'expert opinion', a certified likelihood of death, to be sent to families, many of whom have waited for half a century to learn what became of men whom they last heard of as prisoners in Russian hands. Of the 3.3 million estimated German prisoners-of-war in the Soviet Union, the Red Cross tracing service in Munich now believes that 2.2 million were released, one million died, and the rest stayed on in the Soviet Union.

If forging better links with national societies and establishing a workable partnership with the Federation remains a wearying but crucial task for President Sommaruga, other essential issues are those of education, publicity and relations with the media. The real purpose behind Media Natura's study was to explore ways in which the International Committee could become more open without betraying its mandate of confidentiality. Over education, there is today a sense of urgency, a feeling of subdued desperation that the Red Cross, one of the world's best known symbols, is in danger of completely losing its potency and that desperate measures need to be taken to force governments to carry out energetic programmes of instruction to their armies and in schools on the meaning of the Geneva Conventions and the Red Cross emblem, not helped by calls for a new emblem, without Christian overtones. Delegates specializing in dissemination have been concentrating on working hardest in peacetime, so that when wars break out something at least is known. As with many international agreements, the Geneva Conventions tend to be best known by the armies least likely to violate them in the first place.

Publicity, good contacts with journalists and the placing of stories that will help and not distort International Committee missions, have long lain as a stone at the heart of the organization, many of whose members have chosen to interpret the mandate on confidentiality as an order to say nothing to anyone. In the 1990s this fits ill with a widely accepted view within the humanitarian world in general that the media has become crucial not just to mobilize funds but to focus political will, and real moves are being made inside the International Committee to shake off the old view of the press as something crude, untrustworthy and fickle. A realization of the power of photographs in bringing tragedies to the public eye has led to an internal debate on a revision of the mandate which lays down that the victims of war should not be portrayed as vulnerable and undignified.

Yet a contradiction does remain. While the International Committee retains its unique mandate of being allowed access to places no one else can visit because it is trusted by governments to say nothing in public, this role as sole witness is not an enviable one. Not all the younger delegates have found it bearable to know details of atrocities and not be able to publicize them, so as to put a stop to them. Some, haunted beyond endurance by this inner conflict, have left to seek work with the more straightforwardly campaigning organizations like MSF or Amnesty International. Others have learnt to play what is by now a well-established game, complying to the letter with the mandate while finding ways of letting others benefit from the knowledge they alone possess. On many occasions in recent years, International Committee delegates have acted as the final point of reference, providing confirmation of violations that others can only guess at. This symbiosis, between delegates who know but cannot speak and field workers for campaigning organizations who do not know but can speak, can never be formally acknowledged but is widely agreed to produce results, in the form of accurate and reliable reports, used to bring pressure on despotic governments. Paradoxically, the process is helped by the instructions given to young delegates during their training at Cartigny: 'say what you do and where you go, but not what you have seen'.

Even so, there have been disgruntled defectors from *la maison*, goaded into print by finding these contradictions unacceptable, and Bernard Kouchner is not the only delegate to have attacked the organization from the privileged position of a former insider. In 1983 a one-time delegate called Andreas Balmer published a barely disguised account of life within what he scathingly called '*L'Organization*'. Banned for a while in Switzerland — the International Committee argued that the book was 'scandalous, if not dangerous', in that it put its delegates at risk in the field — *L'Heure de Cuivre* portrayed delegates as full of self-doubt, condemned for their own survival to developing an 'almost scientific attitude' towards their work that soon dehumanized them.

Recently, Laurent Marti, founder of the Red Cross and Red Crescent museum, for almost twenty years a respected delegate, came out with a scabrous volume of memoirs that reduced the International Committee to a stunned silence. Marti's title, *Bonsoir mes victimes* was judged tasteless, but not as unfortunate as a scene in which a young hostage is raped by a colonel, who Marti fears will never again be able to rise to the same pitch of 'animal pleasure' with other lovers. Though Marti did give pseudonyms to the characters he described, they were so minimally disguised as to be offensive. One former envoy to Biafra appears as Hugues Maximillen d'Aarenberg, a man so sexually obsessed with women that his nights in Cotonou were spent prowling for prostitutes. Marti is admired among his colleagues as a man of courage in the field. But he is not liked. His outspoken contempt for the 'antiquated, weighty and anachronistic' articles of the Geneva Conventions has not gone down well among men who have spent a lifetime refining and simplifying ideas of extreme complexity into accessible forms. All the attributes that make the most brilliant of the delegates — bravery, a certain arrogance, independence of mind — are said to be carried in Marti to such excess that they have become repugnant. But there was just enough truth in his portrait of an organization weighed down by form, secrecy and tradition at headquarters, with flamboyant delegates leading exotic lives in the field, to cause a ripple of unease.

When it comes to relations with the media, the years under President Sommaruga have seen a dramatic change, as funds have poured into an expanded information department and into new publications; press officers have been appointed and a web site opened. International Committee missions and work are set to become so transparently accessible that no one will ever again be able to accuse them of secrecy, though Sommaruga insists that reaching victims must never be sacrificed to better public relations. He himself is a master of when and how to use the ultimate sanction which is the International Committee's only real weapon: that of making a public statement when governments refuse again and again to bring about the improvements they have agreed to under the Geneva Conventions. Between 1946 and 1987, the International Committee made seventy-four public appeals; between 1989 and 1996, 104. In the past, these very public leaks, made rarely and without fanfare, attracted little interest. Today, since Sommaruga has spoken out so forcefully on Somalia, Bosnia, Rwanda and most recently the African Great Lakes, people listen.

In the summer of 1996, the question of the concentration camps and the Jews returned to haunt the International Committee. It provided a test for the organization's avowed new spirit of openness; and it passed with distinction.

Formerly secret papers in the American archives in Washington, declassified after fifty years and consulted by researchers from the World Jewish Congress, revealed fresh information about Swiss banks and the laundering of Nazi loot in the Second World War. They showed how the banks had accepted gold stolen from the treasuries of German-occupied Europe and from the private funds and collections of Jewish families, after the German government's own reserves had been depleted, and how they had exchanged it for francs and dollars that went to pay for steel and aluminium. There had even been talk, according to a file codenamed 'Odessa', of setting up a worldwide fund to keep Nazism alive after the war should victory be denied them. What these new documents made plain was that Swiss collaboration with the Germans had in fact been far greater than the public had ever been led to believe. According to the secret papers, Nazis interviewed immediately after the war described to the Allies how the gold from the jewellery and heirlooms had been swiftly melted down and turned into ingots, then stamped with pre-war dates, so that later the Nazis would be able to say that it had come from German funds. As well as Switzerland, routes through Sweden, Portugal, Spain and Turkey had been used to launder the gold, with elaborate legal deceptions and false accounts.

The Allies, through intercepts made by eavesdroppers, had in fact known what was happening just as they had known that the Crèdit Suisse in Zurich and the Union Bank were both systematically violating the Allied Code of Conduct, but they had been unable to prevent the Swiss from accepting the gold and in any case needed Swiss francs themselves. All they could do at the time was to warn the Swiss that they would be liable to 'claims under the terms of the inter-Allied declaration' once the war was over. When peace came, however, there was still nothing they could do to compel the banks to hand over the gold; after many discussions the reluctant Swiss agreed to part with what is now believed to have been about one eighth of all German gold deposits. The question of how to restore the money to its rightful owners, how much to give and to whom, was then simply not pursued.

Behind the furore that broke out in 1996 was the US Republican Senator Alfonse D'Amato, chairman of the Senate banking committee and known for his doggedness in pushing the Whitewater enquiries. D'Amato put a team of researchers to work, digging out further papers and facts, combing the pages of Safehaven, the code name given to some of the files, and opening a site on the Internet, in order to try to trace the living descendants of those whose fortunes had been plundered.

Since then, reacting to the attacks in foreign newspapers, two commissions have been set up in Switzerland, an independent committee composed of bankers and members of the World Jewish Congress and an official one of historians, to clarify exactly what took place and when. The official commission has been given wide powers and is expected to report within three years. The Swiss, though apparently deeply embarrassed by the revelations, are also irritated. They complain that a witch-hunt has been launched, and that far too little is being said by anyone about any possible dirt attached to American and British hands.

All of these new discoveries might well have left the International Committee indifferent had it not been for a particular file discovered in the American archives. This consisted of letters and memoranda written by the American intelligence service, the Office of Strategic Studies, predecessor of the CIA. It contained alarming accusations. According to American agents working in Europe and North Africa during the latter part of the war, International Committee delegates were dealing in money and valuables looted from victims of Nazi persecution. Worse, there were German spies among them and the International Committee itself was seriously thought to have been infiltrated by Nazi agents. There was mention of a Frank Bodo, a Gestapo spy providing information about the British in Palestine, who had used International Committee employees to carry 'enemy-owned jewels' across the Swiss border; of a man named Ehrenhold, 'chief of the International Committee in Marseilles', who had secured secret naval information by interviewing crews as they left their ships; of a Dr Paul Burkhard, 'suspected of working for enemy agents' in Naples. There were also references to invisible ink, shared hotel bedrooms and German agents known only by the letters X, Y and Z.

It might all have been, if not funny, at least fairly absurd, had the International Committee not been acutely sensitive about its wartime past and had a bitter attack on them not been mounted in the newspapers, led in Switzerland by a Jewish journalist called Pierre Hazan, who was once refused a job as delegate and has since been the first to accuse the International Committee of wrong doing whenever the occasion arises. In keeping with their new policy of openness, the Committee announced that it would carry out an immediate investigation, both in its own archives and in those of the various Swiss state papers, though President Sommaruga was at pains to stress that it is important not to suggest that the International Committee felt, or believes itself to be, guilty. The archivists set to work, and in an impressively short space of time, began to issue statements. D'Amato's accusations began to seem something of an anti-climax.

Of the twenty-one names drawn from the OSS documents as having been involved in shady practices, only sixteen are in fact known to have been employed at any time by the International Committee. For fifteen of these, evidence of wrong doing is at best circumstantial. The sixteenth, a man called Giuseppe Beretta, has a case to answer. Beretta, who joined the International Committee in 1942, was sent to Izmir in Turkey to help with the famine in the Aegean islands and transferred to Istanbul the following year to take part in a relief operation for Italian prisoners-of-war in India. He had a Mexican wife and was known to the International Committee to have been investigated by the Swiss police for forgery. Beretta's superior, Gilbert Simond, referred to him in a letter written on 25 August 1943 as an 'intelligent and very capable chap who I am certain will render me valuable service'.

Not everyone, either inside or outside the International Committee, agreed with him.

After diplomatic relations between Germany and Turkey were broken off, the Swiss undertook to look after German interests, setting up a bureau in Istanbul and, it now transpires, smuggling assets from Germany into Turkey and from Turkey into Switzerland, using Swiss couriers. In January 1945, Beretta was placed under investigation by the Turkish police who suspected him of breaking the law over the 'protection of Turkish currency and of having imported certain goods without declaring them to customs'. Raymond Courvoisier, at the time delegate in Istanbul, was also deeply suspicious of Beretta's contacts and later revealed that Beretta had asked him to use his diplomatic passport to smuggle out of Turkey a box of gold ingots. After the Turkish police enquiry, Beretta was compelled by the police to hand over 710 gold coins found in a strongbox rented in his name at the Deutsche Orient Bank. He was recalled to Geneva, where he denied transferring Nazi funds or being a courier but was immediately sacked by the International Committee. He was not, however, prosecuted. In a note dated 23 March 1945, Colonel Brigadier Roger Masson, head of the Swiss Army Intelligence Service, intervened asking the International Committee to treat him with 'benevolent understanding', which suggests that Beretta may in fact have been working for the Swiss all along.

There were accusations against other delegates that have turned out to be accurate, concerning contact with Nazi agents, but they seem to have been made in innocence, as with Pradervand's friend Georges Graz, the mining geologist in Algiers. As for other revelations about spying, neither the International Committee nor anyone else in Switzerland has, at the time of writing, found evidence to suggest anything more than a confusion over names and a misunderstanding about the nature of International Committee work, hardly surprising, perhaps, as the delegates, secretive, asking detailed and sensitive questions, moving around in search of information, must have looked suspicious indeed. And, as the International Committee points out, there were over 3,000 people working for them in Switzerland during the war, up to 180 more in delegations and subdelegations in sixty-one different countries, and several thousand others recruited locally. To find a couple of black sheep among them is hardly a surprise.

More troubling, perhaps, is a new story, unearthed at the end of 1996 by a group of young Swiss journalists and historians and confirmed by a handful of people who survived the experience. It concerns Max Huber.

Huber's father was a respected and successful businessman, with interests in metallurgic and machine tool factories. In 1915, Max took his father's place on the boards of Alusuisse and Oerlikon, becoming vice-president in 1924 and president in 1929. He kept closely in touch with the companies, telling friends that he felt it to be his duty, his father having done so much for Switzerland's economy. As presiden of the International Committee, however, he is said to have agonized over the obvious conflict between the aims of the Red Cross and his involvement with a factory producing arms. When the Second World War broke out, Huber donated his entire salary of 80,000 Swiss francs from Alusuisse to the International Committee. It was a very large sum for the time.

After the war began, Switzerland was faced with a choice. It could work with and for the Germans or come to terms with ever-rising unemployment and economic hardship. The decision was taken to co-operate with Germany and many people to this day are willing to accept that, though unpleasant, this was a reasonable step. What they find harder to accept is what the Swiss were prepared to tolerate in the factories they owned in German-occupied territory; and people who will forgive the banks and insurance companies for their lack of morality, are disgusted by what they are now learning about these factories.

In 1941, after Germany invaded the Soviet Union, Russian and Ukrainian deportees and prisoners-of-war were despatched to work in factories turning out goods for the war effort in the occupied territories. Unpaid and brutally treated, these slave labourers died in their thousands, exhausted, beaten and starved. Half are said not to have survived the war. One of the factories using slave labour was Alusuisse AG, a subsidiary of Alusuisse-Lonza, which had a factory just over the border from Switzerland in a town called Singen. Four hundred prisoners-of-war and 800 deportees arrived to work here, to join many hundreds of others already working for Maggi and Georg Fischer in the same town. Since the slave labourers wore patches on their clothes with the letters OST – for Ostarbeiter, worker from the east – there was no mistaking who they were. Survivors remember watching Swiss managers coming on visits of inspection, walking silently on their rounds and keeping their eyes carefully straight ahead of them, avoiding all contact with the men at the machines who were turning out aluminium and arms for Germany.

In 1945, when peace was signed, the three Swiss factories in Singen appealed to Berne for help; they were sent Swiss flags to prove their neutrality. The French, in whose zone of occupation Singen lay, are believed to have known precisely what had been going on in the Swiss owned factories. But in 1945, Burckhardt was appointed Swiss minister in Paris and in any case Switzerland was important in the new Cold War order against communism. Nothing was said. It had become in no one's interest to say too much about Switzerland's wartime employment record.

Did Max Huber, the man whom every moral decision reduced to anguish, know what was going on in the factories of which he was president? Did he talk to the senior managers when they returned from their visits across the border? As the head of Alusuisse's board, is it possible that he never looked at the accounts, which would have told him precisely how much his company was paying the Nazis for the slave labourers from the east? Could a man who stayed awake all night contemplating the agonies of war have borne to have known so much? Jean Pictet, who knew Huber better than anyone still alive, believes that it is inconceivable that Huber knew anything about it. 'It is not possible,' he says. 'He cannot have known.' Others are not so sure. The truth about the pious and anguished president and his factories, also under investigation today, promises to join the ranks of shadowy questions that have come to traumatize the organization's view of its own past.

The story of the International Committee and its relations with Nazi Germany seems unwilling to go away; fifty-five years after the famous meeting when Burckhardt and Etter persuaded their colleagues that it was not in the best interests of the International Committee or of the victims of war they had been set up to protect to speak out about the concentration camps, the whole subject remains as potent and unsettling as it was in the accusatory days of 1946 and 1947. It represents, wrote Yves Sandoz of the International Committee in the *International Herald Tribune* a few years ago, 'the greatest defeat in the 125-year history of our humanitarian mission. It is a burden we share with many others who could not fathom the unimaginable, for it marked the failure of an entire generation.' Nor, perhaps, should it go away, if only because it serves as a permanent reminder that humanitarian organizations have to be very careful indeed in their choice of friends, that anti-Semitism is insidious and pervasive, and that at the moment when they were most needed, the International Committee lacked courage and imagination. To have acted, to have taken a strong moral line, even if this was not in their mandate, would have expressed the real dream of the Red Cross. In failing to do so, they failed not only the Jews, but themselves.

On 26 January 1995, President Sommaruga, whose openness has included a very real desire to face up properly to the shadows of the past, addressed a meeting of Nobel Peace Prize laureates and heads of state in Kraków's Wawel Royal Palace, on the fiftieth anniversary of the liberation of Auschwitz. 'I am here to honour the memory of all victims and to express admiration and solidarity for those who escaped Auschwitz,' he declared. 'I say it with humility, aware of possible omissions and mistakes of the Red Cross in the past.'

Among some Jewish historians, his words were greeted with pleasure, as a formal apology, a recognition that the International Committee did not do all that it could and should have done during the Second World War. The apology, says Gerhart Riegner, the young wartime secretary of the World Jewish Congress in Geneva, was fine as far as it went but it did not go far enough. Sommaruga's words, he believes, failed to take into account, as all previous quasi-apologies have done, the attitude that suffused the Committee during the war years, which was one of acceptance that at least some aspects of Nazi ideology would be the reality of the new post-war Europe. Nor did it explain why, despite the right of initiative conferred on it by its mandate, the International Committee never chose to stand up to the Nazis, to really press hard to halt the worst atrocities against the Jews. 'One of the International Committee's greatest failures,' says Riegner, 'is that it simply accepted the facts. It never tried to intervene at the highest level.' The International Committee did not want to take the Nazis on over the Jews, just as Huber did not want to know what was taking place in his factories; and no amount of apology today for not having acted then, and no matter how often people point out that the Allies and the Vatican did no better, excuses the stand taken by Huber, Burckhardt and the Committee during the long years of the war.

Every hour, on average, at the end of the 1990s, three people are killed or maimed by a land-mine. In the last few years the International Committee has moved to the front of the vast international campaign to get mines banned from modern warfare, believing that the modifications and restrictions proposed by governments and arms manufacturers — such as recording where mines have been dropped — are meaningless and that only a total ban will put an end to what has become one of the major killers and mutilators of our time. If nuclear weapons were the symbol of the Cold War, mines have become that of the last decade. This 'blind carnage', announced President Sommaruga in the autumn of 1995, 'is an affront to humanitarian values, an affront to civilization.' He has been backed by Archbishop Desmund Tutu and six other Nobel Peace Prize winners. 'You cannot,' says one delegate, 'go on selling mines as if they were chocolates.'

Expanding their expertise in arms and the laws that should govern them, the International Committee has also been instrumental in pushing through, meeting by meeting, a new agreement on the prohibition of laser weapons which cause blindness. In a world of growing indifference to suffering, of the acceptance with ever greater cynicism of cruelties inflicted on soldiers, who are regarded more and more as objects, the International Committee has returned to the philosophy expressed in the St Petersburg Declaration of 1868: 'the progress of civilization must result in the attenuation, as far as possible, of the calamities of war.' In the past, the Committee points out, this sense of civilization led to rules prohibiting certain weapons; today, it leads to research into ever more lethal ones. Within the International Committee there are moves to enter further fields, those of arms dumping and arms transfers as well as that of light weapons, the AK47s whose proliferation around the world is causing untold injury, though there are fears that such a campaign may bring them up against the vested interests of governments and arms manufacturers in ways that the campaign against mines has not. As with many other issues that have faced the Committee over the decades, there are splits in the movement, with some people believing that the

International Committee is morally bound to pursue weapons because it alone has the status and authority to do so and those who fear it will be led too far from its original mandate. These conflicts, between the dreamers and the realists, the Dunants and the Moyniers, are no less sharp today than they were in the 1860s.

The legal department now resounds to debates on such subjects as the growing closeness between human rights, a series of relatively short and simple affirmations of the rights of man based on respect for life and recognition that war itself is a violation of human rights, and humanitarian laws, seen as a way of protecting people from the horrors of war. The Istanbul declaration, adopted at the twenty-first international conference in 1969, laid down that 'man has the right to enjoy lasting peace, and that it is essential for him to be able to live a full and satisfactory life founded on respect of his rights and of his fundamental liberty.' There was, the declaration went on, a 'human right to be free from all fears, acts of violence and brutality, threats and anxieties likely to injure man.' The fundamental principles of the Geneva Convention and those of human rights are natural allies and nowhere more so than in a desire to protect man against the absolute power of an enemy. With the Universal Declaration of Human Rights in 1948, the subject entered the field of international agreements; with Common Article 3 of the Geneva Conventions of 1949, humanitarian law moved into that of internal conflicts. As the world has slowly been consumed by ever greater violence, so the two disciplines have been drawing closer, boosted by the protocols of 1977 which saw humanitarian rules correspond to 'inalienable' rights, what the lawyers in Geneva call the *noyau dur*, the kernel, of man's basic entitlements.

Other legal debates, running now for many decades, concern what remains the most contentious of all the International Committee's mandates, that of the 'right of initiative', the right to offer its services, wherever and whenever it sees fit. Based on the affirmation of the right to life which transcends national borders, this *droit d'ingérence* has been strengthened by successive agreements and UN resolutions. However, it now finds itself challenged and even taken over by other organizations, as the tensions between sovereignty and humanity in countries all around the world become more acute. These newcomers argue that what they do falls under the first Red Cross principle, that of 'preventing and alleviating human suffering wherever it may be found'; they say that they are entitled to take help to victims on the basis of unwritten law even against the will of governments, and that basic rights know no national boundaries. In 1987, at a conference partly organized by Bernard Kouchner, the *droit d'ingérence* was greeted warmly by the French, who had long been talking of trying to get it included under various international agreements. 'The duty not to interfere stops where the risk of failure to assist begins,' the French president declared not long afterwards. Since then, the French have led the field in arguing that a law of humanity should take precedence over the law of nations and humanitarian issues have become a major theme of French diplomacy at the UN. During the late 1980s and early 1990s, prodded by the French, the Security Council passed a number of resolutions about protection and intervention in Iraq and Somalia. The International Committee has not watched the MSF manoeuvrings with indifference and there was a distinct feeling of annoyance when President Mitterrand appointed Kouchner to the post of minister for humanitarian affairs; not only was MSF felt to be jumping on to the Red Cross bandwagon, but to be taking over as spokesman for the world's victims.

In theory, however, interference in the internal affairs of a state is still condemned by international law. The right to offer assistance is broadly recognized but the essence of that right remains that it is subject to permission by the state. The International Committee, under the Geneva Conventions, has a privileged position to do so, but no monopoly, the same right being open to any impartial humanitarian organization. The legal waters are further muddied by an understanding under international law that when a state refuses to allow the *droit d'ingérence*, then the principle of subsidiarity can come into play, a 'substitute' for activities that should have been undertaken by the state for victims abandoned without assistance, the lack of which constitutes a 'threat to human life and an offence to human dignity'. Just where this leaves the International Committee, as well as the vast array of legitimate players and the groups Xavier Emmanuelli, one of the founders of MSF, calls the 'predators of humanitarian action', is far from clear.

Nor is the legal position helped by all the talk, in the 1990s, about how far the Conventions cover the kinds of violations that started to appear only after the drafting of the 1977 protocols I and II, and whether there would be any point in drafting new ones if no one is listening. The protocols, points out Hays Park, one of their greatest critics, remain precisely what they were, proposals and not sanctions. As for the four Geneva Conventions, Hays Park has calculated that there has been 'virtually no implementation of even the most basic requirements' of the treaties in ninety-eight per cent of the 167 nations party to them. Adam Roberts, Professor of International Relations at Oxford University, argues that it is the Conventions that are seen as too idealistic, too complicated, and that all the rhetoric and failure to see them implemented has led to a widespread feeling that the laws are now obsolete and can be ignored with impunity. Nor is the fact that they are seen to emanate from Geneva in the shape of an immutable Gospel helpful. Never, he points out, has effective action to implement the laws of war been more necessary and never have they been so hard to translate into effective policies. In the 150 conflicts that broke out between 1945 and 1995, more than 23 million people died and at least 50 million more were injured.

Not long ago, the International Court of Justice at The Hague announced that the principles of humanity and impartiality, helping others without discrimination as proclaimed by the International Committee, are the touchstones of all humanitarian action. The court did not mention neutrality, the refusal to commit oneself to any one side in controversies, the most hotly discussed of all Red Cross principles, which some today argue has become synonymous with indifference and, since the end of the Cold War, both dated and meaningless in Switzerland, a country no more neutral than many others. It is here that still lies the battle with organizations like MSF, who have led the field in dismissing what they brand as a form of moral paralysis and insist that the provision of relief and the denunciation of human rights violations must go hand in hand; and that without this joint approach, humanitarian work becomes 'little more than a plaything of international politics'. MSF continues to be a constant thorn in the International Committee's side and there was trouble not long ago when it adopted an emblem unashamedly similar to a red cross, then went on teasing the International Committee for months with barely modified alternatives. Romy Brauman, co-founder of MSF but now retired from it, feels that the rivalries that beset the humanitarian world are extremely dangerous in that they will alienate donors, who may prefer to by-pass existing organizations and enter the field directly. He argues that what is needed today are clearly demarcated roles for the various players, and particularly for the long-established ones like the Red Cross and MSF.

The International Committee is not prepared to enter the debate about neutrality, continuing to view it as the very basis of its uniqueness and insisting that its 135-year commitment to evenhandedness and a refusal to act as judge should provide safety for its delegates in the way no amount of armed guards could. In the same way, Sommaruga and his predecessors have clung to the organization's Swiss identity, arguing not on grounds of its Swissness per se – over the years many attempts have been made to proclaim complete independence from the Swiss government, and that independence has, since 1993, been enshrined in a formal document – but for mono-nationality, the only guarantee, as they see it, that the organization will not descend into a UN kind of impotence. To all the attacks currently made on the organization the International Committee has a simple answer: its history is littered with attacks and never are they louder than during times of upheaval.

Just the same, the problems the International Committee faces, as it approaches the twenty-first century, are vast. The battle for protection for vulnerable people, for an acceptable and manageable balance between the principles of humanity and those of necessity and the duty of public authorities to protect the state, defend its territorial integrity and maintain order, has come to preoccupy it more and more. The Geneva Conventions, the two protocols and the whole panoply of international humanitarian law have given it new weapons, but they are proving frail when the Red Cross, as history has made plain, is accepted only when its interests coincide with those of the nation state. The International Committee can ask but it cannot command; even its national societies can reject its suggestions. It can educate, monitor, report, complain, but it cannot force. How is it to work when its delegates are refused access to victims and are themselves made targets for armed gangs who do not want witnesses to the atrocities they commit? When civilians are slaughtered with disregard for all the recent additions to the Geneva Conventions? When the infrastructure of states collapses as the states themselves collapse, destroyed by marauding warlords? When humanitarian organizations are increasingly used by western governments as tokens of their commitment to the resolution of conflicts that only diplomatic pressure and military force can stop? When the nature of modern conflict makes it impossible to tell where war stops and peace begins? When there has been no year – probably no day – since 1914 without conflict, and the best the movement can say about its pacifist role is that its very work is a 'factor for peace'?

The answer lies, believes Yves Sandoz, one of the organization's most respected lawyers, in reaffirming the three clear responsibilities of the International Committee's mandate: as a moral authority against the horrors of war; as an operational agent during armed conflict; and as an expert on humanitarian law. It lies in making certain that the humanitarian voice of the Red Cross is heard, that its proven track record is recognized and its uniqueness respected, says Gian-Battista Bacchetta, one of the senior figures in the International Committee, and by 'jumping over the shadow of inhibition and discretion'. It lies in reminding governments of their responsibilities under the Geneva Conventions, insists President Sommaruga, in concentrating on the International Committee's duties towards all victims of conflict, regardless of their nationality, race, religion and politics, in eschewing politics themselves, while recognizing that humanitarian aid is now so enmeshed in politics that its roots are often hard to find, and in protecting delegates and Red Cross workers even though the sheer complexity of modern wars and the destruction they leave behind are raising serious debates about the very nature of humanitarian aid. 'The world *needs* an International Committee of the Red Cross such as it is,' President Sommaruga said in a speech not long ago. 'Neutral, independent, mono-national and Swiss.'

The International Committee is not of course alone in its inability to ensure compliance with the laws of war, and the bitter realization of how little can be achieved by anyone lies at the heart of the growing calls for an International Criminal Court. The fundamental difference between the International Committee and other humanitarian organizations remains its individual approach: using discretion and requiring consent, falling back on procedures slowly evolved over 135 years – and still evolving its unique mandate to deal directly with governments and ask awkward questions, its personal appeals and approaches, while most of the others pursue 'revolutionary humanitarianism' and rely on both co-operation and confrontation. Amnesty International questions the reasons for continued detention; the Committee the conditions under which detainees are kept. In an age of continuous warfare, the International Committee can and does produce results in a way that rules cannot. To make its uniqueness stand out even more clearly from the rest of the movement, and particularly from the national societies, by their very nature identified with their governments, a new logo, the red cross surrounded by a double circle, has now been put on every International Committee vehicle, building, flag and badge.

That armed humanitarian intervention, as conducted by the UN, is to be avoided in all but exceptional circumstances has become one clear International Committee position even if it admits that it cannot rule out using armed guards itself as a last resort to protect employees and warehouses. Another is a conviction that banditry and the lawlessness of modern conflicts can only be prevented if the causes that lead to them are tackled by world governments, by co-operation and by economic and political means. But the message is not all bleak. Even if respect for international humanitarian law, that last bulwark against barbarity, seems at times to be crumbling under repeated attacks, President Sommaruga, like the senior delegates who run the regional desks at the headquarters in Geneva, is certain that the humanitarian Red Cross model is as valid today as it was in 1863, as long as people remain flexible, constantly adapting as the patterns of war change. 'Every day,' he says, 'we have to find new means of passing on the message.' The late 1990s are to be a time of discussion, analysis, debates on the future of the movement, on how to improve safety, efficiency and effectiveness, and on how to keep on bringing in money, at a time when donor governments are increasingly using humanitarian funds where they will bring in votes. 'I am constantly scared now,' Sommaruga says, 'that the influence of politics on some of the new actors will jeopardize all our work, and that people will confuse us with them.' To deal with the 'situations of internal disturbances and tensions' — riots, disappearances, summary executions or torture — when the International Committee has only tradition and the *droit d'ingérence* to fall back on, the senior lawyer Hans Gasser not long ago proposed a code of conduct for delegates in the field. With its rules to cover what he calls 'extra-Conventional' activities, the code is being greeted throughout the world with some enthusiasm. As part of its recognition of the importance of the United Nations in all questions of international relations in the wake of the Cold War, the Committee also decided to open an office in the United States in 1995.

What of the International Committee itself, born and nurtured out of the tensions between three pairs of people, three dreamers and three practical figures interested in action and political reality: Dunant and Moynier, Clara Barton and Mabel Boardman, Max Huber and Carl-Jacob Burckhardt? The members of the Red Cross today stand at about 220 million people in 169 countries. The Committee's 800 or so delegates visit an average of 100,000 detainees every year, in forty to fifty countries; its staff, under a governing group of the most senior people, merged in 1991 from the executive board and the directorate and headed by the president, and who make the day-to-day decisions, collect and despatch 250,000 tonnes of relief and transmit about a million family messages. The bank of cards in the central tracing agency recently passed 60 million. Databases have transformed some of the most fundamental tasks of the Red Cross and, by the mid-1990s, there were over a million names on disk. The budget is healthy, reaching some 750 million Swiss francs a year, coming from governments, supranational organizations like the European Union, the national societies, public bodies like the Swiss cantons and private ones, and President Sommaruga's hopes to attract ever more private money, especially within Switzerland, are looking promising. Some seventy-nine governments, fourteen of them most significantly – the largest being Switzerland, followed by the US, Sweden and Japan – contribute to funds, all voluntarily, for neither the national societies nor governments are bound by law to support the organization financially, an essential component of the Committee's independence. In the same spirit, the Committee sends its donors detailed information about where and how the money is spent but is subject to supervision by no higher authority and receives no instructions from outside.

Ador spent fifty-eight years on the Committee; Moynier fifty-five. In over 130 years, the Committee has seen only twelve presidents and remains in some respects barely touched by modern times, even if members are now obliged to retire at seventy and are expected to do at least a month's work spread over the year, a considerably greater undertaking than in the days when they came for an afternoon once a month. French is still the main language spoken. *La maison* remains an obedient place in which people accept the doctrine and the credos and make little fuss. Nor is there any difficulty in finding recruits. Even if the social network which once produced most of the delegates has become weaker, there continues to be considerable cachet in becoming a warrior, a *troisième combattant*, and the life that the International Committee can still offer young journalists, bankers, mathematicians, doctors and engineers remains alluring. The time is long past when anyone could contemplate divorcing the International Committee from Geneva and it would be hard to find a city anywhere in the world as clearly stamped by a single organization: avenues, squares, streets, all bear the names of founders.

Even so, admired, envied, criticized, its delegates in danger and its funds competed for, at the mercy of anarchical and brutal conflict, at constant risk of being tarnished by other humanitarian organizations who do not abide by their rules of war, the International Committee looks anxiously at the future, even if the success of the last international conference in 1995 boosted its own position and routed those who still had dreams of shifting power away from Geneva. There was something a little desperate not long ago in the tone of the final declaration of the international conference on the protection of war victims – one of the International Committee's most determined campaigns of the last ten years and one of Sommaruga's most inspired ideas – to help dispel the uncertainty created by the cancellation of the Budapest conference. The words read like a sad hymn to probity, compassion and responsibility. 'We refuse to accept that war, violence and hatred spread throughout the world . . . that the wounded are shown no mercy, children massacred, women raped, prisoners tortured, victims denied elementary humanitarian assistance, civilians starved as a method of warfare . . . populations illegally displaced, and countries laid to waste . . .'

What would the five founders have made of it all? What would that small band of prosperous and responsible Genevans for whom the civilized world barely stretched as far as North America, seated at their solid dining-room tables in their frockcoats and heavy whiskers, have made of a world in which small children are maimed more often than soldiers by mines which go by the name of 'butterfly' and 'frog' and in which governments, basking in the warmth of their own generosity, mindful of the mileage to be gained from a very public response to a crisis, protest more and more loudly about violations, yet do less and less to help prevent them?

General Dufour, the upright old soldier, would look around him with disbelief but conclude that it was his duty to intervene. Louis Appia would probably view the barbarity as a challenge and work ever more frenetically to forge new laws and improve medical treatment. Maunoir would have urged the others on and quietly attempted to control the uncontrollable. Moynier would have been appalled. The world he had known and understood was not filled with senseless savagery but was a place of reason, just as man was ultimately good, once he was taught to see the right way.

And Dunant, the wayward entrepreneur whose energy and enthusiasm sparked off a movement which has no equal in size and commitment outside of organized religion, what would he have made of it? He would have enjoyed the chaos, been entertained by the discussions, taken to the computers and radio links that bring instant news and instant access, risen to the challenge of competitors; and no one would have cared about or indeed noticed his imprudent investments. He could only have been pleased to see his great machine so efficiently at work, delighted that tracing the missing and the relations of prisoners-of-war proved such an inspired idea, gratified that his fundamental question – how to protect people in the hands of the enemy – continues to fly like a flag over the entire organization, and overwhelmed by the numbers of people who have flocked to his dream. But he would have been saddened to see what man has made of war in a little over 130 years: Dunant would not recognize modern conflict. If his conclusion was a little bleak, it would be not so much that the international movement he gave birth to had failed as a recognition that man, in fashioning such wars, had posed challenges it has yet to rise to.

As for Dunant himself, passionate, intemperate, foolhardy but essentially a moral figure, he would have thrived.

APPENDIX ONE

The Geneva Conventions

In 1762 Jean-Jacques Rousseau wrote in *The Social Contract*:

> War is in no way a relationship of man with man but a relationship between states, in which individuals are only enemies by accident, not as men but as soldiers.

Building on this, Henri Dunant proposed two practical measures: an international agreement on the neutral status of medical personnel in the field, and the creation of a permanent organization for practical assistance for the war wounded. The second became the Red Cross. The first led to the adoption, in 1864, of the initial Geneva Convention, followed in the years to come by a series of subsequent Conventions extending its mandate and powers.

On 12 August 1949, four new Conventions were unanimously adopted for the protection of victims of war. The first three cover protection of the wounded and sick, the shipwrecked and prisoners-of-war. The fourth, born out of the atrocities committed against civilians in the Second World War, breaks new ground in that it protects civilians who have fallen into enemy hands from arbitrary treatment and violence. Later, protection under humanitarian law was extended to the victims of civil wars. In 1977, two Protocols were adopted to strengthen the protection of the defenceless: Protocol I with new rules on international armed conflicts; Protocol II with further rules of international humanitarian law governing non-international armed conflicts.

The Geneva Conventions have become the most universal of all international treaties: by the end of 1992 they were binding on 175 states.

APPENDIX TWO

Summary of the Fundamental Rules
of Humanitarian Law
Applicable in Armed Conflicts

1. People *hors de combat*, or not taking part directly in hostilities, are entitled to respect for their lives and physical and moral integrity.

2. It is forbidden to kill or injure an enemy who surrenders or is *hors de combat*.

3. The wounded and sick shall be cared for by the party that has taken them prisoner, while medical personnel and property is protected.

4. The emblem of the red cross — and red crescent, red lion and sun — is a sign of protection.

5. Prisoners-of-war and captured civilians are entitled to respect for their lives, dignity and beliefs. They shall have the right to receive relief and communicate with their families.

6. Everyone shall be entitled to a fair trial.

7. No one shall be subjected to physical or mental torture or cruel or degrading treatment.

8. It is prohibited to use weapons or methods of warfare of a nature to cause unnecessary losses or excessive suffering.

9. Neither civilians nor their property shall be the object of attack.

APPENDIX THREE

Presidents of the International Committee of the Red Cross

Henri Dufour	1863–1864
Gustave Moynier	1864–1910
Gustave Ador	1910–1928
Max Huber	1928–1944
Carl-Jacob Burckhardt	1945–1948
Paul Ruegger	1948–1955
Léopold Boissier	1955–1964
Samuel Gonard	1964–1969
Marcel Naville	1969–1973
Eric Martin	1973–1976
Alexander Hay	1976–1987
Cornelio Sommaruga	1987–

CHRONOLOGY

Historical Background to the International Committee of the Red Cross

1859 Battle of Solferino.

1863 Formation of the International Committee for the Relief of Military Wounded.

1863 Geneva International Conference and the establishment of national committees for the relief of military wounded.

1864 Geneva Convention for the amelioration of the condition of the wounded in armies in the field drafted and approved.

1867 First International Conference of the Red Cross attended by nine governments, 16 national committees.

1876 International Committee for the Relief of Military Wounded renamed the International Committee of the Red Cross or ICRC.

1899 Geneva Convention of 1864 adapted to incorporate maritime warfare (Convention No. III of The Hague).

1906 Revision and development of the Geneva Convention of 1864.

1907 Revised Geneva Convention of 1906 adapted to incorporate maritime warfare (Convention No. X of The Hague).

1919 Formation of the League of Red Cross Societies.

1928 Statutes of the International Red Cross approved (revised in 1952 and 1986).

1929 Revision and development of the Geneva Convention of 1906 for the amelioration of the condition of the wounded and sick in armed forces in the field and the adoption of the Geneva Convention related to the treatment of prisoners-of-war; official recognition of the emblem of the red crescent (first used in 1876).

1949 Revision of the Geneva Conventions of 1929: Convention I – for the amelioration of the condition of the wounded and sick in

armed forces in the field;
Convention II – for the
amelioration of the condition
of the wounded, sick and
shipwrecked members of
armed forces at sea (revision
and development of the Xth
Convention of The Hague of
1907;
Convention III – relative to
the treatment of
prisoners-of-war;
Convention IV – relative to
the protection of civilian
persons in time of war.

1965 Proclamation of the
Fundamental Principles of the
Red Cross: Humanity,

Impartiality, Neutrality,
Independence, Voluntary
Service, Unity, Universality.

1977 Protocols additional to the
Geneva Conventions of 1949:
Protocol I – the protection of
victims of international armed
conflicts;
Protocol II – the protection of
victims of non-international
armed conflicts.

1983 League of Red Cross Societies
re-named League of Red Cross
and Red Crescent Societies.

1986 Statutes of the International
Red Cross and Red Crescent
Movement adopted.

NOTES

1. Tutti Fratelli

The most important sources for Henri Dunant's own writings are:

H. Dunant *A Memory of Solferino*, English edition, Geneva: International Committee of the Red Cross, 1959.

H. Dunant *Mémoires*, Geneva: Institut Henri Dunant, 1971.

Collected Letters by and to Henri Dunant in the private papers of Henri Dunant, Geneva University Archives.

Accounts of the early days of Henri Dunant and the founders of the International Committee of the Red Cross are to be found in:

R. Durand and J. Meuraut (eds.) *Préludes et Pionniers, Les Précursors de la Croix Rouge 1840–60*, Geneva: Société Henri Dunant, 1991.

R. Durand and J. D. Candaux (eds.) *De l'Utopie à la Realité: Actes du Colloque Henri Dunant*, Geneva: Société Henri Dunant, 1988.

A. Jullien *Le Berçeau de la Croix-Rouge*, Geneva: A. Jullien, 1918.

R. Durand (ed.) *Aux Sources de l'idée Croix-Rouge*, Geneva: Société Henri Dunant, 1989.

Further sources for this chapter and other descriptions of the early days came from conversations with Roger Durand of the Henri Dunant Society and André Durand, the International Committee of the Red Cross delegate and historian.

p. 3 'The stillness of the night . . .' Dunant *A Memory of Solferino*, p. 4.

p. 3 'endless, sad creaking . . .' P. Boissier *From Solferino to Tsushima*, Geneva: Institut Henri Dunant, 1985, p. 20.

p. 3 'When the sun came up . . .' Dunant *A Memory of Solferino*, p. 41.

p. 5 'Oh the agony . . .' Dunant *A Memory of Solferino*, p. 60.

p. 6 'When I helped him . . .' Dunant *A Memory of Solferino*, p. 66.

p. 9 'These pages are sublime . . .' E. and J. de Goncourt quoted in Boissier *From Solferino to Tsushima*, p. 41.

2. Inhumanity Under Another Name

For useful accounts of early warfare, see G. Butler and S. Maccoby *The Development of International Law*, London: Longmans, 1928.

R. Gordon *The Alarming History of Medicine*, London: Sinclair Stevenson, 1993.

J. Langendorf *Guillaume Henri Dufour*, Geneva: Editions René Coeckelbergus, 1987.

J. A. Farrer *Military Manners and Customs*, London: Chatto and Windus, 1985.

For accounts of the early days of the International Committee see *Mémorial des Vingt-Cinq Premières Années de la Croix-Rouge 1863–1888*,

International Committee of the Red Cross, October 1888.

p. 27 'died of shock' J. Keegan and R. Holmes *Soldiers: A History of Men in Battle*, London: Hamish Hamilton, 1985, p. 121.

p. 29 'officers and soldiers, who might . . .' Boissier *From Solferino to Tsushima*, p. 151.

p. 30 'Miss Nightingale . . .' Letter to Longmore, 23 July 1864: Florence Nightingale papers, Wellcome Institute, London.

p. 31 'however barbarous it may appear . . .' quoted in B. Oliver *The British Red Cross in Action*, London: Faber & Faber, 1966, p. 42.

p. 31 The best account of Florence Nightingale in the Crimea is to be found in Cecil Woodham Smith's biography *Florence Nightingale*, London: Constable, 1950.

p. 34 'one of the principal gates . . .' *New York Times* 7 May 1861.

p. 35 'timidity and caution . . .' Sanitary Commission Bulletin, January 1865.

p. 35 'no steamer of its own . . .' Quoted in W. M. Howell Reed *Heroic Story of the Sanitary Commission*, New York, 1909, p. 10 and following.

p. 37 'Francis Lieber . . .' A good account of these influences is to be found in R. Durand and J. Meurant (ed.) *Préludes et Pionniers: Les Précurseurs de la Croix Rouge 1840–1860*, Geneva: Sociétié Henri Dunant, 1991.

p. 40 'simple enquiry . . .' Procès-Verbal, *Section Genevoise*, 17 March 1864.

p. 44 'Fouillet: Well then . . .' *Carillon de Saint-Gervais* 20 August 1864.

p. 47 'First meeting. Tuesday . . .' *Carillon de Saint-Gervais* 20 August 1864.

For an account of coverage of the Convention in the newspapers see A. Dunand 'The Geneva Conference as seen by the Geneva Press', *International Review of the Red Cross*, July–August 1989.

3. True Metal and Tinkling Brass

Among the most important of the descriptions of the Franco-Prussian War, the siege of Paris and the role played by the new Red Cross societies are:

F. Bugnion 'The Arrival of Bourbaki's Army at Les Verrières', *Bulletin* March–April 1996.

M. du Camp *La Croix-Rouge en France*, Paris: SF-SBM, 1892.

F. M. Whitehurst *My Private Diary During the Siege of Paris*, London: Tinsley Bros, 1875.

A. Horne *The Fall of Paris: The Siege and the Commune*, London: Macmillan & Co, 1968.

Lady Wantage *Lord Wantage VC, KCB: A Memoir by his Wife*, London: Smith Elder & Co, 1907.

E. M. Pearson and L. E. MacLaughlin *Our Adventures During the War of 1870*, London: Richard Bentley & Son, 1871.

J. Furley *In Peace and War: Autobiographical Sketches*, London: Smith Elder & Co, 1905.

C. E. Ryan *With an Ambulance during the Franco-Prussian War*, London: John Murray, 1896

Durand R. (ed.) *The Birth of Red Cross Solidarity: The Franco-Prussian War of 1870–71*, Geneva: Institut Henri Dunant, 1971.

M. Kranzberg *The Siege of Paris 1870–71: A Political and Social History*, Cornell University Press, 1950.

The archives of the British Red Cross Society contain additional material on the war and in particular numerous references among the Wantage papers. There are also many references to the British and the Franco-Prussian War among the Florence Nightingale papers in the Wellcome Institute.

p. 51 'at all levels of society' Quoted in J. Hutchinson 'Rethinking the Origins of the Red Cross', Paper given to the American Association for the History of Medicine, New Orleans, Louisiana, 5 May 1988, p. 571.

P. 52 'of great merit . . .' Dunant Mémoires, p. 33.

p. 54 'Charity should not . . .' Boissier From Solferino to Tsushima, p. 182.

p. 54 'all classes . . .' C. Tschudi Augusta: Empress of Germany, Berlin: Swan Sonnenshein & Co, 1900, p. 131.

p. 59 'Moynier had come up with . . .' For a good account of these events see Boissier From Solferino to Tsushima, p. 200.

p. 65 'scraps of human corpses . . .' see Boissier From Solferino to Tsushima, p. 258.

p. 73 'He took with him . . .' For the story of the trip see W. Whittle My Journey to Paris with Colonel Loyd-Lindsay in the archives of the British Red Cross.

p. 74 'He himself had "breakfasted" . . .' Lecture given to the British Society for Aid in Boulogne, Wantage papers.

p. 80 'The French, and particularly the Parisians . . .' 27 April 1871, letter from Dunant to his mother, Dunant papers, Geneva University.

p. 83 'The baptism of fire . . .' Bulletin, January 1973.

p. 84 'collected by half-pence . . .' see Woodham-Smith Florence Nightingale, p. 505.

p. 85 'evidence that you have . . .' Letter from Florence Nightingale to Sir John Sutherland, end 1874, Florence Nightingale papers, The Wellcome Institute, London.

4. Stone Heaps Full of Snakes

Among the many books on Clara Barton, Mabel Boardman and the founding of the American Red Cross, the following stand out:

P. Gilbo The American Red Cross: The First Century, New York: Harper & Row, 1981.

M. Curti American Philanthrophy Abroad: A History, Rutgers University Press, 1963.

E. Brown Pryor Clara Barton: Professional Angel, University of Pennsylvania Press, 1987.

C. Barton A Story of the Red Cross, New York: D. Appleton & Co, 1928.

The diaries and papers of Clara Barton and Mabel Boardman are to be found at the American Red Cross and in the Library of Congress.

For good accounts of the Russian famine see R. G. Robbins Jnr Famine in Russia 1891–1892: The Imperial Government Responds to a Crisis, Columbia University Press, 1975, as well as the many reports by Quaker missionaries in Friends House archives in London.

P. 89 'They were enfeebled . . .' Congressional Globe, 5 February 1866.

p. 90 'deserves well of Congress . . .' Congressional Globe, 5 March 1866.

p. 91 'like the old war horse . . .' quoted in Pryor *Clara Barton: Professional Angel*, p. 188.

p. 92 'I have talked . . .' quoted in Pryor *Clara Barton: Professional Angel*, p. 193.

p. 95 ' "friendly" eyes . . .' *New York Tribune*, 6 January 1896.

p. 96 'I am always afraid . . .' quoted in Pryor *Clara Barton: Professional Angel*, p. 213.

p. 96 'In certain parts . . .' *Harpers Weekly*, 23 April 1892.

p. 97 'A Reuters correspondent . . .' *The Times*, 6 January 1892.

p. 98 'It seems like a grim . . .' quoted Curti *American Philanthrophy Abroad*, p. 101.

p. 100 'May the ships . . .' *New York Sun*, 13 January 1896.

p. 102 'I doubt if I will ever . . .' quoted Pryor *Clara Barton: Professional Angel*, p. 296.

p. 106 'to make a nice . . .' quoted Pryor *Clara Barton: Professional Angel*, p. 317.

p. 109 'It is a hard . . .' Diary of Clara Barton, 11 May 1901, Library of Congress, Washington.

p. 110 'Good Lord! . . .' quoted Pryor *Clara Barton: Professional Angel*, p. 332.

5. Rebels, Barbarians and Perjurers

For a real understanding of the International Committee's early years see the *Bulletin*, which later became the *International Review*. Nothing gives a better flavour of the times.

p. 122 'Moynier took the view . . .' *Bulletin*, January 1880.

p. 124 'the Convention is . . .' Procés-verbal, 27 November 1872, ICRC archives, Geneva.

p. 131ff For good accounts of the early British Red Cross Society see D. Anderson *The Balkan Volunteers*, London: Hutchinson, 1968; P. Morris (ed.) *First Aid to the Battlefront: The Life and Letters of Sir Vincent Kennett-Harrington 1844–1903*, London: Alan Sutton, 1992; B. Oliver *The British Red Cross in Action*, London: Faber & Faber, 1966; and particularly the papers of Lord Wantage and J. S. Young at the British Red Cross archives. The British newspapers of the time are also helpful.

p. 137 'At the end of June . . .' *Lancaster Guardian*, 20 June 1885.

p. 138 'red-edged . . .' *Pall Mall Gazette*, 23 February 1884.

p. 139ff The Boer War and the activities of the Red Cross in South Africa are described in I. Hay *One Hundred Years of Army Nursing*, London: Cassell & Co, 1953; H. Hay Harrison *Hedge of White Almonds: South Africa, the Pro-Boers and the Quaker Conscience 1890–1910*, London: Heinemann, 1989; M. Memper *War Impressions*, London: A & C Black, 1901; T. Pakenham *The Boer War*, London: Weidenfeld & Nicolson, London, 1979; B. Roberts *These Bloody Women: Three Heroines of the Boer War*, London: John Murray, 1990; B. Farrell *The Great Boer War*, London: Allen Lane, 1976; S. Burdett–Coutts *The Sick and Wounded in South Africa*, London: Cassell & Co, 1900; J. Furley, 'The Truth About the Conduct of the War: Extracts from the Blue Book', *Peace and War*, London: The Patriotic Association in the British Red Cross archives.

p. 141 'pottering about the wards . . .' Roberts *These Bloody Women*, p. 3.

p. 141 'ladies who think . . .' Wantage papers, British Red Cross archives.

p. 142 'On their return . . .' S. Trombley *Sir Frederick Treves*, London: Routledge, 1989, p. 103.

p. 143 'On the British side . . .' Wantage papers, British Red Cross archives.

p. 145 'What struck her . . .' Pakenham *The Boer War*, p. 507.

p. 145 'policy of genocide . . .' Farrell *The Great Boer War*, p. 424.

p. 146 'In America . . .' J. H. Ferguson *American Diplomacy and the Boer War*, University of Pennsylvania Press, 1990, p. 174.

6. American Angels of Mercy

For much of the material on the origins of the Japanese and Russian Red Cross societies I am indebted to the librarians and archivists of the two societies. Olive Checkland *Humanitarianism and the Emperor's Japan 1877–1977*, London: Macmillan, 1994, gives a comprehensive description of the build-up to the Russo-Japanese war which is also covered in:

L. L. Seaman *The Real Triumph of Japan*, New York: D. Appleton, 1906.

L. L. Seaman *From Tokyo Through Manchuria with the Japanese*, New York: D. Appleton, 1905.

E. McCaul *Under the Care of the Japanese War Office*, Cassell & Co.

Baron Suyematsuy *The Risen Sun*, Archibald Constable & Co, 1905.

Mrs Richardson *In Japanese Hospitals During Wartime*, Blackwood & Sons, 1905.

E. E. P. Tisdall *The Dowager Empress*, Stanley Paul, 1957.

E. M. Almedingen *The Empress Alexandra 1872–1918*, London: Hutchinson, 1961.

S. Buxhoeven *Before the Storm*, London: Macmillan & Co, 1938.

R. Pipes (ed.) *The Russian Intelligentsia*, Columbia University Press, 1961.

The Furley papers in the British Red Cross archives also contain much useful material.

Good accounts of the International Committee and its views on peace, and Henri Dunant and the Nobel Peace prize are to be found in:

P. van den Dungen 'Peace Ideas and Peace Movements of the Mid-Nineteenth Century,' Lecture given to the Henri Dunant Association, May 1905.

A. Durant 'The Development of the Idea of Peace in the Thinking of Henri Dunant,' *International Review*, January 1986.

B. von Suttner *Memoirs*, Boston and London: Ginn & Co, 1910.

p. 155 'please bow . . .' McCaul *Under the Care of the Japanese War Office*, p. 219.

p. 157 'This business-like . . .' F. Treves *The Other Side of the Lantern*, London: Cassell & Co, 1904, p. 402.

p. 161ff Henri Dunant's last years are described in a number of articles in the *Bulletin* and *International Review* and in others collected by the Henri Dunant Society in Geneva.

p. 162 'The world gives us . . .' 29 June 1885, Dunant to his niece, Dunant papers.

p. 162 'The hospital, he wrote . . .' September 1892, Dunant to his brother, Dunant papers.

p. 164 'the Committee voted . . .' Procès-verbal, 10 October 1904, ICRC archives, Geneva.

p. 166 'it is in the ranks . . .' 18 July 1896, Berta von Suttner to Dunant, Dunant papers.

p. 168 'An Austrian, Baron von Horst . . .' *Bulletin*, April 1892.

p. 169 'When all the powers . . .' quoted Boissier *From Solferino to Tsushima*, p. 379.

p. 171 'No event gives . . .' Association des Dames Françaises archives of the French Red Cross.

7. The Little Cushion of Europe

The work done by the International Committee in the First World War is extremely well covered in the *Bulletin* in a special series of reports of the visits carried out by delegates to the various prisoner-of-war camps under the heading 'Documents publiés à l'occasion de la Guerre de 1914–1918,' and in dozens of contemporary memoirs, many of a personal nature. The following files in the ICRC archives in Geneva contain relevant papers: Box 24 III/419, VI, VII/419, X/419 and XX; Box 25 XV and XIX; Box 39 XI/5; Box 43 II/17; Box 47 VI/1 and VI/8; FAW 36, 37 and 10.

p. 178 'From today . . .' *Bulletin*, October 1914.

p. 179 'As the white ship . . .' F. R. Dulles *The American Red Cross*, Harper & Bros, 1950, p. 131.

p. 179 'Soon, newspapers . . .' *American Red Cross Magazine*, December 1916.

p. 189 'The word of an officer . . .' *Bulletin*, October 1917.

p. 189 'particularly gruesome reports . . .' *The History of the War*, vol. 6, London: Times Books, 1988, p. 145.

p. 191 'until 1915, the diet . . .' 'The Diet of Prisoners of War,' *Journal of the American Medical Association*, vol. LXII, No. 19, 1917, p. 1575.

p. 202 'the greatest danger . . .' *Bulletin*, July 1917.

p. 203 'for once, it seems . . .' *Bulletin*, February 1915.

p. 204 'the early spirit . . .' 'Reports on Family Visits to Soldiers Interned in Switzerland,' British Red Cross archives, London.

p. 204 'For the most part . . .' 'Les Oeuvres de Guerre on Suisse,' *Nouvelles de L'Agence Internationale des Prisoniers de Guerre*, No. 50, 30 December 1916.

p. 205 'The Bulletin greeted the New Year . . .' *Bulletin*, January 1917.

8. One of Us, Heart and Soul

No war had ever attracted more volunteers to the Red Cross ideal from every part of the world than the First World War. Dozens, hundreds of the young British women and British doctors who responded to calls for help, left memoirs of their experiences; biographies and historical reminiscences have continued to appear ever since. Among the most interesting and enjoyable are:

L. Macdonald *The Roses of No Man's Land*, London: Michael Joseph, 1980.

D. Stuart *Dear Duchess: Millicent Duchess of Sutherland 1867–1955*, London: Victor Gollancz, 1982.

H. Popham *FANY: The Story of the Women's Transport Service 1907–1984*, London: Secker & Warburg, 1984.

D. Walker *With the Lost Generation 1915–1918*, London: A. Brown & Sons Ltd, 1970.

M. Fedden *Sisters' Quarters: Salonika*,
London: Grant Richards Ltd, 1921.

M. Dearmer *Letters from a Field Hospital*,
London: Macmillan & Co, 1916.

A. Summers *Angels & Citizens 1854–1914*,
London: Routledge & Kegan Paul,
1988.

F. Stark *A Traveller's Prelude*, London:
John Murray, 1950.

B. McLaren *Women of the War*, London:
Hodder & Stoughton, 1917.

M. Krippner *The Quality of Mercy*,
London: David & Charles, 1980.

E. Corbett *The Red Cross in Serbia*,
London: Cheyney & Sons, 1964.

The archives of the British Red Cross
contain numerous personal
accounts as well as the reports of
the Joint War Committee 1914–
1919. *The Red Cross: The Official Journal
of the British Red Cross Society* is also
worth consulting.

p. 210 'a churchgoing Yorkshireman . . .'
J. A. Spender (ed.) *Sir Robert Hudson:
A Memoir*, Cassell & Co, 1930,
p. 134.

p. 212 'busy band of aristocratic
amazons . . .' Popham *FANY*, p. 16.

P. 217 'The Germans, she observed . . .'
Macdonald *The Roses of No Man's
Land*, p. 42.

p. 222 'In the retreat . . .' 'The record of
the First Red Cross Unit for Italy,'
British Red Cross archive, London.

p. 227 'She was fortunate . . .' Krippner
The Quality of Mercy, p. 79.

p. 230 'Calling them by the stranger . . .'
Corbett *The Red Cross in Serbia*,
p. 179.

9. The Greatest Mother in the World

Of the many excellent memoirs of the
Russian Red Cross see in particular:

F. Farmborough *Nurse at the Russian Front:
A Diary 1914–1918*, London:
Constable, 1974.

Like the British volunteers the
Americans who now flocked to the
war were keen diarists. Some of
their writings appeared in the
magazine of the American Red
Cross, or are to be found among
the archives of the American Red
Cross in Washington. The following
were published as memoirs:

E. P. Bickwell *Pioneering with the Red Cross*,
London: Macmillan & Co, 1935.

E. P. Bickwell *In War's Wake 1914–1918*,
Washington: The American Red
Cross, 1935.

L. Binyon *For Dauntless France*, Hodder &
Stoughton, 1930.

G. Atherton *The Living Present*, John
Murray, 1917.

p. 233 'There was no drunkenness . . .'
B. Pares *Day by Day with the Russian
Army 1914–1915*, London: Constable
& Co, 1915, p. xi.

p. 234 'They are matter-of-fact . . .' V.
Thurston *Field Hospital and Flying
Column*, London: C. P. Putnam &
Sons, 1915 and *The People Who run*,
London: C. P. Putnam & Sons, 1916.

p. 234 'In November 1915 . . .' W. Blunt
Lady Muriel, London: Methuen, 1962.

p. 235 'There was some trouble . . .' see
M. Harmer *The Forgotten Hospital*,
London: Springwood Books, 1982.

p. 237 'a "purification" of the
central . . .' *Bulletin*, October 1917.

p. 238 'They bear a heavy . . .' *Bulletin*, January 1918.

p. 240 'No Red Cross aid . . .' Dulles *The American Red Cross*, p. 32.

p. 241 'The Red Cross aid . . .' Dulles *The American Red Cross*, p. 141.

p. 244 'A tearful scandal . . .' Letter from Clara McW. Gracen, American Red Cross archives, November 1917.

p. 244 'was averted by soothing phrases . . .' H. P. Davison *The American Red Cross in the Great War*, London: Macmillan & Co, 1919, p. 25.

p. 244 'I am sustained . . .' *American Red Cross Bulletin*, 28 October 1918.

p. 246 'The True Red Crosser . . .' Dulles *The American Red Cross*, p. 163.

p. 246 'By now, France alone . . .' F. Ames *American Red Cross Work Among the French People*, London: Macmillan & Co. 1921.

p. 247 'As Davison saw it . . .' Davison *The American Red Cross in the Great War*, p. 32.

p. 250 The story of the Russian children is to be found in papers in the archives of the American Red Cross and in F. Muller *The Wild Children of the Urals*, London: Hodder & Stoughton, 1966.

p. 254 'It was a weird sight . . .' C. B. Purdom (ed.) *Everyman at War*, London: J. Dent & Sons, 1930.

p. 256 'a French army major . . .' 'La Paix Par le Droits,' Anonymous report in the French Red Cross archives, undated.

10. The Amiable Gentlemen of Geneva

The story of the birth of the League can be followed in J. F. Hutchinson *Charity, War and the Rise of the Red Cross*, Westview Press, 1996; C. E. Buckingham *For Humanity's Sake*, Washington DC: Public Affairs Press, 1964; and in the papers and correspondence held in the American Red Cross archives in Washington. In May 1919, the first *Bulletin of the League of Red Cross Societies* appeared and was followed in July 1920 by the first volume of the *International Journal of Public Health*. Between them the two publications provide the best overview, year by year, of the League's activities.

p. 259 'What Davison seemed to . . .' Letter, Davison to Harvey Gibson, 22 November 1918, League of Red Cross and Red Crescent Societies archives, Geneva.

p. 260 'At a meeting . . .' Memorandum, 2 December 1918, League of Red Cross and Red Crescent Societies archive, Geneva.

p. 261 'gladly co-operative . . .' Letter from Davison to President Wilson, 2 January 1919, League of Red Cross and Red Crescent Societies archives, Geneva.

p. 266 Accounts of the prisoners-of-war are based largely on the reports and letters sent to Geneva from the International Committee delegates in the field and are to be found in the archives. See *'Secours a l'Ukraine,'* Mis 25 A/5/1 in the ICRC archives, Geneva. See also Mis 1/5; Mis 4/5/624; Mis 25/1/232 and Mis 5/5/1167. There are also extensive papers and descriptions in the archives of the Save the Children Fund and a long description in H. H. Fisher *The Famine in the Soviet Union 1919–23*, London: Macmillan & Co, 1927.

p. 266 'literally abandoned by everybody . . .' Report from E. Frick,

1 November 1919, ICRC archives, Geneva.

p. 270 'By now, Frick . . .' '*Rapports sur la Lutte Contre les Epidemies*,' Mis 16 5/1, ICRC archives, Geneva.

p. 271 'It was not . . .' 'Mission Piaget, Hofer, Hacius, Dr Blanchot 1919,' carton oo Mis, ICRC archives, Geneva.

p. 272 'One of three American . . .' 'The American Red Cross in Russia,' report in the ARC archives.

p. 272 'She was arrested . . .' E. Brandström *Among Prisoners of War in Russia and Siberia*, Hutchinson & Co, 1930.

p. 273 'The current state . . .' 12 January 1920, Simonett to ICRC, ICRC archives, Geneva.

p. 275 'This was only the beginning . . .' Frick papers 1918–19, ICRC archives, Geneva.

p. 275 'Morality complete, collapse . . .' '*Rapport de la Mission de Secours du CICR en Pologne et Galicia*,' Mis 5.5.16, ICRC archives, Geneva.

p. 275 'Its first mission . . .' *League Bulletin*, vol. 1, no. 5, November 1919.

p. 277 'There had been terrible . . .' A. Haines 'The Russian Famine', Temp Ms 590/2, Quaker Friends House, London.

p. 278 'Soon, Wehrlin was . . .', 6 February 1922, Wehrlin to ICRC, ICRC archives, Geneva.

p. 280 'their bodies deformed . . .' Fisher *The Famine in the Soviet Union 1919–23*, p. 89.

P. 281 'The Save the Children . . .' The Eglantyne Jebb and Suzanne Ferrière papers are to be found in the SCF archives.

p. 290 'He wishes,' he said . . .' *Bulletin*, Edmond Boissier, May 1923.

11. The Feet of Little Angels

Good accounts of the Tokyo conference are to be found in the newspapers of the day and in the pages of the *Bulletin* and the League's *Bulletin*. See also: L. E. Gielgud *About It and About: Letters from a Diary of Travel*, Oxford: William Blackwell & Sons, 1938.

The story of the International Committee, the Red Cross societies and the war in Abyssinia is based largely on the reports, letters and telegrams sent by Junod and Brown, on the papers in the ICRC archives and on conversations with Rainer Baudendistel, a former ICRC delegate and author of a forthcoming book on the International Committee and the war. See also file CR 210/1.

The Spanish Civil War is minutely described in the reports, letters and telegrams that went between Spain and Geneva (in particular, files on the Spanish Civil War, CR 212 and C. 3.9) in M. Junod *Le Troisième Combattant*, translated into English by Edward Fitzgerald, London: Jonathan Cape, 1951. I am also indebted to the recollections of Jean Pictet.

p. 292 'All things of this kind . . .' Judge John Barton Payne, 16 May 1934, American Red Cross archive, Washington.

p. 297 'His report . . .' S. Brown 'Mission à Shanghai', *Bulletin*, March 1932.

p. 299 'reports on youth work . . .' *Bulletin*, July 1930.

p. 300 'medical magazines . . .' *Bulletin*, April 1930.

p. 306 'Even as they left . . .' M. Frick Cramer, 9 October 1935, ICRC archives, Geneva.

p. 310 'From the British . . .' J. W. S. Macfie *An Ethiopian Diary: A Record of the British Ambulance Service in Ethiopia*, Liverpool University Press, 1936, p. 79.

p. 314 'It was left to . . .' Minute of meeting, 3 July 1936, ICRC archives, Geneva.

p. 314 'If today . . .' Report 16, 12 May 1936, ICRC archives, Geneva.

p. 314 'He was a very good . . .' Letter, 30 April 1936, Archivio Centrale dello Stato, Groce Rossa Italiana, Basta 189, Fasciculo 9.

p. 319 'If I let people go . . .' Boissier *From Solferino to Tsushima*, p. 329.

p. 323 'Camp in chaos . . .' quoted in Durand (ed.) *History*, p. 359.

p. 326 'We managed to extricate . . .' Junod *Le Troisieme Combattant*, p. 128.

12. Where a Savage Inquisition is Master

Accounts of the German Red Cross in the 1930s come from issues of the *Deutsche Rote Kreuz*, from articles in the *Bulletin* and the League's *Bulletin*, and from reports and correspondence in the ICRC archives (see, in particular, file CROO/4/11 and CR 110/1, 'Guerre civile en Autriche' CR 204), from British and American newspapers of the 1930s, from the *Deutsche Allgemeine Zeitung*. Good accounts appear in *Papers Concerning the Treatment of German Nationals in Germany*, Cmd 6120, London: HMSO, 19xx; I. Cohen 'The Jews in Germany', *Quarterly Review*, Vol 61, July 1933 and in the archives of the Wiener Institute Library.

The Sino-Japanese war and the ICRC is covered in the ICRC archives and reports. See also the Public Record Office, FO 371, 20953, 20966.

p. 330 'back to the spring of 1919 . . .' A very full account of the ICRC's work with political prisoners is to be found in J. Moreillon 'Le CICR et la protection des détenus politiques,' *L'Age de L'Homme*, Lausanne Editions, 1973. I am also indebted to conversations with M. Moreillon on the subject.

p. 332 Much of the material on the Soviet Union is based on the reports, letters and cables exchanged between Wehrlin and the ICRC; on Camps de Concentration: Russia File 21, C archives; R. Conquest *The Harvest of Sorrow, Hutchinson*, 1986 provides a useful overview.

p. 334 'The fact was . . .' Wehrlin to ICRC, 3 April 1922, ICRC archives, Geneva.

p. 334 'The Committee decided . . .' 16 May 1922, Ferrière to Soloviev, ICRC archives.

p. 335 'The number of detained . . .' 19 January 1927, Communiqué from Wehrlin, ICRC archives.

p. 336 'In June . . .' Communique from Wehrlin, 1 June 1939, ICRC archives, Geneva.

p. 336 'From Moscow . . .' Boissier, *From Solferino to Tsushima*, p. 236.

p. 336 'As he put it . . .' 24 January 1935, Private paper by Huber, ICRC archives, Geneva.

p. 340 'from Colonel Draudt . . .' 2 February 1924, ICRC archives, Geneva.

p. 343 'in solitary confinement . . .' 30

July 1933, F. Kahn to ICRC, ICRC archives, Geneva.

p. 343 'a conservative estimate . . .' 9 November 1933, ICRC archives, Geneva.

p. 344 'undoubtedly help . . .' Boissier, *From Solferino in Tsushima*, p. 278.

p. 346 'do not only correspond . . .' 22 October 1934, M. von Beck to Huber, ICRC archives, Geneva.

p. 347 'the answer came back . . .' 31 October 1934, Ferrière to Clouzot, ICRC archives, Geneva.

p. 347 'As a medical and social . . .' see R. J. Lifton *The Nazi Doctors: Medical Killing and the Psychology of Genocide*, New York: Basic Books, 1986; M. Burleigh *Death and Deliverance: Euthanasia in Germany 1900–1945*, Cambridge University Press, 1946; *The Yellow Spot: Collection of Documents on Jewish Persecution*, London: Victor Gollancz, 1936.

p. 348 'A photograph appeared . . .' *Das Deutsche Rote Kreuz*, February 1939.

p. 349 'He wanted to listen . . .' Von Cleve to Sidney Brown, 21 November 1933, ICRC archives, Geneva.

p. 349 'He wanted to think . . .' Minute of meeting, 21 September 1935, ICRC archives, Geneva.

p. 353 'Huber wrote to the Duke . . .' 28 October, 1935, Huber to Saxe-Coburg, ICRC archives, Geneva.

p. 353 'Burckhardt wrote to Saxe-Coburg . . .' 12 December 1935, ICRC archives, Geneva.

p. 353 'Early in 1936 . . .' 20 February 1936, Saxe-Coburg to Burckhardt ICRC archives, Geneva.

p. 356 'He behaved . . .' 'Proceedings for 8 April 1947', *The Trial of German Major War Criminals: Procedures of the International Military Tribunal Sitting at Nuremberg, Germany*, London: HMSO, 1948.

p. 357 'Grawitz wrote a terse . . .' 21 March 1937, ICRC archives.

p. 363ff. The Sino–Japanese war and the ICRC is covered in the ICRC archives and reports. See also FO 371, 20953, 20966, Public Record Office, London.

p. 364 'murder. Murder . . .' *Shanghai Evening Post & Mercury*, 30 August 1937.

p. 366 'We are faced here . . .' 25 March 1938, Calame to ICRC, ICRC archives, Geneva.

p. 367 'All the alley ways . . .' 15 March 1938, Calame, ICRC archives, Geneva.

p. 369 'I am becoming . . .' 19 July 1939, N. Davis, Federation of Red Cross and Red Crescent Societies archives, Geneva.

13. New and Old Instruments of Destruction

The International Committee covered its own activities in the Second World War in detail, in the *International Review*, in special publications and, once the war was over, in a three-volume report. The League and the various national Red Cross societies covered their own activities in their own magazines. Much of the material in this chapter is based on the ICRC archives, on the reports of the various delegates, on the *Journal des délègues* which was started in April 1942, on the archives held by the ARC and BRC societies, on papers in the Public Records Office, on wartime histories and memoirs and on conversations with former delegates. See in particular ICRC file G17/URSS, 49a/500 and G17/134 on Russian prisoners-of-war; G3/27c on Greece; G3/14a on Germany; G3/24b on Italy. In the Public Record Office see FO 916887, FO 916557 and G 3/4 on Poland.

p. 373 'authoritative papers for the *Review* . . .' *Review*, November 1939.

p. 373 'The younger members called him the "brake" . . . Maître Lalive in conversation with the author, July 1995.

p. 379 'Dr Hans Wolf de Salis . . .' For a full account of the Italian delegation see file Italy 194–42, G3/24b, ICRC archives.

p. 379 'Many years before . . .' Conversation between Denise Werner and author, 22 July 1995.

p. 381 'Delegates, Junod . . .' Talk to AGM of Geneva branch of Swiss Red cross, 29 March 1943.

p. 384 'Nothing gives . . .' See the papers and archives of the British Red Cross.

p. 385 'Then there were medicines . . .' Dr Pierre Calpini in conversation with the author, July 1995.

p. 386 'One day . . .' Maître Lalive in conversation with the author, 2 August 1995.

p. 388 'Colonel Frederick Islin . . .' See Public Record Office FO 916113.

p. 390 'A very live wire . . .' FO 916 File 112, Note FO to Wo, 21 February 1941.

p. 391 'more interesting . . .' FO 916113 ICRC.

p. 392 'The blockade . . .' 'Starving for Democracy; Britain's Blockade of and Relief for Occupied Europe 1939–45,' *World Society*, vol. 18, 2 October 1990; see also R.

Courvoisier *Ceux qui ne devaient pas mourir*, Paris: Robert Laffont, 1978.

p. 399 'the report describes . . .' ICRC G/17/13.

P. 400 'systematic and barbarous . . .' 23 April 1940, Norman Davis to Huber, ICRC archives, Geneva.

p. 401 'without positive proof . . .' 22 May 1940.

p. 402 'we should not forget . . .' FO 916563, 21 January 1943.

p. 403 'I feel fairly . . .' FO 916533, 26 January 1943.

p. 405 '1939 came at the end . . .' Barbara Pathé in conversation with author, March 1995.

p. 406 'There had been considerable . . .' G. Karson *At His Side: The Story of the ARC Overseas in the Second World War*, New York: Coward McCann, 1945.

p. 408 'stripped to make way . . .' Mme Schumacher in conversation with author, March 1995.

p. 408 'Searchers, some of them . . .' Melchior Borsinger in conversation with the author, July 1995.

14. Keep the Fires Burning Under Those Old Gentlemen

For a detailed account of the ICRC efforts on behalf of civilians see the file 'Projet d'une convention internationale en faveur des internes civiles 1925–43'.

Of the many books written about the Holocaust, a number have a bearing on the International Committee. Most important is J-C Favez *Une Mission Impossible? Le CICR, les Déportations et les Camps de Concentration Nazis*, Editions Payot Lausanne, 1988. The following provide invaluable insights: W. Lacqueur *The Terrible Secret*, London: Weidenfeld &

Nicolson, 1980 D. Arsenijevic
Voluntary Hostages of the SS, Paris:
Editions France-Empire, 1979.

D. Goldhagen *Hitler's Willing Executioners*,
London: Little, Brown and Co, 1996.

E. Thomas Wood and S. M. Jankowski
Karski *How One Man Tried to Stop the
Holocaust*, New York: Jan Wiley,
1980.

Material for this section is again based
on the ICRC archives, on an
account of the work done on behalf
of civilians published at the end of
the war, and on personal
conversations with J-C Favez, and
Burckhardt's biographer, Dr Paul
Stauffer, and Gerhart Riegner.

Material on Poland comes from Favez,
from conversations with members
of the Polish Red Cross, from
Zamosc's Association of Survivors
and from conversations with Dr
Roman Hrabar and R. Hrabar, Z.
Tokarz and J. Wiczur *The Fate of
Polish Children During the Last War*,
Warsaw: Interpress, 1981.

A. Ben-Tov *Facing the Holocaust in Budapest:
The ICRC and the Jews in Hungary
1943–45*, Geneva: Henri Dunant
Institute, 1988 gives a full account
of the ICRC's work in Hungary. I
am also indebted to long
conversations with Mr Ben-Tov in
March 1993 and with Theo Tschuy,
the biographer of Lutz. See also the
reports of ICRC delegates De Bavier,
Born and Wyerman in the ICRC
archives; Mission Hongrie G3 148 c
111 and Born's report G/45. The
following books and papers are also
relevant:

J. Levai *Eichmann in Hungary*, Budapest:
Pannonia Press, 1961

J Bierman *Righteous Gentile*, London:
Allen Lane, 1981

J. Levai *Hungarian Jewry and the Papacy:
Reports, Documents and Records from
Church and State Archives*, London:
Sands & Co, 1966

E Levai *The Black Book of the Martyrdom of
Hungarian Jewry*, Budapest: Pannarana
Co. Ltd, 1948.

American Red Cross report on
Hungary, 30 June 1943, American
Red Cross archives, Washington.

Many accounts have been written about
the liberation of the camps. For
good material on the ICRC and the
Red Cross see the reports of the
delegates as they entered the camps,
and also Report No. 3, Annexe 27,
23 April 1945 (Kuhne) and the
archives of the British Red Cross
and the American Red Cross. See
also:

E. Bark *No Time to Kill*, London: Robert
Hale, 1960.

A. Pfirter *Memories of a Red Cross Mission to
Belsen*, Geneva: International
Committee of the Red Cross, 1954.

'Belsen: Medical Aspects,' *Journal of the
Royal Army Medical Corps*, February
1984.

'Trials of the German Major War
Criminals: The Medical Cases,'
Nuremburg papers, London: HMSO,
1946.

The Letters of Enid Fernandes about
Belsen, Enid Fernandes papers,
British Red Cross archives, London.

The Terezin Diary of Gonda Redlich,
Gonda Redlich papers, Wiener
Library, London.

p. 412 'worried about the fact . . .'
Commission des civils, 1 June 1931,
ICRC archives, Geneva.

p. 413 'Edmond Boissier's paper . . .' See

file CR 110/1-11, ICRC archives, Geneva.

p. 414 'Burckhardt would note . . .' C. Burkhardt *Ma Mission à Danzig*, Paris: Librairie Arthème Fayard, 1961, p. 138.

p. 419 'In August 1942 . . .' Gerhart Riegner in conversation with the author, 26 July 1995 and 1 January 1997.

p. 420 'At least some of the explanation . . .' See A. Lasserre and E. Payot *Frontières et Camps: Le Refuge en Suisse de 1933 a 1945*, Lausanne, 1980.

p. 424 'In October . . .' Gerhart Riegner in conversation with the author, 1 January 1997.

p. 424 'Squire apparently . . .' See Lacqueur *The Terrible Secret*, p. 63.

p. 433 'order of good blood . . .' C. Henry and M. Hillel *Children of the SS*, London: Hutchinson, 1976. See also C. Clay and M. Leapman *Master Race*, London: Hodder & Stoughton, 1995.

p. 436 'On 25 July . . .' Wanda Cebrykow in conversation with the author, 10 May 1995.

p. 441 'At the beginning of . . .' Eugeniusz Sztomberek in conversation with the author, 6 May 1995.

p. 442 'Race is subordinate . . .' Ben-Tov *Facing the Holocaust*, p. 106.

p. 442 'a square, stocky . . .' Geza Kiss in conversation with the author, June 1995.

p. 444 'the idea of looking on . . .' Born, 10 June 1944, ICRC archives, Geneva.

p. 444 'keep the fires . . .' Ben-Tov *Facing the Holocaust*, p. 189.

p. 449 'to this day . . .' Dr Laszlo Karsai in conversation with the author, 1 June 1995.

p. 454 'As for the Jews . . .' R. Marti, 4 November 1942, ICRC archives, Geneva.

p. 457 'negotiate in a moral . . .' Arsenijevic *Voluntary Hostages of the SS*, p. 142.

p. 458 'For the love of God . . .' Favez *Une Mission Impossible*, p. 347.

p. 459 'There is another . . .' Favez in conversation with the author, 1 January 1997.

p. 460 'On 15 April . . .' American Red Cross field report, 1–31 May 1945, American Red Cross archives, Washington.

p. 467 'it is difficult to refuse . . .' Chenevière, 16 October 1939, ICRC archives, Geneva.

p. 467 'it was thought that . . .' PRO file 70 041.

P. 467 'at this juncture . . .' H. C. Thompson to A. J. Berres, 6 April 1940, American Red Cross archives, Washington.

p. 469 'one way to rehabilitation . . .' see A. Mitscherlich and F. Mielke *Doctors of Infamy: The Story of Nazi Medical Crimes*, New York: Henry Schuman, 1949.

15. Piercing the Darkness

p. 473 'As Dr Paravicini . . .' Boissier *From Solferino to Tsushima*, p. 523.

p. 473 'Europeans in the city . . .' 2 February 1942, ICRC archives, Geneva.

p. 473 'No permission . . .' See ICRC files 'Delegation to China and Shanghai G 17/34; and particularly files from Schweizer and Salzmann; also File Strahler and Junod mission 1943–46, 219 and Delegation to Japan 1945, G8/76 and PROFO 916 1234 and FO 916 113.

p. 477 'In the corridors . . .' See PRO file FO 916 332, ICRC 1942.

p. 477 'I found everybody . . .' Report from Shanghai, 18 July 1942; see also D. Kranzler *Japanese, Nazis and Jews: The Jewish Refugee Community of Shanghai 1936–45*, New York: Yeshsiva University Press, 1976.

p. 484 'A Chinese pastor . . .' See E. Gordon *Miracle on the River Kwai*, London: William Collins, 1963.

p. 484 'described prisoners without shoes . . .' PRO HO 215 95, Siam and Singapore 1944.

p. 486 'slow and painful process . . .' see PRO FO 916 774; see also HO 215 95; FO 916 112, FO 916 332.

p. 486 'a large, soft . . .' 1 January 1944 in PRO FO 916 939; see also papers and reports in ARC archives.

p. 487 'On your attitude . . .' Junod *Le Troisième Combattant*, p. 267.

p. 489 'An extraordinary silence . . .' See Junod 'The Hiroshima Disaster', *International Review*, September– October 1982.

p. 491 'A lot of men . . .' J. Boone, Talk to the ARC, 16 January 1956, American Red Cross archives.

p. 492 'Marie Adams . . .' Report in ARC archives, 7 June 1945.

p. 493 'Lady Mountbatten . . .' Letter to Lady Dunbar-Nasmith, 7 October 1945.

p. 495 'It must have been . . .' PRO FO 916 1438, 8 September 1945.

p. 495 'From Schweitzer . . .' 11 October 1945, ICRC archives, Geneva.

p. 497 'Personnel who . . .' See A. C. Brackman *The Other Nuremberg: The Untold Story of the Tokyo War Crimes Trials*, London: William Collins, 1989 and J. Dower *War Without Mercy*, London: Pantheon, 1986.

p. 499 'It had been the international . . .' *International Review*, April 1945.

16. Surviving the Cold Winter

p. 500 'Europe is on . . .' M. Wyman *DP: Europe's Displaced Persons 1945–51*, Philadelphia: Bailch International Press, 1989, p. 15; see also M. R. Marrus *The Unwanted: European Refugees in the Twentieth Century*, New York: Oxford University Press, 1985; V. Gollancz *In Darkest Germany*, London: Victor Gollancz, 1947; ICRC reports on the activities of the Commission Mixte, PRO file F 1231; The Red Cross and St John: The Official Record of the Humanitarian Services of the War Organization 1939–47, British Red Cross 1949.

p. 501 'Citizenship . . .' Quoted in Wyman *DP*, p. 88.

p. 503 'A British Red Cross . . .' Report 'Over to You', August 1945, British Red Cross archives, London.

p. 504 'Most of them were . . .' Wyman *DP*, p. 88.

p. 505 'Vlotho, a sixteenth-century . . .' N. Burckhardt in conversation with author, July 1995.

p. 507 'grey-skinned people . . .' E. Jorden *Operation Mercy*, London: Frederick Muller, 1957, p. 76.

p. 507: not deliberately . . .' V. Gollancz *Leaving Them to Their Fate*, London: Gollancz, 1946.

p. 508 'Joan Couper . . .' 'Civilian war relief', report in the British Red Cross archives, London.

p. 510 'So far . . .' Report in the American Red Cross archives, October 1946.

p. 512 'Sigrid Bork, born . . .' The archives of the German Red Cross Tracing Department and in particular the Tracing Books; International Tracing Service archives, Arolsen; G. Djurovic *The*

Central Tracing Agency of the ICRC,
Geneva: Henri Dunant Institute,
1986.

p. 516 'Muriel Monkhouse . . .' Muriel
Monkhouse in conversation with
author, 13 June 1995.

p. 523 'Roman Hraber . . .' Roman
Hraber in conversation with author,
16 May 1995; and R. Hrabar, Z
Tokarz and J. Wilczur *The Fate of
Polish Children During the Last War*,
p. 246.

p. 526 'Among Hrabar's contacts . . .' see
ARC, BRC and ICRC archives and
particularly file CR00/4.

p. 527 'Foreigners living . . . ; Princess
Marguerite of Hesse in conversation
with the author, 3 May 1995.

17. One Reference to God

p. 530 'On 8 June . . .' ICRC archives, G
17/51/13.

p. 531 'From Perigueux . . .' 30
September 1945, M. Vienne to
Barbey, ICRC archives, Geneva.

p. 532 'In 1944 . . .' Jean Courvoisier in
conversation with author, 15 July
1995.

p. 535 'Some of this disillusionment . . .'
see ICRC archives G 3/26 h 11.

p. 535 'Mrs McCready . . .' Mrs
McCready to J. P. Pradervand, 13
September 1945, ICRC archives,
Geneva.

p. 536 'These people are dying . . .' de
Reynolds, 1 October 1945, ICRC
archives, Geneva.

p. 536 'Alarming reports . . .' See ICRC
archives G. 8/47 and G. 17/51/13, 9
September 1945.

p. 538 'politics of vengeance . . .' *Combat*,
26 September 1945.

p. 538 'At last, something . . .' See ICRC
archives G. 8/51 and G. 3/26 h; some

of this material is based on a
conversation with M. Pradervand, 29
July 1995.

p. 538 'Reports suggest a minimum . . .'
J. Bacque *Other Losses: An Investigation
into the Mass Death of German Prisoners at
the Hands of the French and Americans
after the Second World War*, Canada:
Stoddart, 1989.

p. 539ff. New material continues to
emerge in 1998 from ICRC archives
and Swiss state papers.

p. 541 'From September on . . .' M.
Kochan *Prisoners in England*, London:
Macmillan Press, 1980, p. 130.

p. 543 'Long before the fighting . . .' E.
Chapuisat 'Le Comité Internationale
de la Croix-Rouge et L'Aide aux
Israelites,' *International Review*,
December 1945; also 'Documents sur
l'Activité du CICR en Faveur des
Civils Détenus dans les Camps de
Concentration en Allemagne 1939–
45,' in the *International Review*, March
–April 1946.

p. 543 'sadly sterile . . .' *International
Review*, 18 September 1944.

p. 544 'last, eloquent speech . . .' To
Swedish Red Cross Society AGM, 1
June 1945.

p. 544 'Jean Pictet . . .' Jean Pictet in
conversation with the author, 31
July 1995, 3 January 1997.

p. 548 'In 1946, I was invited . . .'
Gerhart Riegner in conversation
with the author, 3 January 1997.

p. 550 'friendship and comradeship . . .'
F. Bernadotte *Instead of Arms*,
London: Hodder and Stoughton,
1949, p. 131.

p. 551ff. 'The passions that . . .' For an
excellent appraisal of the 1949
Geneva Conventions see G. Best
War and Law since 1945, Oxford:
Clarendon Press, 1994; D. Forsythe
Humanitarian Politics: The International

Committee of the Red Cross, John Hopkins University Press, 1977; W. Hays Parks 'Air War and the Law of War,' *Air Force Law Review*, vol. 32, 1990. The ICRC have also published numerous documents on the subject.

18. Affairs of the Heart

The account of the International Committee's work in Palestine is based on reports that appeared in the *Review*, others written for the Committee by delegates and conversations with Pierre Gaillard, Dominique Junod, Jean Courvoisier and André Durand.

p. 564 'as G. W. Herron . . .' Quoted in Horden *Operation Mercy*, p. 49.

p. 565 'De Reynier described . . .' Jean de Reynier's report is quoted in D. Junod *The Imperiled Red Cross and the Palestine-Eretz-Israel Conflict 1945–1952*, London: Kegan Paul International, 1966, p. 175.

p. 565 'the right of innocent people . . .' UN document a/648, ICRC archives, Geneva.

p. 567 'Ella Jorden, the intrepid . . .' Jorden *Operation Mercy*, p. 35.

p. 568 'An International Committee nurse . . .' *International Review*, January 1949.

p. 569 'Palestine, the Committee now warned . . .' *International Review*, December 1949.

p. 569 'On 25 June . . .' In 1952 the International Committee put together a long report, 'CICR et le Conflict de Corée: Recueil de Documents'. See also W. Lindsey White *The Captives of Korea: An Unofficial White Paper on the Treatment of War Prisoners*, New York: Charles Scribner & Sons, 1957; 'Ministry of Defence Report into the Treatment of British Prisoners of War,' London; HMSO, 1955; J. M. Meyers and A. D. Biderman *Mass Behaviour in Battle and Captivity: The Communist Soldier in the Korean War*, University of Chicago Press, 1968; 'Concerning Bacteriological Warfare in Korea and China,' report circulated by the Chinese Red Cross, 1953, ICRC archives, Geneva.

p. 570 'O, Excellency . . .' Letter to Korean Ambassador, 11 September 1950, ICRC archives, Geneva.

p. 571 'Communists think only of killing . . .' 'CICR et le Conflict de Corée,' p. 10.

p. 572 'Under the present circumstances . . .' Quoted in Lindsey White, *The Captives of Korea*, p. 140.

p. 573 'a scandalous report . . .' 'CICR et le Conflict de Corée,' p. 10.

p. 574 'We will keep you here . . .' 'Treatment of British Prisoners of War,' p. 2.

p. 575 'Later, in a long document . . .' Chinese Red Cross report, ICRC archives, Geneva. For a further account of the bacteriological claims see S. Bailey *How Wars End*, Oxford: Clarendon Press, 1982.

p. 579 'If Korea had shown . . .' For a detailed account see 'Report on the Relief Action in Hungary, October 1956–June 1957,' ICRC archives, Geneva.

p. 581 'footbridge which continues . . .' *International Review*, November 1956.

p. 581 'Herbert Beckh . . .' see R. Deming *Heroes of the Red Cross*, Geneva: ICRC publications, 1969.

p. 584 'Even Geneva . . .' W. E. Casey

Hungarian Refugee Airlift, British Red Cross Society, 31 December 1956.

p. 585 'France's record with . . .' For monthly coverage of the ICRC in Algeria see the *International Review*. For further background see A. Horne *A Savage War of Peace: Algeria 1954–1963*, London: Macmillan, 1977.

p. 587 'Torture was a subject . . .' Full accounts of torture in Algeria appear in P. Vidal-Naquet (ed.) *Les Crimes de L'Armée Francaise*, Paris: Francois Maspero, 1982 and in *Les Temps Modernes*, No 167–8, February–March 1960. The ICRC's work to combat torture is covered in many position papers; see particularly H. Haug 'Efforts to Eliminate Torture Through International Law,' *Review*, January–February 1989.

p. 588 'It was in 1957 . . .' Laurent Vust in conversation with the author, 22 January 1996.

p. 590 'They were a help . . .' M. Moussaoria in conversation with the author, 16 November 1995.

p. 590 'Had the French . . .' Jacques Moreillon in conversation with the author, 18 January 1996.

p. 591 'Was there really? . . .' Quoted in Horne *A Savage War of Peace*, p. 196.

p. 593 'Not all the Algerians . . .' C. de Saint Salvy 'Crimes Commis Contre les Français Musulmans', 26 March 1963, ICRC archives, Geneva.

19. Men of the Red Cross

The war in the Yemen received extensive coverage month by month in the *International Review*. Good accounts of the background to the Biafran conflict and the International Committee's role in it are to be found in: A. H. M. Kirk-Greene, *Crisis and Conflict in Nigeria*, Oxford University Press, 1972; J. J. Stremlau *The International Politics of the Nigerian Civil War 1967–1970*, Princeton University Press, 1977; P. Harrison and R. Palmer *News Out of Africa: Biafra to BandAid*, London: Hilary Shipman, 1986; S. Cronje *The World and Nigeria: the Diplomatic History of the Biafran War 1967–1970*, London: Sidgwick & Jackson, 1972; J. Freymond 'Nigeria-Biafra: L'Aide aux Victimes de la Guerre Civiles,' *Preuves*, Ier Trimestre, 1970; T. Hentsch *Face au Blocus: La Croix Rouge Internationale dans la Nigerie en Guerre 1967–70*, Geneva: Institut Universitaire des Hautes Etudes Internationales, 1973; J. de St Jorre *The Nigerian Civil War*, London: Hodder & Stoughton, 1972; M. Davis 'Audits of International Relief in the Nigerian Civil War: Some Political Perspectives,' *International Organizations* 29, No. 2, Spring 1975.

For the setting up of Médecins Sans Frontières and Kouchner's relationship with the ICRC see S. Saliege 'Histoire de Médecins sans Frontières', Médecins sans Frontières Internal Paper, Paris: MSF, 1980; B. Kouchner *Charité Business*, Paris: Le Pré aux Clercs, 1986.

p. 600 'André Rochat is one . . .' André Rochat in conversation with the author, 11 April 1996.

p. 603 'Without really understanding . . .' Pierre Gaillard in conversation with author, 6 August 1995.

p. 607 'The International Committee has not wasted . . .' see R. Siegrist

The ICRC in Greece 1967–1971,
Montreux: Editions Corbaz, 1985.

p. 608 'In January 1968 . . .' Laurent
Marti in conversation with the
author, 1 September 1994.

p. 611 'Marti's deputy . . .' Philippe
Grand d'Hauteville in conversation
with the author, 10 April 1996.

p. 614 'In a book published . . .' D.
Forsythe *Humanitarian Politics*, John
Hopkins University Press, 1977.

p. 616 'Dr Bernard Kouchner . . .'
International Review, September 1968.

p. 624 'A humanitarian motivation . . .'
Forsythe *Humanitarian Politics*, p. 196.

p. 625 'There was an arrogance . . .'
Romy Brauman in conversation
with the author, 1 November 1995.

p. 626 'We suddenly found . . .' Charles
Egger in conversation with the
author, 16 January 1996.

p. 630 'They steal our victims . . .'
Laurent Marti in conversation with
the author, 1 September 1994.

p. 631 For comments on the Tansley
report, see repeated articles in the
International Review and particularly
November–December 1978 and
January–February 1979.

p. 634ff Excellent notes on the 1977
Protocols are to be found in W.
Hayes-Park 'Air War and the Law of
War,' *Air Force Law Review.* See also:
G. Abi-Saab 'Wars of National
Liberation in the Geneva
Conventions and Protocols,' *Recueil
des Cours*, 1979, vol. IV, The Hague:
Martinus Nijhoff, 1981; M. A. Meyer
(ed.) *Armed Conflict and the New Law:
Aspects of the 1977 Geneva Protocols and
the 1981 Weapons Convention*, British
Institute of International and
Comparative Law, 1989; A. Roberts
*The Laws of War: Problems of
Implementation in Contemporary Crises*, vol.
1, Official Publications of the

European Communities, 1995; G.
Best *War and Law Since 1945*, Oxford
University Press, 1994.

p. 635 'led by radical states . . .'
Hayes-Park, *Air Force Law Review*,
p. 80.

p. 636 Accounts of torture in Israel
come from conversations with
Stanley Cohen, Dr. Salim Maatouk
and Mohammet Alam of the
Palestinian Red Crescent.

20. La Maison

For good background accounts see
'Kampuchea Back From the Brink',
ICRC Reports on 15 Months Joint
Action with UNICEF in Cambodia
and Thailand, ICRC Library,
Geneva; W. Shawcross *The Quality of
Mercy*, London: Andre Deutsch,
1984; M. Black *The Children and the
Nations: The Story of UNICEF*, New
York: UNICEF, 1986 and *A Cause for
our Times: Oxfam – the First Fifty Years*,
Oxford University Press: 1992.
François Bugnion, Charles Egger,
Francis Amar, Jean-Paul Hocké
provided first-hand descriptions.

p. 641 'Nayan Chandra . . .' quoted in
Shawcross *The Quality of Mercy*,
p. 96.

p. 643 'eyes full of pus . . .' quoted in
Shawcross *The Quality of Mercy*,
p. 122.

p. 643 '*The New York Times* . . .' 8 August
1979.

p. 645 'We have too many . . .' quoted
in Shawcross *The Quality of Mercy*,
p. 83.

p. 645 'One morning, as Amar . . .'
Francis Amar in conversation with
author, 28 July 1992.

p. 650 'I have not seen a situation . . .'

quoted in Shawcross *The Quality of Mercy*, p. 178.

p. 657 'We all learnt this . . .' Charles Egger in conversation with author, 16 January 1996.

p. 658 'Xuan is Vietnamese . . .' Xuan in conversation with author, 23 July 1992.

p. 660 'In 1956, a Hungarian . . .' Nicolas Vecsey in conversation with author, 2 August 1995.

p. 662 'In the 1970s . . .' Massimo Cataldi in conversation with author 17 January 1996.

p. 665 For background to the Iran—Iraq war see S. H. Lamar 'The Treatment of Prisoners-of-War: The Role of the ICRC in the War between Iran and Iraq', *Emory International Law Review*, Spring 1991; I. F. Dekher and H. G. Post (eds.) *The Gulf War of 1980—88*, The Hague: Martinus Nijhoff, 1992; D. Hiro *The Longest War: The Iran—Iraq Military Conflict*, London: Grafton Books, 1989.

p. 666 'In the years leading up to . . .' W. A. Terrill Jr., 'Chemical Weapons in the Gulf War', *Strategic Review*, vol. 14, no. 2, 1986.

p. 668 'Kamal Ketuly . . .' Kamal Ketuly in conversation with author, 25 February 1996.

p. 668 'Then there is Hassan . . .' Hassan in conversation with author, 25 February 1983.

p. 675 'When Philippe Grand d'Hauteville . . .' Philippe Grand d'Hauteville in conversation with author, 10 April 1996.

p. 676 'We prepare them . . .' Dr de Haan in conversation with author, 16 January 1996.

p. 678 'At that moment . . .' Carlos Bauverd in conversation with author, 27 July 1995.

21. The Landscape of War

The recent years have been a time of analysis and re-assessment across the entire humanitarian world, and these concerns have been reflected in almost every issue of the *International Review*. See in particular: J. Blondel 'The Meaning of the Word "Humanitarian" in Relation to the Fundamental Principles of the Red Cross and Red Crescent', *International Review*, November—December 1989; M. Harroff-Tavel 'Neutrality and Impartiality', *International Review*, November—December 1989; D. P. Forsythe 'The ICRC and Humanitarian Assistance: A Policy Analysis', *International Review*, September—October 1996. See also H. Slim 'Doing the Right Thing: Relief Agencies, Moral Dilemmas and Moral Responsibility in Political Emergencies and War', Private Paper from the Scandanavian NGO Workshop on Humanitarian Ethics, October 1996; 'Confronting Total War: A "Global" Humanitarian Policy', *American Journal of International Law*, vol. 67, 1973.

p. 693 Many of its findings . . .' M. Keating *Identity, Image and Communication*, London: Media Natura, 1994. Also Michael Keating in conversation with author, 10 April 1995.

p. 705 'It represents, wrote Yves Sandoz . . .' *International Herald Tribune*, 10 March 1992.

p. 706 'The apology, says Gerhart Riegner . . .' Gerhart Riegner in conversation with author, 2 January 1997.

p. 708 Good background material on

the 'right of initiative' is to be
found in M. Torelli 'Droit
d'Ingérence', *International Review.*
May–June 1992.

p. 710 'Little more than a plaything . . .'
Population in Danger, Paris: MSF, 1995.

p. 710 'Romy Brauman, co-founder . . .'
Romy Brauman in conversation
with author, 1 November 1995.

p. 712 'jumping over . . .' Jean-Battista
Bacchetta in conversation with
author, 6 August 1995.

p. 712 'by reminding governments . . .'
President Sommaruga in
conversation with author, 7 January
1997.

INDEX

Abramowitz, Morton, 651

Abu Ghraib prison (Iraq), 668–9

Abyssinia *see* Ethiopia

Adams, Marie, 492

Addis Ababa, 314–15

Ador, Gustave: as acting secretary, 121; at twenty-fifth anniversary celebrations, 131; on Dunant's death, 173; and Tripoli war (1911), 173; attends 1912 Washington conference, 174; age, 176, 260; career and presidency, 176–7, 714; in World War I, 178, 180, 183–4, 187–8, 193; encourages respect for Geneva Convention, 200–1; insists on neutrality, 202; joins Swiss federal government, 205; and civil wars, 231; and Russian Revolution, 238; and rise of US dominance, 242; attacks use of poison gas, 254–5; relations with League of Red Cross Societies, 263, 265, 289; and repatriation of prisoners, 266; on board of *Union Internationale de Secours aux Enfants*, 281; death, 289; succeeded by Huber, 289; proposes international tribunal of arbitration, 300, 368; and Russian political prisoners, 334–5; and Huber, 595

Afghanistan, 658, 685, 691

Africa: violence in, 691; *see also* individual countries

Ahmed, Hocine Ait, 592

Ahmed, Imam, 598

air warfare: forecast, 169–70; in Tripoli (1911), 173; in Spanish civil war, 322, 326; in Sino-Japanese war, 364, 367; in Poland, 374, 376, 412; in World War II, 374, 376

Akara (radio play), 685

Aldrich, George H., 635

Alexander II, Tsar: reign, 1; convenes conference (1868), 59; supervizes 1874 convention, 124; supports cause of prisoners-of-war, 126, 128

Alexandra of Denmark, Queen of Edward VII (*formerly* Princess of Wales), 39, 137, 171, 178, 209

Algeria: Dunant in, 48; locust plague (1988), 696

Algerian war (1954–62), 585–94

Allard, Abbé, 82

Allen (US journalist), 251–2

Allende, Salvador, 663–4

Aloisi, Count, 311

Altherr, Dr, 161–3

Alusuisse (company), 704–5

Amar, Francis, 645–6

ambulances: used in Franco-Prussian war, 67–8, 77–9; in World War I, 218

American Civil War (1861–65), 32–8, 45

American Expeditionary Force (1917–18), 245

American Red Cross: Clara Barton and, 87, 92–6, 98, 108, 110–13; natural disaster relief, 94–6, 98, 113; and Russian 1891–2 famine, 98–9; and Armenian massacres (1895), 100–2; and Spanish-American war, 104–5; incorporated, 110; Clara Barton resigns from, 112; development and achievements, 113–14; reorganized under Mabel Boardman, 113–15; and San Francisco earthquake, 117–18; sends congratulations to International Committee on twenty-fifth anniversary, 131; recruits to Boer cause masquerade under, 147; aid in Messina earthquake, 159–60; in World War I, 240–2, 245–50, 256, 258; association with military, 242; fund-raising and support, 242–4; and

American Red Cross - *cont.*
  lost children of the Urals (1918), 250–3;
  membership numbers, 256, 292, 544; and
  proposed post-World War I
  international reforms, 258–61; and
  released prisoners in Soviet Russia, 272;
  and post-World War I Russian relief,
  280; annual convention (Ohio, 1921),
  287; lectures and speakers, 287; offers
  aid in World War II, 375; Zollinger
  criticizes, 381; in World War II, 403–7,
  509; at liberation of concentration
  camps, 462–3; and Japanese treatment
  of prisoners, 477, 486, 491–3; post-
  World War II relief, 493, 503, 505,
  509–10; and treatment of German
  prisoners in post-World War II France,
  538; O'Connor succeeds Davis as
  chairman, 548; and accusations of
  bacteriological warfare in Korea, 575; *see
  also* United States of America
American Relief Administration, 279–82
American Sanitary Commission, 33–7,
  45–6, 88, 92
Amnesty International, 561, 606–8, 610,
  630, 698, 713
anaesthesia: development, 28; at Sedan, 72
Anastasia Nikolaevna, Grand Duchess of
  Russia, 234
Angola, 685, 691
antiseptics: development of, 28
Aosta, Duchess of, 160
Appia, Pastor George, 55
Appia, Louis: supports Dunant's battlefield
  proposals, 16–17, 21–2; and war
  surgery, 28; and Schleswig-Holstein war,
  40–2; at 1864 Geneva Diplomatic
  Conference, 44; in 1866 Austro-Italian
  war, 55–6; as Secretary to International
  Committee, 60, 121; in Franco-Prussian
  war, 64–6; diaries, 68; and Clara Barton,
  90–3; memoirs published in *Bulletin*, 120;
  attitude to developing nations, 122;
  defends Geneva Convention, 124; later
  activities, 129–30; and International
  Committee's twenty-fifth anniversary,
  131; death, 171–2; reports, 298, 562; and

modern war, 716; *La Guerre et la Charité*
  (with Moynier), 51, 69
Arab League, 564
Arabs: and partition of Palestine, 568; in
  Six Day War (1967), 636–7; *see also*
  Palestine
Arandora Star (ship), 401
Arendt, Hannah, 501
Argentina: disappeared people in, 663, 665
Armand-Dumaresque, Charles-Edouard, 44
Armenia: massacres (1895) and relief,
  99–103, 418; 1990s fighting in, 691; 1888
  earthquake, 696
arms and armaments *see* war
Arolsen, Germany, 518–22
Arrault, Henri, 26, 28–9
Arrow Cross Party (Hungary), 445–7,
  449–53
Arthur, Chester Alan, 94
Asahi (Japanese officer, Singapore), 481
Ashton (negotiator at Belsen), 460
Atherton, Gertrude, 247–8
atomic weapons: used against Japan,
  488–90; and Geneva Convention
  revisions, 553, 556; Red Cross attacks,
  562
Atterbury, W. H., 246
Audigné, Marquise d', 248
Augusta of Sachsen-Weimar, Queen of
  Prussia (*later* Empress of Germany),
  54–5, 58, 61, 174
Augusta of Schleswig-Holstein, Empress of
  Germany, 179
Augustine of Hippo, St, 23
Auschwitz, 417–18, 418, 443, 460, 468, 469,
  706
Australia: World War I prisoners, 187
Australian Red Cross, 487
Austria (and Austria-Hungary): 1859 war
  with Italy, 1–2; peace settlement, 7;
  war of independence (1743), 24; attacks
  Schleswig-Holstein, 39; war with Prussia
  (1866), 53–4; signs 1864 convention, 54;
  war with Italy (1866), 55–6; declares
  war on and invades Serbia (1914), 174,
  178, 223–4; treatment of World War I
  prisoners, 193; post-World War I

starvation, 274–5; political prisoners and camps in, 345–7; union with Germany ('Anschluss', 1938), 357, 421; Jews persecuted, 358; and relief for Hungary (1956), 580–3

Austrian Red Cross, 191, 274, 346, 357, 583

Austrian Society of Friends of Peace, 165

Awa Maru (ship), 479

Axis pact (Germany-Italy-Japan, 1940), 377

Axson, Stockton, 259–60

Azerbaijan, 691

Bacchetta, Gian Battista, 712

Bachmann, Hans, 458–9

bacteriological warfare, 286; in Korean war, 575–7; *see also* chemical warfare

Bade, Prince de, 81

Baden-Powell, General Robert, lst Baron, 169

Badr, Imam El, 598, 600, 603

Baker, George F., 243

Bakiroff, George, 250

Balfour, Arthur James, 211, 265

Balkan wars: (1875–7), 125–6, 132–3; (1912–14), 173

Balmer, Andreas: *L'Heure de Cuivre*, 699

Bangkok: Tracing Agency, 656

Bangladesh, 627, 696

Barbey, Frédéric, xxv

Barnett, Captain, 484

Barre, Mohamed Ali, 684

Barton, Clara: in American Civil War, 32, 35–6; background, character and career, 87–9, 95, 714; financial difficulties, 89–90, 405; and tracing of missing persons, 89; in Europe, 90–1; health collapse, 91; promotes and runs Red Cross in USA, 92–6, 108–9, 118, 714; honours, 94, 102–3; and 1891–2 Russian famine, 98–9; and Armenian massacres (1895), 100–3; in Cuban revolution (1895), 103–4; and Spanish–American war, 104–5; life in Glen Echo, Maryland, 106, 111–12; in Galveston hurricane relief, 107–8; investigated and criticized by administrators, 109–111; Mabel

Boardman attacks, 110–12; ousted from American Red Cross, 112; death, 113; *The Red Cross or Geneva Conventions*, 92–3; *A Story of the Red Cross*, 103

Barton, Sir Sydney, 306, 314–5

Bashi-Bazouks, 125

Basle: agency established, 64

Bastiat, Frédéric, 122

Basting, S.H.C., 18, 21, 39, 40

Bataan death march (Philippines, 1942), 497

Baumberger, Georg, 163–4

Bauverd, Carlos, 678–81

Bavarian Red Cross, 174

Bavier, Jean de, 439–42

Baxter, William, 143

Bayern (German ship), 159

Beau, Henri, 171

Beaumont, Jacques, 640–1, 643 4, 647–8, 652

Beaunis, Dr, 62

Beauvoir, Simone de, 625

Beck, Baron Max von, 346

Beckh, Herbert, 581–2, 584

Bedford, Adeline, Duchess of, 213

Beer, Henrik, 596

Belgian Red Cross: formed, 39; in Franco-Prussian war, 68; closed by von Bissing in World War I, 208; boycotts tenth Red Cross conference (1921), 284; post-World War II relief, 507

Belgium: World War I refugees, 248; surrenders (1940), 377

Bell, George, Bishop of Chichester, 394

Bellows, Pastor Henry W., 33–4, 92

Belsen concentration camp, 460–2

Ben Bella, Ahmed, 592

Ben-Tov, Arieh, 442

Benin, 691

Benjamin, Cissy, 229

Berchem, René von, 560

Bereczky, Albert, 445

Beretta, Giuseppe, 702–3

Berlin: occupied by Russians, 382; post-World War II refugees and conditions in, 502, 507; International Committee delegates in (post-World War II), 505

Berlin Congress (1878), 135
Berlin Wall: falls, 681, 696
Bernadotte, Count Folke, 457, 546, 549–50; killed, 563–5
Bernard, St. 23
Bernardini, Mgr, 554
Bernhardt, William, 616–17
Berres, A.J., 467
Besange, Père Jacquinot de see Jacquinot de Besange, Père
Best, Geoffrey: *War and Law since 1945*, 558
Biafra: civil war (1967–70), 614–22; effect on International Committee, 622–6, 642, 647, 656; genocide charges, 626–7
Biafran Baby, Operation, 621
Bibesco, Prince, 306
Bicknell, Ernest, 114–15, 117–18, 159–60, 179
Bien-Être du Blessé, Le (organization), 248
Bieri, Alain, 674
Bieri, Frédéric, 570, 573
'Big Study, The' (1975), 631–3
Bilbao, Don Esteban, 318
Bilfinger, Fritz, 487, 489
Bismarck, Prince Otto von, 1, 39, 55, 58, 61, 81–2
Bissing, General von, 208
Blackie, Eileen, 523, 526
Blaine, James G., 93
Blanchot, Dr, 197–9
Blazynska, Marianna, 431
Blum, Léon, 466
Bluntschli, Johann, 124
Boardman, Mabel Thorp: relations with Clara Barton, 87, 109–10, 113; and administration of American Red Cross, 110–15; and San Francisco earthquake, 117–18; and Messina earthquake, 159–60; and outbreak of World War I, 178–9; relegated in World War I, 241; promotes recruitment, 243; replaced as general secretary, 259, 264–5; regains power, 283–4; attends 1934 Red Cross Tokyo conference, 293, 296; and 1938 London conference, 359; on women in American Red Cross, 405; achievements, 714

'boat people' (Vietnamese), 644–5
Bodmer, Martin, 544
Bodo, Frank, 702
Boehringer, Robert, 388, 409
Boer War (1899–1902), 132, 139–44, 146; civilians and prisoners maltreated, 143–8
Bogota: 1991 conference abandoned, 694
Boissier family, 676
Boissier, Edmond, xxiv, 337, 413, 560
Boissier, Léopold, 560, 589; succeeds Huber as president, 596
Boissier, Pierre, 592, 600
Bolshevism, 271–2, 280
Bonigk, Baron Captain von, 190
Bonna, Pierre, 443
Boone, Admiral (USN), 491
Borinowska, Maria, 427
Bork, Sigrid, 512
Born, Frederick, 439, 442–3, 445–54, 584, 661
Boronin, Petro, 250
Borsinger, Melchior, 409–10, 517
Bosnia: revolts against Turks (1875), 125; conflict in, 683, 686–8; and disappeared people in, 692
Bosshard, Walter, 315
Bottini, Marchese, 509
Bouvier, Edmond, 295
Bowles, Charles, 45–6
Bowles, Thomas Gibson, 132
Boxelaere, Wim van, 684
boy scouts, 287
Brandström, Elsa, 193–5, 272–3
Brastagi, Marie, 489
Brauman, Romy, 625, 711
Brazil: Amazonian Indians in, 627; disappeared people in, 663
Breda, Count, 59
Brenier, Baron, 66
Brest-Litovsk, Treaty of (1917/18), 240, 266
Briand-Kellogg Pact (1928), 290
Briquet, Jean, 462
Britain: 19th-century power, 1; reserve at 1864 Geneva Conference, 45–6; and Dunant's proposals for prisoners-of-war, 127–8; and campaign in Sudan (1884),

136−8; and Boer War, 139−40, 144−7; in World War I, 178; and World War I prisoners, 186−7, 192, 196−7; and World War I atrocities, 202; official resistance to Red Cross society, 236, 238; and use of poison gas, 255; and protection of civilians, 369; treatment of World War II prisoners, 379, 402−3, 407; behaviour as prisoners-of-war, 380; World War II blockade, 389−90, 392, 455; International Committee's wartime visits to (1941), 390−1; lifts blockade, 394, 397; practises reprisals, 402−3; and violations of Geneva Convention, 402−3; improved relations with International Committee, 409; donations to post-World War II relief, 511; post-World War II German prisoners in, 541−2; Malaysian conflict, 555; withdraws from Palestine, 564−5; accepts Hungarian refugees (1956), 583−4

British Aid Society see British Red Cross Society

British Broadcasting Corporation (BBC), 626

British Journal of Nursing, 213

British Red Cross Society (*formerly* British Aid Society): in Franco-Prussian war, 68−9, 71, 73−6, 84−6; established, 69−71; reluctant beginnings and development, 131−2; in Russo-Turkish war (1877), 132−5; skills increase, 136; and Sudan campaign (1884), 137−8; criticized for inactivity, 138−9; in Boer War, 139−41, 143, 147; permanent committee approved (1899), 139; reorganized, 171; royal patronage, 171; expansion and activities in World War I, 208−15, 219−26, 256; magazine, 213−14; aid in Russia during World War I, 234−6; rivalry with Save the Children Fund, 282; in Ethiopia (1935−6), 307, 314; at outbreak of World War II, 375; relief operations and supplies in World War II, 384−5; criticized by Commission Mixte, 388; and wartime visits from Geneva, 390−1; at Belsen, 461; and

Japanese treatment of prisoners, 477−8; Lady Mountbatten heads, 493; in liberated Italy, 505; in post-World War II Europe, 505−11; post-World War II tracing programme, 516−17; and Hungarian refugees, 584

Brittain, Vera, 213

Brown, Sidney Hamlet: in Shanghai, 297, 302, 366, 471; background and career, 301−2; in Ethiopia, 304−7, 309−10, 312, 314−15, 376; resignation, 315−16; and Junod, 328; influence, 562; qualities, 603

Brunel, Robert, 392−4, 396−7

Brussels Convention and Declaration Concerning the Laws of War (1874), 124−5

Buchanan, Lady Georgiana, 235

Buchenwald, 156, 462, 469, 521

Budapest: ghetto, 450−1; liberated by Russians, 452−3; in 1956 rising, 581−2; *see also* Hungary

Buenos Aires, 663

Bugnion, François, 640−1, 634−5, 647−9, 652

Buisson, General, 538

Bulgaria: revolts against Turks (1875), 125; joins Axis pact, 377

Bulletin (of International Committee; later *International Review*): launched, 57, 119−20; Appia's memoirs in, 120; on British Red Cross society, 138; on Boer war, 148; on Russo-Japanese war, 156; on relief in natural disasters, 158; on new weaponry, 168; obituary of Dunant, 172; on World War I, 185−6, 188−9, 202−3; retitled *International Review*, 256; outclassed by *The World's Health*, 264; on social welfare, 284; Gorky writes on gas in, 286; on preparations for World War II, 299−300; and use of gas in Ethiopia, 309, 313; ignores mention of concentration camps, 411; and German Red Cross, 467; proclaims humanitarian spirit, 562; on Tansley's 'Big Study', 632

Bülow, General Karl von, 217

Burckhardt, Carl-Jacob: background, xxii, 302−3, 338; as High Commissioner for

Burckhardt, Carl-Jacob - *cont.*
Danzig persecution of Jews, xxii—xxiii,
359, 362, 390, 414, 416, 545; and Nazi
persecution of Jews, xxii—xxiii, xxv, 362,
414, 416—19, 424—5, 439; and Italian war
in Ethiopia, 305, 311—12; and Brown's
resignation, 315; and Spanish civil war,
316; inspects and reports on German
prison camps, 350—8, 360, 463; relations
with Mlle Odier, 372—3, 423; works in
Geneva in World War II, 372, 382; co-
operates with League during World War
II, 386—9; British suspicion of, 390—1;
visits Britain (1941), 391—2, 394;
organizes wartime shipping in Greece,
394; protests against reprisals, 402—3;
position during World War II, 409;
relations with Germans, 414, 416;
administrative qualities, 423—4, and
Hungarian Jews, 446, 453; and
concentration camp victims, 458—60,
463, 705, 707; succeeds Huber as
president, 458; and Karoline von
Lanskoranska, 459—60; and Japanese in
World War II, 486; pleads for
Weizsäcker, 497; on Red Cross
effectiveness in World War II, 499;
appointed Ambassador to France, 543,
705; defends International Committee's
record on concentration camps, 543,
545, 549; and Huber's pessimism, 544;
inaction over Nazi behaviour, 551;
achievements, 714; *Ma Mission à Danzig*,
355, 362
Burckhardt, Charles, 401
Burckhardt, Elizabeth (*née* de Reynold), 303
Burckhardt, Nicholas, 418, 506, 527
Burdett-Coutts, William, 141
Burger, Heinrich, 342
Burkhard, Dr Paul, 702
Burma railway, 483—4, 491, 496
Burnard (Swiss painter), 205
Burnier, Georges, 331, 440
Burundi, 682, 689—91
Butler, Captain, 212
Butler, Lady Constance, 214
Buxton, Dorothy, 281

Cabanella, General, 318
Caffrey, Mrs (of American Red Cross),
510—11
Cairo Postal Convention (1935), 383
Calame, Dr Louis, 365—8, 471, 562
Calpini, Dr Pierre, 385, 538
Calvin, Jean, 10
Calwell, Miss, 227
Cambodia (Kampuchea): war and relief
operations in, 640—57; effect on
International Committee, 656—7, 679;
tracing in, 658—60; casualties, 660
Camp, Maxime du, 85
Campbell-Bannerman, Sir Henry, 145
Canada: World War I prisoners, 187
Canaris, Admiral Wilhelm, 416
Canrobert, Marshal François Certain, 67
Cape Town: in Boer War, 139—42, 145
Carillon de Saint-Gervais (newspaper), 44,
47
Carter, Rosalyn, 651
Cartigny, 699
Casley, W.E., 584
Castiglione, 4—7
Castro, Fidel, 586
Cataldi, Massimo, 663—5, 671
Catholics: excluded from International
Committee, 60, 176
Cavour, Count Camillo Benso, 1
Cazenove, Léonce de, 62
Cebrykow, Wanda, 435—6
Central America, 696
Central Prisoner of War Agency (World
War II), 373, 376
Central Tracing Agency, Geneva, 660; *see
also* tracing service
Chabra, Charles, 674
Chad, 696
Chamberlain, Mrs Dick, 141
Chamberlain, Joseph, 141
Chamousset, Piarron de, 25
Chanda, Nayan, 641
Chang, Marcus, 484
Changi jail, Singapore, 480—3, 485
Chapuisat, Edouard, xxiii, xxv—xxvi, 359,
440, 543
Charles V, Emperor, 24

Charles, Prince of Sweden, 265, 288, 313, 334, 339, 343–4, 544, 546

Chechnya, 682–3, 692

chemical warfare: calls for regulation of, 285, 368; in Ethiopia, 309; Iraqis employ, 666–7; see also bacteriological warfare; gas (poison)

Chenevière, Jacques: joins International Committee, 184, 302; and war in Ethiopia, 305, 311; criticizes Brown, 315; and Spanish civil war, 316; and World War II concentration camps, 346, 350; in World War II, 372–3, 376, 387, 409; hostility to League and Commission Mixte, 387–8, 695; and atrocities against Romanian Jews, 418; complains of organization of International Committee, 423; on German Red Cross, 467; report from Graz, 539; Retours et images, 311

Chesney, Dr Lilian, 226, 228

Chessex, Dr, 359–60

Chicherin, Georghy Vasilievich, 280, 335

children: protection of, 281, 286–8; and totalitarian ideologies, 299–300; in Spanish civil war, 317–18, 321–4; in German famine, 339; Polish (World War II), 427, 429; Germanized under Nazis, 432–6, 522–5; in post-World War II Europe, 503–4, 507, 512–14; stolen and kidnapped in World War II, 522–6; in Cambodia, 658; slaughtered and lost in Rwanda, 689–90; see also Urals: lost children of

Chile, 663–5

China: 1911 revolution, 173; Japanese war and occupation, 297–8, 301, 363–8, 471; accuses International Committee, 570; in Korean war, 570–1, 574–6

Chinese Red Cross society: launched, 208; and burial of dead, 297; and Japanese war, 363–4, requests Calame to leave, 368; accuses UN forces in Korea, 573–4, 575, 578; subordinated to government, 578; disputes with Taiwanese, 596

Chomanand, General Kriangsak, 648

Christian Association of Geneva, 12

Christian Commission (USA), 35

Christian, Princess of Schleswig-Holstein, 70

Christians, Ludwik, 432

Christina (US ship), 455

Churchill, (Sir) Winston S.: appeals to Germany (December 1942), xxvi; approves of economic blockade, 390, 392; at Yalta, 457; sets up committee of surpluses for relief, 502

Ciano, Count Galeazzo, 308

Cilento, Sir Ralph, 567

Ciraolo, Giovanni, 158, 264, 285–6, 287, 302, 334

civil wars: role of Red Cross in, 125, 231, 285, 316, 329, 633–4; in World War I, 184–5, 194–8, 253; discussed after World War II, 553, 555; see also Korean war; Spanish civil war

civilians: treatment of in war, 37; in Russo-Turkish war (1877–8), 136; in Boer War, 144–7; casualties in World War II, 185; Ferrière's concern for, 185, 286, 295, 302; in World War I, 253; discussed at 10th Red Cross conference, 285; Sidney Brown on, 302; in Spanish civil war, 320–1, 326; protection of, 369–70, 375, 411–13; in World War II, 371, 375, 378, 411–12, 552; definitions of, 412; International Committee sets up special commission on internees, 423; Japanese treatment of in World War II, 473, 480–3, 488; covered by 1949 Geneva Convention, 555; flee from Hungary (1956), 581; detained in Algerian war, 586, 590; in Yemen war, 598–9, 602; in modern wars, 692; see also refugees; Tokyo Draft

Clausewitz, Karl von, 25

Clemenceau, Georges, 260

Cleve, von (of German Red Cross), 349

Clifton, Ginger, 229

clinobox, 599

Clouzot, Etienne, 281, 343–4, 346, 357

Cobden, Richard, 122, 165

Cocatrix, Albert de, 464

Cohn, Dr Oscar, 255

Colladon, Germain, 607–8, 611
Colladon, Henri, 11
Colombia: disappeared people in, 663; war
    in, 691
Commer, Paul Louis, 17
Commission Mixte, La (League-
    International Committee), 387–8, 418,
    440
Commission for Political Prisoners (or
    Detainees), 337, 413
Compagnie Génèvoise des Colonnes de
    Sétif, Algeria, 13
concentration camps: in Boer War, 145,
    148, 344; in Nazi Germany, 343–4, 347,
    349–53, 359, 411, 413, 415, 417–18, 496,
    542–3; liberated (1945), 454–65, 514–16;
    medical experimentation in, 469–70;
    surviving records, 521; International
    Committee criticized for failure to
    speak against, 542–5, 548–9, 551, 559,
    700, 705–6
Convention for the Amelioration of the
    Condition of the Wounded in Armies
    in the Field see Geneva Convention
Corbett, Elsie, 226–30; The Red Cross in
    Serbia, 229
Council of Europe, 607–10, 612–13
Couper, Joan, 508–9
Courvoisier, Jean, 531–4, 541, 566, 570, 679,
    703
Courvoisier, Raymond, 325, 396–7
Coventry, 552
Cox, Colonel and Emma, 75
Cramer, Dr Alec, xxiv
Cramer, Marguerite see Frick-Cramer,
    Marguerite
Crédit Genevois, 48–9
Cremonesi, Filippo, 305, 308, 315
Crimean War (1853–5), 30–2, 34
Croatia, 277, 686–7
Cuba: 1895 revolution, 103–4; and
    Spanish-American war, 104–5; Castro
    lands in, 586
Curie, Sir Philip, 101
Custozza, battle of (1866), 55
Cutting, W. Bayard, 159
Czechoslovak Red Cross, 595

Czechs: support White Russians against
    Bolsheviks, 272–3

D-Day (1944) see Normandy landings
Daae, Dr Hans, 167
Dachau, 347, 351, 353, 355, 359–60, 416,
    456, 462, 464, 469, 521
Daily Express: attacks Eglantyne Jebb, 282
Dale, Major General Torstein, 630
Dalton, Hugh, 390
D'Amato, Alfonse, 701–2
Daniel, Louis Octave, 515
Danielsson, Carl Ivar, 445
Danish National Aid Society, 42
Danish Red Cross, 195, 208, 465
Davidson, Randall, Archbishop of
    Canterbury, 334
Davis, George W., 114
Davis, Norman, 359, 361–2, 369–70, 400,
    505; death, 544, 548
Davis, Richard Harding, 244
Davison, Henry P.: chairs war council of
    American Red Cross, 241, 258; in World
    War I, 242, 244, 246–7, 249; institutes
    post-war reforms and forms League of
    Red Cross Societies, 258–65, 282–3;
    plans for post-war Europe, 258; and
    post-World War I repatriations, 266, 274;
    and post-World War I relief
    programmes, 279–80; rivalry with
    International Committee, 282; death,
    283; ideals, 298; Mme Frick-Cramer and,
    306
Davison, Mrs Henry P., 467
Davy, Sir Humphry, 10
Dayton Agreement (1995), 688
Dean, Patrick, 402
Dearmer, Mabel, 207, 225, 227
Declaration of the Rights of the Child, 286
Delcassé, Théophile, 180
Demidoff, Prince Anatole, 20, 26, 28–9,
    126–8
Demolis, Louis, 320
Denikin, General Anton Ivanovich, 273
Denmark: in Schleswig-Holstein war, 39,
    41–2; and Rwandan crisis, 690
Descouedres, Dr, 378

Desfosses, Mme, 171
d'Espine see Espine
Dessonaz, Georges, 278–9
detainees (civilian and political) see political prisoners
Dettingen, battle of (1743), 24
Deutsche Jugend (magazine), 341
Deutsche Röterkreuz (magazine), 349
Devine, Dr Edward, 117–18
Devonshire House, London, 220
Dieppe raid (1942), 402
Diethelm & Co. Ltd., Singapore, 481–2, 483, 485
Dillon, Kathleen, 226, 228–30
'disappeared, the': in Latin America (desparacidos), 662–4; in Bosnia, 692
disarmament, 169; see also peace movement
disasters see natural disasters
displaced persons see refugees
Dixon, Brian, 616
Dmitri Pavlovich, Grand Duke of Russia, 235–6
Doenitz, Admiral Karl, 496
Dollfuss, Engelbert, 345
Draudt, Colonel Paul, 289, 293, 340, 342, 344, 349, 357, 414, 626; death, 544
Drevet, Camille, 350
Drogheda, Henry Moore, 10th Earl of, 389
Dudley, Georgina, Countess of, 209
Dufour, General Guillaume Henri: relations with Napoleon III, 14, 43, 48; supports Dunant's battlefield proposals, 14, 16–20, 43; and Schleswig-Holstein war, 40; at 1864 Geneva Diplomatic Conference, 44–5; and Dunant's finances, 48; and Dunant's resignation, 49; awarded gold medal of 1867 Exhibition, 57; and changes to composition of Committee, 60; death, 129; Geneva statue, 183; and modern war, 716
Duhan (officer enemy of Kenworthy), 143
du Maurier, Guy: The Englishman's Home, 213
Dunand, Georges, 460
Dunant, André, 566
Dunant, Anne-Antoinette (née Colladon; HJD's mother), 11–12

Dunant, Henri Jean: present at Solferino battlefield, 2–7, 27, 693; proposes volunteer battlefield help, 8–9, 14–18, 30, 32, 87; background and upbringing, 11–13; character and appearance, 13; suggests neutral medical personnel, 19–20, 25, 46; and 1863–4 Geneva conferences, 20–3, 29, 38–9, 43–4, 46, 48; ignores work of Arrault and Palasciano, 28; relations with Florence Nightingale, 29–30, 32; and American Sanitary Commission, 36–7; Moynier's attitude to, 38, 50, 57, 126, 128, 164, 172; and Schleswig-Holstein war, 40; on duty of International Committee to report truth, 42; financial problems, 43, 48–9, 57; offers to resign from International Committee, 43; in Paris, 43, 57, 66; Swiss support for, 47; resigns and departs from Geneva, 49–50, 60, 126; on urgency of need to restrict war, 52; on women, 52; ideals, 53, 157, 207, 285, 372, 552, 561, 714; in Berlin after Austro-Prussian war, 54–5; and naval warfare, 56; awarded gold medal of 1867 Exhibition, 57; in Franco-Prussian war, 66; in siege of Paris, 76, 80–2; continues humanitarian work, 126; promotes cause of prisoners-of-war, 126–8, 142; changes name to Henry, 127; relations with Mme Kastner, 128–9; disappears from view, 129; ignored at International Committee's twenty-fifth anniversary, 131; eczema, 161; later movements and activities, 161–3, 173; writes memoirs, 162–3; death and will, 163, 172–3; rediscovered and rehabilitated, 163–4; shares Nobel Peace Prize, 164–5, 167–8; and peace movement, 166–7; and national Red Cross societies in World War I, 207; proposes peacetime activities, 259; celebrated in USA, 287; scorned by International Committee, 289; on work of national societies, 329; and German Red Cross, 340; and conduct of war, 579; monument proposed, 597; and modern war and methods, 716; L'Avenir

Dunant, Henri Jean - *cont.*
  Sanglant, 162; *Charity on the Battlefield*, 165;
  The Empire of Charlemagne Restored, 7; *A
  Memory of Solferino*, 8–10, 14–16, 18, 26,
  29, 33, 47; *Notes on the Regency of Tunisia*,
  12
Dunant, Jean-Jacques (HJD's father), 11
Dunant, Marie (HJD's sister), 128
Dunant, Maurice (HJD's nephew), 173
Dunant, Paul, 465–6
Dunant, Pierre (HJD's brother), 162
Duning, Henry, 538
Dunkirk evacuation (1940), 377
Dunois, Jean, Comte de, 24
Durand, André: *From Sarajevo to Hiroshima*,
  319
Durham, Miss (Egypt 1884), 137
Durham, Miss (US reporter), 240
Dutch Red Cross, 522

earthquakes, 115–18, 287
Eastern Europe: post Soviet conditions,
  696–7
Eden, Anthony (*later* 1st Earl of Avon),
  xxvi, 312, 426, 484
Edward VII, King of Great Britain (*formerly*
  Prince of Wales), 39, 70, 171
Edwards, Miss: in Egypt, 1884, 137
Egger, Charles, 626, 657
Egle, Edouard, 474–9
Egypt: membership of Red Cross, 122; and
  Sudan campaign (1884), 136–8; Turkish
  civilian internees in World War I,
  197–8; soldiers in Yemen, 600–1; Israeli
  prisoners in, 628
Ehrenhold (German intelligence agent), 702
Eichmann, Adolf: and Hungarian Jews,
  441–2, 444, 447, 449–50, 452
Elcho, Francis Charteris, Viscount (*later*
  8th Earl of Wemyss), 127
Eleonora, Queen of Bulgaria, 179, 228
Ellis (brother and sister in Serbia), 227
Elwes, R.E.A., 479
Emmanuelli, Xavier, 710
Ems, Hedwig, 466
epidemics: post-World War I, 270–1; post-
  World War II, 502; in Yemen, 599

Ercoreca, Señor (mayor of Bilbao), 318
Erin (yacht), 226
Eritrea, 658
Esher, Reginald Baliol Brett, 2nd Viscount,
  211
Espine, family d', 177
Espine, Professor A. d', 191
Esterwegen camp (Germany), 351–3, 355
Ethiopia: Italian invasion and war in
  (1935–6), xxii, 301–2, 304–10, 313–14,
  551; Red Cross delegates in, 304–6;
  poison gas used in, 310–12, 355, 368,
  376; and war in Somalia, 684; 1990s
  fighting in, 691
Ethiopian Red Cross, 305, 310, 313–14
'ethnic cleansing': in Palestine, 568; in
  Bosnia, 686
Etter, Philippe, xxiii, xxv, 421–2, 545, 705
Eugénie, Empress of France, 2, 56, 66–7,
  76
Eugster, M.A., 190–1
Europe: conditions and relief after World
  War II, 501–17; *see also* Eastern Europe
European Commission on Human Rights,
  610
European Convention on Human Rights,
  607, 612
Evans, Dr Thomas, 76, 79
Evian conference (1938), 361
Eynard-Lullin, Mme, 20
Eyre, Major General Sir Vincent, 74–5

Faisal, King of Saudi Arabia, 602
Falck, Stella, 513
famines: Russia (1891–2), 96–9; in post-
  World War I Russia, 276–81; Germany
  (1920s), 338–9; in Nigeria (1960s),
  615–18, 622; Somalia, 684, 690
FANY *see* First Aid Nursing Yeomanry
  Corps
Far Eastern Economic Review, 641
Farrell, Dr Livingstone, 260
fascism: rise of, 298, 300, 303
Favez, Jean-Claude, 355, 391, 459–60
Favre family, 177, 302, 676
Favre, Denis, 502
Favre, Colonel Edmond, 60, 171

Favre, Colonel Guillaume, 302, 305, 313, 3155–16, 350, 359–60, 370; death, 560
Favre, Jules, 66, 81
Fawcett, Millicent, 145
Fazy, Jean James, 17
Fedden, Marguerite, 220
Federation of Red Cross Societies see League of Red Cross Societies
Feisel, James, 299
Feller, Harold, 445
Felton, Monica, 574–5
Fernandez, Enid, 462
Ferrière, Emmanuel, 65
Ferrière, Dr F. (Frédéric's nephew), 195
Ferrière, Frédéric: in Franco-Prussian war, 65; writes in Bulletin on nature of war, 119; in Balkan wars, 125; and Boer War, 142; as vice-president of International Committee, 177; concern for civilian protection, 185, 286, 295, 302; in World War I, 193, 253; age, 260; in post-World War I Vienna, 274–5, 281; and Hungarian refugees, 440; and German concentration camp internees, 455
Ferrière, Louis (Frédéric's nephew), 275, 346–7
Ferrière, Suzanne (Frédéric's niece): founds Union Internationale de Secours aux Enfants, 281; and Eglantyne Jebb, 282; and protection of civilians, 295, 411–12; and Spanish civil war, 316; and Nazi Jewish policy, 347, 350, 419; position on Committee, 409; and tracing programme, 516–17; visits Britain, 516
Ferris, Lorna, 227
Fick, Jules-Guillaume, 8, 14
Filliettaz, E., 534
Finland: bombed during World War II, 400
Finnish Red Cross, 178
First Aid Nursing Yeomanry Corps (FANY), 212–13, 218
Fischer, Eugen, 348
Fischer, Georg (company), 705
Flavigny, Comte de, 67, 69, 73, 80–1, 127
Fogg (US delegate to 1864 Conference), 45
Fontrese, Marguerite, 243

Food and Agriculture Organization (UN), 595, 642, 648, 656
Forbes, Archibald, 85
forced labour: in World War II, 415, 429, 447, 704–5
Ford, Henry, 243
Foringer, Alonzo Earl, 243
Forsythe, David, 614, 624
Fosse Argentine massacre (Italy), 379
France: war with Prussia (1870), xxii, 60–8, 71–83, 90–1, 121; war against Austria (1859), 1–3; Prussians threaten, 7; and development of military medicine, 27; reluctance to attend 1864 Geneva diplomatic conference, 39, 43, accepts 1864 Treaty, 52–3; challenges structure of International Committee, 59; inadequate medical services, 62; accused of violations in war with Prussia, 84, 123; losses in 1894 Madagascar campaign, 156; in World War I, 178; treatment of prisoners in World War I, 191–2, 199–200; American Red Cross in during World War I, 244–9; World War I casualties, 246, 256; uses poison gas, 254; and protection of civilians, 369; falls to Germany (1940), 377; treatment of World War II prisoners, 378; post-World War II German prisoners in, 530–8, 540–1, 585; post-World War II economic conditions, 533–4; war trials in, 541; Indochina conflict, 555; and Algerian war, 585–93
Franco, General Francisco, 316–18, 320, 326–7
Frank, Dr, 74
Frank, Hans, 427
Frank, Karl Hermann, 465
Frankh, General (Bavarian Minister of War), 19
Franz-Ferdinand, Archduke of Austria, 174
Franz-Joseph, Emperor of Austria, 2, 6–7, 9
Fraser, Dr Campbell, 134, 448
Frederick II (the Great), King of Prussia, 25

Frelinghuysen, Frederick T., 96
French Provident Association, 80
French Red Cross Society: in Franco-
Prussian war, 62, 66–7, 83; in siege of
Paris, 77, 80; style, 130, 171; in World
War I, 248; boycotts tenth Red Cross
conference (1921), 284; and Algerian
war, 592; promotes right of initiative,
709
Freymond, Jacques, 610, 621, 624
Frick, Edouard, 239–40, 266–7, 269–71,
275, 280, 294, 372
Frick-Cramer, Marguerite (formerly
Cramer): urges saving of concentration
camp victims, xxiv–xxvi, 458; joins
International Committee, 60, 260; and
founding of League, 262; and post-
World War I prisoner relief, 268; at 1934
Tokyo conference, 294; marriage, 294;
and Italian war in Ethiopia, 302, 306; in
World War II, 372, 399; writings, 373;
and protection of civilians, 412
Fujibayashi, Sergeant Major, 481
Furley, Sir John: and Franco-Prussian war,
69–70, 75, 80, 84, 86, 384; enthusiasm,
132; writes on inactivity of British
Society, 138; appointed honorary
secretary of British Society committee,
139; in Boer War, 140, 142; critical of
reorganized British Red Cross Society,
171
Fürstenberg, Captain, 66–7

Gabaria, Father, 323
Gaillard, Pierre, 563, 565–6, 568, 586,
588–9, 594, 603, 605
Galikova, Maria, 250
Gallopin, Roger, 629
Galveston, Texas: 1900 hurricane, 107–8,
112
Gambetta, Léon, 76
Gambia, 628
Gard, Walter, S., 300
Gardner, Harry, 243
Garfield, James Abram, 93
Garibaldi, Giuseppe, 1, 26, 55
Garrett, Dr (of Southampton), 323

Garteiser, Colonel, 418
gas (poison): proposed banning of, 170,
286, 313; effects, 178; used in World War
I, 254–6; peacetime accidents with, 309;
used in Ethiopia, 310–13, 355, 368, 376,
608; used in Yemen war, 602–3; see also
chemical warfare
Gasparin, Comtesse Valerie de, 5, 9
Gasser, Hans-Peter, 635, 713
Gasser, Jack, 574
Gaulle, Charles de, 537, 543, 593
Gaussen, Pastor Louis, 10
Gautier, Auguste, 531
Gebhardt, Karl, 468–70, 498, 515, 526
Geneva: 1942 Hotel Metropole meeting,
xxi–xxvii; character, 9–11, 14; 1863
International Committee conference,
20–3, 28, 36, 38–9; 1864 Diplomatic
Conference and treaty, 43–7; street
named for Croix Rouge, 130; wartime
organizations in, 205; conditions during
World War II, 407–8; attracts opponents
of Nazism, 416; international conference
and protocols (1974–7), 634–5
Geneva Convention: First (1864) on
unjust–just wars, 29; overlooks sea
wars, 56; Supplementary (second
conference, 1868), 58; flouted and
honoured in Franco-Prussian war, 82–3;
criticized as harmful, 123–4; proposed
revisions, 124–5, 169–70; and peace
movement, 167; and Hague
Convention, 170; signatories at outbreak
of World War I, 175; breached in World
War I, 201–2, 206; Davison proposes
changes to, 261; and regulation of
chemical weapons, 285, 368, 667;
expanded (1928–9), 291, 296, 377; and
political prisoners, 330; in World War II,
374, 376, 400, 402–3; Japanese attitude
to, 471–2, 477; breached by French after
World War II, 534-5; proposed post-
World War II revisions, 548, 551–4; 1949
Revisions (four conventions), 554–7,
558; 1949 code in Korean war, 569,
572–3, 577, 579; 1949 code condemns
torture, 587; ratifications and signatories

to 1949 code, 595; knowledge of and obedience to, 604–5, 698; League proposes revision (1970s), 630; and humanitarian law, 708; 1977 protocols, 710; condemned as obsolete, 710; *see also* Prisoner-of-War Code (1929)

Georg, Stefan, 388

Georgia, 691

German Red Cross society: in Franco-Prussian war, 83, 123; sends supplies in Boer War, 142; in Tripoli campaign (1911), 174; in World War I, 189; numerical strength, 208, 243, 256, 341, 349, 467; excluded from Davison's League, 262; proposes ban on bomber aircraft, 309; on food shortages (1920s), 338–40; inter-war development, 340–2; and League of Red Cross Societies, 340, 357–8, 361–2; and political prisoners, 343–4, 352; subordinated to Nazi government, 345, 349, 356–7, 362, 528; actions under Nazism, 347–50; absorbs Austrian society, 357–8; and Nazi persecution of Jews, 363, 425; at outbreak of World War II, 375; in World War II, 382, 467–8; character, 467–8; not tried at Nuremberg, 497; post World War II reform and reorganization, 526–8; in East Germany, 696

German Youth Red Cross, 341

Germany: in World War I, 178; treatment of World War I prisoners, 187–91, 197, 199–200; complains of atrocities in World War I, 201–2; uses poison gas, 254–6; totalitarianism in, 329; post-World War I famine, 338–40; and rise of Nazism, 341–2, 345, 347; prisoners and camps in, 342–4, 347, 349–55, 358–60, 411–13, 415, 417–18, 496; Nazi government takes over Red Cross, 345; pact with USSR (1939), 369; and outbreak of World War II, 371, 374; conduct of and campaigns in World War II, 377; forms Axis (1940), 377; treatment of prisoners-of-war in World War II, 378, 383, 398–400, 415; behaviour

of prisoners-of-war, 381–2; invasion and campaign in USSR, 397; prisoners-of-war in USSR, 398–9, 697; practises reprisals, 402–3; and protection of civilians, 412–13; allows Red Cross parcels to internees, 454; releases camp detainees for payment, 456; and Soviet advance (1945), 464; systematic killings and medical experimentation, 468–70; Allied occupation and administration of, 505 7, post-World War II compensation to deportees, 520; post-World War II prisoners in France, 530–8, 540–1, 585; Swiss co-operation with in World War II, 704–5; *see also* Nazism

Gernet, Dr Rudolph von, 143

Gettysburg, battle of (1863), 33

Gibson, Harvey D., 243, 258, 406

Gielgud, Colonel Lewis, 292–3, 364

Gillman, Kitty, 510–11

Gingins-la-Sarraz, Baron de, 13

Giral, Jose, 320

Girardin, Saint-Marc, 9

Gladstone, Catherine (*née* Glynne), 137

Gladstone, William Ewart, 163

Gleichen, Countess Helena, 223

Glen Echo, Maryland, 106, 111–12

Gloor, Ernest, 544

Gollancz, (Sir) Victor, 503, 507

Gomulka, Wladyslaw, 579

Goncourt, Edmond de, 78–9, 82

Gordon, General Charles George, 136

Gordon, Ernest, 484

Göring, Frau Hermann, 382

Gorky, Maxim, 277, 286, 334

Gouttes, Paul de, xxiv, 176, 313, 359, 375

Gowan, General Yakubu, 615, 617

Graf, Sergeant Josef, 514, 528

Gramont, Antoine Aganor Alfred, Duc de, 60

Grant, Jim, 653

Grant Duff, Lady, 205

Graves, Lucy, 100, 105

Grawitz, Dr Ernst, 356–7, 359, 363, 382, 468–70; suicide, 526

Graz, Georges, 326, 539–40, 703

Great War, 1914–18 *see* World War I
Gredinger (Swiss resident in Greece), 395
Greece: World War II starvation, 392–4,
    397; prison camps in, 395–6; civil war
    (1949), 555; military coup (1967) and
    political prisoners in, 606–13;
    agreement with International
    Committee (1969–70), 610–12
Greek Red Cross: sends supplies in Boer
    War, 142; in World War II, 395–6; and
    tracing of survivors, 522
Grey, Sir Edward (*later* Viscount), 228
Grey, Lady Sybil, 235–6
Griscom, Lloyd, 159
Grossman, Kurt, 343
Gross Rosen concentration camp, 522
Grotius, Hugo, 24
Grotjahn, Alfred, 348
Grueneisen (of German Red Cross),
    531
Guernica, 322, 326
guerrillas: status, 37, 409; in Boer War,
    143–4; *see also* civilians
Guggenheim, Paul, 419, 424–5, 444
Guise, Major, 505
Gulf War (1991), 685, 691, 696
Gunther, Hans, 433
Gustav V Adolf, King of Sweden, 444–5
Guyot, Dr Frédéric, 200
gypsies: persecuted by Nazis, 354, 358, 411,
    414–15, 470

Haan, Dr Barthold Bierens de, 676–7
Habyarimana, General Juvénal, 688
Haccius, Rodolphe, 330–1, 372, 378–9, 390,
    440
Haefliger, Louis, 463, 498
Hague Convention Respecting the Laws
    and Customs of War on Land, 1899 &
    1907, 38, 125, 170, 180, 187, 254
Hague Peace Conference (1898/9), 166,
    169–70
Hahn, Fritz Gebhardt von, 416–7
Hahn, Philippe, 321
Haile Selassie, Emperor of Ethiopia, 306,
    314
Haines, Anna, 277

Hakuai-sha (Philanthropic Society, Japan),
    151
Haldane, Robert, 10
Hall, Sir John, 31
Halleck, General Henry Wager, 37
Haller, Edouard de, xxiv, 443
Hallins, Rodolphe, 268
Halsen, Dr Jacob, 34
Hamburg, 507
Hammond, William A., 35
Hanneken, Elsa von, 195
Harkis (of Algeria), 593–4
Harley, Mrs (*née* French), 225
Harris, Dr Ira, 102
Harrison (US minister in Berne), 442
Hartmann, Walther, 361–2, 399, 414,
    526–8
Hausa people (Nigeria), 614
Haussmann, Baron Georges-Eugène, 79
Haussonville, Comtesse d', 216, 248
Hautville, Philippe Grand d', 611–12, 675
Hawes, Lady Angela, 217
Hay, Alexander, 644, 658, 667, 672–4,
    678–9
Hay, John, 145
Hazan, Pierre, 702
Hedbloom (Swedish Red Cross delegate),
    272
Heiden, Switzerland, 162–4, 173
Heider, Richard, 395
Helmer, Oscar, 584
Henderson, Sir David, 263, 283
Heng Samrin, 640, 644, 648, 656
Henri IV, King of France, 27
Henry XIII, Prince of Reuss, 20, 39
Herbert, Sidney, 1st Baron, 31
Heron, G.W., 564
Hersh, Seymour, 643
Hertz, Alfred, 115
Herzegovina: revolts against Turks (1875),
    125
Heuber, Christine, 529
Heydrich, Reinhard, 345, 350–3, 415, 457,
    466, 468–9
Hiegel, Dr J.P., 652
Hill, Sir Claude, 283, 288
Hill, Norah, 294, 359

Hilton, John, 384
Himmler, Henrich: and Wannsee
    Conference, xxii; principles, 345; on
    breeding Aryan racial elite, 348, 433;
    authorizes Burckhardt's visit to
    concentration camps, 351; appoints
    Grawitz to head German Red Cross,
    356; anti-Semitism, 362, 414; visits
    Zamosc, 428; Germanization
    programme, 433, 435; and repatriation
    of Jews, 456–9; and Theresienstadt
    ghetto, 465; and gas chambers, 468;
    authorizes medical experimentation,
    469; has concentration camp records
    destroyed, 521
Hindenburg, Paul von, 341
Hirayama, Baron, 294
Hirl, Reichsarbeitsführer, 352, 354
Hirohito, Emperor of Japan, 488, 496
Hiroshima, 488–90
Hitler, Adolf: Jewish policy, xxiii, 414–15,
    419, 424, 441; protests to Mussolini over
    Ethiopia, 308; rise to power, 341, 348;
    and Austrian political prisoners, 345;
    inspects German Red Cross, 349; and
    German prison camps, 352–3, 551;
    Burckhardt writes to, 354; supremacy,
    357; annexations, 369; pact with Stalin
    (1939), 369; assurances on restricting
    attacks to military targets, 374; affirms
    humanitarian commitment, 375; and
    Blitz on London, 377; and Nacht und
    Nebel decree, 415, 454; advocates death
    for concentration camp inmates, 456,
    458
Hobhouse, Emily, 144–6
Ho Chi Minh City, 642
Hocké, Jean-Paul: management position in
    International Committee, 623, 647–8,
    653, 655–7; qualities, 671–2; and 1986
    delegates' coup, 678–9; on
    humanitarian aid, 693
Hockmann, Dr (USA): killed in Ethiopia,
    308
Hocquiny, Mlle, 77
Hodgson, Colonel W.R., 554
Hoefliger, Jean, 679

Hoffmann, George, 614, 619
Hohenberg, Sophie (Chotek), Duchess of,
    174
Holland (Netherlands): falls to Germany
    (1940), 377; conflict in Indonesia, 555
Holleben, von (President of German Red
    Cross), 123
Hollings, Nina, 223
Home, Mr (US spiritualist), 75
homosexuals: International Committee
    disapproves of, 316; persecuted by Nazis,
    414–15
Hong Kong, 472–5, 477, 485
Hoover, Herbert, 279–81
Hore-Belisha, Leslie (later Baron), 378
Horst, Baron von, 168
Hort, Robert, 464
Horthy, Admiral Nicholas, 439–40, 442–5
hostages: exchanged in Spanish civil war,
    318–19, 327
Hoten Camp, Seian, 487–8
Howard, Jim, 643
Howard, William W., 109
Howells, William Dean, 33
Hrabar, Roman, 523–6
Hubbell, Julian, 93–4, 98, 100
Huber, Max: and 1942 Geneva meeting,
    xxiii–xxv; character and beliefs, xxvii,
    410, 420, 594–5; succeeds Ador as
    president, 289–91; absent from 1934
    Tokyo conference, 294; on prestige of
    Red Cross, 299; idealism, 300–1; and
    Sidney Brown, 301; and Italian war in
    Ethiopia, 302, 306, 311–12; emphasizes
    neutrality, 313, 373, 410, 422; and
    Brown's recall from Ethiopia, 315–16;
    and Spanish civil war, 317, 319; and
    Soviet political prisoners, 336–7; Duke
    of Saxe-Coburg visits, 342; and German
    political prisoners, 344, 350, 353, 355;
    and politicization of German Red Cross,
    345, 347, 349, 357, 362; and Austrian
    political prisoners, 346; and Nazi
    persecution of Jews, 358, 418, 420; at
    1938 London conference, 359; vetoes
    Lucie Odier's visit to German camps,
    360; and Sino-Japanese war, 364;

Huber Max - *Cont.*
relations with Calame, 365, 367−8;
caution, 370, 410, 439; moves to Geneva
in World War II, 372; at outbreak of
World War II, 373−4; calls for civilian
sanctuaries in World War II, 375;
appeals in World War II, 400−1, 407,
412; ill-health, 409, 423; on role of Red
Cross, 410; refrains from denunciations
and judging, 422; and expansion of
International Committee, 423; and
Hungarian Jews, 440−4; enjoins
belligerents to respect human rights,
454; Burckhardt succeeds as president,
458; and German medical
experimentation, 470; and Japan in
World War II, 486; on nature and effect
of war, 499; on refugees, 512; and post-
World War II German Red Cross,
526−7; justifies International
Committee's actions over Jews and
camps, 543, 545; pessimism, 544; inaction
over Nazi behaviour, 551; proposes
revising Geneva Convention, 552; and
reorganization of International
Committee, 559; on humanitarian role
of Committee, 561; death and tributes,
594; company's involvement in wartime
arms manufacture, 704−5, 707;
achievements, 714; *The Red Cross and
Neutrality*, 313, 373
Hudson, Sir Robert, 210
Hugo, Victor, 9
human rights: legislation, 286, 708; and
laws of war, 560; commissions and
conventions on, 607, 610, 612, 708
Humbert, Aimé, 123
Hun Sen, 641
Hungarian Red Cross: on post-World War
I conditions, 275; and deported Jews in
World War II, 440; accuses USA of
bacteriological warfare in Korea, 575;
and 1956 rising, 580−2
Hungary: ruled by Austria, 1; post-World
War I starvation, 275; communism
under Béla Kun, 330−1; joins Axis pact,
377; Polish refugees in, 387; World War
II Jews in, 439−54; 1956 rising, 579−85
Hutchinson, Dr Alice, 225, 227−8
Huta people (Rwanda), 688−90
Hylander, Major Dr, 305, 307

Ibo people (Nigeria), 614−18, 627
ICRC, the League and the Tansley Report, The
(document), 632
Ieneps, Ferdinand de, 127
illness: in wars, 27, 32; among repatriated
prisoners, 268−70; *see also* epidemics
Imperial Society of the Caucasus, 9
India: internment camps in World War I,
198; prisoners-of-war in, 627−8
Indian Red Cross: and Korean war
prisoners, 578
Indonesia, 555
influenza: post-World War I epidemic, 270
Inglis, Dr Elsie, 224−5
*Institut Universaire de Hautes Etudes
Internationales*, Geneva, 303
insurrections *see* civil wars
Inter-Allied Armistice Commission, 269
Inter-Allied Committee on Post-War
Requirements, 502
internal wars *see* civil wars
International Agency for Aid and
Information on Prisoners of War, 180,
183−4, 205
International Charity Congress, Berlin
(1863), 16, 18
International Committee of the Red Cross
(*formerly* for Relief to the Wounded):
1942 Geneva meeting (Hotel Metropole)
on Jews in Nazi Germany, xxii−xxvii;
composition, xxi, 60, 175−6, 301−2, 372,
420, 560, 628−9, 714−15; moral
leadership in World War II, xxvi−xxvii;
and Nazi persecution of Jews, xxi−xxiv,
358, 419−20, 422, 424−5, 700, 705−7;
neutrality, xxii−xxiv, 561, 569; formed,
17−20; Geneva conference (1863), 20−3,
28, 36, 38−9; proposes diplomatic treaty,
38-9, 41; and Schleswig-Holstein war,
40−2; duty to publish truth, 42−3; on
use of Red Cross emblem, 53, 62; on
national societies during peacetime,

56–7; French challenge to organization, 59; and Franco-Prussian war, 60–1, 63, 76, 82–3; awards medal, 94; moves premises in Geneva (1874), 121; expansion of Red Cross societies, 122; restricts expansion to 'civilized' nations, 122–3; and civil wars, 125, 285, 329; adopts 'Red Cross' into title, 126; twenty-fifth anniversary (1888), 130–1; and Russo-Turkish war (1877–8), 136; on inactivity of British Society, 138; and Boer War, 140, 142, 145–6; and Russo-Japanese war, 150, 156; and Nobel peace prize, 164, 167–8; and revision of Geneva Convention, 170; and deaths of Moynier and Dunant, 172–3; fiftieth anniversary (1914), 174; and outbreak of World War I, 175, 180; work and activities in World War I, 180, 183–4, 187–8, 257; prisoner inspection delegates in World War I, 187–200; and World War I breaches of Geneva Convention, 201–2; awarded Nobel Peace Prizes, 206, 499, 542, 550, 597; relations with national Red Cross societies, 208, 711; on Bolshevik Revolution and reform of Russian Red Cross, 238–40; and internees in World War I, 253; deplores use of poison gas, 254–6, 355; and Davison's formation of League, 259–64, 268; early rivalry with League, 263–4, 280, 282–4, 288; and post-World War I repatriations, 266–70, 273–4; and post-World War I Russian famine, 278–80; reconciliation with League, 289; and Far East conflicts (1930s), 297; and drift to war (1930s), 298–9; non-political stance, 298, 312–13; character and nature of delegates, 301, 304–5, 325, 328, 376, 498, 603–4, 674–7; and war in Ethiopia, 306, 308–9, 311–13, 316, 355; on use of poison gas, 312–13, 602, 608; and Spanish civil war, 316–17, 319–21, 324–7, 382; and political prisoners, 329–34, 337–8, 343–4, 345–6, 349–50, 352–3, 355, 605–6; and German post-World War I

famine, 339–40; and moral leadership, 339, 561; criticized for confusion in 1930s, 368–9; and protection of civilians, 369, 411–13; and outbreak of World War II, 371–6; neglects national societies, 372; World War II co-operation with League, 387; and British economic blockade, 389–90; and transport of prisoners by sea, 401; protests against reprisals, 402–3; World War II meetings, 408–9; defends Jews, 413, 414–15; and Nazi extermination policy, 416; organization and structure in World War II, 422–3; Committee of Co-ordination ('La Maison'), 423, 629, 677; special commission on Prisoners and Civilian internees, 423; and Hungarian Jews, 444, 452–4; sends parcels to German camp internees, 455–6; CCC department (*Colis aux camps de concentration*), 455; and liberation of Nazi concentration camps, 463–4; and Japan in World War II, 473–80, 484–9, 494–5; Allied dissatisfaction with in World War II, 486; achievements in World War II, 498; Relief to the Wounded work at end of World War II, 500–1; and post-World War II Europe, 502–3, 505, 511–12; tracings in post-World War II Europe, 516–19; and post-World War II German Red Cross, 526–7; post-World War II criticisms of, 535, 543–51, 559, 595; and post-World War II German prisoners, 541–2; post-World War II deficit, 543; October 1945 meeting, 547; Riegner attends 1946 meeting, 548–9; and post-World War II revisions to Geneva Convention, 552–3, 559; granted right of initiative under 1949 Geneva Convention, 557; post-World War II reorganization and restructuring, 559–62; and seven 'fundamental principles', 561–2; later relations with League, 564, 582, 629–30, 672–3, 695–7; and Palestine partition and conflict, 565–9; and promoting humanitarian principles, 605; effect of Biafran war on,

Int. Com. of the Red Cross - *cont.*
614, 622–6; and Médécins sans
frontières, 625, 709–11; archives, 629;
status and role challenged, 630;
Tansley's report on ('Big Study', 1975),
631–3; international conference on laws
of war (1974–7), 634–5; relations with
Israel, 637–9; criticized for work in
Cambodia, 650–2, 656; preoccupation
with failure, 658; tracing of
Cambodians, 658; delegates killed,
kidnapped and endangered, 674–5,
682–3, 692–3; putsch by delegates
(1986), 678–81; commissions study by
Media Natura (1993), 693–4; image and
public perception of, 693–4, 697–700;
relations with other humanitarian
organizations, 693–5, 698, 711, 713;
disenchantment with and criticisms of,
698–9; public appeals, 700; and stolen
Jewish gold, 702–3; seeks ban on
modern weapons, 707–8; and right of
initiative (*droit d'ingérence*), 708–9, 713;
future role and conduct, 711–14;
funding, 714; career and service in, 715
International Committee for Russian
Relief, 280
International Court of Justice, The Hague,
710
International Criminal Court: proposed,
712
International Federation for Peace, 166
International Herald Tribune, 706
International League for Peace and
Freedom, 350
International Military Tribunal,
Nuremberg, 124; *see also* Nuremberg
Trials
International Red Cross Committee of
Nanking, 365
International Relief Union, 287
International Review see Bulletin (of
International Committee)
International Tracing Service, Arolsen,
519–22
internees: in World War I, 186, 198, 203–5,
253

Iran: war with Iraq (1980–8), 665–7,
670–1
Iraq: war with Iran (1980–8), 665–7,
670–1; chemical warfare, 666–7; missing
persons, 667–70; in Gulf War, 691
Ireland: political prisoners visited, 332
Irgun Zvai Leumi (Zionist organization),
565
Isabella, Queen of Spain, 9
Islin, Colonel Frédéric, 388
Israel: recognizes Righteous Gentiles, 453;
political detainees in, 606, 628, 636–8;
Six Day War (1967), 636; relations with
International Committee, 637–8
Istanbul Declaration (1969), 708
Italian Red Cross: sends supplies in Boer
War, 142; in Messina earthquake,
158–60; membership increase, 264; and
invasion of Ethiopia, 305; in World War
II, 379–80
Italy: revolts against Austrian rule, 1–2;
north liberated from Austria, 7; 1866
war with Austria, 55–6; and Messina
earthquake, 157; 1911 war with Turkey,
173; treatment of prisoners in World
War I, 188, 191–2, 407; British Red
Cross unit in during World War I,
221–3; American Red Cross in during
World War I, 249; invasion and war in
Ethiopia (1935–6), 301–2, 304, 307–9,
313–14; uses poison gas in Ethiopia,
310–12, 608; totalitarianism in, 329;
forms Axis (1940), 377; prisoners-of-war
in Britain, 379; treatment of prisoners
in World War II, 379; sinks Swedish Red
Cross ship in World War II, 395; post-
World War II relief, 505, 508; tracing
programme in, 517

Jacquinot de Besange, Père, 366–8
Jaegger (Swiss diplomat in Budapest),
445
Jakobkiewicz, Joseph, 276
Jameson Raid (1895), 139, 145
Japan: ratifies Geneva Convention, 123,
150; 1888 celebrations, 131; war with and
victory over Russia (1904–5), 149–57,

231; absorbs foreign influences, 150; in World War I, 178; treatment of World War I prisoners, 196; and lost children of the Urals, 250–2; and Russian civil war, 272; earthquakes (1923), 287; invades Manchuria (1931), 296–8; non-ratification of 1929 Geneva Convention, 296–7, 471; war and occupation of China, 301, 363–8, 471; wartime atrocities, 365–6; and treatment of prisoners in World War II, 376, 407, 471–88, 490–4; joins Axis pact, 377; attitude to humanitarianism, 471; enters World War II, 471–2; dominance in Far East, 472, 476; and Burma railway, 483; International Committee delegates in (1945), 487–9; atom bombs dropped on (August, 1945), 488–90; post-World War II relief measures, 493–4; surrenders (14 August, 1945), 496–7; war criminals tried, 497, 541, 577; civilian casualties in World War II, 552; USSR declares war on (1945), 558; and bacteriological warfare, 577; compensation for Allied prisoners-of-war, 628; funding contributions, 714

Japanese Red Cross society: established, 122–9, 151; strength, organization and conduct, 130, 150–1, 153–7, 243, 256, 292–3; in 1904–5 war with Russia, 153–7; at 1912 Washington conference, 174; in Europe in World War I, 178; and Davison's proposed post-war reforms, 261; hosts 1934 Red Cross conference, 292–6; association with military, 297; character, 471, 476; in World War II, 475, 476–7, 481

Jebb, Eglantyne, 281, 286–8

Jehovah's Witnesses: persecuted by Nazis, 411

Jekyll, Lady, 210

Jerusalem: Avenue of the Righteous, 453; and partition of Palestine, 563–6; see also Israel; Palestine

Jews: denied entry to Switzerland, xxiii, 421–2, 453, 560; International Committee attempts to defend,

xxi–xxvi, 413, 414–15, 543–4, 551; persecuted by Nazis, xxii–xxvi, 342, 347–8, 352, 354–5, 358, 361–2, 413–20, 424–6, 428, 430, 454, 521, 700, 705–6; in concentration camps, 360–1, 411, 413, 466, 700, 705–6; in Italy, 380; in wartime Greece, 396; refugees, 420–2; Hungarian, 439–54; released from Nazi camps for payment, 456; segregated in concentration camps, 458; in Shanghai, 475; numbers killed in World War II, 496; and Palestine settlement, 564–5, 568; stolen gold in Swiss banks, 700–3

Jezler (Head of Swiss Office for Refugees), 421

Johannes, Mrs Pastor, 489

John, Augustus, 210, 322

Johnson and Johnson (medical suppliers), 110

Johnston, Colonel, 461

Jones, Colonel Guy Carleton, 288

Jordan: Palestinian refugees in, 567

Jordanian Red Cross, 567

Jorden, Ella, 507, 567

Journal de Genève, 40, 286, 609

Journal des Débats, 9–10

Jules Verne (French warship), 684

Junior Red Cross movement, 300, 593

Junod, Dominique, 568

Junod, Dr Marcel: in Ethiopia, 305–7, 310, 312, 314–15; in Spanish civil war, 316–21, 324–8, 376; on bombing of Warsaw, 376; in France during World War II, 378, 381; visits Britain (1941), 390–1; organizes wartime shipping to Greece, 394; on Jews in Poland, 417; appointed to Far East in World War II, 487–9, 492, 494–6; and atom bombing of Japan, 489–90; returns to hospital work, 560; influence, 562; qualities, 677; Le Troisième Combatant, 304; Warrior Without Weapons, 320

Kadar, Janos, 584

Kahn, Emile, 342

Kahn, Friedrich, 343

Kallay, Miklos, 440

Kaltenbrunner, Ernst, 457–60, 464–5
Kampuchea see Cambodia
Kant, Immanuel, 165
Karnebeek, Rear-Admiral, 58
Karsai, Laszlo, 449, 452
Karski, Jan, 425
Kastner, Mme Jean-Georges, 127–9
Katanga Red Cross, 674
Kataryzna, Maria, 434
Katyn massacre (1940), 436–7
Kay, Dr Alec, 145
Kelly, (Sir) David, 391
Kenchu, Baron, 150
Kennedy, Sir John, 391
Kennedy, Kenneth, 222–3
Kenworthy, Captain Ernest, 143
Kenya, 684
Keogh, Sir Alfred, 212, 215
Kerensky, Alexander F., 237
Ketuly, Jamal, 668
Ketuly, Kamal, 668–9
Khartoum, 136
Khider, Mohammed, 592
Khmer Rouge, 640–1, 643–9, 651–2,
   654–5, 658–60
Khomeini, Ayatollah, 665–6
Kigali, Rwanda, 688, 693
Kikava, Marie, 332
Kingston, Beattie, 75
Kiss, Geza, 442, 448
Kitchener, Field Marshal Horatio Herbert,
   1st Earl, 141, 144, 146, 148, 178, 211
Klopsch, Louis, 104
Knocker, Mrs, 219
Koestler, Arthur, 320, 336
Kolchak, Admiral Alexander Vasilievich,
   272
Komoly, Otto, 445, 453
Königgrätz see Sadowa
Korean war (1950–53), 569–79;
   International Committee accused of
   partiality in, 642
Kouchner, Dr Bernard, 624–5, 699, 709
Kristallnacht (1938), 361, 363, 421
Kun, Béla, 330–1, 334, 372
Kurds, 663
Kwai, river, 483; see also Burma railway

Laar, Madame P.A. van, 541
Lachert, Waclaw, 427, 436–8
Lador-Lederer, Joseph, 498
Lafontaine (Belgian League of Nations
   delegate), 278
La Lèche League, 651
Lalive, Maître, 386–8, 560
Lambert, André, 395–6
Landa, Dr, 21
landmines: cleared by German prisoners
   in France, 534; worldwide spread and
   proposed ban on, 692, 707
Lane, Franklin, 263
Lang, Cosmo, Archbishop of Canterbury,
   306, 359, 377
Langleben, Chaim, 515
Lansdowne, Maud Evelyn, Marchioness of,
   209–10
Lanskoranska, Countess Karoline von,
   459–60
Laporte, Mme (of French Red Cross), 592
laser weapons, 707
Latin AmericaL 'disappearing' of unwanted
   people, 662–4
law of nations, 24
Lawson, Thomas, 33
Layard, Mary Evelyn (Lady), 135
Le Boeuf, Marshal Edmond, 62
League of Nations: and US entry into
   World War I, 261; and League of Red
   Cross Societies, 262, 265; and
   repatriation of prisoners, 274; and
   Russian famine, 277–8; and Japanese
   invasion of Manchuria, 296, 298; and
   Italian use of gas in Ethiopia, 312–13;
   and open cities, 320; decline, 369; co-
   operation with International
   Committee in World War II, 375, 387;
   investigated in 'Big Study' (1975), 631
League of Red Cross Societies (later
   Federation): formed, 261–4; early
   rivalry with International Committee,
   263–4, 280, 282–4, 288; first Conference
   (Geneva, 1920), 265; post-World War I
   problems and relief programmes, 274,
   276, 279–80; reform and move to Paris,
   284; defines role and functions, 289–90;

reconciliation with International Committee, 289; and German famine (1920s), 339; and Nazi German Red Cross, 340, 357–8, 361; moves to Geneva in World War II, 374; World War II co-operation with International Committee, 386; at end of World War II, 501; post-World War II status and reputation, 546–7, 559; July 1946 meeting (Oxford), 548; attends Swiss 1949 conference 554; co-operates with International Committee in Palestine, 564; later relations with International Committee, 564, 582, 629–30, 672–3, 695–7; and Hungarian rising (1956), 582; acts in Algerian war, 592–3; reorganization and restructuring, 596, 630; shares 1963 Nobel peace prize with International Committee, 597; questions role of Red Cross, 630; Tansley proposes merging with International Committee, 632; disclaims Tansley's recommendations, 633; renamed Federation (1991), 695; relief activities in 1988, 696

Lehmann, Dr, 43
Lehmann, Kaspar, 25
Lehner, Dr Otto, 382, 465, 573
Lenin, Vladimir Ilich 238, 249
Lenz, Fritz, 348
Leo XIII, Pope, 163
Leopold III, King of the Belgians, 377, 466
Leopold of Hohenzollern-Sigmaringen, Prince, 60
Leopold, Louis, 330
Leslie, Dr Armand, 133
Leuschner, Pastor, 531
Leveson-Gower, Lord Alistair, 217
Levsky, Dr, 238
Lewis, Miss (of Cairo prison camp), 197–8
Lewis, Anthony, 647
Ley, Robert, 425
Liberia, 628, 691
Lichtenberg camp (Germany), 351
Lie, Trygve, 567
Lieber, Francis, 37–8
Lieber, Hamilton, 37

Lieber, Norman, 38
Lillers, Marquis de, 362, 374
Lincoln, Abraham, 33–4, 89, 113
Lindt, August, 619–20, 699
Lipton, Sir Thomas, 226–7
Lisbon: wartime imports through, 388
Lissa, battle of (1866), 56
Lister, Joseph, 1st Baron, 28
Litvinoff, Maxim, 334
Lloyd George, David (later 1st Earl), 145, 260
Loeffler, Dr (of German Red Cross), 356
Loeffler, Frederick, 44
Logan, Mrs John, 112
Long, Olivier, 387
Longfellow, Commodore Wilbert E., 241
Longmore, Sir Thomas, 30, 47, 51
Look magazine, 610
Loritz (German prison camp commandant), 351–3, 355
Louis-Napoleon see Napoleon III, Emperor of the French
Louise, Princess of Great Britain, 70
Louise, Princess of Prussia, 61, 91
Loyd-Lindsay, Colonel Robert James (later Baron Wantage): and aid in Franco-Prussian war, 69–70, 73–4, 84–5; chairs British Red Cross Society, 73; and siege of Paris, 80; and Russo-Turkish war (1877), 131–4; and idea of neutrality, 133, 135; appointed chairman of permanent committee, 139; and Boer War, 141; death, 172
Luard, Nurse K.R., 219
Ludwig, Prince of Hesse, 527
Lullin and Sautter (banking house), 11, 13
Lundström (Swedish driver): killed in Ethiopia, 307
Luther, Martin, 24
Lutz, Carl, 445–6, 449–51, 453, 584
Lutz, Gertrude, 445
Lvov, Prince George, 232, 237
Lyon, France, 532
Lyttelton, Oliver, 394

MacArthur, General Douglas, 490
MacAulay, John, 596

McCaul, Ethel, 154
MacCormac, Sir William, 72, 142, 147
McCready, Mrs, 535
Macfie, Dr, 306–7, 310
MacKenzie, H.F., 485
McKinley, William, 103, 110–11
MacLaughlin, Louise: *Our Adventures During the War of 1870* (with Emma Thomson), 71–3
MacLelland, Rosswell, 416
MacMahon, Marshal Marie Edmé Patrice Maurice de, Duke of Magenta, 7
McPhail, Private, 189
McPherson, Bimbashi, 220
Macrae, Miss (of British Red Cross), 509
Madagascar: French campaign in (1894), 156
Magen David Adom (Red Shield of David), 564, 638
Magenta, battle of (1859), 1, 3
Maggi (company), 705
Mahoney, Dr Margaret, 118
Maine, USS, 104
Majdanek (Polish concentration camp), 428, 430–2
Mak Monn camp (Cambodia), 651
Malaysia, 555
Maleter, Colonel Pál, 580
Mali, 696
Malta, Knights of, 25
Man, Isle of, 196–7, 379
Manchester Guardian Weekly, 355
Manchuria: and Russo-Japanese war, 150; Japan invades (1931), 296, 471
Manley, William George Nicholas, VC, 86
Margarita, Dowager Queen of Italy, 179
Margol, Marianna, 434
Marguerite, Princess of Hesse, 527
Maria Feodorovna, Empress of Russia, 152, 163, 195, 231
Maria Nikolaevna, Grand Duchess of Russia, 234
Marie, Queen of Romania, 179, 220
Markpress (public relations company), 616–17, 626
Marreco, Anthony, 610

Marti, Laurent, 630, 672; *Bonsoir mes victimes*, 699
Marti, Dr Roland: and Spanish civil war, 324–7; and German concentration camps, 377–8, 417–18, 454, 458, 462; on Russian prisoners-of-war, 397–8; on administrative faults in International Committee, 423; requests supplies of tobacco, 456; in Middle East, 564; in Greece, 608–12
Martin, Dr Eric, 629, 631
Martin, Revd Jacques, 196–7
Martineau, Harriet, 84
Marx, Karl, 176
Mary, Princess of Teck (*later* Queen of George V), 70
Masarykova, Dr, 359
Mason, Ernest, 100, 102
Masson, Brigadier Roger, 703
Massu, General Jacques, 588, 591
Matsukata, Count Masayoshi, 153
Maunoir, Dr Theodore: supports Dunant's battlefield proposals, 16–18; at 1864 Geneva Diplomatic Conference, 44; and Dunant's resignation, 49; death, 60; and modern war, 716
Maurer, Victor, 462
Maurice, Frédéric, 682–3, 688
Maurice, Colonel J., 137
Mauritania, 696
Mauthausen concentration camp, 463
Mayo, Dr, 86
Mazoon, Mrs, 252
Mazuet, Claudius, 6
Médécins sans frontières (MSF), 615, 630, 650, 698, 709–11
Media Natura (organization), 693–4, 697
Medical Association of Stuttgart *see* Württenburg Red Cross Society
medical experimentation: Germany practises on prisoners, 469–70, 515, 520
Mehlhose, Wolfgang, 514, 528
Meledine, M., 120–1
Melly, Dr, 306, 308, 314
Menpes, Mortimer, 141
Merrick, Joseph ('the Elephant man'), 142
Merrill, John, 292

Mesopotamia, 220—1
Messina: 1908 earthquake, 157—60, 264
Mexico: 1911 revolution, 173
Meyer, Dr Hans, 498
Millerand, Alexandre, 180
Milson, Georges, 386, 388
Milutin, General D.A., 59
Minnucci, Vittorio, 547
missing persons *see* tracing service
Missouri, USS, 497
Mitterrand, François, 709
Modoux, Alain, 672
Moens, Colonel, 220—1
Mogadishu, 684
Mohr, Adelaide, 293
Mola, General Emilio, 318
Moller, Mrs K., 489
Mollet, Guy, 588
Moltke, Field Marshal Helmuth von, Count, 62
Monde, Le (newspaper), 589—91, 625, 636
Monkhouse, Muriel, 516—17, 660
Mons-Djemila, Algeria, 7, 14, 161
Montadon, Georges, 283
Montebello, battle of (1859), 1, 3, 26
Montenegro, 125, 187
Montreuil Bellay camp, France, 530
Morando, Bernardo, 428
Moreillon, Jacques, 590, 611, 672, 674, 678—80
Morell, Dr Theodor, 469
Moroccan Red Crescent, 593
Morocco: World War I prisoners in, 199
Morra, Dr (of Italian Red Cross), 380
Motta, Giuseppe, 334, 337, 560
Mountbatten, Edwina, Countess, 493
Mouravieff (of Far East Section), 479, 481—2
Moussaoria (Algerian nationalist), 590
Moynier, Gustave: supports Dunant's battlefield proposals, 15—19, 25; at 1863 Geneva meeting of International Committee, 20—1, 23, 28, 38; and American Sanitary Commission, 36—7; animosity towards Dunant, 38, 50, 57, 126, 128, 164, 172; and 1864 Geneva Diplomatic Conference, 43—4, 46, 48; encourages Dunant, 43; accepts Dunant's resignation, 49—50; ideals, 53, 285, 561, 714; on need for preparedness, 54; awarded gold medal of 1867 Exhibition, 57; and disputes over structure of organization, 58—9; resists review of First Geneva Convention, 58; status in Committee, 60; and Franco-Prussian war, 61, 68, 82—3; and tracing of missing soldiers, 63—4; achievements and reputation, 87, 149, 172, 714; and Clara Barton, 91, 94; and *Bulletin*, 119; urges humanizing of war, 121; restricts expansion of Red Cross to 'civilized' nations, 122—3, 157; proposes 'league' of societies, 123; defends Geneva Convention, 124, 552; on Balkan wars, 125; and prisoners-of-war, 127; as President of International Committee, 129; and International Committee's twenty-fifth anniversary, 130—1; proposes international arbitration tribunal, 139, 148, 165, 167, 368; and Russo-Japanese war, 150; and Dunant's nomination for Nobel peace prize, 164, 167; death, 172—3; and non-interference, 208; proposes peacetime activities, 259; and modern war, 716; *La Guerre et la Charité* (with Appia), 51, 69
Mozambique, 685, 691
Muller, de (Red Cross delegate in USSR), 273, 275
Muller, Rudolf, 167, 173
Mundy, Baron, 80
Muralt, Dr de, 547
Murmansk railway, 194
Murphy, Grayson M.P., 242, 245
Mussolini, Benito: and war in Ethiopia, 308, 311, 355, 551; and Brown's criticisms, 316; political deportees, 368; attacks Ruegger, 550
Musy, Jean-Marie, 456
Mvoczek, Jan, 432

Nadolny, Rudolph, 527
Nagasaki, 488—90
Nagy, Imre, 581, 584

Nakagawa, Prince of Japan, 293
Namur, Belgium, 216
Nanking, 365–6, 471, 497
Nansen, Fridtjof, 274, 280–2
Napoleon III, Emperor of the French (*formerly* Louis-Napoleon): alliance with Italy against Austria, 1; Solferino victory, 2–3, 6–7; and Dunant, 3, 7, 163; as pupil of Dufour, 14, 43; frees Austrian surgeons after Montebello, 26; and Schleswig-Holstein war, 40; Dufour pleads for help for Dunant, 48; in Franco-Prussian war, 60–1; objects to nominee to Spanish throne, 60; wounded and captured, 63, 76
Narval, Dr de, 192
Nasser, Gamal Abdel, 602
National First Aid Association (USA), 112
National Women Association of the Red Cross (Germany), 356
natural disasters: Red Cross aid for, 87, 93–4, 264, 287, 596
natural law, 24
naval warfare: covered by Geneva Convention, 56; and breaches of Geneva Convention, 202
Naville family, 676
Naville, Adrien, 5
Naville, Edouard, 177, 192, 196–7, 205, 260, 560
Naville, Marcel, 622, 627–9, 642
Nazism: anti-Semitism and racial theories, xxvi, 347–8, 352, 354, 358, 413–19, 424–6, 428, 430, 432–3, 454, 468, 496; rise of, 341–2, 345, 347; medical ethics, 348–9; and extermination of 'undesirables', 414–16, 418, 432; and stolen Jewish gold, 700–3; International Committee's acceptance of, 706–7; *see also* Germany
Neckerman, Kay, 495
Needham, Joseph, 576
Nepal, 696
Nesmith (US Senator), 90
Nessi, Serge, 62⁻ 3
Neue Zürcher Zeitung, 417

Neuengamme concentration camp, 469, 515–16
Neutral Nation Repatriation Committee (Korean war), 578
neutrality: as Red Cross principle, xxii, 561, 569; of medical personnel, 19–20, 25–6, 41, 58; and 1864 Geneva Convention, 45, 46; US attitude to in World War I, 242
New Statesman and Nation (journal), 343
New York Evening Post, 471
New York Herald, 34
New York Times, 603, 643, 647
Nicholas II, Tsar, 156, 165–6, 169, 236
Nicholas, Grand Duke of Russia, 232
Nick, Henri, 13, 48
Niemöller, Pastor Martin, 362–3
Niger, 696
Nigeria: and Biafran war, 614–24; famine, 615–18, 621
Nigerian Red Cross, 616, 622
Nightingale, Florence: achievements, 29–30, 32, 34, 36; on 1864 Geneva Diplomatic Conference, 47; encourages action in Franco-Prussian war, 69–70, 86; criticizes British Red Cross activities in Franco-Prussian war, 74, 85; on contributions to British Red Cross in Franco-Prussian war, 84; honours, 85; and Clara Barton, 87–8; praises Dunant, 127; on British Aid Society committee, 137; in Dunant's memoirs, 163; death, 172; commemorative medal, 174
Ninagawa, Dr Arata, 261–2
Noailles, Adrien Maurice, Duc de, 24
Noailles, Marchioness de, 294
Nobel, Alfred, 164–5, 167
Nobel Peace Prize, 164, 167–8, 206, 542, 550, 597
Nodia, Michel, 332
Nordling, Paul, 457
Norfolk, Henry Howard, 15th Duke of, 128
Norman, Florence Priscilla, Lady, 217
Normandy landings (D-Day, 1944; 'Operation Overlord'), 405–6, 502, 505

Northcliffe, Alfred Harmsworth, 1st
    Viscount, 210
Northcliffe, Dame Mary Elizabeth,
    Viscountess (later Lady Hudson), 210
Norwegian Red Cross, 630
Nuremberg Laws (1935), 347, 413
Nuremberg Trials (1945–6), 349, 469, 497,
    517, 541, 558
Nyerere, Julius, 616

Oba, T., 477
O'Brien, Conor Cruise, 526
O'Connor, Basil, 548
Odier family, 177
Odier, Edouard, 170, 239
Odier, Lucie: at Geneva meeting (1942),
    xxi; attends 1934 Tokyo conference, 294,
    296; and Italian war in Ethiopia, 302,
    305; and commitment to silence, 314;
    and Spanish civil war, 316; at 1938
    London conference, 359; withdraws
    from visit to German concentration
    camps, 360; relations with Burckhardt,
    372–3, 423; in World War II, 381, 385,
    387; visits Britain (1941), 390; on
    International Committee, 409; and Nazi
    Jewish policy, 419; and German
    concentration camp internees, 155
Oertzen, Luise von, 356
Office of Strategic Studies (USA; later
    Central Intelligence Agency), 498, 540,
    702
Ofuna prison camp, Japan, 492
Ogaden, 658
Ojukwu, Colonel Odumegwu, 615, 617
Oldenburg, Grand Duchy of, 39
Oldenburg, Prince Pyotr Alexandrovich,
    Duke of, 233
Olds, Robert, 252, 260–1, 265
Olivet, Georges, 674
Olmstead, Frederick Law, 34–5
open cities, 320
Orgaz, General, 316
Orlando, Vittorio Emanuele, 260
Orleans, siege of (1429), 24
Osborne, Major, 246
Ossietsky, Karl von, 351–2

Ottoman Empire see Turkey
Oxfam: beginnings, 394, 560; relations with
    International Committee, 630; in
    Cambodia, 643–4, 648–9, 652, 655
Oyama, Marchioness, 155

Pagan, Jean-Roger, 539–40
Paget, Charles, 68, 271
Paget, Lady Muriel, 224–6, 228, 234–6, 240,
    293
Paget, Sir Ralph, 224–5
Paget, Sir Richard, 235
Pakistan: prisoners in, 627
Palasciano, Dr Ferdinando, 26, 28–9, 58
Paléologue, Maurice, 233
Palestine: refugees, 563, 566–9; partition
    and conflict, 564–9; see also Israel;
    Jerusalem
Palestinians, 694–5
Palestro, battle of (1859), 1
Papadopoulos, Colonel George, 610–11
Paravicini, Dr Fritz, 196, 294, 472–5, 481,
    486–7, 498
Paré, Ambroise, 27
Pares, Bernard, 233, 234
Paris: Treaty of (1856), 19; siege of (1870),
    76–82; Commune (1871), 81–2, 91;
    Clara Barton in, 91
Paris Peace Agreement (1995), 688
Park, W. Hays, 636, 710
Parry, Frédéric, 127
partisans: status, 409; see also resistance
    movements
Pasquier, André, 679–81
Passy, Frédéric, 166, 168–9
Pathe, Barbara, 405–6, 463
Payne, John Barton, 283, 289, 292–3, 299
peace movement, 165–9, 295, 298–9
Peacock, Andrew, 649
Pearl Harbor (1941), 404, 471–2
Pehle, John, 455
Pelc, Helena, 434
Percival, General Arthur Ernest, 472,
    487–8
Percy, Pierre-François, Baron, 25, 58
Perrot, Max, 13
Pershing, General John Joseph, 245

Peru, 685, 691

Peshkova, Catherine, 334

Peter I, King of Serbia, 228

Peter-Ciller-Kohler (chocolate company), 205

Pfeiffer, J., 502

Pfister, Amy, 461–2

Pfister, Willy, 464

Philippines, 628, 696

Phillips, Captain, 144

Phnom Penh, 640, 642–4, 646–8, 652–3, 656, 658–9

Pictet, Jean: on Burckhardt's manner, 303; on danger to civilians in wartime, 369; at outbreak of World War II, 371, 376; on Chenevière, 373; on Huber, 410, 594, 705; prepares document on humanitarian commitments, 420; on German Red Cross, 467–8; on hostility to International Committee, 544–5; appointed to International Committee, 560; draws up seven 'fundamental principles', 561; on tone of 1930s Committee, 563; teaches humanitarian law, 605; on shooting of Red Cross delegates in Biafran war, 626; declines presidency, 629

Piedmont, 1

Pietczyk, Barbara, 470

Pilger, John, 643–4, 647

Pinochet, General Augusto, 663–5

Pires, Harry, 462–3

Pirogov, Nicolai, 28

Pius XII, Pope, 443–4

Plas, Comdt des, 515

Pless, Prince of, 61, 73, 81

Plevna, battle of (1877), 134

Plymouth, Robert Windsor-Clive, 1st Earl of, 209

Pochkammer, Captain, 192

Podbielski, Peter, 513, 528

Poe, Major, 137

Poincaré, Mme Raymond, 179

Pol Pot, 641, 643

Poland: post-World War I conditions, 265, 275–6; political prisoners visited, 332; and Gorky's Political Red Cross, 334; Germans invade and occupy (1939), 371, 374, 412, 426–8; bombed, 374, 376, 412; prisoners-of-war (1939–45), 383, 399–400; refugees, 387; mental patients shot, 415; government in exile, 426–7; Nazi extermination policy in, 426, 428–32; German resettlement policy, 428–31, 434; Germanization of children and women, 432–6, 524–6; Jewish casualties, 501; Gomulka sets up socialist state (1956), 579; see also Katyn massacre

Polish Red Cross society, 426–7, 432, 436–8, 463, 527

political prisoners and detainees: International Committee's access to, 329–37, 342–3; in Nazi Germany, 345–7, 349–55; in Algerian war, 586, 592; in Greece, 605–13; in Israel, 606, 628, 636–8; visited by delegates, 628; in Chile, 663–4; in Iraq, 667–70

Political Red Cross, 334

Poncet, Jean-François, 648

Ponchard, François: *Cambodge: Année Zéro*, 641

Poppendick, Dr, 356

Port Arthur, Manchuria, 150, 153, 155–6

Portales, Horace, 372, 379

Portugal: and Boer War, 140, 146; in World War I, 193

Portuguese Red Cross, 388

Pradervand, Jean-Pierre, 535, 537–40

Preah Vinear, Cambodia, 645, 654

Preval (French delegate, 1863), 21

Priestly, Major, 190

Princess Christian (hospital train), 140, 147

Prisoner of War Bread Fund, Berne, 205

Prisoner-of-War Code (Geneva Convention, 1929), 377

prisoners-of-war: and 1863 discussions, 20, 26, 28; reported in Franco-Prussian war, 64; Dunant promotes cause of, 126–8; in Boer War, 142, 147–8; in Russo-Japanese war, 155–6; International Agency set up (1914), 180, 183; in World War I, 180, 183–99; Japanese attitude to and treatment of in World War II,

190—4, 197, 376, 471—3, 476—88; and
'captivity neurosis', 196; reprisals over,
199—200; post-World War I repatriation
problems, 266—74; diseases and
epidemics, 268—71; protection under
1928—9 Geneva Convention revision,
291, 296—7, 377; in Spanish civil war,
324—5; in Sino-Japanese war, 365; World
War II agency for, 373, 376; in World
War II, 378—86, 397—9, 407; national
characteristics, 380—1; food and relief
parcels for, 383—6; studies and reading,
385—6; transported by sea, 401;
International Committee sets up special
commission on (1942), 423; released at
end of World War II, 500; post-World
War II German, 530—8, 540—1; increased
protection under 1949 Geneva
Convention, 554; in Korean war, 571 4,
577—8; in Franco-Algerian war, 586—90;
in Yemen, 600—1; in Iraq-Iran war,
666—7, 670; missing German (World
War II), 697; see also Prisoner-of-War
Code; tracing service

Privat, Ami, 60

Pro Juventute (Swiss organization), 299—300

Protecting Powers: in World War I, 188

protection papers, 270

Prussia: war with France (1870), xxii, 60—8,
71—83, 121; threatens France, 7;
appoints Red Cross society, 39; attacks
Schleswig-Holstein, 39—41; war with
Austria (1866), 53—4; army medical
services, 61—2; besieges Paris (1870),
77—8; see also Germany

Public Welfare Society, Geneva, 15—16

Pullman, George H., 100, 109

Pye, Edith, 394

Rada Glowna Opiekuncza (RGO; Polish
General Welfare Council), 427

Rädda Barnen, 692

Rainer, Archduke of Austria, 19

Rakowsky, Christian, 295

Ramsbottom, Dr (of Orange Free State),
147

Rappard, William, 263

Rasputin, Grigory Efimovich, 235—6

Ravensbruck concentration camp, 456,
464, 469—70

red crescent: adopted as emblem, 126

Red Crescent societies, 295, 598

Red Cross: neutrality, xxii, 561, 569;
adopted as emblem, 45, 53, 62; early
spread of movement, 51—2, 56; emblem
misused in Franco-Prussian war, 66—7,
82, 86, 123; foreign societies participate
in Franco-Prussian war, 68, 83;
intervention in domestic disasters and
problems, 103, 118; expansion restricted
to 'civilized' nations, 122; emblem
abused in 1875 Balkan wars, 126;
attitude to peace, 166, 289—9; personnel
detained and imprisoned in World War
I, 185—6; national societies' activities in
World War I, 207—9; posters, 243;
rivalries with other organizations, 282;
publicity methods, 287—8; character and
anonymity of delegates, 301, 304—5, 325,
328, 376, 498; violated in Ethiopian war,
307—10; and politicization of national
societies, 329, 344—5, 369, 578, 696;
emblem ignored in Sino-Japanese war,
364; food and relief operations in World
War II, 383—5; wartime shipping and
transport, 388—9, 394; in post-World
War II Europe, 503—11; post-World War
II criticisms and dissensions, 544—8,
595 6, emblem violated in World War
II, 553; ideological differences between
national societies, 578—9; co-operation
over help for Hungary (1956), 580—1;
centenary (1963), 596; role and purpose
questioned (1975; 'the Big Study'),
630—3; public image, 693—4; knowledge
of, 697—8; humanitarian principles, 709,
713; total membership numbers, 714; see
also International Committee of the Red
Cross

Red Cross International Conferences: 1st
(Paris, 1867), 58; 2nd (Berlin, 1869), 58,
63; 3rd (Geneva, 1885), 96, 129; 4th
(Karlsrühe, 1887), 129; 6th (Vienna,
1884), 138; 7th (St Petersburg, 1902), 110,

Red Cross Int. Con. - *cont.*
148, 164; 9th (Washington, 1912), 174,
176, 187, 231, 257, 288, 555; 10th
(Geneva, 1921), 284—5, 331, 344; 11th
(Geneva, 1923), 287; 15th (Tokyo, 1934),
292—9; 16th (London, 1938), 358—9; 17th
(Stockholm, 1948, earlier proposed for
1942), 359, 549—51, 553, 587; 18th
(Toronto, 1952), 551, 570, 595; 20th
(Vienna, 1965), 605; 21st (Instanbul,
1969), 708; 25th (Geneva, 1986), 673, 694;
(26th, Budapest, 1991; cancelled), 694;
26th (Geneva, 1995), 715

Red Cross and Red Crescent Day (8 May
1991), 685

Red Cross and Red Crescent Museum,
699

Red Cross Youth: First International
Assembly (Prague, 1923), 286—7

Reformation: spiritual and temporal
division in, 24

refugees: in Franco-Prussian war, 66, 91;
International Committee on, 91; in
World War I, 185, 248; discussed at
tenth Red Cross conference (1921), 285;
in China during Japanese occupation,
366—7; in World War II, 377, 387, 422;
Jewish, 420—2; in post-World War II
Europe, 500—4, 506—8, 511—13; as world
phenomenon, 547; Palestinian, 563,
566—9; in Hungarian rising (1956),
583—4; in Algerian war, 592—3;
Cambodian, 644—52, 654—5; in former
Yugoslavia, 686; in Rwanda, 688, *see also*
tracing service

Renan, Ernest, 9

Renard, Lieut.-General (of Belgium), 39

repatriations: in World War I, 186; post-
World War I, 266—74; in World War II,
456, 458—9; in Iran-Iraq war, 670

reprisals, 402

resistance movements: prisoners covered
by 1949 Convention, 554

Reutinger, Anna, 272

Reveil movement (Geneva), 10, 12

Revue de l'Enfance, La, 286

Reynier, Jacques de, 563, 568, 570—1, 573

Reynold, M. de (Red Cross delegate),
530—1, 536

Reynold, Cronach de, 303

Rhee, Syngman, 569

Rhodesia (*later* Zimbabwe), 674—5

Ribbentrop, Joachim von, 352, 371, 403, 457

Ribot, Alexandre Félix Joseph, 180

Richardson, Mrs (nurse), 154

Riegner, Gerhardt, xxii, 419, 423—5, 443—4,
446, 458—9, 461, 548, 551, 706

Rietmann, Otto, 163

Rive, Louis Michel de la, 60

Rivoire, Etienne, 9

Robert, Charles, 7

Roberts, Lt. Col., 481—2

Roberts, Adam, 710

Roberts, Field Marshal Frederick Sleigh,
1st Earl, 143

Roberts, Nora, Lady, 143

Roberts, Walter, 392, 402—3

Robins, Raymond, 249

Rochat, André, 600—4, 609, 678

Rockwell, Norman, 404

Rohner, W., 387, 418

Roja Cruz International (Spain), 320

Rolland, Romain, 184

Romania: Jews persecuted in, 418

Romanian Red Cross, 135

Romeo, Dr Aurelio, 317

Roon, Albrecht Theodor Emil, Count
von, 19

Roosevelt, Eleanor, 247, 523

Roosevelt, Franklin Delano, xxvi, 361, 371,
444, 455, 457

Roosevelt, Theodore, 110-12, 117—18, 159

Root, L.R., 112

Rosen, Count Carl Gustav von, 307—8,
310, 621

Rossel, Dr, 465

Rothmund, Heinrich, 421—2

Rothschild, Nathan Meyer, 1st Baron,
215—16, 218

Rotta, Angelo, 445—6, 448—50

Rougé, Bonabes de, 369, 386, 388, 547,
596

Rousseau, Jean-Jacques, 10, 17; *The Social
Contract,* 25

Rouvier, Bernard, 283
Rozanec, Poland, 434–5
Rubli, Dr Jean-Maurice, 463
Ruegger, Paul, 550, 560, 565, 570, 574, 586, 605
Russell, Bertrand: *Conquest of Happiness*, 480
Russell, (Sir) William Howard, 30–1
Russia (and USSR): accepts 1864 treaty, 52–3; 1891–2 famine, 96–9; proposals on prisoners-of-war, 126, 128; war with Turkey (1877), 132–6; war with Japan (1904–5), 149–57, 231; mobilizes for World War I, 178; treatment of prisoners in World War I, 193–6; conduct of World War I, 232–6; British medical aid in during World War I, 234–6; Soviet regime, 239–40, 332–8; peace settlement (1917/18), 240; civil war in (1918–20), 249, 272–3; and lost children of Urals, 250–3; World War I casualties, 256; post-World War I prisoner repatriations, 266–9; Bolshevism in, 271–2, 280; post-World War I treatment of prisoners-of-war, 272–4; post-World War I famine and relief, 276–82; Red Crescent societies, 295; totalitarianism in, 329; political prisoners and persecution under communists, 332–8; pact with Germany (1939), 369; treatment of prisoners in World War II, 377, 398–9; occupies Berlin (1945), 382; German invasion and campaign in, 397, non-signatory of 1929 Geneva Convention, 397, 550; prisoners of Germans in World War II, 397–9, 415, 549; and Katyn massacre, 437–8; liberates Budapest (1945), 452–3; suspects International Committee of espionage, 452; World War II casualties, 496; post World War II relief in, 509; post-World War II criticism of International Committee, 549–51; attends Swiss 1949 conference on revisions to Geneva Convention, 554; condemns protection of victims of civil wars, 555; declares war on Japan (1945), 558; suppresses Hungarian rising (1956),

580–2, 584; missing German prisoners in, 697
Russian Red Cross society: in 1891 famine, 97–8; under Empress's patronage, 130, 152; in 1877 war with Turkey, 133; composition and organization, 151–2, 179, 232; in 1904 war with Japan, 152–3; in World War I, 179, 232–3; formed (1867) and developed, 231–2; reformed in 1917 Revolution, 237–8; criticized by Rouvier, 283; exiled HQ in Paris (1921), 332; post-war attack on International Committee, 546; *see also* Soviet Red Cross
Russian Revolution (1917), 231, 236–8
Rutherford, Dr (British deputy inspector of hospitals), 21, 45
Rwanda, 628, 683, 688–91
Ryan, Charles, 72
Rzegotta, Irmgard, 529
Rzegotta, Siegfried, 513, 529

Sa Kaeo camp (Cambodia), 650–1
Saddam Hussein, 665, 667–70
Sadowa (Königgrätz), battle of (1866), 53–4, 61
St Clair Stobart, Mabel, 224, 226, 228–9
St John Ambulance Association, 209
St John of Jerusalem, Order of: at 1863 Geneva meeting, 20; in Schleswig-Holstein war, 41
St Jorre, John, 620
St Petersburg Declaration (1868), 59, 707
Saint-Aulaire, Comtesse de, 52
Salan, General Raoul, 585
Salis, Dr Hans Wolf de, 379–80
Sallal, Abdallah, 598
Salonika: Jews deported, 425
Salzmann, Werner, 483–4, 491
Sams, Colonel, 489
San'a, Yemen, 598
Sandbostel concentration camp, Germany, 514
Sandoz, Yves, 706, 712
San Francisco: 1906 earthquake, 115–18
Sannomiya, Baroness, 155
Sano, Count Tsunetami, 151

Santiago, Chile, 663–4
Sarajevo: 1914 assassinations, 174; in Bosnian conflict, 682, 687
Sargent, John Singer, 210
Sartre, Jean-Paul, 590, 625
Satoh, Miss (Egle's Japanese assistant), 475
Satterlee, Dr (in American Civil War), 34
Savak (Iranian secret police), 665
Save the Children Fund, 281–2, 288, 503, 690
Save Europe Now campaign, 503
Saxe-Coburg, Carl-Edouard, Duke of, 293, 341, 345, 350, 353, 356–7, 467, 526
Saxony, John, King of, 19
Schellenberg, Walter, 457
Schindler, Dietrich, 560
Schirmer, Robert, 444–5
Schleswig-Holstein: attacked (1864), 39–42
Schlossmacher (German Red Cross member), 342
Schmitz (mayor of San Francisco, 1906), 116–17
Schoch, E., 197
Schöling, Anton, 341, 527–8
Scholtz-Klink, Gertrud, 356
Schulten-Schindler, Dr de, 193
Schulter, Edouard, 419
Schumacher, Madame, 408
Schwarz, Bruno, 513, 529
Schwarz, Theresa, 529
Schwarze Korps, Das (SS journal), 347
Schwarzenberg, Jean de, 388, 425, 446, 455–6, 458
Schweizer, H.M., 480–4, 490–1, 495, 498
Scutari, 30–2
Seaman, Louis Livingstone, 155–6
Secours aux Blessés (organization), 216
Sedan, battle of (1870), 71–2, 74–6
Selborne, William Waldegrave Palmer, 2nd Earl of, 202
Semenov, General, 272
Sendero Luminoso (Peru), 685
Serbia: and start of World War I, 174, 178; non-ratification of Hague regulations, 187; reports Belgrade hospital bombed in 1914, 201; World War I campaign, 223–30; typhus in, 225, 227; deplores Russian famine, 277
Serbs: in 1875 revolt against Turks, 132–3; in former Yugoslavia conflict, 686–8
Serurier, Jean-Mathieu-Philibert, Count, 58
Sethe, Dr, 418, 454
Sétif, Algeria, 13
Sevenheck (German Red Cross member), 342
SHAEF (Supreme Headquarters, Allied Expeditionary Force), 502, 517
Shamir, Yitzhak, 564
Shanghai, 297, 363–7, 472, 474–5, 478
Shanghai International Red Cross Committee on Refugee Problems, 367
Shatt-al-Arab waterway, 665
Shawcross, William: The Quality of Mercy, 656–7
Shigemitsu, General Maroru, 486
Shiloh, battle of (1862), 33
Shimadzu, Prince, 476, 481, 494
Shiro, Ishii, 576–7
Shōken, Empress of Japan, 151, 154–5, 174
Siam see Thailand
Sicily: and Messina earthquake, 157–9
Siegrist, Roland, 613
Sierra Leone, 628
Simond, Gilbert, 703
Simonett (Red Cross delegate in USSR), 273
Sinclair, Sir John George Tollemache, 74, 84
Singapore, 472, 480–2, 491
Singen, Germany, 705
Siordet, Frédéric, 452, 543, 549, 557, 629
Six Day War (1967; Israeli-Arab), 636
slave labour see forced labour
Slovenia, 277, 686
Smiley, Samuel, 250
Smith, Charles Emory, 97
Sobibor concentration camp, 460
Solferino, battle of (1859): xxi, 1–7, 27–8, 693; site revisited (1948), 542
Solovieff, Zenoby Petrovitch, 252, 333–5
Somali Red Crescent, 684
Somalia, 658, 683–6, 690

Somerset, Edward Adolphus Seymour,
12th Duke of, 128

Sommaruga, Cornelio, 678–81, 683, 686–7,
691, 697, 700, 702, 706–7, 711–14

Sonderegger, William, 161–2

South Africa: political detainees in, 606;
apartheid in, 673, 693

South African conciliation committee, 144

South African Red Cross, 673–4

Southampton: Spanish children removed
to, 321–3

Soviet Red Cross: established and
recognized, 237–8, 252, 333; and
political prisoners, 332–4; see also
Russian Red Cross

Soviet Union see Russia

Spain: and Cuban revolution, 103; war
with USA, 104–5; second Carlist war
(1872), 231

Spanish civil war (1936–9), xxii, 301,
316–28, 329, 382

Spanish Red Cross: sends supplies in Boer
War, 142; in civil war, 317

Speiser, Dr, 199

Spirgi, Dr Edwin, 615

Squire, Paul, 424–5

Srebrenica, Bosnia, 687–8

Sri Lanka, 628, 691

Stadler, Max, 612

Stalin, Josef: pact with Hitler (1939), 369;
son killed, 398; at Yalta, 457

Stalingrad, battle of (1942–3), 398, 424

Stanley, Sir Arthur, 259, 289, 306, 375

Stanley Camp, Hong Kong, 477–8

Stanley, Major, 221

Stark, Freya, 221, 223

Starkenborgh, General, 487

State of Texas (ship), 105

Staudinger, Professor, 255

Stauffer, Dr Paul, 303, 311, 355, 391,
424

Steffen, Charles, 463

Stephan, Ziprian, 268

Stephens, W.A., 510

Stern Gang, 564–5

Sternberg, George M., 105

Storey, Dr Russell, 250

Stowe, Harriet Beecher, 12, 29

Straehler, Marguerite, 479, 487–8, 494

Stringer, Guy, 649

Stureborg (Swedish ship), 394–5

Stuttgart, 552

Suarez, François: De Legibus ac Deo Legislatore,
24

submarines, 202

Suchard, Philippe, 4

Sudan, 136–8, 628, 691

Sudetenland, 369

Suez crisis (1956), 586

Suffolk, William de la Pole, 4th Earl (later
1st Duke) of, 24

Sumner, Charles, 165

Surbek (delegate in Sumatra), 474, 476

Sutherland, George Granville Leveson-
Gower, 2nd Duke of, 128

Sutherland, Millicent, Dowager Duchess
of, 216–18

Suttner, Bertha, Baroness von, 165–6,
168–9; Down with Arms, 166

Suyematsu, Baron, 157

Sweden: uses Red Cross emblem, 53; aid
for concentration camp detainees, 457;
funding contributions, 714

Swedish Red Cross: and Russian prisoner-
of-war camps in World War I, 195; in
Ethiopia, 305, 307, 313; in World War II,
394, 457; in post-World War II
Germany, 507

Swierdoff (of Russian Red Cross), 261

Swift, Ernest, 317, 343, 361–2, 374; death,
544

Swinburne, Dr, 79

Swiss Women's Civilian Service, 385

Switzerland: denies entry to Jewish
refugees, xxiii, 421–2, 453, 560;
constitution, 11; humanitarianism, 11,
14–16; and twenty-fifth anniversary of
Red Cross, 131; internment and refuge
in during World War I, 186, 203–5;
neutrality threatened in World War I,
203; and founding of League of Red
Cross Societies, 263; supports
International Committee in World War
II, 373, 375; relations with Nazi

Switzerland - *cont.*
Germany, 420, 439, 551; official relations with International Committee, 545, 679, 711; convenes 1949 conference on revising Geneva Convention, 553–4; banks hold looted Jewish gold, 700–3; co-operation with Germany in World War II, 704–5; funding contributions, 714
Sydow, Baron von, 69
Syria: Israeli prisoners in, 628
Sythe, Mrs Carlyle, 294
Szalasi, Ferenc, 445, 449–50
Szamosi, Laszlo, 448
Sztelho, Gaber, 445
Sztojay, Döme, 440
Sztomberek, Eugeniusz, 427, 432, 438
Szymanik, Boleslaw, 430–1

Taft, William Howard, 110, 115, 117, 174, 179
Tait, Agnes, 243
Taiwan, 673
Taiwanese Red Cross, 596
Talmage, Revd T. Dewitt, 100
Tansley, Donald, 630–3, 693–4
Tarnogot, Poland, 430
Tat. Die (newspaper), 608
Tatiana Nikolaevna, Grand Duchess of Russia, 234
Taverna, Signor (of Italian Red Cross), 159
Taylor, Telford, 557
Tegetthof, Admiral Wilhelm von, Baron, 56
Terrell, Alexander, 99
terrorism: growth of, 558; in Palestine, 564; covered by 1977 protocols, 633, 636; and weapons, 681
Tewk Pasha, 101
Thai Red Cross, 491, 596
Thailand (Siam): World War II prisoners in, 483, 491; and war in Cambodia, 641, 644–50, 654, 658; 1991 coup, 685
Thatcher, Margaret, Baroness, 691
Theresienstadt concentration camp, 456–7, 465–6

Thompson, H.C., 467
Thomson, Emma: *Our Adventures During the War of 1870* (with Louise MacLaughlin), 71–3
Thoré camp, France, 537–8
Thormeyer, F., 195, 197, 237–8
Thorold, Mrs (of British Red Cross), 509
Thurstan, Violetta, 234
Tieche, André, 674–5
Tiffany, Mrs Belfont, 247
Times, The: and Crimean War, 30–1; on 1891 Russian famine, 97; reports Boer War, 141; opens Red Cross Fund (1914), 210; on British women in World War I, 216; appeals for motor cars in World War I, 218; on war in Ethiopia, 308–9; and Spanish child refugees in Southampton, 323; on end of World War II, 500; on British arms in Biafran war, 620
Timperleey, H.J., 366
Tocqueville, Alexis de: *Democracy in America*, 15
Togo, 691
Tokugawa, Prince, 476
Tokunaga, Colonel, 478
Tokyo: earthquake (1923), 287; *see also* Red Cross International Conference, 15th (1934)
Tokyo Draft (1934), 295, 321, 374, 412, 415, 552, 558
Tokyo War Trials (1946–8), 497, 541, 577
Tolstoy, Count Leo, 99, 168
torture: in Algerian war, 587–92; in Greek military coup (1967), 607–10; modern spread of, 613; Israel accused of, 636–8; in Cambodia, 643, 645
tracing service: of missing soldiers, 63–4; of prisoners-of-war, 89, 180, 183–6; post-World War II, 515–23, 528, 543, 650–1; in Cambodia, 658–60; development of, 660–2; of Latin American 'disappeared', 662–5; of Iraqis, 667–9; in Bosnian conflict, 687–8; in Rwanda, 690; of post-World II German prisoners in Russia, 697; scale of, 714

Transvaal Red Cross, 143

Traz, de (of Commission Mixte), 440

Treblinka concentration camp, 460

Trevelyan, George, 221, 223

Treves, Sir Frederick, 142, 147, 157, 209–10, 213

Tripoli: war in (1911), 173–4

Trochu, General Louis Jules, 66, 76

Tronchu, Mme, 80

Trotsky, Leon, 249, 276

Tschiffli, A., 628

Tsushima, battle of (1905), 156

Tufnel, Caroline, 228

Turckneik concentration camp, 464

Turkey (and Ottoman Empire): ratifies 1864 treaty, 52; and Armenian massacres, 99–103; suppresses Balkan revolt (1875), 125–6, 132; war with Russia (1877), 132–6; Ottoman Empire dismembered (1878), 135; war with Italy (1911), 173; in World War I, 178; civilians interned in World War I, 197–8; war against Kurds, 663; and Beretta, 702–3

Turkish Red Crescent, 394

Turner, Miss (of British Red Cross in Italy), 508

Tutsi people (Rwanda), 688–9, 691

Tutu, Desmond, Archbishop of Cape Town, 707

typhus: in World War I Serbian campaign, 225, 227; among post-World War I repatriated prisoners, 270–1

Uganda, 691

Ugria, Colonel, 327

Uniacke, Captain, 86

UNICEF see United Nations Children's Fund

Union Internationale de Secours aux Enfants, 281

Unit 731 (Japanese bacteriological warfare), 576–7

United Nations: relations with League of Red Cross Societies, 548; and international co-operation, 558–9; in Korean war, 569–75, 577, 579; peacekeeping in Somalia, 685; and Rwanda crisis, 688–9; resolutions on intervention in Iraq and Somalia, 709; armed intervention by, 713

United Nations Children's Fund (UNICEF): in Biafran war, 626; in Cambodia, 641, 643, 645–9, 651–7

United Nations High Commissioner for Refugees (UNHCR), 512, 583, 650, 654, 662, 691

United Nations Relief to Palestinian Refugees (UNRPR), 568

United States of America: army instructions, 37–8; reserve at 1864 Geneva Conference, 45, 90, 92; helpers in Franco-Prussian war, 72; residents in siege of Paris, 79; ratifies Geneva Convention, 93–4, 113; natural disasters, 94–6; and 1891–2 Russian famine, 98–9; and Armenian massacres, 99–102; war with Spain (1898), 104–5; medical aid in Russo-Japanese war, 155; sends aid to Messina earthquake, 159–60; and outbreak of World War I, 179; as Protecting Power in World War I, 193; enters World War I, 240–2, 244–5; women Red Cross helpers, 246–8, 405; and proposed reform of Red Cross movement, 258–60; and relief of Russian post-World War I famine, 278–82; isolationism, 298; aid for Germany (1920s), 339; wartime susicions of International Red Cross delegates, 392; gives relief before entry into World War II, 403–4; aid for concentration camp detainees, 455–6; protests about Japanese in World War II, 477; transfers German prisoners to France, 535–7; accused of bacteriological warfare in Korea, 575–6; attitude to Greek colonels' coup, 612, 614; and 1977 protocols, 635–6; bombs Cambodia, 642; pursues stolen Jewish gold in Swiss banks, 701–2; funding contributions, 714; see also American Civil War; American Red Cross

Universal Alliance for Order and Civilization, 127

Universal Declaration of Human Rights (1948), 708
Universal Exhibitions: Paris (1867), 57; Vienna (1873), 151
UNRRA (United Nations Relief and Rehabilitation Administration), 502–4, 506, 510–12, 517–19, 523–4, 526
Uqhd, Arabia, 599
Urals: lost children of, 150–3
Uruguay: disappeared people in, 663
US Military Railroad in France, 246
USSR see Russia

VAD scheme (Voluntary Aid Detachments; Britain), 212–13, 220–1
Vaillant, Marshal Edouard Marie, 43
Van Buren, Dr William, 34
van de Velde, Captain, 40–2, 44, 68, 120, 562; death, 171–2
Vattel, Emmerich de: Droit des Gens, 25
Veale, Dr (of Transvaal), 143
Veale, Mrs (of British Red Cross), 509
Vecsey, Nicholas, 661–2
Veesenmayer (German ambassador in Budapest, 1944), 442, 444
Verney, Emily, 74
Verney, Sir Harry, 30, 70
Verolino, Gennaro, 445
Versailles: in Franco-Prussian war, 73, 81
Versailles, Treaty of (1919), 266
Victor Emmanuel II, King of Italy, 9, 55, 159
Victoria, Queen: rebukes women visitors to Boer War, 14; becomes patroness of British Red Cross society, 70; sends gifts for Sudan campaign relief, 137
Vienna, Congress and Treaty of (1815), 11, 53
Viet-Minh, 555
Vietnam: and war in Cambodia, 640–5, 652, 656; boat people, 644–5; attacks Cambodian refugee camp, 654
Vinci, Count Guido, 315
Vischer, Betsy, 495–6
Vischer, Dr Matthaeus, 474, 476, 495–6
Visser't Hooft, Pastor, 418
Vitoria, Francisco de, 24
Viviani, René, 180

Vladivostok, 151, 249, 272
Vlotho, Germany, 505–6, 510
Vogue, Marquis de, 180
Volkonsky, Prince and Princess, 234
Voltaire, François Marie Arouet de, 10
Voronzov-Dachkov, Count, 152
Voss, Gertrude, 529
Vukovar, Bosnia, 687
Vust, Laurent, 588, 590–1, 594, 598, 602

Wagner, Pastor (of Stuttgart), 129
Wagnière, Georges, xxi, xxiv
Wainwright, General Jonathan Mayhew, 487
Waldheim, Kurt, 647–8
Walinger, G.A., 479
Wallenberg, Raoul, 445–6, 449–53, 584
Wannsee conference (1942), xxii, 415, 420
Wantage, Baron see Loyd-Lindsay, Colonel Robert James
war: and 'just cause', 23; 'laws' of, 24–6, 122, 124, 170, 560, 633–5, 691; conduct of, 29; and modern communications, 51; changing nature and weapons, 119, 168–9, 173–4, 177, 254, 369, 707–8; moves to end, 285; condemned by Briand-Kellogg pact, 290; total, 555; nature of after 1945, 558–9; of liberation, 633–5; character in 1990s, 692; see also civil wars
war crimes see Nuremberg Trials; Tokyo War Trials
War Office (British), 211–12
War Refugee Board (USA), 455
Warner, Sidney Jeanetta, 477, 506–7, 516
Warsaw: bombed (1939), 374, 376
Washington, DC: International Committee in, 714
Washington Conference (1912) see Red Cross International Conference
Wasserfuhr, Dr Auguste, 25
Watteville, Charles de, 364–5
weapons see war
Weck, René de, 418
Wehrlin, Voldemar, 278, 332–7, 399
Weidman (delegate in Sumatra), 474, 476
Weizsäcker, Ernst von, xxii, 414, 416

Wellington, Arthur Richard Wellesley, 2nd Duke of, 128
Wells, H.G., 184
Werner, Denise, 379—80
Werner, George, 286
Wernher, Alice, Lady, 211
Western Sahara, 658
Westminster, Constance, Duchess of, 217
Westphalia, Treaty of (1648), 11
Weyerman, Hans, 453
Wharton, Edith, 250
White Russians, 272—4, 276
Whitehurst, Felix, 78
Whitman, Walt, 35
Whittle (Loyd-Lindsay's manservant), 73—4
Wilbur, Lawrence, 404
Wildboz, Colonel, 339—40
Wiles, Staff-Surgeon, 86
Wilhelm I, King of Prussia (later Emperor of Germany), 1, 54—5, 81, 113
Williams, Dr Maurice, 322
Wilson, Woodrow, 241, 243, 259—61, 280
Windsor, Edward, Duke of, 110
Wingate, Catherine, Lady, 210
Winnington, Alan, 574
Wolf, Norbert, 513, 528
Wolmer, Lady Maud, 137
women: insignificance in early Red Cross movement, 52; activities in Franco-Prussian war, 85—6; participation in Red Cross societies, 130, 171, 179; in Boer War, 140, 144—7; in Japanese Red Cross, 151; at 1912 Washington conference, 174; excluded from early International Committee, 176; in World War I, 179—80, 184, 205, 209, 212—29, 246—8, 256; Russian, 233—4; in American Red Cross, 246—7, 405—7; first appointment to International Committee, 260; at 1934 Tokyo conference, 294; in Spanish civil war, 318; in German Red Cross, 341, 356; in World War II, 405; Nazi medical experimentation on, 469—70; in Japanese prison camps, 480; tracing expertise, 518; in Israel, 638
Women's Central Association (USA), 35

Women's National Relief Organization (USA), 93
World Food Programme, 648, 651
World Jewish Congress, xxii, 444, 459, 700—1
World Refugee Year (1959), 595
World War I (1914—18): International Committee's achievements in, xxii, 257; American Red Cross and, 115, 240—2, 245—50, 256; outbreak, 174, 175, 178; nature of, 177—8; women in, 179—80, 184, 205, 209, 212—29, 246—8, 256; conduct and campaigns, 180, 200, 219; prisoners, 180, 183—99; repatriations, 186; USA enters, 240—2, 244—5; atrocities and breaches of Convention, 253; ends, 256, 265; estimated casualties, 256
World War II (1939—45): Red Cross neutrality debated in, xxi—xxii; relief operations in, xxii, 382—6; outbreak, 371; conduct and campaigns, 374, 377, 424; prisoners in, 377—82; casualties, 496, 552; aftermath, 500—6
World's Health, The (magazine), 263—4, 284
Wrba, Rudolf, 443
Württenburg, 39
Württenburg Red Cross Society, 340

Xuan (Cambodian Veitnamese), 658—60

Yalta conference (1945), 457
Yemen: civil war in, 598—603; Egyptians in, 600—1; detainees in, 628; Somali refugees in, 684
Yen, Dr F.C., 363
Yokohama: earthquake (1923), 287
Yomei Maru (ship), 251—3
Young, Geoffrey Winthrop, 223
Young, Colonel J.S., 136—40
Young, Oran, 629
Younger, Sir Allen, 136
Yugoslavia (former), 686—8, 695
Yusupov, Prince Felix, 235—6

Zafari, Madame, 395
Zaire, 689—90

Zamosc, Poland, 428–32, 434–6
Zamoyski, Count, 435
Zangger, Heinrich, xxv
Zemstvos, Union of (Russia), 232–3, 237
Zhou, Enlai, 570, 577
Ziereis, Colonel Franz, 463
Zimbabwe see Rhodesia

Zimmerman, Anna, 91
Zindel (delegate in Hong Kong), 474–5,
    477–8, 485, 494–5
Zohnes, Edouard, 336
Zollinger, Alfred, 381, 405
Zweig, Stefan, 184
Zwierzyniec, Poland, 435–6